The Business Environment

The Business
Environment
Adrian Palmer & Bob Hartley
Fifth Edition

The McGraw·Hill Companies

London	Boston	Burr Ridge, IL	Dubuque, IA	Madison, WI	New York
St. Louis	San Francisco	Bangkok	Bogotá	Caracas	Kuala Lumpur
Lisbon	Madrid	Mexico City	Milan	Montreal	New Delhi
Santiago	Seoul	Singapore	Sydney	Taipei	Toronto

The Business Environment
Adrian Palmer and Bob Hartley
ISBN-13 9780077109905
ISBN-10 0077109902

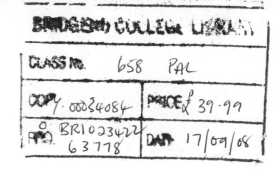
Published by McGraw-Hill Education
Shoppenhangers Road
Maidenhead
Berkshire
SL6 2QL
Telephone: 44 (0) 1628 502 500
Fax: 44 (0) 1628 770 224
Website: www.mcgraw-hill.co.uk

British Library Cataloguing in Publication Data
A catalogue record for this book is available from the British Library

Library of Congress Cataloging-in-Publication Data
The Library of Congress data for this book has been applied for from the Library of
Congress

Acquisitions Editor: Kirsty Reade
Development Editor: Rachel Crookes
Marketing Manager: Alice Djuiser
Senior Production Editor: Beverley Shields

Text design by SCW
Cover design by Paul Fielding Design
Printed and bound in the UK by Bell & Bain Ltd., Glasgow

ISBN-13 9780077109905
ISBN-10 0077109902

Brief Table of Contents

Detailed Table of Contents

Contents

Contents

Contents

Contents

CASE STUDIES

Preface

Business organizations exist in an environment that is becoming increasingly complex and competitive. The firm in its business environment is essentially similar to any living organism in the natural environment – survival and prosperity come to those that are best able to adapt to their environment.

This book explores the complexity of forces that make up the business environment. In particular, it aims to understand the impact of these forces on the activities of business organizations, and the nature of the decisions that organizations must take if they are to survive and prosper in a changing environment.

The book is structured in five parts. The first part provides contexts by analysing the general nature of the business environment. The key elements and forces in the environment are discussed within a systems framework.

In the second part, we focus on the external environment and explore in more detail the environmental elements and forces introduced in Part 1. Dividing the business environment into a number of distinct areas inevitably involves some fairly arbitrary boundaries and the chapters in this part continually seek to provide links to other chapters. Part 2 begins with a review of the political environment. The social, technological and legal environments are explored in subsequent chapters.

Part 3 switches the focus of attention inward by looking at how organizations cope with external change. The aim here is to understand the internal factors that can facilitate or inhibit response to a changing external environment. A review is made of the different types of organization that exist in the business environment, their objectives and internal processes. Part 3 concludes with a review of the increasingly important topic of the social responsibilities of business and the duties owed by business organizations to multiple stakeholder groups.

Part 4 focuses on markets. Markets are the means through which organizations satisfy consumers' needs and provide signals that should channel an organization's resources to serving groups with the greatest opportunity. We begin this part with a discussion of the economic environment of business organizations, first at the micro level of market competition and, second, at the macro level of national economic policy. Basic principles of micro- and macroeconomics are introduced. With the increasing globalization of business, a chapter on firms' international environment sets markets in this broader context.

Having explored individual elements of the business environment introduced in Part 1, the final part returns to a more holistic perspective of the business environment. In this part we look at methods of analysing a complex environment and making decisions about future business strategy. Great attention is given to the role of information gathering, data analysis and the ways in which change can be implemented. Further integration of the business environment is provided through five case studies.

This fifth edition has itself responded to changes in the business environment, with strengthened coverage of topics of contemporary concern. There is greater coverage of the impacts on business of ecological change, especially global warming. In the light of corporate scandals such as Enron and Parmalat, and stakeholders' ever-increasing expectations of business organizations' behaviour, corporate responsibility is given greater coverage.

Learning throughout the book is supported in a number of ways. Each chapter contains a number of thought-provoking vignettes based on contemporary examples. In addition, each chapter has a mini-case study with review questions and a further series of chapter review questions. Key terms are introduced and defined in a glossary. Suggestions are made for further reading and each chapter concludes with a list of websites that will allow the reader to pursue issues raised in the chapter. All the websites listed in this book were freely accessible at the time of writing. The authors invite comments about any of the material contained in this book.

Adrian Palmer
mail@apalmer.com

Bob Hartley
bob.hartley@northampton.ac.uk

About the Authors

Adrian Palmer is Professor of Services Marketing, University of Gloucestershire Business School, Cheltenham, UK

Bob Hartley is Associate Dean, Northampton Business School, The University of Northampton, UK

Specialist contributor on the legal environment: **Mary Mulholland** is Principal Lecturer in Law, De Montfort University, Leicester, UK

Guided Tour

Chapter Objectives

This chapter will explain:

■ the elements that make up an organization's macro-, micro- and i
environments

■ the complex interdependencies that exist in the business environr

CHAPTER OBJECTIVES
Each chapter opens with a set of objectives, summarizing what readers should learn from each chapter.

Key Terms

Act of Parliament	(49)	European Union (EU)	(58)	Pressure groups	(78)
Best value	(71)	Executive	(50)	Public Finance Initiative	
Cabinet	(51)	Ideology	(43)	(PFI)	(74)
Charter Mark	(69)	Judicial review	(53)	Public–private partnership	
Civil service	(51)	Judiciary	(52)	(PPP)	(74)
Directives	(51)	Legislature	(48)	Quango	(73)
European Commission	(61)	Lobbying	(49)	Regional government	(54)
European Council of		Local government	(57)	Regulation	(75)
Ministers	(61)	Non-Departmental Public		Social exclusion	(45)
European Court of Justice	(61)	Bodies (NDPBs)	(73)	Task forces	(71)
European Economic		Outsourcing	(72)		

KEY TERMS
These are highlighted throughout the chapter and listed at the end of each chapter for quick reference. A glossary at the back of the book aids revision.

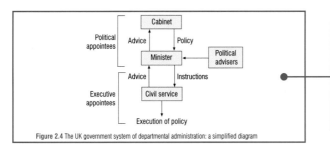

Figure 2.4 The UK government system of departmental administration: a simplified diagram

FIGURES AND TABLES
Each chapter provides a number of figures and tables to help you to visualize the various models, and to illustrate and summarize important concepts.

SUMMARY

The political environment impinges on so many other aspects of an organization environment, for example change in the dominant poltical ideology can result i significant changes in the economic environment. Businesses dislike uncertainty i the political environment and monitoring and understanding it is useful to pick u early signs of change. This chapter has explored the basis of government in th United Kingdom and the respective roles of national, regional, local and uropea government. Although examples have been taken from the UK, the elements of th political environment described here are similar in most Western democrat countries. A two-way interaction occurs between government and business, i which business organizations monitor changes in the political environment, but also see to influence the environment through lobbying. Pressure groups represent an increas ingly important element of the political environment, working from outside the form

SUMMARY
This briefly reviews and reinforces the main topics you will have covered in each chapter to ensure you have acquired a solid understanding of the key topics, as well as linking.

CHAPTER REVIEW QUESTIONS & ACTIVITIES
The questions encourage you to review and apply the knowledge you have acquired from each chapter, while the activities suggest practical projects for group or solo study.

CHAPTER REVIEW QUESTIONS

1 (a) Explain briefly what you understand by the 'environment' of a business.
   (b) Prepare a list of recommendations which would aid a business to address change in its technical environment.
   (*Based on CIM Marketing Environment Examination*)

2 Suppliers and intermediaries are important stakeholders in the microenvironment of the business.

3 Using a company of your choice, produce and justify an environmental set. You should include and rank at least five factors in your set.

ACTIVITY
Develop a checklist of points that you consider to be important indicators of whether an organization is responsive to changes in its business environment. Why

CASE STUDIES
Each chapter includes one case study designed to test how well you can apply the main techniques learned. At the back of the book, you'll find a section of five extra in-depth cases.

CASE STUDY

CRISIS SPREADS FROM THE FIELDS OF INDIA TO THE SUPERMARKET SHELVES OF SHEFFIELD
Businesses involved in food production have faced a number of challenges in their business environment. In addition to the usual issues of securing profitability in commodity-type market, the past two decades have seen growing concerns about food safety. For many consumers, food standards have been declining, as factory farming and mass production have led to a succession of food scares – salmonella in chickens, BSE in cows, chemicals in 'pure' bottled water, to name but a few. Whether food standards have actually been going down or whether it is consumers' perceptions that have been changing is less clear. Media reports about food scares may convey the impression that food standards are out of control, but the very fact that newspapers are reporting them suggests how unusual they are. It is easy to overlook the hugе

FURTHER READING
Each chapter includes the latest recommended reading, covering journal articles, textbooks and other essential sources.

Further Reading
A good starting point for understanding competitive advantage of firms and the role of value chains in achieving this is provided in Michael Porter's frequently cited book:
Porter, M.E. (1985) *Competitive Advantage: Creating and Sustaining Superior Performance*, Free Press.
This has been brought up to date to take account of the World Wide Web in the following:
Porter, M.E. (2001) 'Strategy and the Internet', *Harvard Business Review*, March, pp. 63–78.
There is now an extensive literature on the

Varey, R.J. (2002) *Relationship Marketing: Dialogue and Networks in the E-commerce Era*, Chichester, Wiley.
A good analysis of networks between companies is provided in the following:
Batonda, G. and Perry, C. (2003) 'Approaches to relationship development processes in inter-firm networks', *European Journal of Marketing*, Vol. 37 (10), pp. 1457–84.
Healy, M., Hastings, K., Brown, L. and Gardiner, M. (2001) 'The old, the new and the complicated: A trilogy of marketing relationships', *European Journal of Marketing*,

USEFUL WEBSITES
At the end of each chapter you'll find a list of useful websites for finding extra information on the topics covered, ideal for writing essays and revising.

Useful Websites

Biz/Ed
Biz/ed is a business and economics resource for students, teachers and lecturers and includes news and case studies:
http://www.bized.ac.uk

Supply chain management discussion group
List for all aspects of purchasing and supply chain management, and interorganizational theory. The list supports the networking and collaborative activities of the IPSERA association

Newspaper websites
The quality daily newspapers have websites and these are a useful source of information about the business environment:
Financial Times: **http://www.ft.com**
Telegraph: **http://www.Telegraph.co.uk**
Guardian: **http://www.Guardian.co.uk**
The Times: **http://www.the-times.co.uk**
The Sunday Times: **http://www.the_sunday-times.co.uk**

Technology to Enhance Learning and Teaching

Online Learning Centre (OLC)

After completing each chapter, log on to the supporting Online Learning Centre website. Take advantage of the study tools offered to reinforce the material you have read in the text, and to develop your knowledge in a fun and effective way.

Resources for students include:

- revision notes
- weblinks
- self-text questions
- glossary.

Also available for lecturers:

- lecturer manual
- PowerPoint slides
- testbank.

For lecturers: Primis Content Centre

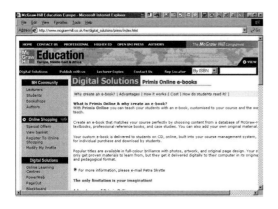

If you need to supplement your course with additional cases or content, create a personalized e-Book for your students. Visit www.primiscontentcenter.com or e-mail primis_euro@mcgraw-hill.com for more information.

Study Skills

We publish guides to help you study, research, pass exams and write essays, all the way through your university studies.

Visit **www.openup.co.uk/ss/** to see the full selection and get £2 discount by entering promotional code **study** when buying online!

Computing Skills

If you'd like to brush up your Computing skills, we have a range of titles covering MS Office applications such as Word, Excel, PowerPoint, Access and more.

Get a £2 discount on these titles by entering the promotional code **app** when ordering online at www.mcgraw-hill.co.uk/app

Acknowledgements

Our thanks go to the following reviewers for their comments at various stages in the text's development:

Alexander Noble, Surrey University

Andrea Beetles, Cardiff University

Rishma Dattani, Wolverhampton University

Martin Holmes, Wolverhampton University

Douglas Chalmers, Glasgow Caledonian University

Frank Auton, Westminster Business School

James Cunningham, NUI Galway

Nicholas Perdikis, University of Aberystwyth

Steve Millard, Buckinghamshire Chilterns University College

Walter Cairns, Manchester Metropolitan University

Philip Drummond-Thompson, Kingston University

Part 1

Contexts

Chapter 1
What is the Business Environment?

Chapter 1

What is the Business Environment?

Chapter Objectives

This chapter will explain:

- the elements that make up an organization's macro-, micro- and internal environments

- the complex interdependencies that exist in the business environment

- the concept of a value chain

- models for viewing the business environment as a system

1.1 DEFINING THE BUSINESS ENVIRONMENT

What do we mean by the term business environment? In its most general sense, an environment can be defined as everything which surrounds a system. The environment of a central heating system, for example, comprises all of those phenomena which impact on the system's ability to operate effectively. The environment would therefore include such factors as the external air temperature, the insulation properties of the rooms being heated, the quality and consistency of fuel supplied etc. A business organization can similarly be seen as a system, whose performance is influenced by a whole range of phenomena in its environment. However, while a central heating system may be said to be a *closed* system, the business organization and its environment is an *open* system. For the central heating system, all elements of the system can generally be identified, but for business organizations, it can be difficult to define what makes up the system, and even more difficult to define the elements of their environment. Some elements may seem quite inconsequential today, but may nevertheless have potential to critically affect a business organization in future years. The test of a good business leader is to be able to read the environment and to understand not only how business systems and their environments work today, but also how they will evolve in the future. Society's rising expectations with regard to the ethical behaviour of business organizations is an example of an environmental factor that has emerged as an increasingly critical factor to the survival of business organizations. After studying this book, you should have a better idea of the complexity of the business environment.

Business organizations exist to turn inputs from their environment (e.g. materials, labour and capital) into goods and services which customers in the environment want to purchase. This transformation process adds value to the inputs, so that buyers are prepared to pay more to the business organization than the cost of resources that it has used up in the production process. This is the basis of a simple model of the organization in its environment, illustrated in Figure 1.1. This transformation process within the organization cannot be seen as a steady state, because external environmental influences have a tendency to be continually shifting, having the effect of undermining the current balance within the system. Just as the central heating thermostat has to constantly react to ensure a balance between its inputs (the energy source) and its outputs (the required amount of heat), so too organizations must constantly ensure that the system continues to transform inputs into higher-value outputs.

Of course, the organizations which form the centre of this transformation process take many

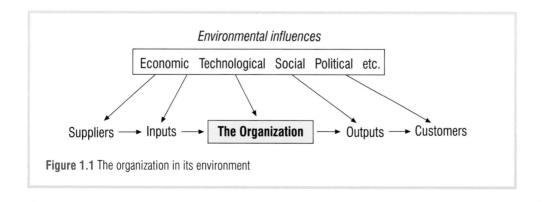

Figure 1.1 The organization in its environment

shapes and forms, from a small sole trader through to a large multinational organization. The nature of the organization greatly affects the way in which it can adapt to its external environment. We will explore the great diversity of organizational types later, in the context of their ability to respond to environmental change.

Throughout this book, we are going to disaggregate a business organization's environment into a number of components. For now, we will introduce three important groups of components, which we will classify under the following headings:

- the macroenvironment
- the microenvironment
- the internal environment.

These are introduced schematically in Figure 1.2.

The external environment comprises all of those forces and events outside the organization that impinge on its activities. Some of these events impinge directly on the firm's activities – these can be described as forming an organization's microenvironment. Other events that are beyond the immediate environment nevertheless affect the organization and can be described as the macroenvironment. As well as looking to the outside world, managers must also take

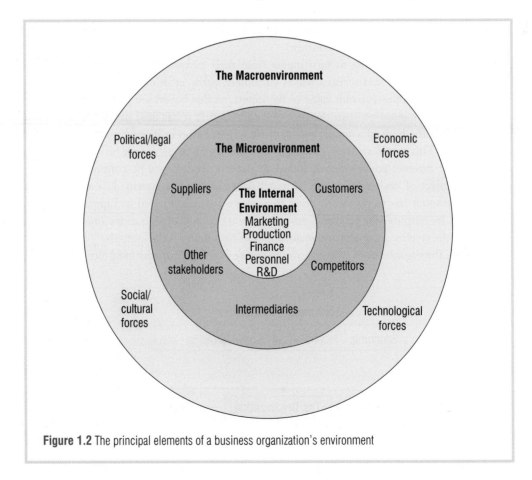

Figure 1.2 The principal elements of a business organization's environment

account of factors within other functions of their own firm. This is referred to as the internal environment.

The macroenvironment comprises a whole set of factors that can indirectly affect an organization's relationship to its markets. The organization may have no direct relationships with legislators as it does with suppliers, yet their actions in passing new legislation may have profound effects on the markets that the organization is able to serve, as well as affecting its production costs. The macroenvironmental factors cover a wide range of nebulous phenomena. They represent general forces and pressures rather than institutions with which the organization relates.

The microenvironmnent, by contrast, is concerned with actual individuals and organizations (such as customers, suppliers and intermediaries) that a company deals with. It may currently deal directly with some of these, while others exist with whom there is currently no direct contact, but could nevertheless influence its policies. An organization's competitors could have a direct effect on its market position and form part of its microenvironment.

1.2 WHY STUDY THE BUSINESS ENVIRONMENT?

History is full of examples of organizations that have failed to understand their operating environment, or simply failed to respond to change in the environment. The result has been a gradual decline in their profitability, and eventually they may cease to exist as a viable business unit. Theodore Levitt called this 'marketing myopia' and cited the example of railway companies that focused their vision on providing railway services, but failed to take account of the development of road transport (Levitt 1960). Consider the following more recent examples.

- The retailer Marks & Spencer assumed that its position was unassailable, but failed to take account of the great improvements in value being offered by its competitors. The result was that many of Marks & Spencer's loyal customers deserted it, leading to a sharp fall in profitability.
- Healthy eating became an important issue in the early twenty-first century. The profits of the fast food company McDonald's fell and it was forced to close branches worldwide as consumers sought more healthy convenience food, before the company belatedly responded to change with healthier menu items.
- The Shell oil company alienated many people with its proposal to dump the *Brent Spar* oil platform at sea, ignoring changing public attitudes towards the ecological environment in favour of its own technical analysis of the merits of dumping at sea.

On the other hand, there have been many spectacular successes where organizations have spotted emerging trends in their business environment, and capitalized on these with new goods and services, or new ways of operating their business, in order to meet the new opportunities presented within the environment. Consider the following examples.

- In the airline market, companies such as Ryanair and easyJet spotted the opportunities represented by government deregulation and offered profitable low-cost 'no frills' air services, often aimed at people who would not previously have flown.
- Many supermarkets and farmers have noted consumers' concern for the purity of the food we eat, and this, combined with rising incomes, has led them to successfully develop ranges of organic foods.

■ Many of the UK's brewers have identified changing social behaviour, with fewer people using pubs as a regular venue primarily for beer drinking, but much greater levels of dining out for social purposes. This has led breweries to increase their profits by reconfiguring their pubs as restaurants.

There is every indication that the pace of change in most organizations' business environment is speeding up and it is therefore increasingly important for organizations to have in place systems for monitoring their environment and, just as importantly, for responding appropriately to such change. There is evidence that successful organizations are not so much those that deliver value to customers today, but those that understand how definitions of value are likely to change in the future. A company may have been very good at creating value through the typewriters that it made, but it may nevertheless have failed to deliver value into the future had it not understood the impact of information technology. In the eyes of customers, the company's traditional products would no longer represent good value when compared with the possibilities presented by the new technologies.

Of course, it is much more difficult to predict the future than to describe the past. A stark indication of the rewards of looking forwards rather than backwards is provided by an analyst who studied stock market performance. If a cumulative investment of $1 had been invested from 1900 on 1 January each year in the stock that had performed best in the *previous* year, and then reinvested the following year, the accumulated value in 2000 would have been just $250. However, if it had been invested each year in the stock which performed best in the *year ahead*, the accumulated value would be over $1 billion. Successful companies have often been those that understand their business environment and have invested in growth areas, while cutting back in areas which are most likely to go into decline. Being first to market when trends are changing can be much more profitable than simply reacting to a market trend. However, predicting future trends can be very difficult and can involve a lot of risk. The aim of this book is to provide frameworks for making well-informed judgements about the likely future state of the business environment, based on a sound analysis of emerging trends.

1.3 THE MACROENVIRONMENT

While the microenvironment comprises individuals and organizations with whom a company interacts, the macroenvironment is more nebulous. It comprises general trends and forces that may not immediately affect the relationships that a company has with its customers, suppliers and intermediaries but, sooner or later, macroenvironmental change will alter the nature of these relationships. As an example, change in the population structure of a country does not immediately affect the way in which a company does business with its customers but, over time, it may affect the numbers of young or elderly people who it is able to do business with.

Most analyses of the macroenvironment divide the environment into a number of areas. The principle headings, which form the basis for chapters of this book, are described below. It must, however, be remembered that the division of the macroenvironment into subject areas does not result in watertight compartments. The macroenvironment is complex and interdependent and these interdependencies will be brought out in later chapters. The subheadings of the sections that follow are also those that are commonly used in macroenvironmental analysis.

THINKING AROUND THE SUBJECT:
BIG MAC, BIG BUSINESS, BIG PROBLEM?

Television images of young people joining protest marches against world capitalism have featured on our television screens recently. But just how hostile is the environment to business organizations? Large, successful companies, it seems, just have to accept that they will never please some people, who hold large corporate organizations responsible for all of the world's problems.

A report by the Future Foundation appears to challenge the idea that young people are becoming more hostile towards big business. According to a 2001 study by the organization, 16 to 24 year olds have more positive feelings towards multinationals than older groups, with the original protest generation, those who came of age in the 1960s, least likely of all to trust multinationals.

In the wake of violent protests surrounding recent World Trade Organization meetings, the research revealed that younger generations are less inclined towards direct action than their parents and grandparents. Nearly half of all 16 to 34 year olds claimed they would not demonstrate if a multinational company had done something wrong. Further confounding the myth of young people wanting to change the world was the statistic that fewer than one in twenty strongly agreed that they 'would not buy the products of a large multinational company that had done something wrong'. A third of teens and twentysomethings agreed to preserving the power of multinational companies and a further one in ten believed that multinationals are 'ultimately for the good of consumers' and should be encouraged to grow. By contrast, two-thirds of their grandparents – those aged 55 and above – claimed they would boycott goods to punish companies they considered guilty of corporate crimes. Even the issue of genetic engineering failed to provoke a strong response from young people, with only four in ten mistrusting the claims of the multinationals, compared to six in ten of their parents and grandparents.

Does this research indicate the ultimate supremacy for big business, where the golden arches of McDonald's and the Nike 'swoosh' are symbols of its global sovereignty? Should they feel safe in the knowledge of this study, or do they still need to be alert to possible trouble in the future? And even if a high proportion of young people support the idea of capitalism and big business, can such firms afford to ignore the vociferous and extreme minority whose direct action and boycotts can do costly and long-lasting harm to a firm's image?

1.3.1 The political environment

Politicians are instrumental in shaping the general nature of the external environment as well as being responsible for passing legislation that affects specific types of organization. The political environment can be one of the less predictable elements in an organization's marketing environment, and businesses need to monitor the changing political environment for a number of reasons.

- At the most general level, the stability of the political system affects the attractiveness of the business environment. Companies are likely to be reluctant to invest in a country with an unstable government, for fear that the law would not protect their investment.
- Governments pass legislation which directly and indirectly affects firms' business opportunities. There are many examples of the direct effects on business organizations, for example

laws giving consumers rights against the seller of faulty goods. At other times, the effects of legislative changes are less direct, as where legislation outlawing anti-competitive practices changes the nature of competition between firms within a market.

■ Government is responsible for formulating policies which can influence the rate of growth in the economy and hence the total amount of spending power. It is also a political decision as to how this spending power should be distributed between different groups of consumers and between the public and private sectors.

■ Governments are responsible for protecting the public interest at large, imposing further constraints on the activities of firms (for example, controls on pollution which may make a manufacturing firm uncompetitive in international markets on account of its increased costs).

■ Increasingly, the political environment affecting business organizations includes supranational organizations which can directly or indirectly affect companies. These include trading blocs (e.g. the EU, ASEAN and NAFTA) and the influence of worldwide intergovernmental organizations whose members seek to implement agreed policy (e.g. the World Trade Organization).

1.3.2 The social and cultural environment

Culture is concerned with a set of shared values which are passed down between generations. It is crucial for businesses to fully appreciate the cultural values of a society, especially where an organization is seeking to do business in a country which is quite different to its own. Attitudes to specific products change through time and at any one time can differ between groups in society.

Even in home markets, business organizations should understand the processes of gradual change in values and attitudes and be prepared to satisfy the changing needs of consumers. Consider the following examples of contemporary social change in Western Europe and the possible responses of businesses.

■ Leisure is becoming a bigger part of many people's lives, and businesses have responded with a wide range of leisure-related goods and services.

■ Attitudes towards the work/life balance change. The nature of work relationships can affect company profits; for example, the formal clothing retailer Moss Bros claimed that the popularity of 'dress-down Friday' and more casual dressing in the workplace had badly affected its profits in 2002, as its customers switched to more casual clothes.

■ The role of women in society is changing as men and women increasingly share expectations in terms of employment and household responsibilities. This is reflected in the observation that women made up 47 per cent of the UK paid workforce in 2001, compared with 37 per cent in 1971. Examples of business responses include cars designed to meet the aspirational needs of career women and ready prepared meals which relieve working women of their traditional role in preparing household meals.

■ Greater life expectancy is leading to an ageing of the population and a shift to an increasingly 'elderly' culture. This is reflected in product design which emphasizes durability rather than fashionability.

■ The growing concern with the environment among many groups in society is reflected in a variety of 'green' consumer products.

In Chapter 3 we look in detail at consumers' values, attitudes and lifestyles, and the processes of gradual change in these. That chapter also explores the issue of 'cultural convergence', referring to an apparent decline in differences between cultures.

1.3.3 The demographic environment

Changes in the size and age structure of the population are critical to many organizations, for predicting both the demand for their products and the availability of personnel required for production. Analysis of the demographic environment raises a number of important issues. Although the total population of most Western countries is stable, their composition is changing. Most countries are experiencing an increase in the proportion of elderly people. Organizations have monitored this growth and responded with the development of residential homes, cruise holidays and financial portfolio management services aimed at meeting the needs of this growing group. At the other end of the age spectrum, the birth rate of most countries is cyclical. The decline in the birth rate in the United Kingdom in the late 1970s initially had a profound effect on those manufacturing and services organizations providing for the very young, such as maternity wards in hospitals and kindergartens. Organizations that monitored the progress of this diminished cohort were prepared for the early 1990s when there were fewer teenagers requiring high schools or wanting to buy music from record shops. Companies that had previously relied on the supply of teenage labour to provide a cheap input to their production process would have been prepared for the downturn in numbers by substituting the quantity of staff with quality and by mechanizing many jobs previously performed by this group.

Other aspects of the demographic environment that organizations need to monitor include the changing geographical distribution of the population (between different regions of the country and between urban and rural areas) and the changing composition of households (especially the growing number of single-person households).

1.3.4 The technological environment

The pace of technological change is becoming increasingly rapid and marketers need to understand how technological developments might affect them in four related business areas.

Figure 1.3 Changing family structures and growing career orientation among women have led many people to seek outside childcare services, rather than caring for children entirely within the family unit. Some cultures may regard childcare as central to family life, and would therefore provide few opportunities for a commercial childcare service. Attitudes in Western countries have changed, and a growing proportion of people would regard it as quite normal to buy in professional help to look after their children. Many service providers, such as this one, have emerged to satisfy this growing market.

1 New technologies can allow new goods and services to be offered to consumers – Internet banking, mobile Internet and new anti-cancer drugs, for example.

2 New technology can allow existing products to be made more cheaply, thereby widening their market through being able to charge lower prices. In this way, more efficient aircraft have allowed new markets for air travel to develop.

3 Technological developments have allowed new methods of distributing goods and services (for example, Amazon.com used the Internet to offer book buyers a new way of browsing and buying books).

4 New opportunities for companies to communicate with their target customers have emerged, with many financial services companies using computer databases to target potential customers and to maintain a dialogue with established customers. The Internet has opened up new distribution opportunities for many services-based companies. The development of mobile Internet services offers new possibilities for targeting buyers at times and places of high readiness to buy.

1.3.5 The ecological environment

Issues affecting our natural ecology have captured the public imagination in recent years. The destruction of tropical rainforests, and the depletion of the ozone layer leading to global warming have serious implications for our quality of life, not necessarily today, but for future generations. Business organizations are often seen as being in conflict with the need to protect the natural ecology. It is very easy for critics of commercial organizations to point to cases where greed and mismanagement have created long-lasting or permanent ecological damage. Have rainforests been destroyed partly by our greed for more hardwood furniture? More locally, is our impatience for getting to our destination quickly the reason why many natural habitats have been lost to new road developments?

Commercial organizations cannot ignore threats to the natural ecology for two principal reasons.

1 There has been growing pressure on natural resources, including those that are used, directly or indirectly, in firms' production processes. This is evidenced by the extinction of species of animals and depletion of hardwood timber resources. As a result of overuse of natural resources, many industry sectors, such as North Sea fishing, have faced severe constraints on their production possibilities.

2 The general public has become increasingly aware of ecological issues and, more importantly, some segments have shown a greater willingness and ability to spend money to alleviate the problems associated with ecologically harmful practices (see Laroche *et al.* 2003).

We will return to issues of the ecological environment in Chapter 9.

1.3.6 The economic environment

Businesses need to keep an eye on indications of a nation's prosperity. There are many indicators of a nation's economic health, of which two of the most common are measures of gross domestic product (GDP) and household disposable income. Many of these indicators tend to follow cyclical patterns related to a general economic cycle of expansion followed by contraction.

Throughout the economic cycle, the consumption of most goods and services tends to increase during the boom period and to decline during recessionary periods. The difficulty in forecasting the level of demand for a firm's products is therefore often quite closely linked to the difficulty of forecasting future economic prosperity. This difficulty is compounded by the problem of understanding the relationship between economic factors and the state of demand – most goods and services are positively related to total available income, but some, such as bus services and insolvency practitioners, are negatively related. Furthermore, while aggregate changes in spending power may indicate a likely increase for goods and services in general, the actual distribution of spending power among the population will influence the pattern of demand for specific products. In addition to measurable economic prosperity, the level of perceived wealth and confidence in the future can be an important determinant of demand for some high-value goods and services.

THINKING AROUND THE SUBJECT:
'NEW MAN' FOR A 'NEW ECONOMY'?

In the late 1990s it became fashionable to talk about a 'new economy'. The environment of business organizations was to be changed for ever in a brave new world in which 'new' Britain was ruled by 'New' Labour, inhabited by 'new' man, who works in the 'new' economy and learns about the world through 'new' media. Electronic commerce would allow for almost infinite communication possibilities, breaking down international trade and cultural barriers in the process. Monopolies would be broken by the powerful forces of global competition facilitated by the Internet, and our neighbours would become not the person who lives next door, but a person anywhere in cyberspace who shares our interests and lifestyle. As the world entered the new millennium, it seemed that the business environment would never be the same again, or at least that is what many people thought.

Of course, many 'big ideas' have a habit of imploding and we need to ask whether any of the promises of the 'new world' have been delivered, or are ever likely to be. The idea that the 'new economy' had banished the economic cycle of prosperity and recession appeared to be dubious as the United States economy entered recession in 2001 after a prolonged period of expansion. Many questioned the myth of 'new man' as something which was more talked about in glossy magazines than experienced in everyday life.

Many of the 'new' world phenomena which helped to define the new economy soon began to lose their sparkle, leaving observers wondering whether there really was anything new. As an example, many commentators were excited by the prospects of new media advertising, and justified this by pointing to Procter & Gamble's decision to direct 80 per cent of its promotion budget to new media. But old media has a habit of fighting back hard, as witnessed by the huge amount of advertising by the new media owners themselves in traditional newspapers and on television channels.

It soon became recognized that the 'new' economy is very dependent upon the 'old' economy. Electronic communication may be fine in theory as a means of improving global competition, but somebody still has to manufacture goods and deliver them, invariably using 'old economy' methods.

Had the whole structure of the business environment changed, or was it simply transient details which had caused such excitement? Should we be wary of any proclamations of 'new' ways of doing business, or do we ignore changes in the business environment at our peril?

An analysis of the economic environment will also indicate the level of competitor activity – an oversupply of products in a market sector normally results in a downward pressure on prices and profitability. Competition for resources could also affect the production costs of an organization, which in turn will affect its production possibilities and pricing decisions. Rising unemployment may put downward pressure on wage rates, favouring companies that offer a labour-intensive service.

1.4 THE MICROENVIRONMENT

The microenvironment of an organization can best be understood as comprising all those other organizations and individuals who directly or indirectly affect the activities of the organization. The microenvironment comprises actual people and organizations. The company may be dealing with these organizations today, or may potentially deal with them in the future. It may have no intention of dealing with other companies in its microenvironment (such as competitors), but these can nevertheless have a major impact on the activities of an organization. The following key groups can be identified in most companies' microenvironments.

1.4.1 Customers

Customers are a crucial part of an organization's microenvironment. Quite simply, in a competitive environment, no customers means no business. An organization should be concerned about the changing requirements of its customers and should keep in touch with these changing needs by using an appropriate information gathering system. In an ideal world, an organization should know its customers so well that it is able to predict what they will require next, rather than wait until it is possibly too late and then follow.

But we need to think beyond this simplistic model of customers expressing their preferences and businesses then satisfying them. First, the people who buy a company's products are not necessarily the same as those who consume them. Any good book on consumer behaviour will describe a range of influencers, users, deciders and 'gatekeepers' who have a bearing on whether a company's product is bought. Second, does the customer always know what is best for them, and should organizations think wider about their customers' long-term interests? There have been many examples of situations where customers' long-term interests have been neglected by companies, including the following.

- In 2002, the Consumers Association launched a campaign against financial services companies which, it claimed, had mis-sold endowment policies to individuals. A salesperson may have been tempted by a high level of commission to sell a policy which the customer did not understand and that clearly was not in their best interest (for example, a policy which would only pay out some time after the customer's mortgage was due to be paid off).
- Manufacturers of baby milk that failed to make mothers aware of the claimed long-term health benefits of using breast milk rather than manufactured milk products.
- Car manufacturers that add expensive music systems to cars as standard equipment but relegate vital safety equipment such as passenger airbags to the status of optional extras.

In each of these cases, most people might agree that, objectively, buyers are being persuaded to make a choice against their own long-term self-interest. Consumer groups have an increasing tendency to highlight mis-selling of products which are against the best long-term interests of customers, and the results of such actions range from bad publicity to expensive product recalls and litigation. We will return to the issue of ethical behaviour in Chapter 9.

1.4.2 Suppliers

Suppliers provide an organization with goods and services that are transformed by the organization into value-added products for customers. Very often, suppliers are crucial to an organization's marketing success. This is particularly true where factors of production are in short supply and the main constraint on an organization selling more of its product is the shortage of production resources. For example, in 2004, world steel prices rose following an increase in demand relative to the available capacity. Some businesses in the engineering sector were forced to reduce their production because of difficulties in obtaining supplies of steel. For companies operating in highly competitive markets where differentiation between products is minimal, obtaining supplies at the best possible price may be vital in order to be able to pass on cost savings in the form of lower prices charged to customers. Where reliability of delivery to customers is crucial, unreliable suppliers may thwart a manufacturer's marketing efforts.

There is an argument that companies should act in a socially responsible way to their suppliers. Does a company favour local companies rather than possibly lower-priced overseas producers? (For example, Marks & Spencer prided itself on sourcing nearly all of its supplies through long-standing supply arrangements with a number of UK manufacturers, so many suppliers felt let down when it started placing a high proportion of its orders with lower-cost overseas producers.) Does it unfairly use its dominant market power over small suppliers (an accusation that has been made against UK supermarkets for their treatment of their small farm suppliers)? Does it divide its orders between a large number of small suppliers, or place the bulk of its custom with a small handful of preferred suppliers? Does it favour new businesses or businesses representing minority interests when it places its orders?

Taking into account the needs of suppliers is a combination of shrewd business sense and good ethical practice. In business-to-business marketing, one company's supplier is likely to be another company's customer, and it is important to understand how suppliers, manufacturers and intermediaries work together to create value. The idea of a value chain is introduced later in this chapter.

1.4.3 Intermediaries

These often provide a valuable link between an organization and its customers. Large-scale manufacturing firms usually find it difficult to deal with each one of their final customers individually, so they choose instead to sell their products through intermediaries. The advantages of using intermediaries are discussed below. In some business sectors, access to effective intermediaries can be crucial for marketing success. For example, food manufacturers who do not get shelf space in the major supermarkets may find it difficult to achieve large volume sales.

Channels of distribution comprise all those people and organizations involved in the process of transferring title to a product from the producer to the consumer. Sometimes, products will be transferred directly from producer to final consumer – a factory selling specialized kitchen units direct to the public would fit into this category. Alternatively, the producer could sell its output through retailers or, if these are considered too numerous for the manufacturer to handle, it could deal with a wholesaler that in turn would sell to the retailer. More than one wholesaler could be involved in the process.

Intermediaries may need reassurance about the company's capabilities as a supplier that is capable of working with intermediaries to supply goods and services in a reliable and ethical manner. Many companies have suffered because they failed to take adequate account of the needs of their intermediaries (for example, Body Shop and McDonald's have faced protests from their franchisees where they felt threatened by a marketing strategy which was perceived as being against their own interests).

1.4.4 Competitors

In highly competitive markets, keeping an eye on competitors and trying to understand their likely next moves can be crucial. Think of the manoeuvring and out-manoeuvring which appears to take place between competitors in such highly competitive sectors as soft drinks,

THINKING AROUND THE SUBJECT: COMPETITION FOR THE WRITTEN WORD?

Putting the spoken word into print has seen a quickening pace in the technologies available that can do the job speedily and accurately. Typewriter manufacturers didn't last for long after the appearance of mass market computers, which provided fierce competition because they were able to do most of the functions of a typewriter and often at lower cost. Although computers got a lot quicker, there was still the time-consuming task of inputting information to a computer. In the 1990s, a number of new online services appeared that offered to take customers' speech and turn it into printed text. These initially set out to compete with conventional typing bureaux and secretarial support services. But how long would this new kind of online typing service last before it too was overtaken by changes in the competitive environment brought about by new technology?

A UK company called Speech Machines (www.speechmachines.co.uk) uses computers to receive dictation over the telephone or as voice messages sent through the Internet by email. The dictation is transcribed automatically by computer with a claimed 95 per cent accuracy. Specially written software manages the incoming dictation and automatically sends the transcribed document to one of the contract typists the company uses for checking and correction of the final manuscript. It is then sent back to the customer via the Internet. The service has found a useful niche in the USA with the legal and medical professions, offering a speedy and efficient alternative to employing a secretary in-house.

Within 10 years of creation, the company was facing a new competitive threat from increasingly reliable, user-friendly and inexpensive voice recognition systems. Some, such as IBM's ViaVoice program, were selling below £100 and were achieving very high levels of reliability. The small business owners that had previously sent typing through the Internet were in danger of being lost to these new self-service technologies. The company had to move on, and in 2001 was acquired by the American company MedQuist. How could the company overcome the technological threat to its core service? Could it reposition itself to provide a broader range of services to meet its customers' requirements?

budget airlines and mobile phones. But who are a company's competitors? *Direct* competitors are generally similar in form and satisfy customers' needs in a similar way. *Indirect* competitors may appear different in form, but satisfy a fundamentally similar need. It is the indirect competitors that are most difficult to identify and to understand. What is a competitor for a cinema? Is it another cinema? A home rental movie? Or some completely different form of leisure activity which satisfies similar underlying needs?

1.4.5 Government

The demands of government agencies often take precedence over the needs of a company's customers. Government has a number of roles to play as stakeholder in commercial organizations.

■ Commercial organizations provide governments with taxation revenue, so a healthy business sector is in the interests of government.

■ Government is increasingly expecting business organizations to take over many responsibilities from the public sector, for example with regard to the payment of sickness and maternity benefits to employees.

■ It is through business organizations that governments achieve many of their economic and social objectives, for example with respect to regional economic development and skills training.

As a regulator which impacts on many aspects of business activity, companies often go to great lengths in seeking favourable responses from such agencies. In the case of many UK private-sector utility providers, promotional effort is often aimed more at regulatory bodies than final consumers. In the case of the water industry, promoting greater use of water to final consumers is unlikely to have any significant impact on a water utility company, but influencing the disposition of the Office of Water Regulation, which sets price limits and service standards, can have a major impact.

1.4.6 The financial community

This includes financial institutions that have supported, are currently supporting or may support the organization in the future. Shareholders – both private and institutional – form an important element of this community and must be reassured that the organization is going to achieve its stated objectives. Many market expansion plans have failed because the company did not adequately consider the needs and expectations of potential investors.

1.4.7 Local communities

Society at large has rising expectations of organizations and market-led companies often try to be seen as a 'good neighbour' in their local communities. Such companies can enhance their image through the use of charitable contributions, sponsorship of local events and being seen to support the local environment. Again, this may be interpreted either as part of a firm's genuine concern for its local community, or as a more cynical and pragmatic attempt to buy favour where its own interests are at stake. If a fast-food restaurant installs improved filters on its extractor fans, is it doing it to genuinely improve the lives of local residents, or merely in an attempt to forestall prohibition action taken by the local authority?

1.4.8 Pressure groups

Members of pressure groups may never have been customers of a company and are never likely to be. Yet a pressure group can detract seriously from the image that the company has worked hard to develop. Many businesses have learnt to their cost that they cannot ignore pressure groups. It seems that, in Britain, fewer people may be voting in elections but this is more than offset by a greater willingness of people to make their voice heard through pressure groups.

1.5 THE INTERNAL ENVIRONMENT

We must remember that the structure and politics of an organization affect the manner in which it responds to environmental change. We are all familiar with lumbering giants of companies which, like a supertanker, have ploughed ahead on a seemingly predetermined course and had difficulty in changing direction. During the late 1990s such well-respected companies as Sainsbury's and Marks & Spencer were accused of having internal structures and processes which were too rigid to cope with a changing external environment. Simply having a strong marketing department is not necessarily the best way of ensuring adaptation to change. Such companies may in fact create internal tensions which make them less effective at responding to changing consumer needs than where marketing responsibilities in their widest sense are spread throughout the organization.

The internal culture of an organization can greatly affect the way it responds to organizational change. In the case of Sainsbury's, its culture was probably too much based on hierarchy and tradition, which can be a weakness in a rapidly changing external environment. Organizational culture concerns the social and behavioural manifestation of a whole set of values which are shared by members of the organization. Cultural values can be shared in a

---

THINKING AROUND THE SUBJECT:
BOYCOTTS MAY COST PROTESTORS VERY LITTLE, BUT THEY CAUSE BIG LOSSES FOR COMPANIES

They may never buy a litre of petrol, but protesters have the power to change the policies of oil company giants. Pressure groups have criticized the Esso company (Exxon Mobil) for opposing government policies that would encourage renewable energy and reduce dependency on fossil fuels. The company has been accused of putting its shareholders' interests before the interests of ecological sustainability.

A pressure group (www.stopesso.com) has sought to change the behaviour of Esso through boycotts and demonstrations, among other things. In 2003, the Stop Esso campaign reached new heights when Greenpeace activists abseiled on to the roof of the company's UK headquarters in Surrey, shutting it down in protest against the firm's environmental policies. About 100 Esso garages were closed for a few hours as activists dressed as tigers chained themselves to the pumps.

Other oil companies have taken the hint and responded with initiatives such as support for research on hydrogen fuel cells. How much pressure would it take before Esso found the bad publicity and boycotts eating into its profits? Or should it stick to its principles and offer its customers what a majority appear to want most – the cheapest possible oil to support their chosen lifestyles?

number of ways, including: the way work is organized and experienced; how authority is exercised and delegated; how people are rewarded, organized and controlled; and the roles and expectations of staff and managers.

For many organizations, employees are the biggest item of cost and potentially the biggest cause of delay in responding to environmental change. Having the right staff in the right place at the right time can demand a lot of flexibility on the part of employees. Many organizations have sought to improve the effectiveness of their employees through a programme of 'internal marketing'. Internal marketing came to prominence during the 1990s and describes the application of marketing techniques to audiences within the organization. A central feature of internal marketing is to develop values in employees which are aligned with organizational values. That way, if change is required, employees are more likely to share in the threats and opportunities which environmental change presents, and to change their behaviour more enthusiastically.

Every organization can be considered to comprise an internal marketplace where diverse groups of employees engage in exchanges between each other. These internal exchanges include relationships between front-line staff and the backroom staff, managers and the front-line staff, managers and the backroom staff and, for large organizations, between the head office and each branch. It is not uncommon to find organizations where relationships between these different groups are characterized by distrust, lack of communication and even hostility, making it difficult for the organization to respond to environmental change in a rapid and co-ordinated manner. In Chapter 8 we will look in more detail at the effects of internal management structure on an organization's ability to respond to external environmental change.

1.6 CONTEXTUAL ISSUES IN A DYNAMIC ENVIRONMENT

So far in this introductory chapter, we have broken the business environment down into a number of component parts. These are the basic building blocks that we will come back to throughout the book. However, the key to analysing the business environment is to see the links between these component parts. A number of these linkages have already been mentioned, for example how the political environment affects the nature of the economic environment that the business faces. Within the microenvironment, members of the local community may also be customers of an organization. Community groups may influence government agencies, which in turn affect the activities of business organizations.

As well as taking a snapshot of the interdependency between elements of the business environment, we also need to consider their dynamic interaction. Successful business organizations have spotted trends, especially the interaction between trends in the different environments. For example, one trend in the social environment has been an increasing fear of crime, especially against children. Another trend in the technological environment has been the falling cost and increasing sophistication of mobile telephony. By putting these two trends together, businesses have developed novel products, for example mobile phones that can track children and automatically send warning messages if the child strays beyond a predetermined zone.

We have introduced the main levels of the business environment in a manner which provides a foundation for the structure of this book. We will begin by looking at the macroenvironment before moving on to the micro- and internal environments. But the point cannot be stressed enough that the different elements of an organization's environment are very much interrelated and, in order to stress this interrelatedness, we will now briefly examine some common themes which run through all levels of the environment. We will focus on information and communication as two crucial elements which run through an organization's environment. We will then consider some simple frameworks that integrate the elements of the business environment, beginning with identification of the members of an organization's 'environmental set'. We will then integrate these within the concept of a 'value chain'. and move on to take a dynamic look at these relationships and the emergence of power within them.

1.6.1 The information environment

Let us first consider the subject of the information environment. Information represents a bridge between the organization and its environment and is the means by which a picture of the changing environment is built up within the organization. Knowledge is one of the greatest assets of most organizations and its contribution to sustainable competitive advantage has been noted by many. In 1991, Ikujiro Nonaka began an article in the *Harvard Business Review* with a simple statement: 'In an economy where the only certainty is uncertainty, the one sure source of lasting competitive advantage is knowledge' (Nonaka 1991). A firm's knowledge base is likely to include, among other things, an understanding of the precise needs of customers; how those needs are likely to change over time; how those needs are satisfied in terms of efficient and effective production systems and an understanding of competitors' activities.

Information about the current state of the environment is used as a starting point for planning future strategy, based on assumptions about how the environment will change. It is also vital to monitor the implementation of an organization's corporate plans and to note the cause of any deviation from plan, and to identify whether these are caused by internal or external environmental factors. Information allows management to improve its strategic planning, tactical implementation of programmes, and its monitoring and control. In turbulent environments, having access to timely and relevant information can give a firm a competitive advantage. This can be manifested, for example, in the ability to spot turning points in the business cycle ahead of competitors; to respond more rapidly to customers' changing preferences; and to adapt manufacturing schedules more closely to demand patterns, thereby avoiding a build-up of stocks.

Information collection, processing, transmission and storage technologies are continually improving, as witnessed by the development of electronic point of sale (EPOS) systems. These have enabled organizations to greatly enhance the quality of the information they have about their operating environment. However, information is becoming more accessible, not just to one particular organization, but also to its competitors. Attention is therefore moving away from how information is collected to who is best able to make use of the information.

Large organizations operating in complex and turbulent environments often use information to build models of their environment, or at least sub-components of it. Some of these can be quite general, as in the case of the models of the national economy which many large companies have developed. From a general model of the economy a firm can predict how a specific item of government policy (for example, increasing the rate of Value Added Tax on luxury goods) will impact directly and indirectly on sales of its own products.

THINKING AROUND THE SUBJECT:
SPOTTING DISSENT THROUGH THE INTERNET

The Internet is not just a tool that organizations can use to send messages to customers, suppliers and intermediaries – it is increasingly being used by organizations to monitor their business environment. Monitoring chat groups and critical websites has become an important activity for organizations and their public relations agencies, anxious to spot any general shifts in attitudes and specific comments which may harm the organization. News now crosses geographical frontiers quicker than a blink of the eye and corporate reputations can be savaged as disgruntled customers and shareholders swap comments on the World Wide Web. Thorns in the side of PR people include the McSpotlight site (www.mcspotlight.org) which carries information critical of McDonald's restaurants, and the Boycott Shell site (www.essential.org/action/shell). Such sites can be created without the companies' knowledge if they are not monitoring, and contributing to, the forums and chat rooms. And it can end up as a damaging mix of rumour and untruths.

PR agencies that have the technical expertise have set up monitoring services. One PR consultancy, Edelman, monitors the Internet, checking on 33,000 user groups and bulletin boards, and regularly preparing web pages for its clients in anticipation of crises. These are then 'hidden' on the website, ready to be activated if needed.

Businesses have had to face up to the new realities of the Internet. Response times need to be immediate, with no specific deadlines that are typical of conventional published media. But, at the same time, activists are changing the nature of the game they have to deal with. When environmental activists staged a sit-in at Shell's London offices in 1999, the group broadcast the protest live to the Internet and emailed the press using a digital camera, laptop computer and mobile phone.

Quite aside from the battle of information technology is the fundamental question: why did a company allow itself to get into the position of exposing itself to criticism? Could this not have been foreseen? If there is little for people to campaign about, the dissident websites would probably lose much of their support.

We look in more detail at the ways in which information technology influences firms' business environment in Chapter 4, and explore the implications of information for firms' responses to environmental change in Chapter 13.

1.6.2 The communication environment

Communications bring together elements within a firm's environmental set. With no communication, there is no possibility for trading to take place. Although we talk today about a communications 'revolution', businesses in previous centuries have faced the challenge of rapid developments in communication. Consider the following historic developments in communications and their impacts on businesses.

- The development of canals and railways during the industrialization of nineteenth-century England allowed manufacturers to communicate with customers who had previously been impossible or very expensive to reach. Manufacturers used improved communications to exploit emerging mass-production techniques which allowed them to compete in distant markets with relatively low-priced mass-produced goods.

■ The development of steamships allowed companies to communicate with distant parts of the world, opening up new markets for their finished products and allowing new sources of supply of raw materials. British manufacturers of consumer goods exploited new markets in parts of the Empire served by the new shipping lines.

■ The absence of a reliable postal and telephone system has often been cited as a reason for the failure of businesses to grow in less developed parts of the world.

Today, the Internet has emerged as a versatile tool in an organization's relationship with its business environment, combining a communication function with a distribution function. The ability of companies to rapidly exchange information with their suppliers and intermediaries has allowed for the development of increasingly efficient supply chains, initially using EDI (Electronic Data Interface) systems but more recently using Internet, intranet and extranet-based systems. Without efficient communication systems, attempts to introduce just-in-time production systems and rapid customer response are likely to be impeded.

The Internet has an increasing role in allowing companies to communicate with their final consumers using email and SMS text messaging. Some companies have used the Internet to cut out intermediaries altogether through a process of 'disintermediation', although in reality the Internet has allowed a new generation of 'information intermediary' (e.g. Expedia.com and esure.com) to appear in large numbers. As a promotional medium, a great strength of the Internet is to target promotional messages which are directly relevant to the user, so, for example, a train operator's website may give information relating to a specific journey that the user had enquired about. Websites are increasingly being enabled to allow immediate fulfilment of a request, such as confirmation of a hotel booking or reservation of a plane ticket. The Internet and 3G mobile phones have narrowed the gap between a potential buyer receiving a message and being able to act upon it.

1.6.3 The environmental set of an organization

A firm's microenvironment is distinguished from its macroenvironment by comprising actual individuals and organizations with whom the firm does business, or at least may potentially do business. The people and organizations within a particular company's business environment that are of particular relevance to it are sometimes referred to as its environmental set. An example of an environmental set for a car manufacturer is shown in Figure 1.4.

The relationship between set members is likely to be complex and constantly changing. Change can take a number of forms, including:

■ shifts in the balance of power between members of the environment (e.g. retailers becoming more dominant relative to manufacturers)

■ the emergence of new groups of potential customers or suppliers

■ fringe pressure groups may come to represent mainstream opinions, in response to changes in social attitudes.

Understanding the relationship between members of an organization's environmental set is a crucial part of environmental analysis which we will consider further below.

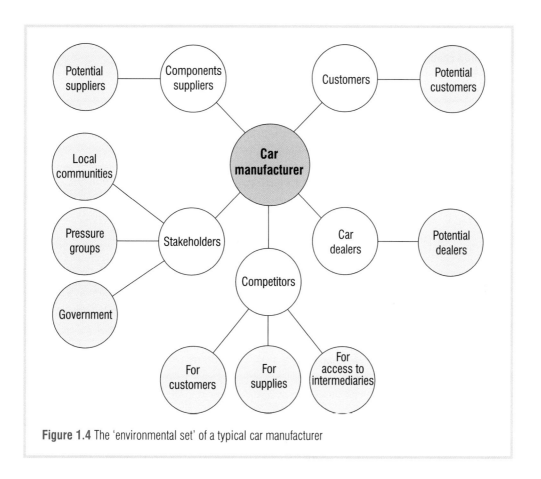

Figure 1.4 The 'environmental set' of a typical car manufacturer

1.6.4 Value chains

It was noted at the beginning of this chapter that the purpose of organizations is to transform inputs bought from suppliers into outputs sold to customers. In carrying out such a transformation, organizations add value to resources. In fact, the buyer of one firm's output may be another firm that treats the products purchased as inputs to its own production process. It in turn will add value to the resources and sell on its outputs to customers. This process can continue as goods and services pass though several organizations, gaining added value as they change hands. This is the basis of a value chain.

An illustration of the principles of a value chain can be made by considering the value-added transformation processes that occur in the process of making ice cream available to consumers. Figure 1.5 shows who may be involved in the value-adding process and the value that is added at each stage.

The value of the raw milk contained in a block of ice cream may be no more than a few pennies, but the final product may be sold for over £1. Customers are happy to pay £1 for a few pennies' worth of milk because it is transformed into a product that they value and it is made available at a time and place where they want it. In fact, on a hot sunny day at the beach, many buyers would be prepared to pay even more to a vendor that brings cold ice cream to

Value chain member	Functions performed
Farmer	Produces a basic commodity product – milk
Milk merchant	Adds value to the milk by arranging for it to be collected from the farm, checked for purity and made available to milk processors
Ice cream manufacturer	By processing the milk and adding other ingredients, turns raw milk into ice cream. Through promotion, creates a brand image
Wholesaler	Buys bulk stocks of ice cream and stores in warehouses close to customers
Retailer	Provides a facility for customers to buy ice cream at a place and a time that is convenient to them rather than the manufacturer

Figure 1.5 A value chain for ice cream

them. Value – as defined by customers – has been added at each stage of the transformation process.

Who should be in the value chain? The ice cream manufacturer might decide that it can add value at the preceding and subsequent stages better than other people are capable of doing. It may, for example, decide to operate its own farms and produce its own milk, or sell its ice cream direct to the public. The crucial question to be asked is whether the company can add value more cost-effectively than other suppliers and intermediaries. In a value chain, it is only value in the eyes of customers that matters. If high value is attached to having ice cream easily available, then distributing it through a limited number of company-owned shops will not add much value to the product.

The process of expanding a firm's activities through the value chain is often referred to as vertical integration where ownership is established. Backward vertical integration occurs where a manufacturer buys back into its suppliers. Forward vertical integration occurs where it buys into its outlets. Many firms expand in both directions.

With service being used as an increasingly important basis for differentiation between competing products, it is important that an organization looks not only outward at the value chain, but also inward at its own service–profit chain. The concept of the service–profit chain is based on the idea that employee satisfaction and productivity feeds into customer satisfaction and loyalty, thereby improving profitability. Profitability in turn can help create a more productive and satisfying work environment (see Figure 1.6).

The Internet has led to the development of a modified form of 'virtual value chain' to try to

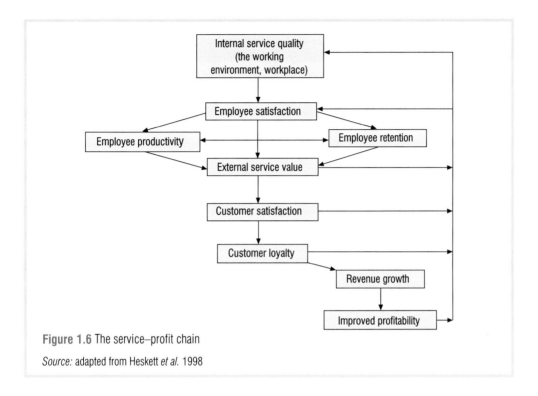

Figure 1.6 The service–profit chain

Source: adapted from Heskett *et al.* 1998

explain how information-based industries operate a value chain which is distinct from traditional models based on raw materials, production and distribution. While the traditional value chain may be applicable to industries involved in the movement of goods through a tangible, physical marketplace, other information-based industries (such as financial services) operate in a market 'space'. It has been argued that, for these companies, the value chain consists of content, infrastructure and context. The content is what is being offered, the infrastructure is what exists to enable transactions and the context is how the goods are offered.

1.6.5 The development of close business relationships

The discussion of value chains indicated that members of an organization's business environment are often being brought closer together to act co-operatively rather than in confrontation with each other. There is nothing new in the way that firms have sought to develop ongoing relationships with their customers and suppliers. In simple economies where production of goods and services took place on a small scale, it was possible for the owners of businesses to know each customer personally and to come to understand their individual characteristics. They could therefore adapt their product offer to the needs of individuals on the basis of knowledge gained during previous transactions, and could suggest appropriate new product offers. They would also be able to form an opinion about customers' creditworthiness. Networks of relationships between buyers and sellers are still the norm in many Far Eastern countries and many Western exporters have found it difficult to break into these long-standing, closed networks.

With the growth in size of Western organizations, the personal contact that an organization can have with its customers, suppliers and intermediaries has been diluted. Instead of being able to reassure customers on the basis of close relationships, organizations in many cases have sought to provide this reassurance through the development of strong brands. Recent resurgence of interest in close buyer–seller relationships has occurred for a number of reasons.

1 In increasingly competitive markets, good products alone are insufficient to differentiate an organization's products from those of its competitors. For example, in the car sector, manufacturers traditionally differentiated their cars on the basis of superior design features such as styling, speed and reliability. Once most companies had reached a common standard of design, attention switched to differentiation through superior added-service facilities, such as warranties and finance. Once these service standards became the norm for the sector, many car manufacturers sought to differentiate their cars on the basis of superior relationships. Therefore, most major car manufacturers now offer customers complete packages which keep a car financed, insured, maintained and renewed after a specified period. Instead of a three-yearly one-off purchase of a new car, many customers enter an ongoing relationship with a car manufacturer and its dealers which gives the customer the support they need to keep their car on the road and to have it renewed when this falls due (see Figure 1.7).

2 Developments in information technology have had dramatic effects in developing close buyer–seller relationships. The development of powerful user-friendly databases has allowed organizations to recreate in a computer what the individual small business owner knew in his or her head. Large businesses are therefore now able to tell very quickly the status of a particular customer, for example their previous ordering pattern, product preferences and profitability. Developments in information technology have also allowed companies to enter individual dialogues with their customers through direct mail and increasingly through electronic means. Increased production flexibility based on improved technology allows many manufacturers and service organizations to design unique products that meet the needs of individual customers, rather than broad groups of customers.

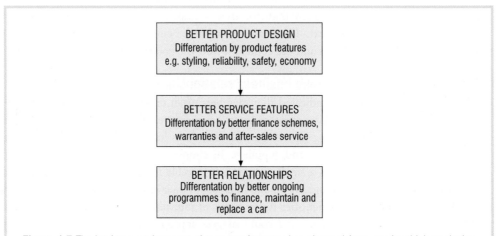

Figure 1.7 The business environment of car manufacturers has changed from one in which marketing activities emphasise differentiation through tangible desing features, to one where differentiation is based on the quality of ongoing buyer–seller relationships.

3 Just-in-time (JIT) production methods have become very widespread in Western countries, thanks to the lead given by Japanese manufacturing companies. It often makes sense for a manufacturer to keep its holdings of component parts down to an absolute minimum. This way, it ties up less capital, needs less storage space and suffers less risk of stocks becoming obsolete. Instead of keeping large stocks of components 'just in case' they are needed, manufacturers arrange for them to be delivered 'just in time' for them to be used in their production process. It is not uncommon to find car manufacturers receiving batches of components which, within an hour, are incorporated into a car. JIT systems demand a lot of cooperation between supplier and customer, which cannot easily be achieved if each transaction is to be individually bargained. Some form of ongoing relationship between the two is essential.

Movement towards integrating the different stages of a value chain has occurred in a number of ways. In its most simple form, integration can occur through agreement over operational matters – standardization of pallet sizes and packaging methods to suit the needs of manufacturer, wholesaler and retailer is one example. More recently, bar coding of products has allowed all intermediaries to process goods by a common standard much more efficiently. Sometimes, the agreement takes the form of a voluntary buying chain set up to act as a wholesaler on behalf of a group of retailers; Londis and Nisa are examples. Companies have also sought to develop closer relationships by: recording information about buyers' preferences, which allows their needs to be satisfied more effectively on future occasions; offering incentives to reward loyalty; and undertaking new product research with key customers.

THINKING AROUND THE SUBJECT: LOYALTY TO A MOTORWAY?

Getting closer to customers has been a key challenge for many businesses in recent years, and one outcome of this process should be customers who are loyal to a company. But just because customers repeatedly come back to a company does not necessarily mean that they have a loyal relationship with that company. This point was made, tongue-in-cheek, during the continuing war of words between British Airways and Virgin Atlantic Airways. The latter had objected to BA's use of the advertising slogan 'The world's favourite airline'. Statistically, it was true that more passengers travelled internationally with British Airways than with any other airline, but surveys of airline users had consistently put Virgin ahead of BA in terms of perceived quality of service. Virgin's Richard Branson claimed that on BA's logic, the M25, London's notorious orbital motorway, could be described as the world's favourite motorway. Despite coming back to the motorway day after day, few motorists could claim to be loyal to it – they simply have no other choice.

The spat between BA and Virgin serves to underline the point that close buyer–seller relationships are about more than mere repetitious buying. True loyalty involves customers becoming enthusiastic advocates of a company.

1.6.6 Power in the environmental set

All the members of an organization's environmental set are not equal in terms of their power. Some are likely to have great power over the others and, moreover, it is quite likely that shifts in power between members of the set will occur over time. In many markets, a small number of suppliers may dominate and exert power over a large number of fragmented buyers. In the UK, the growing strength of grocery retailers has put them at the focal point of a value chain. By building up their own strong brands, large retailers are increasingly able to exert pressure on manufacturers in terms of product specification, price and the level of promotional support to be given to the retailer. It is estimated that, in Britain, the four largest grocery retailers may account for over half of the sales of a typical manufacturer of fast-moving consumer goods. The dependency is not reciprocated, with very few retailers relying on one single supplier for more than 1 per cent of their supplies. Most countries have legislation which prevents one company having dominant power in a market, unless there are public interest benefits.

There is plenty of evidence of the growing power of retailers. Following the Barclay brothers' acquisition of the Littlewoods retail chain from the Moores family in 2002, the 189-shop chain wrote to its suppliers, informing them of the outcome of an 'initial trading review' which demanded a 2 per cent price cut from all suppliers to the Littlewoods retail chain, or lose all future orders (Fletcher 2002a). Similarly, the new owner of the Arcadia fashion chain imposed a retrospective 1.25 per cent price cut on suppliers to the high-street group that owns Top Shop and Dorothy Perkins. With an estimated £60 million worth of outstanding invoices, the power of the retailer to make a unilateral decision and to apply the discount retrospectively netted it a 'windfall' in the region of £8 million (Fletcher 2002b).

In Chapter 10 we review market structure and the lengths that regulatory authorities go to in order to prevent distortion of markets caused by power imbalances.

In Chapter 2, we discuss the power of government. In some industries in some countries, the need for a licence (or in some cases the need to pay a bribe to a government official) can make government the most dominant element in a firm's environmental set.

1.6.7 Shared codes of conduct

All systems need rules if they are to operate efficiently and effectively. This can be observed in any marketplace, whether it is a fruit and vegetable market or a stock market. The market only functions because all participants conduct their actions according to a shared set of rules. These rules can either be informal or based on formal regulation. In many less developed economies, the dominant basis for rules is focused on embedded codes of trust. Increasingly in Western societies, commercial relationships are governed by formality and regulation. Of course, informal rules in a market may not always be in consumers' best interests, as sometimes happens when suppliers have formal or informal understandings about how they can restrict the level of competition between themselves.

In Western societies there is increasing concern that relationships between members of the environmental set should be conducted in an ethical manner. Ethics is essentially about the definition of what is right and wrong. However, a difficulty occurs in trying to agree just what is right and wrong. No two people have precisely the same opinion, so some critics would argue that ethical considerations are of little interest to business. It can also be difficult to dis-

> **THINKING AROUND THE SUBJECT:**
> **AN ETHICAL CUP OF COFFEE?**
>
> The Starbucks Coffee Company has developed a distinctive position in the market that it serves. Part of the chain's success is attributed to sharing the values of the company with its employees through its mission statement. This is operationalized through a series of guiding principles which seek to balance in the minds of employees (or 'partners') the mutually supportive aims of achieving profits, satisfying customers, and serving the interests of the wider communities in which the company operates. Starbucks has developed a loyal following of customers for whom the atmosphere of its stores warrants a premium price. The company is conscious of critics who point to low prices paid to producers, and addresses this by offering 'Fairtrade' certified coffee. Fairtrade seeks to improve the lives of coffee growers by ensuring that they receive a fair price for their harvest. For many Western consumers, this ethical positioning is a basis for differentiating Starbucks from other coffee shops.

tinguish between ethics and legality, for example it may not yet be strictly illegal to exploit the gullibility of children in advertisements, but it may nevertheless be unethical.

Today, ethical considerations are present in many business decisions. An example of a current issue is whether soft drinks and confectionery manufacturers should sponsor school activities – is it ethical to expose children to subconscious positive messages about junk food at a time of increasing obesity?

Culture has a great effect in defining ethics, and what is considered unethical in one society may be considered perfectly acceptable in another.

With expanding media availability and an increasingly intelligent audience, it is becoming easier to expose examples of unethical business practice. Moreover, many television audiences appear to enjoy watching programmes which reveal alleged unethical practices of household-name companies. To give one example, the media has on many occasions focused attention on alleged exploitative employment practices of suppliers used by some of the biggest brand names in sportswear.

We return to the subject of ethics in Chapter 9.

1.6.8 Systems theory, complexity and chaos

Systems theory was proposed in the 1940s by the biologist Ludwig von Bertalanffy. It is the interdisciplinary study of the abstract organization of phenomena, and investigates both the principles common to all complex entities and the models which can be used to describe them. More recently it has been applied to mathematics, computing and ecological systems. Some elements of systems theory have been applied to the modelling of relationships within the environmental sets that we discussed earlier.

Although a number of attempts have been made to apply the principles of systems theory to the business environment, there are major differences between scientific models and the business environment. Very often, the natural sciences deal with closed systems in which all the parameters are known, and each can be monitored and controlled. Admittedly, this is not always true; for example, in some ecological studies it may not be possible to identify all life forms which might possibly migrate into a system. By contrast, the business environment is essentially an open system in which it is very difficult to place a boundary round the environment and to identify the complete set of components within the system. Elements may come or go from the system and a researcher generally has no control over these elements in the way that a laboratory-based scientist could carry out controlled experiments.

Two developments of systems theory are complexity theory and chaos theory. Complexity theory is concerned with the behaviour over time of certain kinds of complex system. The systems of interest to complexity theory, under certain conditions, perform in regular, predictable ways; under other conditions they exhibit behaviour in which regularity and predictability is lost. Almost undetectable differences in initial conditions lead to gradually diverging system reactions until eventually the evolution of behaviour is quite dissimilar.

Chaos theory describes the dynamics of sensitive systems which are mathematically deterministic but nearly impossible to predict, due to their sensitivity to initial conditions. The weather is an example of a chaotic system. In order to make long-term weather forecasts it would be necessary to take an infinite number of measurements, which would be impossible to do. Also, because the atmosphere is chaotic, tiny uncertainties would eventually overwhelm any calculations and defeat the accuracy of the forecast. One of the most widely quoted examples of chaos theory is the butterfly which flaps its wings and in doing so creates destabilizing forces which trigger subsequent events, resulting in a hurricane on the other side of the world.

Many business environments may be considered as chaotic in that it can be very difficult to predict the sequence of events following an initial disturbance to equilibrium. In Chapter 13 we return to the subject of risk and turbulence in the business environment.

1.6.9 Business cycles

The business environment is rarely in a stable state, and many phenomena follow a cyclical pattern. Companies are particularly interested in understanding business cycles and in predicting the cycle as it affects their sector. We return to the subject of business cycles in Chapter 11. Although the business cycle is widely talked about, there are other cyclical factors evident in the business environment. The interaction between supply and demand can result in a cycle of high prices, leading to new entrants coming into the market, which leads to lower prices, which makes the market less attractive, so companies leave the market, so prices begin to rise, which attracts new entrants to the market, and the cycle repeats itself.

As well as cycles affecting tangible resources, it is also possible to identify cycles in *ideas* about how the business environment operates.

There have been many studies of how ideas grow to become mainstream and the critical factors involved in this process. Chaos theory and the study of mimetics has offered an explanation of how, through random events, a small local idea can develop into a global paradigm. An analysis by Gladwell discusses how reaching a critical point is facilitated by the existence of 'connectors', 'mavens' and the 'stickiness' of an idea (Gladwell 2000). One such idea that took hold in the 1990s was 'relationship marketing' as a method of conducting exchanges between a company and its customers. It followed a long series of 'big new ideas' which have risen and fallen over time.

1.6.10 Risk and uncertainty

The business environment for most organizations is rarely in a stable state. There is no certainty that the future will follow the pattern of the recent past. For companies operating in a low-tech, low-scale environment, adaptation to change may be quite easy. But for a large organization which has to invest heavily for the future, risks can be enormous. For very large projects, such as the construction of the new European Airbus 'super jumbo' aircraft, the risk and uncertainty is great not only for one company to take upon itself, but the consortium of companies that makes up Airbus. Apart from uncertainty about the technology, and the risk of cost overruns, there is considerable risk concerning the business environment of airlines which would be customers for the Airbus. Will passengers want to fly between a small number of very large airports in very large aircraft? Or would they prefer the alternative model of the future which sees larger numbers of smaller aircraft flying between a much bigger network of smaller airports? What will happen to fuel prices? Will long-term real increases in fuel prices put up air fares to the point where the long-term growth rate in passenger traffic is slowed down? Will government introduce new taxation on aviation fuel, again possibly slowing down demand for air travel? And there is always the threat of terrorism, which caused such uncertainty following 11 September 2001 and which could recur at any time.

All aspects of the business environment which have been introduced in this chapter carry an element of uncertainty. Within the microenvironment, what is the risk of a new, well-resourced competitor emerging? What if a strategic supplier goes out of business or is acquired by a firm's competitor? What happens if government introduces new legislation or imposes new taxation? Within the macroenvironment, there is continual uncertainty for most companies about the future state of the economy and the impact of changes in disposable income on consumer expenditure. What would happen if a new government was elected with a radically different political agenda? And in the internal environment, what is the risk of not being able to recruit the skilled employees the company needs? What would be the effect of new legislation on the recruitment and payment of employees?

There are many models for trying to comprehend the complexity of the business environment, and to attach risk levels to the different elements of it. In Chapter 13, we will look in more detail at some of these methods, including cross-impact analysis and environmental threat and opportunity profiles. We will also discuss the development of scenarios, which is an attempt to paint a picture of the future. It may be possible to build a small number of alternative scenarios based on differing assumptions. This qualitative approach is a means of handling environmental issues that are hard to quantify because they are less structured, more uncertain and may involve very complex relationships. Scenarios may paint a picture of a major crisis or source of turbulence facing a company. For an airline, this could be a renewed terrorist threat elsewhere in the world, or the crash of one of its own aircraft. Although it may not be possible to predict the exact detail of the event, the company could establish a set of guidelines for what it should do in the event that a scenario comes true. For example, following 11 September 2001, the airline Virgin Atlantic rapidly downsized its fleet and laid off staff. It had seen the future where a major incident caused a rapid fall in passenger traffic, before consumers regained confidence and returned in their previous numbers.

THINKING AROUND THE SUBJECT:
CRISES AND REPUTATIONS

A crisis can hit even the best-run company, with events such as a train crash, wrongdoings of its directors and pollution incidents undoing a company's hard-earned good reputation. Cultivating a good image with the public in general can help to protect a company's image from such shocks. Close relations with the media built over a period of time can ease the process of restoring a company's reputation. Many of the best-run companies practise their response to a simulated crisis so that, when one occurs, their response can be fast and coordinated.

NEW REVELATIONS ABOUT HALTON CHEMICAL ESCAPE

New revelations have emerged about the activities of some of Callaghan Surfactant's key employees at the time of the explosion which rocked the company's Halton plant. Carcinogenic material was released into the atmosphere in what was one of the region's worst ever pollution incidents.

At the time of the explosion, the evening shift was 12 staff short of its rostered duties, leaving the remaining 35 staff to cover their duties, including vital safety checks. Now it has been revealed that many staff had taken time off to go and support the company's staff football team, which was playing a crucial match in their league. Moreover, management of the company had laid on drinks and snacks for all supporters who attended.

CASE STUDY

CRISIS SPREADS FROM THE FIELDS OF INDIA TO THE SUPERMARKET SHELVES OF SHEFFIELD

Businesses involved in food production have faced a number of challenges in their business environment. In addition to the usual issues of securing profitability in a commodity-type market, the past two decades have seen growing concerns about food safety. To many consumers, food standards have been declining, as factory farming and mass production have led to a succession of food scares – salmonella in chickens, BSE in cows, chemicals in 'pure' bottled water, to name but a few. Whether food standards have actually been going down or whether it is consumers' perceptions that have been changing is less clear. Media reports about food scares may convey the impression that food standards are out of control, but the very fact that newspapers are reporting them suggests how unusual they are. It is easy to overlook the huge improvement in standards that has taken place over the past hundred years.

In February 2005 the newspapers found themselves reporting another food scare, this time of contaminated chilli powder which had made its way into hundreds of manufactured foods. An analysis of this incident reveals a lot about the nature of value chains, interorganizational relationships and risk.

Events began in India in 2002 where chillies were grown, harvested and dried. Thousands of small-scale farmers were involved in growing chillies, which were sold to spice mills where they were ground and an illegal red dye, called Sudan 1, was added. This dye adds colour to chilli powder, and is normally used to colour wax and floor polish. Labora-tory experiments involving rats had shown the presence of cancer-causing toxins in Sudan 1. There was argument about just how real the risk was to humans when taken in very small doses, but nevertheless the Food Standards Agency had banned the dye from all food products sold in the UK.

The adulterated chilli powder was purchased by an unknown trader in 2002. At this stage, it was a commodity product, worth a few pennies per kilogram. The consignment was then purchased by Clacton-on-Sea-based East Anglia Food Ingredients, a wholesaler of basic raw materials for the food industry. It then sold the consignment to Unbar Rothon, an Essex-based food processor which adds value to raw materials by providing graded ingredients to the food manufacturing industry.

The contaminated chilli powder was then sold to Premier Foods, a major manufacturer of foods to the consumer and food-processing sector. One of the products it used the chilli powder in was its Crosse & Blackwell Worcestershire sauce. Some of these bottles of Worcestershire sauce went to supermarkets and were purchased by consumers. Further catering packs were sold to wholesalers, who subsequently sold them to manu-facturers of a wide range of value-added food products. The list of products included Pot Noodle, Walkers Worcestershire sauce crisps, Sainsbury's 'Taste the Difference' sausages, and a chicken and vegetable casserole ready meal made by Unilever but sold with the Tesco brand name. From a basic raw material costing a few pence, the chilli powder had become a value-added component of a wide range of food products, with mass distribution across the UK (see Figure 1.8).

A widespread product recall followed the discovery of the contaminated batch of chilli powder, covering more than 420 individual food items. Would such a recall have hap-pened just two or three decades earlier?

The business environment of food producers has changed considerably. Traceability of food was very limited 20 or 30 years ago, but in this case detailed records allowed each transaction in the value chain to be identified. The prospect of identifying specific batches of over 420 final consumer products which might have been contaminated would previ-ously have been very difficult.

Consumers' perceptions of risk had also changed. The actual risk to a human being of consuming several tiny doses of the dye Sudan 1 was minimal, and experts rated the chance of death resulting from it as being considerably less than the chance of death from being struck by lightning. But consumers had come to distrust the food industry, and were now more susceptible to stories of food scares. Many were ready to believe extreme stories printed in the media. Had food manufacturers done nothing, they might have been perceived as uncaring companies that tried to cover up a potential problem. Consumers had previously punished companies such as the tyre company Bridgestone, which failed to immediately own up to problems. On the other hand, companies such as Perrier, which immediately took decisive action when faced with potential contamination of its bottled water, have been rewarded by long-term customer loyalty.

The regulatory environment had moved on. The UK Food Standards Agency now had a

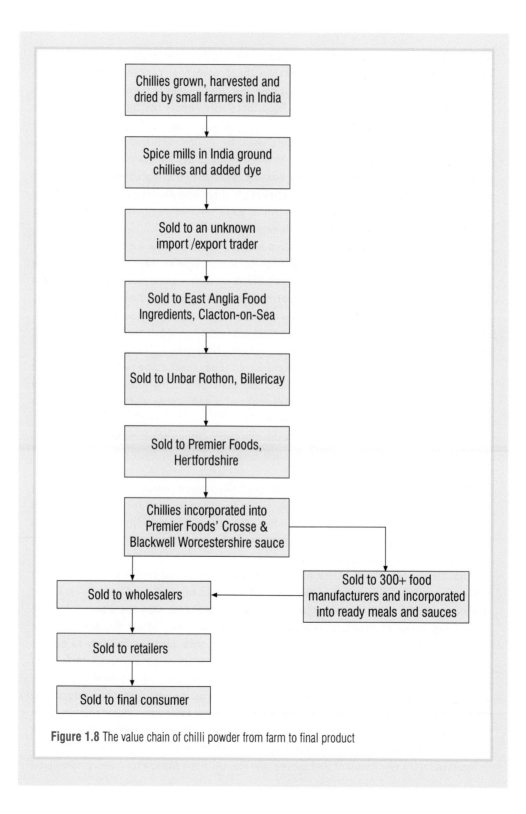

Figure 1.8 The value chain of chilli powder from farm to final product

long list of products which research had shown to be potentially harmful to human health. Moreover, it now works much more closely with EU institutions (the source of increasing numbers of EU-wide food regulations) to monitor international flows of food ingredients. In fact, the problem of the contaminated Sudan 1 first appeared in France when French authorities spotted the dye in a routine test of British food. This triggered a Europe-wide alert.

The public face of Sudan 1 was limited to the branded manufacturers who unwittingly incorporated the dye into their final value-added products. These companies had invested heavily in their brands which had earned the trust of consumers. Simply being associated with a food scare was potentially harmful for these companies, mindful that consumers have increasing choice on the shelves of supermarkets. Few consumers will have heard of the traders who initially brought the dye into the country. Nevertheless, food brokers and processors must earn the trust of the manufacturers that they supply. The small contaminated batch of chilli powder, sold for just a few hundred pounds in the early stages of the value chain, led to the recall of millions of pounds' worth of final products, costing firms further down the value chain not only their reputation, but also the costs of recalling and destroying the value-added products.

QUESTIONS

1 Critically analyse the concept of 'value added' in the context of this case study.
2 Identify sources of risk in the business environment discussed in this case study. How can members of the value chain manage their exposure to risk?
3 Briefly summarize the macroenvironmental factors that have led to change in the nature of value chains for food products.

SUMMARY

This chapter has reviewed the complex nature of an organization's business environment. The environment can be analysed at three levels: the microenvironment, comprising firms and individuals that an organization directly interacts with (or that directly affect its activities); the macroenvironment, comprising general forces that may eventually impact on the microenvironment; and the internal environment, comprising other functions within the organization.

This chapter has stressed the interrelatedness of all elements of the business environment. Although the social environment and technological environment are identified as separate elements, the two are closely linked (for example, technology has resulted in mass ownership of cars which has in turn affected social behaviour).

Subsequent chapters pay attention to each of the elements of the business environment, but the complexity of linkages must never be forgotten. Chapter 13 seeks to integrate these elements within dynamic analytical frameworks, which can be used to develop holistic forecasts of the future business environment.

Key Terms

Buyer–seller relationships (24)	Internal environment (5)	System (28)
Channels of distribution (13)	Macroenvironment (4)	Transformation process (3)
Environmental set (20)	Microenvironment (4)	Value chain (21)
Information environment (18)	Organizational culture (16)	
Intermediaries (13)	Stakeholders (15)	

CHAPTER REVIEW QUESTIONS

1 (a) Explain briefly what you understand by the 'environment' of a business.

(b) Prepare a list of recommendations which would aid a business to address change in its technical environment.

(*Based on CIM Marketing Environment Examination*)

2 Suppliers and intermediaries are important stakeholders in the microenvironment of the business.

(a) Explain the evolving role and functions of these stakeholders in the marketing-orientated business of the 1990s.

(b) With examples, comment on the growing importance of relationship marketing in this regard.

(*Based on CIM Marketing Environment Examination*)

3 Using a company of your choice, produce and justify an environmental set. You should include and rank at least five factors in your set.

ACTIVITY

Develop a checklist of points that you consider to be important indicators of whether an organization is responsive to changes in its business environment. Why did you choose these indicators? Now apply your checklist to three selected organizations: one a traditional manufacturing industry, the second a service-based commercial organization, and the third a government organization that serves the public. What, if anything, should your chosen organizations do to become more responsive to changes in their business environment?

Useful Websites

Biz/ed

Biz/ed is a business and economics resource for students, teachers and lecturers, and includes news and case studies.

http://www.bized.ac.uk

Supply chain management discussion group

List for all aspects of purchasing and supply chain management, and interorganizational theory. The list supports the networking and collaborative activities of the IPSERA association.

http://www.jiscmail.ac.uk/lists/purchasing-supply-chain.html

Newspaper websites

The quality daily newspapers have websites and these are a useful source of information about the business environment.

Financial Times: http://www.ft.com

Telegraph: http://www.Telegraph.co.uk

Guardian: http://www.Guardian.co.uk

The Times: http://www.the-times.co.uk

The Sunday Times: http://www.the_sunday-times.co.uk

Further Reading

A good starting point for understanding competitive advantage of firms and the role of value chains in achieving this is provided in Michael Porter's frequently cited book:

Porter, M.E. (1985) *Competitive Advantage: Creating and Sustaining Superior Performance*, Free Press.

This has been brought up to date to take account of the World Wide Web in the following:

Porter. M.E. (2001) 'Strategy and the Internet', *Harvard Business Review*, March, pp. 63–78.

There is now an extensive literature on the development of close buyer–seller relationships. A good summary of the principles can be found in the following two texts:

Christopher, M., Payne, A. and Ballantyne, D. (2001) *Relationship Marketing: Creating Stakeholder Value*, London, Butterworth-Heinemann.

Varey, R.J. (2002) *Relationship Marketing: Dialogue and Networks in the E-commerce Era*, Chichester, Wiley.

A good analysis of networks between companies is provided in the following:

Batonda, G. and Perry, C. (2003) 'Approaches to relationship development processes in inter-firm networks', *European Journal of Marketing*, Vol. 37, No. 10, pp. 1457–84.

Healy, M., Hastings, K., Brown, L. and Gardiner, M. (2001) 'The old, the new and the complicated: a trilogy of marketing relationships', *European Journal of Marketing*, Vol. 35, No. 1, pp. 182–93.

This chapter has provided a general overview of the components that make up the business environment. Suggestions for further reading on each of these components are given in later chapters.

References

Fletcher, R. (2002a) 'Barclay brothers to net £15m from suppliers', *Sunday Telegraph* (London, England), 24 November.

Fletcher, R. (2002b) 'Green nets £8m from Arcadia suppliers', *Sunday Telegraph* (London, England), 3 November.

Gladwell, M. (2000) *The Tipping Point: How Little Things Can Make a Big Difference*, New York, Little Brown & Co.

Heskett, J.L., W.E. Sasser and L.A. Schlesinger (1998) 'The service–profit chain: how leading companies link profit and growth to loyalty, satisfaction and value', *International Journal of Service Industry Management*, Vol. 9, No. 3, pp. 145–76.

Laroche, M., Bergeron, J. and Goutaland, C. (2003) 'How intangibility affects perceived risk: the moderating role of knowledge and involvement', *Journal of Services Marketing*, Vol. 17, No. 2, pp. 122–40.

Levitt, T. (1960) 'Marketing myopia', *Harvard Business Review*, July–August, pp. 45–56.

Nonaka, I. (1991) 'The knowledge-creating company', *Harvard Business Review*, Vol. 69, No. 6, pp. 96–104.

Part 2
The Macroenvironment

Chapter 2
The Political Environment

Chapter Objectives
This chapter will explain:

- the nature of the political environment

- the structure and processes of local, regional, national and supranational government

- political ideologies and their effects on government policy and implications for business organizations

- the two-way influence between business organizations and government

- the role of pressure groups in the political process

2.1 DEFINING THE POLITICAL ENVIRONMENT

All aspects of an organization's business environment are interrelated to some extent, and this is especially true of the political environment. Interlinkages occur in many ways. Here are some examples.

- Political decisions inevitably affect the economic environment, for example in the proportion of GDP accounted for by the state and the distribution of income between different groups in society (Chapter 11).
- Political decisions also influence the social and cultural environment of a country (Chapter 3). For example, governments create legislation, which can have the effect of encouraging families to care for their elderly relatives or allowing shops to open on Sundays. In short, the actions of politicians are both a reflection of the social and cultural environment of a country and also help to shape it.
- Politicians can influence the pace at which new technologies appear and are adopted, for example through tax concessions on research and development activity (Chapter 4).

The political environment is one of the less predictable elements in an organization's business environment. Although politicians issue manifestos and other policy statements, these have to be seen against the pragmatic need of governments to modify their policies during their period in office. Change in the political environment can result from a variety of internal and external pressures. The fact that democratic governments have to seek re-election every few years has contributed towards a cyclical political environment. Turbulence in the political environment can be seen by considering some of the major swings that have occurred in the political environment in the United Kingdom since the Second World War.

- During the late 1940s, the political environment stressed heavy government intervention in all aspects of the economy, including ownership of a substantial share of productive capacity.
- During the 1950s, there was a much more restrained hands-off approach in which many of the previously nationalized industries were deregulated and sold off.
- During the 1960s and 1970s the political environment oscillated in moderation between more and less government involvement in the ways businesses are run.
- The 1980s saw a significant change in the political environment, with the wholesale withdrawal of government from ownership and regulation of large areas of business activity.
- During the 1990s political commentators detected a shift away from the radicalism of the 1980s to more middle-of-the-road policies based on a social market economy.
- With the election of a Labour government in 1997, there has been a gradual retreat from the free market idealism of previous Conservative governments.

2.2 POLITICAL SYSTEMS

Throughout most of this chapter, we will be describing political systems based on the type of democracy which is prevalent in Western countries. However, there is great diversity in political systems. At one extreme is a political system based on an open system of government which is democratically elected by the population of a country. The other extreme may be represented by totalitarian systems of government in which power derives not from popular representation, but is acquired by a select group. This may be in the form of communism, or may be based on the interests of sectional groups, often militarily based, which acquire power through force or tradition.

The link between the dominant political system, economic growth and the nature of the business environment is an interesting and often complex one. There has been a lot of research into the relationship between democracy and economic prosperity. The idea that autocratic regimes have an advantage in economic development was once quite fashionable. The plausibility of such a notion lies in the advantages such regimes were said to have in forcing through development in the long term. There is some evidence for this in the way that countries go about the construction of major transport infrastructure projects. In Western countries with open democratic governance, a lengthy process of consultation is likely to take place before a new road is built, and there are likely to be extensive checks and balances to prevent the interests of individuals or groups being threatened or unduly favoured. In countries with less democratic traditions, government is more likely to go ahead regardless of objections. Some commentators have attributed part of the rapid economic development of South-east Asia during the 1980s and 1990s to the absence of democratic government in the Western tradition.

An alternative view is that democracy is likely to foster economic development. The political institutions critical to economic development are more likely to exist and function effectively in democratic systems. These institutions include a legal system which protects property rights, individual liberties which encourage creativity and entrepreneurship, the freedom of expression which facilitates the flow of information in an economy, and institutional checks and balances that prevent the theft of public wealth often observed in totalitarian systems. There is a suggestion of a nonlinear relationship in which greater democracy enhances growth at low levels of political freedom but depresses growth when a moderate level of freedom has already been attained. Improvements in the standard of living, health services and education may subsequently raise the probability that political freedom will grow.

Corruption remains a barrier to economic development in many countries. Some companies may survive and prosper by bribing government officials, but the success and growth of such companies is not necessarily based on the value they create for consumers. In many cases, they have simply bought themselves a dominant position in a market which the government is happy to allow them to exploit, in return for a payment which is made. In government systems with poor accountability, such payments may not be made for the public good, but instead just add to the private wealth of government officials.

The statistical evidence of a link between democracy and economic growth is mixed. One study of economic growth data for 115 countries from 1960 to 1980 found that countries with high degrees of political openness achieved an average annual real per capita growth rate of 2.53 per cent, compared with 1.41 per cent in more closed political systems. This implies that more democratic countries may grow 80 per cent faster than less democratic countries. However, other studies have given more ambiguous results, including some that reported a weak negative overall effect of democracy on economic growth (Barro 1996).

Figure 2.1 reports data for a selection of countries, linking annual GDP per capita with an index of political freedom within the country (for example, the extent of universal voting rights); a ranking of economic freedom (for example, the ease with which new entrants can enter a market); and ranking of corruption. A casual glance at this table will reveal that many of the poorest countries of the world are associated with lower levels of political freedom and a high level of corruption.

Countries	Per Capita GDP $ (2004 estimate)	Index of Freedom (1997)	Ranking of Economic Freedom (1999)	Ranking of Corruption (1998)
Tanzania	700	10	90	81
Zambia	900	9	75	52
Nigeria	1,000	13	95	81
Zimbabwe	1,900	10	124	43
Pakistan	2,200	9	97	71
India	3,100	6	120	66
Philippines	5,000	5	48	55
China	5,600	14	124	52
United Kingdom	29,600	3	7	11
Canada	31,500	2	14	6
Ireland	31,900	2	25	14
Switzerland	33,800	2	5	10
Hong Kong	34,200	9	1	16
Norway	40,000	2	27	8

Figure 2.1 National indices for selected countries linking GDP per capita, political freedom, economic freedom and corruption

Source: Based on United Nations, *Human Development Report 1998*; World Bank, *World Development Report 1996*; Freedom House, *Freedom in the World 1997/98*; Bryan Johnson *et al.*, *Index of Economic Freedom 1999*; Transparency International, 'Corruption Perceptions Index 1998'; World Factbook 2005 (http://www.cia.gov)

Note: The measure of political freedom comprises a composite of two separate indicators: political rights and civil liberties. The combined score is between 2 and 14, 2 being the freest and 14 being the most unfree. The organization Freedom House considers countries with scores of between 2 and 5 'free'; those scoring between 6 and 10 as 'partly free'; those scoring between 11 and 14 as 'unfree'.

The ranking of economic freedom consists of one index in which the freest economy (Hong Kong) is ranked 1 and the least free economy (North Korea) ranks 170.

Ranking of corruption is based on data provided by Transparency International (1998), with the least corrupt country being ranked 1.

A further intriguing issue concerns the role of political systems relative to transnational organizations. It has been suggested that the increasing volume of business transactions which take place across the borders of nation-states is eroding the efficiency of national governing structures, especially democratic ones. Many multinational corporations have a turnover that is much larger than that of small less developed countries. When one of these countries relies on the multinational company for a lot of its income (a situation which is common in many economies dependent on natural resources), some would argue that the power of the people to control their government is less than the power of the multinational company (Rodrik 2002).

2.3 THE IMPORTANCE OF MONITORING THE POLITICAL ENVIRONMENT

We now move on to explore the reasons why business organizations should constantly monitor their political environment, whether this be a totalitarian or democratic system, or a system that is in the process of changing from one type of system to another. It must not be forgotten that within the past couple of decades businesses have observed and reacted to some dramatic changes in political systems, for example the transformation of former communist Eastern European countries into fledgling democracies. Even here, the ending of communism was only the beginning of a process of political change. In many Eastern European countries, the early days of *laissez-faire* capitalism (described by Joseph Stiglitz as 'market bolshevism', in which unregulated free markets were forced on these countries) was replaced over time with calls for more rather than less state involvement. Governments gradually recognized the need to intervene to counteract market failures by creating enforceable laws and collectable taxes, among other things (Stiglitz 2000).

Change in the political environment can impact on business strategy and operations in a number of ways.

■ At the most general level, the stability of the political system affects the attractiveness of a particular national market. While radical change rarely results from political upheaval in most Western countries, the instability of governments in many less developed countries leads to uncertainty about the economic and legislative framework in which goods and services will be provided.

■ At a national level, governments pass legislation that directly affects the relationship between the firm and its customers, relationships between itself and its suppliers, and between itself and other firms and individuals. Sometimes legislation has a direct effect on the organization, for example a law giving consumers rights against the seller of faulty goods. At other times, the effect is less direct, as where changes in legislation concerning anti-competitive practices alter an organization's relative competitive advantage in a market.

■ As employers, governments see business organizations as an important vehicle for social reform through legislation which affects employment relationships. During the previous 30 years, organizations have been affected by a wide range of employment legislation, affecting, among other things, discrimination against disadvantaged groups, minimum wages and more stringent health and safety requirements.

■ The government is additionally responsible for protecting the public interest at large, imposing further constraints on the activities of firms, for example where the government lays down design standards for cars to protect the public against pollution or road safety risks.

■ The economic environment is influenced by the actions of government. It is responsible for formulating policies that can influence the rate of growth in the economy and hence the total amount of spending power. It is also a political decision as to how this spending power should be distributed between different groups of consumers and between the public and private sectors.

■ Government at both a central and local level is itself a major consumer of goods and services, and accounts for about 40 per cent of the UK's gross domestic product.

■ Government policies can influence the dominant social and cultural values of a country, although there can be argument about which is the cause and which is the effect. For example, UK government policies of the 1980s emphasized wealth creation as an end in itself and these policies also had the effect of generating a feeling of confidence among consumers. This can be directly linked to an increase in consumer spending at a higher rate than earnings growth, and a renewed enthusiasm for purchasing items of ostentatious consumption.

It should be remembered that organizations not only monitor the political environment – they also contribute to it. This can happen where organizations feel threatened by change and lobby government to intervene to pass legislation that will protect their interests. The role of lobbying and pressure groups will be discussed later in this chapter.

2.4 POLITICAL IDEOLOGIES

It was noted earlier that political ideologies in the UK have changed through a series of cycles during the post-Second World War period. It is important to consider the issue of dominant political ideologies, as they can have such a major impact on the business environment. At one extreme, the ideology of the immediate post-war Labour government placed great importance on the role of the state, and this resulted in many private-sector organizations being taken into state ownership. The political ideology of the incoming Conservative government in 1979 was very different on this and many other issues. As a consequence of this shift in ideology, large parts of state control of business were dismantled and nationalized industries sold off. For business organizations, understanding shifts in dominant ideologies can be crucial to understanding the future nature of their business environment. Two important and recurring ideological issues which affect business organizations are the distribution of wealth between different groups in society and the role of the state versus the private sector in delivering goods and services. Political parties represent the gathering of individuals who share a political ideology.

2.4.1 Political parties

Most Members of Parliament belong to a political party. In general, the views of members of political parties cross a range of policy issues, so political parties can be distinguished from single-interest groups such as the League Against Cruel Sports. The existence of political parties makes the management of parliamentary business more efficient, because party leaders can generally be assured of the support of their members when passing new legislation. Parties also provide a hierarchical organization through which MPs can become junior ministers and eventually take a place in the executive.

From the perspective of the electorate, belonging to a political party identifies an individual candidate with a known set of values. There is a lot of evidence that when voting for a Member of Parliament, a substantial proportion of voters are guided primarily by the party affiliation of a candidate, rather than the personal views and characteristics of the candidate.

Political parties represent an ideological point of view, although it has been noted that in recent years the ideological gap between the main UK parties has been reducing. Some cynics suggested that the incoming New Labour government in 1997 shared many ideological values of the previous Conservative government and was far removed from the ideological zeal with which the post-Second World War Labour government took office. The main parties have tended to converge on a relatively moderate ideology, leaving extreme parties such as the

British National Party and Socialist Workers Party to pursue more radical ideologies. Of course, the prevalence of an ideology represents shifts in the value of society as a whole. The radical free market ideology of the incoming Conservative government of 1979 found a ready reception by an electorate that had come to see the shortcomings of the previous Labour government. This was seen by many as being too restrictive and closely aligned with the inflexible attitudes of trades unions. The fact that extreme ideologies have not found great recent support in the UK, and the fact that the difference between the two main parties has been narrowed, is a reflection of relatively moderate political values held by the population as a whole, and possibly contentment with increasing personal wealth and living standards.

Because political parties represent a diverse range of ideological issues, it is not surprising that party leaders often find it difficult to gain the unanimous support of all members on all issues. In the United Kingdom, members of the main political parties are divided on issues such as the level of involvement with the European Union, defence expenditure and educational policy. Nevertheless, a political party stands for a broad statement of ideological values which its members can identify with. In the United Kingdom, the Conservative Party has traditionally been identified with such core values as the self-reliance of individuals, less rather than more government and the role of law and order. The Labour Party, by contrast, has traditionally stood for state intervention where market failure has occurred, protection of the weak in society from the strong and efforts to reduce inequalities in wealth. The Liberal Democrat Party has traditionally appealed to people who believe in open democratic government in a market economy with government intervention where market mechanisms have produced inequalities or inefficiencies.

The Conservative Party has traditionally been seen as the party of business and the Labour Party as the party of organized labour. This is true as far as the funding of the parties goes, with the Conservative Party receiving sizeable donations from business organizations while many Labour MPs are sponsored by trades unions (although the number of donations by business to New Labour has increased in recent years). In general, the free market enterprise values of the Conservative Party would appear to favour the interests of businesses, while the socialist values of the Labour Party would appear to be against business interests. Historically, business has been worried at the prospect of a Labour government, as witnessed by the fall in stock market prices which has often followed a Labour Party election victory. However, the United Kingdom, like many Western countries, has seen increasing levels of convergence between parties which makes business leaders very uncertain about just what makes a party's policies distinctive. For example, the UK Labour Party has traditionally been opposed to privatization of public utilities, but the New Labour government elected in 1997 had no immediate plans to renationalize previously privatized companies, and indeed has subsequently privatized London Underground and the air navigation services. As political parties have targeted the crucial middle-ground 'floating voter', their underlying ideologies have become increasingly indistinguishable.

The UK political environment has traditionally been dominated at a national level by two major parties. By contrast, most other European countries have a long tradition of multiple parties which represent different shades of opinion and each send small numbers of members to their legislative body. The result is often that no one party is able to form an executive with an outright majority of members, so executives based on a coalition of parties must be formed. The difference in electoral outcomes between the two systems reflects the method by which the election is conducted. In the UK, the party with the most MPs elected within individual constituencies takes power. In most European countries it is the percentage of total votes which determines the number of representatives of each party. Within the Scottish Parliament (see below) proportional representation has resulted in a coalition of Green MSPs (Members of the Scottish Parliament) together with an ideological Scottish Socialist Party.

There is an argument that diversity of parties in the legislature (something which is generally favoured by 'proportional representation' electoral systems) allows for a wide range of political views to be represented in the government, in contrast to two-party systems where minority opinions can easily be lost. Against this, the reality is often that a minority party is able to hold power which is disproportionate to its size, by threatening to withhold its membership of a coalition. Coalition governments (which are common in some European countries such as Italy and Germany) also have a tendency to be unstable and withdrawal of one party may bring down an executive. Radical change which occurred with the strong single-party governments of the Conservative Party in the 1980s may be much more difficult where a coalition government has to broker a compromise between all parties.

2.4.2 Social exclusion

Political parties have often based their principal ideology on a desire to see a more equitable distribution of wealth and life chances within society. Some great revolutions in history have been brought about by the socially excluded using force to overturn the power of an elite. The New Labour government of 1997 set about reducing social exclusion in a more low-key manner, but nevertheless as an important part of its election promise.

Social exclusion is a shorthand term for what can happen when people or areas suffer from a combination of linked problems such as unemployment, poor skills, low incomes, poor housing, high-crime environments, bad health and family breakdown. In the past, governments have had policies that tried to deal with each of these problems individually, but there has been little success at tackling the complicated links between them or preventing them from arising in the first place.

In response to these problems, the UK government created the Social Exclusion Unit in 1997. Its remit has been to help improve government action to reduce social exclusion by producing 'joined-up solutions to joined-up problems'. Most of its work is based on specific projects, which the Prime Minister chooses following consultation with other Ministers and suggestions from interested groups. The Unit is staffed by a combination of civil servants and external secondees. They come from a number of government departments and from organizations with experience of tackling social exclusion – the probation service, housing, police, local authorities, the voluntary sector and business.

One of the Unit's early reports focused on problems caused by housing estates which had become 'sink areas'. Numerous government agencies had tackled the problems but more concerted collective action was needed if significant results were to be achieved. The Unit's report on neighbourhood renewal was published in September 1998. It gave a detailed picture of the concentration in poor neighbourhoods of a range of interlocking problems such as high levels of unemployment, crime and ill-health, and poor education. It showed how the gap with the rest of the country had widened, and analysed why previous initiatives to deal with the problems had failed. The report set out a range of issues on which urgent policy work was needed, with the aim of bridging the gap between the poorest neighbourhoods and the rest. The Social Exclusion Unit set up 18 Policy Action Teams (PATs) to work on solutions, bringing together civil servants and outside experts to develop a National Strategy for Neighbourhood Renewal. Alongside the publication of the report, the £800 million 'New Deal for Communities' programme was announced, providing intensive support to some of the poorest neighbourhoods, beginning with 17 Pathfinder areas.

2.4.3 Redistribution of wealth

Left to market forces, numerous studies have suggested that the wealthier members of a society would continue to get richer, while the poor would find it difficult to escape from their relative poverty. Karl Marx's analysis predicted the end of capitalism on the basis that without the spending power of the poor, the wealthy owners of resources would have no markets for their products which they made profits from. In reality, Marx's thesis was weakened by new overseas opportunities to recirculate capital owners' wealth. During the twentieth century, progress towards a more egalitarian distribution of the wealth was slow and required intervention by governments.

Governments with socialist leanings have recognized that there is nothing inherently just in the pattern of market rewards that reflects the accidents of heredity and the labour skills that happen to be in demand at the time. A distinguishing feature of the Left in politics is often its belief in a positive role for government. However, redistribution has acquired a bad name because it has been associated with the politics of envy. It has also sometimes been carried out in such a way as to interfere unnecessarily with incentives.

Under previous Labour governments, taxation on marginal income has exceeded 90 per cent. This has invariably entrenched the position of those who already own wealth or who can take their rewards in the form of professional perks, while discouraging those who want to better themselves without the aid of tax advisers.

Actually getting benefits to lower-income groups can pose a challenge for policy makers. Minimum wage legislation, introduced in the UK in 1999, may provide guaranteed levels of income for the poorest members of society, but higher-earning individuals invariably seek to maintain differentials, leaving minimum wage employees in a position of relative poverty, and possibly putting an employer at a competitive disadvantage compared to companies located in low-wage economies. An alternative approach to redistribution has been to increase the benefits paid to individuals who are not in work. But this has often led to a 'poverty trap' whereby it is not financially advantageous for an individual to enter employment, because the benefits that they are giving up are greater than the wages that they will earn. There are a number of structural issues that governments have sought to tackle in order to improve the relative economic standing of disadvantaged groups. As an example, many single parents have found it uneconomic to enter the labour market because the loss of benefits and costs of childcare are greater than their earnings.

Pursuing full employment may be an admirable goal as a means of reducing poverty. But public perceptions of government programmes to get people off benefits and into employment can very easily change from enlightenment to harassment once pressure is put on people, whether they be the well-meaning unmarried mother or the workshy who would rather claim benefit than work.

It seems that even a socialist government dedicated to reducing social inequality cannot easily eliminate inequality. According to a report by the Office of National Statistics, the income of the richest and poorest 10 per cent of the population had each grown by around 5 per cent between 1997 (the date when a Labour government was elected) and 2003. But in absolute terms, the gap between rich and poor had widened. The poorest 10 per cent had seen a £28 a week rise, compared to the richest 10 per cent, which had seen a rise of £119. Furthermore, the wealthiest 1 per cent of the population had prospered. In 1996, they owned 20 per cent of the nation's wealth, but by 2002 the figure had grown to 23 per cent. A large part of this growth was attributed to a rise in house prices (Office of National Statistics 2004).

It has often been argued that the surest way out of inequality is through education, but the report found that children's chances of doing well in exams depended enormously on their parents' qualifications and jobs. In 2002, more than three-quarters of children with parents in higher professional occupations achieved five or more GCSEs at grades A to C. Less than a third of children with parents in manual or clerical jobs achieved this.

Even when the government takes proactive measures to help disadvantaged groups, these may backfire. In 2001, the government abolished entrance fees to national museums, arguing that high charges were deterring poor people from sharing the nation's heritage and learning from it. After the abolition of charges, museum attendance figures rose. However, a subsequent report by the National Audit Office indicated that it was relatively wealthy middle-class parents who were now making more visits to museums, and disadvantaged groups were still underrepresented in the admission figures. Worse still, many of the middle-class parents who were now making more visits to state-subsidised museums now made fewer visits to privately owned museums, many of which were forced to cut back their expenditure and reduce the number of staff they employed.

What policies can in practice be used to overcome social inequality? Given the importance of education as a means of reducing inequality, what can governments do to encourage people from disadvantaged backgrounds to take part in higher education? Even in higher education, is government policy sometimes contradictory, as evidenced by the introduction of tuition fees which may deter groups in society that have traditionally been afraid of getting into debt?

2.5 THE STRUCTURE OF GOVERNMENT

To understand the nature of the political environment more fully, and its impact on business organizations, it is necessary to examine the different aspects of government. Government influence on businesses in the United Kingdom can be divided into the following categories:

- central government
- regional government
- local government
- European Union (EU) government
- supranational government.

Most countries have hierarchical levels of government which follow a roughly similar pattern. The UK will be used to illustrate the principles of multi-level government influences on businesses, with reference to comparable institutions in other countries.

2.6 CENTRAL GOVERNMENT

The central government system of most countries can be divided into four separate functions. The United Kingdom is quite typical in dividing functions of government between the legislature, the executive, the civil service and the judiciary. These collectively provide sovereign government within the United Kingdom although, as will be seen later, this sovereignty is increasingly being subjected to the authority of the European Union.

2.6.1 Parliament

Parliament provides the supreme legislative authority in the United Kingdom and comprises the Queen, the House of Commons and the House of Lords. The House of Commons is the most important part of the legislature as previous legislation has curtailed the authority in Parliament of the monarch and the House of Lords. It is useful to be aware of the procedures for enacting new legislation so that the influences on the legislative process can be fully understood (see Figure 2.2).

New legislation starts life as a Bill and passes through parliamentary processes to the point

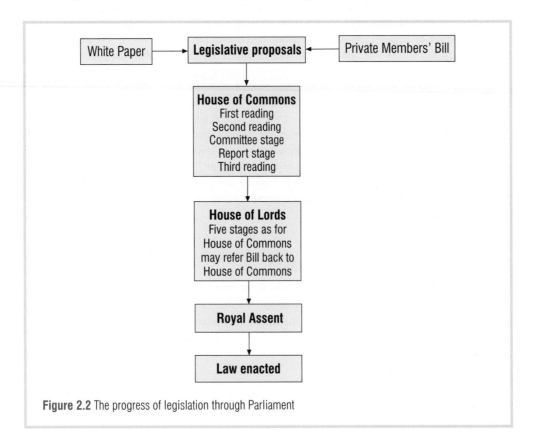

Figure 2.2 The progress of legislation through Parliament

where it becomes an Act of Parliament. Most Bills that subsequently become law are government sponsored and often start life following discussion between government departments and interested parties. On some occasions these discussions may lead to the setting up of a Committee of Enquiry or (less frequently) a Royal Commission which reports to the government. The findings of such a committee can be accepted, rejected or amended by the government which puts forward ideas for discussion in a Green Paper. Following initial discussion, the government would submit definite proposals for legislation in the form of a White Paper. A Parliamentary Bill would then be drafted, incorporating some of the comments that the government has received in response to the publication of the White Paper. The Bill is then formally introduced to Parliament by a first reading in the House of Commons at which a date is set for the main debate at a second reading. A vote is taken at each reading and, if it is a government Bill, it will invariably pass at each stage. If it passes the second reading, the Bill will be sent to a Standing Committee for a discussion of the details. The Committee will in due course report back to the full House of Commons and there will be a final debate where amendments are considered, some of which originate from the Committee and some from members of the House of Commons in general. The Bill then passes to the House of Lords and goes through a similar five stages. The Lords may delay or amend a Bill, although the Commons may subsequently use the Parliament Act to force the Bill through. Finally, the Bill goes to the monarch to receive the Royal Assent, upon which it becomes an Act of Parliament.

This basic model can be changed in a number of ways. First, in response to a newly perceived problem, the government could introduce a Bill with very few clauses and with the agreement of party managers could cut short the consultation stages, speed up the passage of the Bill through its various stages and provide Royal Assent within a matter of days, instead of the months that it could typically take. This has occurred, for example, in the case of a one-clause Bill to prohibit trade in human organs, a measure that had received all-party support. A second variation on the basic model is provided by Private Members' Bills. Most Bills start life with government backing. However, backbench Members of Parliament can introduce their own Bills, although the opportunities for doing this are limited and if they do not subsequently receive government backing, their chances of passing all stages of the Parliamentary process are significantly reduced.

The lobbying of Members of Parliament has become an increasingly important activity, brought about by individuals and pressure groups to try to protect their interests where new legislation is proposed which may affect them. Typical of tasks for which professional lobbyists have been employed in recent years are:

- a major campaign by tobacco companies against a Bill which would have limited their ability to sponsor sporting events
- the insurance industry lobbied hard against a clause in a Finance Bill which would introduce a new Insurance Premium Tax on insurance policies
- the British Roads Federation regularly lobbies for greater expenditure on roads, and seizes opportunities presented by relevant new Bills to include provisions which are more supportive of increased expenditure on roads
- each year, prior to the Chancellor of the Exchequer's annual Budget speech (which forms the basis of a Finance Act), considerable lobbying is undertaken by vested interests that appeal for more public spending to be directed to their cause and/or less taxation to be imposed on it.

If organizations are to succeed in influencing their political environment, they need to identify the critical points in the passage of a Bill at which pressure can be applied and the critical members who should form the focus of lobbying (for example, the members of the Committee to which the Bill is sent for detailed examination). As we will see later, much legislation which passes through the UK parliament is enacting EU legislation. At this stage it may be too late for lobbyists to achieve significant change in the overall policy underlying the Bill, although it may still be possible to amend details of its implementation.

Political parties typically make bold promises in their election manifestos. If elected, they may promptly enact legislation that formed the flagship of their campaign. However, after a honeymoon period, governments must set to work addressing structural issues in the economy which will take some time to make good. This may involve painful economic measures in the short term, but the payoff is improved economic performance in a few years' time. With a five-year election cycle for Parliament in the United Kingdom, it is often claimed that voters have short memories and will forget austere economic conditions of two or three years ago. What matters at election time is the appearance that economic conditions are getting better. Therefore, government economic planning may try to achieve falling unemployment, stable prices and a consumer boom just ahead of a general election. This may itself lead to structural problems which must be sorted out after the election, leading to a repeat of this cyclical process (see Figure 2.3). The existence of the political cycle frequently impacts on the economic environment, with periods of increased expenditure just before an election and reduced expenditure shortly after. Organizations may acknowledge this cycle by gearing up for a boom in sales just ahead of a general election.

2.6.2 The executive

Parliament comprises elected representatives whose decisions, in theory, are carried out by the executive arm of government. In practice, the executive plays a very important role in formulating policies which Parliament then debates and invariably accepts. In the United Kingdom, the principal elements of the executive comprise the Cabinet and Ministers of State.

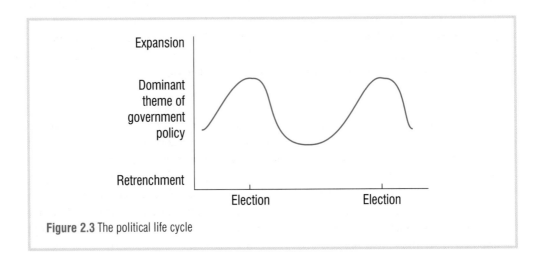

Figure 2.3 The political life cycle

The Cabinet

The main executive element of central government is made up of the Prime Minister and Cabinet (comprising 26 members), who determine policy and who are responsible for the consequences of their policies. The Cabinet is headed by the Prime Minister who has many powers, including the appointment and dismissal of ministers and determining the membership of Cabinet committees, chairing the Cabinet and setting its agenda, summarizing the discussions of the Cabinet and sending directives to ministers. The Prime Minister is also responsible for a variety of government and non-government appointments and can determine the timing of a general election. Many have argued that Britain is moving towards a system of presidential government by the Prime Minister, given the considerable powers at his or her disposal. There are, however, a number of constraints on the power of the Prime Minister, such as the need to keep the loyalty of the Cabinet and the agreement of Parliament, which may be difficult when the governing party has only a small majority in the House of Commons.

In practice, the Prime Minister is particularly dependent upon the support of a small inner cabinet of senior colleagues for advice and assistance in carrying policy through the party. In addition to this small inner cabinet surrounding the Prime Minister, recent years have seen the development of a small group of outside advisers on whose loyalty the Prime Minister can totally rely. Some are likely to be party members sitting in Parliament, while others may be party loyalists who belong to the business or academic community. There have been occasions when it has appeared that the Prime Minister's advisers were having a greater influence on policy than their Cabinet colleagues.

The ideological background of the Prime Minister and the composition of the government may give some indication of the direction of government policy. On government attitudes towards issues such as competition policy and personal taxation, organizations should study the composition of the government to try to predict future policy.

Ministers of State

The government of the country is divided between a number of different departments of state (see Figure 2.4). Each department is headed by a Minister or Secretary of State who is a political appointee, usually a member of the House of Commons. They are assisted in their tasks by junior ministers. The portfolio of responsibilities of a department frequently changes when a new government comes into being. Ministers are often given delegated authority by Parliament, as where an Act may allow charges to be made for certain health services, but the minister has the delegated power to decide the actual level of the charges.

2.6.3 The civil service

The civil service is the secretariat responsible for implementing government policy. In the United Kingdom, civil servants are paid officials who do not change when the government changes, adding a degree of continuity to government (although in some countries, such as the United States, it is customary for senior officials to be political appointees and therefore replaced following a change of government). Although, legally, civil servants are servants of the Crown, they are technically employed by a separate government department and are responsible to a minister. Each department is generally headed by a Permanent Secretary, responsible to the Public Accounts Committee of Parliament. The Permanent Secretary is a

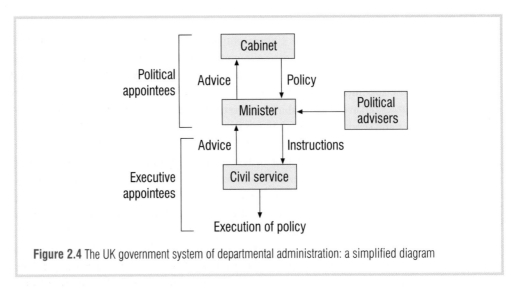

Figure 2.4 The UK government system of departmental administration: a simplified diagram

professional administrator who gives advice to his or her minister, a political appointee who generally lacks expertise in the work of the department.

The fact that civil servants are relatively expert in their areas and generally remain in their posts for much longer than their minister gives them great power. A delicate relationship develops between the Permanent Secretary and the minister, based on sometimes conflicting goals. The minister may view an issue in terms of broader political opportunities while the civil servant may be more concerned about his or her status and career prospects resulting from a change affecting his or her department.

The nature of the career civil servant is changing with the emergence of Non-Departmental Public Bodies (NDPBs) to take over many of the activities of civil service departments (see below). In theory, these new executive agencies should be much freer of ministerial control, meeting longer-term performance standards with less day-to-day ministerial intervention as to how this should be achieved.

Organizations seeking to influence government policy must recognize the power that civil servants have in advising their minister, especially on the details of proposed legislation. Civil servants are usually involved in consultation exercises, for example on the details of proposed food regulations. In some countries, business may seek to influence the policy-making process at this stage through overt or covert bribery. This is not a feature of most mature democracies such as Britain, and business seeks to exert influence in a more mutually co-operative manner. Civil servants require information on the background to policy and need to understand its possible implications. A close dialogue between the business community and civil servants can increase the chances of civil servants' policy recommendations being based on a sound understanding of business needs, rather than ignorance.

2.6.4 The judiciary

Most democratic systems of government provide a number of checks and balances against the abuse of executive power. The judiciary is independent of government, and judges in the United Kingdom are answerable to the Crown and not to politicians. Through the court

THINKING AROUND THE SUBJECT:
MINISTER FOR SPIN?

Britain's system of government has often been held out as an example of good governance. Politicians decided policy and if the electorate didn't like their policies, they could be thrown out of office at the next election. Civil servants were the loyal servants of politicians who got on and implemented their masters' policies. Because the electorate could not throw out a civil servant directly, ministers took responsibility for the actions of their civil servants. Carefully honed sets of procedures and codes of conduct were developed which made the UK civil service an example to the world of professionalism.

What then are we to make of recent developments which would appear to blur the distinction between elected politicians and an appointed civil service? The 1990s saw a big growth in policy advisers who report to the Prime Minister or other senior ministers, but who are still technically civil servants. These special advisers are overtly chosen by ministers on the basis of their political views, breaking the tradition of neutrality within the civil service. They have often been given the label of 'spin doctor' for the way in which they represent the views of their minister. Do these advisers debase the whole principle of a politically neutral civil service? Are they one step towards the development of a presidential style of government on the American model? Are 'spin doctors' merely providing a substitute for substantive actions by the politicians? Against this, isn't good government all about strong leadership? Could these special advisers be beneficial in the way that they cut through the delaying tactics of the civil service machinery in their efforts to see the politically accountable executive's wishes implemented?

The blurred distinction between functions doesn't end with special policy advisers. Governments have been increasingly enthusiastic about the use of 'task forces' and so-called policy 'csars' to implement policy in such areas as crime, education, housing and environmental protection. These may draw on individuals' special skills, or draw membership from a wide range of interests, but they are invariably political appointments and not democratically accountable in the way that a civil servant is accountable to their minister. Are the possible benefits for good government worth the possible price of less accountability to the electorate?

system, citizens can have some redress against a legislature, executive or civil service that acts beyond its authority. If complainants believe that they have suffered because a government minister did not follow statutory consultation procedures, they may apply to the courts for a judicial review of the case. A court may order that ministers reconsider the matter by following statutory procedures.

Business organizations have become increasingly willing to use the courts to challenge allegedly incorrect government procedures which have put them at a disadvantage. The proliferation of industry sector regulators in the UK has created many opportunities for aggrieved business organizations to challenge the processes of the regulator. As an example, the UK National Lottery regulator Oflot was challenged in the High Court during 2000 by Camelot – the existing Lottery franchise holder – when it alleged that it had been procedurally incorrect in the manner that it granted a new franchise to the rival People's Lottery. The Court instructed the regulator to reconsider its decision.

2.7 REGIONAL AND NATIONAL GOVERNMENT

Although many European countries, such as Germany and France, have had some degree of regional government, this has been largely absent in the UK. The end of the 1990s saw a potentially fundamental change in the structure of government in the UK with the emergence of regional elected government.

2.7.1 Scotland

Scotland was granted devolution by the passing of the Scotland Act in 1998 which means that Scotland has a parliament with 'devolved' powers within the United Kingdom. Any powers which remain with the UK Parliament at Westminster are 'reserved', and set out in Schedule 5 of the Scotland Act. Essentially the powers of the Scottish Parliament are defined by what it does not have legislative competence in rather than in what it can do. Devolved powers include matters such as education, health and prisons. Reserved powers comprise all other areas of decision making. Those decisions which have a UK-wide or an international impact are reserved and dealt with at Westminster.

The Scottish Parliament is made up of 129 Members (MSPs), one of whom is elected by the Parliament to serve as the Presiding Officer. Like the UK Parliament, the Scottish Parliament passes laws. It also scrutinizes the work and policies of the Scottish Executive. The Scottish Parliament is staffed by civil servants who serve the Parliament and, like the Presiding Officer, they must remain neutral.

The Scottish Executive is the government in Scotland for all devolved matters. It is formed from the party or parties holding a majority of seats in the Parliament. The Executive is led by the First Minister, who appoints other ministers and is supported by six administrative departments staffed by Civil Servants.

The Scottish Assembly has powers to vary income tax by plus or minus up to 3p in the pound to spend as it wishes. This, combined with the Scottish Parliament's ability to alter Scots law increasingly leads to disparities, such as on anti-smoking legislation, care of the elderly and student fees.

The UK government continues to appoint a Secretary of State for Scotland, who remains a member of the UK Cabinet and is responsible for reserved items of government within Scotland.

2.7.2 Wales

In Wales, the National Assembly for Wales consists of 60 members elected throughout Wales. The Welsh Assembly is responsible for developing and implementing policies and programmes for all issues that have been devolved to Wales, which include agriculture; ancient monuments and historic buildings; culture; economic development; education and training; the environment; health services; highways; housing; industry; local government; social services; sport and leisure; tourism; town and country planning; transport and roads; and the Welsh language. The First Minister leads the Assembly and chairs a Cabinet of eight other ministers. All Ministers are accountable to the Assembly and its committees for their actions. Unlike the Scottish Parliament, the Welsh Assembly has no tax-raising powers.

2.7.3 Northern Ireland

In Northern Ireland, an Assembly was established as part of the Belfast (or 'Good Friday') Agreement. Northern Ireland had previously had a high level of devolved administration through the UK government's Northern Ireland Office, and the Good Friday Agreement sought to re-establish a form of Parliament which had previously been suspended during two decades of the 'Troubles'. The newly established Northern Ireland Assembly consists of 108 elected Members – six from each of the 18 Westminster constituencies. Its role is primarily to scrutinize and make decisions on the issues dealt with by government departments and to consider and make legislation. A First Minister and a Deputy First Minister are elected to lead the Executive Committee of Ministers. Due to the history of divisions within Northern Ireland society, a complicated system was set up whereby the First Minister and Deputy First Minister must stand for election jointly and, to be elected, they must have cross-community support. Decisions in the Assembly are taken by a 'parallel consent formula', which means that a majority of both the members who have designated themselves Nationalists and those who have designated themselves Unionists, and a majority of the whole Assembly, must vote in favour. The Northern Ireland Assembly assumed responsibility for government functions previously handled by the UK government's Northern Ireland Office, and allocated its block allocation of government expenditure. The Northern Ireland Assembly had a troubled history and was suspended in October 2002, when the Secretary of State for Northern Ireland assumed responsibility for the direction of the Northern Ireland Departments.

2.7.4 London

In London, a referendum established the Greater London Authority. This provides for a directly elected mayor (Ken Livingstone was the first mayor elected in 2000, and re-elected in 2004), who has the role of a policy leader and Champion for London. The mayor's office is the executive of London's government – managing a budget of over £8 billion, and having revenue-raising powers (e.g. the London Congestion Charge is determined by the mayor). The London Assembly – an elected body – scrutinizes the mayor's policies, decisions and budget.

The Greater London Authority is made up of the mayor, the London Assembly and a team of over 600 staff supporting their work to develop and implement London-wide policies in respect of transport; policing; fire and emergency services; economic development; planning; culture and the environment. The mayor works closely with, and sets budgets for, Transport for London (TfL), the London Development Agency (LDA), the Metropolitan Police Authority (MPA), and the London Fire and Emergency Planning Authority (LFEPA). The Mayor also works closely with London's borough councils, which are responsible for providing many local services. The Mayor works with the boroughs to ensure that local and London-wide policies work together for maximum effect.

2.7.5 Other regional assemblies

The UK government published a White Paper on regional governance in 2002. It proposed to strengthen the existing regional institutions in England and take forward the government's manifesto commitment on elected regional government in England. However, a number of anomalies have arisen with the piecemeal development of regional government in the UK. The

THINKING AROUND THE SUBJECT:
POLITICAL VISION HELPS WIN OLYMPIC GAMES FOR LONDON

It has been claimed that having an elected mayor and assembly greatly assisted London in its successful bid to host the 2012 Olympic Games. At a time when much of the country was ambivalent about bidding for the Games, the mayor provided a focal point for championing the interests of London. The Games would bring more than 28 days of sporting activities, and provide a lasting legacy in terms of economic growth and social regeneration. The Games would also create opportunities for businesses, large and small, bringing thousands of new jobs in sectors ranging from construction, hospitality, media and environmental services. As well as leaving behind great sporting facilities, including swimming pools, a velodrome and hockey facilities, it was hoped that the games would inspire a new generation to greater sporting activity and achievement.

The mayor agreed with the government a funding package of up to £2.375 billion to help meet the costs of staging the Olympics. The first £2.050 billion would be met, with up to £1.5 billion from the Lottery and up to £550 million from London council tax, which would cost the average London household £20 a year, or 38p a week.

parliamentary arrangements for Scotland, Wales, Northern Ireland and London are all different. While all the regions have power to make local legislation, they all still elect MPs to the UK national Parliament, which can vote on legislation affecting England. England remains the only region without its own parliament and legislator.

Advocates of regional government argue that it will allow legislation and economic policy to be developed that is better suited to the needs of their area. Critics would argue that regional government creates more bureaucracy, which will cost businesses time and money. Instead of devolving powers down from central government, a Local Government Association study in 2004 suggested regional assemblies would actually lead to the transfer of authority upwards from local authorities to the new regional government bodies. There has been a muted response to the proposals and, in 2005, a referendum to establish a regional assembly in northeast England overwhelmingly rejected the proposal.

Delays in implementing policies may occur where the aims of national and regional governments differ, but co-operation between the two is essential if a regional policy is to be implemented successfully. Legal challenges by the London Assembly against the Department of Transport, Environment and Regions over privatization of the London Underground demonstrated that interdependencies between regional and national governments are likely to remain strong.

The likely effects of regional governments on business organizations is ambiguous. On the one hand it can be argued that increasing amounts of UK legislation are merely enactments of EU directives, which would need to be enacted regardless of whether it is the UK Parliament or regional assembly which assumes the responsibility. On the other hand there are many areas of discretion, which can lead to differences between regions. Where it has tax-raising powers, regional assembly funds can be directed towards what are considered to be regionally important social goals. As an example of differences which can emerge, the Scottish Parliament voted in 2001 to fund long-term care for elderly people, something which was not available in England, and thereby opening up business opportunities in Scotland which were not available in England.

2.8 LOCAL GOVERNMENT

Local authorities in the United Kingdom are responsible for a wide range of services, from social services and education to refuse collection and street cleaning. The structure of local government that was implemented in 1974 divided the largely rural areas of England into counties ('shire counties'), each with a County Council. The chief responsibilities of these County Councils included education, social services, emergency services, highways and refuse disposal. Shire counties were further subdivided into District Councils (sometimes designated as Borough or City Councils) which had responsibilities for housing, leisure services and refuse collection. Districts in rural areas were usually further divided into parishes with a Parish Council (sometimes designated as a Town Council) responsible for local matters such as the maintenance of playing fields.

In the larger conurbations, Metropolitan District Councils had greater functions than their shire county counterparts, for example they were additionally responsible for education and social services. Following the abolition of Metropolitan County Councils in 1986, responsibility for conurbation-wide services (such as public transport and emergency services) passed to a series of joint boards governed by the District Councils. In London, the pattern of government has been broadly similar to that of metropolitan areas, although there is now an assembly for the capital (see above). In Scotland, the structure of local government has been based on a two-tier system of Regional and District Councils.

From the mid-1990s, the basic structure of local government set up by the 1974 Act has been changed further by the appointment of commissions to study the needs of local government in individual areas. This has led to the emergence of 'unitary' authorities that combine functions of District and County Councils. Many large urban areas, such as Leicester, Nottingham and Bristol, have gained their own unitary authorities, in the hope that previous duplication of facilities provided by District and Council Councils can be avoided. As an example, the new 'unitary' authority for Leicester combines previous City Council functions of housing, refuse collection and car parking (among others) with responsibilities transferred from Leicestershire County Council for education, social services and highways.

Arguments for large County Councils based on economies of scale and centralized provision have given way to a philosophy based on small, locally responsive units acting as enablers for services provided by subcontracted suppliers. Even a small, recreated county such as Rutland, it is argued, can provide many services previously considered too complex for such a small unit, by buying them in from outside suppliers, or by acting in partnership with other local authorities.

2.8.1 The relationship between central and local government

It has been argued that local government in Britain is losing its independence from central government, despite claims by successive governments that they support a philosophy of less government and a decentralization of powers. There is a great deal of evidence of this erosion of local autonomy.

■ Over half of local government income now comes in the form of grants from the Department of Environment, Transport and Regions.

■ Local authorities have had the ability to set rates on business premises taken away from them altogether and these are now determined by central government.

■ Furthermore, central government has the power to set a maximum permitted total expenditure for a local authority and to set a maximum amount for its council tax due from householders.

In addition, legislation setting performance standards in education and social services (among others) has limited the independence of local government to set locally determined standards. Local authorities now have less local discretion in determining what is an acceptable standard for services in its area and in deciding between competing priorities.

Local authorities have had increasing numbers of functions removed from their responsibility and placed with Non-Departmental Public Bodies (NDPBs) which are no longer answerable to the local authority (for example, colleges of further education now have their own governing bodies).

2.9 THE EUROPEAN UNION

The European Union (EU), formerly known as the European Community (EC), has its origins in the European Coal and Steel Community. The EC was founded by the Treaty of Rome, signed in 1957 by the original six members of the ECSC – France, West Germany, Italy, Belgium, the Netherlands and Luxembourg. Britain joined the EC in 1972, together with Ireland and Denmark, to be joined by Greece in 1981, Spain and Portugal in 1986, and Austria, Finland and Sweden in 1995. A more significant expansion to the EU occurred in May 2004 when 10 countries of Central and Eastern Europe joined – Cyprus, the Czech Republic, Estonia, Hungary, Latvia, Lithuania, Malta, Poland, Slovakia and Slovenia. The additions brought the EU's population to 450 million in 25 countries. Romania and Bulgaria are expected to join the EU in 2007, and Turkey has begun accession talks.

The European Community linked with five of the seven members of the European Free Trade Association (EFTA) to create the European Economic Area (EEA). Three of these members subsequently became full members of the EU. The EEA agreement extended the four basic freedoms of the European Community to EEA members, that is, freedom of movement of services, freedom of movement of capital, freedom of movement of goods and freedom of movement of workers. Details of EU and EEA member states are shown in Figure 2.5.

2.9.1 Aims of the EU

The Treaty of Rome initially created a Customs Union and a Common Market. The creation of a Customs Union has involved the introduction of a common external tariff on trade with the rest of the world and the abolition of tariffs between member states. When the United

EU	Population, millions (2003)
Austria	8.1
Belgium	10.4
Cyprus	0.7
Czech Republic	10.2
Denmark	5.3
Estonia	1.3
Finland	5.2
France	59.6
Germany	82.5
Greece	11.0
Hungary	10.1
Ireland	3.9
Italy	57.3
Latvia	2.3
Lithuania	3.4
Luxembourg	0.4
Malta	0.4
Netherlands	16.2
Poland	38.2
Portugal	10.4
Slovakia	5.4
Slovenia	2.0
Spain	40.6
Sweden	8.9
United Kingdom	59.3
TOTAL	464.0
European Economic Area	
Iceland	0.3
Norway	4.5

Figure 2.5 Population of member states of the EU and EEA at 2003

Source: Population Statistics, Eurostat, Brussels 2004

Kingdom joined the EC, tariffs tended to encourage trade with Commonwealth countries at the expense of European countries. In particular, the UK had been able to obtain a source of relatively cheap agricultural produce from Commonwealth countries but, on joining the EC, was forced to phase in a common tariff for agricultural products imported from outside the EC.

An important aim of the Treaty of Rome was the creation of a common market in which trade could take place between member states as if they were one country. The implication of a common market is the free movement of trade, labour and capital between member states. Agriculture was the first sector in which a genuinely common market was created, with a system of common pricing and support payments between all countries and free movement of produce between member states. Further development of a common market has been impeded by a range of non-tariff trade barriers, such as national legislation specifying design standards, the cost and risk of currency exchange and the underlying desire of public authorities to back their own national industries. The creation of the Single European Market in January 1993 removed many of these barriers, but many practical barriers to trade still remain, of which differences in language and cultural traditions are probably the most intractable.

There is considerable debate about the form that future development of the EU should take and, in particular, the extent to which there should be political as well as economic union. Debate continues about the future of the EU and in recent times has focused on the following issues.

■ The creation of a common unit of currency has been seen by many as crucial to the development of a single European market, avoiding the cost and uncertainty for business and travellers of having to change currencies for cross-border transactions. The launch of the single European currency (the euro, now adopted by the 15 pre-2004 EU countries except the UK and Denmark) in 1999 has reduced transaction costs for trade between member states and has allowed member states' central banks to reduce their holdings of foreign currency. Within the UK, opposition to monetary union has been based on economic and political arguments. Economically, a common currency would deny to countries the opportunity to revalue or devalue their currency to suit the needs of their domestic economy. This lack of flexibility implies a political sacrifice, as control of currency is central to government management of the economy (although it should be noted that the UK government has handed over control of monetary policy to the Bank of England in an attempt to de-politicize financial policy). During 2001 so-called Eurosceptics seized on guidance given by the European Central Bank to the Irish government. Irish inflation was approaching upper limits set by the ECB, and in asking the Irish government to take fiscal measures to reduce inflation, this was seen as interfering in a very successful national economy.

Regardless of whether the UK government formally adopts the euro, businesses may start using the currency, in much the same way as non-USA companies often trade in US dollars. It will gain acceptability if businesses perceive the currency as being stable and widely accepted.

■ Argument continues about the amount of influence the EU should have in nation-states' social and economic policy. For example, previous UK governments have shown reluctance to agree to EU proposals which would harmonize personal taxation and social welfare benefits. The UK government has supported the idea of 'subsidiarity' whereby decisions are taken at the most localized level of government that is compatible with achieving EU objectives. Cynics have, however, pointed out that the UK government has not always been willing to practise this principle at home, as witnessed by the gradual erosion of the powers of local authorities in favour of central government.

■ There is concern that enlargement of the EU to include the less developed economies of Central and Eastern Europe could put strains on EU budgets. Many have argued that enlargement should allow the EU to become a loose federation of states, rather than a centralizing bureaucracy, which many critics claim it has become.

■ The principle of free movement of people across borders remains controversial in view of the possibility of large numbers of refugees or economic migrants being admitted by one state and then being automatically allowed to migrate to other member states.

■ Member states still have difficulty formulating a coherent foreign policy for the EU as a whole, as has been seen in the fragmented approach taken towards the 2004 invasion of Iraq.

■ There remains widespread concern about the lack of democratic accountability of EU institutions, not helped by allegations of excessive bureaucracy and corruption.

■ In order to meet the challenges posed by growth in the EU, a new constitution has been developed which will formalize the rights and responsibilities of member states. Inevitably, member states have widely differing experiences of written constitutions, and there has, not surprisingly, been a lot of debate about what such a constitution should cover (see below).

2.9.2 The structure of the EU

The Treaty of Rome (as modified by the Treaty of Maastricht) developed a structure of government whose elements reflect, in part, the structure of the UK government. The executive (or Cabinet) is provided by the European Council of Ministers; the secretariat (or Civil Service) is provided by the European Commission; while the legislature is provided by the European Parliament. The judiciary is represented by the European Court of Justice.

The Treaty of Rome places constraints upon the policies that the institutions of the EU can adopt. The European Court of Justice is able to rule that an action or decision is not in accordance with the Treaty. In some cases, such as competition policy, the Treaty is quite specific, for example Articles 85 and 86 which define the basic approach to be adopted in dealing with cartels and monopoly power. On the other hand, the Treaty says little more on transport policy than that there should be a common policy, giving the community institutions considerable power to develop policies.

The activities of the EU are now directly funded from income received from customs duties and other levies on goods entering the EU from non-member countries. In addition, a value added tax collected by member states on purchases by consumers includes an element of up to 1.45 per cent which is automatically transferred to the EU budget. More recently, a new resource transfer payment between member states and the EU has been introduced which is based on the gross domestic product of each member state. The United Kingdom remains a net contributor to the EU budget.

New legislation is increasingly the result of co-operation between the various institutions of the EU. The process of co-operation is shown in Figure 2.6 and the role of the principal institutions described below. There have been attempts to simplify this process following expansion of the EU from 15 to 25 members.

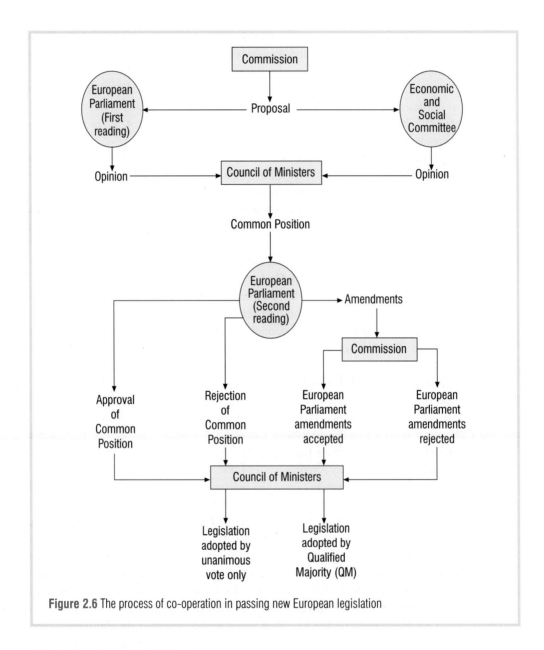

Figure 2.6 The process of co-operation in passing new European legislation

2.9.3 The Council of Ministers

The Council of Ministers represents the governments of member states and can be regarded as the principal lawmaker of the EU, although it can act only on proposals submitted by the Commission. It has powers to:

- adopt legislation
- ratify treaties after consultation with the European Parliament
- ask the Commission to undertake studies and to submit legislation
- delegate executive and legislative powers to the Commission.

Each member state sends one minister to the European Council of Ministers. Which minister attends will depend on the subject being discussed – for example, agriculture ministers would be sent if the Common Agricultural Policy were being discussed. The ministers of foreign affairs, of agriculture, and those with budgetary responsibilities meet more frequently, making a senior body within the Council, sometimes called the General Council. The chairmanship or presidency of the Council of Ministers rotates between countries in alphabetical order, with each period of presidency lasting for six months (see below for proposed constitutional changes in the method of selecting the President).

The Council of Ministers adopts new legislation either by simple majority, qualified majority or unanimity.

- Simple majority gives each minister one vote and is used for proposals such as procedural rules for the convening of intergovernmental conferences.
- Qualified majority voting is based on a weighted voting system where member states' votes are roughly proportional to their size and economic strength. Qualified majority voting prevents smaller states being consistently outvoted and eliminates the risk of two of the larger member states constituting a blocking majority. Examples of applications of this method of voting include legislation on completion of the internal market; the freedom to provide professional services across national borders; and measures to free up the movement of capital within the EU.
- Unanimity is required on issues that are fundamental to individual member states' interests, such as enlargement of the EU, harmonization of taxation and extension of EU powers.

In 2000 an intergovernmental conference of ministers agreed to reduce the number of areas in which unanimity was required, to be further codified by a proposed EU constitution (see below). With the prospect of enlargement, achieving unanimity between all member states has become increasingly difficult.

The Council of Ministers can generally pass laws even if the European Parliament disagrees with them, unlike the practice within the UK and other national parliamentary systems where ministers must obtain the approval of a majority of Members of Parliament. There are two main exceptions to this authority of the Council. First, the European Parliament has power to approve or reject the EU budget (see below). Second, the Single European Act introduced a system of legislative co-operation between the Council and Parliament, obliging the Council and the Commission to take Parliament's amendments to proposals into consideration, although a unanimous vote by the Council of Ministers retains ultimate authority.

The Committee of Permanent Representatives (Coreper) complements the work of the Council of Ministers. Because ministers have responsibilities to their own national governments as well as to the European Union, they cannot give a continuing presence. To make up for this, each member state sends one ambassador to the Committee, which is based in Brussels. Proposals are discussed in Coreper and its sub-committees before they reach ministers. If Coreper reaches full agreement on the matter, it is empowered to pass it through the Council without further debate, but where disagreement occurs it is left for ministers to discuss.

2.9.4 The European Commission

Each member state sends one commissioner to the Commission (the larger members send two), each appointed by the member government for a renewable term of four years. They are supported in their work by a staff of about 14,000 civil servants, divided between 23 directorates-general and mainly based at the Commission's headquarters in Brussels. Each commissioner is given responsibility for a portfolio which could be for a policy area such as transport, or for administrative matters such as the Commission's relations with the Parliament, while others are given a combination of responsibilities in their portfolio. Unlike the Council of Ministers, all members of the Commission are supposed to act primarily for the benefit of the Union as a whole, rather than the country that they represent. This is spelt out in Article 157 of the Treaty of Rome, which states that commissioners 'shall neither seek nor take instruction from any other body'.

The Commission has an initiation, mediation and implementation role. As an initiator, it is the task of the Commission to draft proposals for legislation which the Council of Ministers has to consider. If the Council does not accept a proposal, it can only alter the draft by a unanimous vote. If unanimity cannot be achieved, the proposal has to go back to the Commission for it to draft a revised proposal which will be acceptable to the Council of Ministers.

As a mediator, the Commission can intervene in disputes between member states to try to find a solution through negotiation. The Commission has frequently acted as mediator in trade disputes between members, avoiding recourse to the European Court of Justice. As an implementer, the Commission undertakes the day-to-day administration of the EU. This involves monitoring the activities of member states to ensure that they do not conflict with community policy. In addition, the Commission implements community policies such as the Regional Development Fund and Common Agricultural Policy.

2.9.5 The European Parliament

Unlike the UK Parliament, the European Parliament is primarily consultative and has relatively little power. Its main function is to monitor the activities of other EU institutions. It can give an opinion on Commission proposals but has powers only to amend, adopt or reject legislation, especially the EU budget. It also has the theoretical power to dismiss the entire Commission, for which a censure motion must be passed by a two-thirds majority of members. Although it can dismiss the entire Commission, the Parliament has no control over the selection of new commissioners to replace those who have been dismissed. It does not yet have the power to initiate and enact legislation.

Members of the European Parliament are now directly elected by the constituents of each country, with countries returning members roughly in proportion to their populations. The European Parliament generally meets in Strasbourg, but Parliamentary Committee meetings are held in Brussels and in Luxembourg, where the Parliament's Secretariat is mainly based. Members of the European Parliament increasingly belong to political rather than national groupings (e.g. the British Conservative MEPs sit in the European People's Party).

2.9.6 The European Court of Justice

The supreme legislative body of the EU is the Court of Justice. Article 164 of the Treaty of Rome gave the Court the task of 'ensuring that the law is observed in the interpretation and implementation of the Treaty'. It is the final arbiter in all matters of interpreting community treaties and rules on disputes between member states, between member states and the Commission, and between the Commission and business organizations, individuals or EU officials. Although the Court can condemn violations of the Treaty by member governments, it has no sanctions against them except goodwill. The European Court of Justice can investigate complaints that the Commission has acted beyond its powers and, if upheld, can annul decisions of the Commission.

The European Court of Justice is composed of 15 judges, assisted by nine advocates-general. Each is appointed by common agreement between the member states on the basis of their qualifications and impartiality, for a renewable six-year term of office. Members of the Court must put European interests before national interests. The Court can be called upon to settle disputes where the persuasion and negotiations of the Commission have failed to yield results. For example, in the area of competition policy, the Commission may by decision forbid an anti-competitive practice or impose a fine. The companies concerned can appeal to the European Court of Justice for the decision to be set aside. In one case, several dye producers appealed to the European Court of Justice against the fines imposed on them for an alleged price cartel.

2.9.7 The EU constitution

The European Union is in a state of flux. Its main institutions – the commission, the Council of Ministers and the European Parliament – remain widely unloved and vulnerable to charges of inefficiency and lack of transparency. But, paradoxically, the EU is in many respects more active than ever before.

The administration of the EU has subtly changed as the EU has matured. The initiative for many new proposals has been the European Council – summits of EU leaders held three or four times a year. By contrast, the European Commission has tended to become more of an administrator of programmes rather than the bold innovator that launched the single market in the 1980s. It was badly demoralized in March 1999 when the 20-strong commissioners headed by Jacques Santer resigned after a critical report alleging nepotism, fraud and mismanagement. At the Nice summit in 2000, the leaders of member states identified the urgent task of defining how powers would be divided between Brussels and national governments, and aimed to achieve this at an intergovernmental conference in 2004. The result was a proposed constitution for the EU. This had become urgently needed because the expansion of the EU to 25 member states in 2004 had threatened to slow down the process of decision making to the speed of the slowest country.

The treaty to establish a constitution for Europe was agreed by EU heads of government in June 2004, but rejected in May 2005 by referenda of voters in France and the Netherlands.

The proposed constitution brought together for the first time the many treaties and agreements on which the EU is based. It sought to define the powers of the EU, stating where it can act and where the member states retain their right of veto. It also defines the role of the EU institutions.

Although the proposed EU constitution may have suffered a setback following its rejection by French and Dutch voters, the pressure to modernize and formalize EU administration remains. The constitution sought to apply the principle of voting by qualified majority, as it was recognized that, otherwise, getting the agreement of all 25 members would stifle progress. However, member states remain keen to retain a veto, especially in areas of foreign policy, defence and taxation. There is pressure for the European Parliament to have an equal say on decisions requiring majority voting.

There has also been pressure for the appointment of a President of the EU for a term longer than the current rotating six-month presidency. A permanent President would potentially have much greater influence inside and outside the EU.

2.9.8 Relationship between the EU and the United Kingdom government

A distinction needs to be drawn between primary and secondary legislation of the EU. Primary legislation is contained in the Treaty of Rome (and subsequent treaties agreed by an intergovernmental conference) and takes precedence over national legislation, although national legislation may be required to implement it. Primary legislation can be altered only by an intergovernmental conference of all members. Secondary legislation is made by the Council of Ministers and the Commission under authority delegated to them by the treaties. Secondary legislation affects member states in several forms.

- Regulations automatically form part of the law of member states and apply directly to every individual in the EU. They give rights and duties to individuals that national courts must recognize.
- Directives are mandatory instructions to member states, which must take steps to implement them through national legislation. For example, national laws concerning vehicle safety have varied from state to state and, as a result, trade across frontiers may be impeded. One solution has been to harmonize standards between all member states by means of a directive. The directive will require member states to amend their national legislation governing the design of cars. Individuals will then have to obey the modified national law.
- Decisions of the EU are directly binding on the specific individuals or organizations to whom they are addressed, as where the Commission intervenes in a proposed merger between organizations.

2.9.9 Effects of EU membership on UK business organizations

The EU is having an increasingly important effect on business organizations in the United Kingdom. The relationship between a company and its customers is increasingly being influenced by EU regulations and directives, for example in the provision of safety features in cars and the labelling of foods. The influence extends to the relationship between the firm and the public at large, as where the EU passes directives affecting advertising standards and pollution controls. Business organizations must monitor proposed EU legislation not only to spot possible changes in legislation which will eventually be implemented through national legislation, but also to lobby to bring about a desired change in EU law. To an increasing extent, lobbying of the UK parliamentary process is becoming less effective as the United Kingdom is bound to implement legislation emanating from the EU.

The extent to which the Single European Market legislation will further affect business organizations is open to debate. The EU has already had the effect of removing tariff barriers within the Community and great progress has been made on EU legislation specifying common product design standards. Firms are increasingly seeing Europe as one market and

**THINKING AROUND THE SUBJECT:
EU DIRECTIVES CAUSE A HEADACHE FOR MANUFACTURERS OF HERBAL
REMEDIES**

The importance of understanding the complexities and different levels of political environments was illustrated by the case of a new EU directive affecting food supplements and herbal remedies that was scheduled to come into force in 2005.

The EU had earlier passed two directives which would place all herbal medicines and vitamin and mineral supplements on the same regulatory basis as medicines. More than 300 widely used 'natural remedies' would be banned altogether and the cost of licensing each product – estimated at up to £2000 per product – would be beyond the means of many of the small producers that dominated the market for natural remedies. The big pharmaceutical companies had been lobbying the EU hard to get such a change, citing 'adverse reactions' from many herbal remedies and vitamin supplements such as vitamin B6. Of course, they knew that driving thousands of small herbal producers out of business would draw customers to the pharmaceutical companies' mass-produced products. The natural remedy producers were much more fragmented than the large pharmaceutical companies and were slow to get their lobbying together. In November 2002, the sector presented to the UK government a petition protesting about the proposed changes. It contained over 1 million signatures, including those of Sir Paul McCartney and Sir Elton John, but it was too late because the directives had already been passed by the EU and there was now little discretion left for the UK government. The lobbyists of the pharmaceutical industry seemed to have outsmarted the lobbyists of the natural remedy firms and understood where and when to apply pressure.

In this case, the herbal remedy industry portrayed the EU as a remote and bureaucratic institution which was harming the interests not only of producers, but also customers who bought its products. However, at other times, businesses have been avid supporters of greater European integration, although sceptics have pointed out that a lot of this may be opportunistic. As an example, brewers have in the past condemned the European Commission's plans for tighter control over the labelling of beer, claiming their national beer is unique, but this has not prevented them also campaigning for a harmonization of taxes where the tax paid in their own country is higher than the EU average.

The EU is accounting for an increasing proportion of the legislation that affects UK businesses. Should the herbal remedy producers have recognized this, and applied their pressure to the EU at an early stage in the drafting of the directives, rather than wait to apply pressure to the UK government?

designing standardized products which appeal to consumers in a number of EU states. Many would argue that overseas investors, especially American firms, have always regarded Europe as one market and developed products as varied as soft drinks and cars to satisfy the whole European market. However, no amount of legislation is likely to overcome the hidden barriers to trade provided by language and by ingrained market characteristics such as the UK practice of driving on the left and using electrical plugs that are not used elsewhere in Continental Europe.

The UK was not among the initial group of countries that launched the single European currency. Shortly after launch, the value of the euro fell sharply against sterling, making exports from the UK to the rest of the EU more expensive (and competitors' imports to the

UK cheaper). The high value of sterling was blamed by many manufacturing companies for decisions to move operations to within the euro area, or to not make further investments in the UK. However, there was little evidence of actual amounts of inward investment falling during the period that the value of sterling remained high. Many firms benefited from the high value of sterling, as imported components became less expensive. The subject of the impact of the euro on business is considered further in Chapter 12.

2.10 SUPRANATIONAL GOVERNMENTAL ORGANIZATIONS

National governments' freedom of action is further constrained by international agreements and membership of international organizations. In general, although the treaties of the EU impose duties on the UK government which it is obliged to follow, membership of other supranational organizations is voluntary and does not have binding authority on the UK government.

Probably the most important organization which affects UK government policy is the United Nations (UN). Its General and Security Councils are designed as fora in which differences between countries can be resolved through negotiation rather than force. In the field of international trade, the UN has sought to encourage freedom of trade through the United Nations Conference on Trade and Development (UNCTAD). In matters of national security, the United Kingdom is a member of the North Atlantic Treaty Organization (NATO), whose role is changing following the end of the 'Cold War'.

Because the importance to the United Kingdom of international treaties and organizations lies to such a great extent in their benefits for international trade, they are considered in more detail in Chapter 12.

2.11 IMPROVING THE STANDARDS OF GOVERNMENT ADMINISTRATION

There have been a number of government initiatives to improve the standards of public-sector services which are provided in an environment where there is no market discipline. These generally use a combination of carrot and stick approaches, offering rewards to those public bodies that are performing well, while taking funds away from those that are failing.

In this section, we will consider a number of recent UK government initiatives – performance measures, 'best value indicators' and the sometimes elusive aim of bringing about 'joined-up government'.

2.11.1 Government performance targets

Government organizations have been set increasingly detailed performance targets, for example the waiting time for a hospital appointment, the percentage of household waste that is recycled, and the time taken to process a passport application. Managers are often paid a bonus based on their achievement of targets. Of course, such micromanagement by government through targets can lead to dysfunctional outcomes. It was famously noted that when the centralized Russian government set output targets for state-owned nail factories by weight, the factories simply produced very large nails which few people wanted. To overcome this problem, targets need to be specified in more detail, resulting in a greater data collection burden for managers.

An alternative approach is to encourage public-sector organizations to achieve status labels based on their performance. The Charter Mark is a UK government award scheme which aims to recognize and encourage excellence in public service. It also plays a powerful role as a quality improvement tool, focusing on customer service and service delivery. Unlike many quality management tools adopted by the private sector (which essentially focus on production processes), the Charter Mark is unique among quality schemes in the way it concentrates on results: the service the user actually receives. Achieving the Charter Mark standard is an indication that a government department or agency has put its users first.

All public-sector organizations that deal directly with the public are eligible to apply for a Charter Mark. The scheme is also extended to voluntary organizations providing a service to the public and receiving at least 10 per cent of their income from public-sector funds. Government subcontractors can apply as long as they provide a service to the public, which is provided elsewhere by another public-sector organization.

A wide range of government organizations have been successful in applying for a Charter Mark, including branches of the Benefits Agency and courts services, and local HGV testing stations. The Trading Standards Service of West Sussex had its Charter Mark status renewed in 2004, having first been awarded it in 2000.

In local government, the Beacon Council Scheme was set up to facilitate the sharing of excellent practice among local authorities by holding out such authorities as exemplars to be followed by others. Each year the government selects themes for the beacon scheme which are important to improving the quality of life in local communities. Beacon status is granted to those authorities that can demonstrate a clear vision, excellent services and a willingness to innovate within a specific theme. However, to obtain beacon status, applicants must also demonstrate that they have good overall performance, and not just in the service area for which beacon status is awarded. All authorities can apply to become a beacon, and the final decision is made by government ministers based on recommendations of an independent advisory panel. Authorities hold the status for a year and share their good practice through a series of learning exchanges, open days and other learning activities. As an example, Bexley Council was chosen in 2004 as a Beacon Council for its success in cutting anti-social behaviour and crime.

2.11.2 Obtaining best value in local government

Given that local authorities account for a high proportion of total public expenditure, central government has been increasingly determined to ensure that authorities spend their money wisely and do not exceed total public-sector spending limits. During the 1980s the UK government introduced Compulsory Competitive Tendering (CCT) for a range of services provided by local authorities. This required an ever-increasing range of services which had been provided internally by an authority to be given to a private- or public-sector organization that could provide the service at the lowest cost. From relatively straightforward services such as refuse collection, the scope of CCT eventually extended to many professional services provided by local authorities, including accountancy and legal services. By the 1990s it had become apparent that CCT's emphasis on cost reduction had done little to improve the quality of services provided by local authorities. Moreover, the process of competitive tendering consumed large amounts of staff time and the financial savings resulting from tendering were becoming more illusory.

THINKING AROUND THE SUBJECT:
HOW GOOD IS THE NATIONAL HEALTH SERVICE?

One of the recurring problems of public-sector services is monitoring their performance, in an environment where market mechanisms alone will not reward the good performers and punish the bad. The UK has prided itself on a centralized National Health Service (NHS) which is free to consumers, and paid for largely out of government taxation. But how do you measure the performance of doctors, either individually or in teams? The NHS has focused its efforts on quality of service issues. It routinely monitors a number of quality of service indicators, for example the waiting time to see a consultant or to have elective surgery undertaken. But even such apparently simple indicators can hide a lot of problems. What does it mean when one consultant is shown to keep their patients waiting for longer than another consultant? To many people, a long waiting list may be a sign of a top-rated consultant who is very popular with patients, rather than a failing professional who cannot keep up with the demands put on them. And then, of course, figures for waiting time can often be manipulated, scrupulously or unscrupulously. For example, Accident and Emergency departments use triage nurses to assess new patients upon arrival, thereby keeping within their Patients' Charter target for the time taken to initially see a new patient. However, the hospital may be slower to provide actual treatment. In 2003, a number of ambulance services were reprimanded for trying to make their response times appear better than they actually were, by measuring the response time from when an ambulance set out, rather than when a call for help was received.

Attempts to measure doctors' medical performance are much less developed, with debate about the most appropriate methodologies for assessing the efficacy of an operation or clinical diagnosis. Many medical outcomes cannot be assessed simply on the basis of success/failure, but require more subjective quality of life assessments to be taken into account. Nevertheless, in the UK's private healthcare sector, BUPA announced in 2004 that it would publish statistics showing patients' recovery rates for its named doctors. Meanwhile, the National Health Service was keeping its eyes on developments.

Some doctors have expressed a concern that merely publishing performance indicators pushes up users' expectations of service delivery, so that in the end they may become more dissatisfied even though actual performance has improved. Is there a case for treating doctors as professionals whose professional ethics leads them to do their very best for their patients? Or is this inward-looking approach to professional standards becoming increasingly untenable in an era of well-informed consumers who know their rights and have high expectations?

An alternative approach was adopted by the Local Government Act 1999, which introduced the concept of 'best value' in specified local authorities. The Act places on authorities a duty to seek continuous improvement in the way they exercise their functions. At the heart of best value is a statutory performance management framework. This provides for a set of national performance indicators and standards set by the government. In order to ensure the best value performance indicators give a balanced view of performance, the government has adopted five 'dimensions' of performance. These are as follows.

1 Strategic objectives: why the service exists and what it seeks to achieve.
2 Cost/efficiency: the resources committed to a service and the efficiency with which they are turned into outputs.

3 Service delivery outcomes: how well the service is being operated in order to achieve the strategic objectives.
4 Quality: the quality of the services delivered, explicitly reflecting users' experience of services.
5 Fair access: ease and equality of access to services.

A series of best value performance indicators has been set by the government. The Best Value Corporate Health indicators provide a snapshot of how well the authority is performing overall. These indicators are designed to reflect the underlying capacity and performance of local authorities and other public bodies responsible for managing a significant share of public expenditure. Best Value Service Delivery indicators are designed to enable comparisons to be made between the performances of different authorities, including different types of authorities and within an authority over time. Authorities need to set targets for all indicators that are relevant to the services they provide.

2.11.3 Joined-up government

Central, regional and local government can at times seem an amorphous mass of departments, each not appearing to know what the others are doing. There have been many documented cases where different government departments have taken completely opposing policy directions, thereby cancelling each other out (see 'Thinking around the subject' on p. 72).

The UK government sought to overcome such problems with the publication in 1999 of a White Paper on modernizing government. As a result of this, a government task force asked groups of public-sector volunteers, called integrated-service teams, to put themselves in the position of a member of the public experiencing one of a number of major life events, such as leaving school, becoming unemployed, changing address, having a baby or retiring. Team members contacted the relevant departments and agencies direct, and their research gave insights into the problems resulting from the way services are organized, and what might be done to improve things. The study found, for example, that people had to give the same information more than once to different – or even the same – organizations: for example, Housing Benefit and Income Support forms both ask for very similar information.

Having identified the problems, Service Action Teams (SATs) were created to look into particular life episodes that caused most problems in dealing with multiple departments and agencies. Early evidence of the move to joined-up government was seen in the trial integration of previously separate agencies dealing with finding employment and the payment of unemployment benefits.

Creating 'joined-up' thinking is never easy, even within profit-orientated private-sector organizations. In seeking to achieve integration within government, the administration must balance the need to share responsibilities with the need to hold manageable-sized units accountable for their actions.

2.12 IMPACTS OF GOVERNMENT ON BUSINESS OPERATIONS

We will now return to impacts of the political environment on business organizations and discuss three levels of effect:

1 the transformation of many government departments into 'Non-Departmental Government Bodies', so that they act more like a business organization rather than a government department

2 the outsourcing of many government functions through public–private partnerships (PPPs)

3 the effects of government legislation on business operations.

THINKING AROUND THE SUBJECT:
DOES THE LEFT HAND KNOW WHAT THE RIGHT HAND IS DOING?

The government of a large modern economy necessarily involves dividing responsibilities between departments, each of which is given increasingly clear aims and objectives, as well as what are usually vague objectives 'to co-ordinate their activities with other departments'. But despite talk about 'joined-up government', evidence of disjointed government is often all too clear to see. Consider the following cases.

Farming in Britain and the EU has traditionally relied on high levels of government intervention and farmers have often spotted inconsistencies in government policy. For a period during the 1990s, the Department of Agriculture was paying farmers to drain wetlands to turn into farmland. At the same time, the Department of Environment was paying landowners to create ponds and marshland from farmland in order to foster wildlife.

The Department of Education has promoted the recruitment of students from overseas, which is good for the national economy, and the longer-term cultural benefits of having students study in the UK. However, in 2004, the Home Office announced that it was doubling the fee for issuing visas to overseas students, and the number of overseas student applications subsequently fell. Were the government and the country any better off as a result of these apparently conflicting actions?

In 2004, the problem of 'binge drinking' late at night in town centres became a priority area for the Home Office. It was particularly concerned by pubs' practice of offering a 'happy hour' in which drinks were sold at a reduced price, leading to problems of drunkenness. The Home Office urged pubs to drop their happy hours. In one Essex town, pub landlords met under the auspices of their Licensed Victuallers Association and agreed with the Home Office that the happy hour should be abolished. The pub landlords realized that it would be pointless for just one pub to abolish it, because customers would simply go to those pubs which retained cheap drinks. They therefore agreed collectively to abolish the happy hour for all pubs in the town. But this upset another government agency, the Office of Fair Trading, which claimed that the pub landlords were in danger of prosecution for breaching competition law which made any agreement between suppliers to fix prices illegal.

Some businesses have exploited gaps in government thinking to their own advantage. However, to many businesses, such as the well-meaning pub landlords, the appearance that the left hand of government doesn't know what the right hand is doing can be very frustrating. But how in practice can such a large institution as a national government be made to be entirely consistent in the diverse objectives which its departments set?

2.12.1 Non-Departmental Public Bodies (NDPBs)

The 1990s saw significant developments in the delegation of powers from government organizations to 'arm's length' executive agencies, often referred to collectively as quasi-autonomous non-governmental organizations (Quangos) or, more correctly, Non-Departmental Public Bodies (NDPBs). In Britain, quasi-governmental bodies exist because direct involvement by a government department in an activity is considered to be inefficient or undesirable, while leaving the activity to the private sector may be inappropriate where issues of public policy are concerned. The quasi-government body therefore represents a compromise between the constitutional needs of government control and the organizational needs of independence and flexibility associated with private-sector organizations.

There is nothing new in arm's length organizations being created by governments, for example the Arts Council has existed since before the Second World War. As the size of the state increased in the early post-Second World War period, there was concern that government departments were becoming overloaded. In 1968 the Fulton Committee came out in favour of 'hiving off' some government activities and NDPBs were one means of doing this.

A flood of NDPBs created during the 1970s (e.g. the Equal Opportunities Board, Regional Tourist Boards and the Civil Aviation Authority) led to Opposition calls for a cut in their number. However, the incoming Conservative government of 1979 soon began adding to their number, after a token culling of a few unpopular bodies. In particular, the privatization programme led to the creation of regulators for the utilities. These are non-ministerial government departments, but with built-in independence from ministerial control. The Conservative governments from the 1980s onwards were responsible for a significant increase in the number of NDPBs , which had reached 5500 by 1994. In that year they accounted for £46.4 billion of expenditure, equivalent to about one-third of total government expenditure.

Many aspects of government have been devolved to NDPBs. These are some examples:

■ regulatory bodies (e.g. Ofcom, Ofwat and Ofgem)
■ Regional Development Agencies
■ the Driver and Vehicle Licensing Agency.

NDPBs enjoy considerable autonomy from their parent department and the sponsoring minister has no direct control over the activities of the body, other than making the appointment of the chairman. The minister therefore ceases to be answerable to Parliament for the day-to-day activities of the body, unlike the responsibility that a minister has in respect of a government department. The responsibilities of NDPBs vary from being purely advisory to making important policy decisions and allocating large amounts of expenditure. Their income can come from a combination of government grant, precepts from local authorities and charges to users.

The main advantage of delegation to NDPBs is that action can generally be taken much more quickly than may have been the case with a government department, where it would probably have been necessary to receive ministerial approval before action was taken. Ministers may have less time to devote to the details of policy application with which many NDPBs are often involved, and may also be constrained to a much greater extent by broader considerations of political policy. Being relatively free of day-to-day political interference, NDPBs are in a better position to maintain a long-term plan free of short-term diversions which may be the result of direct control by a minister who is subject to the need for short-term political popularity.

Against the advantages, NDPBs have a number of potential disadvantages over government departments. It is often argued that NDPBs are not sufficiently accountable to elected representatives for their actions. This can become an important issue where an NDPB is responsible for developing policy or is a monopoly provider of an essential service. Many have also questioned the actual independence of NDPBs from government, as many are still dependent on government funding for block grants. NDPBs can easily become unpopular with the public, especially where senior managers are seen paying themselves high salaries as they take 'business-like' decisions to cut back on services that they provide to the public.

A major objective of delegation to NDPBs has been to ensure that services are provided more in line with users' requirements rather than political or operational expediency. High-level appointments to NDPBs have been made from the private sector with a view to bringing about a cultural change that develops a customer-focused ethos. For the marketing services industry, the development of NDPBs has resulted in many opportunities as they increasingly use the services of market research firms, advertising agencies and public relations consultants.

2.12.2 Public–private partnerships (PPPs)

Throughout Europe, collaborative partnerships between the public and private sectors have become increasingly popular. In the UK, public-private partnerships (PPPs) is the umbrella name given to a range of initiatives which involve the private sector in the operation of public services. The Private Finance Initiative (PFI) is the most common initiative but PPPs could also extend to other forms of partnership, for example joint ventures. The key difference between PFI and conventional ways of providing public services is that the public sector does not own the asset. The authority makes an annual payment to the private company, which provides the building and associated services.

Traditionally, government has procured facilities and services which the private sector has supplied under contract to the public sector. For example, under the traditional route, a private-sector contractor would build a new school to a Local Education Authority's (LEA) specification, with associated maintenance and services then being provided by a range of private companies and the LEA itself. With PPPs, one contractor provides the school and then operates a range of specific services such as maintenance, heating and school meals on behalf of the LEA through a long-term contract. This new way of working allows the private sector to contribute its expertise to the process, so as to find innovative solutions and secure better value for money. A typical PFI project will be owned by a company set up especially to run the scheme. These companies are usually consortia including a building firm, a bank and a facilities management company. While PFI projects can be structured in different ways, there are usually four key elements: design, finance, build and operations. In the case of new hospitals funded by PFI schemes, the clinical, medical and nursing services continue to be provided by the NHS, while the private sector finances the building of the new hospital and runs the non-clinical services in it such as maintenance, cleaning, portering and security.

The most significant benefits to government of PPP come through transferring risk to the private sector. This means that should a project under the PPP overrun its budget, the government and taxpayers should not be left to pick up the bill. Contrast this with a major project taken forward under direct contract to the public sector, such as London Transport's Jubilee

Line Extension. This overran its planned budget by around £1.4 billion and opened nearly two years late, forcing the government to use taxpayers' money and grant additional funds to get the project completed.

In principle, a PPP will result in a lower level of government borrowing and it should also achieve best value. A public-sector comparator is developed in order to establish whether the PPP represents better value than government providing the service by itself. It will show the overall cost of raising the finance and actually doing the work under a wholly public-sector arrangement.

Critics of PPPs argue that the price of involvement by the private sector inevitably includes a high premium to cover the risk of a budget overrun which could come about for a variety of extraneous reasons. Although the government is saved the initial capital expenditure, over the longer term it has to pay rental charges for the use of facilities, which could work out more expensive than undertaking the whole task itself. The private sector borrows at higher rates of interest than the public sector, and this cost has to be passed on to the purchasing government department. Audit Scotland has calculated these costs as adding £0.2–£0.3 million each year for every £10 million invested. PFI projects can also have high set-up costs due to lengthy negotiations involving lawyers and consultants employed by both sides. It has been reported that the first 15 NHS trust hospital PFIs spent £45 million on advisers, an average of 4 per cent of the capital value.

There is growing evidence that PFI projects escalate both in scale and cost, reflecting not just inflation but the very nature of PFI itself. In many cases, the PFI agreement places some responsibility for cost overruns with the government rather than the private sector, especially where specifications have changed during the duration of the contract. The higher costs can lead to an affordability gap for the procuring authority that is met by reductions in services and capacity.

There have been casualties among PFI providers. In 2005, Jarvis, a major provider of PFI schemes to schools, hospitals and fire stations, narrowly avoided bankruptcy which had been threatened by cost overrun in a number of its PFI projects. A secondary market in PFI projects had developed, and Jarvis concluded agreements to transfer its interest in most of its remaining projects.

2.12.3 Impacts of government legislation on business operations

Very few governments, whether free market or interventionist, would claim to have made life more difficult for businesses to operate. Yet a frequent complaint of many businesses, especially small business owners, is that government expects them to do too much administration on behalf of the government. Despite frequent high-profile government campaigns against 'red tape', the volume of regulation continues to have a major impact on the costs of business organizations. While large organizations may be able to afford specialists to handle administrative matters and can spread the cost over large volumes of output, government regulation can hit small businesses very hard. Consider some of the following examples of regulations that have added to the costs of business organizations in recent years.

■ Value added tax (VAT) effectively makes most business organizations tax collectors on behalf of government, and small business owners must become familiar with complex sets of regulations.

■ Legislation to give additional rights to employees bears down particularly heavily on small businesses. Granting maternity rights to new mothers may be easily absorbed by large organizations, but a small business may experience great difficulties when one person who represents a large and critical part of the workforce decides to exercise their rights.

■ The mounting volume of consumer protection and health and safety legislation has a particularly big impact on small businesses which do not generally have the expertise to readily assimilate the provisions of new regulations.

A number of attempts have been made to quantify the costs to business organizations of government regulation. The British Chamber of Commerce's 'Burdens Barometer' is independently compiled by the London and Manchester Business Schools. Its Barometer for 2005 indicates that the cost of 46 major regulations introduced by the UK government since 1998 resulted in annual costs to business of over £15 billion. Figure 2.7 shows a sample of these 46 regulations and the calculated resulting financial burden on business (BCC 2005).

It appeared to many that even the introduction of the Internet, which was supposed to simplify many administrative tasks, led to new government-imposed burdens on businesses. Worried at the prospect of organized crime using the Internet, the government passed the controversial Regulation of Investigatory Powers (RIP) Act. This was bitterly contested by business for its provisions enabling the interception of emails and electronic correspondence.

The incoming New Labour government of 1997 set out − as with many previous governments − on a mission to reduce unnecessary regulation, by creating the Better Regulation Task Force. The task force has produced a number of recommendations to government about ways in which the administrative burden could be reduced, but in reaching its recommendations it has to balance efficiency improvements against the often opposing need for greater protection of individuals which regulations provide.

The work of the task force can be seen in its impact on regulation governing the use of electronic signatures over the Internet. While the RIP was viewed as interventionist and heavy-handed, the Electronic Communications Act, passed in 2000, has been broadly accepted as positive and light of touch. The Act allows companies and individuals to use electronic signatures to conduct their business, and accredits organizations providing encryption services. Industry welcomed the move as it will enable companies to take advantage of technology to speed up their legal transactions. Moreover, the government listened to industry and the Better Regulation Task Force, and adopted a hands-off solution to regulation − saying it would not intervene in accreditation if the industry came up with an effective self-regulation system before 2005.

2.13 INFLUENCES ON GOVERNMENT POLICY FORMATION

Political parties were described earlier as organizations that people belong to in order to influence government policy, generally over a range of issues. Political parties aim to work within the political system, for example by having members elected as MPs or local councillors. A distinction can be drawn between political parties and pressure groups or interest groups. These latter groups seek to change policy in accordance with members' interests, generally advancing a relatively narrow cause. Unlike members of political parties, members of pressure groups generally work from outside the political system and do not become part of the political establishment.

Regulation	Date of first implementation	Estimated annual recurring cost to UK business (£m)	Cumulative cost to UK businesses from date of introduction to July 2005 (£m)
The Working Time Regulations 1999	1999	2,300	13,608
Employment Act 2002	2002	530	645
Flexible Working (Procedural Arrangements) 2002	2003	240	760
The Maternity and Parental Leave (Amendment) Regulations 2001	2001	32	180
The Money Laundering Regulations 2003	2004	106	154
The Consumer Credit Regulations 2004	2004	102	375
The Tax Credit Acts 1999 and accompanying Regulations	1999	100	565
The Part-time Workers (Prevention of Less Favourable Treatment) Regulations 2000	2000	27	139
The Stakeholder Pensions Schemes Regulations 2000	2000	76	423
The Disability Discrimination (Providers of Services) (Adjustments to Premises) Regulations 2001	2001	211	1,208
The Animal By-products Regulations 2003	2003	100	240
The Consumer Credit Regulations 2004	2004	102	375

Figure 2.7 Estimated costs to UK businesses of compliance with selected regulations.

Source: adapted from British Chambers of Commerce 'Burdens Barometer', 2005

Note: Figures show estimated annual administrative and financial costs to UK businesses, calculated in 2004.

2.13.1 Pressure groups

Pressure groups can be divided into a number of categories. In the first place there is a division between those which are permanently fighting for a general cause, and those which are set up to achieve a specific objective and are dissolved when this objective is met – or there no longer seems any prospect of changing the situation. Pressure groups set up to fight specific new road building proposals fit into the latter category.

Pressure groups can also be classified according to their functions. Sectional groups exist to promote the common interests of their members over a wide range of issues. Trades unions and employers' associations fall into this category. They represent their members' views to government on diverse issues such as proposed employment legislation, import controls and vocational training. This type of pressure group frequently offers other benefits to members such as legal representation for individual members and the dissemination of information to members. Promotional groups, on the other hand, are established to fight for specific causes, such as animal welfare, which is represented by, say, the League Against Cruel Sports.

Not all pressure groups represent a widespread body of grass-roots public opinion. Businesses also frequently join pressure groups as a means of influencing government legislative proposals that will affect their industry sector. An example of a powerful commercial pressure group is the British Road Federation, which represents companies with interests in road construction and lobbies government to increase expenditure on new road building.

Pressure groups can influence government policy using three main approaches.

1 The first, propaganda, can be used to create awareness of the group and its cause. This can be aimed directly at policy formers, or indirectly by appealing to the constituents of policy formers to apply direct pressure themselves. This is essentially an impersonal form of mass communication.

2 A second option is to try to represent the views of the group directly to policy formers on a one-to-one basis. Policy formers frequently welcome representations that they may see as preventing bigger problems or confrontations arising in the future. Links between pressure groups and government often become institutionalized, such as where the Department of Transport routinely seeks the views of the Automobile Association and RAC Foundation on proposals to change road traffic legislation. Where no regular contacts exist, pressure groups can be represented by giving evidence before a government-appointed enquiry or by approaching sympathetic MPs or by hiring the services of a professional lobbyist.

3 A third approach used by pressure groups is to carry out research and to supply information. This has the effect of increasing public awareness of the organization and usually has a valuable propaganda function. The British Road Federation frequently supplies MPs with comparative road statistics purporting to show reasons why the government should be spending more money on road building.

Pressure groups are most effective where they apply pressure in a low-key manner, for example where they are routinely consulted for their views. Lobbying of MPs – which combines elements of all three methods described above – has become increasingly important over recent years.

Sometimes pressure groups, or sectional interests within them, recognize that they are unlikely to achieve their aims by using the channels described above. Recent years have seen an increase in 'direct action' by pressure groups, or breakaway sections of mainstream groups, against their target. Campaigners for animal rights, or those opposed to the use of genetically modified crops, have on occasions given up on trying to change the law and have instead sought to disrupt the activities of organizations giving rise to their concerns. Organizations targeted in this way may initially put a brave face on such activities by dismissing them as inconsequential, but often the result has been to change the organization's behaviour, especially where the prospect of large profits is uncertain. Action by animal rights protestors contributed to the near collapse of Huntingdon Life Sciences (an animal testing laboratory), and many farmers were discouraged from taking part in GM crop trials by the prospect of direct action against their farms.

It is not only national governments to which pressure groups apply their attention – local authorities are frequently the target of pressure groups over issues of planning policy or the provision of welfare services. Increasingly, pressure is also being applied at EU level. Again, the European Commission regularly consults some groups while other groups apply direct pressure to members of the Commission.

Business organizations have achieved numerous reported triumphs in attempting to influence the political environment in which they operate. The pressure group representing the tobacco industry – the Tobacco Advisory Council – had a significant effect in countering the pressure applied by the anti-tobacco lobby, represented by Action on Smoking Health. Legislation to ban cigarette advertising was delayed, and the pressure group has lobbied against a proposed ban on smoking in public places.

Pressure groups themselves are increasingly crossing national boundaries to reflect the influence of international governmental institutions such as the EU and the increasing influence of multinational business organizations. Both industrial and consumer pressure groups have been formed at a multinational level to counter these influences – a good example of the latter is Greenpeace.

2.13.2 Role of the media

The media – press, radio, television and increasingly the Internet – not only spread awareness of political issues but also influence policy and decision making by setting the political agenda and influencing public opinion. The broadcast media in the United Kingdom must by law show balance in their coverage of political events, but the press is often more openly partisan. Campaigns undertaken by the press frequently reflect the background of their owners – the *Daily Telegraph* is more likely to support the causes of deregulation in an industry while the *Guardian* will be more likely to put forward the case for government spending on essential public services. It is often said that *The Times* and the BBC Radio 4 *Today* programme set the political agenda for the day ahead.

SHOULD GOVERNMENT BE RUNNING THE RAILWAYS?

Railways throughout the world have traditionally been owned and operated by governments. There have been good social arguments for state ownership, especially in communities where a railway represents a vital lifeline. The sheer costs and risks involved in building and operating a railway have deterred private investors, mindful of many bankruptcies that have occurred during earlier 'railway booms'.

Britain led the way in privatizing its railways during the 1990s, and many other governments have followed by loosening their countries' railway links with government. But, 10 years on, Britain's railways have been treated as a political football, and questions have been raised about the relative merits of state ownership and privatization. Along the way, there have been many opportunities, and headaches, for private-sector organizations that have been attracted to the sector.

Britain's railways came into public ownership because they had ceased to make profits for their private owners in the 1920s and 1930s. They became starved of new investment and this was seen as a major hindrance for the post-war Labour government's national reconstruction plans. It is true that the great modernization plan of the post-war period did see a lot of new investment in the railways, for example new signalling and the replacement of steam trains with diesel and electric trains. Unfortunately, much of this investment was not customer-focused and customers increasingly voted with their wallets by going elsewhere. Passengers deserted in large numbers to the private car, coach services and, to an increasing extent, domestic air services. Freight customers found the cost, speed and reliability of road haulage gaining an edge over the railways.

To the Conservative government of the 1990s, British railways were suffering from a lack of entrepreneurship which could be overcome by replacing public-sector employees and finance with new ideas and new capital brought in from the private sector. Ownership and maintenance of the track passed to Railtrack, whose shares were offered to the public. Railtrack in turn subcontracted much of its maintenance work to other private companies. The train operation was sold off to 26 franchised companies, which leased trains from three privatized rolling stock companies. All of these were regulated by the Office of the Rail Regulator (Ofrail).

Privatization, and opposition to it, appeared to be driven as much by dogma as the operational realities of running a railway. The fragmentation of the industry track operator, rolling stock owners and franchise operators was driven by a desire for competition. Even the idea of having integrated regional organizations which would be responsible for the track, the rolling stock and operations was seen by the Conservative government as inherently anti-competitive and avoided almost as a dogmatic belief. During discussion of rail privatization, the opposition Labour Party appeared to be equally dogmatically opposed to it. Some of the party's more left-wing members were opposed to any diminution in the role of the state. The party's transport spokesperson vowed to renationalize railways if and when it came back into government but, paradoxically, this simply frightened off potential investors who could pick up shares in railway assets at knock-down bargain basement prices.

It didn't take long for the critics of privatization to argue that the railways were now in worse shape than they ever were under state ownership. There was often a suspicion that when things went wrong, companies simply passed the blame to one another. Train operators accused Railtrack if a train was late and Railtrack may have blamed a train operator for causing a blockage on its lines. This fragmentation was felt most seriously where accidents occurred and it was difficult to pin down responsibility. Worryingly, it seemed that the service quality improvements sought from privatization had actually gone into reverse. During the year ended September 2004, just 76.4 per cent of Virgin Cross-Country trains arrived on time or within 10 minutes of the scheduled time. The UK rail sector as a whole achieved only 81.2 per cent on-time arrivals in that period, lower than pre-privatization levels of reliability (90 per cent in 1992–93), despite longer scheduled journey times on many routes. Astonishingly, an international comparison found the Pakistan Railways route from Lahore to Karachi achieving 88 per cent reliability. Even the steam-hauled trains operating from Accra to Kumasi in Ghana beat Virgin's reliability, at 85 per cent. Critics of privatization argued that private companies were too concerned with cutting costs in order to meet their shareholders' expectations. Cost cutting and poor communications between companies were highlighted following a number of serious rail crashes. With most companies having franchises of only around seven years, cost reduction rather than investment was seen as the best way of improving profitability.

At the same time as service quality was evidently deteriorating, the cost to the government of subsidizing train services had increased sharply. Research carried out by rail journalist Roger Ford, and published in *The Rising Cost of Britain's Railways* by pressure group Transport 2000, showed that total government subsidy to Britain's railways in 2003/04 was expected to total £3.84 billion. By comparison, in British Rail's last year as operator of an integrated railway (1993–94) the total subsidy was £1.325 billion (at 2003–04 prices).

The Labour Party, when in opposition, had failed to reverse rail privatization. However, the incoming Labour government of 1997 realized that undoing the process would be prohibitively costly and the government had much more pressing priority areas to spend the billions of pounds that rail nationalization would have cost. Nationalization would probably cause even more disruption to travellers in the process. The track operator, Railtrack, had become a popular scapegoat for the railway's problems, despite investing record amounts of private capital in the network. In 2002, the government used its powers to place Railtrack in administration, and gave responsibility for the track to a new not-for-profit organization, Network Rail. Two years later, it sacked the operator of the South Central franchise – Connex – and replaced it with a new company directly answerable to the government's previously created Strategic Rail Authority. Was this Labour Party dogma reasserting itself in a gradual manner, or was it a simple realization that the private sector is not capable of running a complex system such as the rail network? Meanwhile, political uncertainty had caused a lot of harm in the rail sector. Faced with short-term franchises, most train operators were initially reluctant to order new rolling stock, resulting in a drastic reduction in the UK's train-building capacity as manufacturers closed down or relocated their facilities overseas. Many suppliers to the industry could survive happily in either a state-owned or privatized system of ownership, but the worst situation for them was political uncertainty.

QUESTIONS

1 Summarize the effects of political ideology on the management and ownership of railways in Britain.
2 What public interest is served by government involvement in the management and ownership of railways?
3 What are likely to be the key differences between the objectives of a railway in private ownership and a railway in state ownership?

SUMMARY

The political environment impinges on many other aspects of an organization's environment; for example change in the dominant political ideology can result in significant changes in the economic environment. Businesses dislike uncertainty in the political environment, and monitoring and understanding it is useful to pick up early signs of change. This chapter has explored the basis of government in the United Kingdom and the respective roles of national, regional, local and European government. Although examples have been taken from the UK, the elements of the political environment described here are similar in most Western democratic countries. A two-way interaction occurs between government and business, in which business organizations monitor changes in the political environment, but also seek to influence the environment through lobbying. Pressure groups represent an increasingly important element of the political environment, working from outside the formal political system.

The overlaps between the political environment and other aspects of a firm's marketing environment are covered in following chapters. Politicians have a significant impact on the national economic environment (**Chapter 11**) and indeed respond to changes in it. The level of competition within any market can be influenced by government policies on anti-competitive practices (**Chapter 10**). Government policy is translated into legislation (**Chapter 5**) and influences standards of behaviour expected from business (**Chapter 9**).

Key Terms

Act of Parliament	(49)	European Union (EU)	(58)	Pressure groups	(78)
Best value	(71)	Executive	(50)	Private Finance Initiative	
Cabinet	(51)	Ideology	(43)	(PFI)	(74)
Charter Mark	(69)	Judicial review	(53)	Public–private partnership	
Civil service	(51)	Judiciary	(52)	(PPP)	(74)
Directives	(51)	Legislature	(48)	Quango	(73)
European Commission	(61)	Lobbying	(49)	Regional government	(54)
European Council of		Local government	(57)	Regulation	(75)
Ministers	(61)	Non-Departmental Public		Social exclusion	(45)
European Court of Justice	(61)	Bodies (NDPBs)	(73)	Task forces	(71)
European Economic		Outsourcing	(72)		
Area (EEA)	(58)	Political parties	(43)		

CHAPTER REVIEW QUESTIONS

1 Against the background of a worldwide trend towards privatization and deregulation, prepare a report for an industry association of your choice, assessing the potential threats and opportunities arising for your sector. (*Based on CIM Marketing Environment Examination question*)

2 Prepare arguments for and against greater control being exercised over business and marketing practices by government. (*Based on CIM Marketing Environment Examination question*)

3 Briefly identify the main areas of attention which the marketing manager of a UK bicycle manufacturer is likely to give to his or her political environment.

4 For a newspaper lobbying against government proposals to impose value added tax on newspaper sales, identify the key points within the government system to which lobbying could be applied.

5 For a British manufacturing company, briefly summarize the principal problems and opportunities presented by the development of closer economic and political union within the EU.

6 What measures can a large multinational business take to monitor the political environment in its various operating areas?

ACTIVITY

Take three of the recent regulatory burdens on business which are listed in Figure 2.7. Discuss whether these are unfair burdens on business, or a real and worthwhile net benefit for customers, employees and society as a whole.

Useful Websites

UK government gateway

This is an important access point to UK government websites. Links are provided to many local and national government sites.

http://www.open.gov.uk/

UK Parliament

Provides information about the House of Commons and the House of Lords including details of committees, Acts, Bills, elections, Members of Parliament and publications.

http://www.parliament.uk/

UK political parties

Websites of the main UK political parties can be found at the following addresses:

Labour: http://www.labour.org.uk

Conservative: http://www.conservative-party.org.uk

Liberal Democrat: http://www.libdems.org.uk

Best value in local government

A forum for the UK local government (including police and fire) best value initiative. It allows researchers and practitioners working with both pilot and non-pilot authorities to discuss how best value – economic, efficient and effective delivery of services – can be achieved.

http://www.jiscmail.ac.uk/lists/best-value-uk-local-government.html

European Union online

A useful entry point for information about the European Union. Provides information on the Parliament, the Council, the Commission, the Court of Justice, the Court of Auditors and other bodies of the European Union.

http://europa.eu.int/index_en.htm

Fact sheets on the European Union

A comprehensive guide to how the European Community works, the single market, common policies, economic and monetary union and EU external relations.

http://europa.eu.int/

EUsceptic.org

A website providing links to various organizations sceptical of the European Union.

http://www.eusceptic.org/

Further Reading

For an overview of how government is managed in the UK, the following provide a useful insight:

Bogdanor, Vernon (2005) *Joined-up Government*, Oxford University Press.

Bovaird, Tony and Loeffler, Elke (eds) (2003) *Public Management and Governance*, Routledge.

Van Der Waldt, Gerrit (2004) *Managing Performance in the Public Sector: Concepts, Considerations and Challenges*, Juta & Company, Ltd.

The following provide a more specific focus on local government:

Bogdanor, Vernon (2001) *Devolution in the United Kingdom*, Oxford University Press.

Stoker, G. (1999) *The New Management of British Local Governance: Government Beyond the Centre*, Palgrave.

For a discussion of devolved government in Scotland, consult the following:

Adams, John and Robertson, Peter (2002) *Devolution in Practice, Public Policy Differences within the UK*, IPPR.

Hassan, Gerry and Warhurst, Chris (2002) *Anatomy of the New Scotland: Power, Influence and Change*, Edinburgh, Mainstream.

To many, the workings of the European Union are extremely complex and the following texts provide a general overview:

Green-Cowles, Maria and Dinan, Desmond (eds) (2004) *Developments in the European Union 2*, Palgrave Macmillan.

McCormick, John (2002) *Understanding the European Union*, 2nd edn, Palgrave Macmillan.

Teasdale, Anthony and Bambridge, Timothy (2004) *The Penguin Companion to European Union*, Penguin Books.

The following official publications of the EU are also useful for monitoring current developments:

Basic Statistics of the Community

Bulletin of the European Commission of the European Communities

Finally, there is extensive coverage of the functions of pressure groups. The following texts are useful for highlighting their relationship to business organizations:

Coxall, B. (2001) *Pressure Groups in British Politics*, Longman.

Grant, W. (2000) *Pressure Groups and British Politics*, Palgrave.

References

Barro, Robert J. (1996) 'Democracy and growth', *Journal of Economic Growth*, Kluwer Academic Publishers, Vol. 1, No. 1, pp. 1–27.

BCC (2005) 'Burdens Barometer', London, British Chamber of Commerce.

Office of National Statistics (2004) *Focus on Social Inequalities*, London.

Rodrik, D. (2002) *Feasible Globalization*, Working Paper, Harvard University, May.

Stiglitz, Joseph (2000) 'Whither reform? Ten years of the transition', in B. Pleskovic and J. Stiglitz (eds) *Annual World Bank Conference on Development Economics 1999*, Washington, DC, World Bank, pp. 27–56.

Chapter 3

The Social and Demographic Environment

Chapter Objectives

This chapter will explain:

- how changing attitudes and lifestyles affect business organizations

- the changing demographic composition of society and its effects on business organizations

- change in family composition and household structure

- the effects on business of greater ethnic diversity

- the two-way relationship between society and business

3.1 SOCIAL CHANGE AND ITS EFFECTS ON BUSINESS ORGANIZATIONS

Consider the following recent social changes that have occurred in the UK and many other Western countries:

- an increasing ethnic diversity, which is manifested in Asian and Indian communities in many towns of the UK
- a rising divorce rate, which is manifested in a rising number of single-person households and single-parent families
- a desire for instant gratification, manifested in individuals' desire to obtain goods and services 24 hours a day.

These are typical of changes that have concentrated the minds of business organizations as they attempt to supply goods and services which are of continuing relevance to the population. Companies that continue to base their efforts on the assumption of a typical white family unit which is prepared to wait for a long time before a product is delivered may find themselves targeting an increasingly small market segment.

As a result of social change, we have seen many goods and services become redundant, as they no longer satisfy a population whose needs, attitudes, values and behaviour have changed. The following are typical of goods and services which have disappeared or been greatly reduced in sales as a result of social change.

- Traditional drinking pubs have reduced in number as patterns of social relationships change and individuals seek more family-friendly pubs which serve food in a pleasant environment.
- The number of butchers' shops has been sharply reduced as consumers opt for a healthier lifestyle, based on foods which do not contain meat.
- Rural bus services have gone into decline as they fail to cater for a lifestyle in which an individual's community comprises not just their immediate neighbours, but people who may live many miles away.

On the other hand, social change has resulted in a tremendous growth in the following goods and services.

- Microwave cookers and portable televisions have benefited from a move towards a 'cellular' household in which each member of the family operates in a much more independent manner than has traditionally been the case.
- Gyms and leisure facilities have benefited from individuals' increasing concern for health and personal fitness.
- The sale and use of cars has expanded in response to individuals' desire for a lifestyle in which their friends, workplace and leisure activities may be geographically dispersed.

It is very easy for an individual to take for granted the way they live. Furthermore, young people may imagine that people have always lived their lives that way. Taking one year with the next, social change may seem quite imperceptible, but when life today is compared with what it was like 10 years ago, noticeable changes begin to appear. If comparisons are made with 20 or 50 years ago, it may seem as if two entirely different societies are being compared. Simply by looking at an old movie, big differences become apparent, such as attitudes to the family, leisure activities and the items commonly purchased by consumers.

Change in society is also brought about by changes in its composition. Much recent attention has been given in many Western European countries to the effects of an ageing population on society. Taken to an extreme, some commentators have seen major problems ahead as an increasingly large dependent population has to be kept by a proportionately smaller economically active group in society. Some see this as challenging basic attitudes that individuals have towards the community and the family. At the very least, business organizations should be concerned about the effects of demographic change on patterns of demand for goods and services and the availability of a workforce to produce those goods and services.

It is bad enough not to recognize social change that has happened in the past. It is much worse to fail to read the signs of social change that is happening now and to understand the profound effect this could have on the goods and services that people will buy in the future.

This chapter begins by examining what can loosely be described as a society's social and cultural values. These are what make people in the United Kingdom different from how they were 20 years ago, or different from how people in Algeria or Indonesia are today. Social and cultural differences between countries focus on differences in attitudes, family structures and the pattern of interaction between individuals. Business organizations should understand the

THINKING AROUND THE SUBJECT:
GOVERNMENT'S OFFICIAL SHOPPING BASKET REFLECTS SOCIAL CHANGE

New evidence of changing lifestyles sometimes emerges from the most unlikely sources. One interesting insight comes from the regular updating of the UK's Consumer Prices Index (CPI), which is used by many organizations as a benchmark for inflation in the national economy.

In principle, it is quite easy to take a typical shopping basket of consumers' purchases and to monitor what happens to the price of this basket from one year to the next. A problem occurs, however, because the contents of the basket are constantly changing as consumers' preferences change and products with low prices are substituted for more expensive ones.

In 2001 the Office for National Statistics (ONS), which records the CPI (previously called the Retail Prices Index), took a periodic look at the contents of its average shopping basket of 650 goods and services to reflect changes in national spending habits. The ONS takes advice from retail analysts, consults the diaries of families participating in regular shopping surveys and scrutinizes trade figures. The basket was amended to include for the first time organic food, salmon fillets, energy drinks, herbal teabags, cereal snacks and sunscreen lotion. Out went salad cream, rainbow trout, leeks, sterilized milk, doorstep-delivered milk – a victim of the steady increase in supermarket sales of milk from the shelves – and the household bread bin. The disappearance of the bread bin may reflect a change in habits away from buying standard loaves of bread in favour of a desire to experiment with specialist bread such as baguettes.

In an increasingly service-orientated culture, the CPI reflects the growing importance of services in a typical individual's spending pattern. From 2001 the shopping basket was amended to include health club membership, catering costs and bank overdraft charges.

Some items of fashion enter the shopping basket but may soon disappear. Cardigans have been entering and leaving the CPI as fashions change. In 2001, alcopops, baseball caps and laminate flooring joined, but are just as likely to go the way of women's ski pants and leave again if fashions change.

consequences of what may appear nebulous social changes for the types of things that consumers are likely to buy in the future.

3.1.1 Social influences on behaviour

The way an individual behaves as a consumer is a result of their unique physical and psychological make-up on the one hand, and a process of learning from experience on the other. The debate about the relative importance of nature and nurture is familiar to social psychologists. This chapter is concerned with the effects of learned behaviour on individuals' buying behaviour.

An individual learns norms of behaviour from a number of sources (see Figure 3.1):

- the dominant cultural values of the society in which they live
- the social class to which they belong
- important reference groups, in particular the family.

Culture can be seen as an umbrella within which social class systems exist and reference groups exert influence on individuals or groups of individuals. The following sections consider the effects of each of these influences.

3.2 THE CULTURAL ENVIRONMENT

The *Oxford English Dictionary* defines culture as a 'trained and refined state of understanding, manners and tastes'. Central to culture is the concept of learning and passing down of values

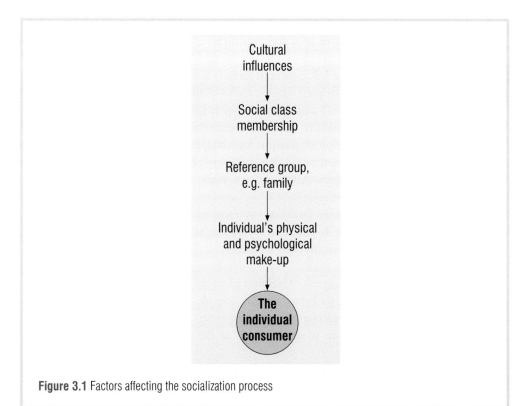

Figure 3.1 Factors affecting the socialization process

from one generation to the next. A culture's values are expressed in a complex set of beliefs, customs and symbols which help to identify individuals as members of one particular culture rather than another. The following are typical manifestations of cultural identity.

■ Shared attitudes, for example towards the role of women or children in society.

■ Abstract symbols and rituals, which can be seen in historic cultures by such events as religious practices, harvest festivals and maypole dancing, and in more modern times by support for local football teams.

■ Material manifestations, for example the literature and art of a culture or the style of decorations used in private houses.

It is common to distinguish between 'core' and 'secondary' cultural values.

■ Core cultural values tend to be very enduring over time. In Britain, for example, the acceptance of monogamy represents a core belief and one that very few people would disagree with.

■ Secondary cultural values are more susceptible to change over time. While there may be a core belief in the family, this does not prevent changes in attitudes towards the form that families should take, as is evident from the growing incidence of divorce and the increasing number of single-parent families. It is shifts in these secondary cultural values that are particularly important for business organizations to monitor.

3.2.1 Effects of culture on business organizations

It is crucial for business organizations to fully appreciate the cultural values of a society, especially where an organization is seeking to do business in a country that is quite different from its own. The possible consequences of failing to do this can be illustrated by the following examples.

■ When McDonald's entered the UK market, it initially found hostility from the British, who did not appreciate the brash, scripted 'Have a nice day' mentality of its staff. The company subsequently adapted its style of business to cater for British preferences.

■ The UK retailer Sainsbury's failed to replicate supermarkets on the British model in Egypt, a country which had no tradition of supermarket shopping. Worse still, at the height of a Palestinian uprising, a story went round that Sainsbury's had Jewish connections, a rumour encouraged by local shopkeepers. After just two years, and losses of over £100 million, Sainsbury's pulled out of Egypt.

■ Many UK businesses have set up operations overseas and gone about business in an open and above-board manner, only to find that corruption and the use of bribes is endemic in the local culture and essential for business success.

Cultural sensitivity affects many aspects of business planning and operations.

■ Understanding processes of buyer behaviour (for example, the role of men in buying routine household goods varies between countries, leading sellers to adjust their product specification and promotional efforts to meet the needs of the most influential members of the buying unit).

■ Some products may be unacceptable in a culture and must be adapted to be culturally acceptable (e.g. the original formulation for the McDonald's 'Big Mac' is unacceptable in Muslim cultures).

- Symbols associated with products, such as the design and colour of packaging, may be unacceptable in some cultures (e.g. the colour white is associated with pureness in most West European cultures, but in others it is associated with bereavement).
- Distribution channel decisions are partly a reflection of cultural attitudes and not just economics and land use. Retailers and wholesalers may be seen as a vital part of a culture's social infrastructure and individuals may feel a sense of loyalty to their suppliers. Although it may appear economically rational for shoppers to buy in bulk, small local shops opening long hours may be seen by consumers as an extension of their pantry.
- Advertising messages do not always translate easily between different cultures, reflecting culturally influenced standards of what is considered decent and appropriate.
- Methods of procuring resources can vary between cultures. In some Far Eastern countries, it is essential to establish a trusting relationship with a buyer before the buyer will even consider placing an order. Sometimes, it is essential to personally know the key decision maker or to offer a bribe, which is considered routine business practice in some cultures.
- Obtaining good-quality staff can be influenced by cultural factors. The notion of punctual timekeeping and commitment to the employer is often an unfamiliar set of values in cultures where commitment to the family comes very strongly first and timekeeping has little meaning.

Even in home markets, business organizations should understand the processes of gradual cultural change and be prepared to satisfy the changing needs of consumers. The following are examples of contemporary cultural change in Western Europe and the possible business responses.

- Women are increasingly being seen as equal to men in terms of employment expectations and household responsibilities. According to the Office for National Statistics, women in 2003 represented 56 per cent of graduates in the UK and 47 per cent of the workforce (compared with 37 per cent in 1971). Examples of business responses include variants of cars designed to appeal to career women and ready prepared meals which save time for busy working women who need to juggle work, family and social roles.
- Greater life expectancy is leading to an ageing of the population and a shift to an increasingly 'elderly' culture. This is reflected in product design which reflects durability rather than fashionability.
- Leisure is becoming an increasingly important part of many people's lives, and businesses have responded with a wide range of leisure-related goods and services.
- Increasing concern for the environment is reflected in a variety of 'green' consumer products.

3.2.2 Cultural convergence

There has been much recent discussion about the concept of cultural convergence, referring to an apparent decline in differences between cultures. It has been argued that basic human needs are universal in nature and, in principle, capable of satisfaction with universally similar solutions. Companies have been keen to pursue this possibility in order to achieve economies of scale in producing homogeneous products for global markets. There is some evidence of firms achieving this, for example the worldwide success of Coca-Cola and McDonald's. In the case of fast food, many Western chains have capitalized on deep-seated habits in some Far Eastern

THINKING AROUND THE SUBJECT:
NEW MAGAZINES FOR NEW MEN?

Until a few years ago, the shelves of most newsagents would have been loaded with many general interest women's magazines (e.g. *Woman's Own*, *Woman's Weekly*, *Cosmopolitan*), but very few general interest magazines aimed at men. Why? Some cynics might have argued that women were more likely to have spare time at home and could sit around reading, while 'busy' men were out at work, in the pub, or watching sport and did not have time to read magazines. There may just have been a bit of truth in this, but the main reason has been that women's magazines have been popular with advertisers, who generally provide a high proportion of total income for a magazine publisher. In the traditional household, it has been women who have made decisions on a wide range of consumer goods purchases. Advertising the benefits of toothpaste, yoghurt or jam would have been lost on most men, who had little interest in which brand was put in front of them and played little part in the buying process.

Take a look at the newsstand now and it will carry a wide range of men's general interest magazines, such as *FHM*, *Maxim*, *Nuts* and *Zoo*. Why have they suddenly mushroomed in number and in readership? Again, the answer lies in their attractiveness to advertisers. Talk of a male identity crisis may have spurred some sales. More importantly, it is evident that men are now involved in a much wider range of purchasing decisions than ever before, and therefore likely to be of much greater interest to advertisers. While some 'new men' may be taking a more active interest in the household shopping, many more are marrying later and indulging themselves in personal luxuries, an option which is less readily available to their married counterparts. With support from advertisers, the leading men's magazine in the UK, *FHM*, had a circulation of 601,166 copies per issue in 2004 (Audit Bureau of Circulation), overtaking the leading women's monthly magazine, *Cosmopolitan*, which had a circulation of 478,394. Advertising to men had never before looked so attractive.

countries of eating from small hawkers' facilities by offering the same basic facility in a clean and hygienic environment.

The desire of a subculture in one country to imitate the values of those in another culture has also contributed to cultural convergence. This is nothing new. During the Second World War, many individuals in Western Europe sought to follow the American lifestyle, and nylon stockings from the United States became highly sought-after cultural icons by some groups. The same process is at work today in many developing countries where some groups seek to identify with Western cultural values through the purchases they make. Today, however, improved media communications allow messages about cultural values to be disseminated much more rapidly. The development of satellite television and the Internet hastens the process of creating shared worldwide values.

It can be argued that business organizations are not only responding to cultural convergence, they are also significant contributors to that convergence. The development of global brands backed up by global advertising campaigns has contributed to an increasing uniformity in goods and services offered throughout the world. Many commentators have described an 'MTV' generation which views global satellite television channels and who converge in their

Figure 3.2 How can Coca-Cola be sure that its brand name and product offer will be the object of aspiration for the dominant groups in a country, rather than a hated symbol of an alien system of capitalism? Coca-cola has been challenged by numerous functionally similar cola drinks, which seek to appeal to consumers' emotions. By rejecting Coca-cola in favour of Qibla Cola (shown here), individuals are making a statement about their sense of cultural identity.

attitudes to consumption. The Internet is contributing to this process of apparent global homogenization.

Critics of the trend towards cultural convergence have noted individuals' growing need for *identity* in a world which is becoming increasingly homogenized. Support for regional breakaway governments (e.g. by the Kurdish and Basque people) may provide some evidence of this. During the build-up to the Iraq war in 2003, many consumers in Arab countries used purchases of Muslim products to identify themselves with an anti-American cause. Many Western service brands have become despised by some groups as symbols of an alien identity. Banks in many Muslim countries have reported increased interest in syariah-based banking services (*This is Money*, 2005).

In some countries, cultural convergence has been seen as a threat to the sense of local identity that culture represents. Governments have therefore taken measures in an attempt to slow down this process of cultural homogenization. This has achieved significance in France where legislation requires the use of the French language – an important means of creating identity for any culture – in packaging and advertising for products.

3.2.3 Multicultural, multi-ethnic socities

The United Kingdom, like many Western countries, is increasingly becoming a culturally and ethnically diverse society (see Figure 3.3). By ethnicity, we are talking about groups based on their common racial, national, tribal, religious, linguistic or cultural origin. An important reason for increasing ethnic diversity in most Western countries is the growing numbers of immigrant people from overseas cultures, attracted, among other reasons, by economic prosperity in the host country, and motivated to leave their native country by the relative lack of available opportunities. Immigrants bring with them a distinctive set of cultural and religious values and adapting to the values of the host country can be a difficult task. In some countries, church and state may be closely linked, leading to an expectation that religious principles should be the basis for governance. For some religious groups, the power of a religious leader transcends any government institution. A lack of understanding from members of the host country may cause some immigrants to be seen as arrogant, lazy or lacking in humour by the standards of the host culture, but they may nevertheless be perfectly normal by the standards of their home culture. Where members of ethnic minorities are concentrated into distinct areas (such as certain suburbs of London, Leicester and Bradford), their traditional cultural values may be strengthened and prolonged by mutual support and the presence of an infrastructure (such as places of worship and specialized shops) to support the values of the culture.

The presence of concentrations of ethnic subcultures in a town presents opportunities for businesses that cater for distinctive cultural preferences. In many towns catering for people of Asian origin, these include halal butchers, bureaux for arranged marriages and travel agents specializing in travel to India. In some cases, completely new markets have emerged

Religion	Number (000)	% of total population	% of non-Christian religious population
Christian	37,046	71.8	
Muslim	1,547	2.8	51.9
Hindu	552	1.0	18.3
Sikh	329	0.6	11.0
Jewish	260	0.5	8.7
Buddhist	144	0.3	4.9
Others	89	0.3	5.2
All non-Christian religions			100.00
No religion	7,274	15.1	
Not stated	4,453	7.8	
TOTAL	57,100	100.00	

Figure 3.3 Population of Great Britain by religion, 2001

Source: based on Census of Population, 2001

specifically for ethnic minorities, such as the market for black sticking plasters. It has some-times proved difficult for established businesses to gain access to immigrant segments. Many established companies have not adequately researched the attitudes and buying processes of these groups, with the result that, in markets as diverse as vegetables, clothing and travel, ethnic minorities have supported businesses run by fellow members of their minority group

The report *Marketing to Ethnic Minorities*, published by Interfocus in 2001, identified a number of issues, such as differing household structures and value systems, which pose new challenges and opportunities for businesses arising from increasing cultural diversity. The report found that consumers from this group are typically younger, more likely to own a business than others, tend to live in large urban centres – creating opportunities for cost-effective marketing – and are close-knit, making word-of-mouth recommendation a powerful force. However, they tend to be very fragmented, with intergenerational differences, requiring that businesses com-mission professional research to gain in-depth understanding of their target markets.

Members of ethnic minorities have contributed to the diversity of goods and services avail-able to consumers in the host country. The large number of Indian restaurants in Britain, for example, can be attributed to the entrepreneurial skills of immigrants, while many food prod-ucts (such as kebabs and Chinese food) have followed the example of immigrants.

On the supply side, immigrants have tended to be of working age and have filled a vital role in providing labour for the economy. Moreover, some Asian groups have brought vital entre-preneurial skills to the economy, often at a high cost economically and socially to the less developed countries that they have left.

It must be noted that there are great differences between ethnic sub-groups. Entrepreneur-ship is much greater among the Chinese group, where 22 per cent were classified as self-employed by the Office of Population Censuses and Surveys in 1996/7, compared to 19 per cent for Pakistanis and Bangladeshis, but only 7 per cent for black groups. The comparable figure was 12.5 per cent for whites. The age structure of ethnic minority groups gives rise to differences in the proportion that are dependent. Within the Bangladeshi group, for example, 42 per cent are under 16 (compared to a comparable figure of 20 per cent for whites), while only 20 per cent are in the economically most active group of 35–64 (compared with 37 per cent for whites). These figures are reversed for the Chinese community, where only 17 per cent are under 16 and 38 per cent are between 35 and 64.

3.2.4 Social class

In most societies, divisions exist between groups of people in terms of their access to privileges and status within that society. In some social systems, such as the Hindu caste system, the group that an individual belongs to exerts influence from birth and it is very difficult for the individual to change between groups. Western societies have class systems in which individuals are divided into one of a number of classes. Although the possibilities for individuals to move between social classes in Western countries is generally greater than the possibilities of move-ment open to a member of a caste system, class values tend to be passed down through families. The very fact that it is seen as possible to move classes may encourage people to see the world in a different way from that which has been induced in them during their years of socialization.

While some may have visions of a 'classless' society which is devoid of divisions in status and privileges, the reality is that divisions exist in most societies and are likely to persist in some

THINKING AROUND THE SUBJECT:
HOW FAR CAN HALAL FOOD GO?

One consequence of increasing cultural diversity in the UK is the emergence of a market in halal fresh meat and processed foods, which Mintel estimated to be worth £460 million in 2001 (Mintel 2002). Halal means 'lawful and permitted' and, in food terms, products are not halal if they contain alcohol, any part of a pig, carnivorous animal meat or blood. Foods are also not halal if meat has not been slaughtered according to Islamic law.

The main market for halal food in the UK is the estimated 1.9 million Muslims who account for about 3.2 per cent of the population. However, Muslims have a varied ethnic background and in Britain are mainly drawn from Pakistan, Bangladesh, India and the Middle East, each with their own food preferences. Those from the Indian sub-continent are known to prefer hot, spicy food, while those from the Middle East have blander tastes, similar to native British people.

For butchers, who have had a hard time following a series of food scares and an increase in vege-tarian consumers, the emergence of the halal market is a welcome opportunity. Mintel estimated that halal fresh meat accounted for 11 per cent of the value of all meat sales in the UK, but it appeared that just 3.2 per cent of the population was accounting for a disproportionate volume of halal meat sales.

Small independent butchers' shops have dominated halal meat sales. There have been problems in verifying the authenticity of halal meat, so trust is an important element of fresh meat supply, and it is likely that independent butchers' shops are used regularly as consumers have learned to trust the meat that they buy. This is particularly true of older and more traditional Asian shoppers, who are much less likely to use supermarkets. Mintel observed that a large proportion of Muslim women play the traditional role of home-maker, which means that they have more time available for shop-ping in independent outlets – particularly those where their native language is spoken – and for preparing meals from scratch. However, it is unlikely that third-generation Muslims onwards will be satisfied with such a lifestyle. Third-generation Muslim women are more likely to have careers, and their busy lifestyles are likely to lead them to seek the convenience of one-stop shopping at super-markets and online rather than using specialist small suppliers. They are also more likely to seek the convenience of ready prepared meals, rather than cooking from raw ingredients as their parents did.

Already, halal brands have emerged, including Tahira (frozen, chilled, ambient foods) and Maggi (sauces and seasonings). Could other convenience food retailers further develop this market? Fast-food chains such as McDonald's are already experienced in catering for Muslim consumers in coun-tries such as Malaysia – would there be a market for a halal burger in the UK?

Another intriguing question is whether the cultural traditions of Muslims may spread to the popu-lation generally. After all, Indian and Chinese restaurants now appeal to the UK population at large, rather than the narrow groups they initially served. Could halal food become mainstream rather than a niche market? One opportunity arises among the 3.4 million vegetarians in the UK, to whom meat-free halal foods are ideally placed to appeal.

form. It is common in Western societies to attribute individuals with belonging to groups that have been given labels such as 'working class' or 'middle class'. This emotional language of class is not particularly helpful to businesses that need a more measurable basis for describing differences within society.

Why do business organizations need to know about which social grouping an individual belongs? The basic idea of a classification system is to identify groups that share common attitudes and behaviour patterns, and access to resources. This can translate into similar spending patterns. There are, for example, many goods and services that are most heavily bought by people who can be described as 'working class', such as the *Daily Star* newspaper and betting services, while others are more often associated with 'upper-class' purchasers, such as Jaguar cars, the *Financial Times* and investment management services.

Businesses need to take note of the changing class structure of society. As the size of each class changes, so market segments, which are made up of people who are similar in some important respects, also change. In the United Kingdom during the 1960s and 1970s it has been observed that more people were moving into the 'middle classes'. The effects of taxation, the welfare state and access to education had flattened the class structure of society. For car manufacturers, this translated into a very large demand for mainstream middle-of-the-road cars. However, during the 1980s and 1990s, both the upper and lower classes tended to grow in what had become a more polarized society. In terms of car sales, there was a growing demand for luxury cars such as Jaguars and BMWs at one end of the market and cheaper cars such as Ladas at the other.

3.3 THE FAMILY

The family represents a further layer in the socialization process. It is important that business organizations understand changes in family structures and values because change in this area can impact on them in a number of ways. Consider the following impacts of families on business organizations.

■ Many household goods and services are typically bought by family units, for example food and package holidays. When family structures and values change, consumption patterns may change significantly.

■ The family is crucial in giving individuals a distinctive personality. Many of the differences in attitude and behaviour between individuals can be attributed to the values that were instilled in them by their family during childhood. These differences may persist well into adult life.

■ The family has a central role as a transmitter of cultural values and norms, and can exercise a strong influence on an individual's buying behaviour.

3.3.1 Family composition

Many people still live with the idea that the typical family comprises two parents and an average of 2.4 children. In many Western European countries this is increasingly becoming a myth, with single-person and single-parent households becoming increasingly common. The following factors have contributed to changes in family composition:

■ an increasing divorce rate, with about one-third of all marriages in the United Kingdom now ending in divorce

■ marriage and parenthood are being put off until later; the average age of marriage has increased by around five years since 1961, to 30 for men and 28 for women (based on UK 2001 Census)

■ the gap between people leaving school, settling down to get married and starting a family has grown steadily, and young people are now enjoying freedom from parental responsibility for longer than ever before

■ more people are living on their own outside a family unit, either out of choice or through circumstances (e.g. divorce, widowhood)

■ family role expectations have changed with an increasing number of career-oriented wives.

Changes in family composition have led firms to develop new goods and services that meet the changing needs of families, such as crèche facilities for working mothers and holidays for single parents. Advertising has increasingly moved away from portraying the traditional family group which many individuals may have difficulty in identifying with. Recent examples that portray the new reality include an advertisement for McDonald's in which a boy takes his separated father to one of the company's restaurants, and one for Volkswagen in which a career-minded woman puts her car before her husband.

3.3.2 Family roles

As well as changing in composition, there is evidence of change in the way that families operate as a unit. Many household products have been traditionally dominated by either the male or female partner, but these distinctions are becoming increasingly blurred as family roles change.

A report by the Future Foundation showed that, in the UK, the proportion of couples in which the man has the final say in big financial decisions has fallen from 25 per cent in 1993 to 20 per cent in 2003 (Future Foundation 2004). This reflects an increase in the number of couples who claim that they have an equal say from 65 per cent to 69 per cent. The data also show that the number of couples where the female partner has the final says has risen from 10 per cent to 12 per cent.

Men still make the major financial decisions in 40 per cent of couples aged over 65. Conversely, in couples under the age of 35, the woman is not only more likely to control the day-to-day financial management, but also likely to claim to control major financial decisions. However, women still have the main responsibility for shopping in 47 per cent of couples, compared with 11 per cent of couples where men do it. Future Foundation's research showed that 62 per cent of couples agreed that, aside from joint expenses, each person should have the right to spend their own money without asking their partner first.

The scope for individual freedom of expenditure has increased significantly, and increasing affluence has widened the scope for discretionary spending in general. There are a number of markets, such as clothing, that benefit from this independent spending, although this finding is not consistent across the different age groups. Among couples aged over 65, a majority of men said their partner has at least an equal influence in the clothes they wear. This is lower in couples aged under 45, with only 19 per cent of men claiming that their partner mainly chooses their clothes for them. On the other hand, none of the women surveyed by Future Foundation said that their partner always chooses their clothes and a very small number indicated any significant influence.

The Future Foundation also highlighted a number of other changes in roles within family units.

■ Cooking is still dominated by women, although men are increasingly sharing the task of preparing the main evening meal.

■ Although men may say they believe household tasks should be shared, only 1 per cent say they always do the washing and ironing. Household cleaning is carried out mainly by women in nearly two-thirds of households, and this proportion has been falling gradually over the last two decades.

■ The view that a man's task is to earn money, while a wife's job is to look after the family and home, has fallen consistently over the last decade.

■ More women are stating that work and careers are more important than home and children.

There has been much debate about the fragmentation of families into cellular households in which family members essentially do their own activities independently of other members. This is reflected in individually consumed meals rather than family meals, and leisure interests that are increasingly with a family member's peer groups rather than other family members. Businesses have responded to the needs of the cellular household with products such as microwave cookers and portable televisions which allow family units to function in this way. It can also be argued, however, that new product developments, combined with increasing wealth, are actually responsible for the fragmentation of family activities. The microwave cooker and portable television may have lessened the need for families to operate as a collective unit, although these possible consequences were not immediately obvious when they were launched. The family unit can expect to come under further pressures as new products, such as online entertainment and information services, allow individual members to consume in accordance with their own preferences rather than the collective preferences of the family.

THINKING AROUND THE SUBJECT:
POCKET-MONEY PESTER POWER PACKS A PUNCH

What role do children play in the purchase of goods which they ultimately consume? In the UK, children aged just 7 to 14 years old receive an estimated £1.5 billion in pocket money and financial handouts, according to a report by Mintel (Mintel 2004). There has been considerable debate about the extent of 'pester power', where parents give in to the demands of children. Increasingly, advertisers are aiming their promotional messages over the heads of adults and straight at children. The ethics of doing this have been questioned by many, and some countries have imposed restrictions on television advertising of children's products. However, even with advertising restrictions, companies have managed to get through to children in more subtle ways, for example by sponsoring educational materials used in schools and paying celebrities to endorse their products. When it comes to such items as confectionery and toys, just what influence do children exert on the purchase decision? And when football clubs deliberately change their strip every season, is it unethical for the clubs to expect fanatical children to pester their parents to buy a new one so that they can keep up with their peer group? And does the role of children in influencing purchase decisions say a lot about the structure of a society? In some cultures, children should be 'seen but not heard', but in others children may be treated as responsible adults from a much earlier age.

3.4 REFERENCE GROUPS

The family is not the only influence on an individual as they develop a view of the world. Just as individuals learn from and mimic the values of parents and close relations, so too they also learn from and mimic other people outside their immediate family. Groups that influence individuals in this way are often referred to as reference groups. These can be one of two types.

1 Primary reference groups exist where an individual has direct face-to-face contact with members of the group.

2 Secondary reference groups describe the influence of groups where there is no direct relationship, but an individual is nevertheless influenced by the group's values.

3.4.1 Primary reference groups

These comprise people with whom an individual has direct two-way contact, including those with whom an individual works, plays football and goes to church. In effect, the group acts as a frame of reference for the individual. Small groups of trusted colleagues have great power in passing on recommendations about goods and services, especially those where a buyer has very little other evidence on which to base a decision. For many personal services, such as hairdressing, word-of-mouth recommendation from a member of a peer group may be a vital method by which a company gains new business. If an individual needs to hire a builder, the first thing they are likely to do is ask friends if they can recommend a good one on the basis of their previous experience. For many items of conspicuous consumption, individuals often select specific brands in accordance with which brand carries most prestige with its primary reference group.

3.4.2 Secondary reference groups

These are groups with whom an individual has no direct contact, but which can nevertheless influence a person's attitudes, values, opinions and behaviour. Sometimes, the individual may be a member of the group and this will have a direct influence on their behaviour patterns, with the group serving as a frame of reference for the individual member. Individuals typically belong to several groups which can influence attitudes and behaviour in this way, for example university groups, trades unions and religious organizations. A member of a trades union may have little active involvement with the organization, but may nevertheless adopt the values of the union, such as solidarity.

At other times, an individual may not actually be a member of a group, but may aspire to be a member of it. Aspirational groups can be general descriptions of the characteristics of groups of people who share attitudes and behaviour. They range from teenage 'wannabes' who idolize pop stars through to businessmen who want to surround themselves with the trappings of their successful business heroes. It can be difficult to identify just which aspirational groups are highly sought at any one time. In the 1980s, the 'yuppie' was considered an aspirational group by many, but then largely disappeared in the recessionary period of the early 1990s. Middle-aged marketers marketing youth products may find it difficult to keep up with which pop stars and fashion models are currently in favour with teenagers.

Although a person may not be influenced by all the attitudes or behaviour patterns of a particular reference group, the fact that such influence occurs at all makes it important for businesses to try to identify the reference groups of the target markets they are selling to.

The importance of secondary group influences tends to vary between products and brands. In the case of products that are consumed or used in public, group influence is likely to affect not only the choice of product but also the choice of brand. (For example, training shoes are often sold using a 'brand spokesperson' to create an image for the shoe. There are some people who are so influenced by the images developed by famous athletes wearing a particular brand that they would not want to be seen wearing anything else.) For mass-market goods which are consumed less publicly (e.g. many grocery items), the effects of reference groups are usually less.

3.5 VALUES, ATTITUDES AND LIFESTYLES

Many organizations have recognized that traditional indicators of social class are of little relevance in understanding buyer behaviour. Instead of monitoring changes in such indicators, an analysis of changing attitudes, values and lifestyles is considered to be more useful. Changes in attitudes may be behaviourally manifested by changes in lifestyles.

3.5.1 Values

Values represent an individual's core beliefs and tend to be deep-seated and relatively enduring. They tend to be learnt at an early age and passed on through generations. They form an underlying framework which guides an individual's construction of the world, and their response to events in it. Typical underlying value systems may include the belief that it is wrong to get into debt; a belief that family is more important than work; and that it is important to be the winner in any competitive event.

The term values should be distinguished from value. Economists describe value as the ratio of the benefit arising from a product relative to its cost. The distinction between values and value is that an individual's value system influences the value they place on any particular object. A person with a value system that rates security and reliability highly may place a high value on a car that is solidly built but not particularly attractive. Another person whose value system ranks recognition by others as being more important may place a higher value on a car which is not necessarily reliable, but has 'street credibility'.

Although value systems tend to be deeply ingrained, they have a tendency to change through an individual's life cycle. So it follows that the value system of a teenager is likely to be different to that of a young adult parent, and different again to an elderly retired person.

3.5.2 Attitudes

Compared to values, attitudes are relatively transient sets of beliefs. Attitudes should be distinguished from the behaviour that may be manifested in a particular lifestyle. An individual may have an attitude about a subject, but keep their thoughts to themselves, possibly in fear of the consequences if these do not conform to generally accepted norms. A man may believe that it should be acceptable for men to use facial cosmetics, but unwilling to be the first to actually change behaviour by using them.

It is important for businesses to study changes in social attitudes, because these will most likely eventually be translated into changes in buying behaviour. The change may begin with a small group of social pioneers, followed by more traditional groups who may be slow to change their attitudes and more reluctant to change their behaviour. They may be prepared to change only when something has become the norm in their society.

Businesses have monitored a number of significant changes in individuals' attitudes in Western Europe, for example:

■ healthy living is considered to be increasingly important
■ consumers have a tendency to want instant results, rather than having to wait for things
■ attitudes are increasingly based on secular rather than religious values.

Business organizations have been able to respond to these attitude changes creatively, for example:

■ demand for healthy foods and gymnasium services has increased significantly; at first, it was only a small group of people whose attitude towards health led them to buy specialist products – now it is a mainstream purchase
■ the desire for instant gratification has been translated into strategies to make stock always available, next-day delivery for mail-order purchases, instant credit approval and instant lottery tickets
■ supermarkets in England have capitalized on the secularization of Sunday by opening stores and doing increasing levels of business on Sundays.

3.5.3 Lifestyles

Lifestyles are the manifestation of underlying value systems and attitudes. Lifestyle analysis seeks to identify groups within the population based on distinctive patterns of behaviour. It is possible for two people from the same social class carrying out an identical occupation to have very different lifestyles that would not be apparent if businesses segmented markets solely on the basis of easily identifiable criteria such as occupation. Consequently, product development and marketing communications have often been designed to appeal to specific lifestyle groups. This type of analysis can be very subjective and quantification of numbers in each category within a population at best can only be achieved through a small sample survey.

Studies have indicated a number of trends in lifestyles which have impacts on business organizations.

■ A growing number of individuals are becoming money rich, but time poor. Such individuals quite commonly seek additional convenience from their purchases, even if this means paying a premium price. Businesses have responded with such products as gourmet ready prepared meals.
■ As individuals become financially more secure, their motivation to buy products typically changes from a need for necessities to a desire for the unusual and challenging. Businesses have responded with ranges of designer clothes, adventure holidays and personalized interior design services.
■ With the increase in numbers of single-person households, the symbolic meaning of the home has changed for many people. Businesses have responded with a range of home-related products such as widescreen home cinema systems and gas-fired barbecues.

Gaining knowledge of the current composition and geographical distribution of lifestyle segments is much more difficult than monitoring occupation-based segments, for which data are regularly collected by government and private-sector organizations. This is discussed again later in this chapter.

THINKING AROUND THE SUBJECT:
A PENNY FOR YOUR THOUGHTS?

Values and attitudes can be a key to understanding likely future changes in lifestyles. We may have an attitude about something, but be unable to act on it, perhaps because of a lack of resources or the perceived risk of changing established patterns of bahaviour. Given the importance of attitudes, how can businesses find out about what customers are really thinking? Can consumers be trusted to tell the truth? There are countless cases where companies have carried out conventional marketing research, using surveys, focus groups and observation, then used the results to plan for the future, only to find that their planning has been a complete failure. This is evidenced by claims that roughly 80 per cent of all new products fail. Customers may be quite happy to say that they would find a proposed new product desirable, and may claim that they would even buy it. But when it is launched, they actually do something else.

Businesses have become increasingly interested in individuals' deep-seated unconscious emotions, on the basis that these are much better guides to how they will actually behave than their considered responses to questions. Enter the brave new world of 'neuro-marketing' which seeks to go straight to individuals' brains, rather than understanding them through what they say. One American organization, the Bright House Institute for Science, has used Magnetic Resonance Imaging (MRI) to try to learn more about how marketing cues activate different parts of the brain.

The idea of trying to understand how people's brains function is not new and has occupied scientists and criminologists, among others, for some time. The debate about the relative power of nature (a hard-wiring of the brain) versus nurture (the effects of socialization processes on our behaviour) is a long-running one. Marketers have already found some limited role for experimental methods of understanding deep-seated processing, for example research into advertising effectiveness has used tachistoscopes to record individuals' conscious eye movements.

Should neuro-marketing be regarded as a great hope for the future? Or is it overhyped? Critics have been quick to argue that it is one thing being able to identify a pattern of brain activity but quite another to be able to infer causative links between brain patterns and buying behaviour. Some have dismissed neuro-marketing as a management fad, and a device used by research companies to get their foot in the door of the client, but then sell more conventional research.

Is neuro-marketing ethical? To many people, neuro-marketing sounds like an Orwellian nightmare which could play straight into the hands of the 'thought police'. Could an understanding of people's deep-seated thought processes potentially allow companies to wrongly exploit emotions which are against a consumer's best interest? Could food companies exploit an emotional need for high-calorie 'comfort' food at the expense of a more considered need for healthy food? At a broader level, what are the implications for democracy if politicians can understand and manipulate individuals' deep-seated attitudes?

3.6 IDENTIFYING AND MEASURING SOCIAL GROUPS

So far we have discussed the changing composition of society in general terms, but now we need to turn our attention to possible methods by which organizations can identify specific groups within society. This is important if business organizations are to be able to target differentiated goods and services at groups that have quite distinctive sets of attitudes and lifestyles.

THINKING AROUND THE SUBJECT:
COMPLICATED LIFESTYLES

Some indication of the minutiae of changing lifestyles, and their implications for marketing, was revealed in the report *Complicated Lives II – The Price of Complexity*, commissioned by Abbey National bank from the Future Foundation. The report brought together quantitative and qualitative research with extensive analysis of a range of trends affecting families and their finances. The findings show that between 1961 and 2001:

- the average time women spent in a week doing cleaning and laundry fell from 12 hours and 40 minutes to 6 hours and 18 minutes
- the average time that parents spent helping their children with homework had increased from 1 minute a day to 15 minutes
- time spent caring for children increased from 30 minutes a day to 75 minutes
- the average amount of time spent entertaining went up from 25 minutes to 55 minutes
- time spent cooking has decreased for women, down from more than 1 hour and 40 minutes to just over an hour (73 minutes) per day; at the same time, men marginally increased their time in the kitchen from 26 to 27 minutes per day.

Figure 3.4 The growing number of money-rich, time-poor households presents new opportunities for businesses to provide convenient solutions to this group at a premium price. Sainsbury's was an early retailer to identify this opportunity and has developed a home delivery service which delivers customers' shopping to their home or place of work. The service has proved particularly popular with families who have difficulties in finding childminders, thereby avoiding the need to drag children round a supermarket. Nevertheless, such groups, for whom shopping has been transformed into a leisure experience may enjoy shopping for non-household goods such as clothes.

The aim of any system of social classification is to provide a measure that encapsulates differences between individuals in terms of their type of occupation, income level, educational background and attitudes to life, among other factors. There are three theoretical approaches to measuring social groupings.

1 **By self-measurement:** Researchers could ask an individual which of a number of possible groups they belong to. This approach has a number of theoretical advantages for organizations, because how an individual actually sees him or herself is often a more important determinant of behaviour than an objective measure. If people see themselves as working class, they are probably proud of the fact and will choose products and brands that accord with their own self-image. The danger of this approach is that many people tend to self-select themselves for 'middle of the road' categories. In one self-assessment study, over two-thirds of the sample described themselves as 'middle class'.

2 **By objective approaches:** These involve the use of measurable indicators about a person, such as their occupation, education and spending habits, as a basis for class determination. A number of these are discussed below.

3 **By asking third parties:** This combines the objective approach of indicators described above with a subjective assessment of an individual's behaviour and attitudes.

Social scientists have traditionally used the second of these approaches as a basis for defining social groupings, largely on account of its objectivity and relative ease of measurement. However, organizations must also recognize that an individual's attitudes can be crucial in determining buying behaviour, and have therefore been keen to introduce more subjective and self-assessed bases for classification. In the following sections we will review some bases commonly used by businesses for identifying social groups.

3.6.1 IPA classification system

One of the most long-standing and still widely used bases for social classification is the system adopted by the Institute of Practitioners in Advertising (IPA). It uses an individual's occupation as a basis for classification, on the basis that occupation is closely associated with many aspects of a person's attitudes and behaviour. The classes defined range from A to E, and Figure 3.5 indicates the allocation of selected occupations to groups.

Such an attempt to reduce the multidimensional concept of social grouping to a single measure is bound to be an oversimplification which leads to limited usefulness of the measure for business organizations. A person's occupation is not necessarily a good indicator of their buying behaviour, which was the reason for the classification system being created in the first place. For example, the owner of a large scrap metal business and a bishop would probably be put in the same occupational classification, but there are likely to be very significant differences in their spending patterns and the way they pass their leisure time. Nevertheless, the classification system described above is widely used. Newspapers regularly analyse their readership in terms of membership of these groups and go out of their way to show how many of the highly prized A/B readers they have.

3.6.2 Classification used for the UK Census

The data sets used by many organizations import data collected by the UK's Census of Population. Since 1921, government statisticians have divided the population into six classes, based

Class category	Occupation
A	Higher managerial, administrative or professional
B	Intermediate managerial, administrative or professional
C1	Supervisory or clerical, and junior managerial, administrative or professional
C2	Skilled manual workers
D	Semi- and unskilled manual workers
E	State pensioners or widows (no other earners), casual or lower grade workers, or long-term unemployed

Figure 3.5 IPA basis for social classification

simply on their occupation. But the expansion of workers in traditionally middle-class jobs such as finance and management led the government to increase the number of classes and to look more critically at an occupational title in terms of the life opportunities that it offers.

The Standard Occupational Classification used for the Census was first published in 1990 and updated in 2000. It uses two main concepts for classifying individuals:

1 the kind of work performed (that, is the job description)
2 the competence level required for the tasks and duties (the required skills for the job).

Changes introduced in 2000 reflected the need to improve comparability with the International Standard Classification of Occupations and the changing needs of users of census data, who were becoming increasingly dubious about the existing bases of classification. Revisions were influenced by innovations associated with technological developments and the re-definition of work, reflecting the educational attainment of those entering the labour market. The main features of the revision included:

■ a tighter definition of managerial occupations
■ a thorough overhaul of computing and related occupations
■ the introduction of specific occupations associated with the environment and conservation
■ changes linked to the de-skilling of many manufacturing processes
■ the recognition of the development of customer service occupations and the emergence of remote service provision through the operation of call centres.

The major occupational groups defined by the census are shown in Figure 3.6.

Each of these nine groups is broken down into further sub-groups so, for example, major group 2 (professional occupations) has a sub-major group (21) of science and technology professionals, which is broken down into a minor group (211) of science professionals, from which a unit (2111) of scientists can be identified.

1 Managers and senior officials

2 Professional occupations

3 Associate professional and technical occupations

4 Administrative and secretarial occupations

5 Skilled trades occupations

6 Personal service occupations

7 Sales and customer service occupations

8 Process, plant and machine operatives

9 Elementary occupations

Figure 3.6 Major occupational groups used in UK Census data collection

In this revised system of classification there were risers and fallers. Teachers, librarians, nurses and police officers were among the risers, based on the skills and security of their job. Workers in call centres fell according to this system of classification.

3.6.3 Geodemographic classification systems

A lot of research has shown a correlation between where a person lives and their buying behaviour. The type of house and its location says much more about an individual than occupation alone can. Income, the size of the family unit and attitudes towards city life/country living, as well as occupation, are closely related to residence. The classification of individuals in this way has come to be known as geodemographic analysis. A number of firms offer a geodemographic segmentation analysis, which allows a classification of small geographical pockets of households according to a combination of demographic characteristics and buying behaviour.

A widely used classification system is ACORN (ACORN is an acronym of A Classification Of Residential Neighbourhoods). ACORN is a geodemographic segmentation method, using census data to classify consumers according to the type of residential area in which they live. Each postcode in the country can, therefore, be allocated an ACORN category. This classification has been found to be a more powerful differentiator of consumer behaviour than traditional socio-economic and demographic indicators. The ACORN categories, and their components, are described in Figure 3.7.

Another widely used application of geodemographic analysis is MOSAIC, offered by Experian Ltd. By analysing a lot of sales data from people in each postcode area, it is possible to build up a good picture of the lifestyle and spending patterns associated with each classification. It is also possible to see how the distribution of the population between different classifications changes over time (see Figure 3.8).

3.6.4 Lifestyle bases of classification

Geodemographic classification systems tell business a lot more about individuals than their occupation alone can, but this still misses much detail about the lifestyle of particular individuals, or the size of groups that share a similar lifestyle. A starting point for lifestyle segmentation is to understand where an individual is located in the family life cycle. Traditional

Group A – Thriving (Approx 20% of population)	Wealthy achievers, suburban areas Affluent greys, rural communities Prosperous pensioners, retirement areas
Group B – Expanding (Approx 11% of population)	Affluent executives, family areas Well-off workers, family areas
Group C – Rising (Approx 8% of population)	Affluent urbanites, town and city areas Prosperous professionals, metropolitan areas Better-off executives, inner-city areas
Group D – Settling (Approx 25% of population)	Comfortable middle-agers, mature home-owning areas Skilled workers, home-owning areas
Group E – Aspiring (Approx 13% of population)	New homeowners, mature communities White-collar workers, better-off multiethnic areas
Group F – Striving (Approx 21% of population)	Older people, less prosperous areas Council estate residents, better-off homes Council estate residents, high unemployment Council estate residents, greatest hardship People in multiethnic, low-income areas

Figure 3.7 ACORN classifications

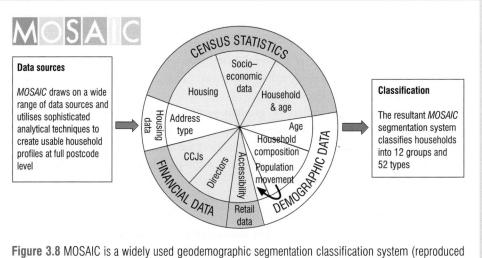

Figure 3.8 MOSAIC is a widely used geodemographic segmentation classification system (reproduced with permission of Experian Ltd)

Life stage groups	
Pre-family	those aged under 35 who are not parents
Family	those aged 15–54 with at least one child aged under 16 still at home
Empty nesters	no family/empty nesters aged 35–54 with no children (aged under 16)
Post-family	post-family/retired, those aged over 55/not working
Special category groups	
Benefit dependents	Es aged 35+ – those who are reliant solely on state benefits (around 10% of the adult population)
Families on a tight budget	working C2Ds with at least one child aged under 16 in the household – the majority have limited incomes which must be spent on a relatively large household (around 10% of the adult population)
Better-off families	working ABC1s with at least one child aged under 16 in the household (around 9% of the population)
Better-off empty nesters	ABC1s aged 35–64 who are working with no children (aged under 16) living at home. They are, therefore, the classic no family/empty nesters with probably a high income that can be spent on themselves rather than on family (around 8% of the adult population)
Working managers	working ABs (around 9% of the population)
Working women	women in part- or full-time employment (around 21% of the adult population)

Figure 3.9 Consumer life stage and special categories as identified by Mintel

models of family life cycles have portrayed individuals as going through a number of distinct and sequential stages from dependent child, through young adults, adults with dependent children, then with no dependent children ('empty nesters'), to solitary survivors. However, such simple linear models are no longer considered relevant to an increasing number of individuals who break this pattern through divorce, single parenthood, remarriage etc. The research company Mintel, for example, has advanced from the traditional family lifecycle model by identifying a number of special categories which typify consumer habits in the early 2000s (see Figure 3.9). Unlike the life stage groups, these groups represent only sections of the population and do not account for all adults.

Many research companies have developed much more subjective bases for defining lifestyle groups, which rely on a verbal description of the groups. Information to support the validity of these groups is hard to come by and generally relies on small sample surveys of the population. For this reason, such ideal-type classification systems are less well suited to monitoring social change than more objective systems based on quantifiable data.

Because of their subjectivity, there is a wide variety of lifestyle segmentation models which tend to reflect the needs of the companies that created them. For example, one model developed by Young & Rubicam described four lifestyle groups to which members of a population could be allocated.

1 Conformers, comprising the bulk of the population, who typically may live in a suburban semi-detached house, drive a Vauxhall Astra, shop at Sainsbury's and book a Thomsons package holiday.

2 Aspirers, a smaller group who are ambitious, innovative and keen to surround themselves with the trappings of success. This group may typically live in a trendy mews house, drive a GTI car, shop for brand-name clothes and take adventure holidays.

3 Controllers, by contrast, are comfortable in the knowledge that they have made it in life and do not feel the need to flaunt their success. They are more likely to live in a comfortable detached house, drive a Volvo, shop at Marks & Spencer and book their holiday through the local travel agent they trust.

4 Reformers have a vision of how life could be improved for everybody in society. At home they may be enthusiastic about DIY and energy conservation. They may see their car more as a means of transport than a status symbol and buy own-label brands at the Co-op.

Of course, these are ideal types, and very few people will precisely meet these descriptions. However, they are a useful starting point for trying to understand who it is that a company is targeting. The numbers in each category have undoubtedly risen and fallen in the recent past. Aspirers seemed to appear in great numbers during periods of economic boom, but become less conspicuous at the onset of a recession.

Many more informal, almost tongue-in-cheek, bases for segmenting lifestyle groups are commonly used. It has in the past, for example, been common to talk about lifestyle groups that have been labelled yuppies (young, upwardly mobile professionals), dinkys (dual income, no kids yet) and bobos (burnt out, but opulent), to name but a few. New descriptions emerge to describe new lifestyles. Again, these classifications are not at all scientific, but they give market researchers a chance to describe target markets.

3.7 DEMOGRAPHY

Demography is the study of populations in terms of their size and characteristics. Among the topics of interest to demographers are the age structure of a country, the geographic distribution of its population, the balance between males and females, and the likely future size of the population and its characteristics.

3.7.1 The importance of demographic analysis to business organizations

A number of reasons can be identified why business organizations should study demographic trends.

THINKING AROUND THE SUBJECT: SANDWICH STATEMENT

What does an individual's choice of sandwich say about them? The retailer Tesco undertook research that showed how complex the market for ready-made sandwiches had become, with clear segments emerging of people who sought quite different types of sandwiches. In an attempt to define and target its lunch customers more precisely, the company found that well-paid executives invariably insisted on 'designer' sandwiches made from ciabatta and focaccia with sun dried tomatoes and costing about £2.50. Salespeople and middle-ranking executives were more inclined to opt for meaty triple-deckers. Upwardly mobile women aged 25–40 chose low-calorie sandwiches costing around £1.49. Busy manual workers tended to grab a sandwich that looked affordable, simple and quick to eat, such as ploughman's sandwich that Tesco sold for £1.15. Tesco's research claimed that sandwiches have become an important statement made by individuals and need to be targeted appropriately. What do your snack meals say about *you*?

1 First, on the demand side, demography helps to predict the size of the market that a product is likely to face. For example, demographers can predict an increase in elderly people living in the United Kingdom and the numbers living in the south-west region of the country. Businesses can use this information as a basis for predicting, for example, the size of the market for retirement homes in the south-west.

2 Demographic trends have supply side implications. An important aim of business organizations is to match the opportunities facing an organization with the resource strengths that it possesses. In many businesses, labour is a key resource and a study of demographics will indicate the human resources that an organization can expect to have available to it in future years. Thus a business that has relied on relatively low-wage, young labour, such as retailing, would need to have regard to the availability of this type of worker when developing its product strategy. A retailer might decide to invest in more automated methods of processing transactions and handling customer enquiries rather than relying on a traditional but diminishing source of relatively low-cost labour.

3 The study of demographics also has implications for public-sector services, which are themselves becoming more marketing orientated. Changing population structures influence the community facilities which need to be provided by the government. For example, fluctuations in the number of children have affected the number of schools and teachers required, while the increasing number of elderly people will require the provision of more specialized housing and hospital facilities suitable for this group.

4 In an even wider sense, demographic change can influence the nature of family life and communities and ultimately affects the social and economic system in which organizations operate. The imbalance that is developing between a growing dependent elderly population and a diminishing population of working age is already beginning to affect government fiscal policy and the way in which we care for the elderly, with major implications for business organizations.

Although the study of demographics has assumed great importance in Western Europe in recent years, study of the consequences of population change dates back a considerable time. T.R. Malthus studied the effects of population changes in a paper published in 1798. He predicted that the population would continue to grow exponentially, while world food resources would grow at a slower linear rate. Population growth would only be held back by 'war, pestilence and famine' until an equilibrium point was again reached at which population was just equal to the food resources available.

Malthus's model of population growth failed to predict the future accurately and this only serves to highlight the difficulty of predicting population levels when the underlying assumptions on which predictions are based are themselves changing. Malthus failed to predict, on the one hand, the tremendous improvement in agricultural efficiency which would allow a larger population to be sustained and, on the other hand, changes in social and cultural attitudes that were to limit family size.

3.7.2 Global population changes

Globally, population has been expanding at an increasing rate. The world population level at AD 1000 has been estimated at about 300 million. Over the next 750 years, it rose at a steady rate to 728 million in 1750. Thereafter, the rate of increase became progressively more rapid, doubling in the following 150 years to 1550 million in 1900 and almost doubling again to 3000 million in the 62 years to 1962. The United Nations estimated total world population in 2003 to be 6.5 billion, and predicted that this would rise to 9.1 billion by 2050 (UNFPA 2004). The growth of world population has not been uniform, with recent growth being focused on the world's poorer countries, especially Korea and China, as well as South America. Within the EU countries, the total population in recent times has increased at a natural rate of about 1 per 1000 population (that is, for every 1000 deaths, there are 1001 births). However, this hides a range of rates of increase with, at each extreme, Ireland having a particularly high birth rate and Germany a particularly low one. This has major implications for future age structures and consumption patterns (see below). Much faster population growth is expected to occur in Africa and Latin America.

An indication of the variation in population growth rates is given in Figure 3.10. It should, however, be noted that there is still considerable debate about future world population levels, with many predictions being revised downwards.

A growth in the population of a country does not necessarily mean a growth in business opportunities, for the countries with the highest population growth rates also tend to be those with the lowest gross domestic product per head. Indeed, in many countries of Africa, total GDP is not keeping up with the growth in population levels, resulting in a lower GDP per head. On the other hand, the growth in population results in a large and low-cost labour force, which can help to explain the tendency for many European-based organizations to base their design capacity in Europe but relatively labour-intensive assembly operations in the Far East.

3.7.3 Changes in UK population level

The first British Census was carried out in 1801 and the subsequent 10-yearly census provides the basis for studying changes in the size of the British population. A summary of British population growth is shown in Figure 3.11.

The fluctuation in the rate of population growth can be attributed to three main factors: the

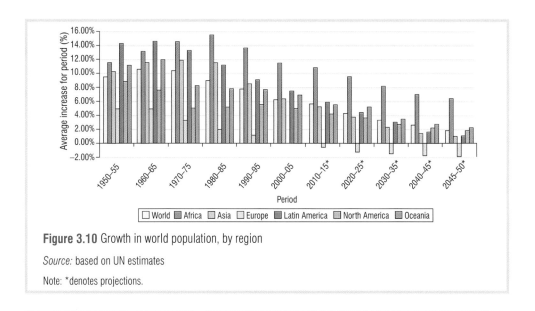

Figure 3.10 Growth in world population, by region

Source: based on UN estimates

Note: *denotes projections.

Year	Population of England, Wales and Scotland (000)	Average increase per decade (%)
1801	10,501	13.9
1871	26,072	9.4
1911	40,891	4.5
1941	46,605	5.8
1971	54,369	0.8
1981	54,814	2.4
1995	56,957	3.4
2011	58,794	1.7 (estimated)
2031	58,970	−0.5 (estimated)

Figure 3.11 Population growth, England, Wales and Scotland, 1801–2031

Source: based on *Annual Abstract of Statistics*, Government Actuary's Department and population censuses

birth rate, the death rate, and the difference between inward and outward migration. The fluctuation in these rates is illustrated in Figure 3.12. These three components of population change are described below.

3.7.4 The birth rate

The birth rate is usually expressed in terms of the number of live births per 1000 population. Since the Second World War, the birth rate of the UK has shown a number of distinct cyclical tendencies. The immediate post-war years are associated with a 'baby boom', followed by a

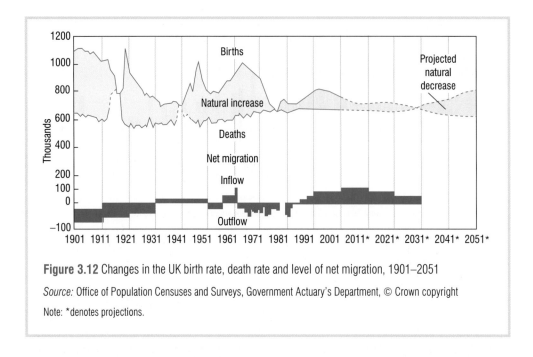

Figure 3.12 Changes in the UK birth rate, death rate and level of net migration, 1901–2051

Source: Office of Population Censuses and Surveys, Government Actuary's Department, © Crown copyright

Note: *denotes projections.

steady decrease in the number of births until 1956. Following this, the rate rose again until the mid-1960s during a second, but lesser, baby boom. The birth rate then fell until the mid-1970s, rising again in recent years. Worldwide, the United Nations has estimated that the average birth rate per female has fallen from 5 in 1953 to 2.65 in 2003 (UNFPA, 2004). Of the 44 countries in the developed world, all except Albania were reported to have birth rates below the natural replacement rate of 2.1 per female (the level needed to maintain a stable population level).

In order to explain these trends, it is necessary to examine two key factors:

1 the number of women in the population who are of child-bearing age
2 the proportion of these women who actually give birth (this is referred to as the fertility rate).

The peak in the birth rate of the early 1960s could be partly explained by the 'baby boom' children of the immediate post-war period working through to childbearing age. Similarly, the children of this group have themselves reached childbearing age, accounting for some of the recent increase in the birth rate. Greater doubt lies over reasons for changes in the fertility rate, usually expressed in terms of the number of births per 1000 women aged between 16 and 44. This has varied from a peak of 115 at the beginning of the century to a low point of 56.8 in 1983 (see Figure 3.13).

There are many possible explanations for changes in fertility rates and it is our difficulty in understanding the precise nature of these changes that makes population forecasting a difficult task. Some of the more frequently suggested causes of the declining fertility rate are listed below.

1 A large family is no longer seen as an insurance policy for future parental security. The extended family has declined in importance and state institutions have taken over many of the welfare functions towards elderly members of the family which were previously expected of children. Furthermore, infant and child mortality has declined and consequently the

need for large numbers of births has declined. Alongside this falling need for large numbers of children has come a greater ability to control the number of births.

2 Children use household resources that could otherwise be used for consumption. The cost of bringing up children has been increasing as a result of increased expectations of children and the raising of the school leaving age. Although in many Western countries this is partly offset by financial incentives for having children, the cost of child rearing has increased relative to consumer purchases in general. According to a study by the US Department of Agriculture, it costs a family earning $54,100 (£28,000) a year $178,000 (£93,000) at 2004 prices to raise a child from birth to 18 (US Department of Agriculture 2004).

3 In addition to diverting household resources from the consumption of other goods and services, caring for children also has the effect of reducing the earning capacity of the household. Women may also seek additional status and career progression by having fewer children or spacing them over a shorter period of time.

4 Birth rates tend to be related to current economic conditions, falling significantly in response to temporary economic recession and rising in response to a period of economic boom.

The effects of variation in birth rates can be felt for a long time after the variation itself. In the UK, a post-war peak in births resulted in a large 'baby boomer' generation having a high number of children in the 1960s, and their children in turn made up a large cohort of mothers who raised the birth rate again when they had children 20 to 30 years later. Although these cycles become progressively less pronounced over time, businesses should nevertheless be able to predict them and adjust their capacity accordingly.

3.7.5 The death rate

Death rates are normally expressed as the number of people in the country that die in a year per 1000 of the population. This is sometimes called the crude death rate; the age-specific death rate takes account of the age of death and is expressed as the number of people per 1000 of a particular age group that die in a year.

Year	Fertility rate
1900	115.0
1933	81.0
1951	73.0
1961	90.6
1971	84.3
1981	62.1
1991	64.0
2001	54.5

Figure 3.13 General fertility rate: total births per 1000 women aged 15–44, United Kingdom

Source: based on OPCS/Census of Population data

In contrast to the volatility of the birth rate during the post-war period, the death rate has been relatively stable and has played a relatively small part in changing the total population level. The main feature of mortality in the United Kingdom has been a small decline in age-specific death rates, having the effect of increasing the survival chances of relatively old people. The age-specific death rate of women has fallen more significantly than for men. The main reasons for the decline in age-specific death rates are improved standards of living, a better environment and better awareness of health issues, and an improvement in health services. While age-specific death rates have been falling in most advanced industrial countries, the United Kingdom has generally experienced a slower fall than most other EU member states.

3.7.6 Migration

If immigration is compared with emigration, a figure for net migration is obtained. In general, net immigration tends to be greatest during periods of economic prosperity, while net emigration tends to be greatest during periods of economic recession. During most periods of the twentieth century, the United Kingdom experienced a net outflow of population, the main exceptions being the 1930s, caused by emigrants to the Commonwealth returning home during the depression; the 1940s when a large number of refugees entered the United Kingdom from Nazi Europe; and the late 1950s/early 1960s when the prosperity of the British economy attracted large numbers of immigrants from the new Commonwealth. Emigration has tended to peak at times of economic depression in the United Kingdom. The prosperity of the UK during the 1990s increased the number of immigrants (and to most other EU countries).

3.7.7 The age structure of the population

It was noted earlier that the total population of the United Kingdom – and indeed most countries of the EU – is fairly stable. However, within this stable total, there has been a more noted change in the composition of particular age groups, with Ireland having a particularly high birth rate and Germany a particularly low one (see Figure 3.14). This has major implications for future age structures and consumption patterns. By 2030, people over 65 in Germany will account for almost half the adult population, compared with one-fifth in 2000. And unless the country's birth rate recovers from its present low of 1.3 per woman, over the same period its population of under-35s will shrink about twice as fast as the older population will grow. The net result will be that the total population, now 82 million, will decline to 70–73 million, and the number of people of working age will fall by a quarter, from 40 million today to 30 million. In Japan, the population will peak in 2005, at around 125 million, and by around 2030, the share of the over-65s in the adult population will have grown to about half (*The Economist* 2001).

The changes that have affected the size of age-specific segments in the UK are illustrated in Figure 3.15.

What are the implications for business organizations of an ageing of the population structure?

■ There is a growing imbalance between the shrinking size of the working population and an increasingly large dependent population. Government statistics show that between 1961 and 1996, the number of people of working age in the UK available to support the retired

THINKING AROUND THE SUBJECT:
HOW TO DEFUSE A DEMOGRAPHIC TIME BOMB

The term demographic time bomb is often used to describe the effects of the increasing average age of populations in the EU. What will the effects of this 'time bomb' be on the business environment?

In 2005, the European Commission published a Green Paper on demographic change which claimed that from 2005 until 2030 the EU would lose 20.8 million (6.8 per cent) people of working age. By 2030, Europe would have 18 million fewer children and young people than in 2005. By 2030, the number of 'older workers' (aged 55 to 64) would have risen by 24 million as the baby boomer generation become senior citizens and the EU would have 34.7 million citizens aged over 80 (compared to 18.8 million in 2005). Average life expectancy has also risen by five years since 1960 for women and nearly four years for men. The number of people aged 80+ is expected to grow 180 per cent by 2050. At the same time, the EU's fertility rate fell to 1.48 in 2003, below the level needed to replace the population (2.1 children per woman). As a result of these demographic changes, the proportion of dependent young and old people in the population will increase from 49 per cent in 2005 to 66 per cent in 2030.

For many people, the most pressing consequence of an ageing population focuses on pensions provision, but according to the European Employment and Social Affairs Commissioner, Vladimir Spidla, the looming crisis raises issues that are much broader. 'This development will affect almost every aspect of our lives, for example the way businesses operate and work is organized, our urban planning, the design of houses, public transport, voting behaviour and the infrastructure of shopping possibilities in our cities,' he said.

The EU report noted that modern Europe has never experienced economic growth without rising birth rates, and suggested that 'ever larger migrant flows may be needed to meet the need for labour and to safeguard Europe's prosperity'.

How can Europe increase the size of its working population to serve the growing proportion of the population that is dependent? One strategy is to ensure that all people who are of working age and able to work actually do so. This would entail eliminating unemployment through retraining and changes to government social payments. Another strategy to increase long-term employment levels is to promote a higher birth rate. But there is an apparent contradiction here, because there is evidence that pressure on families to work harder has been having the effect of reducing the birth rate. The EU report found that Europe's low birth rate is largely the result of constraints on families' choices – late access to employment, job instability, expensive housing and lack of family-focused incentives (such as parental leave and childcare). Incentives of this kind can have a positive impact on the birth rate and increase employment, especially female employment.

A further way of expanding the workforce is to rely on immigration, but this raises a number of issues. First, there is the emotive issue to many people of diluting a national culture. More significantly, from a demographic perspective, what happens when these immigrant workers themselves get old and become dependent? They will need yet more immigrants to look after them. There is also a moral issue associated with immigration, because a common source of immigrants is the developing world. Given that many immigrants are the better-educated members of the society that they come from, is it morally right for the prosperous West to deprive developing countries of trained staff, such as doctors and nurses?

In presenting the EU report, Commissioner Spidla noted that 'Politics alone cannot solve the problem ... they have to go hand in hand with a picture in society that does not stamp women who re-enter the labour market after maternity leave as "bad mothers" and men that take care of children as "softies".' Why do some cultures find this challenge insurmountable, whereas others readily accept working mothers as a valuable addition to the workforce? Is this the best way to defuse the 'demographic time bomb'?

Country	Total population 2001 (000)	% aged 0–14	% aged 15–24	% aged 25–64	65+
Austria	8,128	16.5	11.8	56.1	15.5
Belgium	10,263	17.6	12.1	53.5	16.9
Czech Republic	10,287	16.1	14.8	53.5	13.8
Cyprus	671	22.7	15.4	60.7	12.1
Denmark	5,355	18.7	11.2	55.3	14.8
Estonia	1,364	17.6	14.7	52.4	15.3
Finland	5,188	18.0	12.7	54.3	15.1
France	59,191	18.8	13.0	52.0	16.2
Germany	82,349	15.4	11.3	56.4	16.9
Greece	10,538	15.3	14.1	53.5	17.1
Hungary	10,187	16.5	14.3	54.0	15.2
Ireland	3,838	21.4	17.2	43.4	11.2
Italy	57,844	14.4	11.4	56.0	18.2
Latvia	2,355	17.0	14.6	53.0	15.4
Lithuania	3,477	19.3	14.5	52.1	14.1
Luxembourg	441	18.8	11.5	55.7	14.0
Malta	393	19.5	15.0	53.1	12.5
Netherlands	16,043	18.0	11.9	56.1	14.1
Poland	38,641	18.5	17.0	52.1	12.4
Portugal	10,299	16.0	14.2	53.4	16.5
Slovakia	5,391	19.0	16.9	52.2	11.4
Slovenia	1,992	15.6	14.3	55.8	14.3
Spain	40,265	14.6	13.8	54.6	17.0
Sweden	8,896	18.3	11.6	52.9	17.2
United Kingdom	59,755	18.9	12.1	53.3	15.6

Figure 3.14 A comparison of the population structure of EU member countries

Source: compiled from National Statistical Office sources

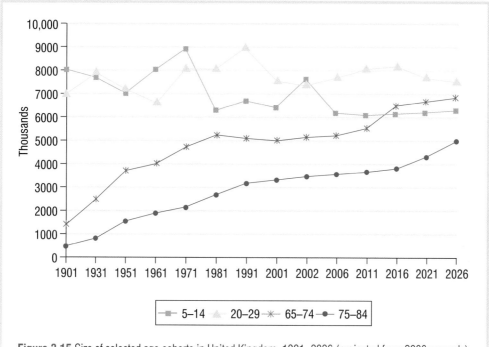

Figure 3.15 Size of selected age cohorts in United Kingdom, 1901–2026 (projected from 2006 onwards)

Source: based on Office of Population Censuses and Surveys estimates

population decreased from 4.1 per pensioner to 3.3. This figure is expected to fall again slightly to 2020 but then fall again sharply as those in the baby boom generation start to become eligible for their pensions. The ratio of those contributing to the pensions that sustain the retired population is smaller still, to take account of the fact that although many people of working age are available to work, many are either unemployed or pay no taxes. By 2020, each pensioner will be supported by the contributions of two tax-paying workers. This is expected to fall to 1.6 by 2040.

- For businesses that have offered their employees a 'final salary' pension scheme, the cost of paying pensions has increased markedly, as longevity has resulted in a lengthening stream of pension payments. The current profitability of many companies has been reduced as they divert profits to fill this pension gap.

- With younger people declining as a proportion of the workforce, employers are increasingly looking to older people to fill their vacancies.

- The growing proportion of older people in the population may change the values of a youth-orientated culture. For example, the emphasis on fashion and short-life products may give way to an emphasis on quality and durability as the growing numbers in the older age groups increasingly dominate cultural values.

THINKING AROUND THE SUBJECT:
THE COMPLEXITIES OF FORECASTING FUTURE DEMAND FOR CARE HOMES

Ageing of the population is a major opportunity for many organizations. However, the link between growth in size of the elderly population and demand for a company's products can be complex. Nursing homes may expect a boom in demand as the population ages. However, during the period 1995–2004, the number of elderly people in residential care in the UK fell and many care homes and their operators went out of business, despite a growth in the number of elderly people during this period. Trying to forecast future demand for care homes is complicated by uncertainty over the future health needs of elderly people – will elderly people of the future be healthier and able to look after themselves longer? Will they make greater efforts to live in their own homes, rather than in a residential care home? Some care homes, such as this one, have spotted this trend and now offer an outreach service to care for people in their own homes. Costs of operating residential care homes are likely to increase, fuelled by increasing government regulations, and wages rising in real terms, reflecting a scarcity of people of working age relative to the number of elderly people. How much will elderly people and their relatives be able or willing to pay for residential care home accommodation? How much will the government be prepared to pay towards care? The Scottish Parliament announced in 2003 that it would provide financial support for elderly people in residential care homes, making the sector more attractive to operators in Scotland compared with the rest of the UK.

3.7.8 Household structure

Reference was made earlier in this chapter to the changing role and functions of family units, and this is reflected in an analysis of household structure statistics. A number of important trends can be noted.

1 First, it was noted above that there has been a trend for women to have fewer children. From a high point in the 1870s, the average number of children for each woman born in 1930 was 2.35, 2.2 for those born in 1945 and it is projected to be 1.97 for those born in 1965. There has also been a tendency for women to have children later in life. In the United Kingdom, the average age at which women have their first child has moved from 24 years in 1961 to 28 in 2001. There has also been an increase in the number of women having no children. According to the Office of Population Census and Surveys, more than one-fifth of women born in 1967 are expected to be childless when they reach the age of 40, compared with 13 per cent of those born in 1947.

2 Alongside a declining number of children has been a decline in the average household size. The total number of dwellings in the UK is estimated to have risen by 9 per cent between 1992 and 2002, significantly outstripping population growth, which was 2.3 per cent for the same period. The result is a falling number of people per household, falling continuously from an average of 3.1 people in 1961 to 2.4 in 2001 (Mintel 2003). There has been a particular fall in the number of very large households with six or more people (down from 7 per cent of all households in 1961 to under 2 per cent in 2001) and a significant increase in the number of one-person households (up from 14 per cent to 30 per cent over the same period). A number of factors have contributed to the increase in one-person households, including the increase in solitary survivors, later marriage and an increased divorce rate. The business implications of the growth of this group are numerous, ranging from an increased demand for smaller units of housing to the types and size of groceries purchased. A single-person household buying for him or herself is likely to use different types of retail outlet compared to the household buying as a unit – the single person may be more likely to use a niche retailer than the (typically) housewife buying for the whole family whose needs may be better met by a department store. Mintel showed a number of ways in which the spending patterns of single-person households deviate from the average. For example, compared to the British average, a person living in a single-person household spends 49 per cent more on tobacco, 26 per cent more on household services and 23 per cent less on meat (Mintel 2003).

3 There has been an increase in other forms of household that vary from traditional life cycle patterns. Households comprising lone parents with children have increased, and in 2001, 20 per cent of all households in England and Wales with dependent children comprised only one adult. Further variation is provided by house sharers who live independent lives within a household, pragmatically sharing the cost of many household items, while retaining the independence of mind more typical of a single-person household. The number of shared households has increased as young people find themselves priced out of the property market, and shared ownership (or shared rental) offers lifestyle opportunities which may be otherwise closed to a single person. In some cases, two families have shared the cost of a house, living as separate units within it.

4 Very significant differences occur throughout the EU in home ownership patterns, with implications for demand for a wide range of home-related services. The proportion of households living in rented accommodation ranges from 21 per cent in Spain to 53 per cent in West Germany, while the proportion with a mortgage ranges from 8 per cent in Spain to 44 per cent in the United Kingdom (Eurostat 2004).

3.7.9 Geographical distribution of population

The population density of the United Kingdom of 231 people per square kilometre is one of the highest in the world. However, this figure hides the fact that the population is dispersed very unevenly between regions and between urban and rural areas. The distribution of population is not static.

Regional distribution

The major feature of the regional distribution of the United Kingdom population is the dominance of the south-east of England with 30 per cent of the population, and the industrial regions of the West Midlands, Lancashire and Yorkshire. By contrast, the populations of Scotland, Wales and Northern Ireland account in total for only 17 per cent of the UK population.

Movement between the regions tends to be a very gradual process. In an average year, about 10 per cent of the population will change address, but only about one-eighth of these will move to another region. Nevertheless, there have been a number of noticeable trends. First, throughout the twentieth century there has been a general drift of population from the north to the Midlands and south. More recently, there has been a trend for population to move away from the relatively congested south-east to East Anglia, the south-west and the Home Counties. This can be partly explained by the increased cost of industrial and residential location in the south-east, the greater locational flexibility of modern industry and the desire of people for a pleasanter environment in which to live. The inter-regional movement of population is illustrated in Figure 3.16.

Urban concentration

Another trend has been a shift in the proportion of the population living in urban areas. Throughout most of Western Europe, the nineteenth and twentieth centuries have been associated with a drift from rural areas to towns. In the United Kingdom, this has resulted in the urban areas of Greater London, Greater Manchester, Merseyside, Greater Glasgow, the West Midlands, West Yorkshire and Tyneside having just one-thirtieth of the United Kingdom's surface area, but nearly one-third of the total population. From the 1960s, the trend towards urbanization was partly reversed, with many of the larger conurbations experiencing a decline in population, combined with a deterioration in many inner-city areas. Those moving out have tended to be the most economically active, leaving behind a relatively elderly and poor population. Much of the movement from the conurbations has been towards the rural areas just beyond the urban fringe. For example, London has lost population to the Home Counties of Berkshire, Buckinghamshire, Hertfordshire and Essex. The increasingly large dormitory population of these areas remains dependent on the neighbouring conurbation. Movement from urban to rural areas has brought about a change in lifestyle which has implications for businesses. Higher car ownership in rural areas has led more households to make fewer shop-

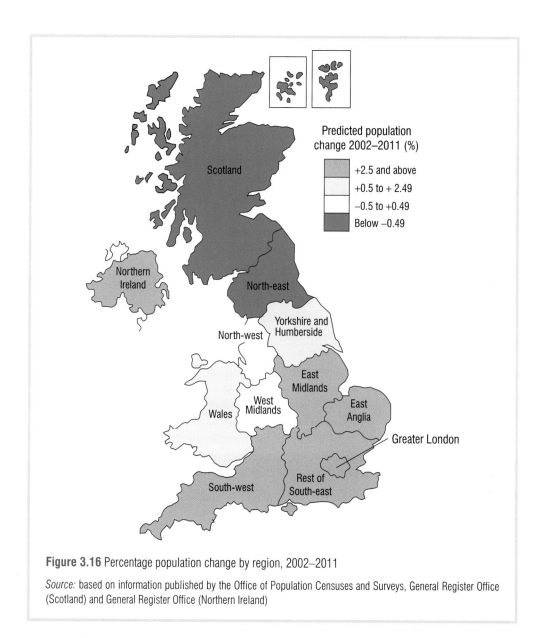

Figure 3.16 Percentage population change by region, 2002–2011

Source: based on information published by the Office of Population Censuses and Surveys, General Register Office (Scotland) and General Register Office (Northern Ireland)

ping trips for household goods, to travel further to the shop that best suits their lifestyle and to spend more on each trip. In this changed shopping pattern, the decision-making unit may comprise more members of the household than in an urban area where the (typically) wife may have made more frequent trips to the local supermarket by herself.

More recently, there has been a trend for young professional people to move back into town centres. For this group, having the facilities of a town centre close at hand without the need for increasingly expensive and time-consuming commuting has proved attractive. Town centres which were once deserted in the evening have often been brought back to life, helped by this group's patronage of wine bars, restaurants and all-night convenience stores.

The geographical distribution of the population differs between EU member states. For example, EU statistics show that the proportion of the population living within metropolitan areas varies from 13 per cent in Italy to 44 per cent in France. The resulting differences in lifestyles can have implications for goods and services as diverse as car repairs, entertainment and retailing.

CASE STUDY

A JOURNEY THROUGH LIVERPOOL – EUROPEAN CAPITAL OF CULTURE 2008
By Damian Gallagher, Liverpool Hope University

To many people, Liverpool's culture is characterized by the 'Scouser', an individual with a jovial happy-go-lucky sense of humour, a strong, distinct accent and sense of community spirit. The Scouser's love of music and entertainment is epitomized by Liverpool being the birthplace of the Beatles, and home to one of the world's greatest football teams. But scratch beneath the surface of Scouser culture and you will find a number of subcultures. It has always been that way, and a historical excursion through the city's culture demonstrates how the evolution of Scouser culture has influenced the business environment of Liverpool.

In 1660, the population of Liverpool was a modest 1200 but over the course of the next three centuries this was to change dramatically in the face of unrelenting urban and commercial growth. By 1775 the culture of Liverpool was dominated by commerce and the population had increased to 35,000; by 1801 this had doubled to more than 82,295 as more people were drawn to its ever developing port facilities and transport links as it grew to become one of the most important ports in the world, trading in almost everything, including sugar, tobacco, grain, cotton and even people.

As well as growing in size, the population had grown in its cultural diversity. Between 1830 and 1930 Liverpool became a centre for transcontinental migration as almost 9 million people used its port as a gateway to a new life. Many sought escape from the events of their own countries of origin such as the Irish Famine and social unrest in Eastern Europe via emigration to Canada, the USA, Australia, New Zealand, South Africa and South America. Many immigrant seafarers settled in the area and others moved from neighbouring agricultural areas attracted by the work available. Between 1845 and 1849 1.25 million Irish people used Liverpool in this way, but many had to stay, as they could not afford to go any further. By 1851, 25 per cent of Liverpool's population was Irish.

By the mid-nineteenth century, Liverpool had become a city of social extremes. There was a distinctly unequal distribution of wealth headed by the wealthy elite of merchant traders, bankers and shipping agents who benefited from Liverpool's prospering port and invested heavily in the city's architecture, but very little in the education, housing or healthcare of its workers. This allowed for ghetto-like segregation to develop in the city with lots of poverty and deprivation. As the population increased the city's boundaries expanded but its infrastructure struggled to cope with the sheer number of people and many poor Irish, Caribbean, Chinese, Dutch, German, Jewish, Welsh, Filipino and African working-class slum areas developed around the Scotland Road and Sebastapol Dock areas. Houses built to accommodate 19 were often found to contain over 90 people where typhus, dysentery, cholera and lack of adequate sanitation saw average life expectancy at only 38 for women and 37 for men compared to the national averages of 42 and 40 respectively.

In the years prior to World War Two, Liverpool's population peaked at 867,000. However, the twentieth century saw massive changes in the world's economic order, with many political and commercial changes having a negative impact upon Liverpool. As the century drew to a close the last of the working docks had closed and the once thriving port was a ghost of its former self. The population fell to 439,473, with many having chosen to leave the city in the face of rising unemployment.

High unemployment has often played a major role in the life of Liverpool. Manufacturing, which had boomed in the early post-war years, declined in the 1970s and 1980s. The docks were also shrinking rapidly and many of the inner-city docks closed, with the once strong workforce being replaced by machinery and new technologies. This led to much social and political unrest as answers and solutions were sought by the 22 per cent of the male population who were unemployed (compared to the national average of 10 per cent). In some areas of Liverpool, unemployment was as high as 90 per cent. In 1981, social unrest exploded into the notorious Toxteth riots. While racial tensions between the police and black youths provided the spark, it is now widely accepted that this was not a 'race riot'. Many underlying social issues lay at the heart of the problems in the form of chronic unemployment, bad housing and poor education. Many white youths from neighbouring areas saw the riots as an excuse to vent their frustrations and joined in the fierce battles that raged for most of that summer, causing millions of pounds worth of damage and leading to over 500 arrests.

Many people in these areas also blamed the recently elected Thatcher government for making their problems worse, seeing no role for the working classes in its policies of free market enterprise and the reduced role of trades unions. This gave birth in the mid-1980s to a radical militant local government in the city. Based on the Far Left of the Labour Party, it was seen by many as a revolt against Thatcherism as it embarked upon largely confrontational policies that were detached from the central Conservative government. In challenging the Conservative government's house-building policies, among others, the socialist government of Liverpool appeared to be riding on a wave of popular support from the disadvantaged Scousers who had lost out in the economic and social reforms of the Thatcher government.

This militancy was seen by many as a hangover from the working-class labour organizations of the Docks that were opposed to the aims of the Conservative government. Negative media images of a city with many social and economic problems did little to attract inward investment to the city or alleviate the sense of decline felt by its inhabitants.

By the 1990s, while the extremes of wealth and poverty still existed in Liverpool, though perhaps not as pronounced as in earlier years, a substantial middle-class population had also emerged. A new generation of young affluent and well-educated professionals with ambition and drive for success helped to fuel the social and economic regeneration of the city – some even point out with irony that these were the products of the Thatcherism that was once so reviled by the traditional Scouser. The smart coffee bars that this group gravitates to today are in another world compared with the rough pubs and ale houses of their predecessors.

An aerial view of Liverpool today reveals a city that is symbolized by its two cathedrals, one Catholic and one Anglican, standing at opposite ends of Hope Street. However, this hides the underlying multicultural make-up of the city that remains from its days as a successful trading port. The Irish influence on the city remains strong, with many Scousers being fourth- and fifth-generation Irish and the city often referred to as the 'capital of Ireland'! Muslims, Jews, Hindus, Sikhs, Buddhists and Taoists of Europe's second largest Chinese community still play a substantial role in the city. Many businesses specifically target these ethnic and cultural groups, whose cultures are celebrated in events such as the annual Chinese New Year celebrations, the Irish Festival, the Caribbean Carnival and the Liverpool Welsh Choral Union, as well as the recent Gay, Lesbian, Bisexual and Transsexual Homotopia festivals.

In June 2003, the city of Liverpool was named European Capital of Culture for 2008. Liverpool was looking to its Capital of Culture celebrations as a key driver for economic and social regeneration in the same way as previous hosts have experienced (e.g. Glasgow saw 50 per cent economic growth in 1990). With unemployment at its lowest rate for 30 years as a good starting point, the city saw many benefits to be obtained by 2008; 11.1 million tourists are projected to visit and spend £547 million, leading to the creation of 14,000 new jobs. The docks area that temporarily lay derelict has been subject to regeneration and redevelopment and is now home to many expensive luxury apartments and trendy bars, shops, restaurants and cafes, art galleries and museums. In 2004, Liverpool's Pier Head was even designated a UNESCO World Heritage site. Will such an influx bring about further change in the composition of Liverpool's cultural groups? And will the traditional working-class solidarity derived from the days of the docks survive in an era of consumerism and competitive service industry employment?

QUESTIONS

1 Summarize the changes in the cultural composition of Liverpool that have occurred during the last two centuries, and explain why business organizations should be interested in understanding these changes.
2 The case describes periods of social unrest in Liverpool which resulted from rising levels of unemployment following the decline of many traditional industries. Should business organizations seek to address issues of social exclusion such as that which occurred in Liverpool in the 1980s? If so, how could they help?
3 Identify the possible effects on businesses in Liverpool resulting from its nomination as European Capital of Culture 2008.

SUMMARY

Societies are not homogeneous and this chapter has explored the processes by which individuals develop distinct social and cultural values. The concepts of social class, lifestyles, reference groups, family structure and culture are important reference points for businesses and change in these must be monitored and addressed. Population totals and structures change and this chapter has reviewed the impact of demographic change on the marketing of goods and services. A changing population structure also has implications for the availability of employees.

There is a close link between this chapter and **Chapter 9** where we look at the social responsibility of businesses. As attitudes change, there has been a trend for the public to expect business organizations to act in a socially more acceptable manner. There are close links between the social environment and the political environment **(Chapter 2)**, with the latter reflecting changes in the former. It has also been noted that technology can have a two-way effect with the social environment, and understanding the complexity of society's changing needs calls for an information system that is comprehensive and speedy **(Chapter 4)**. When a company enters an overseas market, it is likely to face a quite different set of cultural values **(Chapter 12)**.

Key Terms

Age structure	(116)	Demography	(110)	Migration	(116)
Attitudes	(101)	Ethnic minorities	(95)	Reference groups	(100)
Birth rate	(113)	Family roles	(98)	Roles	(99)
Cellular household	(99)	Geodemographic analysis	(107)	Social class	(95)
Census of Population	(105)	Household structure	(121)	Subculture	(92)
Cultural convergence	(91)	Life stages	(109)	Values	(101)
Culture	(89)	Lifestyle	(102)		

CHAPTER REVIEW QUESTIONS

1 (a) Discuss the likely impact of ageing on the labour market.

   (b) What recommendations would you make to a business currently reliant on recruiting large numbers of school leavers to meet its labour needs?

   (*Based on CIM Marketing Environment Examination*)

2 'Businesses will have to cope with changes in demand patterns as older consumers become more significant in their markets and younger people less so.' Explain, with examples, some of the opportunities provided by these changing demand patterns and how the marketer should address this buyer segment.

   (*Based on CIM Marketing Environment Examination*)

3 'Ageing is one of the few trends that can be forecast with confidence.' Briefly explain why this is so, and suggest two forecasting approaches, showing how they might enable the marketer to forecast the future with greater confidence.
(*Based on CIM Marketing Environment Examination*)

4 In what ways do you think the different culture of a less-developed country may affect the marketing of confectionery that has previously been marketed successfully in the United Kingdom?

5 In what ways are the buying habits of a household with two adults and two children likely to change when the children leave home?

6 Critically assess some of the implications of an increasingly aged population on the demand for hotel accommodation in the United Kingdom.

ACTIVITY

Postcodes can reveal a lot about the social and economic composition of an area. If you live in England, Scotland or Wales, go to the Up My Street website (www.upmystreet.com) and enter a selection of postcodes that you are familiar with. You will be given a range of information about each area, for example house prices, nearby schools and crime levels. Click on the demographics button and you will be presented with a description of the area based on its ACORN code classification.

Useful Websites

ESRC Archive

A data archive of social sciences and humanities, providing links to many social sciences resources.

http://dawww.essex.ac.uk

Organization for Economic Co-operation and Development (OECD)

This site provides a summary of member states' population statistics.

http://www.oecd.org/publications/figures/ 2005/english/Demography.pdf

Social Science

A listing of social sciences resources, listed by subject heading.

http://www.sosig.ac.uk

Statbase

UK National Statistics' website, with summaries of numerous surveys of population characteristics, lifestyles and attitudes.

http://www.statistics.gov.uk/statbase/ mainmenu.asp

Up My Street

An interactive site which highlights differences between areas in terms of social structures. Enter a postcode or name of a town and a page will appear that displays data on that area. Data include unemployment statistics, house prices, council rates and local community services.

http://www.upmystreet.com

World Population

World population data from the US Census.

http://www.census.gov/ipc/www/world.html

Further Reading

Social classification has been discussed widely and the following texts are useful in a marketing context:

Grusky, D. (2001) *Social Stratification*, Westview Press.

Savage, M. (2000) *Class Analysis and Social Transformation: Sociology and Social Change*, Open University Press.

Sivados, E., Matthews, G. and Curry, D. (1997) 'A preliminary examination of the continuing significance of social class for marketing: a geodemographic replication', *Journal of Consumer Marketing*, Nov–Dec 1997, Vol. 14, No. 6, pp. 463–77.

Worsthorne, P. (1998) 'Chain of being', *New Statesman*, 16 October 1998, Vol. 127, No. 4407, pp. 54–55 (article about UK social class hierarchy).

Distinctive aspects of business within ethnic minority groups are discussed in the following:

Light, I.H. and Gold, S.J. (2000) *Ethnic Economies*, Academic Press.

For further discussion of market segmentation methods, the following texts build on the previous references:

Ehrenberg, A. (2002), 'More on modeling and segmentation', *Marketing Research*, Vol. 14, No. 3, p. 42.

Gonzalez, Ana M. and Bello, Laurentino (2002) 'The construct "lifestyle" in market segmentation: the behaviour of tourist consumers', *European Journal of Marketing*, Vol. 36, No. 1/2, pp. 51–85.

McDonald, M. and Dunbar, I. (1998) *Market Segmentation*, Basingstoke, Palgrave.

For statistics on the changing structure of UK society and its habits, the following regularly updated publications of the Office for National Statistics provide good coverage:

Family Expenditure Survey, a sample survey of consumer spending habits, providing a snapshot of household spending, published annually.

Social Trends, statistics combined with text, tables and charts which present a narrative of life and lifestyles in the UK, published annually.

Regional Trends, a comprehensive source of statistics about the regions of the UK, allowing regional comparisons.

Population Trends, statistics on population, including population change, births and deaths, life expectancy and migration.

References

The Economist (2001) 'The new demographics', Vol. 361, Issue 8246, 11 March, Special Section, pp. 5–8.

Eurostat (2004) *Eurostat Yearbook 2004*, Luxembourg, Statistical Office of the European Communities.

Future Foundation (2004) *Changing Lives*, London, Future Foundation.

Mintel (2002) *Halal Foods – UK*, London, Mintel.

Mintel (2003) *British Lifestyles*, London, Mintel.

Mintel (2004) *Pocket Money – Food and Drink in the UK 2004*, London, Mintel.

Office for National Statistics, *Social Focus on Women*, London, The Stationery Office, 1998.

This is Money (2005) 'Banking fit for Muslim faith', 14 June.

UNFPA (2004) *State of World Population Report 2004*, New York, United Nations Population Fund.

US Department of Agriculture (2004) *Annual Report*, 'The Cost of Raising a Child', Washington, US Department of Agriculture.

Chapter 4
The Technological and Information Environment

Chapter Objectives

This chapter will explain:

- the diversity of technological impacts on business

- the increasing speed of technological development

- innovation as a source of companies' and countries' competitive advantage

- the effects of the social environment on technology acceptance

- the impact of the Internet on communication between organizations and their environment

4.1 WHAT IS TECHNOLOGY?

The word 'technology' can easily be misunderstood as simply being about computers and hi-tech industries such as aerospace. In fact, technology has a much broader meaning and influences our everyday lives. It impacts on the frying pan (Teflon-coated for non-stick), the programmable central heating timer, cavity wall insulation, the television, DVD player, washing machine, car – in fact, just about everything in the home. The impact at work can be even greater, as technology changes the nature of people's jobs, creating new jobs and making others redundant. It influences the way we shop, our entertainment, leisure, the way we work, how we communicate, and the treatment we receive in hospital. The aim of this chapter is to explore the many ways in which technology impacts on business, and will focus on:

- the development of new or better products
- reduction in the cost of making existing products
- improvements in the distribution of goods and services
- new methods of communicating with customers and suppliers.

Technology is defined in the *Longman Modern English Dictionary* as 'the science of technical processes in wide, though related, fields of knowledge'. Technology therefore embraces mechanics, electrics, electronics, physics, chemistry and biology, and all the derivatives and combinations of them. The technological fusion and interaction of these sciences is what drives the frontiers of achievement forward. It is the continuing development, combination and application of these disciplines that give rise to new processes, materials, manufacturing systems, products and ways of storing, processing and communicating data. The fusion and interaction of knowledge and experience from different sciences is what sustains the 'technological revolution' (see Figure 4.1).

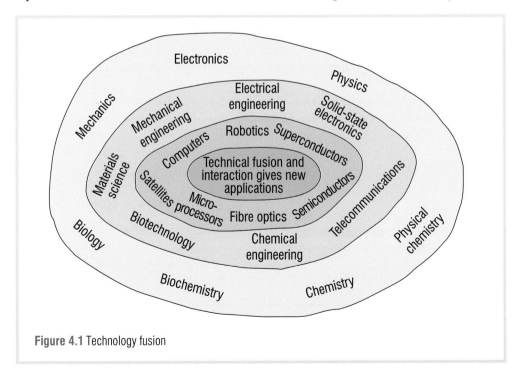

Figure 4.1 Technology fusion

Kotler (1997) has used the term demand-technology life cycle to help explain the relevance to businesses of technological advances. Products are produced and marketed to meet some basic underlying need of individuals. An individual product or group of products may be only one way of meeting this need, however, and indeed is likely to be only a temporary means of meeting this need. The way in which the need is met at any period is dependent on the level of technology prevailing at that time. Kotler cites the need of the human race for calculating power. The need has grown over the centuries with the growth of trade and the increasing complexity of life. This is depicted by the 'demand life cycle' in Figure 4.2, which runs through the stages of emergence (E), accelerating growth (G_1), decelerating growth (G_2), maturity (M) and decline (D).

Over the centuries, the need for calculating power has been met by finger-counting, abacuses, ready-reckoners, slide rules, mechanical adding machines (as big as an office desk), electrical adding machines (half the size of an office desk), electric calculators (half the size of a typewriter), battery-powered hand calculators and now palm-sized computers. Kotler suggests that 'each new technology normally satisfies the need in a superior way'. Each technology has its own 'demand-technology life cycle', shown in Figure 4.2 as T_1 and T_2, which serves the demand cycle for a period of time. Each demand-technology life cycle will have a history of emergence, rapid growth, slower growth, maturity and decline, but over a shorter period than the more sustainable longer-term demand cycle.

Business organizations should watch closely not only their immediate competitors but also emerging technologies. Should the demand technology on which their product is based be undermined by a new demand technology, the consequences may be dire. If the emerging demand technology is not recognized until the new and superior products are on the market, there may be insufficient time and money available for the firm to develop its own products using the competing technology. Companies making mechanical typewriters, slide rules, gas lights and radio valves all had to adjust rapidly or go out of business. One way executives can scan the technological environment in order to spot changes and future trends is to study technology transfer.

The term technology transfer can be used in a number of contexts. It is used to refer to the transfer of technology from research establishments and universities to commercial applica-

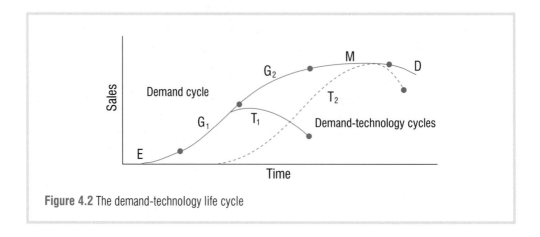

Figure 4.2 The demand-technology life cycle

tions. It may also be used in the context of transfers from one country to another, usually from advanced to less advanced economies. Transfers also occur from one industry to another; technology then permeates through the international economy from research into commercial applications in industries that can sustain the initially high development and production costs. As the costs of the new technology fall, new applications become possible. Thus, the technology permeates through different industries and countries. Applications of technology first developed for the US space programme, for example, may now be found in many domestic and industrial situations. NASA (the National Aeronautics and Space Administration) established nine application centres in the United States to help in transferring the technology that was developed for space exploration to other applications.

4.2 TECHNOLOGY AND SOCIETY

The rate at which technology is being enhanced and the rate at which it permeates through the world economy is of importance to business organizations. Product life cycles are typically becoming shorter. Expertise in a particular technology may no longer be a barrier preventing competitors from entering an industry. New entrants into an industry may benefit from the falling costs of technology or may be able to bypass the traditional technology by using some new and alternative technology.

Businesses managers should be interested in the degree to which technology influences their business. As we have learned, the environment is always changing and throwing up new challenges. Consider some historical antecedents: Bic produces a disposable plastic razor to challenge Wilkinson and Gillette; the fountain pen is challenged by the ball-point, and in turn the ball-point is challenged by the fibre-tip. Failure to identify changes in technology soon enough may cause severe and sometimes terminal problems for companies. Although there can be sudden changes in technology that impact on an industry, it is the gradual changes that creep through the industry that may be harder to detect. Companies that anticipate, identify and successfully invest in emerging technologies should be able to develop a strategic advantage over the competition. As the demand-technology life cycle goes through the stage of rapid growth, they will grow with it. As growth slows and the cycle matures, competitors will find it increasingly hard to gain a foothold in the new and by now dominant technology.

Our lives are affected by the interaction between technological changes and the social, economic and political systems within which we live and work. Over the last half-century the life of a mother has changed dramatically. With washing machines, tumble dryers, dishwashers, fridge-freezers and microwave cookers, modern textiles which are easier to wash and iron, convenience foods, and possibly the use of a car, the time devoted to household chores is much reduced. Partly as a result of these innovations, women are better educated and more likely to be in paid employment and thus contributing to an increased disposable income. Also flowing from these developments, shopping patterns change from daily shopping in small local shops, limited to what can be carried and with transport via the bus, to weekly shopping (perhaps even on a Sunday or in the middle of the night) using the car or online grocery shopping with home delivery. The lives of schoolchildren also change, with even the youngest being introduced to the computer. Business people now have a truly mobile office with a laptop computer, PDA and mobile phone, which in turn are being integrated into a single unit. They may be working from the car, from home, or even from a client's office. We are experiencing the casualization of communications, with people using personal phones, faxes, email and SMS text messages and expecting immediate responses but of a less formal nature. Within the family, life can become more dysfunctional as individual members pursue their own lives and activities. With more TV channels and choice, so there is a greater need for additional TVs, at least one of which is likely to be linked to a games machine. Space will also need to be found for at least one computer. There will be more phones around the home and not just line extensions; additional numbers and personal phones will be the norm.

4.2.1 Technology and consumer adoption

Many new technologies experience initial scepticism from consumers. At first, many thought that the technology of bank ATM machines would never become popular with bank customers, who would prefer to deal with bank staff face to face. Of course, ATMs have now become the routine method of withdrawing cash from a bank account. Similar voices of scepticism were raised with Internet banking. So how does a company try to predict the take-up of new technologies by consumers?

Parasuraman (2000) developed a Technology Readiness Index, designed to assess the likelihood of consumers adopting new technologies on the basis of four dimensions: their optimism, innovativeness, discomfort and insecurity. It has been noted that consumer adoption of self-service technologies is likely to be facilitated where the technology fits in with their existing lifestyle and they have a low perception of risk (Bobbit and Dabholkar 2001). Models of technology adoption have their origins in the disciplines of psychology, information systems and sociology. The Technology Acceptance Model (TAM) (Davis, Bagozzi and Warshaw 1989), based on the Theory of Reasoned Action (Ajzen and Fishbein 1980; Fishbein and Ajzen 1975), has become well established as a model for predicting acceptance of new IT-based services. The model (Figure 4.3) introduces two specific beliefs that are relevant for technology usage, namely perceived usefulness (U) and perceived ease of use (E). Actual behaviour is determined by behavioural intention (BI); however, behavioural intention is jointly determined by the individual's attitude towards a technology (A) and perceived usefulness (U). Finally, perceived ease of use (E) is a direct determinant of attitude (A) and perceived usefulness (U). In the case of older bank customers, where there is often nothing to be gained by switching to computer-mediated banking because other banking methods are available, it is likely that perceived ease of use would have a stronger influence on behavioural intentions than would perceived usefulness. However, in a business banking context, perceived usefulness is likely to be a stronger predictor of behavioural intention than attitude. There is considerable evidence that young people have been more ready to adopt new technologies than older people (O'Cass and Fenech 2003).

In some newly emerging countries people would view the rush in Western economies to automated self-service as perplexing. In India and other Asian countries, where labour is cheap and plentiful, the rising incomes of the middle classes would be used to employ more domestic help rather than buying a washing machine or vacuum cleaner, for example. Consumers in different parts of the world will have different priorities according to wealth and circumstances. In China, where the opportunity to buy your own home or car is more limited than in the UK, consumers with rising incomes are more likely to spend on TVs and mobile phones.

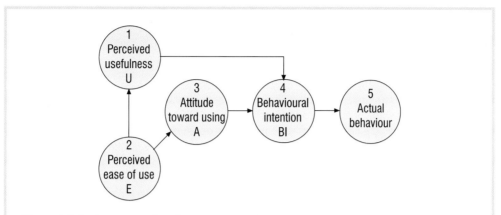

Figure 4.3 Services companies often encourage their customers to adopt new self-service technologies, thereby reducing their costs, especially staffing costs. They may also promote the fact that service users can obtain additional benefits by using an automated form of service delivery. However, many service users may remain deeply sceptical, failing to see the benefits to themselves, and influenced by horror stories in the media of how the new technology has previously let customers down (for example, many people remain cautious about giving their credit card details over the Internet, although, rationally, this is safer than giving details over the telephone). When planning the expansion of self-service facilities, companies need to be able to estimate the take-up rate, so that queues do not form or capacity remain unused. This model has been developed to explain the influences of perceived usefulness and attitude on consumers' intention to use, and actual use of new technology.

Source: based on Davis, Bogazzi and Warshaw 1989, p. 985

4.3 EXPENDITURE ON RESEARCH AND DEVELOPMENT

Research and development (R&D) expenditure is often classified into three major types: basic, applied and experimental.

1 Basic or fundamental research is work undertaken primarily for the advancement of scientific knowledge without a specific application in view.

2 Applied research is work undertaken with either a general or specific application in mind.

3 Experimental development is the development of fundamental or applied research with a view to introduction of new, or the improvement of existing, materials, processes, products, devices and systems.

Classification is also often carried out on a sectoral basis, e.g. public or private, and by type of industry. The International Standard Industrial Classification Code (ISIC) is often used.

International comparisons of R&D expenditure should be used with caution. Difficulties in comparing statistics stem from:

■ differences in the basic definitions of R&D and the boundaries between R&D and education, training, related scientific expenditure and administration costs

■ differences in counting numbers employed in R&D; e.g. definitions of full-time/part-time, directly or indirectly employed, qualifications and occupation

THINKING AROUND THE SUBJECT:
TOO MANY CHIPS IN THE KITCHEN?

How does a company developing high-technology consumer products predict whether a new product is going to be a hit with consumers or a miserable failure? One very simple, but naïve, solution would be to ask target consumers whether they would purchase the proposed new product. But, for radically new technologies, consumers may have very little idea of what the product involves and how it would fit into their lives. They would probably have difficulty articulating their thoughts about the product to a researcher. Is it any wonder then that an estimated 80 per cent of new products fail?

One method used by companies to try to better predict the likely take-up of new products is based on ethnographic research. This involves supplying participating households with prototype versions of the product and watching how they actually use and interact with the product. In return for an incentive, a family may be filmed and a diary recorded of their activities, typically over a two- or three-week period.

Researchers have been curious to understand how automation, and the Internet, can be brought into the domestic kitchen. The Korean firm LG developed an 'intelligent fridge' that used bar code readers to record items put into the fridge, and then taken from it and used up. This was linked to a simple stock control programme, which drew up a shopping list for the household, which in turn could be sent through the Internet to the household's preferred online grocer. In principle, the household need not worry about shopping or running out of any of its favourite grocery items. But the developers of the intelligent fridge didn't take account of the loss of a sense of control felt by the household. Ethnographic researchers pointed out that what appeared to be a technologically neat solution did not meet the lifestyle requirements of households.

The electronics companies Electrolux and Ericsson joined forces for another study involving human guinea pigs and their use of domestic refrigerators. They wanted to test the concept of a 'screen fridge' which allowed the user to download recipe ideas from the Internet, store shopping lists and had a built-in video camera to record messages. Among the questions that they sought answers to were: To what extent are households adventurous in their use of recipes? What is the typical number of recipes that a household relies on when cooking family meals? Who would show most interest in the technology – male members of the household who like gizmos, or the women who do most of the cooking?

The idea of being watched by television cameras throughout the house might seem very Orwellian. However, a rash of reality television shows such as *Big Brother* have made many people more open to the idea of being watched. But the question is often asked – as it has been for the *Big Brother* series – whether what is being seen is reality or the actions of a self-selecting idiosyncratic group who like to be watched? There is apparently no shortage of individuals and households who are willing to be filmed, and stories abound of semi-professional people who make a decent part-time living through such research. But is this really research which represents the population as a whole?

Source: based on Helen Jones (2004) 'Up Close and Personal',
The Marketer, Issue 7, November

■ discrepancies in the sources and destination of funds; e.g. private and commercial organizations receive some public funds, but public bodies also receive some funding from private sources; this makes it difficult to calculate the proportion of R&D expenditure financed by governments as compared to that financed by the private sector; university expenditure is typically a mix of the two, for instance

■ difficulties in distinguishing the R&D element of large-scale defence programmes

■ difficulties in assessing R&D funds flowing between countries, particularly between the components of multinational firms (Young 1993); the consolidated accounts of a multinational may show R&D expenditure, but in which country was it spent?

■ R&D expenditure undertaken by small firms is not usually recorded by government agencies (Lopez-Bassols 1998).

In order to overcome these difficulties, economists at the OECD issue guidelines in the form of the *Frascati Manual* for use by government statisticians. This helps to ensure that statistics are collected by each country on a similar basis, thereby aiding international comparison. The Frascati standards have now spread to most industrialized countries in the world, thus improving the reliability of comparable statistics. The manual is also updated regularly to take account of new issues, such as software R&D expenditure, for example.

These internationally agreed definitions aid comparison between nations, although caution still needs to be exercised when using international statistics. The variations in the exchange rate, purchasing power of the currency in the domestic market, and the reliability and comparability of the statistics all give grounds for caution.

For some countries the proportion of government R&D expenditure directed at defence remains high, the USA, UK and France being by far the biggest spenders, with 54 per cent, 39.5 per cent, and 24.8 per cent, respectively, of the government's R&D budget going to defence. Some emerging countries have robust and growing budgets for R&D; for example, according to the Organization for Economic Co-operation and Development (OECD), China doubled its spending on R&D as a percentage of GDP between 1995 and 2002.

The UK's R&D figures do not make happy reading for the country's industrialists and politicians. The figures for the UK's R&D expenditure in manufacturing are particularly bad, with a decline in expenditure in almost every sector. In real terms the UK's R&D expenditure has declined in recent years in mechanical engineering, electronics, electrical engineering, motor vehicles and aerospace. Increases in expenditure have occurred in chemicals, other manufactured products and non-manufactured products, reflecting the decline of the UK manufacturing industry. The United Kingdom is well down the international league table on expenditure. Add to this the controversy surrounding cuts in science research budgets affecting UK universities and the picture looks even worse. Research and development is the seedcorn for the new technologies, processes, materials and products of the future. Failure in this area is likely to mean that UK companies are less competitive in the future.

According to the OECD the UK's expenditure on R&D between 1981 and 2003 declined from 2.4 per cent of gross domestic product (GDP) to 1.9 per cent (*OECD Factbook* 2005). The United Kingdom's ranking against other major industrial nations (Group of Seven, or G7, nations) has slipped (see Figure 4.4).

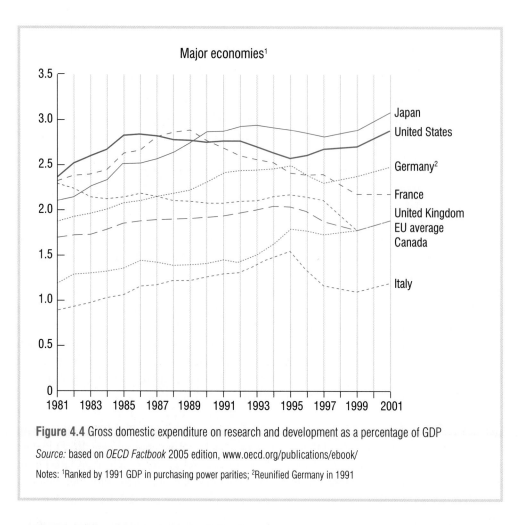

Figure 4.4 Gross domestic expenditure on research and development as a percentage of GDP

Source: based on *OECD Factbook* 2005 edition, www.oecd.org/publications/ebook/

Notes: [1]Ranked by 1991 GDP in purchasing power parities; [2]Reunified Germany in 1991

Spending on research and development is not the only indicator, however, when looking for evidence of healthy innovative activity. The number of patents registered in a country is also a reflection of a healthy R&D culture and advanced economy. As might be expected, Japan with 415,698 is ahead, with the USA having 230,336, Germany 134,775 and the UK 117,506 (OECD 2000). However, with multinationals conducting research in many countries and with multiple international registrations, it is becoming more difficult to track expenditure and patents by country. The OECD also collects data on the wider 'Investment in Knowledge', which includes public spending on education and software development, as well as the expenditure on R&D (see Figure 4.5).

Having taken the broad macro view of technology thus far, the rest of this chapter looks more specifically at how technology impacts on a business and where it may be applied to improve business operations. The following areas of technology application will be discussed: product design, manufacturing and processing systems, storage and distribution, order and payment processing, materials handling, document handling, computerized information and communications, and office automation (see Figure 4.6).

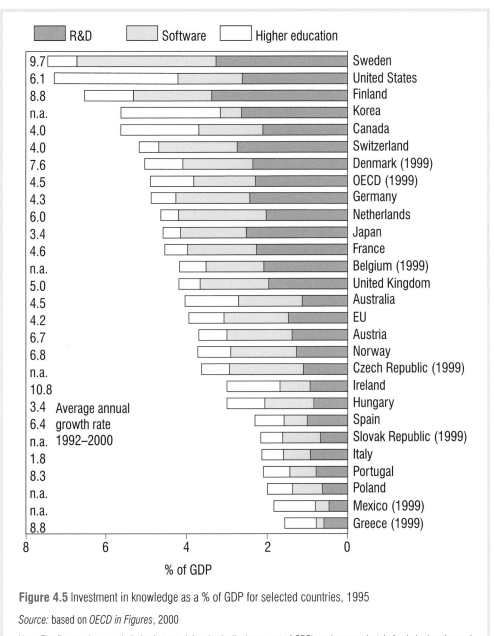

Figure 4.5 Investment in knowledge as a % of GDP for selected countries, 1995

Source: based on *OECD in Figures*, 2000

Note: The figures above exclude business training (typically 1 per cent of GDP), and some privately funded education and expenditure on market research.

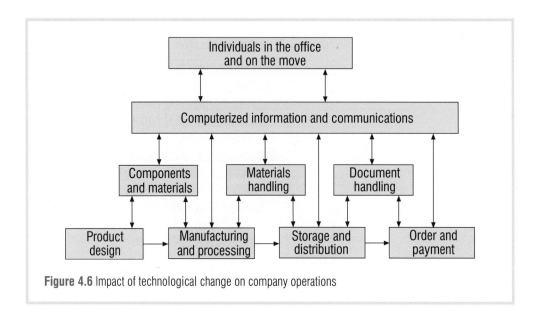

Figure 4.6 Impact of technological change on company operations

4.4 PRODUCT DESIGN AND DEVELOPMENT

It is often argued that the life expectancy of products has generally tended to shorten as technology has advanced. It took radio 30 years, from 1922 to 1952, to reach 50 million users. Television required 13 years to do the same thing. Cable television became available in 1974 and achieved this level of worldwide take-up in 10 years. It took the Internet approximately five years to reach an estimated 100 million users (*Harris Interactive*, www.harrisinteractive.com). The product life cycle (PLC) is a means of plotting sales and profits of a product over time (see Figure 4.7) in such a way that different stages in the life cycle can be identified and appropriate marketing strategies thus applied.

Five stages in the product life cycle can be identified, as follows.

1 Product development prior to launch: at this point, sales are zero and development and investment costs are rising.

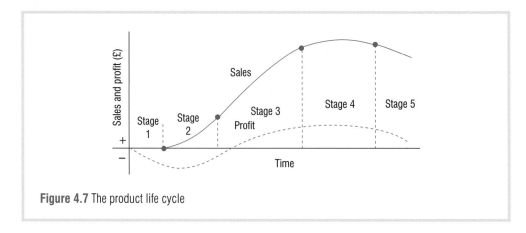

Figure 4.7 The product life cycle

Patents grant their owner a limited monopoly on the 'idea' defined by the patent. Such monopoly rights restrict competition for the length of the patent, which some may argue is socially harmful (the example of drugs companies pricing AIDS-related drugs out of the reach of most people in developing countries is often mentioned). On the other hand, a patent helps the owner to achieve a return on research expenditures which went into the discovery of the patented idea. This makes large expenditures for easily copied products, such as pharmaceuticals, easier to justify, arguably increasing research and development activity throughout an industry.

But could granting of patents slow down, rather than encourage, technological development? And are there cases where it may be considered immoral to grant patents for knowledge which should be freely available to all?

One of the biggest public concerns voiced in recent times against the patent system is in relation to the granting of patents by the United States Patent Office (USPTO) for inventions in biotechnology, especially those based on genetic information. The Human Genome Project has sought to identify the structure of DNA, sometimes referred to as the building blocks of life. An understanding of human genes offers the prospect of new medical treatments. But can and should gene sequences be patented? It is reported that, by 2005, four leading private companies had already patented about 750 human genes between them and had applications for a further 20,000 pending. If all of these pending patents were awarded (which is unlikely), those four private companies could own half of the human genome.

There have been conflicting results in studies of the impact on research of gene patents. Is there a risk that a lack of reasonable access to the genetic codes will stifle further basic research? Will it slow down the development of commercial products? In one study, it is reported that 25 per cent of United States university and commercial laboratories were refraining from providing genetic tests or continuing with some of their research for fear of breaching patents or because they lacked the funds to pay licence fees or royalties. Patents appeared to be challenging the traditional academic approach to a shared community of knowledge (Press and Washburn 2003).

On the other hand, turning genetic research into marketable treatments implies a long-term investment, for which there is no certainty of success. In a report on genetics patents, the OECD suggested that patents have the effect of making 'knowledge a tradeable commodity which both encourages the circulation of new information and promotes a division of labour'. It found little evidence that growth in the number and complexity of biotechnology patents had caused a breakdown in the patent system or prevented access to inventions by researchers and health service providers. In fact patents and licences for genetic inventions appeared to have stimulated research, knowledge flows and the entry of new technology into markets (OECD 2002)

2 Introduction of the product into the market: this means expensive launch costs and promotion. Profitable sales may take some time to develop.

3 Growth stage: this is when the product is fully accepted into the market and healthy profits begin to materialize on the strength of increasing sales.

4 Maturity: this refers to the period over which sales growth begins to slow and eventually stop. Profits may begin to decline as increasing competition puts pressure on prices and forces up promotional expenses to defend the market share.

5 Decline: at this point sales begin to fall off and profits decline due to a lower volume of production.

A distinction can be made between product category (say computers), product forms (e.g. networked, desktop PC, laptop, notebook and PDA) and brands (individual product brands offered by particular manufacturers such as Dell, Toshiba and Apple). According to Kotler (1977), product categories tend to have the longest life cycles and stay in the mature stage for very long periods. They may begin to decline only with significant and fundamental changes in technology (as when typewriters come to be replaced by personal computers) or shifts in consumer preferences. Product forms tend to show a more classical PLC, with each subsequent form showing a similar history to the previous one. For example, manual typewriters moved through the stages of introduction, growth and maturity, and entered decline as electronic typewriters were introduced. These then followed a similar history until they began to decline as personal computers were introduced. The old product category is now entering a decline stage as the new product category of personal computers has gone through a growth stage, and indeed into maturity. Individual brands follow the shortest PLC, as companies are constantly attempting to update their products to keep abreast of changes in technology, fashion, customer preferences and competitors' offerings. Rapid advances in technology may mean shortening product life cycles in some industries. In consumer electronics, for example, advances in technology have allowed manufacturers to add more and more product features and to reduce prices as costs have fallen. Brands in this product category may have a life expectancy of only 18 months before they are withdrawn and replaced.

Managing the development of new products is a complex and risky business. While many textbooks will identify a linear process, usually comprising about five stages, the reality involves a complex interaction between a number of forces. These external forces comprise technological developments, market demand, competitor activity, and possibly government influence. The internal organizational factors include management culture, R&D capabilities, engineering skills, production experience, management competence, access to finance, and marketing ability.

The linear model of the new product development (NPD) process can be seen in Figure 4.8.

The process starts with idea generation which involves the search for new ideas. The next step is then evaluation and screening during which the ideas are assessed for potential. If the company has a short-term planning horizon and a conservative culture then revolutionary and innovative ideas may be dropped at this stage. As the company focuses on the short term and operates in its comfort zone it may reduce risks but it may also be producing 'me too' products. In doing so it may also miss innovative developments and technological shifts and, as a result, jeopardize its long-term competitive position or even its survival. The purpose of this stage is

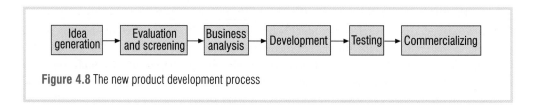

Figure 4.8 The new product development process

to reduce the number of ideas and to focus on further development of those with potential. Before engaging in expensive research and development an initial business analysis should be undertaken to assess the market potential of new ideas. For products involving minor innovation, and aimed at an existing well-defined market, estimating total market potential should be relatively straightforward. But what will be the share taken by a completely new product, especially if it is aimed at a new group of buyers? How will consumers take to the new product? Will distributors like the product? How will competitors react? Will competitors launch a similar product? What price should be charged and how will this affect demand? Is the new product likely to cost more, the same or less than the existing product to make? These are all questions that need to be considered when calculating the potential sales and profit.

For those products remaining, the next stage is development. This is where the expenses, mainly associated with research and development and/or engineering, are heaviest. Can the idea and new technology be developed into a workable product which can be produced in volume, at a reasonable cost, and which is practicable for the consumer? The testing stage may involve a number of activities. Testing the functional capabilities of the product may include technical tests, reliability tests and performance tests. Market testing involves testing consumers' and dealers' attitudes to the product. The final decision as to whether to launch the product is made at this stage.

Commercializing is the last stage and involves the highest expenditure as the product is prepared for manufacture and launch into the market. Decisions on expected sales, what volume to manufacture, what to contract out and what to manufacture in-house can all be critical. Product decisions such as the final form of the product, the number of variants to offer, features, size, colours, branding and packaging all have to be made, as have decisions on pricing and dealer margins. Promotional strategies have to be finalized and the timing and logistics of the launch planned.

These stages are often presented as sequential linear activities with one stage being completed before the next commences. In reality not all of the new product ideas come together and start the process at the same time. Ideas are generated at odd times and come from a wide variety of sources. The company needs to capture and evaluate these as and when they arise. From here on the company will have a number of products at different stages in the process at any one time. The development of some may be speeded up or slowed down as priorities are reassessed. Neither is the process completed in discrete stages as described above. Some new ideas may come from the company's blue-sky (speculative) research, so a certain amount of 'development' will have been done before the 'evaluation and screening' stage. 'Testing' is likely to begin before the 'development' stage is finished, and planning for 'commercialization' will commence before 'testing' is finished. The important point to note is that there should be formal reviews and reappraisal at regular intervals. Transition between the stages identified in the NPD process are appropriate times for such reviews.

There are of course internal barriers to the adoption of new technology. Individuals may be resistant to change in the organizational setting. They may have a fear of new technology itself, or for their job, or the disruption that change may bring. Change may disturb existing management structures, departmental power bases, individual authority and working relationships.

Products should be designed with a view to keeping material, manufacturing, handling and storage costs to a minimum. These issues should be considered at the outset of the design brief and not as an after-thought. Reducing product costs by 5 or 10 per cent can mean huge savings over the life of a product. In many industries computer-aided design (CAD) gives more flexibility and a speedier response to customer needs. As production methods may now give greater flexibility, it is possible to produce a wider variety of styles, colours and features based on a basic product. These planned variations should be designed in at the initial design stages, even though they may not be incorporated until much later.

The new service development process can be extremely complex, with many examples of cost overruns and delayed results (Kim and Wilemon 2003). A key to more effective new service development activity is close working relationships between marketing and operational functions. Even simple administrative matters such as rapid communication following the results of one stage can help to speed up the new product development process. The complexity of the new service development process has often led to companies outsourcing the whole process to specialist companies that have developed an expertise in product development and market testing (Howley 2002). The use of an outside consultancy can also be useful where a company's ethos is production orientated and it seeks to bring on board broader marketing skills. It has been noted that brilliant inventors do not necessarily make good marketers of a new product (Little 2002).

4.5 FORECASTING NEW TECHNOLOGIES

Over the longer term one of the difficulties is forecasting technological developments. This is key for the health of a nation's economy. Those nations and companies that are first to develop a technological lead will grow, as the technology is embedded in new industries and products. Early developments in biotechnology in the USA and UK, for example, in the mid-1980s have developed into a billion-dollar global industry impacting on agriculture, pharmaceuticals, health and chemicals. Developments in the software industry transformed Silicon Valley, California, in the 1980s and 1990s, just as the car industry transformed Detroit, USA, in the 1950s. The interaction between a favourable political and social climate, higher education and research, and entrepreneurial individuals, may transform a whole economy and have a global impact. For this reason governments are supporting partnerships between industry and academia in an attempt to predict future trends and developments.

The UK government has introduced the 'Foresight Programme', which was first announced in the 1993 White Paper *Realising our Potential*. The programme brings together industry, academia and government to consider how the UK can take advantage of opportunities to promote wealth creation through innovation.

Foresight, and its associated 'horizon scanning centre', aims to provide challenging visions of the future, and to develop effective strategies for meeting them. It does this by providing a core of skills in science-based future projects and access to leaders in government, business and science.

The most recent round of Foresight – launched in April 2002 – operates through a rolling programme that looks at three or four areas at any one time. The starting point for a project area is either a key issue where science holds the promise of solutions, or an area of cutting-edge science where the potential applications and technologies have yet to be considered and articulated. The current projects focus on brain science, addiction and drugs, detection and identification of infectious diseases, and intelligent infrastructure systems.

THINKING AROUND THE SUBJECT:
SOAP POWDER COMPANIES – ALL WASHED UP?

The soap powder companies are popularly attributed with having invented modern marketing and have continuously been at the forefront of new sales and marketing techniques. But could their progress be undone by recent developments in technology? A South Korean company, Kyungwon Enterprise Company, is reported to have developed a washing machine which does not use detergent to clean clothes.

According to the company, a device inserted into a washing machine is able to transform water into electrically charged liquid that cleans with the same results as a conventional synthetic detergent. Water is transformed inside the machine by forcing it through layers of special catalysts planted between electrodes. The system utilizes the natural tendency of water to return to a stable state and harnesses it for laundering, deodorizing and killing viruses. The system also promises to cut water consumption and to reduce the growing problem of water pollution by detergents. The developers of the system have applied for patents in over 60 countries. How are existing washing machine and detergent manufacturers likely to react? The washing machine manufacturer Hotpoint is reported to have been monitoring developments closely and would doubtless seek a licence to use the technology, or develop an alternative technology not covered by patent. But what about the detergent manufacturers? Their market is unlikely to disappear overnight. The new system has still to be proven and even if it is shown to be effective, important segments for detergent could remain out of inertia or simply because the new technology does not cope with all tasks as well as traditional methods. The detergent companies may also embrace the new technology by developing ranges of complementary products, such as fragrant conditioners. Another possibility is that the detergent companies might seek to buy the patents to the new process and then not use them. The inventor of the technology would receive a payout and the detergent companies would continue to sell detergent, but what would be the effects on consumers?

4.6 MANUFACTURING AND PROCESSING

Technology impacts on manufacturing and processing systems, particularly in computerized numerical control (CNC) machine tools, computer-aided manufacturing (CAM), integrated manufacturing systems (IMS) and just-in-time (JIT) systems. With CNC, the machine tool is directly linked to a microprocessor so that the instructions can be created and stored. This gives greater reliability and quicker changeover times. Previously, the machine would have been controlled by punch cards or cassette tapes. CAM involves linking computers to a number of machine tools and assembly robots that are interfaced with computer-controlled material handling systems. Sections of the manufacturing process are thus integrated into the same production control system. CAD/CAM (computer-aided design/computer-aided manufacturing) is where parts designed on the computer can be programmed directly into the machine tool via the same computer system. These systems can save hundreds of hours over previous methods involving the separate activities of design, building models and prototypes and then programming separate machines for production.

Integrated manufacturing systems (IMS) enable a number of CAM sub-systems to be integrated together within a larger computer-controlled system. A number of manufacturers are attempting to integrate the total manufacturing process. This, however, is very difficult to do in practice, as plant and equipment are often of different ages, were designed by different companies and use different control systems. While it is possible to design a total IMS from scratch, the investment costs are likely to be prohibitive for most companies.

JIT systems are designed to limit stockholding and handling costs. A supplier is often expected to deliver components to the right delivery bay, at a specific day and time. There may be heavy penalties for failing to deliver on time. Components can then be moved directly on to the production floor ready for use on the line. This requires close co-operation between the manufacturer and supplier, and usually is made possible only by the use of computerized information systems and data links.

These developments in technology impact on small companies and large, and on traditional industries such as textiles and shoes as well as on new ones. Generally speaking, modern manufacturing systems allow production lines to be run with greater flexibility and higher quality, making it easier to produce product variations and allowing a speedier changeover between products, thus minimizing down-time.

Developments in production technology present companies with a number of opportunities for gaining a competitive advantage. First, developments in these areas are likely to contribute to a reduction in costs. Aiming to be a low-cost manufacturer should help in achieving a higher return on investment by allowing a higher margin and/or a higher volume of sales at lower prices. Second, modern manufacturing techniques allow for greater flexibility in production; thus, a wider variety of product variations may be produced without incurring onerous cost penalties. Third, lead times between orders and delivery can be improved. Finally, it is possible to ensure that the quality of the products is more consistent and of a higher standard. Recent advances in integrated manufacturing systems using computer-controlled industrial robots have meant that car-markers, for example, can produce totally different models on the same production line. Thus, low-volume/high-value cars can be produced more cheaply by utilizing an automated line previously set up for the high-volume output of another model. The company can take a higher profit margin or pass on lower prices to its customer, or a combination of both.

4.7 SUPPLY CHAIN MANAGEMENT

The storage and distribution of goods has also benefited from advances in technology. In particular, the increased capacity and reliability of computerized data processing and storage combined with improved data transmission and computer-controlled physical handling systems have led to reductions in costs and improvements in service. It is now possible to hold less stock at all stages in the distribution chain for a given product variety. From the retailer's perspective they can reduce the amount of stock on the sales floor and in the back room.

As companies come to rely very heavily on IT systems, any problems in the system can have an adverse effect on logistical and financial operations. During 2001, the children's goods retailer Mothercare opened a new UK distribution centre at Daventry. The aim was to increase the efficiency and effectiveness of deliveries to the company's nationwide store network. In reality, poor implementation of IT systems caused stock to be lost within its system instead of getting 'hot' products to the shelves where customers were eager to buy them. By the time they had arrived, market preferences had changed and goods had to be sold at discounted 'clearance' prices. As a direct result of its distribution problems, the company was forced to issue a series of profit warnings and its share price slumped, threatening the continued independent existence of the company (Keers 2002).

Retail groups acquiring competitor companies now face a much more difficult task in integrating the newly acquired stores. Previously the takeover required re-branding with the new company's logo and house style; selling off old stock and replacement with new; and refurbishment of some stores. Now all tills and local computer systems are likely to need replacing; the newly acquired stores must be networked into the group computer, information and communication systems; and staff need to be trained in the new systems (see Figure 4.9).

4.7.1 Efficient consumer response

Partnerships between producers and intermediaries are evident in the Efficient Consumer Response (ECR) initiative. This involves members of the total supply chain working together to respond to customers' purchasing patterns, thereby ensuring the right products are delivered to store shelves on time. The ECR Scorecard Group (1996) describes the moves made by the manufacturer Johnson & Johnson. These include: agreeing with major retail customers to optimize categories in order to drive mutual business needs; focusing on consumer research in conjunction with retailers; and providing promotional activities that suit target consumers' particular needs. The implications of ECR for IT in enhancing the flow of information between participants are discussed later in this chapter. However, it should be noted that the implementation of ECR could require considerable investment from manufacturers to change corporate structures and culture, and to improve IT links between participants.

4.7.2 Just-in-time production

The just-in-time (JIT) philosophy is based on the view, commonly attributed to the Japanese, that inventory is waste and that large inventories merely hide problems such as inaccurate

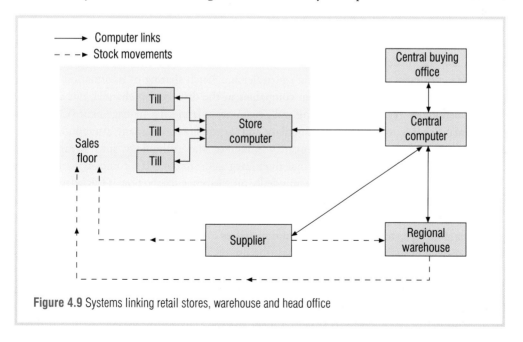

Figure 4.9 Systems linking retail stores, warehouse and head office

forecasts, unreliable suppliers, quality issues and production bottlenecks. The JIT concept aims to eliminate any need for safety stock, with parts for manufacture (or goods for reselling) arriving just as they are needed. As a result, small shipments must be made more frequently. Order requirements can specify the exact unloading point and time of day, with suppliers having to respond accordingly. For example, Toyota schedules its production to minimize sharp fluctuations in daily volume, and to turn out a predicted number of each model every day. Suppliers are automatically notified of orders and given a stable production schedule so they will not deliver the wrong components on the date of final assembly. This level of planning also occurs with retailers such as Marks & Spencer stipulating delivery 'windows' for carriers. In the fast-changing world of personal computers, many companies have followed the lead of Dell, which builds computers to customers' specific requirements. This reduces the risk of obsolescence, but requires carefully planned logistics if promised delivery dates are to be met.

Successful implementation of JIT systems relies on high levels of co-operation between supplying and buying organizations, supported by IT systems which can be shared by all organizations in the distribution chain.

4.7.3 Managing customer relationships

Finally, improved information through a supply chain can allow individual organizations to gain a better understanding of their markets and performance. Traditionally, a retailer would not disclose information about their customers to a supplier, on the bases that they 'owned' the customer and the revenue benefits that derived from this. In some supply chains, there has been a very real possibility of the supplier using customer information collected by the retailer to go direct to the customer next time, and cut out the intermediary. Intermediaries as diverse as travel agents and car dealers have jealously guarded information about their customers in order to prevent their role in the supply chain being reduced. Many members of supply chains now recognize that, within the confines of the Data Protection Act, it makes sense to co-operate and share data. Car dealers now routinely pass on information about their customers to the car manufacturer. The car manufacturer can in turn communicate directly with car owners, and the virtuous circle is completed by communications from the manufacturer which encourage customers to visit their local car dealership. Such sharing of information demands not only trusting relationships between companies in the distribution channel, but also compatible technology. When it is working well, customer relationship management (CRM) can bring great benefits to supplier, intermediary and customer. Sadly, many attempts at implementing CRM have failed to adequately integrate the technology into organizational processes, leading to disintegration rather than integration of data. If a company is not led by senior management that focuses single mindedly on customer satisfaction, a CRM system will probably not achieve very great benefits in the company's dealings with customers.

Shared information through a distribution channel can also help to improve each member's measurement of business performance. Intermediaries can conduct direct product profitability (DPP) analysis of individual items, through the use of EPOS data. DPP attempts to identify all the costs that are attached to a product or an order as it moves through the distribution channel. Thus, after the gross margin has been calculated, costs such as warehousing, transportation, retail space allocation and stocking labour are subtracted to give the product's net profit contribution to a business. It is in a manufacturer's interest to determine how it might

---

**THINKING AROUND THE SUBJECT:
ANY EXCUSE FOR A PINT?**

Companies are able to capture ever-increasing amounts of information in order to build up a better picture of their customers. The retailer Tesco is one of many companies that gather large volumes of data from till receipts, loyalty card data and other bought-in data, to give previously unimaginable insights into consumer behaviour. Using data-mining techniques, one discovery that is reported to have intrigued the company's analysts was the apparent correlation between sales of beer and sales of nappies. The two products were not in any way complementary to each other, so why should their sales appear to be associated? Was this just another spurious correlation, to be binned along with other gems of information such as a previously reported correlation between an individual's shoe size and their propensity to use a gym? The company didn't give up, and refined its analysis to study the correlation for different categories of store and by different times of day. Where it also had details of customers' demographic characteristics (gathered through its Clubcard loyalty programme) it was able to probe for further insights. The company was edging towards a better understanding of why the sales of these two products should be closely correlated, but it took further qualitative analysis techniques to provide a fuller explanation. It appeared that men were offering to run a household errand to the shops in order to buy babies' nappies. This was an excuse to leave the family home in order to buy more beer for their own consumption. The company learnt from this exercise and subsequently positioned the two products closer together in selected stores.

But should it take data mining to reveal these insights to buyer behaviour? The landlord of the traditional Irish pub spotted this type of behaviour long ago, with pubs doubling up as the local post office, bookseller or grocer, giving the Irish drinker plenty of good reasons for visiting the pub. He would have had none of the technology available to today's businesses, just a good set of ears and eyes. Do we sometimes look for complex technological solutions to problems when the answer might be much easier to find using more traditional judgements?

---

lower the cost element to the retailer by, say, redesigning a product's packaging, and thus influencing the retailer's purchase decision more favourably. Because shelf space is often a limiting factor, the key performance measure becomes DPP per square metre. A typical store may find that the figure for ready prepared meals is over twice that of basic items such as rice.

4.7.4 Article numbering/bar codes

Efficient response to consumer demands depends on each individual product having a unique code number and the equipment at the point of sale being able to read that number. Manufacturers, retailers and other interested parties co-operated under the auspices of the global umbrella of GS1 (formed from an alliance of the Article Number Association, Electronic Commerce Association and e-Centre UK) to devise an article numbering system, to allocate numbers and set standards for the use of what have become known as 'bar codes'. GS1 is a non-profit-making member organization with representation globally. It works with manufacturers, retailers, system companies and governments to set 'cross-sector supply chain standards from bar coding to electronic business communications' (www.gs1uk.org, 29 May 2005). The aim is to improve intercompany logistics and increase efficiency of trade. This global system is also referred to as EAN.UCC (European Article Numbering/Uniform Code Council). Recently the organization has also extended the work to radio frequency identification (RFI) for use in tracking goods in transit. According to GS1, over 1 million organizations in 133 countries adhere to these standards.

GS1 'issues its members with sets of globally unique numbers which form the basis of this identification and communication system'. Each product item is allocated a unique global traded item number (referred to as the GTIN), so that each product variation by size and colour can be identified by the manufacturer. For example, a 430g can of peas has a different number from a 300g can; a tin of blue paint has a different number from the same size can of red paint. Nearly 100 per cent of grocery products now carry a bar code on the packaging, and over 50 per cent of general merchandise. Membership of the ANA now totals over 7000 firms, and the association has recently merged with the Electronic Commerce Association to form the Association of Standards and Practices in Electronic Trade which trades under the name of e-Centre UK.

At first bar codes were read by light pens and were only suitable for outlets with a medium volume of daily sales such as clothing retailers. Very high-volume outlets such as supermarkets had to wait for the development of the laser scanner, which can now be seen in most grocery stores. The product is simply passed over the scanner at the checkout so that the computerized till can read the bar code. It is these systems that provide itemized till receipts. Developments in Radio Frequency Identity (RFId) technology is allowing tags to be attached to products, transmitting information to nearby receivers without the need for a bar code to be manually scanned. RFId tags were first used to track bulk containers and cartons of products, but falling costs and improved reliability are allowing individual products to be fitted with tags. This has potential to remove the need to manually scan groceries at a supermarket checkout, as the tag would immediately transmit full details of products contained in a shopping basket.

For a national clothing retailer, improved service and reduction in costs are achieved by linking computerized tills to a central computer and stock control system which connects all stores and warehouses (Figure 4.10). In many cases large suppliers are linked directly into the system. Items purchased are read with a laser scanner at the till which, in addition to logging the price, identifies the item. At the end of the day's trading, or periodically during the day, the central computer checks on the sales through each till. Replacement orders can then be

- One number for global identification
- Automatic scanning at point of sale/use
- Automatic identification on a global scale
- Assisted stock/inventory control
- Increased market information
- Assisted traceability
- Meets customer demand and legislation

Figure 4.10 Benefits of article numbering

Source: www.gs1uk.org

placed with the nearest warehouse, and if necessary the warehouse stock will be replenished by calling off further orders from the supplier. In the warehouse, orders can be processed overnight or the next day and delivered the following evening or early the next morning. On delivery to the store, most of the items will be placed directly on to the sales floor, thus considerably reducing the need for back-room storage. This allows for a greater range of items to be stocked in a given floor space, as the stock held for each item is reduced. The space previously given over to backroom storage (up to a third of the total space in a high-street store) can now be opened up as part of the sales floor. Thus, the total selling space is increased, sales turnover per square metre is increased and the range of items carried is increased. There is less overstocking, fewer out-of-stock situations and less shrinkage. Immediate price changes can be introduced and there is generally tighter price control. The tighter financial control, higher sales turnover and increased profits help pay for the investment in computers, new out-of-town warehousing, transport and physical handling systems. The systems that are dependent on these computerized tills are known as electronic point of sale (EPOS), and are discussed later in the chapter.

Other benefits to these systems derive from the sales information which is collected and stored. Sales of individual product items can be analysed. For fast-moving fashion items, this is vital information. In the past, a whole season's estimated sales had to be ordered in advance from the supplier – a risky business in the fashion world. Now initial orders from the supplier

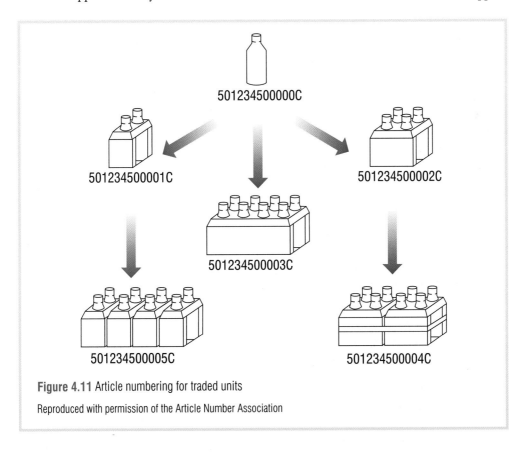

Figure 4.11 Article numbering for traded units

Reproduced with permission of the Article Number Association may be kept relatively low. Fast-selling lines can be identified using sales data and projections of sales made; further orders can then be placed with the supplier. This may be based on the first few days of a line being placed on sale. The whole process of business is thus speeded up. The links between store, warehouse, buying office and supplier become much more dynamic. Stockholding by the individual store may be as low as two days' sales, compared with a week in the late 1970s.

Bar code scanning systems are used throughout the distribution chain. Outer cases are referred to as 'traded units' and can include pallets. GS1 UK co-ordinates the allocation of numbers that are used for traded units as well as consumer units. These bar codes for the 'traded units' are also machine-readable, so the outer case can be controlled more effectively at every stage in the distribution channel, from the manufacturer to the retailer or customer; every traded unit which differs by the nature or quantity of its contents must have a different number (see Figure 4.11).

Bar codes are now used in every stage of manufacture, warehousing, transport and retail. Each individual item has a code, as products are packed each case is numbered, and finally each pallet or Logistic Unit (items packed for transport) is coded. Throughout the distribution chain the Logistic Unit can be tracked by its unique numbered bar code. According to GS1, 'By scanning the item, case or pallet as it leaves the warehouse, the distributor can capture information and match it to a purchase order message. Details of the shipment items (cases, quantities, identification number etc.) are sent to the buyer using a despatch advice message.' At each stage of the distribution process electronic communications between seller, distributor and buyer keep all the individual organizations' systems up to date. Electronic despatch documents, shipping documents and goods received documents form the basis of electronic invoicing and payment systems.

These systems are not only invaluable in tracking items through the supply chain but can be used to trace products in the event of a product recall. This is known as 'traceability' and is an essential requirement in a world of global trade. The safety of consumers is paramount and

THINKING AROUND THE SUBJECT: TRACEABILITY AND PRODUCT RECALLS

Assume you are working for a multinational manufacturer of electrical goods. Your main retailer in the UK has had a number of your vacuum cleaners returned recently with a serious malfunction. It appears to be a problem with the on/off switch. The product is assembled at the company's plant in Spain, but the on/off switch is manufactured in China. However, the miniature circuit board in the vacuum could have been made in Japan or Korea (two suppliers). It may be just one batch of switches or circuit boards that was faulty. To recall all the products sold in the UK in recent months would be extremely expensive. Also it is not known as yet if the vacuums sold in other countries are affected, or if other products (such as hair dryers) use the same switch or other switch designs with the same circuit board.

How would you trace the identity of the batch of vacuums and other products affected before enacting a product recall?

with products and processed food manufactured from components and ingredients sourced throughout the world, traceablity back through the supply chain is necessary to isolate the cause of any problems.

4.8 POINT OF SALE, ORDER AND PAYMENT PROCESSING

This chapter continues to explore specific methods by which technology has been used to improve the efficiency and effectiveness of transactions within a supply chain. In particular, organizations must aim to cut the cost of stockholding, yet still be able to respond efficiently and effectively to customers' requests.

In a previous section we considered the impact of computer systems and data links on storage and distribution. The combination of bar codes, laser scanners, computerized tills, data links and powerful computers with remote terminals has much improved the control of stock. Systems are constantly being improved, as is the reliability and speed with which the systems operate. These systems are also expensive to install and run. However, as the technology improves and competition increases between suppliers of systems, we can expect the costs to come down.

EPOS (electronic point of sale) systems allow each till to total the goods purchased by individual customers and record the transaction in the normal way. In addition to the daily cash analysis, however, EPOS systems may provide stock reports and an analysis of sales figures, and improve control over each till and the staff using it. The retailer no longer has to price each individual item, as the price needs to be displayed only on the shelf or the rack. This saves labour and allows for easier price changes. The customer benefits from itemized till receipts, a faster checkout, greater choice and fewer items out of stock (Figure 4.12).

EFTPOS (electronic funds transfer at point of sale) extends the benefits of EPOS to include electronic funds transfer. This means that the computerized till is now fitted with a card reader, and data links into the banking system can transfer funds electronically. The customer's payment card, such as MasterCard or Visa, is presented in the normal way, the cashier swipes this through the card reader, the till prints out the slip for signature and the customer retains the top copy. Alternatively the customer may be asked to enter their PIN rather than sign a slip. The customer's credit card or current account (depending on the card used) is debited with the sale and the retailer's account is credited. The convenience for customers and retailers is enhanced, the accuracy of transactions is increased, cash handling is reduced and the costs of processing the sale are also significantly reduced (Figure 4.13).

In business-to-business transactions the speed at which orders can be captured and processed by a company's systems is related to the speed at which orders and invoices can be despatched and payment collected. Closely associated and inseparable from the ordering system is a document handling system, which includes orders, manufacturing dockets, picking notes, despatch/delivery notes, invoices and statements. Advances in technology will continue to influence all these aspects of the business.

Golden Wonder Crisps, a UK manufacturer of crisps and snacks, provides an example of how business-to-business transactions have been transformed in recent years. Its van sales representatives take orders from local shops and drop off the goods. Orders are entered in the van sales representative's portable computer or PDA, which will then print out a delivery note to leave with the buyer. Until recently, the van salespeople would have connected their computer

| **Improved management information** |
| Store-by-store comparison of sales |
| Direct product profitability analysis |
| Sales-promotion effectiveness |
| **Operational efficiency** |
| Better stock control |
| Quicker stocktaking |
| Reduced shrinkage |
| No item pricing |
| Faster price changes |
| **Improved customer service** |
| Faster checkout service |
| Fewer queues |
| Itemized sales receipts |
| Reduced operator error |

Figure 4.12 Benefits of EPOS

Source: adapted from Fletcher 1995, p. 367

to the telephone line when they got home in the evening, and downloaded their sales data to the office mainframe computer. The mainframe draws out the sales data and passes back any messages. Next day the invoice is raised by the head office computer and posted so as to arrive the third day after delivery. Improved mobile technology is now allowing almost real-time transmission of data back to the mainframe through a 'permanently on' mobile data service.

When these systems were first developed in the early 1980s, it would take up to 20 minutes to download this data. Today it takes only a few seconds with new portable computers and broadband Internet connections, and the data transmission is much more of a two-way process. It is possible for the mainframe to input into the representative's portable computer the sales journey cycles for the coming weeks, relevant customer information, updates on products and prices, notes on special promotional deals and messages from the manager.

This system is now being used for the direct sales force serving the larger retailers and cash-and-carries. Orders received one day are downloaded to the mainframe the same evening. Overnight or the next day (day 2), the mainframe raises the picking and despatch notes. On day 3 the order is despatched, and the invoice is printed and posted.

In the late 1970s the time taken between an order being placed and delivery fulfilled was between seven and ten days. Now, next-day delivery following an order is more normal.

Benefits to retailers

Reduced paperwork

Single system for all cards

Reduction in volume and cost of cash handling

Reduced security risk

Reduction in fraud

Faster checkout time

Faster payment into retailer's account

Benefits to customers

Less need to carry large amounts of cash

More choice in methods of payment

No £50 limit as with cheques

Itemized receipts and statements easy to check

Faster checkout time

Figure 4.13 Benefits of EFTPOS

Source: adapted from Fletcher 1995, p. 367

4.9 THE INTERNET AND ELECTRONIC BUSINESS

We may be tempted to think that the use of information technology to communicate between organizations began with the development of the Internet. In fact, organizations had already developed proprietary systems through which orders and payments could be processed. In this section, we will explore the diversity of forms of electronic business. One underlying theme of the development of electronic business has been the reduced cost of handling transactions electronically, rather than through paper-based systems. Alongside this, the speed of communication has allowed business to be transacted much quicker, and the data generated through electronic business systems has given managers a much better understanding of the marketing and operational aspects of their organization.

4.9.1 The Internet

The Internet, or World Wide Web (www), is an open system that anyone can log on to via a computer and a modem. No one person, organization or government controls or owns the Internet. It developed as a means of transferring large volumes of information between academic and government research centres in the USA. Soon people were sending messages via electronic-mail (email). More universities hooked up and commercial companies became involved, as did the telecommunications giants. As the personal computer developed so did the software, netware, browsers, search engines etc., to interface between the user and the Internet. Messages and information are relayed quickly via servers and hubs to their final destination.

Initially the system was used by technical experts to send data, and text messages followed subsequently. Commercial companies began to post web pages on the Internet so those interested could browse through the information. Soon websites were developed which provided more information and eventually led to the development of interactive sites. With the development of protocols for encoding financial and other sensitive information the Internet can now be used to purchase services and products using a credit card. Latest developments mean that the screen can be integrated with a telephone call so that the web page can be viewed at the same time as using the phone to talk to the telesales operator. The system is now popular with business-to-business users and individual consumers. It is borderless and cheap to use. The advance of the Internet as a distribution channel has been affected by the speed with which consumer and commercial buyers have adopted the medium.

Of course, it is not just in business-to-consumer markets that the Internet is reshaping distribution channels. In business-to-business channels, the Internet (and intranets and extranets) has replaced previous Electronic Data Interchange (EDI) systems for handling transactions between businesses. Government and not-for-profit organizations have also incorporated the Internet into their distribution channels, both for procuring purchases (Timmins 2003) and making services available to users (e.g. NHS Direct makes medical advice available to the public through call centres and the Internet).

Intranet systems are private internal systems (as opposed to open and public systems) constructed using Internet and web technology. They are internal to an organization and can be accessed and used only with permission and passwords. These systems provide a similar function to the older EDI systems, but are more flexible and user friendly. A company's intranet system can link together an organization that is geographically dispersed and facilitate links between an organization and its business partners such as suppliers and distributors. Such a system is often described as an 'extranet'.

The deregulated nature of the Internet, operating across international boundaries, poses new challenges as it develops from an information service, to a promotional tool, and finally a sales and distribution channel facilitating transactions. Concerns have been expressed in four areas: confidentiality of individual information; consumer protection for those purchasing goods and services; under which legal system a transaction takes place; and concern over the difficulty of governments collecting sales taxes.

The OECD Sacher Report identified three priority areas for governments. The first is for governments to actively support the development of electronic commerce by encouraging the development of the infrastructure. Governments have traditionally controlled telecommunications and television industries by either direct ownership or licensing. Technologies in computing, telecommunications, data networks and television are now converging rapidly. The report recommends that governments should encourage this by modifying regulatory regimes where necessary and by working to commonly agreed international protocols.

The second recommendation was that all governments should 'raise the visibility of electronic commerce and promote new partnerships with the private sector in order to co-ordinate technical, economic and political choices'. It is suggested that governments may seek to appoint a Chief Information Officer to co-ordinate these activities.

The third recommendation was that governments themselves should acquire the skills to participate in the electronic information age. Regulatory issues need to be dealt with urgently and as they arise. Legal issues surrounding the 'definitions, practices and structures' of electronic commerce are now being addressed. International protocols need to be further developed for dealing with consumer protection, fraud, crime prevention, the protection of intellectual property, electronic identity, definitions of residence, liability, auditing, and the control, unauthorized use and protection of databases. The issue of taxation is also of concern, particularly for taxes based on sales. Sales taxes are often refunded to exporters at despatch but re-applied on receipt in the country of importation. These issues have not been fully resolved for Internet transactions.

The Economist Intelligence Unit (EIU), working in collaboration with IBM's Institute for Business Value, provides a benchmark for countries to compare how they fare against others. Its E-readiness Rankings survey published in April 2003 showed the UK to have held on to its ranking of third among the 60 countries surveyed. It defines 'E-readiness' as the extent to which a country is conducive to Internet-based opportunities, and takes into account a wide range of factors including the quality of its information technology infrastructure, the ambition of government initiatives and the degree to which the Internet is helping businesses to become commercially efficient. The 2003 E-readiness survey showed that, for the first time, Europe had overtaken the United States. Sweden was the most e-ready, with Denmark in second place. It seemed that what set Scandinavia apart was its wholehearted embrace of the information society. Sweden also had among the lowest broadband prices in Europe and the highest levels of broadband Internet access. The UK government was praised for its UK Online for Business initiative, an innovative government project supporting e-business, which was launched in September 2000.

4.9.2 The EU and the development of a knowledge-based economy

At the 2000 summit of EU leaders held in Nice, leaders stated their intention for Europe 'to become the most competitive and dynamic knowledge-based economy in the world'. A programme of action included the creation of a fully integrated and liberalized telecoms market by the end of 2001; a single market for financial services by 2005; making all EU public services, including tenders, available on the Internet; an EU regulatory framework and common security standards for e-commerce; connecting all schools and training centres to the Internet; and creating an IT 'passport' of specific skills.

Since the summit, there has been a flurry of activity: an accelerated effort to boost national programmes for promoting e-business and getting schools online; and new laws and directives governing e-business. However, although the pace of change may be more brisk than before, those used to the rapid speed of developments in the Internet world still find EU processes very slow. Business is particularly frustrated by EU-wide government inaction in terms of creating a better environment for e-commerce to flourish in.

Can the EU rhetoric be matched by reality? A report by the UK research and consultancy group Gartner identified a number of pressing challenges for the EU in its attempts to create an e-commerce friendly environment.

■ Anti-trust authorities will have to resolve, more rapidly than at present, complex competition issues raised by mergers in the media and telecoms sectors, electronic marketplaces, wireless portals and public service providers.

■ Enterprises will need more flexible employment schemes and laws to cope with skill shortages in the information technology sector. Employers need the ability to import and outsource skills as required and a clearer legislative framework for teleworking.

■ Tax regulations need to be brought up to date to recognize the presence of Internet transactions. The Gartner study predicted that the difference between European and US Internet tax schemes would become a major source of friction in international trade.

■ In order to boost consumers' trust in e-commerce and reduce legal uncertainty for enterprises, governments need to develop privacy laws which are relevant to the Internet.

The report painted a picture of national governments throwing money at the microenvironment of electronic commerce (e-commerce), such as grants for computer training, often displacing money that could readily be provided by the private sector. Developing the macroenvironment for e-commerce throughout the EU is a much bigger challenge.

If the e-commerce-friendly business environment is achieved, the savings to the EU administration are likely to be considerable, with one estimate that the EU will save $700 billion (£500 billion) each year by moving more government transactions on to the Internet. In Berlin, for example, city officials have predicted savings of €7.8 billion (£5 billion) if only 50 per cent of administrative procedures could be transacted online by 2005.

The question remains as to just what it is possible for governments to do to create an e-commerce-friendly environment. Is responsibility for achieving it best left to the EU rather than national governments? Or is even the EU too small a unit for making decisions, when the Internet is progressively breaking down national boundaries?

4.9.3 E-business

E-business embraces many aspects of business that are moving closer together and which require integration. Terminology is constantly changing as the technology and concepts develop and managers and academics from differing functions interact. It is helpful to make a distinction between e-business and e-commerce. E-business may be defined as:

> ... the ability to integrate local and wide area networks through the use of Internet protocols to effectively remove the barriers between businesses, their customers and their suppliers in global markets. (National Computing Centre 2001)

This is a broader definition than that usually attributed to the narrower function of e-commerce, which has been defined as:

> ... transactions of goods or services for which payment occurs over the Internet or other wide area networks. (Chaffey *et al.* 1999)

Using the Internet for conducting business activities generally offers the following benefits.

■ Retailers can be linked with other branches/suppliers, thus improving the supply chain and reducing the amount of time to process transactions.

■ Red tape and administration can be reduced when systems are established.

■ Efficiency can be increased in the company's operations.

■ Services of the company can be extended to add value for the customer.

■ Customer profiles can be established and exploited to develop better marketing and business strategies.

■ New technology can be integrated with existing sales and inventory infrastructure, such as payment and distribution systems.

■ Cross-selling of products can be generated via advertising and promotional activities.

■ Sales can be safeguarded by identifying alternatives when a requested item is unavailable or would require time to deliver.

■ Customers can be targeted with promotions based on the customers' individual interests and preferences.

There are some limitations that can be summarized as follows.

■ Systems often require high capital outlay, and there may be a slow return on investment.

■ Perceived security risks regarding sensitive data such as credit card numbers have to be overcome.

■ Compatibility within the technological architecture can be a limitation.

■ Technological delays and failures continue to pose a risk.

■ A poor online storefront can be a deterrent for potential customers.

Many of these limitations have been experienced by companies, particularly those 'dotcom' companies which do not have established high-street business operations. Many new pure Internet businesses have closed.

In the early stages of Internet development, the technology has been used to provide a modest incremental improvement on what was previously possible using voice telephone or postal services. With increasing sophistication, possibilities arise for the Internet to provide additional benefits which are not possible using more traditional distribution methods. Personalization of websites can facilitate re-ordering of routinely purchased services (e.g. an airline site which opens with previously recorded preferences). Many websites are now linked with other complementary value-adding services (e.g. an airline's website which has links to national and regional tourist board websites).

E-procurement by businesses has become established and early adopters claim improved supply chain management and 50 per cent savings on purchasing costs (Whittle 2001). Research by Dynamic Markets Ltd, reported in Whittle, suggests that 76 per cent of respondents felt it was the way forward, 72 per cent thought it would bring significant benefits, and 68 per cent thought that companies that do not use it will lose out.

4.9.4 E-retailing

The trend towards direct delivery from producer to consumer has been speeded up by the growth of Internet access. As a communication medium with customers, email (and SMS text messaging) extends the profiling and interactivity features of direct mail. An accurate database of customers' preferences is essential if email messages are not to be discarded as junk messages. The prospect of email to individuals' mobile phones raises the prospect of a huge amount of low-cost messages being targeted at individuals, and senders of messages must ensure that their messages stand out from competitors' and have immediate relevance to the recipient.

Although 'bricks and mortar' companies may have been a little late into the fray, they are now

THINKING AROUND THE SUBJECT:
THE INTERNET AND THE LAW OF UNINTENDED CONSEQUENCES

'The world will never be the same again.' This was the bold message being proclaimed by many pundits at the dawn of the Internet age. In one sense, these pundits were quite right, because the Internet has had significant effects on how individuals have gone about their lives. Business processes have been transformed, often resulting in great cost savings and improvements in service to customers. But in many respects the nature of the change that has resulted from the development of the Internet has not quite been what was expected. The complex interaction between the technological, social and economic environments has produced some unexpected consequences of technological development.

Consider the following predictions which were made in 2000 when 'dotcom' mania was at its height.

■ Predictions were made that there would be less commuting as people work from home using the Internet to communicate with their work colleagues. Traffic congestion would disappear and commuter rail services would lose customers. In fact, technology has allowed many people to choose a pleasant residential environment and to live much further away from their work, because they now have to travel to the office on only a couple of days each week rather than every day. Overall, the travelling distances of many people in this situation have actually increased, resulting in more rather than less total commuting.

■ Conferences were predicted to disappear in favour of video conferencing. Why bother travelling to a meeting or conference when you could meet 'virtually' from the comfort of your own desk or armchair, and at lower cost? However, face-to-face conferences have continued to prosper. The technology which causes many people to work in isolation may have indirectly contributed to a desire to counter this with more face-to-face meetings with a greater social content.

■ High-street shops were being written off in 2000 when, quite extraordinarily, the pure Internet company Lastminute.com had a market capitalization value far in excess of the 110-outlet Debenhams store. The convenience of shopping in the high street or at out-of-town shopping centres and the problems of arranging home delivery of Internet suppliers were underestimated by advocates of Internet-based shopping.

■ Pre-dating all of these predictions has been the expectation that we will need to work fewer hours, as we live in a world of leisure where machines do the work, leaving consumers with more leisure time. In reality, average working hours have tended to increase in recent years, not fall.

We seem to have an inherent tendency to overstate the short-term effects of technological change, but to understate the long-term effects on our behaviour. With the development of new technologies enabling high-speed mobile Internet services, further predictions were being made in 2005. Would we really want to download full-length feature films to watch on our mobile phones? Would we really want to surf the net while travelling on a train? Would there be unforeseen 'killer applications' such as SMS text messaging, which was almost left out of the specification of first-generation mobile phones because no useful role for it was foreseen? Perhaps the long-term effects of the Internet may be more subtle by contributing to individuals' sense of connectedness with narrowly selected commercial and social groups, no matter where they may be located, while the sense of community with diverse groups of people forced to live together in close proximity may be reduced.

The unforeseen consequences of the Internet emphasize how difficult it can be for organizations to understand the consequences of new technologies. These examples demonstrate the importance of understanding the linkages between different elements of the business environment, so developments in the technological environment can only be sensibly understood in conjunction with changes in the social environment.

Figure 4.14 The Internet has opened up a powerful distribution channel by which a company can communicate directly with each of its customers, providing rapid, low-cost distribution which need not involve intermediaries. The budget airline easyJet has embraced the Internet and claims to be the 'web's favourite airline', with about 90 per cent of customers using the company's website for booking their tickets. The company is proud of the fact that it does not pay commission to intermediaries, and can pass on these savings in the form of lower ticket prices. (Reproduced with permission of easyJet Airline Company Ltd)

doing well compared to some dotcom start-ups. According to research carried out in 2002 by MMXI Europe, six of the top ten UK retail sites were traditional 'bricks and mortar' retailers. Many high-street names are transforming themselves into 'clicks and mortar' companies, including Argos (general household catalogue sales), Tesco (grocery supermarket), Dixons (household electrical), Comet (electrical appliances), PCWorld (computers), WHSmith (books and stationery). According to Forrester Research, Internet sales accounted for less than an estimated 5 per cent of retail sales in Western countries in 2003, but reached 20 per cent in some sectors, including travel and tourism services, and music. Although research estimates and sales forecast vary widely, most agree that travel is the largest e-retailing sector.

The traditional problems of home shopping and delivery remain:

- small orders
- high transport costs
- goods not compatible with the letter/mail box
- inability to offer a timed delivery window
- most economical delivery times for companies are 9 a.m. to 5 p.m. Monday to Friday, when the customer is most likely to be out
- difficulty of returning goods.

The delivery of goods to the final consumer has not shown the productivity gains that Internet-based ordering has achieved (see Yrjölä 2001). This is probably not surprising when it is remembered that home delivery remains a labour-intensive activity in which two of the main costs – labour and transport – are likely to continue to increase in real terms. We should not forget that in the UK the milkman has almost disappeared because efficiency of delivery could not be improved relative to the cost of consumers collecting milk from large, efficient supermarkets. The logistics function must also face the challenge of being able to deliver goods when somebody is at home, or of providing alternative secure storage arrangements (de Koster 2002).

There are also many high-involvement goods where buyers feel more comfortable being able to see and feel the goods before they commit to a purchase. The failed Internet clothes retailer boo.com encountered the reality that many people would probably find it much easier and reassuring to try on clothes in a shop rather than relying on a computer image, thereby ensuring a continuing role for traditional high-street retailers (although 'bricks and clicks' retailers such as Next have quietly developed a substantial level of clothes sales via their websites).

In addition, customer expectations of 'e-tailers' have risen. When ordering online, customers expect to have prices and stock confirmed as well as a delivery date and preferably the time. Customers are also expecting to be told of any delays, particularly when they are waiting in for the delivery.

Some retailers have closed a number of branches or reduced their sales force and instead offer customers access to their product range via a website. Several UK suppliers of books, music, computer games and flowers have the logistical support to develop their business on the Internet. In the longer term, it is possible that fmcg suppliers may use the Internet to regain some of their lost power in channel relationships. Car manufacturers are recognizing the impact of the Internet on their traditional dealership-based channels of distribution, with evidence that the Internet is increasingly being used for selecting new cars. To some car buyers, the dealership has become little more than a delivery point (Morton 2003).

However, while the Internet may facilitate direct communication between producers and end-consumers, the chances of dialogue actually taking place are lessened by the proliferation of content on the Internet, which presents a bewildering array of choice to consumers. The response has been the development of a new breed of information intermediary, or 'infomediary'. This type of channel intermediary gathers information about customers and sells access to them to companies seeking to promote their products. The new generation of infomediaries has effectively become a new form of value-adding member in a virtual value chain. Within the travel and financial services sectors, airlines' and insurance companies' attempts to create direct dialogue with customers have often been overshadowed by the development of powerful infomediaries such as Lastminute.com, expedia.com and e-sure.com

WILL 3G PHONE COMPANY LEARN FROM A RABBIT?

CASE STUDY

The mobile telephone sector hardly existed just 20 years ago, but during its short history it has grown phenomenally to the point where, in 2004, over two-thirds of the UK population owned a mobile phone. The pace of growth posed enormous risks for the companies involved, especially where new technologies displaced the technology which went before them, calling for ever-increasing capital investment, and no chance of a return from consumers until long after the initial investment has been made in new capacity.

Many commentators saw third-generation (or '3G') technology as the key to a whole new world of mobile telephony in which the mobile phone would be positioned not just as a device for voice communication, but as a vital business and information tool. In 2000 the UK government held an auction for five new 3G mobile telephone licences, and the mobile phone companies paid a total of £22 billion for them. Would they get back their huge investment, not only in licences but also in the infrastructure that was needed to support the new 3G networks?

During 2003, the Hong Kong-based Hutchison Whampoa became the first company to launch a 3G service in the UK, with its '3' network. The launch was accompanied by endless hype about the wireless Internet and video links. The world was going to be transformed by streaming of video and football clips live to customers' mobile phones, and a whole new world of mobile advertising media would open up. Location-Based Services (LBS) had been a small but growing sector of the mobile phone industry. A report by Concise Insight (2004) noted that Vodafone UK's mobile content reached 1.9 per cent of total service revenue for March 2004, almost double the 1.0 per cent a year before. It seemed that location technology was underpinning value-added data services. Even the emergency services stood to benefit from 3G's ability to precisely pinpoint a caller's location. By 2004, 60 per cent of calls to the UK emergency services were made from mobiles, but in many instances callers didn't know exactly where they were, and ambulances and fire brigades had only very approximate locations.

But after long delays in rolling out the new phones and networks, followed by sluggish uptake of the early services, 3 found itself in 2004 focusing on more mundane marketing issues, such as the cost of old-fashioned voice calls. The costs of recruiting new customers were high, with Mark James, telecoms analyst at Japanese investment bank Nomura, estimating that 3's customer acquisition costs in its first year were £600 per customer – around four times the European average.

Initially, technical glitches, the high price of handsets and poor customer service were compounded by a phone shortage. But 3 was on a mission to grab market share ahead of the launch of its rivals' 3G services, seemingly almost regardless of the cost. During 2003 its 'land grab' programme received a boost with the launch of a highly desirable light-weight silver clamshell-style phone manufactured by LG. Just a year previously, one of these cost more than £400, but now 3 was giving them away for free on the back of generous tariffs that offered consumers 500 or 750 voice minutes to any network for £25 or £35 a month respectively.

Analysts estimated that Hutchison, which had placed a US$22 billion bet on the fledgling technology, was seeing a worldwide 3G cash-burn of about HK$100 million ($12.8 million) per day, and market concern about its 3G exposure was beginning to depress the group's share price. By June 2004, the company had already lost one of its key shareholders – Japanese heavyweight NTT DoCoMo – which sold its 20 per cent stake in 3 UK back to Hutchison at a 90 per cent loss on its initial investment. However, Hutchison Whampoa had deep pockets to fund an expensive launch – although it had net borrowings, most of those were long-term debts, and disposals during 2003/4 meant it had HK$111 billion (£8 billion) of cash on its balance sheet.

More worrying to many commentators was the effects of Hutchison's tactics on the fledgling 3G industry. At the time of launch, 3 emphasized its 'gee-whiz' features. But after only a year, it was increasingly emphasizing the more mundane affordability of its calling plans. Rival operators that were preparing their own 3G launches would aim to start by pricing the technology at a premium. But their problem was that 3 was already pricing its phones and services – which offered ITN News and Premiership football clips, among other features – at cut-throat prices. Their best hope was that 3's model would prove unsustainable. After all, anyone can get customers if they effectively give their product away.

Hutchison is not new to taking big risks in the mobile phone market. It was behind the 'Rabbit' network of semi-mobile Telepoint phones launched in the UK in the 1980s. These allowed callers to use a compact handset to make outgoing calls only, when they were within 150 metres of a base station, these being located in public places such as railway stations, shops, petrol stations etc. As in the case of many new markets that suddenly emerge, operators saw advantages of having an early market share lead. Customers who perceived that one network was more readily available than any other would – all other things being equal – be more likely to subscribe to that network. Operators saw that a bandwagon effect could be set up – to gain entry to the market at a later stage could become a much more expensive market challenger exercise.

Such was the speed of development that the Telepoint concept was not rigorously test-marketed. To many, the development was too much product led, with insufficient understanding of buyer behaviour and competitive pressures. Each of the four companies forced through their own technologies, with little inclination or time available to discuss industry-standard handsets which could eventually have caused the market to grow at a faster rate and allowed the operators to cut their costs.

The final straw for the Rabbit network came with the announcement by the UK government of its proposal to issue licences for a new generation of Personal Communications Networks – these would have the additional benefit of allowing both incoming and outgoing calls, and would not be tied to a limited base station range. While this in itself might not have put people off buying new Rabbit handsets, it did have the effect of bringing new investment in the network to a halt, leaving the existing networks in a state of limbo.

Could the point about leapfrogging technology – which had wiped out Hutchison's Rabbit network – happen again with 3G technology? By 2004 the next generation of mobile phone services was under development, with Japanese trials of 4G well under way and already promising even greater functionality and transfer rates. The International Telecommunication Union (ITU) defined 4G as providing a minimum stationary data rate of 1Gbps and a moving (say in a car or a train) data rate of around 100Mbps. In field tests held in Kanagawa, the Japanese telephone company NTT achieved up to 300Mbps at 30kmh and an average moving transfer rate of 135Mbps up to 1 kilometre from the base station. Could 3G become old hat before it had even had a successful and profitable launch?

Or should Hutchison point to its record with another of its previous ventures – the launch of the UK Orange network in the early 1990s, which critics initially dismissed as a costly failure, but which went on to become one of the UK's strongest mobile phone brands?

QUESTIONS

1 Review the launch of Telepoint in the context of the 'demand-technology life cycle'. Where would '3G' mobile phones fit in this life cycle?

2 Summarize the environmental factors that contributed to the demise of Telepoint services. What are the main environmental challenges facing 3G phones?

3 How would the launch of 3G services differ in a less developed country with a less sophisticated telecommunications infrastructure?

SUMMARY

This chapter has considered technological change from the macro perspective and examined the impact of technology on different aspects of the business at the micro level. In both instances the relevance of technological change to business success has been stressed. At the macro level of technological change, the key points to remember concern the demand-technology life cycle. This will be influenced by the level of research and development expenditure, not only in a particular industry but also in related and sometimes unrelated industries. The fusion and interaction of different technologies results in new applications and processes which eventually may give rise to whole new industries. Technology permeates through from academic and research institutions into industry, from one industry to another, and from one economy to another. However, if the UK manufacturing sector has become a follower rather than a leader, then it will have lost a much-needed competitive advantage in world markets. Managers should be just as concerned with the long-term prospects of their company as with yesterday's sales. Research and development is too important to be left to the technical experts. Production, finance and marketing people need to be involved in the R&D process, along with the scientists and development engineers and senior board members. The board of directors needs to show serious interest and should be seen to be giving R&D the priority it requires.

At the micro level, this chapter has considered the impact of technology on the company's products and operations: product design and development, manufacturing and processing; storage and distribution; order and payment processing; and information and communication systems via electronic business. With regard to the specific areas of business operations referred to throughout the chapter, marketing managers and other executives may look to the medium-term horizon for planning purposes. The aim is not only to improve efficiency of business operations but also to ensure that the benefits are passed on to the customer. These customer benefits may include better pre-order services such as product availability and specification, information, faster quotations and quicker design customization. Improved post-order services may include shorter delivery times, delivery to just-in-time (JIT) requirements, installation, training, electronic data interchange (EDI), the Internet, and itemized till receipts.

The technological environment is a constantly changing environment. In many industries during the 2000s and beyond, change will be the norm rather than the exception. Companies that focus on customer needs, competitor activity and technological developments, rather than simply aiming to sell what the factory makes, are more likely to succeed.

The dynamics of the information, communications and technology revolution are impacting on all organizations in the developed world – new and old, large and small, commercial and governmental. The business environmental forces are pushing towards increased globalization and competition. Organizations are under pressure to reduce costs, increase profitability, enhance quality and improve customer service. Investment in IT and communications systems can be relatively inexpensive for small businesses. But for large, well-established, organizations that have to re-engineer all their business processes, the costs and time involved are substantial. Customers, suppliers and internal departments demand real-time information and immediate responses to queries. Increasingly, customers expect an organization that trades under one corporate name to be a seamless organization.

The challenge for many organizations is to integrate their internal systems (discussed in **Chapter 2**) within a local area network/intranet, and to patch these into the Internet via the web. This will require careful strategic thought. For most established organizations implementation would take some time, would have to be in stages and would be expensive in the short term. Long-term benefits will accrue to the winners, no doubt, both to the organization and the customers. IT and communication systems are now of strategic importance and a means by which to establish a competitive advantage. They determine the cost base, and now influence how an organization is structured and run, and how it communicates to its suppliers and customers. More available information will result in increasing power for the customers who are interested in convenience, speed, control, choice and comparability, in addition to demanding world-class quality products and service.

The interrelationship between technology and society is stressed in **Chapter 8** and this chapter has explored not only technology's response to changes in society, but also the effects of changing technology on social values.

Technology has opened up many opportunities for businesses to enter global markets, and these are discussed in more detail in **Chapter 12**.

Finally, issues of privacy and security surrounding new technologies have attracted the attention of the law (**Chapter 5**) and parliamentary legislators.

Key Terms

Article numbering	(149)	Electronic Data Interchange		Product life cycle	(140)
Computer-aided		(EDI)	(156)	Research and development	
manufacturing (CAM)	(145)	Electronic point of sale		(R&D)	(135)
Computer-aided design		(EPOS)	(151)	Technological fusion	(131)
(CAD)	(144)	Internet	(155)	Technology transfer	(132)
Demand-technology life		Just-in-time (JIT) systems	(145)		
cycle	(132)	New product development			
Electronic commerce	(158)	(NPD) process	(142)		

CHAPTER REVIEW QUESTIONS

1   Should the United Kingdom be concerned about its relatively poor showing (compared with its main competitor countries) in research and development?

2   Should marketing managers be involved in the R&D process and, if so, what should their role be?

3 Can you identify any product class that has recently been affected by changes in the demand-technology life cycle and, if so, what has been the impact of the change?

4 Identify some recent technological developments and discuss the benefits these have brought to the consumer.

5 How have recent advances in technology helped companies improve their marketing operations?

6 What are the ingredients that led to the successful development and implementation of 'article numbering' in the United Kingdom?

7 Have governments a role to play in fostering an R&D culture and in encouraging technological development?

8 What are the main differences between EDI and the Internet?

9 How might the development of e-commerce via the Internet affect our future?

ACTIVITY

In the pub one Friday evening two men were overheard discussing electronic shopping. Both men worked in the computer industry, had lots of 'kit' at home, and had been connected to the World Wide Web for some time. They were exchanging views about the latest developments on the Internet and getting quite excited about the possibilities of buying their weekly groceries over the net and having them delivered. This would take the drudgery out of supermarket shopping they agreed. Both men worked long hours and when asked the last time they had seen the inside of a supermarket, neither could remember. Both were married. One wife, although quite capable of holding a good job, did not work at all, had no need to work, and was quite happy to look after the family (two children) and do the supermarket shopping. The other was in a very similar position, although she had taken up part-time work, as the children were a little older. Neither woman was much taken with computers and thought that being tied to a computer all day and half the evening would be a life of drudgery.

Questions:

1 Examine the situation from:
   (a) the point of view of the working men
   (b) the point of view of the housewives
   (c) from a marketing perspective (target markets, cost factors, sales potential etc.).

2 Do you think that shopping for groceries via the Internet will become a mainstream activity and, if so, by when?

3 Discuss the advantages and limitations of setting up the system to operate from existing supermarket outlets in contrast to establishing new warehouses and home delivery systems to cater for Internet shopping.

Useful Websites

CBI Innovation Trends Survey

A review of the CBI's survey on companies' perceptions of innovation.

http://www.cbi.org.uk/innovation/

European Assistance Network

Assistance with article numbering, bar codes and Radio Frequency Identification.

http://www.ean.be

GS1

Global organization for e-business standards including article numbering, bar codes, Radio Frequency Identification.

http://www.gs1uk.org

http://www.your-barcodes.co.uk

IBM E-Commerce Case Studies

Contains news and e-commerce case studies.

http://www2.software.ibm.com/casestudies/swcs.nsf/topstories

OECD Electronic Commerce site

Site maintained by the OECD on electronic commerce. Includes news releases, conference reports, policy analysis and statistical work.

http://www.oecd.org/dsti/sti/it/ec/

UK Foresight programme

Provides a review of the UK government's technology foresight programme.

http://www.foresight.gov.uk

Vanderbilt University's eLab

eLab was founded by Vanderbilt University in 1994 to study the business implications of commercializing the World Wide Web. It has emerged as one of the premier research centres in the world for the study of Electronic Commerce.

http://ecommerce.vanderbilt.edu/

Virtual Society Research Programme

An ESRC-funded programme at Oxford University into the sociology of electronic technologies. Useful social sciences links and research.

http://www.virtualsociety.org.uk

Further Reading

The following provide contemporary insights into the role of innovation in organizations and the relationship between business and R&D:

Christensen, Clayton M., Anthony, Scott D. and Roth, Erik A. (2004) *Seeing What's Next: Using the Theories of Innovation to Predict Industry Change*, Harvard Business School Press.

Kim, J. and Wilemon, D. (2003) 'Sources and assessment of complexity in NPD projects', *R&D Management*, Vol. 33, No. 1, pp. 16–30.

Tidd, J., Bessant, J. and Pavitt, K. (2001) *Managing Innovation*, 2nd edn, Chichester, John Wiley.

Trott, Paul (2004) *Innovation Management and New Product Development*, London, FT Prentice Hall.

There are now lots of books about e-business, ranging from textbooks to quick 'how to' books:

Beynon-Davies, P. (2005) *E-Business*, Basingstoke, Palgrave.

Chaffey, D. (2003) *E-business and E-commerce Management*, London, FT Prentice Hall.

Chan, H., Lee, R. and Dillon, T. (2001) *E-Commerce: Fundamentals and Applications*, Chichester, John Wiley.

Jackson, P., Eckersley, P. and Harris, L. (2003) *E-Business Fundamentals*, London, Routledge.

References

Ajzen, I. and Fishbein, M. (1980) *Understanding Attitudes and Predicting Social Behaviour*, Englewood Cliffs, New Jersey, Prentice Hall.

Bobbit, L. and Dabholkar, P.A. (2001) 'Integrating attitudinal theories to understand and predict use of technology-based self-service: the Internet as an illustration', *International Journal of Service Industry Management*, Vol. 12, No. 5, pp. 423–50.

Chaffey D., Bocij, P., Greasley, A. and Hickie, A. (1999) *Business Information Systems: Technology Development and Management*, London, FT Prentice Hall.

Concise Insight (2004) *European Location-Based Services 2004 Report*, www.Concise-Insight.com.

Davis, F.D., Bagozzi, R.P. and Warshaw, P.R. (1989) 'User acceptance of computer technology: a comparison of two theoretical models', *Management Science*, Vol. 35, No. 8, pp. 982–1003.

de Koster, R.B.M. (2002) 'Distribution structures for food home shopping', *International Journal of Physical Distribution and Logistics Management*, Vol. 32, No. 5.

Economist Intelligence Unit (2003) *E-Readiness Rankings*, London, EIU.

ECR Scorecard Group (1996) *ECR Scorecard: a UK Perspective*, Watford, ECR UK.

Fishbein, M. and Ajzen, I. (1975) *Belief, Attitude, Intention and Behaviour: An Introduction to Theory and Research*, Reading, Massachusetts, Addison-Wesley.

Fletcher, K. (1995) *Marketing Management and Information Technology*, 2nd edn, Prentice Hall.

GS1 online at www.gs1uk.org, accessed 29 May 2005.

Howley, M. (2002) 'The role of consultancies in new product development', *Journal of Product and Brand Management*, Vol. 11, No. 6/7, pp. 447–58.

Keers, H. (2002) 'Mothercare slips into red as warehouse woes grow', *Daily Telegraph*, 22 November.

Kim, J. and Wilemon, D. (2003) 'Sources and assessment of complexity in NPD projects', *R&D Management*, Vol. 33, No. 1, pp. 16–30.

Kotler, P. (1997) *Marketing Management: Analysis, Planning, Implementation and Control*, 9th edn, Englewood Cliffs, NJ, Prentice-Hall.

Little, G. (2002) 'Inventors don't always make great marketers', *Design Week*, Vol. 17, No. 27, p. 15.

Lopez-Bassols, V. (1998) *The OECD Observer*, No. 213, August–September, pp. 16–19.

Morton, R. (2003) 'Some pick-up in online sales . . . however, most customers still prefer to buy from showrooms', *Financial Times*, 4 March, p. 5.

National Computing Centre (2001) *Survey of IT Spending*, London, NCC.

O'Cass, A. and Fenech, T. (2003) 'Web retailing adoption: exploring the nature of Internet users' web retailing behaviour', *Journal of Retailing and Consumer Services*, Vol. 10, No. 2, pp. 81–94.

OECD (2000) *OECD in Figures 2000*, Paris, Organization for Economic Co-operation and Development.

OECD (2002) *Short Summary of the Workshop on Genetic Inventions, Intellectual Property Rights and Licensing Practices*, Paris, OECD.

OECD (2005) *OECD Factbook*, 2005 edition, www.oecd.org/scienceandinnovation.

Parasuraman, A. (2000) 'Technology readiness index (TRI): a multiple-item scale to measure readiness to embrace new technologies', *Journal of Service Research*, Vol. 2, No. 4, pp. 307–20.

Press, E. and Washburn, J. (2003) *Secrecy and Science*, The Atlantic Online, www.theatlantic.com/issues/2000/03/press2.htm, accessed April 2005.

Timmins, N. (2003) 'A bid to save money for the government: online auctions', *Financial Times*, 29 January, p. 12.

Whittle, S. (2001) 'Early adopters are sold on online purchasing', *Computing* (UK), 1 February, p. 39.

Young, A. (1993) 'What goes into R&D?', *OECD Observer*, No. 183, August–September.

Yrjölä, H. (2001) 'Physical distribution considerations for electronic grocery shopping', *International Journal of Physical Distribution and Logistics Management*, Vol. 31, No. 10, pp. 25–38.

Chapter 5
The Legal Environment

Chapter Objectives
This chapter will explain:

- the key legal challenges and opportunities facing business organizations, in respect of their relationships with customers, suppliers, employees and intermediaries

- sources of law – common law and statute law

- the basic principles of law – contract and tort

- legal processes

- quasi-law based on voluntary codes of conduct

- legal protection of intellectual property

5.1 INTRODUCTION

It was noted in the first chapter that all societies need some form of rules which govern the relationship between individuals, organizations and government bodies. In the absence of rules, chaos is likely to ensue, in which the strongest people will survive at the expense of the weakest. Businesses do not like to operate in environments in which there are no accepted rules of behaviour, because there is no guarantee that their investments will be protected from unauthorized seizure. This may partly explain why some countries of central Africa which have been regarded as lawless areas without proper government have failed to attract significant inward investment by businesses.

However, a system of rules does not necessarily imply a formal legal system. Many less developed economies manage with moral codes of governance which exert pressure on individuals and organizations to conform to an agreed code of conduct. In such countries, the shame inflicted on the family of a trader who defrauds a customer may be sufficient to ensure that traders abide by a moral code of governance.

In complex, pluralistic societies, moral governance alone may be insufficient to ensure compliance from business organizations. The tendency therefore has been for legal frameworks to expand as economies develop. One observer has pointed out that the Ten Commandments – a biblical code for governing society – ran to about 300 words. The American Bill of Rights of 1791 ran to about 700 words. Today, as an example of the detailed legislation which affects our conduct, the Eggs (Marketing Standards) Regulations 1995 runs to several pages. The law essentially represents a codification of the rules and governance values of a society, expressed in a way that allows aggrieved parties to use an essentially bureaucratic system to gain what the society regards as justice. The legal environment of Western developed economies is very much influenced by the political environment, which in turn is influenced by the social environment. In this sense, the law does not exist in a vacuum. Developments in the business environment have led to changes in the law affecting businesses, and the law in turn has affected the activities of business organizations.

In previous chapters we have considered the relationship between elements of an organization's micro- and macroenvironments at a fairly abstract level. In reality, these relationships are governed by a legal framework which presents opportunities and constraints for the manner in which these relationships can be developed.

We can identify a number of important areas in which the legal environment impinges on the activities of business organizations.

■ The nature of the relationship between the organization and its customers, suppliers and intermediaries is influenced by the prevailing law. Over time, there has been a tendency for the law to give additional rights to buyers of goods and additional duties to the seller, especially in the case of transactions between businesses and private individuals. Whereas the nineteenth-century entrepreneur in Britain would have had almost complete freedom to dictate the terms of the relationship with its customers, developments in statute law and common law now require, for example, the supplier to ensure that the goods are of satisfactory quality and that no misleading description of them is made. Furthermore, the expectations of an organization's customers have changed over time. Whereas previous generations may have resigned themselves to suffering injustice in their dealings with a business, today the expectation is increasingly for perfection every time. Greater awareness of the law on the part of consumers has produced an increasingly litigious society.

■ In addition to the direct relationship that a company has with its customers, the law also influences the relationship that it has with other members of the general public. The law may, for example, prevent a firm having business relationships with certain sectors of the market, as where children are prohibited by law from buying cigarettes or drinking in public houses. Also, the messages that a company sends out in its advertising are likely to be picked up by members of the general public, and the law has intervened to protect the public interest where these messages could cause offence (adverts that are racially prejudicial, for example).

■ Employment relationships are covered by increasingly complex legislation which recognizes that employees have a proprietary interest in their job. Legislation seeks to make up for inequalities in the power between employers and employee.

■ The legal environment influences the relationship between business enterprises themselves, not only in terms of contracts for transactions between them, but also in the way they relate to each other in a competitive environment. The law has increasingly prevented companies from joining together in anti-competitive practices, whether covertly or overtly.

■ Companies need to develop new products, yet the rewards of undertaking new product development are influenced by the law. The laws of copyright and patent protect a firm's investment in fruitful research.

■ The legal environment influences the production possibilities of an enterprise and hence the products that can be offered to consumers. These can have a direct effect − as in the case of regulations stipulating car safety design requirements − or a more indirect effect − as where legislation to reduce pollution increases the manufacturing costs of a product, or prevents its manufacture completely.

The legal environment is very closely related to the political environment. In the UK, law derives from two sources: common law and statute law.

■ The common law develops on the basis of judgments in the courts − a case may set a precedent for all subsequent cases to follow. The judiciary is independent of government and the general direction of precedents tends gradually to reflect changing attitudes in society.

■ Statute law, on the other hand, is passed by Parliament and to a much greater extent reflects the prevailing political ideology of the government.

We can draw a distinction between *civil* law and *criminal* law. Civil law provides a means by which one party can bring an action for a loss which it has suffered as the direct result of actions by another party. A party who is injured by a defective vehicle, or has suffered loss because a promised order for goods has not been delivered can use the civil law to claim some kind of recompense against the other party. By contrast, criminal law is invoked when a party causes harm to society more generally. In this case, it is the government that brings a claim against a wrongdoer and punishment generally takes the form of a fine or a prison sentence. Most of the subjects covered in this chapter are concerned with the civil law − that is, relationships between an organization and other individuals and organizations in their business environment. However, business organizations are increasingly being prosecuted for breaches of criminal law. Cases discussed in this chapter include: breaches of food safety law; breaches of health and safety law; and providing misleading price information.

The law is a very complex area of the business environment. Most businesses would call upon expert members of the legal profession to interpret and act upon some of the more complex elements of the law. The purpose of this chapter is not to give definitive answers on aspects of the law as it affects business organizations – this would be impossible and dangerous in such a short space. Instead, the aim is to raise awareness of legal issues in order to recognize in general terms the opportunities and restrictions that the law poses, and the areas in which business organizations may need to seek the specialized advice of a legal professional.

This chapter will begin by looking at some general principles of law: the law of contract, the law relating to negligence and the processes of the legal system in England. Although the detail will describe the legal system of England, many of the principles apply in other judicial systems. The chapter will then consider the following specific areas of applications of the law, which are of particular relevance to businesses:

- dealings between organizations and their customers for the supply of goods and services
- contracts of employment
- protection of intellectual property rights
- legislation relating to production processes
- legislation to prevent anti-competitive practices.

5.2 THE LAW OF CONTRACT

A contract is an agreement between two parties where one party agrees to do something (e.g. supply goods, provide a service, offer employment) in return for which the other party provides some form of payment (in money or some other form of value). A typical organization would have contracts with a wide range of other parties, including customers, suppliers, employees and intermediaries.

There can be no direct legal relationship between a company and any of these groups unless it can be proved that a contract exists. An advertisement on its own only very rarely creates a legal relationship. The elements of a contract comprise: offer, acceptance, intention to create legal relations, consideration and capacity. We will consider these in turn.

5.2.1 Offer

An offer is a declaration by which the offeror indicates that they intend to be legally bound on the terms stated in the offer if it is accepted by the offeree. The offer may be oral, in writing or by conduct between the parties, and must be clear and unambiguous. It may be made to a particular person or to the whole world. It is extremely important that it be distinguished from an invitation to treat, which can be defined as an invitation to make offers. Normally, all advertisements are regarded as invitations to treat, as is illustrated in a case in which a man was charged with offering for sale live birds, bramble finches (Partridge v. Crittendon [1968] 1 WLR 286). A person reading the advert wrote, enclosing money for a bird, which was duly sent. The advertiser was charged with the offence of offering wild birds for sale, but it was held that the advertisement was not an offer but an invitation to treat and therefore he escaped the charge.

In the context of sales to customers it is important to note that priced goods on display in supermarkets and shops are not offers, but invitations to treat. Therefore, if a leather jacket is priced at £20 (through error) in the shop widow, it is not possible to demand the garment at that price. As the display is an invitation to treat, it is the consumer who is making the offer, which the shopkeeper may accept or reject as he wishes.

5.2.2 Acceptance

Acceptance may be made only by the person(s) to whom the offer was made, and it must be absolute and unqualified; i.e. it must not add any new terms or conditions, for to do so would have the effect of revoking the original offer. Acceptance must be communicated to the offeror unless it can be implied by conduct. In the case of Carlill v. Carbolic Smoke Ball Co. ([1893] 1 QB 256 CA), the defendants were the makers of a smoke ball which was purported to prevent influenza. The advertisement stated that £100 would be given to any person catching influenza after having sniffed their smoke ball in accordance with the instructions given. The manufacturers deposited £1000 at a bank to show that their claim was sincere. Mrs Carlill bought a smoke ball in response to the advertisement, complied with the instructions but still caught influenza.

In Mrs Carlill's case, her purchase implied her acceptance, for this was an offer to the world at large and it was not therefore necessary to communicate her acceptance in person to the offeror. She sued for the £100 and was successful. It was argued by the defence that the advertisement was an invitation to treat, but in this rare instance it was held to be an offer.

5.2.3 Intention to create legal relations

The above case turned on the third element of a contract – the intention to create legal relations. It was held that, because the company had deposited the £1000 in the bank, this was evidence of its intention to be legally bound and therefore the advertisement constituted an offer. Generally, in all commercial agreements it is accepted that both parties intend to make a legally binding contract and therefore it is unnecessary to include terms to this effect.

5.2.4 Consideration

This factor is essential in all contracts unless they are made 'under seal'. Consideration has been defined as some right, interest, profit or benefit accruing to one party or some forbearance, detriment, loss or responsibility given, suffered or undertaken by the other – i.e. some benefit accruing to one party or a detriment suffered by the other. In commercial contracts generally, the consideration takes the form of a cash payment. However, in contracts of barter, which are common in some countries, goods are often exchanged for goods.

5.2.5 Capacity

The final element is that of capacity. Generally, any person or organization may enter into an agreement which may be enforced against them. Exceptions include minors, drunks and mental patients; for this reason, companies usually exclude people under 18 from offers of goods to be supplied on credit. Limited companies must have the capacity to make a contract identified in their Objects clause within their Articles and Memorandum of Association (see Chapter 6).

An offer may be revoked at any time prior to acceptance. However, if postal acceptance is an acceptable means of communication between the parties, then acceptance is effective as soon as it is posted, provided it is correctly addressed and stamped.

5.2.6 Misrepresentation

Generally, it is assumed that statements which are made at the formation of a contract are terms of that contract, but many statements made during the course of negotiations are mere representations. If the statement is a term, the injured party may sue for breach of contract and will normally obtain damages that are deemed to put him or her in the position they would have been in if the statement had been true. If the statement is a mere representation, it may be possible to avoid the contract by obtaining an order – known as rescission – which puts the parties back in the position they were in prior to the formation of the contract. Even though the essential elements of a contract are present, the contract may still fail to be given full effect.

THINKING AROUND THE SUBJECT:
IS A BUSINESS RELATIONSHIP A CONTRACT?

One of the trends in the business environment that we discussed in Chapter 1 is towards closer relationships between companies in a supply chain. So, instead of buying 'job lots' of components and raw materials from the cheapest buyer whenever they are needed, a buyer and seller will come to an arrangement for their supply over the longer term. The parties may not be able to specify the precise products or volumes that they will need to buy, but just by understanding each other's processes and likely future requirements, the supply chain can be made more efficient and effective.

Many of these business relationships are based on 'gentlemen's agreements' with little formal specification in writing. So is this a contract? Can either party unilaterally end a gentleman's agreement?

The question was tested in 2002 in the case of Baird Textile Holdings Ltd v. Marks & Spencer plc (M&S). Baird had been making lingerie, women's coats and men's clothes for M&S for over 30 years and had largely built its business round the retail chain's requirements. However, the parties had resisted formalizing the arrangement in order to maintain maximum flexibility in their relationship. But increased competition in the high street had led M&S to look for cheaper sources of manufacturing overseas, and Baird was told that with immediate effect its goods were no longer required by M&S.

Baird argued that although there was no written contract governing their relationship, there was an implied term that either party would give reasonable notice of any change to the relationship. The supplier claimed for damages of £53.6 million, which included a £33 million charge to cover redundancy payments, and a further £21.4m loss in respect of asset write-downs, including IT equipment it used to help fulfil its M&S clothing orders. The claim was intended to put Baird back into a position it would have been in had M&S given it three years' notice, rather than suddenly terminating its agreement. But did the agreement between the two constitute a contract?

The Court of Appeal held that the long-term arrangements between Baird and M&S did not constitute a contract. It stated that there was a clear mutual intent not to enter into a legal agreement and this view was supported by the absence of any precise terms. Both parties clearly wished to preserve flexibility in their dealings with each other. A contract existed only in respect of individual orders when they were placed, but there was no contract governing the continuity of orders.

5.3 NON-CONTRACTUAL LIABILITY

Consider now the situation where a consumer discovers that goods are defective in some way but is unable to sue the retailer from which they were supplied because the consumer is not a party to the contract (which may occur where the goods were bought as a gift by a friend). The product may also injure a completely unconnected third party. The only possible course of action here has been to sue the manufacturer. This situation was illustrated in 1932 in the case of Donaghue v. Stevenson, where a man bought a bottle of ginger beer manufactured by the defendant. The man gave the bottle to his female companion, who became ill from drinking the contents, as the bottle (which was opaque) contained the decomposing remains of a snail. The consumer sued the manufacturer and won. The House of Lords held that on the facts outlined there was remedy in the tort of negligence.

To prove negligence, there are three elements that must be shown:

1 that the defendant was under a duty of care to the plaintiff
2 that there had been a breach of that duty
3 that there is damage to the plaintiff as a result of the breach which is not too remote a consequence.

In the case, Lord Atkin defined a duty of care thus:

> A manufacturer of products, which he sells in such a form as to show that he intends them to reach the ultimate consumer in the form in which they left him with no reasonable possibility of intermediate examination, and with the knowledge that the absence of reasonable care in the preparation or putting up of the products will result in an injury to the consumer's life or property, owes a duty to the consumer to take reasonable care. You must take reasonable care to avoid acts or omissions which you can reasonably foresee would be likely to injure your neighbour. Who then is my neighbour? The answer seems to be persons who are so closely and directly affected by my act that I ought reasonably to have them in contemplation as being so affected when I am directing my mind to the acts or omissions which are called in question.

The law of negligence is founded almost entirely on decided cases, and the approach adopted by the courts is one that affords flexibility in response to the changing patterns of practical problems. Unfortunately, it is unavoidable that with flexibility comes an element of uncertainty. Whether or not liability will arise in a particular set of circumstances appears to be heavily governed by public policy, and it is not clear exactly when a duty of care will arise. At present, the principles, or alternatively the questions to be asked in attempting to determine whether a duty exists, are:

■ is there foreseeability of harm and, if so,
■ is there proximity – a close and direct relationship – and, if so,
■ is it fair and reasonable for there to be a duty in these circumstances?

Having established in certain circumstances that a duty of care exists, defendants will be in breach of that duty if they have not acted reasonably. The question is: What standard of care does the law require? The standard of care required is that of an ordinary prudent man in the circumstances pertaining to the case. For example, in one case it was held that an employee owed a higher standard of care to a one-eyed motor mechanic and was therefore obliged to provide protective goggles – not because the likelihood of damage was greater, but because the consequences of an eye injury were more serious (Paris v. Stepney BC [1951]). Similarly, a higher standard of care would be expected from a drug manufacturer than from a greetings cards manufacturer because the consequences of defective products would be far more serious in the former case.

Where a person is regarded as a professional – i.e. where people set themselves up as possessing a particular skill, such as a plumber, solicitor, surgeon – then they must display the type of skill required in carrying out that particular profession or trade.

With a liability based on fault, the defendant can be liable only for damages caused by him or her. The test adopted is whether the damage is of a type or kind that ought reasonably to have been foreseen even though the extent need not have been envisaged. The main duty is that of the manufacturer, but cases have shown that almost any party that is responsible for the supply of goods may be held liable. The onus of proving negligence is on the plaintiff. Of importance in this area is s. 2(1) of the Unfair Contract Terms Act 1977, which states: 'a person cannot by reference to any contract term or notice exclude or restrict his liability for death or personal injury resulting from negligence'. Also s. 2(2): 'in the case of other loss or damage, a person cannot so exclude or restrict his liability for negligence except in so far as the contract term or notice satisfies the test of reasonableness'. Thus, all clauses that purport to exclude liability in respect of negligence resulting in death or personal injuries are void, and other clauses, e.g. 'goods accepted at owner's risk', must satisfy the test of reasonableness.

5.4 LEGAL PROCESSES

It is not only changes in the law itself that should be of concern to businesses but also the ease of access to legal processes. If legal processes are excessively expensive or time-consuming, the law may come to be seen as irrelevant if parties have no realistic means of enforcing the law. In general, developed economies have seen access to the law widened, so that it is not exclusively at the service of rich individuals or companies. As well as individuals and companies having the right to protect their own legal interests, a number of government agencies facilitate enforcement of the law.

In England, a number of courts of law operate with distinct functional and hierarchical roles.

■ The Magistrates' Court deals primarily with criminal matters, where it handles approximately 97 per cent of the workload. It is responsible for handling prosecutions of companies for breaches of legislation under the Trade Descriptions and the Consumer Protection Acts. More serious criminal matters are 'committed' up to the Crown Court for trial.

■ The Crown Court handles the more serious cases that have been committed to it for trial on 'indictment'. In addition, it also hears defendants' appeals as to sentence or conviction from the Magistrates' Court.

■ The High Court is responsible for hearing appeals by way of 'case stated' from the Magistrates' Court or occasionally the Crown Court. The lower court, whose decision is being challenged, prepares papers (the case) and seeks the opinion of the High Court.

■ The Court of Appeal deals primarily with appeals from trials on indictment in the Crown Court. It may review either sentence or conviction.

- County Courts are for almost all purposes the courts of first instance in civil matters (contract and tort). Generally, where the amount claimed is less than £25,000, this court will have jurisdiction in the first instance, but between £25,000 and £50,000, the case may be heard here, or be directed to the High Court, depending on its complexity.

- When larger amounts are being litigated, the High Court will have jurisdiction in the first instance. There is a commercial court within the structure which is designed to be a quicker and generally more suitable court for commercial matters. Bankruptcy appeals from the County Court are heard here.

- Cases worth less than £5000 are referred by the County Court to its 'Small Claims' division, where the case will be heard informally under arbitration, and costs normally limited to the value of the issue of the summons. The object of the Small Claims Court is to remove the disincentive to litigate due to the fear of High Court costs.

- The Court of Appeals' Civil Division hears civil appeals from the County Court and the High Court.

- The House of Lords is the ultimate appeal court for both criminal and domestic matters. However, where there is a European Issue, the European Court of Justice will give a ruling on the point at issue, after which the case is referred back to the UK court.

In addition to the court structure (see Figure 5.1), there are numerous quasi-judicial tribunals which exist to reconcile disagreeing parties. Examples include Rent Tribunals (for agreeing property rents), Valuation Tribunals (for agreeing property values) and Employment Tribunals (for bringing claims covered by employment legislation).

Despite the existence of legal rights, the cost to an individual or a firm of enforcing its rights can be prohibitive, especially where there is no certainty that a party taking action will be able to recover its legal costs. For a typical inter-company dispute over a debt of £50,000, the party suing the debtor can easily incur legal expenses of several thousand pounds, not counting the

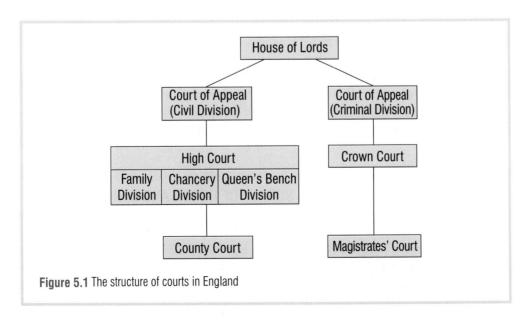

Figure 5.1 The structure of courts in England

cost of its employees' time. Where a case goes to the Court of Appeal, a company could be involved in inestimable costs. The legal process can also be very slow. In the case of an inter-company debt claim, a case may take up to 10 years between the first issue of a writ and com-pensation being finally received.

Numerous attempts have been made to make the legal system more widely accessible, such as the small claims section of the County Court which handles claims of up to £5000 in a less formal and costly manner than a normal County Court claim. There have also been attempts to reduce the risks to individuals by allowing, in certain circumstances, solicitors to charge their clients depending upon results obtained in Court (often referred to as a 'no win, no fee' system). There is a strong feeling that costs of running the courts system could be greatly reduced by reducing many bureaucratic and restrictive practices within the legal profession.

Despite moves to make legal remedies more widely available, access to the law remains unequal. Among commercial organizations, a small under-resourced firm may be unable to put money up-front to pursue a case against a larger company which could defend itself with an army of retained lawyers. Similarly, private consumers are unequal in their access to the law. It has often been suggested that easy access to the law is afforded to the very rich (who can afford it) and the very poor (who may be eligible to receive legal aid). An apparent paradox of attempts to make the law more accessible is that these attempts may themselves overwhelm courts with cases with which they are unable to cope. Recent restrictions on funding for legal aid reflect the fact that there can be almost unlimited demand for legal remedies, but finite judicial capacity.

Central and local government is increasingly being given power to act as a consumer cham-pion and to bring cases before the courts which are in the interest of consumers in general. Bodies that pursue actions in this way include the following.

- Trading Standards Departments which are operated by County Councils (by Borough Councils in Metropolitan areas). They have powers to investigate complaints about false or misleading descriptions of prices, inaccurate weights and measures, consumer credit and the safety of consumer legislation. Consumers' knowledge of their rights has often stretched the resources of Trading Standards Departments so that, at best, they can only selectively take action against bad practice.
- Environmental Health Departments of local authorities deal with health matters such as unfit food and dirty shops and restaurants. A consumer who suspects that they have suffered food poisoning as a result of eating unfit food at a restaurant may lodge a complaint with the local Environmental Health Department, which may collate similar complaints and use this evidence to prosecute the offending restaurant or take steps to have it closed down.
- Utility regulators have powers to bring action against companies that are in breach of their licence conditions.

5.5 LEGISLATION AFFECTING THE SUPPLY OF GOODS AND SERVICES

Prior to 1968, there was very little statutory intervention in the contractual relationship between business organizations and their customers, with a few exceptions such as those that came within the scope of the Food and Drugs Act 1955. Since the 1960s there has been an increasing amount of legislation designed to protect the interests of private consumers, who legislators have seen as unequal parties to a contract. In recent years EU directives have been incorporated into UK legislation to provide additional duties for suppliers of goods and services. It should be

THINKING AROUND THE SUBJECT:
WHO BENEFITS FROM A 'COMPENSATION CULTURE'?

Are we becoming a litigious society, dominated by a 'compensation culture'? Newspapers are continually reporting claims made by individuals which at first may seem quite trivial and not warranting legal intervention. Recent claims which some would argue typify a compensation culture include a teacher who won £55,000 after slipping on a chip, and the parents of a Girl Guide who sued after she was burnt by fat spitting from a sausage. Aggrieved parties may have been spurred on by the rise of 'personal injury advisers' who offer to take on a claim at no risk to the claimant. They have sometimes been referred to as 'ambulance chasers' for the way they pursue injured parties, making them aware of the possibility of claiming for a loss or injury, which they may otherwise have written off in their minds as unfortunate bad luck. If their claim is rejected by the court, the claimant will pay nothing. If it succeeds, they pay the company handling the claim a percentage of the damages awarded. Such companies have been accused of unrealistically raising clients' expectations of damages, and looking for confrontation where alternative methods of reconciliation may be more effective. The business practices of some companies have been criticized, and one company, the Accident Group, went out of business in 2004 after accumulating large debts and failing to deliver promised benefits to many of its customers.

Is the compensation culture necessarily a bad thing for society? Defending cases costs companies time and money, which will inevitably be passed on in the form of higher prices charged to consumers. Claims against companies sometimes even lead to goods or services no longer being made available to consumers because of an open-ended risk of being sued if there is a problem with the product.

But shouldn't consumers expect businesses to deliver their promises in a responsible manner? Is a compensation culture essentially about redressing the balance between relatively weak consumers and more powerful organizations? If those organizations did their job properly, would there be no case for even talking about a compensation culture? If the cost of obtaining justice made it difficult for aggrieved customers to bring a claim against a company, would the company simply carry on acting irresponsibly because it realized it was beyond reproach? In the case of very dubious claims, such as a customer who sued a restaurant because their cup of coffee was 'too hot', could the company attract sympathy from the majority of its customers, who might regard such a claim as frivolous?

---

noted that much of the legislation applies only to business-to-consumer contracts and not business-to-business contracts. In the latter case, legislation has often presumed that parties have equal bargaining power and therefore do not need additional legislative protection.

In this section, we consider the following important pieces of statute law which have an impact on the relationship between an organization and its customers:

■ the Trade Descriptions Act 1968
■ the Sale of Goods Act 1979
■ the Misrepresentation Act 1967
■ the Consumer Protection Act 1987
■ the Consumer Credit Act 1974.

In addition, this section reviews a number of quasi-legal codes of conduct operated by industry bodies.

5.5.1 Trade Descriptions Act 1968

The Trade Descriptions Act 1968 makes it an offence for a person to make a false or misleading trade description and creates three principal offences, as described below.

A false trade description to goods

Under s. 1, this states that 'a person who, in the course of business, applies false trade descriptions to goods or suppliers or offers to supply goods to which a false description has been applied is guilty of an offence'. Section 2 defines a false trade description as including 'any indication of any physical characteristics such as quantity, size, method of manufacture, composition and fitness for purpose'.

A description is regarded as false when it is false or, by s. 3(2), misleading to a material degree. In one case it was held that to describe as 'new' a car that had sustained damage while in the manufacturer's compound was not an offence because of the excellent repair work carried out on the car which rendered the vehicle 'good as new' (R. v. Ford Motor Co. Ltd [1947] 3 All ER 489).

In some cases consumers are misled by advertisements that are economical with the truth. A car was advertised as having one previous 'owner'. Strictly this was true, but it had been owned by a leasing company who had leased it to five different users. The divisional court held this was misleading and caught by s. 3(2) of the Trade Descriptions Act (R. v. South Western Justices ex parte London Borough of Wandsworth, Times [20 January 1983]).

A false statement of price

Section 11 makes a false statement as to the price an offence. If a trader claims that his prices are reduced, he is guilty of an offence unless he can show that the goods have been on sale at the higher price during the preceding six months for a consecutive period of 28 days (more specific requirements concerning pricing are contained in the Price Marking Order 2004).

A false trade description of services

Section 14 states that it is an offence to make false or misleading statements as to services. An example of this is illustrated in the case of a store that advertised 'folding doors and folding door gear − carriage free'. This statement was intended to convey to the consumer that only the folding door gear would be sent carriage-free on purchase of the folding doors. It was held that the advert was misleading and that it was irrelevant that it was not intended to be misleading (MFI Warehouses Ltd v. Nattrass [1973] 1 All ER 762).

Defences under the Trade Descriptions Act are set out in s. 24(i):

(a) that the commission of the offence was due to a mistake or to reliance on information supplied to him or to the act or default of another person, an accident or some other cause beyond his control; and

(b) that he took all reasonable precautions and exercised all due diligence to avoid the commission of such an offence by himself or any person under his control.

For the defence to succeed, it is necessary to show that both sub-sections apply. In a case concerning a leading supermarket, a brand of washing powder was advertised as being 5p less than the price marked in the store. The defendants said that it was the fault of the store manager who had failed to go through the system laid down for checking shelves. The court held that the defence applied; the store manager was another person (s. 24(i)(a)) and the store had taken reasonable precautions to prevent commission of the offence (Tesco Supermarkets Ltd v. Nattrass [1971] 2 All ER 127).

5.5.2 Sale of Goods Act 1979

What rights has the consumer if on purchase he discovers that the goods are faulty or different from those ordered? The Sale of Goods Act (SOGA) contains implied terms specifically to protect the consumer. The term 'consumer' is defined by s.20(6) of the Consumer Protection Act 1987 which states:

(a) in relation to any goods, [consumer] means any person who might wish to be supplied with the goods for his own private use or consumption;

(b) in relation to any service or facilities, [consumer] means any person who might wish to be provided with the service or facilities otherwise than for the purposes of any business of his; and

(c) in relation to any accommodation, [consumer] means any person who might wish to occupy the accommodation otherwise than for the purposes of any business of his.

Section 13 of the Sale of Goods Act 1979 states that 'Where there is a contract for the sale of goods by description there is an implied condition that the goods will correspond with the description.' The sale is not prevented from being a sale by description even if the goods are on display and selected by the buyer. It is important to note that s. 13 applies to sales by private individuals and businesses.

In a case concerning a 1961 Triumph Herald, advertised for sale in the paper, it was discovered that the car was made up of two halves of different Triumph Heralds, only one of which was a 1961 model, and in the Court of Appeal the plaintiff's claim for damages was upheld (Beale v. Taylor [1967] 1 WLR 1993).

The goods must, for example, be as described on the package. If a customer purchases a blue long-sleeved shirt and on opening the box discovers that it is a red short-sleeved shirt, then he is entitled to a return of the price for breach of an implied condition of the contract.

An example that illustrates the operation of s. 13 is a case concerning the sale by one art dealer to another of a painting that both assumed genuine. It later transpired that the painting was a forgery. The buyer brought an action relying on a breach of s. 13(1) and s. 14(2) of SOGA. It was, however, held that the contract was not one for the sale of goods by description within s. 13(1) because the description of the painting as regards its author did not become a term of the contract. It was clearly fit for the purpose for which art is commonly bought and therefore of merchantable quality. In this case, 'by description [it] was held to imply that the description must have been so important a factor in the sale to become a condition of the contract' (Harlingdon & Leinster Enterprises Ltd v. Christopher Hull/Fine Art Ltd [1990] 1 All ER 737).

Section 14(2) as amended by the Sale and Supply of Goods Act 1994 states:

Where the seller sells goods in the course of a business, there is an implied term that the goods supplied under the contract are of satisfactory quality.

Section 14(2A) gives a definition of satisfactory quality which now replaces the term 'merchantable quality':

> For the purposes of this Act goods are of satisfactory quality if they meet the standard that a reasonable person would regard as satisfactory, taking account of any description of the goods, the price (if relevant) and all other relevant circumstances.

This definition is further expanded by s. 14(2B) as follows.

> For the purposes of this Act, the quality of goods includes their state and condition and the following (among others) are in appropriate cases aspects of the quality of the goods:
> (a) fitness for all the purposes for which goods of the kind in question are commonly supplied,
> (b) appearance and finish,
> (c) freedom from minor defects,
> (d) safety, and
> (e) durability.

Section 14(2C) states:

> The term implied by subsection (2) above does not extend to any matter making the quality of goods unsatisfactory:
> (a) which is specifically drawn to the buyer's attention before the contract is made,
> (b) where the buyer examines the goods before the contract is made, which that examination ought to reveal, or
> (c) in the case of a sale by sample, which would have been apparent on a reasonable examination of the sample.
> (The moral for the consumer is therefore: examine thoroughly or not at all.)

The implied term of unsatisfactory quality applies to sale goods and second-hand goods, but clearly the consumer would not have such high expectations of second-hand goods. For example, a clutch fault in a new car would make it unsatisfactory, but not so if the car were second-hand. In a second-hand car – again, depending on all the circumstances – a fault would have to be major to render the car unsatisfactory. Thus, the question to be asked is, 'Are the goods satisfactory in the light of the contract description and all the circumstances of the case?'

It is often asked for how long the goods should remain merchantable. It is perhaps implicit that the goods remain merchantable for a length of time reasonable in the circumstances of the case and the nature of the goods. If a good becomes defective within a very short time, this is evidence that there was possibly a latent defect at the time of the sale.

In one case, a new car which on delivery had a minor defect that was likely to, and subsequently did, cause the engine to seize up while the car was being driven was neither of merchantable quality nor reasonably fit for its purpose under s. 14. The purchaser could not, however, rescind the contract and recover the price because it was held that he had retained the car 'after the lapse of a reasonable time' without intimating to the seller that he had rejected it even though the defect had not at that time become obvious (Berstein v. Pampson Motors (Golders Green) Ltd [1987] 2 All ER 220 N3). It was held that s. 35(1) of SOGA did not refer to a reasonable time to discover a particular defect: rather, it meant a reasonable time to inspect the goods and try them out generally. Thus, the owner, having been deemed to have accepted the car, was entitled to damages to compensate him for the cost of getting home, the loss of a tank of petrol and the inconvenience of being without a car while it was being repaired. Had there been any evidence that the car's value had been reduced as a result of the defect, he would have been entitled to damages for that too. The moral here is to examine thoroughly immediately on purchase.

Under s. 14(3), there is an implied condition that goods are fit for a particular purpose:

> Where the seller sells goods in the course of a business and the buyer, expressly or by implication, makes known to the seller any particular purpose for which the goods are being bought, there is an implied condition that the goods are reasonably fit for that purpose, whether or not it is a purpose for which goods are commonly supplied, except where the circumstances show that the buyer does not rely, or that it is unreasonable for him to rely, on the skill or judgement of the seller.

Thus, if a seller, on request, confirms suitability for a particular purpose and the product proves unsuitable, there would be a breach of s. 14(3); if the product is also unsuitable for its normal purposes, then s. 14(2) would be breached too. If the seller disclaims any knowledge of the product's suitability for the particular purpose and the consumer takes a chance and purchases it, then if it proves unsuitable for its particular purpose there is no breach of s. 14(3). The only circumstance in which a breach may occur is, again, if it were unsuitable for its normal purposes under s. 14(2).

In business contracts, implied terms in ss. 13–15 of the Sale of Goods Act 1979 can be excluded. Such exclusion clauses, purporting, for example, to exclude a term for reasonable fitness for goods (s. 14), are valid subject to the test of reasonableness provided that the term is incorporated into the contract (i.e. that the buyer is or ought reasonably to be aware of the term).

Where consumer contracts are concerned, then such clauses that purport to limit or exclude liability are void under s. 6(2) of the Unfair Contract Terms Act 1977. Obviously, the goods purchased must come within the scope of consumer goods, and thus items such as lorries or machinery would take the transaction outside the scope of a consumer sale.

The case of R & B Customs Brokers Co Ltd v. United Dominions Trust Ltd ([1988] 1 All ER 847) is of some importance to the business world. Here, a company operating as a shipping broker and freight forwarding agent purchased a car for use by a director in the business. The sale was held to be a consumer sale within the meaning of s. 12 of the Unfair Contract Terms Act 1977 (UCTA); therefore, a term for reasonable fitness for purpose under s. 14 of SOGA 1979 could not be excluded from the contract of sale (s. 6(2) of UCTA). The Court of Appeal followed the decision in a Trade Descriptions Act case in which a self-employed courier traded in his old car in part-exchange for a new car. The milometer registered 18,100 miles, but it was evident that the true mileage was 118,000 miles. The owner was therefore prosecuted for having applied a false trade description to the car and was convicted by the magistrates' court. The division court allowed the appeal on the grounds that the vehicle was not disposed of in the course of a business – the point on which the prosecution turned. Lord Keith held that the expression 'in the course of a trade or business' in the context of an Act having consumer protection as its primary purpose conveys the concept of some degree of regularity. He said that the requisite degree of regularity had not been established here because a normal practice of buying and disposing of cars had not been established at the time of the alleged offence in the case. From this it follows that, had R & B Custom Brokers been dealing in cars, then the purchase of a director's car would not have been a consumer purchase. It is clear then that the self-employed – the sole traders – who no doubt assume that they are dealing in the course of a business are extremely well protected under the Sale of Goods Act and the Trade Descriptions Act. How anomalous it is when one considers that R & B Customs Brokers would no doubt be horrified if the Inland Revenue held that it was not operating in the course of a business and refused capital allowances on the director's car.

Where the buyer is dealing otherwise than as a consumer, any exclusion or limitation clause will be valid subject to the tests of reasonableness contained in s. 11 and schedule II of the Unfair Contract Terms Act 1977.

The Supply of Goods and Services Act 1982 (SGSA) offers almost identical protection where goods are passed under a Supply of Goods and Services contract in s. 3 (which corresponds to s. 13 of SOGA) and s. 4 (which corresponds to s. 14 of SOGA). Where exclusion clauses are incorporated that relate to the supply of goods, then s. 7 of the Unfair Contract Terms Act replaces s. 6, previously discussed.

Section 13 of SGSA provides that, where the supplier of a service under a contract is acting in the course of a business, there is an implied term that the supplier will carry out the service with reasonable care and skill. Reasonable care and skill may be defined as 'the ordinary skill of an ordinary competent man exercising that particular act'. Much will depend on the circumstances of the case and the nature of the trade or profession.

5.5.3 Misrepresentation Act 1967

The Misrepresentation Act 1967 provides remedies for victims of misrepresentation. For the purpose of the Act, an actionable misrepresentation may be defined as 'a false statement of existing or past fact made by one party to the other before or at the time of making the contract, which is intended to, and does, induce the other party to enter into the contract'.

Since the 1967 Act, it has been necessary to maintain a clear distinction between negligent misrepresentation and wholly innocent misrepresentation.

Section 2(1) states:

> Where a person has entered into a contract after a misrepresentation has been made to him by another party and as a result has suffered loss, then, if the person making the representation would be liable to damages in respect thereof had the misrepresentation been made fraudulently, that person shall be so liable not withstanding that the misrepresentation was not made fraudulently, unless he pleads that he had reasonable grounds to believe and did believe up to the time the contract was made that the facts represented were true.

Section 2(2) states:

> Where a person has entered into a contract after a misrepresentation has been made to him otherwise than fraudulently, and he would be entitled, by reason of the misrepresentation, to rescind the contract, then if it is claimed, in any proceedings arising out of the contract, that the contract ought to be or has been rescinded, the court or arbitrator may declare the contract subsisting and award damages in lieu of rescission, if of the opinion that it would be equitable to do so having regard to the nature of the misrepresentation and the loss that would be caused by it if the contract were upheld, as well as to the loss that rescission would cause to the other party.

The 1967 Act introduced a different type of misrepresentation (negligence under s. 2(i)), but this is misleading because negligence does not have to be proved, as Bridge LJ held in Howard Marine and Dredging Co Ltd v. Ogden and Sons (Excavations) Ltd:

> The liability of the representor does not depend on his being under a duty of care, the extent of which may vary according to the circumstances in which the representation is made. In the course of negotiations leading to a contract the 1967 Act imposes an absolute obligation not to state facts which he cannot prove he had reasonable grounds to believe.

Section 2(2) empowers the court to refuse rescission or to reconstitute a rescinded contract and award damages in lieu.

To sum up, rescission is a remedy for all three types of misrepresentation. In addition to rescission for fraudulent misrepresentation, damages may be awarded under the tort of fraud, and in respect of negligent misrepresentation damages may be awarded under s. 2(1) of the 1967 Act. Under s. 2(2) damages may also be awarded at the discretion of the court, but, if so, these are in lieu of rescission.

The Property Misdescriptions Act 1991 built on the Misrepresentation Act and created a strict liability criminal offence of making, in the course of an estate agency or property development business, a false or misleading statement about a prescribed matter (s. 1(1)) to be specified in an order by the Secretary of State (s. 1(5)). The most common complaints from estate agents' (mis)descriptions include incorrect room sizes, misleading photographs and deceptive descriptions of local amenities. In one case, the agents blocked out in the photograph an ugly gasworks which overshadowed a house they were trying to sell.

5.5.4 The Consumer Protection Act 1987

The Consumer Protection Act 1987 came into force in March 1988 as a result of the government's obligation to implement an EU directive, and provides a remedy in damages for anyone who suffers personal injury or damage to property as a result of a defective product. The effect is to impose a strict (i.e. whereby it is unnecessary to prove negligence) tortious liability on producers of defective goods. The Act supplements the existing law; thus, a consumer may well have a remedy in contract, in the tort of negligence or under the Act if he or she has suffered loss caused by a defective product.

A product is defined in s. 12 as 'any goods or electricity'; s. 45(1) defines goods as including substances (natural or artificial, in solid, liquid or gaseous form), growing crops, things compressed in land by virtue of being attached to it, ships, aircraft and vehicles.

The producer will be liable if the consumer can establish that the product is defective and that it caused a loss. There is a defect if the safety of the goods does not conform to general expectations with reference to the risk of damage to property or risk of death or personal injury. The general expectations will differ depending on the particular circumstances, but points to be taken into account include the product's instructions, warnings and the time elapsed since supply, the latter point to determine the possibility of the defect being due to wear and tear.

The onus is on the plaintiff to prove that loss was caused by the defect. A claim may be made by anyone, whether death, personal injury or damage to property has occurred. However, where damage to property is concerned, the damage is confined to property ordinarily intended for private use or consumption and acquired by the person mainly for his or her own use or consumption, thus excluding commercial goods and property. Damage caused to private property must exceed £275 for claims to be considered. It is not possible to exclude liability under the Consumer Protection Act.

The Act is intended to place liability on the producer of defective goods. In some cases the company may not manufacture the goods, but may still be liable, as follows.

- Anyone carrying out an 'industrial or other process' to goods that have been manufactured by someone else will be treated as the producer where 'essential characteristics' are attributable to that process. Essential characteristics are nowhere defined in the Act, but processes that modify the goods may well be within the scope. It is important to note there that defects in the goods are not limited to those caused by the modifications, but encompass any defects in the product.
- If a company puts its own brand name on goods that have been manufactured on its behalf, thus holding itself out to be the producer, that company will be liable for any defects in the branded goods.
- Any importer who imports goods from outside EU countries will likewise be liable for defects in the imported goods. This is an extremely beneficial move for the consumer.

The Act is also instrumental in providing a remedy against suppliers who are unable to identify the importee or the previous supplier to them. If the supplier fails or cannot identify the manufacturer's importee or previous supplier, then the supplier is liable. It should be noted that if the product itself is defective, the remedy lies in contract (usually SOGA 1979).

5.5.5 Consumer Credit Act 1974

This is a consumer protection measure to protect the public from, among other things, extortionate credit agreements and high-pressure selling off trade premises. The Act became fully operational in May 1985, and much of the protection afforded to hire purchase transactions is extended to those obtaining goods and services through consumer credit transactions. It is important to note that contract law governs the formation of agreements coming within the scope of the Consumer Credit Act. Also, the Act is applicable only to credit agreements not exceeding £25,000 or where the debtor is not a corporate body.

Section 8(1) states:

A personal credit agreement is an agreement between an individual ('the debtor') and any other person ('the creditor') by which the creditor provides the debtor with credit of any amount.

Section 8(2) defines a consumer credit agreement as a personal credit providing the debtor with credit not exceeding £25,000.

Section 9 defines credit as a cash loan and any form of financial accommodation.

There are two types of credit. The first is a running account credit (s. 10(a)), whereby the debtor is enabled to receive from time to time, from the creditor or a third party, cash, goods and services to an amount or value such that, taking into account payments made by or to the credit of the debtor, the credit limit (if any) is not at any time exceeded. Thus, running account credit is revolving credit, where the debtor can keep taking credit when he or she wants it subject to a credit limit. An example of this would be a credit card facility, e.g. Visa or MasterCard.

The second type is fixed-sum credit, defined in s. 10(b) as any other facility under a personal credit agreement whereby the debtor is enabled to receive credit. An example here would be a bank loan. The Act then covers hire purchase agreements (s. 189), which are agreements under which goods are bailed or hired in return for periodical payments by the person to whom they are bailed or hired and where the property in the goods will pass to that person if the terms of the agreement are complied with and one or more of the following occurs:

- the exercise of an option to purchase by that person
- the doing of any other specified act by any party to the agreement
- the happening of any other specified event.

In simple terms, a hire purchase agreement is a contract of hire which gives the hirer the option to purchase the goods. The hirer does not own the goods until the option is exercised.

In addition to hire purchase agreements, also within the scope of the Act are conditional sale agreements for the sale of goods or land, in respect of which the price is payable by instalments and the property (i.e. ownership) remains with the seller until any conditions set out in the contract are fulfilled, and credit sale agreements, where the property (ownership) passes to the buyer when the sale is effected.

Unrestricted use credit is where the money is paid to the debtor direct and the debtor is left free to use the money as he or she wishes. Restricted use credit is where the money is paid direct to a third party (usually the seller), e.g. via Barclaycard.

Debtor-creditor supplier agreements relate to the situation where there is a business connection between creditor and supplier – i.e. a pre-existing arrangement – or where the creditor and the supplier are the same person. Section 55 and ss. 60–65 deal with formalities of the contract, their aim being that the debtor be made fully aware of the nature and the cost of the transaction and his or her rights and liabilities under it. The Act requires that certain information must be disclosed to the debtor before the contract is made. This includes total charge for credit, and the annual rate of the total charge for credit which the debtor will have to pay expressed as a percentage. All regulated agreements must comply with the formality procedures and must contain:

- names and addresses of the parties to the agreement
- amount of payments due and to whom payable
- total charge for credit
- annual rate of charge expressed as a percentage
- debtor's right to pay off early
- all the terms of the agreement
- the debtor's right to cancel (if applicable).

If a consumer credit agreement is drawn up off business premises, then it is a cancellable agreement designed to counteract high-pressure doorstep salesmen. If an agreement is cancellable, the debtor is entitled to a cooling-off period, i.e. to the close of the fifth day following the date the second copy of the agreement is received. If the debtor then cancels in writing, the agreement and any linked transaction is cancelled. Any sums paid are recoverable, and the debtor has a lien on any goods in his or her possession until repayment is made.

5.5.6 Codes of practice

Codes of practice do not in themselves have the force of law. They can, however, be of great importance to businesses. In the first place, they can help to raise the standards of an industry by imposing a discipline on signatories to a code not to indulge in dubious marketing practices, which – although legal – act against the long-term interests of the industry and its customers. Second, voluntary codes of practice can offer a cheaper and quicker means of resolving grievances between the two parties compared with more formal legal channels. For example, the holiday industry has its own arbitration facilities which avoid the cost of taking many cases through to the courts. Third, business organizations are often happy to accept restrictions imposed by codes of practice as these are seen as preferable to restrictions being imposed by laws. The tobacco industry in the UK for a long time avoided statutory controls on cigarette advertising because of the existence of its voluntary code which imposed restrictions on tobacco advertising.

The post of Director General of the Office of Fair Trading is instrumental in encouraging trade associations to adopt codes of practice. An example of a voluntary code is provided by the Vehicle Builders and Repair Association, which, among other items, requires members to: give clear estimates of prices; inform customers as soon as possible if additional costs are likely to be incurred; complete work in a timely manner. In the event of a dispute between a customer and a member of the Association, a conciliation service is available which reduces the need to resort to legal remedies. However, in April 2005, the National Consumer Council accused the motor industry of failing to adequately regulate itself, by providing 'shoddy services and rip-off charges'. The council pledged to submit a 'super complaint' to the Office of Fair Trading (OFT), which would force the OFT to investigate its allegations, unless the industry took prompt remedial action. This raised the possibility of a licensing system for car repairers, something which the industry had resisted so far and realized would be more onerous than a voluntary code of conduct.

Useful leaflets published by the Office of Fair Trading giving information regarding codes of practice can be obtained from local Consumer Advice Bureaux.

5.5.7 Controls on advertising

There are a number of laws that influence the content of advertisements in Britain. For example, the Trade Descriptions Act makes false statements in an advertisement an offence, while the Consumer Credit Act lays down quite precise rules about the way in which credit can be advertised. However, the content of advertisements is influenced just as much by voluntary codes as by legislation.

In the UK, the codes for advertising are the responsibility of the advertising industry through two Committees of Advertising Practice: CAP (Broadcast) and CAP (Non-broadcast). CAP (Broadcast) is responsible for the TV and radio advertising codes and CAP (Non-broadcast) is responsible for non-broadcast advertisements, sales promotions and direct marketing. Both are administered by the Advertising Standards Authority (ASA). The Office of Communications (Ofcom) is the statutory regulator for broadcast advertising in the UK and has delegated its powers to the ASA, which deals with all complaints about such advertising (until 2004, the television advertising code was administered by the Independent Television Commission).

The ASA codes are subscribed to by most organizations involved in advertising, including the Advertising Association, the Institute of Practitioners in Advertising and the associations representing publishers of newspapers and magazines, the outdoor advertising industry and direct marketing.

The Code of Advertising Practice (Non-broadcast) requires that all advertisements appearing in members' publications should be legal, honest, decent and truthful. Thus, an advertisement by a building society offering 'free' weekend breaks was deemed to have broken the code by not stating in the advertisement that a compulsory charge was made for meals during the weekend. An advert by the fashion retailer H & M Hennes depicting a reclining female model dressed in underwear with the caption 'Last time we ran an ad for Swedish lingerie 78 women complained – no men' was held to be offensive, inaccurate and sexist.

Although the main role of the ASA is advisory, it does have a number of sanctions available against individual advertisers that break the code, ultimately leading to the ASA requesting its media members to refuse to publish the advertisements of an offending company. More often, the ASA relies on publicizing its rulings to shame advertisers into responding.

The advertising codes are continually evolving to meet the changing attitudes and expectations of the public. Thus, restrictions on alcohol advertising have been tightened up, for example by insisting that young actors are not portrayed in advertisements and by not showing them on television when children are likely to be watching. On the other hand, advertising restrictions for some products have been relaxed in response to changing public attitudes. Television adverts for condoms have moved from being completely banned to being allowed, but only in very abstract form, to the present situation where the product itself can be mentioned using actors in life-like situations.

Numerous other forms of voluntary controls exist. As mentioned previously, many trade associations have codes which impose restrictions on how they can advertise. Solicitors, for example, were previously not allowed to advertise at all, but now can do so within limits defined by the Law Society.

The Control of Misleading Advertisements Regulations 1988 (as amended) provides the legislative back-up to the self-regulatory system in respect of advertisements which mislead.

The Regulations require the Office of Fair Trading (OFT) to investigate complaints, and empower the OFT to seek, if necessary, an injunction from the courts against publication of an advertisement. More usually it would initially seek assurances from an advertiser to modify or not repeat an offending advertisement. Before investigating, the OFT can require that other means of dealing with a complaint, such as the ASA system mentioned above, have been fully explored. Action by the OFT therefore usually results only from a referral from the Advertising Standards Authority where the self-regulatory system has not had the required impact.

In general, the system of voluntary regulation of advertising has worked well in the UK. For advertisers, voluntary codes can allow more flexibility and opportunities to have an input to the code. For the public, a code can be updated in a less bureaucratic manner than may be necessary with new legislation or statutory regulations. However, the question remains as to how much responsibility for the social and cultural content of advertising should be given to industry-led voluntary bodies rather than being decided by government. Do voluntary codes unduly reflect the narrow financial interests of advertisers rather than the broader interests of the public at large? Doubtless, advertisers realize that if they do not develop a code which is socially acceptable, the task will be taken away from them and carried out by government in a process where they will have less influence.

5.6 STATUTORY LEGISLATION ON EMPLOYMENT

Employment law is essentially based on the principles of law previously discussed. The relationship between an employer and its employees is governed by the law of contract, while the employer owes a duty of care to its employees and can be sued for negligence where this duty of care is broken. Employers are vicariously liable for the actions of their employees, so if an employee is negligent and harms a member of the public during the course of their employment, the injured party has a claim against the employer as well as the employee who was the immediate cause of the injury.

The common law principles of contract and negligence have for a long time been supplemented with statutory intervention. Society has recognized that a contract of employment is quite different from a contract to buy consumer goods, because the personal investment of the employee in their job can be very considerable. Losing a job without good cause can have a much more profound effect than suffering loss as a result of losing money on a purchase of goods. Governments have recognized that individuals should have a proprietary interest in their jobs and have therefore passed legislation to protect employees against the actions of unscrupulous employers who abuse their dominant power over employees. Legislation has also recognized that employment practices can have a much wider effect on society through organizations' recruitment policies.

In this section we consider some of the areas in which statutory intervention has affected the environment in which organizations recruit, reward and dismiss employees. The information here cannot hope to go into any depth on particular legislative requirements, as legislation is complex, detailed and continually changing. There is also considerable difference between countries in terms of legislation that affects employment. The following brief summary can only hope to identify the main issues of concern covered by legislation, in England specifically. This chapter should also be read in conjunction with Chapter 8 on the internal environment.

In that chapter we look in general terms at issues such as the need for flexibility in the workforce. This chapter identifies particular legal opportunities and constraints, which help to define an organization's internal environment.

5.6.1 When does an employment contract occur?

It is not always obvious whether a contract of employment exists between an organization and individuals providing services for it. Many individuals working for organizations in fact provide their services as self-employed subcontractors, rather than as employees. The distinction between the two is important, because a self-employed contractor does not benefit from the legislation which only protects employees. There can be many advantages in classifying an individual as self-employed rather than as an employee. For the self-employed, tax advantages result from being able to claim as legitimate, business expense items that in many circumstances are denied to the employee. The method of assessing National Insurance and income tax liability in arrears can favour a self-employed subcontractor. For the employer, designation as self-employed could relieve the employer of some duties that are imposed in respect of employees but not subcontractors, such as entitlement to sick pay, notice periods and maternity leave.

There was a great trend towards self-employment during the 1990s, encouraged by the trend towards outsourcing of many non-core functions by businesses (see Chapter 8). Not surprisingly, the UK government has sought to recoup potentially lost tax revenue and to protect unwitting self-employed individuals, by examining closely the terms on which an individual is engaged. The courts have decided the matter on the basis of, among other things, the degree of control that the organization buying a person's services has over the person providing them, the level of integration between the individual and the organization, and who bears the business risk. If the organization is able to specify the manner in which a task is to be carried out, then an employment relationship generally exists. If, however, the required end result is specified but the manner in which it is achieved is left up to the individual, then a contract for services will exist – in other words, self-employment. There is still ambiguity in the distinction between employment and self-employment, which has, for example, resulted in numerous appeals by individuals against classification decisions made by the Inland Revenue.

5.6.2 Flexibility of contract

Organizations are increasingly seeking a more flexible workforce to help them respond more rapidly to changes in their external environment. In Chapter 8 we see some of the benefits to an organization of developing flexible employment practices.

Short-term employment contracts are becoming increasingly significant in a number of European countries, partly due to the existence of labour market regulations that make it difficult for employers to recruit and dismiss permanent staff. Within Europe, there has been a tendency for national legislation to reflect EU directives by imposing additional burdens on employers of full-time, permanent employees. This can affect the ease with which staff can be laid off or dismissed should demand fall – for example, in Germany, the Dismissals Protection Law (*Kundigungsschutzgesetz*) has given considerable protection to salaried staff who have been in their job for more than six months, allowing dismissal only for a 'socially justified' reason.

The move towards short-term contracts is a Europe-wide phenomenon. In 2000, it was estimated that a third of the Spanish workforce was employed on short-term contracts that last up to three years compared with less than 16 per cent 15 years previously, while in France the proportion of short-term contracts climbed from 6.7 per cent in 1985 to more than 13 per cent by 2000 (see Figure 5.2). But even in European countries with less restrictive employment laws, such as the Netherlands, short-term contracts have become more popular. The spread of short-term contracts is most apparent among young workers employed in insecure and highly mobile areas of the labour market such as the retail, distribution, communication and information technology sectors.

The European Union and most member state governments have been keen to ensure that workers on short-term contracts enjoy similar legal rights as those in full-time, permanent employment. In the UK, the Employment Relations Act 1999 requires the trade and industry secretary to make regulations to ensure that part-time workers are treated no less favourably than full-time workers. These regulations include provisions to implement the EU-level social partners' agreement and subsequent Council Directive on part-time work (97/81/EC). In the UK a worker must generally be employed for at least 12 months on a contract to secure such rights.

Despite imposing additional burdens, many European governments have encouraged the greater use of short-term contracts as a way of improving the flexibility of their national economies, for example through changes in welfare benefits which do not penalize short-term working.

5.6.3 Terms of the contract of employment

Under the Employment Rights Act 1996 it is required that an employer must issue its employees within 13 weeks of the date they start work the written terms and conditions of their employment in detail. The details can, however, be placed on a staff noticeboard at a

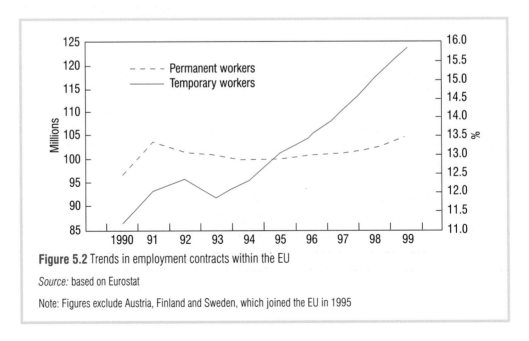

Figure 5.2 Trends in employment contracts within the EU

Source: based on Eurostat

Note: Figures exclude Austria, Finland and Sweden, which joined the EU in 1995 point where every member of the workforce concerned can read them. In the statement there should be references to the following:

1 the job title
2 which individuals or groups the document is addressed to
3 the starting date of the employment
4 the scale of wages and the calculations used to work this out
5 the periods in which wages are paid
6 hours of work and the terms and conditions
7 holidays and holiday pay
8 sickness and sickness pay
9 pensions and pension schemes
10 how much notice the employee must give upon leaving and how much notice the company has to give the employee when terminating employment
11 rules for discipline procedures
12 to whom any grievances are to be made, and procedures.

The terms of contract cannot be altered until both parties have discussed and agreed the new conditions.

5.6.4 Minimum acceptable contract terms

Legislators have recognized that employee and employer possess unequal bargaining power in the process of forming a contract of employment. Legislation therefore protects the interests of the weaker party – generally the employee – against the use of their power by unscrupulous employers. The following are examples of statutory intervention that protect employees' rights. Some would argue that intervention of this type has the effect of increasing the costs of businesses, thereby reducing their competitive advantage. However, as we see in Chapter 8, a lot of statutory intervention is merely spreading current best practice to all employees.

Health and safety legislation

There is a wide range of regulations governing employers' duty to provide a safe working environment. Most health and safety legislation is based on the Health and Safety at Work Act 1974 which provides a general duty to provide a safe working environment. The Act makes provision for specific regulations to be issued by government ministers and these detailed regulations can have significant impacts on businesses. The following are some recent examples of regulations:

■ the Control of Major Accident Hazards Regulations 1999
■ the Control of Substances Hazardous to Health Regulations 1999
■ the Lifts Regulations 1997
■ the Railway Safety (Miscellaneous Provisions) Regulations 1997.

The Health and Safety Executive oversees enforcement of these regulations.

Minimum wage legislation

The national minimum wage came into force in the UK in 1999, implementing an earlier EU directive. In 2005, this rate was set at £5.05 per hour (rising to £5.35 in October 2006) for workers aged 22 and over, and £4.10, rising to £4.25 for 18 to 21 year olds. There is provision for annual revision. Most adult workers in the UK must be paid at least the national minimum wage. This includes part-time workers, temporary or short-term workers, homeworkers, agency workers and casual labourers. An employee cannot be forced by an employer to accept a wage that is below the minimum wage and can claim compensation if they are sacked or victimized because they sought to enforce their right to the national minimum wage.

THINKING AROUND THE SUBJECT:
TAKE RISKS AND GO TO JAIL?

One of the defining characteristics of a limited liability company (discussed in Chapter 6), is the separation of the company from its owners. So, in general, if the company breaks the law, whether civil law or criminal, the directors of the company can protect themselves behind a 'veil of incorporation'. Furthermore, many of the punishments available under the criminal law would at first sight seem to be inappropriate to business organizations. How, for example, can an organization be sent to prison for a serious breach of the criminal law? The question has arisen following a number of high-profile cases where a business has caused harm to the general public, but the directors of the company responsible for the wrongdoing have escaped relatively lightly. The *Herald of Free Enterprise* tragedy in 1987, and the Ladbroke Grove train accident of 1999 raised issues about senior management's culpability in these two serious transport accidents. In the first case, questions were raised about unreasonable pressures that management had put on staff loading vehicles on to ferries, one of which subsequently capsized. In the second case, questions were raised about the suitability of staff training programmes, which management, and ultimately the board of directors, was responsible for. Relatives of victims who died in both of these incidents claimed that they were not accidents at all, but the combination of negligent actions by senior management. In both cases, initial blame was focused on relatively lowly paid, junior staff who made a mistake. But was senior management responsible for expecting too much of its junior staff? In both these cases, attempts were made to bring charges of manslaughter against the directors of the companies involved, but due to the complexity of the cases, and the diffuse lines of responsibility within their organizations, there was insufficient evidence to successfully bring a case. According to the Centre for Corporate Accountability, only 11 directors were successfully prosecuted for manslaughter in the 30 years to 2005. Most of these have been small company directors; for example, in January 2005, the managing director of a building contractor was sentenced to 16 months in jail after a roofing worker died after falling through a poorly protected roof light. Campaigners for a law on corporate manslaughter have argued that it is much more difficult to pin down responsibility in a large organization, but this is no reason for not trying to make senior staff personally accountable for their actions. Would directors of a company be so keen to pursue potentially dangerous efficiency-gaining strategies if they thought there was a risk that they might personally end up in prison? Or would a corporate manslaughter law stifle initiatives by directors, fearful that, if anything went wrong, there could be very serious consequences for them personally?

Working hours

The EU's Working Time Directive of 1993 was implemented in the UK by the Working Time Regulations of 2000. By these regulations, workers cannot be forced to work for more than 48 hours a week on average. However, there are various exclusions to this time and workers can cancel any opt-out agreement whenever they want, although they must give their employer at least seven days' notice, or longer (up to three months) if this has been agreed.

5.6.5 Discrimination at work

Companies sometimes find themselves being required to recruit their second choice of staff in order to comply with legislation against racial and sexual discrimination. For example, one UK airline found through its research that the majority of its customers preferred its cabin crew to be female and subsequently recruited predominantly female staff for this role. The airline was fined for unlawful discrimination against men, even though it had been innovative in appointing women to the traditionally male job of pilot. Legislation seeks to protect disadvantaged groups that may be discriminated against simply out of employers' ignorance.

The Sex Discrimination Act 1975 (SDA) prohibits discrimination against women, and men, on the grounds of sex or of being married. The SDA makes the distinction between the concepts of direct and indirect discrimination. Direct sex discrimination occurs when an employee is treated less favourably because of her, or his, sex. Indirect discrimination occurs when a requirement or condition – which may seem 'neutral' in terms of how it impacts upon men and women – in fact has an adverse effect on women, or men, in general (for example, specifying a dress code which is more onerous on women than men). The Equal Pay Act 1970 requires that a woman is entitled to the same pay (and other contractual conditions) as a man working for the same employer, provided they are doing similar work or work of equal value.

The legislation dealing with race discrimination derives from the Race Relations Act 1976 (RRA). By this Act, a person is guilty of race discrimination if 'on racial grounds he treats [a] person less favourably than he treats or would treat other persons'. Like the SDA, the RRA makes it illegal to discriminate directly or indirectly against a person on racial grounds. Research and official statistics demonstrate that people from ethnic minorities continue to experience severe discrimination in the field of employment. A report by the Joseph Rowntree Foundation found particularly high levels of unemployment among Africans, Pakistanis and Bangladeshis (Berthoud 2005).

5.6.6 Termination of contract

The proprietary interest of employees in their jobs is recognized by legislation which restricts the ability of an employer to terminate an employee's contract of employment.

Termination may come about because an individual's position is no longer required and the individual is declared redundant. The Employment Rights Act 1996 defines the circumstances in which redundancy takes effect and a sliding scale of payments which an employee is entitled to if they are made redundant by their employer.

In circumstances other than redundancy, employers may not terminate a contract in a way which constitutes unfair dismissal. Under the Employment Relations Act 1999, employees are not entitled to claim unfair dismissal until they have accumulated one year's service. Dismissal may be considered fair where an employee has not acted in good faith and/or has failed to observe previous warnings about poor conduct. Employment tribunals judge whether a dismissal is fair or not, and judgment frequently centres on procedural issues. A finding of unfair dismissal may lead to an order for compensation and a request for reinstatement.

5.6.7 Rights to workers' representation

The political environment and the dominant political ideology have had a very close bearing on legislation regulating the activities of trades unions. Traditionally, Labour governments have sought to advance the cause of organized labour, while Conservative governments have taken a more individualist approach to relationships between employers and employees. The incoming Conservative government of 1979 dismantled much of the legislation which had been passed by the previous Labour government to give greater rights for trades unions and greater duties for employers. The incoming Labour government of 1997 has gone some way to restoring trades union rights. This government inherited the 1993 Trade Union Reform and Employment Rights Act and the Trade Union and Labour Relations (Consolidation) Act 1992. The essence of this legislation was to make trades unions more accountable to their members and to reduce the risks to employers of loss resulting from politically inspired disputes. The following were key features covered by the legislation:

- individuals affected by industrial action are able to seek an injunction to prevent unlawful industrial action taking place
- seven days' notice must be given by trades unions of ballots and of industrial action
- individuals have a right to challenge collective agreements
- employers may refuse to recognize a trade union in specified circumstances
- all industrial action ballots must be postal and subject to independent scrutiny.

The Employment Relations Act 1999 amends a number of provisions of the previous legislation. For trades unions, the key element of the Act is a statutory procedure through which independent unions are able to seek recognition for collective bargaining from employers with more than 20 employees. The Act amends previous legislation to enable employees dismissed for taking part in lawfully organized official industrial action to take cases of unfair dismissal to an employment tribunal where the dismissal occurs within eight weeks of the start of the action.

The Transnational Information and Consultation of Employees Regulations 1999 came into force in the UK in January 2000, implementing the EU Directive on European Works Councils. The Directive covers undertakings which have more than 1000 employees in member states and more than 150 employees in each of two member states and sets out procedures for giving employees a statutory right to be consulted about a range of activities affecting the organization. From April 2005, the legislation has given employees a legal right to know about, and be consulted on, an organization's plans that affect them. This can cover anything from the economic health of the business to decisions likely to cause redundancies or changes in how work is organized. This requirement applies initially only to larger organizations – those with 50 or more employees. However, from 2007, the threshold will be lowered to 100 employees and, in 2008, lowered again to 50 or more employees.

5.7 THE HUMAN RIGHTS ACT

The Human Rights Act came into force in the UK in 2000 and has presented a number of new legal challenges for business organizations. The Act incorporates the European Convention on Human Rights into domestic law. The Convention is a 50-year-old code of basic rights drawn up in the aftermath of the Second World War and covers such rights as that to a family life, to privacy and a fair trial. Prior to 2000, although UK courts could take note of the rights identified by the Convention, they could not be directly enforced. So aggrieved parties often had to take cases to the European Court of Human Rights for a remedy – a lengthy and costly process.

The Act incorporates only part of the European Convention and does not incorporate any of the procedural rights of the Convention. However, it does include all of the following substantive rights:

- to life
- to freedom from torture or inhuman or degrading punishment
- to freedom from slavery, servitude, enforced or compulsory labour
- to liberty and security of the person
- to a fair trial
- to respect for private and family life
- to freedom of thought, conscience and religion
- to freedom of expression
- to freedom of assembly and association
- to marry and found a family
- to education in conformity with parents' religious and philosophical convictions
- to freedom from unfair discrimination in the enjoyment of these rights.

Many of the wider rights enshrined in the Human Rights Act are already protected by the UK's domestic legislation, e.g. Sex Discrimination Act 1975. From 2000, courts in the UK have been able to issue injunctions to prevent violations of rights, award damages and quash unlawful decisions. Individuals are now able to use the Act to defend themselves in criminal proceedings. The Act does not make Convention rights directly enforceable in proceedings against a private litigant, nor against a 'quasi-public' body unless that body is acting in a public capacity. However, private individuals and companies have to take the Convention into account because the courts will be obliged to interpret the law so as to conform to it wherever possible.

In the early days of the Act a number of examples illustrated its possible impact on business organizations, including challenges about the legitimacy of local authority planning procedures and privacy of personal information. Despite early fears that the Human Rights Act would add significantly to business organizations' costs, it would appear that more recent cases have taken a balanced view on what is reasonable and in the public interest.

5.8 PROTECTION OF A COMPANY'S INTANGIBLE PROPERTY RIGHTS

The value of a business enterprise can be measured not only by the value of its physical assets such as land and building: increasingly, the value of a business reflects its investment in new product development and strong brand images. To protect a company from imitators reaping the benefits of this investment but bearing none of its cost, a number of legal protections are available. The most commonly used methods are patents and trade marks, which are described below. Intellectual property can also be protected through copyright (for example, the unauthorized copying and sale of DVD films is a breach of copyright).

5.8.1 Patents

A patent is a right given to an inventor which allows him or her exclusively to reap the benefits from the invention over a specified period. To obtain a patent, application must be made to the Patent Office in accordance with the procedure set out in the Patents Act 1977. To qualify for a patent, the invention must have certain characteristics laid down – it must be covered by the Act, it must be novel and it must include an inventive step.

Nowhere does the Act define what is patentable, but it does specify what is not, under s. 1:

- s. 1(2)(a) discoveries, scientific theories or mathematical methods
- s. 1(2)(b) literacy, dramatic, musical or artistic works or any other aesthetic creations (obviously, works such as these are protected by copyright)
- s. 1(2)(c) schemes, rules or methods for performing a mental act, playing a game, doing business; or a program for a computer
- s. 1(2)(d) the presentation of information.

Obviously, to qualify for a patent the invention must be novel in that it does not form part of the state of the art at the priority date (i.e. the date of filing for a patent, not the date of invention).

State of the art (s. 2(2)) comprises all matter that has at any time before that date been made available to the public anywhere in the world by written or oral description, by use or in any other way.

An inventive step (s. 3) is apparent if it is not obvious to a person skilled in the art having regard to the prior art other than co-pending patent applications which are deemed to be prior art for the purpose of testing for novelty only.

The effect of the Patents Act 1977 has been only to bring UK patent law more into line with that of the EU in accordance with the provisions of the European Patent Convention. As a result of the implementation of the Convention, there are almost uniform criteria in the establishment of a patent in Austria, Belgium, Switzerland, Germany, France, the United Kingdom, Italy, Liechtenstein, Luxembourg, the Netherlands and Sweden. A European Patent Office has been set up in Munich which provides a cheaper method to obtain a patent in three or more countries, but it should be noted that, if the patent fails as a result of an application to the European Patent Office, the rejection applies to all member states unless there is contrary domestic legislation which covers this part.

5.8.2 Trade marks

The Trade Marks Act 1994, which replaced the 1938 Act, implemented the Trade Marks Harmonization Directive No. 89/104/EEC, which provides protection for trade marks (they are also protected under the common law of passing off). A trade mark is defined as any sign capable of being represented graphically which is capable of distinguishing goods or services of one undertaking from those of other undertakings (s. 1(1)).

Any trade mark satisfying these criteria is registerable unless prohibited by s. 3(1) which prevents registration if:
(a) the signs do not satisfy the requirements of s. 1(1)
(b) trade marks are devoid of any distinctive character
(c) trade marks consist exclusively of signs or indications which may serve, in trade, to designate the kind, quality, quantity, intended purpose, value, geographical origin, the time of production of the goods or of rendering of services, or other characteristics of goods or services
(d) trade marks consist exclusively of signs or indications which have become customary in the current language or in the bona fide and established practices in the trade.

However, a trade mark shall not be refused registration by virtue of paragraph (b), (c) or (d) above if before the date of application for registration it has in fact acquired a distinctive character as a result of the use made of it.
A sign shall not be registered as a trade mark if it consists exclusively of (s. 3(2)):
(a) the shape which results from the nature of the goods themselves
(b) the shape of goods which is necessary to obtain a technical result
(c) the shape which gives substantial value to the goods.

In addition, a trade mark shall not be registered if:
(a) it is contrary to public policy or accepted principles of morality (s. 3(3))
(b) it is of such a nature as to deceive the public (for instance as to the nature, quality or geographical origin of the goods or service)(s. 3(3))
(c) its use is prohibited in the UK by any enactment or rule of law (s. 3(4))
(d) it is defined as a specially protected emblem (s. 3(5))
(e) an application to register is made in bad faith (s. 3(6)).

If a trade mark is infringed in any way, a successful plaintiff will be entitled to an injunction and to damages.

5.8.3 Law and the Internet

The development of the Internet does not change the basic principles of law, but the law has on occasions become ambiguous in the light of technological developments.
Unlawful copying of material downloaded from the Internet (images, documents and particularly music) has focused attention on issues of ownership of intellectual property. Section 17 Copyright, Designs and Patents Act 1988 provides that:

(2) Copying in relation to a literary, dramatic, musical or artistic work means reproducing the work in any material form. This includes storing the work in any medium by electronic means.

Copying, therefore, includes downloading files from the Internet or copying text into or attaching it to an email. Given the ability to copy material virtually instantaneously to potentially huge numbers, the Internet presents a serious risk of copyright infringement liability.

Just what constitutes 'public domain' information, and can therefore lawfully be copied, has been raised in a number of cases.

In addition to copyright issues, the international nature of communications on the Internet makes it essential not to overlook questions such as where is the contract concluded, when is it concluded, what law governs it and where will any subsequent dispute be decided? Unexpected additional obligations may arise as a result of statements made during contract negotiations, for example by a salesperson to a customer. Even where the final written contract expressly excludes such representations, courts may be prepared to find that a collateral contract came into existence through the exchange of email messages.

EU countries have begun to introduce into national legislation a 1999 EU directive on electronic signatures. The directive comprises two major advances: the legal recognition of electronic signatures, which provide reliable identification of the parties engaged in an online transaction; and encryption, which enables companies to electronically protect documents liable to be intercepted during transmission, by wire or over the air. These measures will help companies doing business over the Internet to verify with accuracy the identity of their contracting partners and to improve online security standards for international business.

5.9 THE LAW AND PRODUCTION PROCESSES

As economies develop, there is a tendency for societies to raise their expectations about firms' behaviour, particularly where they are responsible for significant external costs (see Chapter 9). The result has been increasing levels of legislation that constrain the activities of firms in meeting buyers' needs. Some of the more important constraints that affect business decisions are described below.

■ Pollution of the natural environment is an external cost which governments seek to limit through legislation such as the Environmental Protection Act 1995, the Environment Act 1990 and the Water Resources Act 1991. Examples of impacts on firms include requirements for additional noise insulation and investment in equipment to purify discharges into watercourses and the atmosphere. These have often added to a firm's total production costs, thereby putting it at a competitive disadvantage, or made plans to increase production capacity uneconomic when faced with competition from companies in countries that have less demanding requirements for environmental protection.

■ The rights of employees to enjoy safe working conditions have become increasingly enshrined in law as a country develops. In the United Kingdom, it was noted earlier in this chapter that the Health and Safety at Work Act 1974 provides for large fines and, in extreme cases, imprisonment of company directors for failing to provide a safe working environment. Definitions of what constitutes an acceptable level of risk for employees to face change over time. As well as obvious serious physical injury, the courts in England now recognize a responsibility of firms to protect their employees against more subtle dangers such as repetitive strain injury. There has also been debate in cases brought before courts as to whether a firm should be responsible for mental illness caused by excessive stress in a job, and the courts have held that companies should be liable if the employee has suffered stress in the past which the company was aware of.

■ In many cases it is not sufficient to rely on law to protect customers from faulty outcomes of a firm's production. It is also necessary to legislate in respect of the quality of the *processes* of production. This is important where buyers are unable to fully evaluate a product without a guarantee that the method of producing it has been in accordance with acceptable criteria. An example of this is the Food Safety Act 1990 which imposes requirements on all firms that manufacture or handle food products to ensure that they cannot become contaminated (e.g. by being kept at too high a temperature during transport). Many small to medium-sized food manufacturers have closed down, claiming that they cannot justify the cost of upgrading premises. Laws governing production processes are also important in the case of intangible services where customers may have little opportunity for evaluating the credentials of one service against another. For example, to protect the public against unethical behaviour by unscrupulous sales personnel, the Financial Services Act 1986 lays down procedures for regulating business practices within the sector.

The traditional view of legislation on production is that the mounting weight of legislation puts domestic firms at a cost disadvantage to those operating in relatively unregulated environments overseas. Critics of over-regulation point to Britain and the United States as two economies that have priced themselves out of many international markets.

Against this, it is argued that as the economy of a country develops, economic gains should be enjoyed by all stakeholders of business, including employees and the local communities in which a business operates. There are also many persuasive arguments why increasing regulation of production processes may not be incompatible with greater business prosperity.

■ Attempts to deregulate conditions of employment may allow firms to be more flexible in their production methods and thereby reduce their costs. However, there is a suggestion that a casualized workforce becomes increasingly reluctant to make major purchases, thereby reducing the level of activity in the domestic economy. In the United Kingdom, moves during the 1990s to free employers of many of their responsibilities to employees resulted in a large number of casual workers who were reluctant or unable to buy houses, resulting in a knock-on effect on supplies of home-related goods and services.

■ There is similarly much evidence that a healthy and safe working environment is likely to be associated with high levels of commitment by employees and a high standard of output quality. The law should represent no more than a codification of good practice by firms.

■ Environmental protection and cost reduction may not be mutually incompatible, as Chapter 9 demonstrates.

5.10 LEGISLATION TO PROTECT THE COMPETITIVENESS OF MARKETS

Finally, there are presumed benefits of having markets which are competitive and free of harmful monopolistic or collusive tendencies. Because of this, the law of most developed countries has been used to try to remove market imperfections where these are deemed to be against the public interest. We will discuss in Chapter 10 how the common law of England has developed the principle of restraint of trade, through which anti-competitive practices have been curbed.

As the economy has become more complex, common law has proved inadequate on its own to preserve the competitiveness of markets. Common law has therefore been supplemented by statutory legislation. One outcome of statutory intervention has been the creation of a regulatory infrastructure, which in the United Kingdom includes the Office of Fair Trading, the

Competition Commission and regulatory bodies to control specific industries. However, much of the current regulatory framework in the UK is based on the requirements of Articles 85 and 86 of the Treaty of Rome.

In the UK, the 1998 Competition Act and the Enterprise Act 2002 reformed and strengthened competition law by prohibiting anti-competitive behaviour. The 1998 Act introduced two basic prohibitions: a prohibition of anti-competitive agreements, based closely on Article 85 of the EC Treaty; and a prohibition of abuse of a dominant position in a market, based closely on Article 86 of the EC Treaty. The Act prohibits agreements which have the aim or effect of preventing, restricting or distorting competition in the UK. Since anti-competitive behaviour between companies may occur without a clearly defined agreement, the prohibition covers not only agreements by associations of companies, but also covert practices.

Further discussion of the application of legislation concerning anti-competitive practices, and the task of defining the public interest, may be found in Chapter 10.

Further discussion of the application of legislation concerning anti-competitive practices, and the task of defining the public interest, may be found in Chapter 10.

CASE STUDY

LEGISLATION STRENGTHENED IN A BID TO END 'NIGHTMARE' HOLIDAYS

Tour operators have probably felt more keenly than most businesses the effects of new legislation to protect consumers. Because holidays are essentially intangible, it is very difficult for a potential customer to check out claims made by tour operators' advertising until their holiday is under way, when it may be too late to do anything to prevent a ruined holiday. Traditional attitudes of 'let the buyer beware' can be of little use to holidaymakers who have little tangible evidence on which to base their decision when they book a holiday.

Consumers have traditionally had very little comeback against tour operators that fail to provide a holiday which is in line with the expectations held out in their brochure. Their brochures have frequently been accused of misleading customers, for example by showing pictures of hotels which conveniently omit the adjacent airport runway or sewerage works. The freedom of tour operators to produce fanciful brochures was limited by the Consumer Protection Act 1987. Part III of the Act holds that any person, who, in the course of a business of his, gives (by any means whatsoever) to any consumers an indication which is misleading as to the price at which any goods, services, accommodation or facilities are available shall be guilty of an offence. These provisions of the Act forced tour operators to end such practices as promoting very low-priced holidays which in reality were never available when customers enquired about them – only higher-priced holidays were offered. Supplements for additional items such as regional airport departures could no longer be hidden away in small print.

Tour operators see themselves as arrangers of holidays who buy in services from hotels, airlines and bus companies, among others, over whom they have no effective management control. It was therefore quite usual for tour operators to include in their booking conditions an exclusion clause absolving themselves of any liability arising from the faults of their subcontractors. If a customer was injured by a faulty lift in a Spanish hotel, a tour operator would deny any responsibility for the injury and could only advise the holidaymaker to sue the Spanish hotel themselves. For some time, the courts in England recognized that it would be unreasonable to expect UK tour operators to be liable for actions which were effectively beyond their management control. Anyone who had felt unfairly treated by a tour operator had to take the offending company to court personally, often at great expense and inconvenience to themselves.

EU legislation has strengthened the position of consumers. EU Directive 90/314/EEC is designed to protect consumers who contract package travel in the EU. It covers the sale of a pre-arranged combination of transport, accommodation, and other tourist services ancillary to transport or accommodation and accounting for a significant proportion of the package. Consumers will be covered only where at least two of these elements are sold or offered for sale at an inclusive price and the service covers a period of more than 24 hours or includes overnight accommodation.

The Directive contains rules concerning the liability of package organizers and retailers, which must accept responsibility for the performance of the services offered. There are some exceptions, for example cases of 'force majeure' or similar circumstances, which could neither be foreseen nor overcome. However, even in these cases the organizer must use its best endeavours to help consumers.

The Directive also prescribes rules on the information that must be given to consumers. It contains specific requirements with regard to the content of brochures, where these are issued. For example, any brochure made available to consumers must indicate clearly and accurately the price, destination, itinerary and the means of transport used, type of accommodation, meal plan, passport and visa requirements, health formalities, timetable for payment and the deadline for informing consumers in the event of cancellation.

The EU directive (initially implemented in England by the Unfair Terms in Consumer Contracts Regulations 1994) sought to redress the balance by providing greater protection for customers of tour operators. The directive makes all tour operators liable for the actions of their subcontractors. In cases which have been brought before courts in England, tour operators have been held liable for illness caused by food poisoning at a hotel; injury caused by uneven tiles at a swimming pool; and loss of enjoyment caused by noisy building work. To emphasize the effects of the directive, one British tour operator was ordered to compensate a holidaymaker in respect of claims that she had been harassed by a waiter at a hotel which had been contracted by the tour operator.

In the space of less than a decade, the UK tour operating industry has been transformed from relying on exclusion clauses and seeking to govern its dealings with customers through voluntary codes of conduct (especially the code of the Association of British Travel Agents (ABTA)). Many would argue that voluntary regulation had failed to protect consumers in accordance with their rising expectations. Legislation, while it was initially resisted by tour operators, has undoubtedly increased consumers' confidence in buying package holidays and lessened the chances of them buying a holiday from a rogue company, and thereby harming the reputation of the industry as a whole.

1 What factors could explain the increasing amount of legislation which now faces tour operators?

2 Summarize the main consequences of the EU directive referred to above on the marketing of package holidays in the UK.

3 Is there still a role for voluntary codes of conduct in preference to legislation as a means of regulating the relationship between a tour operator and its customers?

SUMMARY

This chapter has noted the increasing effects that legislation is having on businesses. The principal sources of law have been identified. Statute law is becoming increasingly important, with more influence being felt from the EU. Legal processes and the remedies available to a firm's customers have been discussed. Voluntary codes of conduct are often seen as an alternative to law and offer firms lower cost and greater flexibility.

The discussion of business ethics in **Chapter 9** relates closely to the legal environment. To many people, law is essentially a formalization of ethics, with statute law enacted by government (**Chapter 2**). The competition environment (**Chapter 10**) is increasingly influenced by legislation governing anti-competitive practices. We saw in **Chapter 4** that legal protection for innovative new technologies is vital if expenditure on research and development is to be sustained. In addition to the aspects of law discussed in this chapter, legislation affects the status of organizations (**Chapter 6**), for example in the protection that is given to limited liability companies.

Key Terms

Codes of practice	(190)	Duty of care	(177)	Patents	(200)
Common law	(173)	Intellectual property		Statute law	(173)
Contract	(174)	rights	(174)	Tort	(177)
Discrimination	(197)	Misrepresentation	(186)	Trade marks	(200)
Dismissal	(197)	Negligence	(177)		

CHAPTER REVIEW QUESTIONS

1 Briefly identify the main ways in which the legal environment impacts on the activities of the sales and marketing functions of business organizations. (*Based on CIM Marketing Environment Examination*)

2 Giving examples, evaluate the criticism that government legislation primarily impacts on those firms that can least afford to pay for it, mainly the small and the competitively vulnerable.

3 In the light of recent legislation in your own country, assess the extent to which the position of consumers compared to business has improved.

Provide a checklist for your brand manager to ensure that a new product complies with the main consumer legislation in force.
(*Based on CIM Marketing Environment Examination*)

4 Using an appropriate example, evaluate the virtues and drawbacks of using voluntary codes of practice to regulate business activity.
(*Based on CIM Marketing Environment Examination*)

5 Philip, shopping at a large department store, sees a colourful spinning top which he buys for his grandson Harry. While purchasing the toy, he sees a prominent notice in the store which states: 'This store will not be held responsible for any defects in the toys sold.' The box containing the spinning top carries the description 'Ideal for children over 12 months, safe and non-toxic.' (Harry is 15 months old.) Within four weeks the spinning top has split into two parts, each with a jagged edge, and Harry has suffered an illness as a result of sucking the paint. Philip has complained vociferously to the store, which merely pointed to the prominent notice disclaiming liability. Philip has now informed the store that he intends to take legal action against it.

Draft a report to the managing director setting out the legal liability of the store.

6 Zak runs his own painting and decorating business and has been engaged to decorate Rebecca's lounge. While burning off layers of paint from the door with his blowtorch, Zak's attention is diverted by the barking of Camilla's Yorkshire terrier and, as he turns round, the flame catches a cushion on the settee. Within seconds the room is filled with acrid smoke. Both the carpet and settee are damaged beyond repair and the dog, terrified, rushes into the road, where it is run over by a car. Consider Zak's legal liability.

ACTIVITY

Think back to a time when you had a problem with a good or service which didn't meet the agreed specification (e.g. a DVD you ordered didn't have as many tracks as advertised; the seats you ended up with at a rock concert were not as good as the ones you had ordered). Identify the methods of conflict resolution available to you, short of taking legal action. Did the supplier make it easy to resolve the problem? What more could it have done? Is there a voluntary code of conduct or arbitration service that you could have used? Is it easy to use? What factors would encourage or discourage you from taking legal action?

Useful Websites

Lex Mercatoria

A free site which provides information relevant to international law, and the implications of e-commerce.

http://lexmercatoria.org

University of Kent Law School links

A useful page providing links to numerous law-related resources.

http://library.ukc.ac.uk/library/lawlinks/

HMSO

Provides full text of recent Acts of Parliament.

http://www.legislation.hmso.gov.uk/

Business Bureau

A commercial site offering an overview of the legislation with particular relevance to small businesses.

http://www.businessbureau-uk.co.uk/law/law.htm

DTI

The Department of Trade and Industry's website gives the latest employment relations guidance.

http://www.dti.gov.uk/er/regs.htm

National Association of Citizens Advice Bureau

Offers advice on many legal issues.

http://www.nacab.org.uk/

International Labour Organization (ILO)

This website provides information on international work standards and national laws on labour and human rights.

http://www.ilo.org

Health and Safety Executive

http://www.hse.gov.uk/pubns/hazards.htm

Commission for Racial Equality

http://www.cre.gov.uk

Equal Opportunities Commission

http://www.eoc.org.uk

Disability Rights Commission

http://www.disability.gov.uk/

Further Reading

The following books provide a general overview of law as it affects commercial organizations:

Adams, Alix (2003) *Law for Business Students*, London, Longman.

Keenan, Denis and Riches, Sarah (2004) *Business Law*, London, Longman.

Lowe, Robert and Woodroffe, Geoffrey (2003) *Consumer Law and Practice*, London, Sweet & Maxwell.

This chapter has discussed the basics of the law of contract and the following texts provide useful further reading:

Duxbury, Robert (ed.) *Contract Law*, London, Sweet & Maxwell.

Elliott, Catherine and Quinn, Frances (2003) *Contract Law*, London, Longman.

Treitel, G.H. (2004) *An Outline of the Law of Contract*, Lexis Nexis UK.

Trade marks and patent laws are discussed in the following text:

Phillips, J. and Firth, A. (2000) *Introduction to Intellectual Property*, 4th edn, London, Butterworths.

A valuable overview of employment law is provided in the following:

Lewis, David and Sargeant, Malcolm (2004) *Essentials of Employment Law*, London, Chartered Institute of Personnel and Development.

Slocombe, Melanie (2004) *Employment Law Guide*, Law Pack Publishing.

Finally, for a discussion of the legal and ethical basis to business relationships, the following is interesting:

Gundlach, Gregory T. and Murphy, Patrick E. (1993) 'Ethical and legal foundations of relational marketing exchange', *Journal of Marketing*, Vol. 57 (October), pp. 35–46.

Reference

Berthoud, R. (2005) *Incomes of Ethnic Minorities*, Joseph Rowntree Foundation.

Part 3

Firms

Chapter 6
Types of Business Organization

Chapter Objectives

This chapter will explain:

- the diversity of organizational types

- advantages and disadvantages of sole traders, partnerships and limited companies

- the role of public-sector organizations and Non-Departmental Public Bodies

- business format franchising

- the effects of organizational form and size on responsiveness to environmental change

6.1 ORGANIZATIONS AND THEIR ENVIRONMENT

Previous chapters have focused on the external environment which affects business organizations. In this chapter we begin to turn our focus inward, to look at the nature of business organizations. We need to understand the factors that facilitate or inhibit an internal response to external environmental change.

But first, we need to ask a basic question – why do organizations exist? The main reason is that some forms of value creation can be carried out much more efficiently within organizations than by individuals acting alone. Imagine individuals trying to build an aircraft and you can appreciate that they will achieve their objective much more effectively if they come together in some form of organization. However, if a group of individuals want to go into business as household decorators, they might find that the costs of managing the organization put them at a competitive disadvantage compared to individuals acting on their own. Business organizations are extremely diverse in their forms and functions, even within a single business sector. It is therefore difficult to define an 'ideal' organization. Instead, all organizational forms have advantages and disadvantages relative to the environment in which they operate, and successful organizations capitalize on their advantages while recognizing their disadvantages. In a single business sector, there can be a role for both the one-person owner-managed business and the multinational organization. Both can adapt and find a role.

Analogies can be drawn between business organizations and their environment and the animal kingdom. In a natural habitat, the largest and most powerful animals can co-exist with much smaller species. The smaller species can avoid becoming prey for the larger ones by being more agile or developing defences such as safe habitats which are inaccessible to their larger predators. Sometimes, a symbiotic relationship can develop between the two. In a bid to survive, animals soon learn which sources of food are easily obtainable and abandon those that are either inedible or face competition from more powerful animals. In Darwinian terms, the fittest survive, and an ecosystem allows for co-existence of living organisms which have adapted in their own way to the challenges of their environment. As in the business environment, macroenvironmental change can affect the relationships between species as, for example, has occurred with deforestation and the use of intensive farming methods.

Just as any study of the animal world may begin by examining the characteristics of the participants, so an analysis of the business environment could begin by looking at the characteristics of the organizations that make it up. Businesses need to understand the diversity of organizational types for a number of reasons.

1 Different types of organization will be able to address their customers, suppliers and employees in different ways. Lack of resources could, for example, inhibit the development of expensive new products by a small business. Sometimes, the objectives of an organization – either formal or informal – will influence what it is able to offer the public.
2 As sellers of materials to companies involved in further manufacture, a company should understand how the buying behaviour of different kinds of organization varies. A small business is likely to buy equipment in a different way to a large public-sector organization.

3 We should be interested in the structure of business units at the macroeconomic level. Many economists have argued that a thriving small business sector is essential for an expanding economy and that the effect of domination by large organizations may be to reduce competition and innovation. We should therefore be interested in the rate of new business creation and trends in the composition of business units.

6.1.1 Classification of business organizations

There are many approaches to classifying organizations that would satisfy the interests identified above. Organizations are commonly classified according to their:

- size (e.g. turnover, assets, employees, geographical coverage)
- ownership (e.g. public, private, cooperative)
- legal form (e.g. sole trader, limited company)
- industry sector.

A good starting point for classifying business organizations is to look at their legal form. A business's legal form is often closely related to its size, objectives, the level of resources it has available for marketing, and for new product development (the issues of organizational size and objectives are considered in more detail in the next chapter).

This chapter will first consider private-sector organizations, which range from the small owner-managed sole trader to the very large public limited company. It will then review the diverse range of publicly owned organizations which operate as businesses. A third, and growing, group of organizations cannot be neatly categorized into private or public sector and includes Non-Departmental Public Bodies (often referred to as Quangos) and charities. To put the diversity of organizations into context, Figure 6.1 illustrates the types of organization that will be described in this chapter.

6.2 THE SOLE TRADER

The most basic level of business organization is provided by the sole trader. In fact, the concept of a separate legal form does not apply to this type of organization, for the business and the individual are considered to be legally indistinguishable. The individual carries on business in his or her own name, with the result that the individual assumes all the rights and duties of the business. It follows that if the business is sued for breach of contract, this amounts to suing the individual. If the business does not have the resources to meet any claim, the claim must be met out of the private resources of the individual.

Becoming a sole trader requires the minimum of formality and for this reason it can be difficult to tell how many are being created or are in existence at any one time. The most commonly used indication is provided by VAT registrations, although this does not give a complete picture as businesses with a turnover of less than £58,000 (2004/05) do not need to register. Maintaining a business as a sole trader also requires a minimum of formality – for example, there is no obligation to file annual accounts, other than for the assessment of the individual's personal tax liability.

It has been estimated that about 80 per cent of all businesses in the United Kingdom are sole traders, although they account for only a small proportion of Gross Domestic Product. In some sectors of the economy they are a very popular business form and dominate sectors such

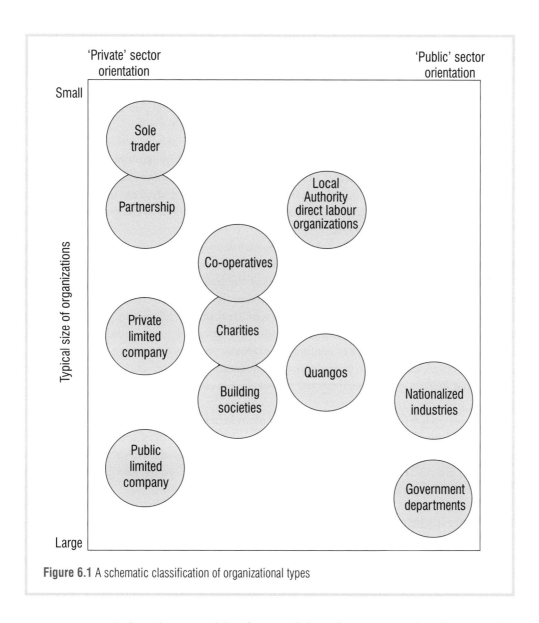

'Private' sector orientation

'Public' sector orientation

Small

Typical size of organizations

Sole trader

Partnership

Local Authority direct labour organizations

Co-operatives

Private limited company

Charities

Quangos

Building societies

Nationalized industries

Public limited company

Government departments

Large

Figure 6.1 A schematic classification of organizational types

as newsagents, window cleaners and hairdressers. Sole traders can grow by taking on additional employees. There is no legal limit on the number of employees that a sole trader may have and there are many examples of sole traders employing over 100 people. At the other extreme, it is sometimes difficult to describe just when a sole trader business unit comes into existence, with many sole traders operating on a part-time basis – some 'moonlighting' without the knowledge of the tax authorities. Estimates of the annual value of this so-called 'black economy' are as high as £200 million per annum.

We should recognize a number of important characteristics of sole traders. First, they tend to have limited capital resources. Risk capital is generally only provided by the sole proprietor or close personal backers and additional loan capital is often only made available against security of the individual's assets. In the field of new product development, this type of business has very often made discoveries, but has been unable to see new products through to production and launch on account of a lack of funds. If a new product does make it into a competitive market, this type of business may face competition in price, promotional effort or product offering from larger and better-resourced firms. The larger firm is likely to have greater resources to mount a campaign to see off a newer competitor.

Being relatively small, the sole trader may suffer by not being able to exploit the economies of scale available to larger firms. On the other hand, many sole traders aim for those sectors where economies of scale are either unimportant or non-existent, for example painting and decorating, hairdressing and outside catering. In many personal services, smallness and the personal touch, plus the fact that many small businesses do not need to charge their customers VAT, can be a strong selling point.

The small sole trader could find that it is too small to justify having its own expertise in many areas. Many do not have specialists to look after the accounting or advertising functions, for example. Furthermore, the goals and policies of the business can become totally dominated by the owner of the business. Although goals can be pursued determinedly and single-mindedly, the sole trader presents a narrower view than may be offered by a larger board of directors. The goals of a sole trader may appear very irrational to an outsider; for instance, many individuals may be happy to continue uneconomic ventures on emotional grounds alone. Many very small caterers, for example, may be financially better off drawing unemployment benefit, but being a sole trader may satisfy wider goals of status or the pursuit of a leisure interest.

Many sole traders fail after only a short time, often because of the lack of management skills of an individual who may well be an expert in his or her own field of specialization. Others continue until they reach a point where lack of expertise and financial resources impose a constraint on growth. At this point, many sole traders consider going into partnership with another individual, or setting up a company with limited liability.

6.2.1 Sole trader or employee?

It can sometimes be difficult to decide whether a person is a self-employed sole trader or an employee of another organization. The distinction is an important one, because a trend in recent years has been for large organizations to outsource many of their operations, often buying in services from apparently self-employed individuals. There can be many advantages in classifying an individual as self-employed rather than an employee. For the self-employed person, tax advantages could result from being able to claim as legitimate some business expense items that are denied to the employee. The method of assessing income tax liability in arrears can favour an expanding small business. For the employer, designation as self-employed could save on National Insurance payments. It also relieves the employer of many duties that are imposed in respect of employees but not subcontractors, such as entitlement to sick pay, notice periods and maternity leave.

The problem of distinction is particularly great in the construction sector and for service sectors (such as market research), which employ large numbers of part-time workers. The courts would decide the matter, among other things, on the basis of the degree of control that the employer has over the employee and their level of integration within the organization. If

One of the biggest complaints from sole traders is the amount of paperwork that they are required by government to complete. Most small business owners have a vision of what they want to do – open a hairdressing salon, install kitchens, run a convenience store or exploit a new invention. But the reality is that they are likely to become bogged down in completing paperwork, some of which they may never have envisaged. According to a NatWest survey, conducted on a quarterly basis by the Open University Business School, the average amount of time that sole traders spend completing paperwork has increased from 6 hours a month in 2000, to 8.3 hours in September 2003. For the average small firm, including limited companies, the average was 23.3 hours a month. More than half the firms surveyed said the cost of employee regulation and paperwork had meant they employed fewer staff than they would like. More than a third said they would avoid employing more people, while 18 per cent said that growing levels of regulation had led them to reduce their workforce. After employment paperwork, main gripes concerned the paperwork associated with VAT, and the form-filling which is associated with health and safety assessments. The Small Business Council has been campaigning to keep paperwork simple and to reduce the time it takes to fill out forms. It has pointed out that, for every hour a sole trader spends filling out forms, they are not able to use the time to sell more products or develop new ones. While large companies may be able to employ specialists to cope with paperwork, for the small business, productivity suffers.

Governments continually say that they wish to reduce the paperwork burden on small businesses, but how in practice can this be achieved?

the employer is able to specify the manner in which a task is to be carried out, and assumes most of the risk in a transaction, then an employment relationship generally exists. If, however, the required end result is specified but the manner in which it is achieved is left up to the individual, who also bears the cost of any budget overrun, then it is most likely that a contract for services will exist – in other words, self-employment.

6.3 PARTNERSHIPS

Two or more persons in partnership can combine their resources and expertise to form what could be a more efficient business unit. The Partnership Act 1890 defines a partnership as 'the relation which subsists between persons carrying on a business with a view to profit'. Partnerships can range from two builders joining together to a very large accountancy or solicitors' practice with hundreds of partners.

Partnerships are generally formed by contract between the parties, although, where this is not done, the Partnership Act 1890 governs relationships between the partners. Among the main items in a Partnership Agreement will be terms specifying:

1 the amount of capital subscribed by each partner
2 the basis on which profits will be determined and allocated between partners and the management responsibilities of each partner – some partners may join as 'sleeping partners' and take no active part in the management of the business

3 the basis for allocating salaries to each partner and for drawing personal advances against entitlement to profits

4 procedures for dissolving the partnership and distributing the assets of the business between members.

Despite this internal agreement between partners, partnerships in England and Wales have not had their own legal personality. As a consequence, the partners incur unlimited personal liability for the debts of the business. Furthermore, each partner is jointly liable for the debts incurred by all partners in the course of business. An added complication of a partnership is that the withdrawal of any one partner, either voluntarily or upon death or bankruptcy, causes the automatic termination of the partnership. A new partnership will come into being, as it would if an additional partner was admitted to the partnership.

Because of the lack of protection afforded to partners, this form of organization tends to be relatively uncommon, except for some groups of professional people, where business risks are low and for whom professional codes of practice may prevent the formation of limited companies. To overcome the problem of limited liability, the Limited Liability Partnerships Act 2000 created a new form of partnership with limited liability. The Act extends limited liability to partnerships in specified circumstances and is most popular with professional partnerships of accountants, solicitors, dentists and opticians.

6.4 LIMITED COMPANIES

It was recognized in the nineteenth century that industrial development would be impeded if investors in business always ran the risk of losing their personal assets to cover the debts of a business over which very often they had no day-to-day control. At the same time, the size of business units had become larger, causing the idea of a partnership to become strained. The need for a trading company to have a separate legal personality from that of its owners was recognized from the Middle Ages, when companies were incorporated by Royal Charter. From the seventeenth century, organizations could additionally be incorporated by Act of Parliament. Both methods of incorporating a company were expensive and cumbersome, and a simpler method was required to cope with the rapid expansion of business enterprises that were fuelling the Industrial Revolution. The response to this need was the Joint Stock Companies Act 1844, which enabled a company to be incorporated as a separate legal identity by the registration of a Memorandum of Association and payment of certain fees. The present law governing the registration of companies is contained in the Companies Act 1985. Today, the vast majority of trading within the United Kingdom is undertaken by limited companies. The legislation of most countries allows for organizations to be created that have a separate legal personality from their owners. In this way, separate legal identity is signified in the United States by the title 'Incorporated' after a company's name, by 'Societie Anonym' (SA) in France, 'Gmbh' in Germany and 'Sdn. Bhd.' in Malaysia.

When a limited company is created under UK legislation, it is required to produce a Memorandum and Articles of Association. The Memorandum regulates the relationships of the company with the outside world while the Articles of Association regulate the internal administration of the company. Most limited companies are registered as private limited companies, indicated in company names by the designation 'Limited'. However, some larger companies choose to register as Public Limited Companies (PLCs) and face tougher regulatory requirements. These are described later in this chapter.

6.4.1 The Memorandum of Association

This is a statement about the company's relations with the outside world and includes a number of important provisions.

1 The first item to be considered is the name of the company. If it is a private limited company, the name must end with the word 'Limited' (or its Welsh equivalent, 'Cyf', for companies registered in Wales). A number of restrictions exist on the company's choice of name – for example, the name must not cause confusion with an existing company or suggest a connection with royalty. The trading name will very often be quite different from the registered name, in which case the company is required to display the name and address of its owner at its business premises, on its business stationery and to customers and suppliers on request.

2 The second important element of the Memorandum is a statement as to whether the liability of its members is limited, and if so what the limit of liability will be in the event of the company being wound up with unpaid debts. The majority of companies are limited by shares. Members' liability to contribute to the assets of the company is limited to the amount – if any – that is unpaid on their shares. An alternative is for companies to be limited by guarantee. In these companies, the liability of each member to make up for any shortfall in assets in the event of the company being wound up is limited to the value of his or her guarantee. This type of company is comparatively rare, being found mainly among non-profit-making organizations, such as professional and trade associations. A further less common type of company occurs where the Memorandum specifies unlimited liability of members. Because the members of such companies have unlimited liability for the company's debts, they are liable to lose their personal assets – a problem that gave rise to the limited liability company in the first place. There has, however, been an increase in the number of unlimited companies since 1967 because the Companies Act of that year exempted them from filing their accounts with the Registrar of Companies, and hence publicizing their financial affairs.

3 The third important element of the Memorandum is the objects clause. This is particularly important because it specifies the scope within which the company can exercise its separate legal personality. There are two principal consequences of having an objects clause. First, the clause protects investors who can learn from it the purposes for which their money is to be used. Second, it protects individuals dealing with the company, who can discover the extent of the company's powers. Any act that the company performs beyond its powers is deemed to be *ultra vires* and therefore void. Therefore, even where the directors of a company are in agreement with a contract which is beyond its powers, the contract itself would be void. The principal of *ultra vires* was amended by the Companies Act 1985, section 35, so that any person who enters into a contract with a company which is outside its objects, but which is sanctioned by the directors of the company, will be able to enforce it against the company, providing that he or she did not know that the contract was beyond the company's powers. In practice, it is common for companies to contain an objects clause that is drafted in a deliberately broad manner, allowing considerable freedom for the directors to move away from their traditional business area.

6.4.2 The Articles of Association

While the Memorandum regulates the relationships of the company with the outside world, the Articles of Association regulate the internal administration of the company, the relations between the company and its members and between the members themselves. The Articles cover such matters as the issue and transfer of shares, the rights of shareholders, meetings of members, the appointment of directors and procedures for producing and auditing accounts.

Companies seeking to expand by acquiring a company may be held back by the target company's Articles of Association. The Articles may, for instance, restrict ownership of shares by any one person to a fixed percentage of the total, as has been the case in many newly privatized companies. Different shares may attract different voting rights, so that, despite acquiring a majority of shares, the acquiring company is not able to acquire effective control of the company. As an example, the Forte Hotel Group (subsequently acquired by the Granada Group) owned a majority of the shares in the Savoy Hotel Group, which it sought to exercise control over. However, most of the shares that it held carried no voting rights and it did not hold a majority of the voting shares. It was therefore frustrated in its efforts to influence the Savoy Group's policy.

6.4.3 Company administration

A company acts through its directors, who are persons chosen by shareholders to conduct and manage the company's affairs. The number of directors and their powers are detailed in the Articles of Association and, so long as they do not exceed these powers, shareholders cannot normally interfere in their conduct of the company's business. The Articles will normally give one director additional powers to act as managing director, enabling him or her to make decisions without reference to the full board of directors.

Every company must have a secretary on whom Companies Acts have placed a number of duties and responsibilities, such as filing reports and accounts with the Registrar of Companies. The secretary is the chief administrative officer of the company, usually chosen by the directors.

6.4.4 Shareholders

The shareholders own the company, and in theory exercise control over it. A number of factors limit the actual control that shareholders in fact exercise over their companies. It was mentioned earlier that the Articles of a company might discriminate between groups of shareholders by giving differential voting rights. Even where shareholders have full voting rights, the vast majority of shareholders typically are either unable or insufficiently interested to attend company meetings, and are happy to leave company management to the directors, so long as the dividend paid to them is satisfactory. In the case of pension funds and other institutional holders of shares in a company, their concern may be mainly with the stability of the financial returns from the business. In most large organizations, private investors are in a distinct minority in terms of the value of shares owned. There has been a tendency in recent years for individual shareholders to use their privileged position to raise issues of social concern at companies' annual shareholders' meetings. For example, small shareholders have used meetings of water companies as a platform to protest about poor levels of service and excessive directors' salaries. In 2001 the annual shareholders' meeting of the BP oil company was presented with a number of motions by individual shareholders disgruntled with the company's environmental policy and involvement in Tibet. Shareholder revolts can have widespread public relations implications for companies.

6.4.5 Company reports and accounts

A company provides information about itself when it is set up through its Memorandum and Articles of Association. To provide further protection for investors and people with whom the company may deal, companies are required to provide subsequent information.

An important document that must be produced annually is the annual report. Every company having a share capital must make a return in the prescribed form to the Registrar of Companies, stating what has happened to its capital during the previous year, for example by describing the number of shares allotted and the cash received for them. The return must be accompanied by a copy of the audited balance sheet in the prescribed form, supported by a profit and loss account that gives a true and fair representation of the year's transactions. Like the Memorandum and Articles of Association, these documents are available for public inspection, with the exception of unlimited companies, which do not have to file annual accounts. Also, most small companies need only file an abridged balance sheet and do not need to submit a profit and loss account.

As well as providing the annual report and accounts, the directors of a company are under a duty to keep proper books of account and details of assets and liabilities.

6.4.6 Liquidation and receivership

Most limited companies are created with a view to continuous operation into the foreseeable future (although, sometimes, companies are set up with an expectation that they should cease to exist once their principal objective has been achieved). The process of breaking up a business is referred to as liquidation. Voluntary liquidation may be initiated by members (for example, where the main shareholder wishes to retire and liquidation is financially more attractive than selling the business as a going concern). Alternatively, a limited company may be liquidated (or wound up) by a court under section 122 of the Insolvency Act 1986. Involuntary liquidation involves the appointment of a receiver, who has authority that overrides the directors of the company. An individual or company that has an unmet claim against a company can apply to a court for it to be placed in receivership. Most receivers initially seek to turn round a failing business by consolidating its strengths and cutting out activities that brought about failure in the first place, allowing the company to be sold as a going concern. The proceeds of such a sale are used towards repaying the company's creditors and, if there is a sufficient surplus, the shareholders of the company. However, many directors who have lost their businesses claim that receivers are too eager to liquidate assets and unwilling to take any risks that may eventually allow both creditors and shareholders to be paid off. The Insolvency Act 1986 allows a period of 'administration' during which a company can seek to put its finances into order with its creditors, without immediate resort to receivership. Section 5.8 of the Act defines the circumstances in which an administration order may be made by a court.

In January 2005, the department store Allders was placed into administration. Like many administrative orders, this one followed poor trading (in this case, lower-than-expected levels of Christmas sales), which left the company short of cash. Krupp was appointed by Allders' bank as administrator, and its first task was to control unnecessary expenditure, resulting in redundancies of staff who were not essential to the continued operation of the chain. The administrator then set about selling the chain as a going concern. Despite expressions of interest from several companies, both trade buyers and venture capital firms, no offers for the whole chain were forthcoming. One complicating factor was the requirement for anybody taking over the whole company as a going concern to assume responsibility for Allders' pension fund deficit, and for making redundancy payments to any staff who they no longer needed after taking over the business. Krupp was mindful that a prolonged search for a buyer would diminish the value of the company, as customers became disillusioned and staff morale sank. It therefore sold bundles of stores to British Home Stores, Debenhams and Primark. Some smaller stores attracted no bids, and the administrator proceeded to close these and to dispose of the assets for the best price possible.

6.4.7 Public limited companies

The Companies Act 1985 recognized that existing company legislation did not sufficiently distinguish between the small owner-managed limited company and the large multinational firm. Thus the concept of the public limited company – abbreviated to PLC – came about. The basic principles of separate legal personality are similar for both private and public limited companies, but the Companies Act 1985 confers a number of additional duties and benefits on public limited companies.

The difference is partly one of scale – a PLC must have a minimum share capital of £50,000 compared to the £100 of the private limited company. It must have at least two directors instead of the minimum of one for the private company. Before a public limited company can start trading, or borrow money, it must obtain a 'business certificate' from the Registrar of Companies, confirming that it has met all legal requirements in relation to its share capital.

Against these additional obstacles of the public limited company is the major advantage that it can offer its shares and debentures to the public, something that is illegal for a private company, where shares are more commonly taken up by friends, business associates and family. As a private limited company grows, it may have exhausted all existing sources of equity capital, and 'going public' is one way of attracting capital from a wider audience. During periods of economic prosperity, there has been a trend for many groups of managers to buy out their businesses, initially setting up a private limited company with a private placement of shares. In order to attract new capital, and often to allow existing shareholders to sell their holding more easily, these businesses have often been re-registered as public companies.

There are a number of additional strengths and weaknesses to PLC status which can be noted. Many companies highlight PLC status in promotional material in order to give potential customers a greater degree of confidence in the company. Another major strength is the greater potential ability to fund major new product developments. Against this, the PLC is much more open to public examination, especially from the financial community. Management may develop business plans that will achieve long-term payback, bringing it into conflict with possibly short-term objectives of City financial institutions. Indeed, a number of companies have recognized this problem of PLC status and reverted to private status by buying back shares from the public – the Virgin airline business, for example, converted back to a private limited company after a few years as a PLC (although the Virgin Mobile business was subsequently floated as a PLC in 2004).

Larger limited companies can sometimes be described as multinational companies. They have operations in many countries, although subsidiaries would usually be registered locally in each country of operation. A multinational company based overseas may register a subsidiary in the UK as a private limited company in which it holds 100 per cent of the shares. UK-based companies which are holding companies for overseas subsidiaries are most likely to be registered as public limited companies.

Today, although public limited companies are in a numerical minority, they account for a substantial proportion of the equity of the limited company sector and cover a wide range of industries which typically operate on a large scale – for example, banking, car manufacture and property development.

6.4.8 Advantages and disadvantages of limited companies

To summarize, comparisons between sole traders and partnerships, on the one hand, and limited companies, on the other, can be made at a number of levels. First, formation of a limited company is relatively formal and time-consuming – for a sole trader there is the minimum of formality in establishing a business. The added formality continues with the requirement to produce an annual return and set of accounts. On the other hand, limited company status affords much greater protection to the entrepreneur in the event of the business getting into financial difficulty. Raising additional funds would usually be easier for a limited company, although personal guarantees may still be required to cover loans to the company. Additional funding which limited company status makes possible, especially public limited company status, allows organizations to embark on more ambitious expansion plans. While a sole trader may concentrate on small niche markets, a limited company may be in a better position to tackle mainstream mass markets.

6.5 SMALL BUSINESSES

So far, we have looked at various forms of private-sector organization ranging from the small sole trader to the possibly very large multinational public limited company. Despite the tendency of firms to grow, there has been renewed interest in the role of small businesses (which can take the legal form of sole trader, partnership or limited company) within the economy. It is suggested that many of Britain's competitors, such as Far Eastern economies, have attributed their growth to a strong small business sector. During recent years, developed economies have seen a significant increase in the number of small businesses, especially in the expanding services sector. By far the majority of business organizations in most Western countries are small, so we will now spend some time looking at the attractions of small business units.

The term 'small business' (or SME, standing for small and medium-sized enterprise) is difficult to define. In an industry such as car manufacture, a firm with 100 employees would be considered very small, whereas among solicitors, a practice of that size would be considered large. The term small business is therefore a relative one, based typically on some measure of numbers of employees or capital employed. Within the European Union, the Eurostat definition of small companies is often used:

Micro-organizations:	0–9 employees
Small organizations:	10–99 employees
Medium-sized organizations:	100–499 employees
Large organizations:	500+ employees

In the United Kingdom, the Department of Trade and Industry's small and medium-sized enterprise statistics highlight a number of features of the small business sector (DTI 2004).

1 There has been a significant growth in the number of business enterprises in the UK, up from around 2.4 million in 1980 to an estimated 4 million in 2003.

2 Of these 4 million businesses, 2.9 million were 'size class zero' businesses, those made up of sole traders or partners without any employees.

3 Businesses with fewer than 50 employees accounted for 99.2 per cent of all businesses. Only 0.2 per cent of all businesses employed more than 250 people.

4 SMEs accounted for 58.2 per cent of all employment and 52.4 per cent of turnover in the UK.

5 The proportion of businesses employing fewer than 50 people was particularly high in agriculture (93.7 per cent) and low in financial services (13.9 per cent).

Advocates of small business argue that they are important to the economy for a number of reasons.

1 They generally offer much greater adaptability than larger firms. With less bureaucracy and fewer channels of communication, decisions can be taken rapidly. A larger organization may be burdened with constraints which tend to slow the decision-making process, such as the need to negotiate new working practices with trades union representatives or the need to obtain board of directors' approval for major decisions. As organizations grow, there is an inherent tendency for them to become more risk averse by building in systems of control which make them slower to adapt to changes in their business environment.

2 It is also argued that small businesses tend to be good innovators. This comes about through greater adaptability, especially where large amounts of capital are not required. The Internet opened many opportunities for small entrepreneurs to establish novel business formats, such as Screwfix.com which developed a home and worksite delivery service for builders requiring small items of building materials. Small firms can also be good innovators where they operate in markets dominated by a small number of larger companies, and the only way in which a small business can gain entry to the market is to develop an innovatory product aimed at a small niche. The soap powder market in Britain is dominated by a small number of large producers, yet it was a relatively small company that identified a niche for environmentally friendly powders and introduced innovatory products to the market.

3 Most large firms started off as very small businesses, so it is important to the health of the economy that there is a continuing supply of growing companies to replace those larger firms that die. According to a report issued by the Small Business Service (*Job Creation by New and Small Firms*) SMEs were responsible for almost three-quarters of the increase in employment between 1995 and 1999 and created 85 per cent of the 2.3 million jobs created in the same period.

The change in the structure and organization of industry and commerce, the growing emphasis on specialized services and the application of new technology have tended to encourage small business. Flexible manufacturing systems are increasingly able to allow a business to function at a much lower level of output than previously. An example is in printing, where new production processes have allowed entrepreneurs to undertake small print runs on relatively inexpensive machinery. The success of the small printer has been further encouraged by the proliferation of small business users of printed material requiring small print runs and a rapid turnaround of work.

The tendency for large companies to outsource functions such as cleaning and catering in order to concentrate on their core business has also given new opportunities to the small business sector. Many catering businesses, for example, have been started when a company's catering staff bought out the operations of their former employer, and now provide their services on a subcontract basis.

It is not only small entrepreneurs that have been creating new small businesses. Larger organizations have also recognized their value and have tried to replicate them at a distance from their own structure. Many large manufacturing organizations operating in mature markets have created autonomous new small business units to serve rapidly developing or specialist niche markets, free of the bureaucratic culture of the parent organization. In the education sector, many universities have established small research companies at arm's length from the universities' organizational structures. In some cases, large organizations with inflexible internal processes have created new small subsidiaries (or acquired existing small businesses) to act as an example to the mainstream business. In the UK bus industry, many large, highly unionized companies acquired or created small coach operators, in order that they could have the operational flexibility that was necessary to enter some markets. They additionally may have expected the culture of flexibility in the smaller business to filter back into the main business.

While small businesses have seen a resurgence in recent years, it should also be recognized that they have a very high failure rate. Conclusive evidence of the failure rate of small businesses is difficult to obtain, especially in view of the problem of identifying new businesses that do not need to register in the first place. However, one indication of failure rates comes from an analysis of VAT (value added tax) registrations, which show that, during the 1990s, only about one-third of businesses set up 10 years previously were still registered.

Further evidence of the high failure rate is provided by Barclays Bank, which noted that in 2003, there were 423,100 new business start-ups in England and Wales. Based on its records of business customers, it estimated that over half of all new firms fail in the first three years (Barclays Bank 2004). Businesses started by 50 to 55 year olds were found to be more likely to survive compared with those begun by people in their twenties.

6.5.1 Government and small business

Governments in many countries have been keen to support small businesses. They have pointed to the successful small-business-led economies of the Far East and sought to emulate their growth through the creation of a strong domestic small business sector. The presence of large numbers of small businesses in a market is also useful for increasing the competitiveness of markets, thereby achieving government objectives of a more flexible economy and lower inflation.

THINKING AROUND THE SUBJECT:
BIG OR SMALL, THE MARKET ACCOMMODATES THEM ALL

In many sectors, the public perception of large, dominant organizations is contrasted by the reality of domination by a large number of small businesses. This is true of the hospitality and accommodation sector, where for every large Hilton or Holiday Inn chain there are hundreds of small guesthouse owners, bed and breakfast businesses, and operators of self-catering accommodation. Small businesses, such as this guesthouse, manage to hold their own against the larger hotel chains for a number of reasons. They generally offer a much more personal and friendly welcome than large hotel chains, especially to guests who tire of the same format of the branded chain hotels. Guesthouses have lower overheads, because the owners often would not employ any staff and this saving can be passed on as lower prices. Many owners of guesthouses would probably not see themselves as being business people at all, but simply earning additional income by taking people into what is, after all, their home. Nevertheless, guesthouses cannot afford to be complacent. The growth of low-cost 'budget' hotel chains, such as Premier Travel Inn, has attracted many guests who would otherwise have chosen the guesthouse on the basis of price. Guesthouse owners must also be alert to changing expectations of customers, for example in the range of in-room entertainment equipment.

Such motivations partly explain some of the concessions that governments have made to the small business sector. These include an exemption on Corporation Tax for all profits below £10,000 (from 2004), and small firms with a turnover of less than £58,000 p.a. (2004/05) are exempt from the need to charge VAT and have often been exempted from statutory duties that apply to larger companies, especially those relating to employment rights. To encourage the development of new businesses, many supportive innovations have been launched by central government, including various training schemes sponsored by Regional Development Agencies.

Small business owners are often sceptical about governments' support for them, pointing out that government legislation often imposes disproportionate burdens on them. Cynics might argue that governments have seen the encouragement of small business as a simple means of getting unemployed people off the list of the unemployed. The British Chambers of Commerce produces an annual *Burdens Barometer* which seeks to assess the cost on business of government regulations (BCC 2005). It worked through over 1100 Regulatory Impact Assessments produced by government departments that evaluate the risks, costs and benefits of new regulatory proposals that have an impact on business, and found that only 50 per cent of all these quantified some benefits that new regulations provide to businesses, consumers, the environment or to government. The burden of regulations falls particularly hard on small businesses, with the report citing VAT – which effectively makes businesses unpaid tax collectors for government – as a particular burden. While larger firms may be able to afford a specialized accounting department, many small business owners are often left to add the submission of VAT returns to their core tasks which they are expected to undertake personally. Government has hoped to stimulate the small business sector through requirements for certain government purchases to be put out to competitive bidding, but often the complexity of regulations governing competitive tenders has put many small businesses off bidding. Many small businesses have found it increasingly difficult to comply with government employment legislation, for example with respect to maternity leave rights. Previous exemptions for small businesses have been steadily removed in recent years. A large business might have the necessary flexibility when one member out of a staff of several hundred employees takes maternity leave, but in a small business, this may be a key person, for whom it may be difficult to recruit a temporary replacement.

Governments frequently declare that they are going to cut the red tape and bureaucracy which impose burdens on small businesses. However, the historic reality has often been in the opposite direction. We saw in Chapter 2 the work of the UK government's Better Regulation Task Force, which has sought to reduce the burden of government on business organizations.

6.6 COMMERCIAL AND QUASI-COMMERCIAL ORGANIZATIONS OPERATING IN THE PUBLIC SECTOR

Government has traditionally been involved in providing goods and services that cannot realistically be provided by market forces – for example defence, education and basic health services. Government involvement has, however, developed beyond providing these basic public services to providing goods and services that could also be provided by private-sector organizations.

Public-sector organizations take a number of forms, embracing government departments and agencies, local government, nationalized industries and all other undertakings in which central or local government has a controlling interest. This chapter will focus on those public-sector organizations that supply goods and services to consumers. Those government organizations that are primarily policy making in nature were considered in more detail in Chapter 2, dealing with the political environment. In between those branches of government responsible for providing goods and services and those responsible for policy are an increasing number that are involved in both. For example, many public services such as National Health Service Trusts are increasingly being required to compete for contracts to provide services, using the price mechanism to allocate resources, rather than centralized planning.

6.6.1 State-owned enterprises

Goods and services provided on a commercial basis have often been provided through state-owned enterprises, often referred to as nationalized industries. Most countries have a state-owned industry sector and the size of the sector generally reflects the political ideology of a nation. The United States has traditionally had very few government-owned business organizations, France has taken nationalization to sectors such as banking, which many would consider a prerogative of the private sector, while Britain has seen a once large state-owned industry sector shrink with changes in political ideology (UK state-owned industries accounted for less than 1 per cent of Gross Domestic Product in 2004, having fallen from 9 per cent in 1979). Throughout the EU, privatization of state-owned enterprises has been occurring, or at least these enterprises are being reorganized to behave more like private-sector organizations. An important item on the agenda of the World Trade Organization is to reduce the power of state-owned industries which can act as a barrier to global competition. This is increasingly the case for the services sector, where many 'utilities' such as gas, water and electricity supply have traditionally been state controlled, preventing global competition in these services. Sceptics have been quick to point out the dangers of the WTO's agenda for developing countries, for example privatization of the Indian Post Office might give new opportunities for Federal Express, but could the Indian Post Office realistically be expected to compete for mail business in the USA?

Governments first became involved in industry for largely pragmatic reasons. In 1913, a key shareholding in the Anglo-Iranian Oil Company – the precursor of British Petroleum – was acquired by the British government to ensure oil supplies to the Royal Navy. During the inter-war years, the Central Electricity Generating Board, the British Broadcasting Corporation and the London Passenger Transport Board were created to fill gaps that the private sector had not been capable of filling. Whereas the reasons for the creation of these early nationalized industries were largely pragmatic, the early post-Second World War period saw a large number of nationalized industries created for increasingly ideological reasons. During the Labour government of the late 1940s, the state acquired control of the coal, electricity, gas and iron and steel industries and most inland transport. Some industries returned to the private sector during the Conservative government of the 1950s, while subsequent Labour governments added others.

The 1980s and 1990s saw a great decline in the role of nationalized industry, not just in the United Kingdom but also throughout the world. Post-war Europe may have needed centralized planning and allocation of resources to facilitate the reconstruction effort, but the mood had changed by the relatively affluent, consumer-orientated years of the 1980s. The view went around that governments were bad managers of commercial businesses and that private-sector organizations were much more capable of giving good value to consumers. In the rush to sell off state-owned industries, privatization was often confused with deregulation. Simply transferring a nationalized industry to the private sector could easily create a private monopoly which was unresponsive to consumers' needs. Consequently, most privatization has been accompanied by measures to deregulate sectors of the economy. Where this has been impractical, government intervention has been retained in the form of regulation of prices and service standards.

Governments have chosen a number of methods to transfer state-owned industries to the private sector (see Figure 6.2). The most common have been the following.

1 **Sale of shares to the public:** Before shares in a state-owned organization can be sold to the public, a limited company with a shareholding must be formed. Initially, all of the new company's shares are owned by the government, and privatization subsequently involves selling these shares to the public. For large privatizations, shares may be targeted at international investors in order to secure the substantial amounts of share capital sought. Sale to the general public has been undertaken where it would be considered politically unacceptable to exclude small investors from the benefits of privatization.

Organization	Date of privatization	Method of privatization
British Aerospace	1981	Public sale of shares
National Freight Corporation	1982	Employee/management buy-out
British Telecom	1984	Public sale of shares
Jaguar	1984	Public sale of shares
Sealink	1984	Trade sale
British Gas	1986	Public sale of shares
British Petroleum	1986	Public sale of shares
BA Helicopters	1986	Trade sale
National Bus Company	1986–91	Trade sales/management buy-outs
British Airports Authority	1987	Public sale of shares
British Airways	1987	Public sale of shares
Rolls-Royce	1987	Public sale of shares
Leyland Bus Company	1987	Trade sale
British Steel	1988	Public sale of shares
Rover Group	1988	Trade sale
Regional Water Companies	1989	Public sale of shares
Regional Electricity Companies	1990	Public sale of shares
Powergen/National Power	1991	Public sale of shares
Scottish Electricity Companies	1991	Public sale of shares
British Coal	1994	Trade sale
British Rail	1994–97	Public sale of shares/trade sales
National Air Traffic Services	2001	Sale of 51% of shares to airline consortium in public–private partnership
London Underground	2001	Franchise-type agreement with private-sector Metronet and Tube Lines to operate and develop infrastructure

Figure 6.2 Methods used in UK privatizations

Note: This is not a complete list. In some cases, the sale of shares was phased over a number of periods.

2 **Trade sale:** Smaller state-owned industries have often been easily sold to other private-sector companies as a complete entity. This happened, for example, in the sale of the then state-owned Rover car company to British Aerospace. Sometimes, parts of nationalized industries have been broken away for sale to private buyers (e.g. the shipping and hotel operations of British Railways were separated from the parent organization for sale to private-sector organizations long before the rail privatization of the 1990s). The administrative costs of this method of disposal are relatively low, but governments are open to allegations that they sold off a private-sector asset too cheaply to favoured buyers (an allegation that was made when British Aerospace subsequently sold Rover to BMW for a much higher price than it had paid for the company).

3 **Management/employee buy-out:** This is often a popular option for people-intensive businesses for which financial institutions may have difficulty in deciding on a value, especially in industries with a history of poor industrial relations. It was used as a method of disposing of the National Freight Corporation and parts of the National Bus Company.

4 **Public–private partnerships:** Sometimes, it may be politically unacceptable, or just impractical, to dispose of government assets into the private sector. Instead, the government may retain ownership of the assets, but pay a contractor to provide services using those assets. Contracts would usually include an incentive for the contractor, so that as their performance rises, the payment that they receive increases. In the UK, much of the management of the motorway network and Royal Navy dockyards is now in the hands of private-sector consortia which receive bonus-related payments in return for work undertaken.

Prior to their privatization, many state-owned organizations have been restructured to make them more attractive to potential buyers. This has typically involved writing off large amounts of debt and offering generous redundancy payments to workers who would not therefore become a liability to a new owner. In doing this, Conservative governments have been accused of providing subsidies for private buyers, although, very often, such action has been essential to provide a buyer with a competitive business proposition.

While governments may be ideologically committed to reducing the role of state-owned industries, it has proved difficult to sell many of them for a variety of practical and ideological reasons. In the case of the Post Office, ideological objections have been raised at the prospect of the Royal Mail letter delivery monopoly being owned by a private-sector company. This has not, however, prevented the Post Office from being reorganized along business lines, with private limited companies being formed for the main business units, one of which – Girobank – was sold off to the Alliance & Leicester Building Society while another – the parcel delivery service – was restructured to act more like one of the private parcel companies with which it is having to compete in an increasingly competitive market. Even the letter business has been opened to competition from 2005.

It is also possible that attitudes towards privatization may be turning and it is now possible to see the problems as well as the benefits. Very few people would advocate turning back the clock in sectors such as telecommunications, where privatization and deregulation have been associated with rapidly falling prices and improving service standards. However, it is more doubtful whether privatization of the bus or water supply industries has been entirely beneficial. Customers of newly privatized train companies have pointed out that punctuality fell sharply in the years immediately after privatization, while public subsidies more than doubled. The complex relationships between companies in the rail industry have led many people to suggest that gaps in safety coverage exist, and that the centralized 'command and control' approach of the former state-owned British Rail offered a safer railway at a lower cost.

The importance of a customer orientation within public corporations has been influenced by the nature of the market in which they operate. Following the nationalizations of the late 1940s, marketing was seen in many of the nationalized industries as being very secondary to production. The relative unimportance of marketing was often associated with some degree of monopoly power granted to the industry. In these circumstances, public corporations could afford to ignore marketing. However, as production of the basic industries caught up with demand and the economy became more deregulated during the 1980s, consumers increasingly had choice between suppliers offered to them. For example, the deregulation of the coach industry in 1981 and the growth in private car ownership placed increasing competitive pressure on British Rail, and hence an increasing importance for the organization to become customer-orientated. British Rail was increasingly set profit objectives rather than poorly specified social objectives.

What could be seen as either a strength or a weakness for the state-owned industries has been finance for investment and new product development. Investment comes from government – either directly or through guarantees on loans from the private sector. Profits earned have not necessarily been ploughed back into the business. The public sector has, since the 1930s, been seen as one instrument for regulating the economy, cutting back or increasing investment to suit the needs of the national economy rather than the needs of the particular market that the corporation is addressing. As well as limiting the amount of investment funds available, government involvement has also been accused of delay caused by the time which it has taken to scrutinize and approve a proposal. By the time approval had been granted, the investment could be too late to meet changed market conditions.

State-owned industries are perceived as an instrument of government and although theoretically they may have an independent constitution, government is frequently accused of exercising covert pressure in order to achieve political favour. Electricity prices, rail fares and telephone charges have all at some time been subject to these allegations, which make life for managers in nationalized industries more difficult because of their confused objectives.

Britain is widely credited with having taken the lead in privatizing state-owned industries, and many countries have followed. The EU has taken action to reduce the anti-competitive consequences of having large subsidized public-sector organizations distorting markets. This has been particularly true in the case of airlines, where some European countries have continued to support loss-making state-owned carriers. In 2005, the EU Transport Commissioner investigated a proposal by the Italian government to rescue the near-bankrupt state-owned airline Alitalia with public money. By EU rules, such funding had to be justified as part of a restructuring process with the objective of returning the airline to profitable private-sector ownership, and could not be allowed as a straightforward operating subsidy.

6.6.2 Local authority enterprise

In addition to providing basic services such as roads, education, housing and social services, local authorities have a number of roles in providing marketable goods and services in competitive markets. For a long time, local authorities have operated bus services and leisure facilities, among others. Initially they were set up for a variety of reasons – sometimes to provide a valuable public service, at other times to help stimulate economic development or to earn a profit to supplement the local authority's income. Sometimes, where a project was too large for one authority and benefited many neighbouring authorities, a joint board would be formed between the authorities. This sometimes happened with local authority-controlled airports, for example East Midlands Airport was formed by a joint board comprising Leicester, Derby, Nottingham, Derbyshire and Nottinghamshire authorities.

Increasingly, UK local authorities are being forced to turn their trading activities into business-like units, separately accountable from the rest of the local authority's activities. In the case of local authority bus and airport operations, the Local Government Act 1988 required local authorities to create limited companies into which their assets are placed. Like any limited company, local authority-owned companies are required to appoint a board of directors and to produce an annual profit and loss statement. By creating a company structure, it becomes easier to introduce private capital, or indeed to sell off the business in its entirety to the private sector. This has occurred in the case of a large number of local authority bus companies and airports (Nottingham East Midlands Airport was initially sold to the National Express group and is now owned by Manchester Airport Group).

Even where separate business units have not been created, local authority services are being exposed to increasing levels of competition. Operations in such areas as highway maintenance, refuse collection and street cleaning must now be assessed to ensure that they offer the 'best value' to the local authority. Local authorities have appointed best value units to monitor their activities against competitive benchmarks, and where necessary put the provision of services out to competitive tender. Where a private-sector company takes over the provision of services for a local authority and takes on its employees, the new employer will generally take on responsibilities for accrued rights to redundancy payments, among other things. Best value requirements were discussed in Chapter 2.

In other non-commercial local authority services, clients are being offered greater choice. With the development of locally managed foundation schools, the governing bodies of schools are adopting – if somewhat grudgingly – a marketing orientation to ensure that the service they are offering is considered better than neighbouring schools that pupils would have the choice of attending. Only by attracting clients can they ensure funding for their school.

6.6.3 Private-sector and public-sector organizations compared

Although public-sector organizations cover a wide range of services operating in diverse environments, a few generalizations can be made about the ways in which their business activities differ from those practised by the private sector.

- The aim of most private-sector organizations is to earn profits for the owners of the organization. By contrast to these quantifiable objectives, public-sector organizations operate with relatively diverse and unquantified objectives. For example, a museum may have qualitative scholarly objectives in addition to relatively quantifiable objectives, such as maximizing revenue or the number of visitors.
- The private sector is usually able to monitor the results of its marketing activity, as the benefits are usually internal to the organization. By contrast, many of the aims that public-

sector organizations seek to achieve are external and a profit and loss statement sometimes cannot be produced in the way that is possible with a private-sector organization operating to narrow internal financial goals.

- The degree of discretion given to a private-sector manager is usually greater than that given to a counterpart in the public sector. The checks and balances imposed on many of the latter reflect the fact that their organizations are accountable to a wider constituency of interests than the typical private-sector organization.

- Many of the marketing mix elements that private-sector organizations can tailor to meet the needs of specific groups of users are often not open to public-sector organizations. For non-traded public services, price − if it is used at all − is a reflection of centrally determined social values rather than the value placed on a service by consumers.

- Public-sector organizations are frequently involved in supplying publicly beneficial services where it can be difficult to identify just who the customer is. Should the customer of a school be regarded as the student, their parents, or society as a whole which is investing in the trained workforce of tomorrow?

- Just as the users of some public services may have no choice in who supplies their service, so too the suppliers may have no choice in who they can provide services to. Within the public sector, organizations may be constrained by statute from providing services beyond specified groups of users. On the other hand, some public-sector organizations may be required by law to supply service to specific groups, even though a market-led decision may lead them not to supply.

6.7 NON-DEPARTMENTAL PUBLIC BODIES

There are many types of organization that do not fit neatly into the private or public sectors. Non-Departmental Public Bodies (NDPBs) is a title given for a type of organization which has traditionally been referred to as a quango ('quasi-autonomous non-governmental organization').

NDPBs have been around in their modern form since before the Second World War and semi-independent public bodies of one sort or another have been part of British governance for 200 years.

NDPBs are used to carry out a variety of trading and policy formulation roles. Their policy-formulation roles are discussed in Chapter 2 and so we briefly note here the reasons why they have become an important type of business-orientated organization.

The following are the most important characteristics of NDPBs.

- They provide services that are considered politically inappropriate for private companies to dominate.

- The assets of the organization are vested in a body whose constitution is determined by government and cannot be changed without its approval.

- Management of an NDPB is generally by political appointees rather than directly elected representatives.

- In theory, NDPBs operate at 'arm's length' from government and are free from day-to-day political interference.

- NDPBs have structures and processes that resemble those of private-sector organizations in terms of their speed and flexibility.

- NDPBs are generally relatively small organizations compared to the larger bureaucracies from which they were separated. Because of their autonomous nature, NDPBs may be financially more accountable than a department within a large government departmental structure. However, many would argue that they are generally much less politically accountable where vital public services are concerned.
- Decisions can generally be made much more speedily by a self-governing organization compared to a unit of a large government department where approval must first be obtained from several layers of a hierarchy.

The following are examples of NDPBs that have recently been created in Britain:

- Housing Associations, which now own and maintain much of the housing stock previously owned by local authorities
- Regional Development Agencies, which have been given, among other things, a remit to encourage inward investment to their areas
- In many areas, organizations with the characteristics of NDPBs have been created to market the areas as tourism destinations.

In all the above examples, bodies are motivated to satisfy the needs of their users more effectively, as users usually have some element of choice. If a local housing association does not score highly on its performance indicators (such as speed of repairing faults or length of time that houses are unoccupied), it may lose funding for future house investment or maintenance.

In practice, the business activities of NDPBs are often highly constrained. Many continue to depend on central or local government for a large part of their income, with no realistic short-term threat of competition for resources. Managers cannot act with as much freedom as their equivalents in the private sector, because the public and local media often take a keen interest in vital public services and are ready to voice their opposition to the activities of a non-elected body responsible for essential services. Another issue that has not been significantly put to the test is what happens to an NDPB if it fails to attract clients and therefore funding. Government would generally not allow such bodies to 'go out of business' in a way that a private-sector organization can go into receivership. Instead, the tendency has been for the assets of a failing NDPB (such as a local tourist board) to be handed over to another body whose management has proved itself to be more capable of meeting clients' needs efficiently and effectively.

6.8 OTHER TYPES OF ORGANIZATION
6.8.1 Co-operative societies

Co-operatives can be divided into two basic types according to who owns them: consumer co-operatives and producer co-operatives.

Consumer co-operative societies date back to the mid-nineteenth century when their aims were to provide cheap, unadulterated food for their members and to share profits among members rather than hand them over to outside shareholders. The number of retail co-operative societies grew during the latter half of the nineteenth century but has declined during recent years as a result of mergers, so that there were fewer than 50 in 2005. Nevertheless, co-operative societies collectively remain the fifth largest retailer in the United Kingdom. Food retail is by far the largest sector of the Co-op in the UK, accounting for almost half of all

THINKING AROUND THE SUBJECT:
THE NATIONAL HEALTH SERVICE GOES TO MARKET

The National Health Service (NHS) is Britain's largest employer and has traditionally operated with a command and control structure. Money was allocated by government and distributed between regions, then between hospitals, and then allocated between wards. There was a sense of security in this centralized planning, and hospitals – even wards – could reasonably expect that their budget in the following year would not be drastically different to the current year. Hospitals developed specialisms and tended to take on a steady workload of patients referred through an established network of consultants and primary care trusts. The development of 'Foundation' status hospital trusts from 2003 and the introduction of a market for hospital services were intended to improve the effectiveness and efficiency with which trusts operated. From 2004, the government introduced privately operated 'treatment centres' to provide a wide range of elective treatment, such as eye cataract operations and MRI scans. These effectively took 'business' away from NHS hospitals, which would in future have to compete for these patients. In the new NHS market, money followed the patients, and patients were given more choice, while family doctors were increasingly being encouraged to take control of their budgets.

But were managers of the traditionally bureaucratic command and control NHS ready for the uncertainty of a market economy? More worryingly, what would happen if a hospital with Foundation Trust status ran out of money? Could it 'go bust'? Foundation Trust hospitals are free-standing businesses that depend on government for their cash flow. Doubts were raised when Bradford Teaching Hospital, one of the first Foundation Trusts, went from a projected surplus of £1 million in 2005 to a potential deficit of £11 million in a matter of months of it coming into existence. At the same time, a number of other Foundation Trusts faced lesser financial difficulties.

The government claimed to have in place procedures for dealing with a failing Foundation Trust hospital. The first resort would be to put in new management. If the failing was more serious, it could be taken over by another Foundation Trust. Ultimately, the Trust could be returned to the Secretary of State's ownership. The government would doubtless be mindful of the political consequences of allowing a hospital trust to close down, or concentrating services in one centralized facility.

In many parts of the country, hospitals provide overlapping services, with very complex sets of relationships with primary care trusts, which do the purchasing of hospital services. In the new NHS market, the financial skills of boards were called for if a chaotic and unstable environment was to be avoided. It was almost unheard of for a British hospital to go out of business but, as the government pursues a market discipline for the NHS, is going out of business a logical consequence that should be shared with the private sector?

turnover, and the Co-operative Group accounts for more than 50 per cent of total co-operative trade. But although food stores are perhaps the most recognizable face of the Co-op, the co-operative societies also comprise travel agencies, funeral homes, the Co-operative Bank, Co-operative Insurance Service (CIS) and car dealerships.

Each co-operative society is registered under the Industrial and Provident Societies Acts, and not the Companies Acts, and has its own legal personality, very much as a private limited company. The main contrast between the two comes in the form of control of the society –

an individual can become a member of a co-operative by buying one share and is entitled to one vote. Further shares can be purchased, but the member still has only one vote, unlike the private limited company where voting power is generally based on the number of shares held. The appeal of a shop owned by customers has declined of late, as customers have been attracted by competing companies offering lower prices and/or better service. So the co-operative movement has responded by taking on many of the values of the private sector, for example through the abolition of 'dividend' payments and advertising low prices for all. However, the movement has tried to capitalize on its customer ownership by appealing to customers on the basis of its social responsibility. Promotion of co-operative retail stores has often sought to stress their 'green' credentials, while the Co-operative Bank has stressed that it does not lend for unethical purposes.

Producer co-operatives are formed where suppliers feel they can produce and sell their output more effectively by pooling their resources, for example by sharing manufacturing equipment and jointly selling output. Producer co-operatives are popular among groups of farmers, allowing individual farmers to market their produce more effectively than they could achieve individually. An example is OMSCo (Organic Milk Supply Company), formed in 1994 when five like-minded organic dairy farmers joined forces to sell their organic milk. Now with around 300 members, OMSCo is the largest and longest established UK organic milk supplier. For the marketing of a producer co-operative to be successful, members need to share a sense of vision and have clear leadership. Where this is lacking, many producer co-operatives may be successful in buying products for their members at a discount, but less successful at marketing their output. There are currently about 1000 producer co-operative societies within the UK, mainly in the farming and fishing sectors. Farmers' co-operatives are much more important in other EU countries such as France where there are many more local, regional and national farmers' co-operatives, the larger of which have diversified into non-farming activities such as banking and transport.

Producer co-operatives may fall foul of legislation to protect the competitiveness of markets where collectively the producers account for a high proportion of sales in the market. However, as most producer co-operatives tend to be quite local in their membership, there is usually the possibility of competition from producers located in other areas.

6.8.2 Charities and voluntary organizations

The aims of this group of organizations can be quite complex. Serving a good cause, such as famine relief or cancer research, is clearly very important. However, these organizations often also set trading objectives, as where charities run shops to raise funds. Often, the way in which such businesses are run is just as important as the funds generated. For example, Dr Barnardos runs coffee shops where providing training for disadvantaged staff is seen to be as important as providing a fast service for customers or maximizing the profits of the outlet.

In the UK, charities that are registered with the Registrar of Charities are given numerous benefits by the government, such as tax concessions (although recent changes in legislation have introduced stricter controls over their activities in order to reduce abuses of their status). Where a charity has substantial trading activities, it is usual for these to be undertaken by a separately registered limited company, which then hands over its profits to the charity.

In some respects, charities have become more like conventional trading organizations, for example in their increasingly sophisticated use of direct marketing techniques. However, in other respects they can act very differently to private- and public-sector organizations. Customers may show a loyalty to the charity's cause, which goes beyond any rational economic explanation. Employees often work for no monetary reward, providing a dedicated and low-cost workforce, which can help the organization achieve its objectives.

6.8.3 Building societies

Building societies are governed by the Building Societies Acts, which have evolved over time to reflect their changing role. They were for some time seen as almost monopoly providers of money for house purchases, with strict regulations on the powers of societies in terms of their sources of funds and the uses for which loans could be advanced. With the liberalization of the home mortgage market, building societies now have wider powers of lending and borrowing and face much greater competition. As a result of this, societies have had to embrace marketing activities more fully. The Building Societies Act 1986 further allowed building societies the possibility of converting to public limited company status, eliminating the remaining controls imposed by the Building Society Acts (Figure 6.3).

Figure 6.3 Public limited companies have grown in number in recent years and added a number of former building societies whose members voted for conversion. Although PLC status does give numerous benefits over mutual status, there are also many benefits of remaining mutual. The Coventry Building Society has stressed the benefits of remaining mutual, arguing that it is achieving high levels of customer satisfaction and a financial performance which matches PLCs and returns the benefits to members. (Picture reproduced with permission of Coventry Building Society)

6.8.4 Franchise organizations

Franchising refers to trading relationships between companies (see Figure 6.4) in which a franchisor grants the right to a franchisee to operate a business using the franchisor's business format. In terms of their legal status, the companies themselves could be any one of the types previously described. The franchisor (which owns the franchise brand name) is more likely to be a public or private limited company, while the franchisee (which buys the right to use the franchise from the franchisor) is more likely to be a sole trader, partnership or private limited company. The franchisor and franchisee have legally separate identities, but the nature of the franchise agreement can make them very interdependent.

Franchising is a rapidly growing type of business relationship. According to the annual NatWest/British Franchise Association survey, the total number of franchise systems in the UK in 2004 was 695. These were linked to a total of 33,800 franchisees, with an annual turnover of £9.65 billion and employed 330,000 people; 95 per cent of franchisees were profitable (British Franchise Association 2004). Franchising offers a ready-made business opportunity for the entrepreneur who has capital but does not want the risk associated with setting up a completely new business afresh. A good franchise operation will have a proven business format and would already be well established in its market. The franchisee would be required to pay an initial capital sum for the right to use the name of the franchisor. This may sometimes seem high, but represents a relatively less risky investment than starting a completely new business. It has been estimated that whereas up to 90 per cent of all new businesses fail within three years of starting up, 90 per cent of all franchisees survive beyond this

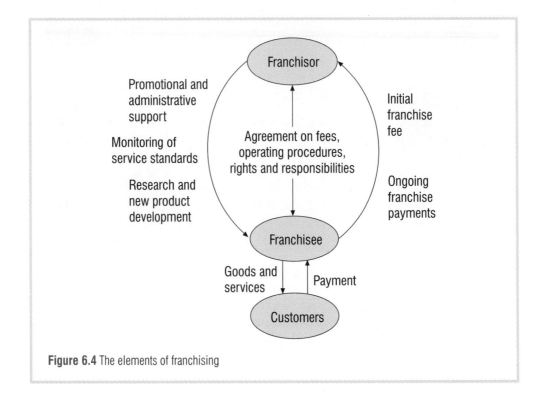

Figure 6.4 The elements of franchising

Figure 6.5 Franchising has firmly taken root in the market for fast printing services, with names such as Prontaprint, Kwik-Print and Kenkos being familiar, well-developed franchise systems. The development of low-cost offset litho and photocopying machines lowered the entry barriers to printing, which had previously confined printing to craft-trained individuals. Prontaprint is typical in selling a franchise to people that can demonstrate commitment to high standards and profitable growth. For a small investor looking for a business of their own, a Prontaprint franchise offers the security of a brand name that customers have come to trust. Like most fast printing companies, Prontaprint's franchisees offer essentially simple, straightforward printing services that can easily be described in a business blueprint. More complex and variable printing services, such as carton printing, tickets and high-volume magazine printing, are less likely to be franchised out.

period (British Franchise Association 2004). Although franchisees are typically small sole traders, in fact they are often large public limited companies. It is quite common for a large company to have a franchise to operate, for example, a number of fast-food restaurants on behalf of the franchise owner.

As well as the initial capital sum, a franchise agreement will usually include provisions for the franchisee to purchase stock from the franchisor and to pass on a percentage of turnover or profit. The franchisor undertakes to provide general marketing and administrative back-up for the franchisees.

Public services are increasingly being delivered by franchised organizations in order to capitalize on the motivation of smaller-scale franchisees (described above). Public-sector franchises can take a number of forms, as described below.

1 The right to operate a vital public service can be sold to a franchisee, which in turn has the right to charge users of the facility. The franchisee will normally be required to maintain the facility to a required standard and to obtain government approval of prices to be charged. In the United Kingdom, the government has offered private organizations franchises to operate vital road links, including the Dartford river crossing, the Severn Bridge and the M6 West Midlands Toll Motorway. In the case of the latter, the Australian-based Macquarie Investment Group acquired the right to collect tolls from motorway users and in return agreed to construct and maintain the road.

2 Government can sell the exclusive right for private organizations to operate a private service which is of public importance. In 2000, the UK government auctioned licences which would allow companies to offer 'third-generation' (3G) mobile phone services. The government raised £22 billion from the sale of these licences and stipulated conditions under which mobile phone services would be provided by the successful bidders. Private-sector radio and television broadcasting is operated on a franchise basis, where the government invites bids from private companies for exclusive rights to broadcast in specified areas and/or times.

3 Where a socially necessary but economically unviable service is provided in a market-mediated environment, government can subsidize provision of the service by means of a franchise. An example of this can be seen in the way subsidies are paid by government to privatized train companies in order to support train services. The award of franchises followed competitive tendering.

4 Even though a public service is not market mediated at the point of delivery, production methods may nevertheless be market mediated and part of the production function may be provided through a franchise agreement. Such an arrangement can have benefits for customers where the franchisee is rewarded partly on the basis of feedback from users. A recent application of this type of franchise can be found in the field of higher education.

5 In the United Kingdom, possibly the longest-established public-sector franchise is seen in the Post Office. In addition to government-owned 'Crown' post offices, 'sub' post offices have traditionally been operated on a franchise basis in smaller towns. Franchises have been taken up by a variety of small shops and newsagents and generally offer a more limited range of postal services compared to Crown offices.

6.9 'VIRTUAL' ORGANIZATIONS

The term 'virtual' organization has been widely used in recent years, and although it does not represent a particular legal basis for an organization, it is nevertheless useful to examine its characteristics.

The virtual organization refers to a network of independent companies, suppliers, customers, even one-time rivals linked by information technology to share skills, cost and access to one another's markets and resources. The network can comprise any combination of legal form of organization, for example multinational airlines may co-operate through virtual organizations to procure engineering resources, while, more locally, many small businesses co-operate through virtual organizations to promote tourism destinations. A characteristic of virtual organizations is that they may have no central office or internal hierarchy. Electronic commerce has facilitated the development of virtual organizations. Hale and Whitlam (1997) define as 'virtual' any organization that is continually evolving, redefining and reinventing itself for practical business purposes. The aim of such organizations is to deliver services through structures and processes that are fast, flexible and flat. Virtual organizations can use computer-mediated communication to become more flexible and responsive than traditional organizational structures. They can allow small businesses to collaborate with minimal bureaucracy and can create value cost-effectively. By drawing together essentially freelance individuals, virtual organizations can benefit from an inherent responsiveness to change in the business environment.

COOKING BY YOURSELF OR WITH COMPANY?

Many people dream about setting up their own restaurant. For somebody who loves food, the prospect of giving up a 9–5 office job and spending all their working life developing new menus may seem irresistible. Sadly, although thousands of people have ventured down the route to becoming a restaurateur, the success rate is low. Estimates vary, but it is generally reckoned that about three-quarters of all new restaurants are not a success, and close within three years of opening. Large corporate restaurant chains generally succeed better, but it is the sole trader that is particularly likely to face problems. Instead of experimenting with new recipes for beef bourguignon or duck a l'orange, the small restaurant owner is likely to spend much of their time on more mundane matters. Filling out the VAT return, recruiting staff, calculating their income tax and paying their National Insurance contributions, keeping abreast of new legislation concerning minimum wage levels, maternity leave, and disability discrimination are all distractions from the kitchen. Then there is the never-ending task of promoting the restaurant. Many restaurateurs think that customers will beat a path to their door, but diners can be fickle and as soon as a new restaurant opens in town, they may be off to try it out.

With so much to do in simply running the business, it is not surprising that many small restaurateurs become disillusioned and move on. Some fail simply because they hadn't developed a realistic business plan. Many of these could have benefited by belonging to a franchise organization, rather than going it alone. In franchised systems, the franchisor typically provides valuable support for administrative and promotional matters, leaving the franchisee to develop their business. Within the restaurant sector, franchising has been relatively slow to take hold at the gourmet end of the market, where the owner's individuality and style can add to the appeal of a restaurant. But in the convenience food sector, franchising has really taken hold and allows dedicated individuals to build a secure and profitable business.

The Domino's Pizza Group has used the energy of talented and hard-working individuals to deliver good financial rewards to its franchisees. Although the company's pizzas may not appeal greatly to people who love fine food, its approach to franchising of food outlets generally offers much more security and profitability than going it alone. In 2004, Domino's reported that 10 of its 100-plus UK and Ireland franchisees owned businesses which were worth more than £1,000,000 each. These figures are based on a

CASE STUDY

standard calculation of twice annual turnover. With an average start-up cost of £183,000 this is a significant return on franchisees' initial investment. How many sole traders running their own restaurant could match this? In 2002, Domino's franchisees earned around £120,000 a year on average (although some considerably more) which was more than three times the average income of a typical business manager (£38,107). Furthermore, no Domino's franchise failed during the year, compared with over 22,000 business failures elsewhere in the UK economy.

Domino's research into the skills set and characteristics of the most successful franchisees both in the UK and internationally had found that the majority of franchisees believed the traditional corporate management career path failed to offer either the scope to succeed or the financial rewards within the time scale they want.

Typical of the hard-working individuals attracted to a Domino's franchise was James Swift. As a 16-year-old delivery driver for Domino's Pizza, Swift spotted the potential to run his own business at an early age. He soon secured a position as the manager of the Domino's branch in Swindon and learned everything there was to know about running a store. This operational experience was critical for learning everything from how to make a pizza to how to manage a big team. It was about three years later that he got the chance to buy a share in the franchise. By the age of 24, he had become co-franchisee of three Domino's outlets in Swindon, Newbury and Bath. He put his success down to sheer hard work and determination, with the backing of a well-known brand and the commitment that only the owner of a business can give.

Maybe one day, James Swift would match the success of Richard P. Mueller, Jr, Domino's Pizza's most successful global franchisee. Mueller joined Domino's in 1967 as a delivery driver and became a franchisee in 1970. By 2003 he owned 158 stores in the USA and employed over 3000 team members. His company sold over 10 million pizzas a year, as many as the entire UK Domino's business. That equated to 5 million pounds of dough, 5 million pounds of cheese and enough pizza sauce to fill a large swimming pool. In the process of growing his business, Mueller had become a millionaire.

Although franchising is important for Domino's, the company retains a proportion of directly managed outlets. As well as providing an internal benchmark against which franchisees can be judged, these outlets are useful for developing new service ideas which may be too risky for individual franchisees to undertake on their own. One outcome of this process has been the development of a bluetooth and GPS-enabled system which can pinpoint a pizza delivery person's exact location via satellite. Information can then be transmitted to the delivery person's bluetooth headset, providing advice of the best route to take to their next customer via the GPRS (General Packet Radio Service) system based at the store. Would such developments be possible without the support of a strong centrally managed franchise?

Source: based on material provided by Domino's (www.dominos.com) and British Franchise Association (www.british-franchise.org) websites

1 Discuss the relative merits of franchising and direct management for restaurants.

2 What problems does a franchisee such as Domino's face in trying to reconcile the individualism of entrepreneurial franchisees with the need for brand consistency?

3 Why do you think that 15 per cent of Domino's outlets are managed directly by the company, rather than by franchisees?

There are numerous ways of classifying business organizations. Classification based on legal status is useful because this is often related to other factors such as size, the ability to raise fresh capital and the level of constraints imposed on marketing managers. Private-sector organizations range from the informality of the sole trader to the formality of the public limited company. In between is a diverse range of organizations, each of which has its role in the business environment. Some of these differences will become apparent in **Chapter 10**, which reviews competition within markets. While small sole traders may be associated with perfectly competitive markets, the reality of most markets is of domination by a small number of public limited companies. This chapter explored the reasons behind the recent resurgence in small business units. The ability to keep in touch with customers and to react to changes in the marketing environment were noted as important advantages. There is also diversity within public-sector organizations, although this group as a whole has tended to diminish in relative importance in most Western countries. **Chapter 2** discussed organizational structures within the public sector by focusing on government bodies that are policy making rather than operational. The following chapter will discuss how organizations grow. This chapter has laid the ground for the following chapter by suggesting that there are differences in organizations' inherent ability to grow.

Key Terms

Building societies	(235)	Liquidation	(219)	Receivership	(219)
Charities	(234)	Nationalized industry	(225)	Share capital	(219)
Co-operative society	(232)	Partnership	(215)	Shareholders	(218)
Franchising	(236)	Privatization	(226)	Sole trader	(212)
Limited company	(216)	Public limited company	(220)	Virtual organization	(238)

CHAPTER REVIEW QUESTIONS

1 (a) Identify the main strengths of two of
        the following types of business
        enterprise:
        - sole trader   - partnership
        - limited company   - PLC
        and assess the extent to which the
        strengths of one form are weaknesses
        of the other.

   (b) Prepare two slides for a business
        presentation comparing the ability of
        the two forms of enterprise to cope
        with a changing environment.
        (*Based on CIM Marketing Environment
        Examination*)

2 In what ways are the marketing efforts of a
   sole trader and a limited company of
   similar size likely to differ?

3 For what reasons might a manufacturer of
   fitted kitchens seek PLC status? What are
   the advantages and disadvantages of this
   course of action?

4 Why have governments found it difficult
   to privatize state-owned postal services?
   Suggest methods by which private-sector
   marketing principles can be applied to
   state-owned postal services.

5 Critically assess the benefits to the public
   of turning branches of the National
   Health Service into self-governing trusts.

6 Why have franchise organizations become
   so important in the United Kingdom?

ACTIVITY

Identify three Non-Departmental Public
Bodies (NDPBs) operating in the following
areas: education, housing and transport.
Critically evaluate the suitability of NDPB
status. Do you think these organizations'
service to the public would be improved if
they were either purely private-sector or
purely public-sector organizations?

Useful Websites

Business Bureau

A commercial site offering an overview of the
legislation with particular relevance to small
business creation and management.

**http://www.businessbureau-uk.co.uk/law/
law.htm**

CBI

The CBI is the premier organization speaking
for companies in the UK. Its website provides
details of CBI surveys and discussion of topical
issues affecting business organizations.

http://www.cbi.org.uk/home.html

British Franchise Association

Useful resources relating to the role of
franchising.

http://www.british-franchise.org/menu.html

Building Societies Association

The Building Societies Association is the trade
association for the UK's building societies. This
site provides useful resources relating to the role
of building societies.

http://www.bsa.org.uk/

Co-operative society links

This site provides links to co-operative societies
throughout the world.

**http://www.jlp86.freeserve.co.uk/pages/links.
html**

Virtual Society Research Programme

An ESRC-funded programme at Oxford
University looking into the impacts of virtual
electronic relationships.

http://www.virtualsociety.org.uk

Further Reading

A useful starting point for further reading is one of a number of books discussing the purpose of organizations and their role in society:

Browning, R. (2003) *Setting Up and Running a Limited Company: A Comprehensive Guide to Forming and Operating a Company as a Director and Shareholder*, How To Books.

Carnall, C. (2002) *Managing Change in Organizations*, London, FT Prentice Hall.

Cyert, R. and March, J. (1992) *A Behavioural Theory of the Firm*, 2nd edn, Oxford, Blackwell.

Salaman, G. (ed.) (2000) *Understanding Business Organizations*, Routledge.

For a review of current statistics on the composition of business units, the following sources are useful:

Department of Trade and Industry, *SME Statistics*, London, The Stationery Office.

Office for National Statistics, *Annual Abstract of Statistics*, London, The Stationery Office.

To gain a further insight into the financing of business organizations and the role of shareholders, the following is useful:

Davis, E.W. (1994) *Finance and the Firm: An Introduction to Corporate Finance*, 2nd edn, Oxford, Oxford University Press.

The following provides a useful background on franchising:

British Franchise Association, *Annual Survey of Franchising*, London, BFA.

The nature of public-sector organizations has changed considerably in recent years and the following provide an overview of this change:

Bovaird, B. and Loeffler, E. (eds) (2003) *Public Management and Governance*, London, Routledge.

Flynn, N. (2001) *Public Sector Management*, 4th edn, London, FT Prentice Hall.

Scholes, K. and Johnson, G. (2000) *Exploring Public Sector Strategy*, FT Prentice Hall.

For a review of 'virtual' organizations and outsourcing, the following are useful sources:

Click, Rick L. and Duening Thomas N. (2004) *Business Process Outsourcing: The Competitive Advantage*, Chichester, John Wiley.

Davidow, W.H. and Malone, M.S. (1992) *The Virtual Corporation*, New York, HarperCollins.

Charities are becoming increasingly involved in business activities and their distinctive characteristics are discussed in the following:

Sargeant, A. (1999) *Marketing Management for Non-Profit Organizations*, Oxford University Press.

References

Barclays Bank (2004) Barclays Small Business Survey, London, Barclays Bank.

British Chambers of Commerce (2005) *Business Burdens Barometer*, London, BCC.

British Franchise Association (2004) *The British Franchise Association Annual Survey of Franchising*, London, BFA.

DTI Small Business Service (2004) *A Government Action Plan for Small Businesses: The Evidence Base*, London, Small Business Service/DTI.

Hale, R. and Whitlam, P. (1997) *Towards the Virtual Organization*, Maidenhead, McGraw-Hill.

Chapter 7

Organizational Objectives, Growth and Scale

7.1 THE OBJECTIVES OF ORGANIZATIONS

All organizations exist to pursue objectives of one description or another. It is important to understand the nature of organizational goals as these will affect – among other things – the way the organization makes purchases, sets prices or pursues a market share strategy. Whether somebody is selling to or competing with another organization, a study of the organization's objectives will help to understand how it is likely to respond to changes in its environment. Think of the difference between the small entrepreneurs who set up Internet businesses as soon as the technology appeared and the established business which they often competed against. The small entrepreneurs may have been more focused on short-term profits but many did not have the resources to see their project through to major growth. The larger established businesses, by contrast, were more likely to focus on maximizing medium- to long-term growth for their shareholders and had sufficient resources to cushion them from the effects of new start-ups. Their objectives could often be met by waiting until the market for Internet services had developed, sometimes acquiring their smaller competitors who had run out of money.

In this chapter we are going to look at organizational objectives, but the link with organizational structure discussed in the previous chapter should never be forgotten. As the example of the dotcom entrepreneur above indicated, the history and structure of an organization can profoundly affect its objectives. Just compare the effects that ownership and objectives have had on the patterns of growth shown by charities, public limited companies and state-owned enterprises.

Very broadly, organizational goals can be classified into a number of categories:

- those that aim to make a profit for their owners
- those that aim to maximize benefit to society
- those that aim to maximize benefits to their members.

Of course, many organizations combine these objectives, as in the case of the trading activities of charities that aim to make the maximum profits which can in turn benefit disadvantaged groups in society. In the following section we look in detail at more specific objectives of business organizations.

7.1.1 Profit maximization

It is often assumed that business organizations will always try to maximize their profits, through a combination of maximizing revenue and minimizing costs. It is usually thought that the pursuit of profit maximization is the unifying characteristic of all private-sector business organizations and, indeed, economic theory is very much based on the notion of the profit maximizing firm.

However, simple models of profit maximization are open to question, even if it is recognized for the moment that profit may be of only marginal relevance to organizations that exist largely for their members' or society's benefit. The following are some of the more important limitations on profit maximizing theories.

1 The profit-maximizing objective must be qualified by a time dimension. A firm pursuing a short-term profit-maximizing objective may act very differently to one that seeks to maximize long-term profit. This may be reflected in a differing emphasis on research and

development, new product development and market development strategies. Whether an organization is able to pursue long-term profit-maximizing objectives will be influenced by the nature of the environment in which it operates. It has frequently been suggested that the financial environment of the United Kingdom and the emphasis on short-term results has caused UK organizations to pursue much more short-term profit goals than organizations in, for example, Japan, where the nature of organizational funding has allowed a longer time for projects to achieve profits. Similarly, an organization operating in a relatively regulated environment – such as patented medicines – will be in a stronger position to plan for long-term profit maximization than one that is operating in a relatively unpredictable and competitive market.

2 A second major criticism of the dominance of profit maximization as a business objective is that maximization is not observed to occur in practice. In most organizations, there is a separation of ownership from management, where the managers of the company have little or no stake in the ownership of the company. Managers may be inclined to pursue policies more in line with their own self-interests, so long as they make sufficient profit to keep their shareholders happy. Instead of pursuing maximum profits, the managers of the company may pursue a policy of maximizing sales turnover, subject to achieving a satisfactory level of profits.

3 In practice, it can be very difficult to quantify the relationship between production costs, selling prices, sales volumes and profit. Managers may have inadequate knowledge about these linkages with which to pursue profit maximization effectively.

7.1.2 Market share maximization

Market share maximization may coincide with profit maximization, in cases where there is a close correlation between market share and return on investment. It has been suggested that this occurs in many sectors, such as UK grocery retailing. There are other instances, however, where there is a less straightforward relationship between market share and profitability. For example, in the UK retail travel agency sector, both the market leader and small specialist retailers have achieved reasonable returns on investment, but many medium-sized firms have faced below average returns.

There are circumstances and reasons why a firm may pursue a policy of maximizing market share independently of a short-term profit-maximizing objective. Domination of a particular market may give stability and security to the organization. This might be regarded as a more attractive option for the management than maximizing profits. Building market share may itself be seen as a short-term strategy to achieve longer-term profits, given that there may be a relationship between the two.

Pursuing a market share growth objective may influence a number of aspects of a firm's business activities, for example it may cut prices and increase promotional expenditure, accepting short-term losses in order to drive its main rivals out of business, leaving it relatively free to exploit its market in the longer term.

7.1.3 Corporate growth

As an organization grows, so too does the power and responsibility of individual managers. In terms of salaries and career development, a growth strategy may appear very attractive to these people, not only for their own self-advancement but also as an aid to attracting and retaining a high calibre of staff, attracted by the prospects of career development. However, such enthusiasm for growth could lead the owners of the business to pursue diversification into possibly unknown and unprofitable areas. As an example, the fashion retailer Next, which is now very successful, earlier came very close to bankruptcy when it expanded too rapidly into relatively unknown activities such as the operation of convenience stores and travel agencies. Shareholders are often happy to back the management and take risks when times are good but may benefit in the longer term by being more cautious and critical of its management's recommendations.

7.1.4 Satisficing

Given that the managers of a business are probably not going to benefit directly from increased profits, the argument has been advanced that managers aim for *satisfactory* rather than *maximum* possible profits. Provided that sufficient profit is made to keep shareholders happy, managers may pursue activities that satisfy their own individual needs, such as better company cars for themselves, or may pursue business activities that give them a relatively easy life or add to their ego. To achieve these diverse individual objectives, part of the organization's profit that could be paid out to shareholders is diverted and used to pay for managerial satisfaction. The extent to which satisficing represents an important business objective can be debated. It can be argued that in relatively competitive markets, competitive pressures do not allow companies to add the costs of these management diversions to their selling prices. If they did, they would eventually go out of business in favour of companies whose shareholders exercised greater control over the costs of their managers. Only in stable and less competitive markets can these implied additional costs be borne by adding to prices.

There has been a growing tendency for the owners of a business to give senior managers of the business contracts of employment that are related to profit performance. While this may lessen the extent of the apparent conflict of objectives for management, a trade-off may still have to be made where, for example, a decision has to be made on whether to spend more money on better company cars for managers. Should they spend the money and get all of the benefit for themselves, or save costs in order to increase profits, of which they will receive only a share?

Satisficing behaviour can have a number of implications for a company's operations. Buying behaviour in any organization is likely to be complex, but companies that are satisficing are likely to attach greater importance to the intangible decision factors such as ease of order, familiarity with a sales representative and the level of status attached to a particular purchase, rather than the more objective factors such as price and quality. There may be a tendency to recruit staff on a more informal basis, with the implication that recruitment is driven by a desire to be surrounded by like-minded people, rather than the type of employee who is most effective at maximizing income from customers.

7.1.5 Survival

For many organizations, the objective of maximizing profit is a luxury for management and shareholders alike – the overriding problem is simply to stay in business. Many businesses have had to close not because of poor profitability – their long-term profit potential may have been very good – but because they ran out of short-term cash. Without a source of finance to pay for current expenses, a longer-term profit-maximizing objective cannot be achieved. Cash flow problems could come about for a number of reasons, such as unexpected increases in costs, a fall in revenue resulting from unexpected competitive pressure or a seasonal pattern of activity that is different to that which was predicted.

Survival as a business objective can influence business decisions in a number of ways. Pricing decisions may reflect the need to liquidate stock regardless of the mark-up or contribution to profit. This was evident during the first Gulf War when many airlines were brought close to bankruptcy by the combination of the falling volume of passenger business and increased fuel prices. In order to survive what many airlines thought would be a temporary blip, many offered very low fares just to keep cash flowing in order to cover their overheads. The need to survive can also affect an organization's promotional activities. An advertising campaign to build up long-term brand loyalty may be sacrificed to a cheaper sales promotion campaign which has a shorter payback period. In order to survive, a firm may impose a 'freeze' on new staff recruitment and capital investment. The company may hope that this will be sufficient to overcome the short-term problem, but it may be creating longer-term problems by weakening the ability of the company to meet customers' needs effectively and profitably.

7.1.6 Loss-making

A company may be part of a group that needs a loss-maker to set off against other companies in the group that are making profits that are heavily taxed by the Inland Revenue. Situations can arise where a subsidiary company makes a component that is used by another member of the group and although that subsidiary may make a loss, it may be more tax efficient for the company as a whole to continue making a loss rather than buying in the product at a cheaper price from an outside organization.

7.1.7 Personal objectives

Many businesses, especially smaller ones, appear to be pursuing objectives that have no economic rationality. They do not pursue maximum profits, and indeed may be quite happy making no profits at all. They may have no desire to grow and may be in no immediate danger of failure. Many small businesses are created to satisfy a variety of personal objectives. This was illustrated by the results of a survey undertaken by NatWest Bank into the reasons why individuals set up their own business. It was claimed by 31 per cent of respondents that their main reason was a desire for independence, while only 32 per cent of entrepreneurs saw maintaining a certain standard of living as the primary motivation. About 15 per cent were tempted into setting up their own business because they had been made redundant. Many new business owners also sought to combine a business with a hobby activity, a desire to remain active and the opportunity for friendly encounters with customers. The survey also showed that although growth is high on the agenda of nearly half the respondents, one-fifth were happy to remain at their current size (NatWest Bank 2004).

Many small businesses are set up by individuals using a capital lump sum which they have received (such as an inheritance or a redundancy payment). Many people in such circumstances have used their lump sum to invest in what are perceived as relatively pleasant and enjoyable businesses, such as antique shops, tea rooms and restaurants. Many fail in a competitive environment where personal objectives cannot be achieved without undue economic sacrifice (e.g. it has been estimated that around three-quarters of all new restaurants fail within two years of opening). However, many others continue to provide goods and services for an acceptable sacrifice from the owners in a marketplace where profit-motivated companies would be unable to meet their objectives. This may partly explain the domination of UK antique shops by small owner-managers and the absence of large chains of profit-motivated businesses.

7.1.8 Social objectives of commercial organizations

Occasionally, commercial organizations have overt social objectives of one form or another, usually alongside a financial objective, for example a requirement that the organization must at least break even. The trading activities of charities such as Oxfam, while having clear objectives in maximizing their revenue, also state their objectives in terms of which groups they seek to benefit. Their social objectives may result in buying supplies from disadvantaged groups, even though this may not be the most commercially profitable option.

Historically, many owners of commercial companies have adopted social objectives. For example, Quakers such as Cadbury and Rowntree sought to maximize the moral welfare of their workforce. In modern times, the Body Shop has an objective of not supporting experiments on animals, an objective that pervades many aspects of the company's business activities, including new product development and promotion. Even organizations which for the most part are pursuing profit objectives may pursue social objectives in some small areas of activity, as where an organization runs a sports or social club for its employees at a loss. The social responsibility of organizations, and the views of critics who are cynical about firms' social objectives, are discussed further in Chapter 9.

7.1.9 Maximizing benefits to consumers

An overriding objective of a marketing-orientated organization is to maximize consumer satisfaction. However, this has to be qualified by a second objective that requires the organization to meet its financial objectives. In the case of consumer co-operatives, maximizing the benefits to their customers has had significance beyond the normal marketing concept of maximizing consumer satisfaction. The co-operative movement was originally conceived to eliminate the role of the outside shareholder, allowing profits to be passed back to customers through a dividend which is related to a customer's spending rather than their shareholding. Any action that maximized the returns to the business by definition maximized the benefits to consumers.

The importance of consumer co-operatives has declined since the 1950s for a number of reasons. Consumer co-operatives could appear very attractive to consumers at a time when firms were essentially production orientated and when the demand for goods exceeded their supply. With the reversal of this situation, other retailers with greater organizational flexibility and a more overt marketing orientation have attracted custom by offering additional services to customers, often associated with lower prices.

During the 1990s, building societies have been keen to promote the fact that they do not have any shareholders to satisfy, and can therefore pass on savings to members. This has led some building societies, such as Nationwide, to argue that they offer consistently lower mortgage rates than those societies that have converted to public limited company status and must therefore meet the profit expectations of shareholders.

The co-operative movement in the UK was founded by the 'Rochdale Pioneers' in 1844. From the very beginning, the objectives of the co-operative retail movement have been dominated by a focus on satisfying consumers' needs in an ethical manner. In the 1840s, this would have led the organization not to put copper dye in its tinned vegetables in order to make them look green. This may have satisfied the objectives of profit-motivated retailers, but it went against the principles of the movement which was to protect the interests of the customers that owned it. Today, the co-operative movement is represented by a number of societies that all share a focus on acting ethically, and can afford to think long term,

without the need to satisfy the short-term interests of shareholders. As an example, the Oxford, Swindon and Gloucester Co-op states that its purpose is to be 'a successful corporate business to enhance the lives of our staff, members, customers and the communities that we serve, and to work towards a better, fairer world'. The society returns surplus profits to its 100,000 members through a dividend, based on members' spending during the previous year. To improve governance of the Co-op, rewards are given to members who attend meetings of the society.

7.1.10 Maximizing public benefits

In many government and charity organizations, it is difficult to talk about the concept of profit or revenue maximization. Instead, the organization is given an objective of maximizing specified aspects of public benefit, or 'externalities', subject to keeping within a resource constraint. Public-sector hospitals are increasingly embracing the philosophy of marketing, but it is recognized that it would be inappropriate for them to be given a strictly financial set of objectives. Instead, they might be given the objective of maximizing the number of operations of a particular kind within a resource constraint. Similarly, a charity campaigning for improved road safety may set an objective of maximizing awareness of its cause among important opinion formers.

There is frequently a gap between the publicly stated objectives of a public-sector organization and the interpretation and implementation of these objectives by the staff concerned. As in a private-sector organization, management in the public sector could promote secondary objectives that add to their own individual status and security, rather than maximizing the public benefit. A manager of a hospital may pursue an objective of maximizing the use of high technology because this may be perceived as enhancing his or her career, even though the public benefit could be maximized more efficiently with simpler technology. Charities have sometimes been accused of becoming self-perpetuating bureaucracies, anxious to protect their organization, rather than being driven primarily by a passion for the cause that they promote.

In recent years, more pressure has been placed on public services such as education and defence to operate according to business criteria. As suppliers of services, public-sector organizations are increasingly being set quantified objectives that reflect the needs of their clients. These are often expressed as service standards, to reduce waiting times for hospital appointments or the turnaround of applications for passports or driving licences, for example. Improved research methods to find out more about client needs and more effective communication of their offering to clients have been part of this process towards a greater business orientation. Many public services have themselves become major consumers of services as peripheral activities such as cleaning and catering have been outsourced. This has resulted in the growth of a market-orientated service sector. Very often, the management and staff previously providing an ancillary service within a public-sector organization have bought out the operation from their employer and now have to sell the service back to the authority. Their objectives have changed from a vague notion of maximizing public benefit to one of maximizing their own profit.

7.1.11 Complexity of objectives

A number of possible objectives for organizations have been suggested above. In practice, an organization is likely to be pursuing multiple objectives at any one time. Furthermore, objectives are likely to change through time. Trying to identify the objectives that are influencing the behaviour of an organization can present a number of practical problems.

The first place to look for a statement of an organization's objectives might be its Memorandum and Articles of Association. In the UK, this statement is required by the Companies Acts for all limited companies and includes an objects clause. In practice, companies frequently draw up their objects clause in a way that is so wide that the company can do almost anything.

A more up-to-date statement of objectives may be found in the annual report and accounts which all companies must produce annually and submit to Companies House where it is available for public inspection. The report includes a Directors' report which may give an indication of the goals that the company is working towards. Many companies publish a mission statement, which gives a broad statement of the anticipated future direction that its business will take. We will return to the subject of mission statements in the following chapter.

Beyond this, the true objectives may be difficult for an outsider to determine. Indeed, clearly stating objectives in too much detail may put a firm at a commercial disadvantage when competitors adapt their behaviour accordingly. Even insiders may have difficulty identifying objectives.

7.2 THE GROWTH OF ORGANIZATIONS

It was noted earlier that organizations, like most living organisms, have an almost inherent tendency to grow. In this section, the reasons for growth and the options for growth that are open to business organizations are explored.

7.2.1 Reasons for growth

An organization can grow in size for a number of reasons.

1 The markets in which the organization operates may be growing, making growth in output relatively easy to achieve. In addition, in a rapidly growing market, if an organization was to maintain a constant output, its market share would be falling. Growth may be considered not so much of a luxury as a necessity if it is to maintain its position in the marketplace. This could be particularly important for industries where economies of scale are an important consideration.

2 A critical mass may exist for the size of firms in a market, below which they are at a competitive disadvantage. For example, a retail grocery chain which is aiming for a broad market segment will need to achieve a sufficiently large size in order to obtain bulk discounts from suppliers which can in turn be passed on in lower prices to customers. Size could also give economies of scale in many other activities such as advertising, distribution and administration. Many new businesses may include in their business plan an objective to achieve a specified critical mass within a given time period.

3 An overt policy of growth is often pursued by organizations in an attempt to stimulate staff morale. A growing organization is likely to be in a strong position to recruit and retain a high calibre of staff.

4 In addition to the formal goals of growth, management may in practice pursue objectives that result in growth. Higher rates of growth can bring greater status and promotion prospects to managers of an organization, even if a more appropriate long-term strategy may indicate a slower rate of growth.

5 Some organizations may grow by acquiring competitors in order to limit the amount of competition in a market where this is considered to be wasteful competition. Many local bus operators in the UK have acquired routes from their competitors for this purpose, although the Competition Commission may impose conditions on such takeovers where there is a serious threat to the public interest. We will return to this subject in Chapter 10.

7.2.2 Leadership

Many of the most successful commercial organizations, including the Virgin Group, Federal Express and McDonald's, attribute their success in part to the quality of leadership within their organizations. The results of poor leadership are evident in many failing organizations, especially within the public sector.

What is good leadership for one organization need not necessarily be so for another. Organizations operating in relatively stable environments may be best suited to a leadership style which places a lot of power in a hierarchical chain of command. In the UK, many banks until recently had leadership styles that had been drawn from models developed in the armed forces, evidenced by some mangers having titles such as superintendent and inspector. Such rigid, hierarchical patterns of leadership may be less effective where the business environment is changing rapidly and a flexible response is called for (as has happened in the banking sector). The literature has developed two typologies of leadership – transactional and transformational – which broadly correspond with control and empowerment respectively, as described in Chapter 8.

What makes a good leader of people? And are leaders born, or can individuals acquire the skills of leadership? On the latter point there is little doubt that development is possible, and successful companies have invested heavily in leadership development programmes. As for what makes a successful leader of organizations, there have been many suggestions of desirable characteristics, including:

- setting clear expectations of staff
- recognizing excellence appropriately and facilitating staff in overcoming their weaknesses
- leading by example
- being able to empathize with employees
- showing adaptability to changing circumstances.

In too many companies, bad leadership is characterized by:

- 'management by confusion' in which expectations of staff are ambiguously stated and management actions are guided by a secretive 'hidden agenda'
- reward systems which are not based on performance and are perceived as being unfair
- the deliberate or inadvertent creation of an 'us and them' attitude
- failing to understand the aspirations of employees
- failing to take the initiative where environmental change calls for adaptation.

THINKING AROUND THE SUBJECT:
SHOP MANAGERS LEAD BY EXAMPLE

Beginning with a small shop in Dundalk in 1960, the Irish grocery retailer SuperQuinn has grown to a successful chain, owning 19 large shops and nine shopping centres, and employing over 2000 people throughout Ireland. A large part of this success has been attributed to the leadership style of the company's founder, Feargal Quinn, and the emphasis on linking employees' activities to excellence in service quality. But what makes such leadership style distinctive?

An important principle is that managers should lead by example and never lose contact with the most important person in the organization – the customer. It is the task of a leader to set the tone for customer-focused excellence. To prevent managers losing sight of customers' needs, Quinn uses every opportunity to move them closer to customers, including locating their offices not in a comfortable room upstairs, but in the middle of the sales floor. Managers regularly take part in customer panels where customers talk about their expectations and perceptions of SuperQuinn. Subcontracting this task entirely to a market research agency is seen as alien to the leadership culture of the company. The company requires its managers to spend periods doing routine front-line jobs (such as packing customers' bags), a practice which has become commonplace in many successful service organizations. This keeps managers close to the company and improves their ability to empathize with junior employees.

Does this leadership style work? Given the company's level of growth, profits and rate of repeat business, it must be doing something right, contradicting much of scientific management theory that management is a specialist task which can be separated from routine dealings with customers and employees.

7.2.3 Organizational life cycles

It is common to talk about products going through a life cycle from launch, through growth and maturity to eventual decline. Many have suggested that organizations also go through a similar type of life cycle. There is evidence that an organization's goals may change over time. It has been argued by Grenier (1972) that periods of steady evolutionary growth are followed by periods of revolutionary development. Periods of crisis exist between states of stability (Hudson 1995). A number of factors trigger the different stages in the organizational life cycle. These can be external threats and opportunities (for example, the emergence of a powerful competitor or the availability of new technology), or the emergence of internal strengths and weaknesses (for example the appointment of a proactive manager or retirement of senior figures).

Within the private commercial sector, new enterprises have been associated with a mission-ary zeal, prompted by the need to survive in a fiercely competitive environment. Over time, an enterprise can establish a niche for itself, allowing it greater control over its markets. This is an invitation for satisficing behaviour by managers, where personal social goals may achieve greater prominence relative to formal corporate goals (Cyert and March 1963; Krabuanrat and Phelps 1998).

One analysis of service organizations, by Sasser, Olsen and Wyckoff (1978), identified a number of stages in the life cycles of organizations.

- Stage 1: **Entrepreneurial** In this stage, an individual identifies a market need and offers a product to a small number of people, usually operating from one location. While most entrepreneurs stay at this stage, some begin to think about growth, often entailing a move to larger and/or additional sites.
- Stage 2: **Multisite rationalization** In this stage, the successful entrepreneur starts to add to the limited number of facilities. It is during this stage that the skills required for being a multisite operator begin to be developed. By the end of this stage, the organization gains a certain degree of stability at a level of critical mass. At this stage, franchising starts to be considered.
- Stage 3: **Growth** Here the company's concept has become accepted as a profitable business idea. The company is now actively expanding through the purchase of competitors, franchising/licensing the concept, developing new company-operated facilities or a combi-nation of the three. Growth is not only influenced by the founder's desire to succeed but also by the pressures placed on the company by the financial community.
- Stage 4: **Maturity** The number of new outlets declines and revenues of individual facilities stabilize and in some cases decline. This tends to be caused by a combination of four factors: changing demographics within the firm's market; changing needs and tastes of consumers; increased competition; and 'cannibalization' of older products by the firm's newer products.
- Stage 5: **Decline/regeneration** Firms can become complacent and, unless new products are developed or new markets found, decline and deterioration soon follows.

7.2.4 Types of organizational growth

Growth of organizations can be analysed in terms of:

1 the object of the growth, which can be defined in terms of the development of new markets and/or new products

2 organizational issues about how the growth is achieved.

The first of these issues can be analysed with the help of growth option matrices. For the second, two basic growth patterns for organizations can be identified – organic growth and growth by acquisition – although many organizations grow by a combination of the two processes.

7.2.5 Product/market expansion

An organization's growth can conceptually be analysed in terms of two key development dimensions: markets and products. This conceptualization forms the basis of the product/market expansion grid (or 'growth matrix') proposed by Ansoff (1957). Products and markets are each analysed in terms of their degree of novelty to an organization and growth strategies identified in terms of these two dimensions. In this way, four types of growth strategy can be identified. The four growth options are associated with differing sets of problems and opportunities for organizations. These relate to the level of resources required to implement a particular strategy and the level of risk associated with each. It follows, therefore, that what might be a feasible growth strategy for one organization may not be for another. The characteristics of the four strategies are described below.

1 **Market-penetration strategy:** This type of strategy focuses growth on the existing product range by encouraging higher levels of take-up among the existing target markets. In this way a specialist tour operator in a growing sector of the holiday market could – all other things being equal – grow naturally, simply by maintaining its current business strategy. If it wanted to accelerate this growth, it could do this, first, by seeking to sell more holidays to its existing customer base and, second, by attracting customers from its direct competitors. If the market was in fact in decline, the company could grow only by attracting customers from its competitors through more aggressive marketing policies and/or cost reduction programmes. A market penetration strategy offers the least level of risk to an organization – it is familiar with both its products and its customers.

2 **Market-development strategy:** This type of strategy builds on the existing product range that an organization has established, but seeks to find new groups of customers for them. In this way a specialist regional ski tour operator that has saturated its current market might seek to expand its sales to new geographical regions or aim its marketing effort at attracting custom from groups beyond its current age/income groups. While the organization may be familiar with the operational aspects of the product that it is providing, it faces risks resulting from possibly poor knowledge of different buyer behaviour patterns in the markets which it seeks to enter. As an example of the potential problems associated with this strategy, many UK retailers have sought to offer their UK shop formats in overseas markets only to find that those features that attracted customers in the United Kingdom failed to do so overseas.

3 **Product-development strategy:** As an alternative to selling existing products into new markets, an organization may choose to develop new products for its existing customers. For example, a ski tour operator may have built up a good understanding of the holiday needs of a particular market segment, such as the 18- to 35-year-old affluent aspiring segment, and then seeks to offer a wider range of services to them than simply skiing holidays. It might offer summer activity holidays in addition, say. While the company minimizes the risk associated with the uncertainty of new markets, it faces risk resulting from

lack of knowledge about its new product area. Often a feature of this growth strategy is collaboration with a product specialist that helps the organization produce the service, leaving it free to market it effectively to its customers. A department store wishing to add a coffee shop to its service offering may not have the skills and resources within its organization to run such a facility effectively, but may outsource to a catering specialist, leaving it free to determine the overall policy that should be adopted.

5 **Diversification strategy:** Here, an organization expands by developing new products for new markets. Diversification can take a number of forms. The company could stay within the same general product/market area, but diversify into a new point of the distribution chain. For example, an airline that sets up its own travel agency moves into a type of service provision that is new to the organization, as well as dealing directly with a segment of the market with which it had previously probably had few sales transactions. Alternatively, the airline might diversify into completely unrelated service areas aimed at completely different groups of customers – by purchasing a golf course or car dealership, for example. Because the company is moving into both unknown markets and unknown product areas, this form of growth carries the greatest level of risk. Diversification may, however, help to manage the long-term risk of the organization by reducing dependency on a narrow product/market area.

An illustration of the framework, with reference to the specific options open to a seaside holiday hotel, is shown in Figure 7.1.

In practice, most growth that occurs is a combination of product development and market development. In very competitive markets, organizations would probably have to slightly adapt their products if they are to become attractive to a new market segment. For the leisure hotel seeking to capture new business customers, it may not be enough to simply promote existing

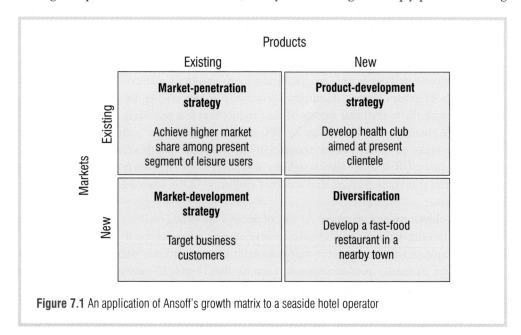

Figure 7.1 An application of Ansoff's growth matrix to a seaside hotel operator

Should a company 'stick to its knitting' and do what it is good at, or search continually for new products and new markets? Countless companies have reported disastrous results after growing into areas they knew very little about. Many UK clearing banks diversified into estate agency but regretted the move later. WHSmith went through bad years in the mid-1990s when the newsagent's diversification into DIY retailing and television, among other things, failed to work. Boots the Chemists bought the Halfords car parts and repair garages, but sold them in 2002 when it realized that Halfords had a poor fit with the rest of the Boots businesses and failed to gain a strong competitive advantage.

But isn't growth into new markets essential for companies, especially those facing static or declining markets? One of the UK's leading grocery retailers, Asda (now a subsidiary of Wal-Mart), would not be where it is today had not the Associated Dairy company taken a risk and set up a retailing operation. The security services company Securicor knew that it was taking a risk when it invested in a joint venture with British Telecom to create the successful Cellnet mobile phone network (now called O_2). And a small manufacturing company called WPP (standing for Wire Plastic Products) took huge risks on its way to becoming the owner of one of the world's leading advertising agencies, J Walter Thompson.

It is fine with hindsight to criticize a firm's decisions about which direction its corporate growth should take. But in an uncertain world, risks have to be taken. A sound analysis of a company's strengths and weaknesses and of its external environment certainly helps, but successful growth also depends on an element of luck.

facilities; in order to meet business people's needs, it might have to offer refurbished facilities to make them more acceptable to business customers and offer new facilities (e.g. the facility for visitors to pay by account).

It has been argued that most successful growth initiatives take place in markets that are adjacent to a company's existing business (Zook 2004). Problems are likely to arise when companies take two or three steps at once, for example offering new customers a new product through a new channel. But even growth into adjacent markets can end in trouble, and a common pitfall occurs where management attention is drawn away from their core business. For example, in the 1990s, the Ford car company expanded into automotive services such as finance and insurance, but it neglected to develop world-class models for its core car business.

7.2.6 Organic growth

Organic growth is considered to be the more natural pattern of growth for an organization. The initial investment by the organization results in profits, an established customer base and a well-established technical, personnel and financial structure. This provides a foundation for future growth. In this sense, success breeds success, for the rate of the organization's growth is influenced by the extent to which it has succeeded in building up internally the means for future expansion. All aspects of the organization can be said to evolve gradually. For example, the accounting and finance function may initially be under the day-to-day control of one person, but as the organization expands, so it becomes necessary to develop specialist areas within accounting, each with its own section head.

An organization may grow organically by tackling one market segment at a time, using the resources, knowledge and market awareness it has gained in order to tackle further segments. A firm may grow organically into new segments in a number of ways. Many retail chains have grown organically by developing one region before moving on to another – Sainsbury's grew organically from its southern base towards the northern regions, while Asda grew organically from its northern base towards the south. Other organizations have grown organically by aiming a basically similar product at new segments of the market – as Thomson Holidays has done over many years in developing slightly differentiated holidays aimed at the youth and elderly markets.

Where new market opportunities suddenly appear, an organization may not have the specialized resources that would allow it to grow organically. Within the financial services sector, a study by Ennew, Wong and Wright (1992) found that many of the assets of companies, such as specialized staff and distribution networks, were quite specific to their existing markets and could not easily be adapted to exploit new markets. Growth by acquisition was in many cases considered to be a better method of expansion.

7.2.7 Growth by acquisition

The rate of organic growth is constrained by a number of factors, for example the rate at which the market that an organization serves is growing. An organization seeking to grow organically in a slowly developing sector such as food manufacture will find organic growth more difficult than an organization serving a rapidly growing sector such as online computer information services. In some cases, organic growth is difficult because of a scarcity of resources (e.g. prime locations for retail sites), and growth by acquiring other companies is the easiest way of acquiring those resources. Also, companies with relatively high capital requirements will find organic growth relatively difficult.

Growth by acquisition may appear attractive to organizations where organic growth is difficult. In some cases it may be almost essential in order to achieve the critical mass which may be necessary for survival. The DIY retail sector in the United Kingdom is one where chains have needed to achieve a critical size in order to exploit economies in buying, distribution and promotion. Small chains have not been able to grow organically at a sufficient rate to achieve critical mass, resulting in their takeover or merger to form larger chains. Sainsbury's, former owner of the Homebase chain of DIY outlets, sought to challenge market leader B&Q. Organic growth would have involved considerable expenditure on new sites in a sector that was becoming saturated. Instead it sought to achieve economies of scale by acquiring its competitor Texas Homecare. Texas had itself grown by acquiring a number of smaller chains, such as Unit Sales. During 2001, the Homebase chain was sold by Sainsbury's, mindful of the fact that it had not achieved the economies of scale required to beat the market leader.

A major problem for firms seeking to grow within the service sector by acquisition lies in the fact that often the main assets being acquired are the skills and knowledge of the acquired organization's employees. Unlike physical assets, key personnel may disappear following the acquisition, reducing the earning ability of the business. Worse still, key staff could defect to the acquiring company's competitors. During the consolidation of the dotcom sector, which occurred during 2000/01, there is evidence that a lot of the acquiring firms' investment in their acquisitions was lost when key personnel left with their list of contacts and specialized knowledge.

Growth by acquisition may occur where an organization sees its existing market sector contracting and it seeks to diversify into other areas. The time and risk associated with starting a new venture in an alien market sector may be considered too great – acquiring an established business could be less risky, allowing access to an established client base and technical skills.

It was noted earlier that growth in itself might be seen as good for developing staff morale in allowing career progression. The organization may formally encourage growth by acquisition for this very reason, while staff may have informal objectives directed towards this end. Acquiring new subsidiaries could satisfy this objective for a company that is operating in otherwise static markets.

Growth by acquisition can take a number of forms. The simplest is the agreed takeover whereby one firm agrees to purchase the majority of the share capital of another company. Payment can be in the form of cash or shares in the acquiring company, or some combination of the two. A takeover can be mutually beneficial where one company has a sound customer base but lacks the financial resources to achieve critical mass while the other has the finance but needs a larger customer base. Many takeovers occur where the founder of a business is seeking to retire and to liquidate the value of the business.

While the majority of takeovers are mutually agreed, circumstances often arise where a takeover is contested. This particularly affects public companies whose shares can be bought and sold openly. Typically a cash-rich firm would identify another company that it recognizes as underperforming because of poor management. Its argument for a takeover is based on the appeal of its proven management style being applied to the underperforming assets of the target company, increasing the profitability of the latter's assets. Disputed takeovers can become very bitter affairs, with each side trying to prove its own performance while denigrating that of the other party. The battle is often made even more vitriolic because of contrasting cultural styles. For the target company, exposure of its management style and practices may be a new and unwelcome event, and represents a desire to remain independent.

During a contested takeover bid, the marketing strategy of both target and bidding companies can be significantly affected during the short term. To prove the ability of the existing management, the target company's marketing programmes may focus on boosting short-term market share, possibly at the expense of long-term brand building. Communication programmes can become aimed at the financial community as much as the final consumer, for example by amending adverts for branded products to include the corporate name, thereby associating the company with a much broader portfolio of brands than may have been appreciated by members of the financial community. New product launches may be brought ahead of the ideal launch date in order to impress the financial community. Contested takeovers can also have a serious effect on staff, and many key employees may fear instability in the future and leave to take up more secure positions.

For public companies, the Stock Exchange imposes strict rules about how a takeover bid may be conducted, covered by the City Code on Takeovers and Mergers and monitored by the Panel on Takeovers. An acquiring company cannot simply quietly acquire shares in a company until it has achieved a majority shareholding. It must declare its holding once it has reached a 10 per cent holding and must make a formal takeover offer once it has acquired 30 per cent. The offer document itself is tightly prescribed in terms of the information that it must contain.

7.2.8 Mergers

A merger is a variation on a takeover where two existing companies agree to set up one new company which issues shares to the shareholders of each of the existing companies in agreed proportions and in exchange for existing shareholdings. Many agreed takeovers show characteristics of a merger and it is difficult to strictly distinguish between the two. Mergers can range in scale from two local solicitors merging their practices, through to multinational mergers characterized by the merger that took place in 2001 between AOL and Time Warner. An important reason for a merger is to allow greater cross-selling opportunities between the two companies' sets of customers and to allow for more efficient sharing of resources. The benefits of a merger can be particularly great where two merging companies have complementary resources. In the case of the AOL–Time Warner merger, AOL gained access to Time Warner's archive of film and published material, while Time Warner gained new channels of distribution for this archive.

As with takeovers, proposed mergers often fail because of cultural differences between the companies involved. During 1998, a proposal to merge Glaxo Wellcome with SmithKline Beecham to create the world's largest pharmaceutical company is reported to have failed because of disagreements among the boards of the two companies about how they would divide their responsibilities after the merger.

Mergers, like takeovers, also run the risk of being blocked by regulatory authorities on the grounds that they may restrict the extent of competition in a market. This is considered further in Chapter 10.

7.2.9 Joint ventures

Diversification into new business areas can be risky, even for a cash-rich business. It may lack the management skills necessary in the market that it seeks to enter, while the barriers to entry may present an unacceptably high level of risk to the company. One way forward is to set up a joint venture, where companies with complementary skills and financial resources join together. A new limited company is usually formed, with shares allocated between the member companies and agreement reached on where the financial and human resources are to come from. There are many examples of joint ventures to be found in new high-technology, high-capital sectors such as telecommunications and broadcasting. Within the mobile phone sector, the Symbian joint venture was established between Psion, Siemens, Nokia, Motorola, Matsushita and Ericsson to reduce the cost of developing new operating systems, and to provide an advanced, open, standard operating system for data-enabled mobile phones which would benefit all members of the joint venture. Joint ventures are a common feature in the aerospace sector, where development costs are high.

A joint venture is commonly used where a company seeking international expansion joins forces with a local or regional company that has a well-developed technology base. This was a foundation for the relationship between America's General Motors and China's Shanghai Automotive Industry (SAIC). Shanghai General Motors Co. Ltd is a 50–50 joint venture

THINKING AROUND THE SUBJECT:
BIG PLANE, BIG RISKS

Developing a new commercial aircraft requires an investment in development costs which is beyond the resources of most individual companies. Furthermore, as projects get bigger and more expensive, the risk to a company can become unacceptable. Even the mighty Rolls-Royce company was brought down by an overrun in the cost of developing its RB211 jet engine in the 1980s. The European civil aviation sector has traditionally been fragmented, with a manufacturer based in each of the main West European countries. Such a fragmented industry provided little opportunity to compete effectively with the American Boeing company, whose access to a large domestic market had propelled it to world leader in the manufacture of large passenger aircraft. In an attempt to challenge this dominance, a number of European manufacturers – initially France's Aerospatiale and Germany's Daimler-Benz Aerospace (later joined by British Aerospace, now BAe Systems, and Spain's Casa) – joined forces to create Airbus, realizing that no single European manufacturer had the resources to overcome the US giants. Each of the joint venture partners has specialized in different components of the Airbus, for example BAe Systems produces wing structures and Aerospatiale manufactures fuselages. The results of such technical specialization and co-operation have been to improve the design quality of Airbus aircraft and, through economies of scale, to lower the manufacturing cost per aircraft. By 2004, worldwide sales of Airbus aircraft had exceeded those of Boeing, something which would have seemed difficult to imagine a couple of decades earlier. Inspired by its success, the Airbus consortium embarked on its greatest joint-venture project to date: the A380 'super jumbo'. With an estimated development cost of €6 billion, this was seen as too much of a risk even for the combined resources of the partners that owned Airbus, and the project proceeded only after government intervention to guarantee part of the project.

between the two companies, formed in 1997 to bring GM's technology to the growing Chinese car market through partnership with a locally based manufacturer.

Where joint ventures are a success, the partners often seek to liquidate their investment by 'floating' the joint venture as a public limited company in its own right. Of course, many joint ventures end in failure, often because of unrealistic expectations of the partners involved. For example, the UK mobile phone company Cellnet (now O_2) invested over £1.5 billion in a joint venture with Dutch Railways to create a new Dutch-based phone operator, Telfort. However, Telfort failed to achieve higher than fifth ranking in the Dutch market and, in April 2003, O_2 admitted defeat and sold its interest in Telfort for just £16 million.

7.2.10 Management buy-outs

Management buy-outs have become popular in recent years. A buy-out is an autonomous company which is created by the management and/or employees of an organization buying part or all of the business of their former employers. Funding a buy-out often leaves the company highly geared, with the management putting in relatively little of their own equity capital relative to the loan capital provided by a merchant bank. Such buy-outs often involve very complex financing, with the merchant bank seeking a route by which its minority share-holding can be liquidated by flotation very quickly afterwards, or assets of the newly formed business sold off to repay the loans. This method of financing growth can be very attractive at a time of an expanding economy and relatively low interest rates. Management use a relatively small amount of their own capital and a relatively high proportion of borrowed capital, but benefit disproportionately from a subsequent increase in the market value of the company. For example, the train-leasing company Porterbrook was bought by its managers from British Rail in 1997, with senior managers investing about £100,000 of their own funds. This was doubtless a big risk to the individuals concerned, who may have had to offer their homes as security for money that they personally borrowed. Further finance for the purchase came from banks using loans which were secured against the assets of the company. Two years after the buy-out, the company was sold to Stagecoach PLC, which acquired all of the managers' shares and assumed responsibility for the bank loans. Individual managers' initial investment of £100,000 was now worth over £5 million each.

Of course, not all management buy-outs are as successful for the managers as the Porterbrook case. A high level of gearing has spelt difficulty for many new buy-outs when the state of the economy turned out to be below expectation and interest rates rose above the level that had been budgeted for. Companies could not defer payment of interest on loans in the way that they could defer paying a dividend to the risk-taking shareholders. In 2004, managers of the Birmingham-based airline Maersk bought out the British operations of the Danish parent company and relaunched the airline with a new name – Duo. The company had underestimated the strength of competition from 'budget' airlines and failed to achieve a high enough number of passengers paying a high enough level of fares to ensure profitability and adequate cash flow. The banks that had supported the management buy-out became concerned at the poor performance of the airline and within three months of launch they withdrew their loan facilities and the airline was grounded. Managers who had invested in the buy-out had lost their entire equity investment.

A management 'buy-in' is a transaction in which an external management team is backed by an investor to acquire a business. In most cases the management buy-in team joins with some of the incumbent management to ensure continuity, so the deal also has an element of a management buy-out.

7.2.11 Horizontal and vertical integration

Amalgamations between firms can take the form of horizontal integration, vertical integration or diversification. Horizontal integration occurs where firms involved in the same stage of manufacture or distribution of a product amalgamate to achieve greater economies of scale and – subject to Competition Commission approval – to reduce the level of wasteful competition in a market. The consolidation which occurred in the UK brewing industry during the late 1990s, when the number of mass-production brewers was cut drastically through mergers, fell into this category. It is increasingly being recognized that growth through horizontal integration can pose serious problems for the competitiveness of a market, which may be good for producers, but may limit choice and/or raise prices for consumers. We will return in Chapter 10 to review the regulatory constraints on this type of growth.

Vertical integration occurs where a company acquires either its suppliers (backward integration) or its distributors (forward integration). Tour operators integrating backwards have ensured provision of aircraft capacity by acquiring or setting up their own airline, while others have integrated forwards by acquiring travel agents. Diversification occurs where firms acquire another firm operating in unrelated business areas, the main purpose of the acquisition often being to spread risk through a balanced portfolio of activities. Figure 7.2 applies this framework of analysis to possible growth patterns for a brewery.

7.2.12 Globalization

Markets are increasingly being affected by globalization, forcing firms in many sectors to see their market not just as the domestic economy, but the whole world. Many industry sectors have witnessed a series of mergers as companies grow in order to achieve economies of scale. In the case of volume car manufacturers, this has resulted in a shrinking number of manufacturers, but those that remain now incorporate a number of brands. Ford, for example, now owns Volvo and Jaguar, while Chrysler and Daimler-Benz merged in 2000 to form a new multinational organization. There are major economies of scale open to car manufacturers. Companies operating at a large scale are able to maintain a cost-effective position at the leading edge of design through investment in research and development, whose cost can be spread over a large volume of output. The Volkswagen group, for example, is able to spread the enormous development costs of a new car 'platform' over four quite distinct brands –

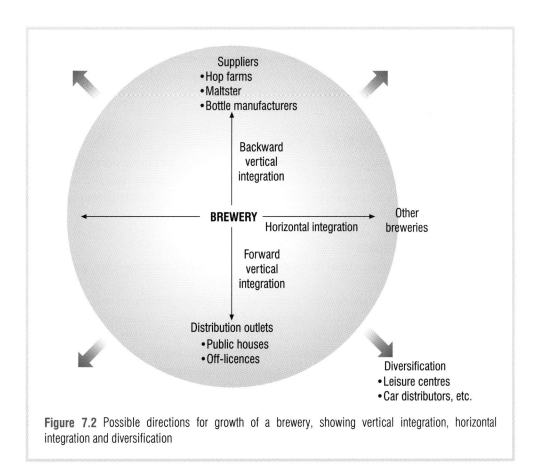

Figure 7.2 Possible directions for growth of a brewery, showing vertical integration, horizontal integration and diversification

Volkswagen, Audi, SEAT and Skoda. If each of these brands had to undertake its own development work, its cars would lose competitive advantage to a company which was able to spread development costs over larger volume.

By expanding overseas, a company that has developed a strong brand can stretch the coverage of that brand. By developing in a foreign market, the company will start with the advantage that some visitors from its domestic market will already understand what the brand stands for. Similarly, for residents of the new market, many may already have become familiar with the brand during visits to the manufacturer's home market. In short, there are economies of scale in promoting a brand in multiple markets simultaneously.

A company may find itself forced to expand into overseas markets because of saturation of its domestic market. Saturation can come about where a product reaches the maturity stage of its life cycle in the domestic market, while being at a much earlier stage of the cycle in less developed foreign markets. The market for cigarettes may be mature in most Western markets, but China represents a new growth opportunity for Western companies.

International markets are becoming increasingly homogenized. The car industry serves as a good example of one where distinctive national preferences have diminished, and companies are able to manufacture one product, with only minor adaptations to make it suitable for the whole world. Instead of talking about market segments defined by national boundaries, companies operating at a global scale increasingly talk about cross-national segments of socio-economic and lifestyle groups. Against this assumption of cultural convergence, many commentators have noted the need for individuals to retain a distinct cultural identity, and this has been seen in the preference of some Muslim consumers for Mecca Cola, as a cultural statement in preference to the global brand values of Coca-Cola.

We will return to look at issues of globalization in more detail in Chapter 12.

7.3 ORGANIZATIONAL SCALE

There is continuing debate about whether there is an 'ideal' size for business organizations. In fact, there are advantages and disadvantages of large firms and they can be found co-existing with much smaller firms in most sectors. This section reviews recent debate about the benefits of large organizations against small business units.

7.3.1 Economies of scale

In many sectors, large organizations have advantages over smaller ones. Here are some of their principal advantages.

1 In some industries there are significant economies of scale in production processes. This is particularly true of industries where fixed costs of production are a high proportion of total costs. Therefore sectors such as car manufacture and banking allow large organizations to spread the high cost of capital equipment over a greater number of units of output, thereby pursuing what Porter (1980) described as a cost leadership strategy. In sectors that use high technology, or that require highly trained labour skills, a learning curve effect may be apparent (also called a cost experience curve). By operating at a larger scale than its competitors, a firm can benefit more from the learning curve and thereby achieve lower unit costs. While this may be true of some industries, others face only a very low critical output at which significant economies of scale occur – plumbing and hairdressing, for example. For organi-

zations in these sectors, cost leadership would be a difficult strategy as many rival firms would also be able to achieve maximum cost efficiency.

2 As well as being more efficient at turning inputs into outputs, larger firms may be able to acquire their inputs on more advantageous terms in the first place. One reason for the success of large-scale retailers is the much greater bargaining power they have over suppliers, compared to smaller retailers. Often, smaller organizations have joined together in voluntary buying chains in order to increase their bargaining power with suppliers. Many farmers' co-operatives realize that a group of farmers can collectively achieve lower prices from suppliers than one farmer negotiating alone. As well as being able to bring greater bargaining power to negotiations with suppliers, buying on a large scale can give savings in the logistical costs of transferring goods from supplier to buyer.

3 Large-scale production can allow for 'economies of scope', by allowing a wider range of goods and services to be offered. This can take the form of additional design features which could not be included if production was on a small scale (e.g. small manufacturers of food products may not be able to afford to spend as much on designing eye-catching packaging as their larger competitors) or additional services that a firm is able to offer (large building societies may, for example, be able to offer a much more comprehensive range of investment services than their smaller competitors).

4 A company's promotion effort can be much more efficient where it is aimed at a large-volume national (or even international) market, rather than a purely local one. National television and press advertising may be an efficient medium for a large-scale national company, which gives it a promotional advantage over smaller-scale local producers that must rely on various local and regional media.

5 Investors generally prefer companies that have a proven track record of stability. By being able to diversify into a number of different products and market segments, companies are able to offer this stability, resulting in 'blue chip' companies being able to obtain equity and loan capital at a lower cost than smaller companies.

6 With relationship marketing becoming an important part of many organizations' strategy, the ability to cross-sell related goods and services becomes crucial. By operating at a larger scale with a broad portfolio of products, cross-selling can be facilitated.

7.3.2 Limits to growth

Most organizations pursue growth to a greater or lesser degree. However, there are limits to how far and how fast a company can grow. Growth by acquisition – being relatively risky – can reveal limits beyond which a company cannot sustain growth. Growth by acquisition is commonly associated with high borrowings resulting in a high level of gearing. The use of relatively cheap debt capital may be attractive while the company is profitable, but can leave the company dangerously exposed when conditions deteriorate. Faced with a fixed charge for interest, the organization may be forced to liquidate some of its assets by disposing of subsidiaries, to raise cash to meet its interest payments. Many Internet companies that grew rapidly during the late 1990s found themselves unable to service debt repayments when the sector faced severe problems from 2000. Organizations that grew organically at a slower rate without reliance on such a high level of borrowed capital rode the subsequent recession better.

The ability of the management structure of a company to respond to growth sets a further limit to growth. Many companies have benefited by having a dynamic personality leading during a period of rapid growth, only to find that a large organization needs a much broader management base once it passes a critical size. Organizations such as Next and Amstrad have had difficult periods in the past where the management structure has not grown to meet the needs of a very different type of organization. If a company does not restructure itself as it grows, diseconomies of scale may set in.

Legislative constraints are increasingly limiting the ability of firms to grow. In industry sectors where there are significant economies of scale in production, and competition takes place at a global level, there is often a great logic behind the motivation to merge and grow. However, the need to compete from a position of strength needs to be balanced against regulators' increasing concern that the competitiveness of markets should be maintained. It can be difficult for regulators to define this balance with government policy objectives often pulling in different directions. Most countries have laws to prevent one firm dominating a market or having undue influence over it and the EU is playing an increasingly important role in this respect. We will return to the subject of legislation governing anti-competitive situations in Chapter 10.

7.3.3 De-mergers

Conglomerates sometimes reach a size and diversity that produce more problems than opportunities for the group as a whole. A number of conglomerates have therefore split themselves up in a reversal of the process of merging, sometimes referred to as de-merging. The initial cause of a de-merger is often the recognition that shareholders' total share value would increase if they had shares in two or more separate businesses rather than the one conglomerate holding company. Stock markets often have difficulty placing a value on the shares of highly diversified companies, and many de-mergers have seen the combined value of the de-merged companies' shares very quickly exceed the previous price of the shares of the former holding company. In an important paper published in 1995, Berger and Ofek found that the US stock market undervalued diversified companies by between 13 and 15 per cent, compared to the value of their component parts. Evidence for a similar but smaller 'diversification discount' was found in the UK and Japan. It has been suggested that this anomaly might arise because managers find it easier to build empires which satisfy their personal goals, rather than maximizing shareholder value. Diversification reduces the transparency of corporate financial reporting.

Some recent UK examples of de-mergers have included the following.

■ BT and Cellnet – BT's landline business served mature markets, in contrast to the high-growth, high-risk nature of the company's Cellnet operation. The latter was de-merged as part of a corporate restructuring to become O_2, with its own Stock Exchange listing.

■ ICI and Zeneca – stock markets had difficulties valuing a company which combined low-risk, low-growth commodity chemicals with high-risk pharmaceuticals. The latter were therefore demerged from ICI to form a new company, Zeneca, which itself was subsequently merged with Astra to achieve economies of scale in the pharmaceutical sector.

■ The Six Continents company (previously called Bass) found itself with a portfolio of hotels and pubs with few synergies between them, and a pessimistic stock market valuation of the whole. The hotels were de-merged to become Inter Continental Hotels, and the pub chain became Mitchells and Butler.

De-merging of activities sometimes follows an investigation by the Competition Commission and may be a condition of a merger between two companies proceeding.

7.4 SOURCES OF FINANCE FOR GROWTH

As far as the private sector is concerned, there are two basic methods of financing growth. On the one hand, companies can raise risk capital (often referred to as *equity* capital) from shareholders for which a relatively high rate of return will be required. To supplement this, companies use a second and relatively less expensive form of *loan* finance. This must be repaid regardless of the fortunes of the company. The relationship between the two is referred to as gearing – a company which has a high amount of loan finance relative to equity capital is said to be highly geared. An optimum balance exists between the two types of finance, although this varies between different industry sectors.

7.4.1 Methods of raising equity capital

One method by which a sole trader or partnership can raise fresh capital is by forming a private limited company and selling shares in the company. For a private limited company, the sale of shares cannot be advertised to the public, so they have to be placed privately. For smaller companies, blocks of shares are often sold to relations or business associates. New opportunities to gain access to equity share capital have been provided through a relatively new type of intermediary – the venture capital company. These intermediaries develop an understanding of the opportunities for investment in smaller private companies and provide the link – and often also the management support – through which investment from cash-rich individuals and organizations such as pension funds is provided.

To gain access to significant amounts of new equity capital from a much wider financial community, a private company may 'go public' by forming a public limited company. Becoming a public company requires a special resolution to be passed by the shareholders and the Articles of Association to be amended to take out those restrictions that apply to a private company (as discussed in Chapter 6).

To acquire a full listing on the Stock Exchange, a considerable amount of time and money must be spent to meet the requirements of the Stock Exchange Council. These essentially aim to ensure that anybody considering buying shares in the company is adequately informed about the record, current position and future prospects of the company. A detailed prospectus, including five years' trading figures, with audited accounts must be produced. The actual sale of shares can take place in a number of ways, the most important of which are:

■ an offer for sale to the general public, where a specified number of shares is offered at a fixed price, usually underwritten to guarantee the share income to the company; this tends to be an expensive method of raising equity capital

■ sale by tender which involves selling the shares to the highest bidders

■ placement with financial institutions without the formality of a public offer for sale.

The cost of raising fresh equity through a share issue can be considerable, reflecting the work of the accountants, bankers, solicitors and underwriters involved. For a typical small share sale valued at £10 million, between 5 and 10 per cent would be lost in issuing expenses.

Obtaining access to equity capital through the stock market can be very expensive for smaller companies, which can be caught in a dilemma. Small, rapidly growing businesses in fast-growing sectors such as bio-technology may need fresh capital to sustain their growth. However, until they have achieved successful operations for a number of years, they cannot seek funding to bring about that growth. The stock markets in many countries have recognized this dilemma by creating secondary markets for companies which fall short of the high standards normally imposed on companies dealing on the main market. At the same time, such secondary stock markets provide opportunities for investors that are more willing to take a speculative risk in a company that could produce a spectacular return, or could just as easily prove to be a complete failure.

In the United Kingdom, an alternative to obtaining a full listing on the Stock Exchange is to seek one on the Alternative Investment Market (AIM). This is much less costly to companies seeking to raise fresh finance. The AIM poses a higher risk for investors as the information companies are required to submit is lower. However, each company must warn potential investors of their risks and must have a nominated adviser approved by the Stock Exchange. The role of the adviser is central to AIM, as the Stock Market does not look at companies' prospectuses. Advisers are required to confirm to the Exchange that the directors of a company have been guided on their responsibilities and obligations in respect of the AIM rules and that the rules have been obeyed. Advisers can be fined for poor performance. The stock markets of many countries have developed similar schemes to promote small, relatively high-risk business ventures (e.g. France's Nouveau Marche).

An alternative method of raising fresh equity capital for an established business is to call on existing shareholders to subscribe for additional shares. This is known as a rights issue and shareholders are given the right to purchase additional shares at a specified price in proportion to their existing shareholding. Where a company is in financial difficulty with excessive debt, it may renegotiate with its creditors to turn some of its loans into equity capital. Shares are then given to creditors in return for cancelling part of the loans outstanding to them. This happened with the financially beleaguered Eurotunnel company, whose shareholders saw the value of their shares fall as new shares were created to pay off debts rather than to invest in new revenue-generating assets.

7.4.2 Retained earnings

Free enterprise idealists would argue that a company's profits should be entirely distributed to its shareholders so that they can decide how they should be reinvested. In practice, companies tend to retain a proportion of profits for reinvestment within the business, encouraged by tax advantages. The amount distributed to shareholders in the form of a dividend tends to be kept at a stable level, meeting a norm for that particular industry and the expectations of shareholders. While retained earnings may seem an easy source of finance for a company, there is a danger that if it does not achieve an adequate internal return on these retained earnings, it may become the subject of a takeover bid from another company that considers it could manage the capital of the business more effectively.

THINKING AROUND THE SUBJECT:
CASH FOR GROWING BUSINESSES

Small businesses often reach a point where they need more capital if they are to expand. The dotcom boom of 2000 produced many small businesses which had been started in the owners' garage or spare room, but soon grew to the point where additional capital became essential in order to sustain growth. But raising additional equity capital can reduce the control the owner has in a business, and cut their share of future profits. Hindsight can be great in deciding when a small business should go to the market to raise additional capital, or indeed to sell out completely to a larger organization which has the resources to exploit the full potential of the company. Some had a lucky break and went to the market at just the right time, raising capital for the company, cash for themselves and still retaining some degree of control. Among the winners were Brent Hoberman and Martha Lane Fox, founders of lastminute.com. The company floated on the London Stock Exchange in March 2000 at the peak of 'dotcom mania'. Shares which floated at £3.70 were down to less than 60p a year later, reducing the value of the company from £140 million to less than £20 million.

Somebody who did less well was Dave Stanworth, who may be quite typical of a new generation of dotcom entrepreneurs in terms of his background. He left school with no qualifications and worked casually in a series of jobs as, among other things, a bricklayer and a bookie. In his spare time he played with the Internet and eventually developed a website called Games Domain. By 1997, it was clear that his venture would need more finance than he had available. He had tried to raise money from venture capitalists, but at this time the hysteria of dotcom frenzy had not yet taken off and he found few backers. Stanworth decided that the best option for him would be to sell out to a better-resourced organization and take a smaller equity stake in the larger organization. In 1997 he sold the business to Attitude Network in return for an equity stake in Attitude. Attitude was itself taken over by theglobe.com, a larger company which was able to raise additional capital through its listing on the US NASDAQ market (a market which is more open to high-risk start-up companies, similar to the UK's AIM). At the height of the dotcom boom, theglobe.com shares peaked at $39.47 and Stanworth's personal stake in the company was valued at more than $3 million. This rags to riches story soon turned to rags again, because just one year later during the 'dotbomb' period, theglobe.com's shares fell to just 31 cents, cutting the value of Stanworth's holding to just $25,000. The company had joined the so-called '90 per cent club' – those companies whose shares had fallen by more than 90 per cent of their peak value. In this, the company was not alone, as the club included such notable names as QXL.com and Amazon.com.

Entrepreneurs starting up a new business frequently complain about the difficulties of obtaining start-up finance, with banks requiring new applicants to submit business plans and then criticizing them as being unrealistic. Many believe that having a good track record and a strong network of contacts is the surest way to raise finance, whatever the amount. This was seen long after the dotcom boom had passed in 2004 when the entrepreneur Phillip Green appeared to have little difficulty in raising £4 billion for his private company to launch an audacious takeover bid for the ailing Marks & Spencer chain. The bid failed, but it did raise the question of how an entrepreneur can raise so much money so quickly when new businesses struggle for their first financial lifeline.

7.4.3 Loan capital

For the small business, loans for expansion may be obtained from family and friends. However, when loan requirements exceed the capabilities of these sources, commercial loans are sought and some form of security against the loan will usually be required. In many cases, the directors of a limited company will have to pledge their personal possessions as security for the company's loans, despite the separate legal identity of the company.

Debentures are loans to a company carrying interest at a fixed rate and are generally repayable on a specified date. Debenture holders receive priority over shareholders for annual income payments and when the assets of the business are liquidated. Some – called mortgage debentures – are backed by a particular fixed asset belonging to the company as security, while others are secured by a floating charge on the company's assets in general. In the event of default on payment, the lender has the right to take over the security offered and sell it in order to repay the outstanding loan. A company may also have unsecured loan stock. Lenders of this stock are in the same position as trade creditors in ranking for repayment in the event of liquidation, although still ahead of shareholders.

7.4.4 Other sources of finance

Shares and debentures provide long-term finance for long-term growth. In the short term, the survival of many companies is influenced by being able to collect money due to them as quickly as possible. Some companies resort to factoring by selling a debt they are owed to a finance company and receiving payment, less a premium, immediately. On the other hand, firms seek to delay paying their debts to suppliers for as long as possible, thereby providing an additional source of short-term finance. Small companies often complain about having to wait for payment from large companies that use smaller businesses as a source of finance for their own operations. Although there are a number of initiatives to 'name and shame' slow payers (for example a list of poor payers is published by the Federation of Small Businesses), some business owners may be so dependent on a customer that they would not wish to stop doing further business with a slow payer.

CASE STUDY

THE CURSE OF SUCCESS?

Companies tend to have a natural life cycle. When small, they are popular with the public they serve, often seen as spirited challengers run by audacious entrepreneurs. When they get bigger, they may have large numbers of fans if they have built up a good name or brand. But when they become the biggest in the market, they can come to be seen as greedy, arrogant monopolists that have become corporate bullies.

One of the problems for companies that have reached a dominant position is that there may be nothing in their history that has prepared their senior management for it. Nowadays, it seems that when a company becomes market leader, it not only has to worry about being resented because of its size – it also stands a good chance of being targeted by anti-globalization protesters, the green lobby, labour activists and government regulators, among others. It may catch the attention of the competition authorities, which are becoming increasingly circumspect about companies with dominant market positions. At that point, senior managers who have spent their working lives learning how to manage and grow their business are suddenly required to become politicians, a role requiring a different set of skills and for which they may be ill-suited. Faced with the 'curse of growth', companies can throw money at the problem by hiring armies of PR people and reputation management consultancies, and may try to defuse criticism by a corporate social responsibility agenda.

The world's biggest retailer, Wal-Mart, has become a target for protesters who have alleged that Wal-Mart underpaid and exploited its US workforce, and employed sweatshop labour overseas, while inflating the US trade deficit by importing most of its goods. It has also been accused of being simply too powerful, squeezing suppliers and driving other retailers out of business. For years, Wal-Mart refused to engage in a discussion about these allegations, sensing that most Americans still shared a pride in the success of the company and the benefits it had brought to ordinary people. But in January 2005, it began a campaign to get its message across with the launch of a website called Wal-Martfacts.com to defend its records on employment, outsourcing and the other allegations that had been made against it.

Could Britain's Tesco suffer the same fate as Wal-Mart? In 2004, Wal-Mart had 8 per cent of all retail sales in the USA, but even the mighty Wal-Mart seemed insignificant in its market share compared to Tesco's 12 per cent share of all retail spending in the UK. When Tesco announced record profits for the year 2004 the company talked down its profit prospects for the year ahead and seemed to go out of its way to avoid antagonizing the apparently growing number of people that resented the 'Tescoization' of Britain. The company had already had skirmishes with farmers' groups over the low price that Tesco was accused of paying farmers for milk, and the large mark-up that Tesco applied when it resold that same milk to customers. It had upset small shopkeepers who felt threatened by Tesco's move into the convenience store sector, following its acquisition of the One Stop chain and the development of its Tesco Express format. Environmental campaigners had protested that the company's trucks unnecessarily transported goods around the country, so that potatoes grown by a farmer just a few miles away from a Tesco store could travel hundreds of miles between distribution centres before they ended up in that store.

It seemed that Tesco was not going to suffer the fate of Wal-Mart. There was none of the triumphalism to antagonize its detractors, conveniently fitting in with a British sense of reserve. The company also had a comprehensive corporate social responsibility agenda, and went out of its way to be seen as a good citizen through sponsorship of good causes.

QUESTIONS

1 What else could Tesco do to avoid being seen as a bully that dominates its suppliers and manipulates its customers?
2 Is it in the public interest that successful companies should be able to grow to a point where they dominate a market?
3 Will Tesco inevitably follow the life cycle of other companies that have fallen out of favour once they have become dominant in their markets?

SUMMARY

Organizations pursue diverse objectives, some formal and others informally held by managers. Most organizations have a tendency to grow, thereby satisfying the needs of a wide range of internal and external interests. It has been noted that certain types of organization, such as public limited companies, have the ability to grow faster than others where availability of external finance imposes a constraint on growth (**Chapter 6**). This chapter has discussed various growth strategies, noting that growth that is too rapid or too dependent on loan capital can be highly risky. For most organizations, the sustainability of growth is highly dependent on the state of the national or international economic environment (see **Chapter 11**).

A large organization is able to achieve numerous advantages over a smaller one, including the ability to invest in new technologies (**Chapter 4**) and the exploitation of overseas markets (**Chapter 12**). In principle, large organizations should be better able to invest in comprehensive information systems (**Chapter 4**), although it must be remembered that size in itself can create barriers between customers and decision makers. Increasing concern about the possible harmful effects for consumers of market domination by large organizations is discussed further in **Chapter 10**.

Key Terms

Acquisition	(258)	Externalities	(250)	Organizational objectives	(245)
Cash flow	(248)	Factoring	(270)	Profit maximization	(245)
Companies Acts	(251)	Flotation	(261)	Prospectus	(267)
Consolidation	(258)	Globalization	(263)	Rights issue	(268)
Co-operatives	(249)	Horizontal integration	(262)	Satisficing	(247)
Debentures	(270)	Joint ventures	(260)	Social objectives	(249)
Directors	(268)	Management buy-out	(261)	Stock Exchange	(259)
Diseconomies of scale	(266)	Mergers	(260)	Takeover	(259)
Diversification	(256)	Mission statement	(251)	Vertical integration	(262)
Economies of scale	(264)	Organic growth	(257)		
Equity capital	(267)	Organizational life cycle	(254)		

CHAPTER REVIEW QUESTIONS

1 (a) Prepare a short report outlining the main reasons why businesses of different sizes exist.

   (b) Are there any relationships between the size of the business and the market in which it operates?

   (*Based on CIM Marketing Environment Examination*)

2 What problems for the management of a furniture manufacturer might arise from rapid growth?

3 In what ways have the objectives of newly privatized industries changed compared to those of the state-owned organizations that they replaced?

4 What are the problems and opportunities for marketing management arising from a policy of growth through diversification?

5 Explain the resurgence of interest in the small business sector.

6 Choose one industry sector with which you are familiar and examine how small and large firms have found roles in which they can co-exist with each other.

ACTIVITY

Get hold of a copy of your local *Yellow Pages* directory. Examine companies advertising under the following business classifications: road haulage services; garden centres; restaurants. What can you tell about the types of organization that operate in each sector? How can you explain why large and small organizations co-exist within the sector?

Useful Websites

Business Bureau

A small-business information resource offering help, advice and guidance for new and expanding businesses.

http://www.businessbureau-uk.co.uk

Small Business Discussion Forum

The aim of this list is to act as a forum for academic discussion relating to small business issues. It is essentially interdisciplinary in nature although the emphasis is placed on the analysis of small-scale enterprise rather than prescriptive or how-to-do-it approaches.

http://www.jiscmail.ac.uk/lists/ small-business-issues.html

Further Reading

Numerous authors have sought to prescribe strategies for successful, profitable growth. The following are classic contributions to the field:

Porter, M. (1980) *Competitive Strategy: Techniques for Analyzing Industries and Competitors*, New York, Free Press.

Ansoff, H.I. (1957) 'Strategies for diversification', *Harvard Business Review*, Vol. 25, No. 5, September–October, pp. 113–24.

Levitt, T. (1960) 'Marketing myopia', *Harvard Business Review*, Vol. 38, No. 4, July–August, pp. 45–56.

Mergers and acquisitions often generate a lot of press coverage when they are contested and a lot can be learnt by following coverage in the *Financial Times*. For a general review of the subject, the following texts are useful:

Harvard Business Review (2001), Harvard Business Review on Mergers and Acquisitions.

Weston, F.J. and Weaver, S. (2004) *Mergers and Acquisitions*, Maidenhead, McGraw-Hill.

Finance for organizational growth can be a complex topic, but the following texts provide a useful insight:

Atrill, P. and McLaney, E.J. (2003) *Financial Management for Non-specialists*, 4th edn, London, FT Prentice Hall.

McLaney, E. (2003) *Business Finance*, 6th edn, London, FT Prentice Hall.

Van Horne, J. (2001) *Financial Management and Policy*, 12th edn, London, FT Prentice Hall.

The following provide a useful set of readings on multinational businesses:

Hood, N. and Young, S. (eds) (1999) *The Globalization of Multinational Enterprise Activity and Economic Development*, Palgrave.

Stonehouse, G.S. (2004) *Global and Transnational Business: Strategy and Management*, Chichester, John Wiley & Sons.

For a review of the role of small businesses and the reasons for their recent resurgence, the following are useful:

Barrow, C. (2002) *The Complete Small Business Guide: Sources of Information for New and Small Businesses*, London, Capstone.

Bridge, S., O'Neill, K. and Cromie, S. (2003) *Understanding Enterprise, Entrepreneurship and Small Business*, Basingstoke, Palgrave.

Williams, S. (2003) *Lloyds TSB Small Business Guide*, 17th edn, Vitesse Media.

References

Ansoff, H.I. (1957) 'Strategies for diversification', *Harvard Business Review*, Vol. 25, No. 5, September–October, pp. 113–24.

Barclays (2004) *Start-ups and Closures*, Barclays Bank SME Market Research Team.

BCC (2005) *Business Burdens Barometer*, London, British Chambers of Commerce.

Berger, P.G. and Ofek, E. (1995) 'Causes and effects of corporate refocusing programs', *Journal of Accounting and Economics*, Vol. 19, No. 2–3, pp. 411–42.

Cyert, R.M. and March, J.G. (1963) *A Behavioural Theory of the Firm*, Englewood Cliffs, NJ, Prentice Hall.

DTI (2004) *SME Statistics UK 2003*, London, Department of Trade and Industry.

Ennew, C., Wong, P. and Wright, M. (1992) 'Organizational structures and the boundaries of the firm: acquisitions and divestments in financial services', *Services Industries Journal*, Vol. 12, No. 4, pp. 478–97.

Grenier, L.E, (1972) 'Evolution and revolution', *Harvard Business Review*, July–August, pp. 37–46.

Hudson, M. (1995) *Managing Without Profit: The Art of Managing Third Sector Organizations*, London, Penguin Books.

Krabuanrat, K. and Phelps, R. (1998), 'Heuristics and rationality in strategic decision making: an exploratory study', *Journal of Business Research*, 1998, Vol. 41, No. 1, January, pp. 83–93.

NatWest Bank (2004) *NatWest/SERTeam Quarterly Survey of Small Business*, Milton Keynes, Open University Business School.

Porter, M. (1980) *Competitive Strategy: Techniques for Analyzing Industries and Competitors*, New York, Free Press.

Sasser, W.E., Olsen, R.P. and Wyckoff, D.D. (1978) *Management of Service Operations: Texts, Cases, Readings*, Boston, Mass, Allyn & Bacon.

Zook, Chris (2004) *Beyond the Core: Expand Your Market Without Abandoning Your Roots*, Harvard Business School Press.

Chapter 8
The Internal Environment

Chapter Objectives
This chapter will explain:

- the link between an organization's external and internal environments

- how organizations organize their structures and processes in order to respond to external demands

- how organizations manage their human resources, so that they have a highly motivated workforce which has the flexibility to respond to environmental change

8.1 THE LINK BETWEEN INTERNAL AND EXTERNAL ENVIRONMENTS

Much of this book has been concerned with the way external environmental forces impinge on an organization's activities. But we must also recognize that the ability of the organization to respond to challenges and opportunities in its external environment is often very dependent on its internal environment. A new development in technology, for example, may present an organization with a major opportunity, but if it has a poorly motivated staff, or if its management structures and processes are ineffective, the opportunity may pass it by. There have been countless examples of companies that have understood their external environment and the change which has been going on in it, but have nevertheless been unable to adapt to the change. The organization's structures and processes may have been so bureaucratic that by the time they had responded to external change, more nimble competitors had already gained a competitive advantage. The slow and bureaucratic organization was left to wither and die. This has been particularly true of public-sector organizations, which have faced newly deregulated markets. The Belgian state-owned airline Sabena, for example, enjoyed protected status from its Brussels base, but when air services were deregulated by the EU in the 1990s, the airline's traditional producer-led approach was not enough to match its leaner and more nimble competitors. The airline was initially taken over, and then went bankrupt in 2001.

But it is not just public-sector organizations that can fail to adapt to a changed environment. Many companies have grown large and complacent, and acquired procedures and structures that have weighed them down when they have needed to change. The supermarket chain Sainsbury's and the computer maker IBM have been accused of losing their market leadership position because of internal complacency.

The concept of a value chain was introduced in Chapter 1, where the chain was seen as something linking organizations. However, the value chain model can be extended to incorporate the internal value-adding activities which occur before a product leaves a company and enters the external value chain.

Every organization can be considered to be a marketplace consisting of a diverse group of employees who engage in exchanges between each other to create value. In order for them to be able to create value, employees are often dependent upon internal services provided by other departments or individuals within their organization. These internal exchanges include relationships between front-line staff and backroom staff, managers and the front-line staff, managers and backroom staff and, for large organizations, between the head office and each branch. In the most general sense, employees have been seen by some as 'consumers' of services provided by their employer, such as a pleasant working environment, provision of a pension scheme and good facilities for performing their tasks.

There is a widely held view that if employees are not happy with their jobs, external customers will never be uppermost in their minds. Researchers have tended to agree that satisfied internal customers are a critical prerequisite to the satisfaction of external customers. Nevertheless, many have recognized the three-way fight between the firm, the employees and the customer. Delivering goods and services is thus a 'compromise between partially conflicting parties' (Bateson 1989). To give an example, it may sound like a good idea to give employees longer rest breaks because this satisfies their needs as internal 'customers'. But longer rest breaks may result in greater waiting time for external customers, as fewer staff are now available to serve them. A fine balance has to be drawn and there is no conclusive proof that in all situations happier employees necessarily result in happier external customers and a more profitable business.

In this chapter, we will look at how organizations organize themselves in terms of their internal structures. Related to this are the internal processes which can help or hinder the task of responding to environmental change, for example if all employees share a sense of trust in management and a shared vision for the future, adaptation to external environmental change should be facilitated. In order to achieve this trust and shared vision, we need to gain a better understanding of the human resource management practices that can facilitate or inhibit this. But first, we go back to the model of a value chain which was introduced in Chapter 1 by extending and applying the framework to the internal environment.

8.1.1 Internal value chains

A value chain describes the process of transforming simple, commodity-type products into goods and services that buyers are prepared to pay a high price for. Think back to Chapter 1 and you will recall that a variety of suppliers, assemblers, manufacturers and distributors are likely to be involved in turning a basic product into a sought consumer item. Some value chains may be quite simple (for example 'pick your own' strawberries sold direct from the farm), but at other times the value chain can be quite lengthy, involving numerous component assemblers, brokers and intermediaries. You may recall from Chapter 1 the lengthy value chain involved in transforming chillies into an ingredient of Worcestershire sauce.

What about the idea of an internal value chain? The principles are similar to the external value chain which has already been discussed. But here we are talking about groups of employees moving a product through a value-creating process, so that basic, low-value items that enter a firm's production process are progressively transformed into high-value products that customers want to buy. Again, internal value chains can be very short, involving only one or two stages. This is typical of companies that focus on a very specialized process. Alternatively, the company may have multiple parallel processes which bring together a variety of basic inputs and combine them to create a complex output. Think of the difference between the internal value chain of a specialist tyre-fitting business and a car manufacturer.

This idea of a value chain and internal trading of goods and services is closely related to the idea of 'Next operation as customer' (NOAC) (Denton 1990). NOAC is based on the idea that each group within an organization should treat the recipients of their output as an internal customer and strive to provide high-quality outputs for them (e.g. Lukas and Maignan 1996). Through this approach, quality will be built into the product delivered to the final customer (Figure 8.1).

Increasingly, organizations are asking internal service departments, such as information technology, human resources, accounting and media services, to be more accountable. In a growing number of instances, organizations have outsourced the services traditionally provided by such internal departments, resulting in extended 'network' or 'virtual' organizations. This has resulted in employees effectively trading services with other employees within their organization. With the development of outsourcing and virtual business relationships, the distinction between internal and external value chains is becoming increasingly blurred.

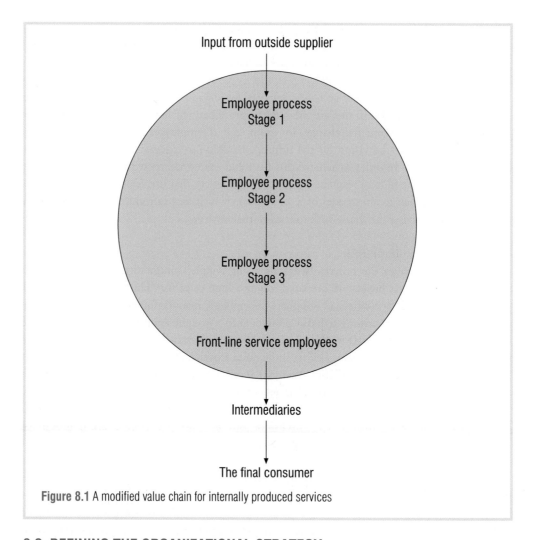

Figure 8.1 A modified value chain for internally produced services

8.2 DEFINING THE ORGANIZATIONAL STRATEGY

Before we begin a detailed discussion of an organization's structures and processes, we need to note that these structures and processes derive from the strategic position that the organization has adopted. Just consider the differences that exist between two airlines that compete with each other for many markets – British Airways and Ryanair. British Airways has a strategy of being a full-service airline, offering customers a comprehensive network of routes with high-quality service at relatively high prices. Ryanair, by contrast, offers a relatively simple series of point-to-point services, a 'no frills' approach to quality, and low prices. British Airways has traditionally moved more slowly than its newer competitors. This is partly due to the size and history of the airline, the extensive network of alliances that it operates with other airlines, which cannot always be changed easily, and the expectations of its customers that it will not chop and change its schedules at short notice. Ryanair, by contrast, is adept at moving into new routes, trying them out and quickly withdrawing them if a better opportunity comes along. It is not surprising that many aspects of the two airlines' employment practices should reportedly differ. For example, while British Airways employs many staff that have been loyal to the company for many years, Ryanair has spotted opportunities for recruiting staff on short-term contracts from low-wage countries. When the company launched domestic services in Italy in 2005, it is reported that the inaugural flight was staffed by a Czech crew.

From an organization's strategy, an organizational culture develops, and it is this culture that contributes to structures and processes. Of course, it could be argued that there is a reciprocal process here, with structures and processes in turn contributing to the organizational culture. We return to this later.

For now, we will focus on an organization's mission statement, which can be seen as an overarching statement of the strategic position that an organization seeks for itself.

A corporate mission statement is a means of reminding everybody within the organization of its essential purpose. Drucker (1973) identified a number of basic questions which management should ask when it perceives itself drifting along with no clear purpose, and which form the basis of a corporate mission statement.

■ What is our business?
■ Who is the customer?
■ What is value to the customer?
■ What will our business be?
■ What should our business be?

By forcing management to focus on the essential nature of the business which they are in and the nature of customer needs which they seek to satisfy, the problem of 'marketing myopia' advanced by Levitt (1960) can be avoided. Levitt argued that in order to avoid a narrow, short-sighted view of its business, managers should define their business in terms of the needs that they fulfil rather than the products they produce. In the classic example, railway operators had lost their way because they defined their service output in terms of the technology of tracked vehicles, rather than in terms of the core benefit of movement which they provided. Accountants learnt the lesson of this myopic example by redefining their central purpose away from a narrow preoccupation with providing 'accounting services' to a much broader mission statement which spoke about providing 'business solutions'. More recently, many freight transport companies have defined their mission in terms of managing customers' complete logistical needs.

In the services sector, where the interface between the consumer and production personnel is often critical, communication of the values contained within the mission statement assumes great importance (see Figure 8.2). The statement is frequently repeated by organizations in staff newsletters and in notices at their place of work.

The nature of an organization's mission statement is a reflection of a number of factors:

■ the organization's ownership, which can lead to marked contrasts in the mission statements of public-sector, private-sector and charity organizations
■ the previous history of the organization, in particular any distinct competencies which it has acquired or images which it has created in the eyes of potential customers
■ environmental factors, in particular the major opportunities and threats which are likely to face the organization in the foreseeable future
■ resources available – without resources available for their accomplishment, a mission statement has little meaning.

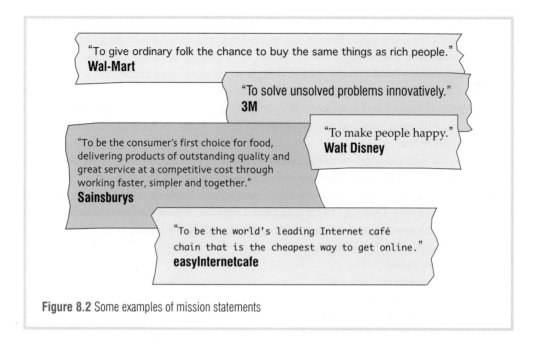

Figure 8.2 Some examples of mission statements

Missions define in general terms the direction in which an organization seeks to move. They contain no quantifiable information which allows them to be operationalized. For this to happen, objectives need to be set.

8.2.1 Organizational culture

Organizational culture concerns the social and behavioural manifestation of a whole set of values which are shared by members of the organization and can be defined as 'some underlying structure of meaning that persists over time, constraining people's perception, interpretation and behaviour' (Jelinek, Smirich and Hirsch 1983). Cultures can be quite enduring, as where new employees soon become aware of the distinctive ways that the organization does things. Cultural values can be shared in a number of ways, including:

- the way work is organized and experienced
- how authority is exercised and delegated
- how people are rewarded, organized and controlled
- the values and work orientation of staff
- the degree of formalization, standardization and control within the organization
- the value placed on structured processes of planning, analysis and control rather than instinct and gut feeling etc.
- how much initiative, risk-taking, scope for individuality and expression is given
- rules and expectations about such things as informality in interpersonal relations, dress, personal eccentricity etc.
- status accorded to senior members of the organization, or particular functions
- expectations for team working or success on the basis of individual efforts.

There are often many visible manifestations of these deep-seated cultural values, including the type of buildings occupied by the organization and the image projected in its publicity and public relations.

An organization's culture may be quite imperceptible; indeed, people who have belonged to it for a long time may not be aware of any alternative way of doing things. Elements of the culture may be questioned where individual or group expectations do not correspond to the behaviours associated with the prevailing values of those who uphold 'the culture'. Central command and control cultures within an organization may become increasingly questioned at a time when other social institutions are embracing more democratic cultures.

Handy (1989) identified four types of organizational culture.

1   The *power culture* is found mainly in smaller organizations where power and influence stem from a single central source, through which all decisions, communication and control are channelled. Because there is no rigid structure within the organization, it is theoretically capable of adapting to change very rapidly, although its actual success in adapting is dependent on the abilities of the central power source.

2   The *role culture* is characterized by a formal, functional organization structure in which there is relatively little freedom and creativity in decision making. Such organizations are more likely to be production orientated and can have difficulty responding to new market opportunities.

3   The *task culture* is concerned primarily with getting a given task done. Importance is therefore attached to those individuals who have the skill or knowledge to accomplish a particular task. Organizations with a task-orientated culture are potentially very flexible, changing constantly as new tasks arise. Innovation and creativity are highly prized for their own sake.

4   The *person culture* is characterized by organizations which are centred on serving the interests of individuals within them. It is a relatively rare form of culture in any market-mediated environment, but can characterize campaigning pressure groups.

As individual organizations develop, it is essential that the dominant culture adapts. While a small business may quite successfully embrace a centralized power culture, continued growth may cause this culture to become a liability. Similarly, the privatization of public utilities calls for a transformation from a bureaucratic role culture to a task-orientated culture.

Within many organizations, it has proved difficult to change cultural attitudes when the nature of an organization's business environment has significantly changed, rendering the established culture a liability in terms of strategic management. As an example, the cultural values of UK clearing banks have for a long time continued to be dominated by prudence and caution when in some product areas, such as insurance sales, a more aggressive approach to marketing management may be called for.

8.3 THE INTERNAL FUNCTIONS OF COMMERCIAL ORGANIZATIONS

For many small businesses, it is often quite possible for one individual to perform all of the main tasks which are necessary to keep the business as a going concern. The task of keeping accounts, seeking new orders and recruiting new staff are typically undertaken by the small business owner, in addition to their main role in producing the goods and services that customers buy. In larger organizations, giving such a wide range of tasks to one individual does

THINKING AROUND THE SUBJECT:
A PUBLIC-SECTOR V. PRIVATE-SECTOR CULTURE GAP?

The gap between the public and private sectors has been narrowing over time, and Chapter 2 noted that many public-sector services have been transformed into agencies modelled more on a private-sector organization than the traditional civil service. However, to many observers, people who work in the public and private sectors could come from different planets. Even their language can differ sharply, as private-sector employees talk about 'customers' while public-sector workers talk about 'users'.

In the UK, public-sector culture has traditionally been characterized by an emphasis on procedure rather than outcome. In a large government bureaucracy, it is necessary to have clearly specified rules and procedures in order to prevent inequitable outcomes. Customers' rights and expectations are often specified in the form of government-inspired standards, so staff have little incentive for innovating and delivering better service to users. Staff promotion within the civil service has often been on the basis of seniority, rather than the ability of an individual to better satisfy the needs of external users. And there has been a belief that public-sector workers are well paid, with generous holidays, and an even more generous final-salary pension scheme. Until a few years ago, it would have been almost unheard of for public-sector employees to lose their jobs through redundancy.

Private-sector employees have been presumed to work harder and to have to think on their feet much more than is the case in the public sector. If the external environment turns against them, they will have to adapt or face the risk of losing their job. In this environment, a concern with outcomes must take priority over internal procedures.

The degree of discretion given to a public-sector manager is usually less than that given to a counterpart in the private sector. Statutorily determined standards generally affect public-sector organizations to a greater extent than the private sector – for example, the provision of educational facilities is constrained by the need to adhere to the national curriculum. Even where a local authority has a significant area of discretion, the checks and balances imposed on many public-sector managers reflect the fact that the public sector is accountable to a wider constituency of interests than the typical private-sector organization.

Managers within the private sector are usually able to monitor the results of their activity as the benefits are usually internal to the organization. By contrast, many of the aims which public-sector organizations seek to achieve are external and a profit and loss statement, or balance sheet, cannot be produced in the way that is possible with a private-sector organization operating to narrow internal financial goals.

Is the apparent cultural gap between private and public sectors narrowing? Many public-sector services such as museums are increasingly being given clearly defined business objectives which make it much more difficult for officers to continue doing what they like doing rather than what the public they serve wants. Many civil servants now work in agencies modelled on the private sector. Even many of the cherished working practices of public-sector workers have come under scrutiny, including government-funded final salary pensions.

The cultural gap appears to have been reduced most in the case of public-sector services which provide marketable goods and services, such as swimming pools and municipal bus services, but is it possible to close the gap where the service is a monopoly provider of a statutory service, such as fire and police services?

not make much sense. The arguments of 'scientific management' would point to the advantages of groups of individuals specializing in doing one function very well, rather than being a 'jack of all trades' and doing all functions only moderately well. So large organizations have evolved with sales functions that can sell better than the organization's competitors, production people that are more productive and accounts people that are more cost-effective.

In the process of specialization of functions, it is possible that as many problems are created as are solved. In addition to the benefits of economies of scale and specialization, problems of integrating the different organizational functions arise. The case of an organization's 'left hand' not knowing what its 'right hand' is doing is sadly all too familiar.

An organization operating in a fiercely competitive environment would typically attach great importance to its marketing department as a means of producing a focused marketing strategy by which it can gain competitive advantage over its competitors. By contrast, an organization operating in a relatively stable environment is more likely to allow strategic decisions to be taken by personnel that are not marketing strategists – for example, pricing decisions may be taken by accountants with less need to understand the marketing implications of price decisions.

In many instances, the main factor governing the success of an organization is its access to key resources and technologies. It is not surprising therefore to find the research and development function being the most important function within such organizations. Responsibilities given to each of the different functions within an organization vary from one organization to another, reflecting the competitive nature of their business environments and also their traditions and organizational inertia.

In a competitive business environment, a guiding influence on organizational design should be the end-customer for whom the organization is creating value. In a truly customer-focused organization, marketing responsibilities cannot be confined to something called a marketing department. In the words of Drucker (1973):

> Marketing is so basic that it cannot be considered to be a separate function. It is the whole business seen from the point of view of its final result, that is, from the customer's point of view.

In competitive business environments, customers are at the centre of all of an organization's activities. The customer is not simply the concern of the marketing department, but also all of the production and administrative personnel whose actions may directly or indirectly have an impact on the goods and services bought by customers. In a typical organization, the activities of a number of functional departments have direct and indirect impacts on customers.

■ Personnel plans can have a crucial bearing on marketing plans. The selection, training motivation and control of staff cannot be considered in isolation from marketing objectives and strategies. Possible conflict between the personnel and marketing functions may arise where, for example, marketing demands highly trained and motivated staff, but the personnel function pursues a policy which places cost reduction above all else.

■ Production managers may have a different outlook compared to marketing managers. A marketing manager may seek to respond as closely as possible to customers' needs, only to find opposition from production managers who argue that a service of the required standard cannot be achieved. A marketing manager of a railway operating company may seek to segment markets with fares tailored to meet the needs of small groups of customers, only to encounter hostility from operations managers who are responsible for actually issuing and checking travel tickets on a day-to-day basis and who may have misgivings about the confusion which finely segmented fares might cause.

■ The actions of finance managers frequently have a direct or indirect impact on marketing plans. Ultimately, finance managers assume responsibility for the allocation of funds which are needed to implement a marketing plan. At a more operational level, finance managers' actions in respect of the level of credit offered to customers, or towards stockholdings, can also significantly affect the quality of service and the volume of customers which the organization is able to serve.

All these departments should 'think customer' and work together to satisfy customers' needs and expectations. There is argument as to what authority the traditional marketing department should have in bringing about this customer orientation. In a truly mature marketing-orientated company, marketing is an implicit part of everybody's job. In such a scenario, marketing becomes responsible for a narrow range of specialist functions such as advertising and marketing research. Responsibility for the relationship between the organization and its customers is spread more diffusely throughout the organization. Gummesson (2001) uses the term 'part-time marketer' to describe staff working in service organizations who may not have any direct line management responsibility for marketing, but whose activities may indirectly impinge on the quality of service received by customers.

It has been argued that the introduction of a marketing department as the principal interface between an organization and its competitive environment can bring problems as well as benefits. In a survey of 219 executives representing public- and private-sector service organizations in Sweden, Grönroos (1982) tested the idea that a separate marketing department may widen the gap between marketing and operations staff. This idea was put to a sample drawn from marketing as well as other functional positions using a Likert-type scale with five points ranging from agreeing strongly to disagreeing strongly. The results indicated that respondents in a wide range of service organizations considered there to be dangers in the creation of a marketing department – an average of 66 per cent agreed with the notion, with higher than average agreement being found among non-marketing executives, and those working in the hotel, restaurant, professional services and insurance sectors.

In the following discussion of organizational structures, we will focus on examples from the private sector, but similar principles apply with public-sector organizations, especially where they operate in a market-based environment. Of course, some functions of public-sector organizations, such as sales management, have little place in a public-sector body that takes its clients as given and, instead of maximizing sales, aims to meet government-specified performance targets.

8.4 BASES FOR ORGANIZING A COMMERCIAL ORGANIZATION

Four basic approaches to allocating management responsibilities within an organization can be identified although, in practice, most organizations use a combination of approaches. The four approaches which will be discussed below are:

1 management by functions performed
2 management by geographical area covered
3 management of products or groups of products
4 management by groups of customers served.

8.4.1 Organization based on functional responsibilities

A traditional and common basis for allocating responsibilities within an organization is to do so on the basis of identifiable functions. In most commercial organizations, a number of core functions can be identified, the most typical being operations, marketing, personnel and finance. The exact title of these functions may vary between organizations, so, for example, personnel is often referred to as the human resources function. In larger organizations, these functions are further sub-divided into areas of specialist responsibility, so, for example, the marketing function would typically be divided into functions covering advertising, sales, marketing research and customer services etc. The nature of an organization's environment will influence the relative size and importance of each of its functional areas of management. The precise division of the functional responsibilities will depend upon the nature of an organization. Buying and merchandising are likely to be an important feature in a retailing organization, while research and development will be an important function for technology-based companies.

The main advantage of allocating responsibilities by function is that it allows individuals and groups of individuals to develop expertise in their functional area. Personnel managers can become expert in the latest employment legislation, or be familiar with the latest thinking on recruitment policies. This expertise may not be developed if personnel management responsibilities were dispersed throughout the organization. A further advantage of functional approaches to management lies in their administrative simplicity. Clearly defined hierarchical structures can allow for rapid identification of lines of authority and responsibility.

Against these advantages, division of responsibilities solely on the basis of functions can have disadvantages. Most seriously, there can be a tendency for corporate goals to become secondary to functional managers' much narrower functional goals. Functions should be seen as a means to an end (in private-sector organizations, this is usually defined in terms of corporate profitability) and should not come to be seen as ends in their own right. It is not uncommon to find destructive rivalry between functional specialists for their share of budgets.

8.4.2 Management by product type

Multi-output organizations frequently appoint a product manager to manage a particular product or group of products. This form of organization does not replace the functional organization, but provides an additional layer of management which co-ordinates the functions' activities. The product manager's role includes a number of key tasks:

- developing a long-range and competitive strategy for a product or group of products
- preparing a budgeted annual plan
- working with internal and external functional specialists to develop and implement programmes, for example in relation to advertising and sales promotion
- monitoring the product's performance and changes occurring in its business environment
- identifying new opportunities and initiating product improvements to meet changing market needs.

A product management organization structure offers a number of advantages.

- The product offering benefits from an integrated cost-effective approach to planning. This particularly benefits minor products which might otherwise be neglected.

- The product manager can, in theory, react quicker to changes in the product's business environment than would be the case if no one had specific responsibility for the product. Within a bank, a mortgage manager is able to devote a lot of time and expertise to monitoring trends in the mortgage market and can become a focal point for initiating and seeing through change when this is required because of environmental change.
- Control within this type of organization can be exercised by linking product managers' salaries to performance.

Against this, product management structures are associated with a number of problems.

- The most serious problem occurs in the common situation where a product manager is given a lot of responsibility for ensuring that objectives are met, but relatively little control over resource inputs which they have at their disposal. Product managers typically must rely on persuasion to get the co-operation of marketing, operations and other functional specialist departments. Sometimes this can result in conflict, for example where a product manager seeks to position a service in one direction, while the advertising manager seeks to position it in another in order to meet broader promotional objectives.
- Confusion can arise in the minds of staff within an organization as to whom they are accountable to for their day-to-day actions. Staff involved in selling insurance policies in a branch bank, for example, may become confused at possibly conflicting messages from an operations manager and a product manager.
- Product management structures can lead to larger numbers of people being employed, resulting in a higher cost structure which may put the organization at a competitive disadvantage in price-sensitive markets.
- Research has suggested that the existence of the optimal product management form is rare and that it is typically associated with an unwillingness of senior management to delegate authority to product managers. While the product management form may be appropriate for a diversified conglomerate, it may be inappropriate for complex multi-output organizations where many functions and products are closely interdependent, allowing very little freedom of action for individual product managers.

8.4.3 Market management organization

Many organizations provide goods and services to a diverse range of customers who have widely varying needs. As an example, a cross-channel ferry operator provides the basically similar service of transport for private car drivers, coach operators and freight operators, among others. However, the specific needs of each group of users vary significantly. A coach operator is likely to attach different importance compared with a road haulier to service attributes such as flexibility, ease of reservations, the type of accommodation provided etc. In such situations, market managers can be appointed to oversee the development of particular markets, in much the same way as a product manager oversees particular products. Instead of being given specific financial targets for their products, market managers are usually given growth or market share targets. The main advantage of this form of organization is that it allows management efforts to be focused on meeting the needs of distinct and identified groups of customers – something which should be at the heart of all truly marketing orientated organization. Market managers can keep a close eye on their market sector and should be in a

THINKING AROUND THE SUBJECT:
CHINESE WALLS PUT BARRIERS BETWEEN STAFF

The idea of an integrated internal work environment may be fine in theory, and may reassure customers that 'the left hand really does know what the right hand is doing'. But in practice, there are many instances where professional codes of conduct require that staff within an organization do *not* talk to each other. This often happens in financial services institutions where one group of employees may have 'inside information' about the shares, activities or financial condition of a company, which, if made public, would be likely to have an effect on the price of that company's shares. As an example, information about a proposed takeover bid for a company may be price-sensitive in relation to other companies in the same sector. This leads many institutions to create 'Chinese walls', which are barriers to the passing of information. They are designed to manage confidential information and prevent inadvertent spread and misuse of information. Many banks have set up global Chinese wall policies. Those areas that routinely have access to inside information (e.g. corporate finance) and are considered 'inside areas', must be physically separated from those areas that deal in or advise on financial instruments (e.g. bonds and shares), which are considered 'public areas'.

Chinese walls are also used by solicitors in cases where they are dealing with clients who may be in dispute with each other. But even a Chinese wall may be insufficient to overcome the conflict of interest which may arise. This was seen in the Court of Appeal's ruling about the solicitor Freshfields Bruckhaus Deringer's role in the 2004 £9 billion takeover bid for Marks & Spencer by Philip Green. The court ruled that Freshfields must not act for the Philip Green consortium in its bid for Marks & Spencer. It held that a potential conflict of interest was likely given that Freshfields had acted for Marks & Spencer in the past in relation to its Per Una clothing line. Despite pledges by Freshfields to increase confidentiality within the firm, this was considered insufficient to prevent a conflict of interest arising.

Other service industries can be identified where similar ethical problems can be lessened by the adoption of a product management structure – accountants selling both auditing services and management consultancy services to a company may be tempted to gain business in the latter area at the expense of integrity in the former. How do large diversified firms convince their customers that information given in confidence to one section of the organization will not be used against them in another?

strong position to respond to environmental change. It is also likely that innovative goods and services are more likely to emerge within this structure than where an organization's response is confined within traditional product management boundaries. Market management structures are also arguably more conducive to the important task of developing relationships with customers, especially for business-to-business services. Where an organization has a number of very important customers, it is common to find the appointment of key account managers to handle relationships with those clients in order to exploit marketing opportunities which are of mutual benefit to both.

Many of the disadvantages of the product management organization are also shared by market-based structures. There can again be a conflict between responsibility and authority, and this form of structure can also become expensive to operate.

8.4.4 Organization based on geographical responsibilities

Organizations providing goods and services to national or international markets frequently organize many of their functions on a geographical basis. This particularly applies to the sales function, although it could also include geographically designated responsibilities for new product development (e.g. a retailer with regional management structures responsible for new store opening) and some local responsibility for promotion.

In most organizations with some form of regional structure, a delicate balance has to be maintained between the responsibilities of the headquarters and the branches. Some delegation of responsibilities to regional branch managers can be vital to secure speedy and effective response to purely local issues. This is especially true of delegated responsibility in overseas markets where headquarters management may have little idea of the cultural factors which affect the dynamics of a distant overseas market. On the other hand, too much delegation can result in inconsistencies in the way that a global brand is developed and promoted.

8.4.5 Integrated approaches

Overall, the management structure of an organization must allow for a flexible and adaptable response to customers' needs within a changing environment, while aiming to reduce the level of confusion, ambiguity and cost inherent in some structures. The differences in organizational structures described above, and their typical application to a car ferry operator, are illustrated in Figure 8.3. The great diversity of organizational structures highlights the fact that there is not one unique structure which is appropriate to all firms, even within the same industry sector. Indeed, most organizational structures exhibit characteristics of all four basic approaches discussed above.

The problem of how to bring people together in an organization to act collectively, while also being able to place responsibility on an individual is one which continues to generate considerable discussion. We will now consider two ideas which seek to integrate these approaches. The first, the matrix approach to management, is essentially about creating a flexible organization based on a combination of the design characteristics discussed above. The second approach – often referred to as business process re-engineering – starts the process of organizational design with a clean sheet of paper and develops structures and processes which are most appropriate for the environment in which an organization operates.

8.4.6 Matrix approach to management

Organizations which produce many different products for many different markets may experience difficulties if they adopt a purely product- or market-based structure. If a product management structure is adopted, product managers would require detailed knowledge of very diverse markets. Likewise, in a market management structure, market managers would require detailed knowledge of possibly very diverse product ranges. The essence of a matrix organization structure is to allow individuals to concentrate on a functional, product, market or geographical specialization and to bring them together in task force teams to solve problems taking an organizational view rather than their own narrow specialist view. Product managers can concentrate on excellence in production, while market managers focus on meeting consumer needs without any preference for a particular product. An example of matrix structures can be found in many vehicle distributors, where market managers can be appointed to identify and formulate a market strategy in respect of the distinct needs of private customers

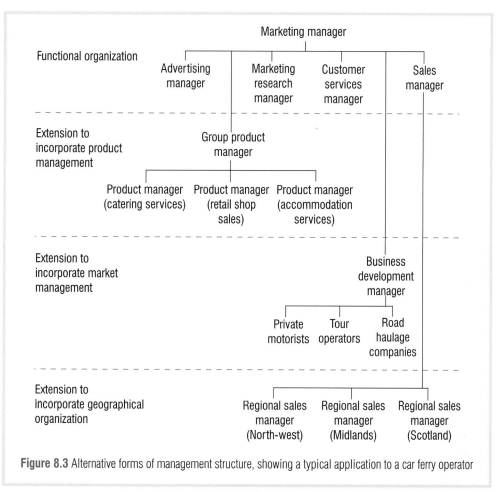

Figure 8.3 Alternative forms of management structure, showing a typical application to a car ferry operator

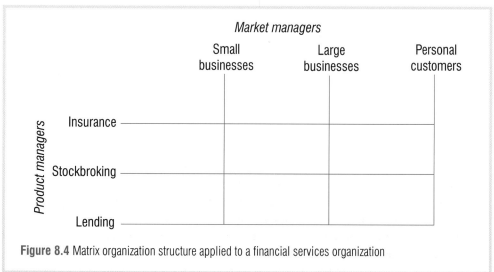

Figure 8.4 Matrix organization structure applied to a financial services organization

and contract hire customers etc., as well as being appointed to manage key customers. Market managers work alongside product managers who can develop specialized activities such as servicing, bodywork repairs and vehicle hire which are made available to final customers through the market managers.

The most important advantages of matrix structures are that they can allow organizations to respond rapidly to environmental change. Short-term project teams can be assembled and disbanded at short notice to meet changed needs. Project teams can bring together a wide variety of disciplines and can be used to evaluate new services before full-scale development is undertaken. A bank exploring the possibility of developing a banking system linked to customers' mobile phones might establish a team drawn from staff involved in marketing to personal customers and staff responsible for technology-based research and development. The former may include market researchers and the latter computer development engineers.

The flexibility of matrix structures can be increased by bringing temporary workers into the structure on a contract basis as and when needed. During the 1990s there was a trend for many organizations to lay off significant numbers of workers – including management – and to buy these back when needed. As well as cutting fixed costs, such 'modular' or 'virtual' organizations have the potential to respond very rapidly to environmental change.

Where matrix structures exist, great motivation can be present in effectively managed teams. Against this, matrix-type structures can be associated with problems. Most serious is the confused lines of authority which may result. Staff may not be clear about which superior they are responsible to for a particular aspect of their duties, resulting in possible stress and demotivation. Where a matrix structure is introduced into an organization with a history and culture of functional specialization, it can be very difficult to implement effectively. Staff may be reluctant to act outside a role which they have traditionally defined narrowly and guarded jealously. Finally, matrix structures invariably result in more managers being employed within an organization. At best this can result in a costly addition to the salary bill. At worst, the existence of additional managers can also slow down decision-making processes where the managers show a reluctance to act outside a narrow functional role.

8.4.7 Business process re-engineering

Most management change within organizations occurs incrementally. The result of this is often a compromised organization structure which is unduly influenced by historic factors which are of no continuing relevance. Vested interests within an organization frequently result in an organization which is production rather than customer focused.

The underlying principle of business process re-engineering is to design an organization around key value-adding activities. Essentially, re-engineering is about *radically* redesigning the *processes* by which an organization does business in order that it can achieve major savings in cost or improvements in output, or both. Seen as a model, the organization which is most effective is the one which adds most value (as defined by customers) for the least cost.

Business process re-engineering focuses on operational aspects of a business, rather than its strategy and starts the design of processes and structures with a clean sheet of paper. This is in contrast to most organizational change which starts with an analysis of the existing structure and attempts to tinker with it. Re-engineering starts by asking 'If we were a new company, how would we organize ourselves?' It follows that re-engineering can stand for a total sudden change, inevitably challenging vested interests of people who are comfortably established within their own departmental boundaries.

To be effective, re-engineering needs to be led by strong individuals who have authority to oversee implementation from beginning to end. They will need a lot of clout because fear, resistance and cynicism will inevitably slow the task down. At first sight, though, this approach to reorganization would appear to be in conflict with the principles of participative schemes that stress employee involvement in change. Successful companies therefore seek to involve their employees in the detail of implementation, even if the radical nature of the agenda is not negotiable.

8.4.8 Outsourcing

In Chapter 6 we discussed the nature of 'virtual' organizations. Outsourcing is an important contributor to virtual organizations and is often a component of business process re-engineering, designed to make an organization's structure more flexible. Many companies that have traditionally employed their own cleaning, catering and security staff now subcontract or 'outsource' these to specialist suppliers. Sometimes, employees of the organization are transferred to the new supplier and hence become employees of the specialist contractor. This contractor then provides an agreed level of service to the organization for a specified contract period. At the end of this period the organization is able to evaluate competing suppliers before placing the next contract. The specialist supplier assumes profit and loss responsibility for the delivery of the service as well as taking on the employment and employment rights of the employees.

Outsourcing has become an acceptable and fashionable way of providing services for both public- and private-sector organizations. Outsourced contracts range from a small factory replacing kitchen assistants with a contract caterer, through to the Greater London Authority's outsourcing of the collection of the London Congestion Charge to Capita plc.

Outsourcing offers many advantages to a company, including:
- allowing a business to focus its operations on its core activities
- giving access to cutting-edge skills that would be difficult for the company to acquire and learn on its own; the company does not have to worry about continually introducing new technologies
- sharing risks of service provision, especially in the case of activities which are new to the company
- improved service quality where a contract provides rewards for good performance
- a company's scarce human resources can be freed up and redeployed in higher-value-adding activities
- cash flow can be freed up, allowing it to be reinvested in core business activities (e.g. an airline outsourcing its maintenance operations can use cash which was previously invested in its maintenance facilities to invest in better aircraft)
- it can make the business more flexible to changes in the external environment.

However, outsourcing does have its disadvantages too.
- Big disruptions can occur if the outsourced service provider ceases to trade (e.g. through bankruptcy).

- Employees may react badly to outsourcing and consequently their quality of work may suffer.
- Outsourcing may involve redundancy costs and bad feeling by employees who remain.
- There may be a career progression problem with the loss of talent generated internally.
- Other companies may also be using the service provider, resulting in a possible conflict of interest by the outsourced service provider.
- The company may lose direct contact with its customers.

Some have argued that outsourcing undermines a coherent internal focus on meeting customers' needs. The outsourced supplier may be so focused on meeting their narrowly defined performance targets that they overlook more qualitative aspects of delivering value to customers. The UK's National Health Service has used outsourcing extensively for cleaning of hospital wards. There may have been significant cost savings from this move, but the cleaners who come in and do their work have been accused of not having the same team spirit as cleaners who are employed by the hospital and directly answerable to the matron. Over time, and through an acculturalization process, a ward-based cleaner may learn to be the eyes and ears of nurses, for example identifying symptoms of medical problems which doctors and nurses may have missed.

Outsourcing has often involved transferring work to overseas companies. Where service operations or manufacturing processes can be broken down into a number of discrete activities, firms have been keen to take advantage of low-wage costs and modern production techniques of relatively labour abundant countries such as China and India. They have typically moved their low-skill-intensive activities abroad, but continued to carry out the high-skill-intensive activities themselves.

8.5 THE FLEXIBLE ORGANIZATION

We have seen how management structures can help or hinder the task of responding to organizational change at a strategic level. We will now consider how organizations can be made more flexible to environmental change at a more short-term or operational level. To continue the analogy with a central heating system and its environment, we will now move from looking at how the system adapts to long-term climatic change, to how it copes with day-to-day changes in weather.

For many organizations, employees are the biggest item of cost and potentially the biggest cause of bottlenecks in responding rapidly to environmental change, especially within the services sector. Having the right staff in the right place at the right time can demand a lot of flexibility on the part of employees. Too often, customers are delayed because, although staff are available, they are not trained to perform the task which currently needs performing urgently. At other times, employees may go about a backroom task oblivious of the fact that delays are occurring elsewhere. Worse still, employees could have a negative attitude towards their job, and see a customer's problem as nothing to do with them and take no interest in finding staff who may be able to help. Many service industries have been notorious in the past for rigid demarcation between jobs which were organization-focused rather than customer-focused. In Britain, train drivers and guards for a long while existed as two separate groups which were not able to stand in for the other. With privatization and increased competition for rail franchises, this mindset has been changed, so that employees who are trained in one area can substitute in the other, if required and suitably trained.

THINKING AROUND THE SUBJECT:
POWERING UP COMPUTERS THROUGH OUTSOURCING

Seeboard, a West Sussex-based energy company that supplies gas and electricity to approximately 2 million customers in the UK identified its core competence as being the distribution of energy at lower prices and with higher customer service levels than its competitors. Of course, low prices and top-quality services can easily lead to a loss, so the company has had to keep a very close eye on its costs, as well as ensuring that the best people deliver its services.

Outsourcing has played an important role for the company. Seeboard began its first outsourcing contract with Accenture in 1993, subsequently adding Siemens to its outsourced suppliers. Since 2001, the company has outsourced the management of its desktop computers and network servers to the specialist IT services company Computacenter.

IT has become increasingly important to Seeboard. Like many companies, Seeboard is web-enabling more and more of its business processes, with recent initiatives including an online service for customers to record and submit their own meter readings. The company also realized that expansion of its IT needs would rapidly outgrow the resources of its in-house team.

Computacenter was brought in to manage Seeboard's computers in a contract which covered 3000 desktops, 400 laptops and 200 servers at various sites across London and the south-east. Computacenter was given responsibility for developing standard desktop builds, configuring servers, rolling out new software and hardware, day-to-day support and the disposal of redundant equipment.

One slight complication of the contract was that care had to be taken to avoid a conflict of interest between Seeboard's power supply operations (Seeboard Power Networks) and its distribution business (Seeboard Energy). The deregulation of the industry had meant that energy companies must avoid taking competitive advantage from their ownership of both supply and distribution operations in an area. Separate service provision to Seeboard Power Networks and Seeboard Energy meant separate support contracts and organizations for each business.

By working with Computacenter, Seeboard was able to access a much wider pool of technical knowledge and benefited from Computacenter's experience gained through other IT projects and outsourcing contracts. As a result, Seeboard benefited from worldwide best practice, requiring fewer staff than if it had carried out the work itself in house, and claimed to have cut its total IT operating costs. Just by implementing a standard desktop configuration, it saw a decrease in support calls and, as a result, support overheads.

It must not be forgotten, however, that Seeboard's aim was not just to cut costs, but also to improve customer service – a vital source of competitive differentiation. A cheap outsourced operation which left the company's websites down for lengthy periods would not be good for customers and profitability. Seeboard used a balanced scorecard system with internal and external users to assess the service level standards, responsiveness, customer satisfaction and project performance, and claimed to be happy with the results.

How far can a company such as Seeboard go in its outsourcing? Like many utility services it saw advantages in supplementing outsourcing with 'offshoring' – moving many of its service processes overseas to lower-cost providers. Some electricity companies have transferred call centres and bill-processing functions to India where a high-quality workforce can usually undertake the job at lower cost. But if it went down this route, would it still be able to maintain high levels of customer service? Would customers be as happy speaking to a call centre worker in Bangalore as a Seeboard worker in Brighton?

To improve their flexibility, many organizations have sought to develop multiple skills among their employees so that they can be switched between tasks at short notice. Within the hotel sector, for example, it is quite usual to find staff multi-skilled in reception duties, food and beverage service and room service. If staff shortages occur within one area, staff can be rapidly transferred from less urgent tasks where there may be sufficient staff coverage anyway. An effective multi-tasking strategy must be backed up by adequate training so that employees can effectively perform all the functions that are expected of them.

Flexibility in working also applies to the rostering of employees' duties. Where patterns of demand are unpredictable, it is useful to have a pool of suitably trained staff who can be called up at short notice. Many service providers therefore operate 'standby' or 'callout' rotas, where staff are expected to be available to go into work at short notice.

A flexible workforce sounds attractive in principle, but there are some drawbacks. Training in multiple skills would appear to be against the principles of scientific management, wherein employees specialize in one task and perform this as efficiently as possible. Multiple skill training represents an investment for firms, and in industry sectors with high turnover, such as the hospitality sector, the benefits of this training may be short lived. Recruiting staff may become more expensive, with staff capable of performing numerous tasks able to command higher salaries than somebody whose background allows them to perform only a narrower range of tasks. Finally, there is also the problem that requiring staff to work flexible hours may make their working conditions less attractive than a job where they had certainty over the days and times that they will be working. Expecting excessive flexibility may be contrary to the principles of internal marketing (discussed later in this chapter), exacerbating problems where there is a shortage of skilled staff. Companies have to compete with other employers for the best staff and if a job is perceived as offering too much uncertainty, staff may prefer to work elsewhere where working conditions are more predictable.

Flexibility within an organization can be achieved by segmenting the workforce into core and peripheral components. Core workers have greater job security and have defined career opportunities within an internal labour market. In return for this job security, core workers may have to accept what Atkinson (1984) termed 'functional flexibility' whereby they become responsible for a variety of job tasks. The work output of this group is intensified, but in order for this to be successful, employees require effective training and motivation which in turn has to be sustained by effective participation methods.

Peripheral employees, on the other hand, have lesser job security and limited career opportunity. In terms of Atkinson's prescription they are 'numerically flexible', while financial flexibility is brought about through the process of 'distancing'. In this situation a firm may utilize the services and skills of specialist labour but acquire it through a commercial contract as distinct from an employment contract. This process is referred to as subcontracting. The principal characteristics of the flexible firm are illustrated in Figure 8.5.

As a strategic tool, the model of the flexible firm has important implications for organizations which operate in an unstable environment. However, critics of the concept have suggested that the strategic role attributed to the flexibility model is often illusory, with many organizations introducing 'flexibility' in very much an opportunistic manner. It has been noted that the opportunities for introducing this model of flexibility are greater in Britain than in most other EU countries, where stricter rules on staff layoffs apply.

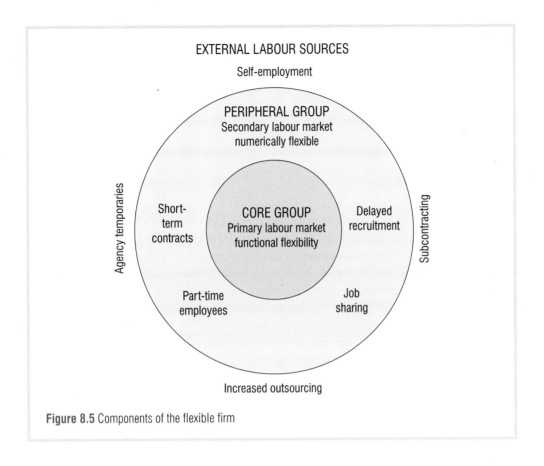

Figure 8.5 Components of the flexible firm

8.6 CREATING INVOLVEMENT BY EMPLOYEES

It can be difficult for an organization to respond to environmental change if it doesn't have the confidence of its employees, for whom change may be viewed with suspicion. While it is probably unrealistic to say that a happy workforce necessarily results in an organization which is more effective at embracing change, there are many things that an organization can do to secure the active participation of its employees in change. We will now review some key elements of the employment relationship which can facilitate this.

8.6.1 Motivating employees

Motivation concerns the choices which employees make between alternative forms of behaviour in order that they as employees attain their own personal goals. The task of management is to equate the individual's personal goals with those of the employing organization – that is, getting employees morally involved with the service which they help to produce. This in turn requires employees to consent to the management of their work activity. Maslow (1943) argued that motivation is based on individuals' desire to satisfy various levels of need. These levels range from the need to realize potential and self-development down to the satisfaction of basic needs such as hunger, thirst and sex. Rewards for reaching goals can be tangible, for example money, or can be intangible (e.g. commendations or awards which add to status or self-esteem). An organization has to bring about congruence between its own goals and those of its employees. This is the basis for designing an appropriate motivation package. Within the UK tourist attractions sector, a comparison can be made between many commercial operations (e.g. Alton Towers and Warwick Castle) where financial incentives are an important motivator and the National Trust, which attracts many unpaid volunteers, motivated by a desire to share in the preservation of historic buildings. Employees' attitudes and opinions about their colleagues and the work environment may make all the difference between workers' merely doing a good job and delivering exceptional service (Arnett, Laverie and McLane 2002).

8.6.2 Consent

The term consent covers a variety of management-led initiatives and strategies which seek to give it authority without actively emphasizing its coercive power. In the UK during the twentieth century there have been various forms of employee participation and involvement designed to aid management in the generation of consent. Such initiatives include scientific management, industrial management, the human relations approach, welfare, paternalism, professionalized and proceduaralized personnel management and, more recently, HRM. Each initiative has its own prescription for the generation of consent.

Scientific management approaches seek co-operation between employer and employee in terms of the division of labour, whereby individual employees work in pre-defined ways as directed by management. Advocates of scientific management see mutual benefits for the employee and employer. For the former, specializing in one work activity would give the opportunity to earn more, especially through piece rate pay systems, while management would benefit through greater work control and higher productivity. What Taylor (1985), the leading advocate of scientific management, did not expect was the hostility of employees to what is often described as the process of de-skilling. Many attempts have been made to de-skill jobs in accordance with the scientific management prescription. However, it is necessary to balance the benefits of specialization and improved efficiency against employees' sense of alienation from their job which occurs where they are involved in only a very small part of a production process.

Paternalism is often associated with Quaker employers such as Cadbury or Rowntree who attempted to show that they were interested in their workforce at home as well as at work. Within the services sector, many retail employers such as Marks & Spencer have taken a paternalistic attitude towards their employees by providing such benefits as on-site welfare services or temporary accommodation for their employees. This and other benefits, such as subsidized social clubs, are designed to encourage employee identification with the company, and therefore loyalty, which legitimizes managerial authority and hence consent to it.

In contrast to the economically based consent strategies of scientific management, the *human relations* approach looks at man as a social animal. Mayo in his study of General Electric in the United States (1933) argued that productivity was unrelated to work organization and economic rewards as suggested by scientific management. Mayo emphasized the importance of atmosphere and social attitudes, group feelings and the sense of identification which employees had. He suggested that the separation of employees which scientific management had created prevented them from experiencing a sense of identification and involvement which is essential for all humans. Hence one solution was to design group structures into production processes. Such processes were thought to assist in the generation of employees' loyalty to their organization via the work group. Mayo's work is similar in focus to that of Herzberg and Maslow. Maslow (1943) suggested that humans have psychological as well as economic needs. Only when the psychological needs have been catered for do the economic needs come into play. To Herzberg (1966), humans have lower- and higher-order needs. The former are the basic economic needs of food and shelter whereas the latter are more psychologically based in terms of recognition and contribution to the group and organization.

All of the management initiatives and strategies described in this section are in part efforts to generate employee consent to management authority without management exercising its authority via coercion. Where this consent is obtained, employees can be motivated by some form of participation in the organization. Such participation gives the employee a small stake in the organization, be it financial or in the form of discretionary control over the performance of their work function.

8.6.3 Participation

An employee's participation in an organization may be limited to purely economic matters – payment is received in return for work performed. Alternatively, participation may manifest itself through more qualitative measures such as employee involvement in decision making through quality circles or team briefings. The process of creating involvement can take the form of devolution of some areas of traditional personnel activity to line management in order that the employees actually doing the work and those responsible for managing particular sections feel that they are somehow involved in it together. This can apply, for example, to selecting, recruiting and appraising employees within a work group.

8.6.4 Communication

Internal communication between management and employees is usually most notable when it is absent. Rumours about revised working arrangements, reductions in the workforce and changes to the terms of employment often circulate around companies, breeding a feeling of distrust by employees in their management. Some managers may take a conscious decision to give employees as little information as possible, perhaps on the basis that knowledge is power. There are sometimes good strategic reasons for not disseminating information to employees (for example business strategy may be a closely guarded secret in order to keep competitors guessing). However, in too many organizations information is unnecessarily withheld from employees, creating a feeling of an underclass in terms of access to information. Such practices do not help to generate consent and involvement by employees.

In good practice organizations, information can be communicated through a number of channels. The staff newsletter is a well-tried medium, but in many instances these are seen as being too little, too late and with inadequate discussion of the issues involved. Many organizations use team briefings to cascade information down through an organization and to permit communication back upwards again. The Internet is developing new possibilities for communicating information to a company's employees and allows much greater personalization to the specific needs of individual employees. External advertising should regard the internal labour force as a secondary target market. The appearance of advertisements on television can have the effect of inspiring confidence of employees in their management and pride in their company.

THINKING AROUND THE SUBJECT:
CUSTOMERS OR EMPLOYEES FIRST?

Many companies have developed a philosophy of putting their employees first. This might at first sound contradictory to the marketing philosophy which puts customers at the centre of a firm's thinking, but there are many examples of companies that have made this proud claim and achieved credible results. The American South Western Airlines has frequently been cited as an advocate of this approach, and has expanded rapidly and profitably. The airline has argued that employees are such a major part of its service offer and that if they are not happy, it is unlikely that the airline's customers will be happy. Being a relatively new airline with no history of poor industrial relations undoubtedly helps employees to identify with the company's mission. Having staff incentive schemes which encourage employees to perform to their best in a highly competitive market also helps. But can this approach of putting employees first work in all situations? If employees do not share a company's mission, management's attempts to put employees first may not be reciprocated in the form of employees' enthusiastic contribution to the business. And if there is very little external competition to spur them on, captive customers may come second best by a long way.

As well as happy staff leading to happy customers, it could also be argued that happy customers lead to happy employees. Sometimes the reverse is true – staff working in one local authority office which handles parking ticket fines suffered a high turnover because angry 'customers' led to unhappiness among the staff.

In reality, it is difficult to talk about employees coming first, if by implication customers come second. They should both be seen as part of a virtuous circle in which attention given to one reinforces attention given to the other.

8.6.5 Strategies to increase employees' involvement

The methods which an organization uses to encourage involvement among its employees are likely to be influenced by the type of person it employs and the extent to which their jobs present opportunities to exercise autonomy (that is, the extent to which employees are able to control their own work processes) and discretion (the degree of independent thinking they can exercise in performing their work).

This section considers various strategies to increase employees' involvement. In practice, organizations are most likely to be concerned with securing greater employee involvement by making individual employee objectives more congruent to those of the whole organization. This type of involvement may be available to all employees but the extent to which their participation is real and effective may well depend on where they are positioned in the employment hierarchy, that is, whether they are within the core or the peripheral groups of workers. Increased participation is brought about by a combination of consultation and communication methods, and team briefings.

- ■ 'Open door' policies encourage employees to air their grievances and to make suggestions directly to their superiors. The aim of this approach is to make management accessible and 'employee friendly'. To be effective, the human relations approach would require employees to feel that they do in fact have a real say in managerial matters. As a consequence, management must appear to be open and interested in employee relations. It is likely that this approach to managerial style and strategy will emphasize open management through some of the methods described below.

■ Team briefings are a system of communication within the organization where a leader of a group provides group members (up to about 20) with management-derived information. The rationale behind briefing is to encourage commitment to and identification with the organization. Team briefings are particularly useful in times of organizational change, although they can be held regularly to cover such items as competitive progress, changes in policy and points of future action. Ideally, they should result in information 'cascading'

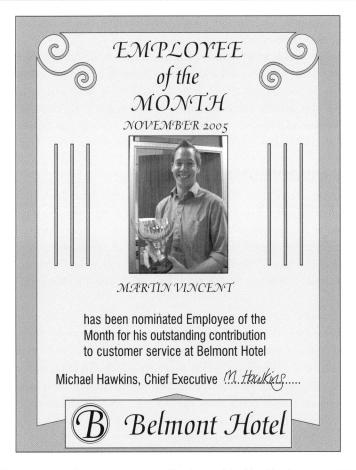

Figure 8.6 Many successful companies operate 'Employee of the Month' schemes to recognize excellent service by staff. Customers may be invited to nominate for the award staff who have served them particularly well, and the employer must then make a judgement about who wins the award. Invariably one of downsides of such schemes can be a feeling of disillusionment on the part of employees who are not selected for an award but who may feel equally deserving. Could the demotivational effect on the 'losers' counterbalance the motivational effect on those who win the award?

down through an organization. The difference between briefing and quality circles (see below) centres on their respective contents. Briefing sessions are likely to be more general and relate to the whole organization, whereas quality circles relate to the specific work activity of a particular group of employees. Any general points of satisfaction or dissatisfaction can be aired in briefings and then taken up in specific quality circles.

■ Quality circles (QCs) are small groups of employees that meet with a supervisor or group leader in an attempt to discuss their work in terms of production quality and service delivery. QCs often work within a total quality management approach. To be successful, the QC leader has to be willing to listen to and act upon issues raised by QC members. This is essential if the QC is to be sustained. Circle members must feel their participation is real and effective, therefore the communication process within the QC must be two way. If quality circles appear to become only a routinized listening session, members may consider it to be just another form of managerial control.

■ The pattern of ownership of an organization can influence the level of consent and participation. Where the workforce owns a significant share of a business, there should in principle be less cause for 'us and them' attitudes to develop between management and the workforce. For this reason, many labour-intensive service organizations have significant worker shareholders and there is evidence that such companies can outperform more conventionally owned organizations.

8.7 TRAINING AND DEVELOPMENT

Training refers to the acquisition of specific knowledge and skills which enable employees to perform their job effectively. The focus of staff training is the job. In contrast to this, staff development concerns activities which are directed to the future needs of the employee, which may themselves be derived from the future needs of the organization. As an example, workers may need to become familiar with personal computers, electronic mail and other aspects of information technology which as yet are not elements within their own specific job requirements.

Training is essential if any process of change is to be actively consented to by the workforce. Initially this may be merely an awareness-training programme whereby the process of change is communicated to the workforce as a precursor to the actual changes. It may involve making employees aware of the competitive market pressures which the organization faces and how the organization proposes to address them. This initial process may also involve giving employees the opportunity to make their views known and to air any concerns they might have. This can help to generate some involvement in the process of change and could itself be the precursor to an effective participation forum.

A practical problem facing many organizations that allocate large budgets to staff training is that many other organizations in their sector may spend very little, relying on staff being poached from the company doing the training. This occurs for example within the banking sector where many building societies have set up cheque account operations using the skills of staff attracted from the 'big four' UK banks. The problem also occurs in many construction-related industries and in the car repair business. While the ease with which an organization can lose trained staff may be one reason to explain UK companies' generally low level of spending on training and development, a number of policies can be adopted to maximize the

THINKING AROUND THE SUBJECT:
DRIVER POWER ON THE BUSES

Many services firms proudly promote the fact that they are owned by their employees. But do they deliver better service quality to customers? Research undertaken by Dolan and Brierley (1992) in the bus sector showed how two companies – People's Provincial of Fareham and Derbyshire-based Chesterfield Transport – had capitalized on their worker ownership to perform better than their more conventionally owned rivals.

To the employees, a financial investment in the two companies studied proved attractive. Over a period of five years, the value of employees' investments in People's Provincial more than doubled, while with Chesterfield Transport it increased over fourfold within two years. Like many employee buy-outs of larger government-owned organizations, takeover bids were attracted from larger bus operators, boosting the value of employees' shareholdings.

The research highlighted four important benefits which had resulted from worker ownership.

1 Traditional hierarchies were broken down, which gave much greater operational flexibility to the companies (for example, inspectors and management would accept it as normal to change their duties and drive buses when the need arose). This was particularly important as the uneven pattern of demand required great flexibility.

2 Costs were held down because staff recognized that they would benefit directly from the resulting increase in profits. Similarly, staff became more willing to pass on ideas about ways in which services could be improved or costs saved.

3 Absenteeism was reduced, as was the need for formal disciplinary measures to be taken. Employees could see the need for a high level of service performance and were able to share in the resulting benefits.

4 All workers had access to financial information, resulting in a more constructive approach to negotiations on work schedules and pay, for example.

The authors concluded that employee ownership – by increasing the level of participation – can give companies a competitive advantage in services industries where flexibility in production and commitment to high standards of service quality are important. But the question remains why so many employee-owned bus companies in the UK have sold out to larger organizations, such as Stagecoach and First Group. Is a one-off cash bonus to employee shareholders more important than involvement in the ownership of their company? And do customers notice any difference once a large company takes over?

benefits of such expenditure to the organization. Training and development should be linked to the generation of loyalty by employees. Where such efforts to increase moral involvement are insufficient to retain trained staff, an organization may seek to tie an individual to it by seeking reimbursement of any expenditure if the employee leaves the organization within a specified time period. Reimbursement is most likely to be sought in the case of expenditure aimed at developing the general abilities of an individual as opposed to their ability to perform a functional and organization-specific task.

Another mechanism which can assist an organization in its goals of recruiting and retaining staff is a clearly defined career progression pathway. Career progression refers to a mechanism which enables employees to visualize how their working life might develop within a particular organization. Clearly defined expectations of what an individual employee should be able to achieve within an organization and clear statements of promotion criteria can assist the employee in this regard. Additionally, the creation and use of an internal labour market, for instance through counselling and the dissemination of job vacancy details, are vital. An organization can introduce vertical job ladders or age- or tenure-based remuneration and promotion programmes to assist in the retention of core employees.

During periods of scarcity among the skilled labour force, offers of defined career paths may become essential if the right calibre of staff are to be recruited and retained. As an example, many retailers which had previously operated relatively casual employment policies introduced career structures for the first time during the tight labour market of the late 1980s. Conversely, during the following period of recession it became very difficult for employers to maintain their promises with a consequent de-motivational effect on staff. In this way, the demise of profitability in UK branch banking in the 1990s brought about considerable disillusionment among core bank employees who saw their career progression prospects made considerably more difficult than they had expected, despite good work performance on their part.

8.8 REWARDING STAFF

The process of staff recruitment and the retention of staff, is directly influenced by the quality of reward on offer. The central purpose of a reward system is to improve the standard of staff performance by giving employees something which they consider to be of value in return for good performance. What employees consider to be a good reward is influenced by the nature of the motivators which drive each individual. For this reason, one standardized reward system is unlikely to achieve maximum motivation among a large and diverse workforce.

Reward systems have been seen by many (e.g. Milkovich and Newman 2002) as an essential tool to link corporate goals, such as customer orientation, with individual and organizational performance. While some studies have demonstrated positive effects of incorporating non-financial measures into employees' reward schemes (e.g. Widmier 2002), many companies have encountered problems in linking pay to customer satisfaction. Reasons for this can be attributed to the measurement of customer satisfaction as well as to the missing link between customer satisfaction and customer retention.

Rewards to employees can be divided into two categories – non-monetary and monetary. Non-monetary rewards cover a wide range of benefits, some of which will be a formal part of the reward system, for example subsidized housing or sports facilities and public recognition for work achievement (as where staff are given diplomas signifying their level of achievement). At other times, non-monetary rewards could be informal and represent something of a hidden agenda for management. In this way, a loyal, long-standing restaurant waiter may be rewarded by being given a relatively easy schedule of work, allowing unpopular Saturday nights to be removed from their duty rota.

Monetary rewards are a more direct method of improving the performance of employees and are a more formal element of human resource management policy. In the absence of more informal and unquantifiable benefits, monetary rewards can form the principal motivator for employees. A number of methods are commonly used by organizations to reward employees financially.

- Basic hourly wages are used to reward large numbers of secondary, or non-core employees. These reflect inputs rather than outputs.
- A fixed salary is more commonly paid to the core workers of an organization. Sometimes the fixed salary is related to length of service – for example, many public-sector service workers in the UK receive automatic annual increments not related to performance. As well as being administratively simple, a fixed salary avoids the problems of trying to assess individuals' eligibility for bonuses, which can be especially difficult where employees work in teams. A fixed salary can be useful to a firm where long-term development of relationships with customers is important and staff are evaluated qualitatively for their ability in this respect rather than quantitatively on the basis of short-term sales achievements. Many financial services companies have adopted fixed salaries to avoid possible unethical conduct by employees who may be tempted to sell commission-based services to customers whose needs have not been properly assessed.
- A fixed annual salary plus a variable commission is commonly paid to service personnel who are actively involved in selling, as a direct reward for their efforts.
- Performance-related pay (PRP) is assuming increasing importance within organizations. PRP systems seek to link some percentage of an employee's pay directly to their work performance. In some ways PRP represents a movement towards the individualization of pay. A key element in any PRP system is the appraisal of individual employees' performance. For some workers, outputs can be quantified relatively easily, for example the level of new accounts opened forms part of most bank managers' performance-related pay. More qualitative aspects of job performance are much more difficult to appraise, for example the quality of advice given by doctors or dentists. Qualitative assessment raises problems about which dimensions of job performance are to be considered important in the exercise and who is to undertake the appraisal. If appraisal is not handled sensitively, it could be viewed by employees with suspicion as a means of rewarding some individuals according to a hidden agenda. However, some form of performance-related pay is generally of great use to organizations. It can allow greater management control and enable management to quickly identify good or bad performers. If handled appropriately, it can also assist in the generation of consent and moral involvement, because employees will have a direct interest in their own performance.
- Profit-sharing schemes can operate as a supplement to the basic wage or salary and can assist in the generation of employee loyalty through greater commitment. Employees can be made members of a trust fund set up by their employer where a percentage of profits are held in trust on behalf of employees, subject to agreed eligibility criteria. Profit-sharing schemes have the advantage of encouraging staff involvement in their organization. Such schemes do, however, have a major disadvantage where despite employees' most committed efforts, profits fall due to some external factor such as an economic recession. There is also debate about whether profit sharing really does act as a motivator to better performance in large companies, or merely becomes part of basic pay expectations. In the UK, examples of profit-sharing schemes have been set up by Tesco, British Gas and Sainsbury's.
- In many service organizations, an important element of the financial reward is derived from outside the formal contract of employment. This in particular refers to the practice of

tipping by customers in return for good service. The acknowledgement of tipping by employers puts greater pressure on front-line service staff to perform well and in principle puts the burden of appraisal directly on the consumer of a service. It also reduces the level of basic wage expected by employees. While customers from some countries – such as the United States – readily accept the principle of tipping, others – including the British – are more ambivalent. In the public sector, attempts at tipping are often viewed as a form of bribery.

Figure 8.7 Labour-intensive service industries have long realized that recruiting, training and motivating the right staff is an important basis for delivering value to customers. In conditions of full employment, companies must sell themselves as a good employer so that they can recruit the people who will ultimately deliver marketers' promises to customers. *The Sunday Times* conducts an annual survey of Britain's best companies to work for, and the shoe repair and key-cutting chain Timpson has scored highly for a number of years. Employee benefits include at least 16 weeks' maternity leave on full pay (compared to statutory minimum of six weeks at 90 per cent pay) and/or at least four weeks' leave above the statutory minimum of four weeks. One sign of the company's success is a low level of staff turnover – at least 40 per cent of its staff have worked at the company for more than five years. Managers are given considerable discretion in how they run their branch, for example the prices that they charge. Customers have come to trust the chain and have rewarded it with sustainable long-term profits. (Reproduced with permission of Timpson)

THINKING AROUND THE SUBJECT:
TRYING TO MEASURE THE LINK BETWEEN EMPLOYEE PERFORMANCE AND
CUSTOMER SATISFACTION

Trying to understand the process of value creation within an organization can be very difficult, involving many linkages between different elements of an internal value chain. Just how much is each individual employee, or groups of employees, worth to a company? Bruhn, Kudernatsch and Tuzovic (2004) reported the case of German bank Direkt Anlage Bank AG (DAB) which used the 'balanced scorecard' (BSC) approach to try to make such estimates. DAB used the BSC to record information down to the lowest level of the command structure, that is, every employee had a personal BSC derived from divisional BSCs, which are in turn derived from the corporate BSC. In 1999 the management of DAB developed a 'theory of business', portrayed as a diagram of supposed cause-and-effect linkages among key performance indicators, including qualitative and quantitative indicators.

To test the theory, DAB developed a monitoring system to collect the necessary data. Since January 2000 DAB had measured all the BSC indicators on a monthly basis. These indicators comprised the four perspectives of the BSC:

1 human resources (global employee satisfaction, recommendation rate of DAB as employer, employee turnover, employee fluctuation, job performance such as number of failures and absence)

2 customers (global customer satisfaction, satisfaction with dimensions and items, intention to remain loyal, recommendation rate of DAB, market share, number of new customers, name recognition rate)

3 processes (cycle time, capacity, number of failures, service level, productivity), and

4 finance (profitability, revenue, cost, shareholder value).

DAB used longitudinal data to develop and estimate a structural equation model of its 'theory of business', enabling the estimation of the direction and strength of the relationships. The model allowed DAB to simulate the effects of changes across linkages, for example how an increase in employee satisfaction would lead to better processes, how this might influence customer satisfaction and, ultimately, the effect on profitability. The development of such a model might seem a remarkable achievement, given the complexity of large organizations. Can quantitative models of employees' contribution to a business ever really hope to capture the more qualitative contributions that can make all the difference in the eyes of customers?

8.9 CONTROLLING AND EMPOWERING STAFF

It follows from the previous discussion of management theories that there are two basic approaches to managing people. On the one hand, staff can be supervised closely and corrective action taken where they fail to perform to standard. On the other hand, staff can be made responsible for controlling their own actions. The latter is often referred to as 'empowering' employees. The problem of control is particularly great in people-intensive service industries where it is usually not possible to remove the results of poor personnel performance before their effects are felt by customers. While the effects of a poorly performing car worker can be concealed from customers by checking his or her tangible output, the inseparability of the service production/consumption process makes quality control in the services sector difficult to achieve.

Should an organization's employees be closely controlled, or should they be empowered to act in the best way they see fit? The degree of empowerment given to employees, or the control exercised over them, depends on the nature of their operating environment. For highly standardized, homogeneous goods and services, employees can be controlled by mechanistic means such as rules and regulations. For high-contact, highly variable services, high levels of empowerment may be more appropriate.

Empowerment essentially involves giving employees discretion over the way they carry out their tasks. One of the underlying assumptions of those advocating empowerment is that employees' values will be in line with those of the organization. Berry (1995, p. 208) noted that empowerment is essentially a state of mind. An employee with an empowered state of mind should experience feelings of: (1) control over how their job is performed; (2) awareness of the context in which the job is performed; (3) accountability for their work output; (4) shared responsibility for unit and organizational performance; and (5) equity in the rewards based on individual and collective performance. Discussion of empowerment frequently stresses the need to share information, so that employees understand the context in which they work. Empowered employees need to be rewarded in a timely fashion and their initiatives, triumphs and achievements acknowledged. Empowerment also implies a culture which encourages employees to experiment with new ideas and can tolerate them making mistakes and learning from them. Such a culture would be more in line with the image of the 'learning organization'. Organizations must be prepared to allow employees the freedom to act and to make decisions based on their own judgement. If an employee is empowered, then that employee must be able to decide how best to deal with the needs of customers and should be accountable and responsible to deal with problems of customer complaints and operational difficulties caused.

Attitudinal changes in employees resulting from empowerment include increased job satisfaction and reduced role stress. A consequence of increased job satisfaction is greater enthusiasm for their job, which can be reflected in increased levels of involvement. Behaviourally, empowerment can lead to quicker response by employees to the needs of customers, as less time is wasted in referring customers' requests to line managers. In situations where customer needs are highly variable, or the nature of demand is highly volatile, empowerment can facilitate rapid response to environmental change.

Advocates of tighter control mechanisms point to the disadvantages of empowerment. One of the consequences of empowerment is that it increases the scope of employees' jobs, requiring employees to be properly trained to cope with the wider range of tasks which they are expected to undertake. It also impacts on recruitment as it is necessary to ensure that employees recruited have the requisite attitudinal characteristics and skills to cope with empowerment. Hartline and Ferrell (1996) found that while empowered employees gained confidence in their abilities, they also experienced increased frustration and ambiguity through role conflict. Additionally, because empowered workers are expected to have a broader range of skills and to perform a greater number of tasks, they are likely to be more expensive to employ because of their ability to command higher rates of pay.

So in what situations should a service provider decide to empower its employees, rather than to tightly control them? A number of authors have suggested a contingency approach to empowerment. Ahmed and Rafiq (2003) have built on the work of Bowen and Lawler (1992) to develop a model of five factors which influence whether a control or empowerment approach is most appropriate, namely: business strategy, tie to the customer, technology, business environment, and types of employee.

1 **Business strategy:** Firms undertaking a differentiation business strategy, or a strategy that involves high degrees of customization and personalization of services, should empower their employees. However, firms pursuing a low-cost high-volume strategy should use a production line approach to controlling employees.

2 **Tie to the customer:** Where service delivery involves managing long-term relationships with customers rather than just performing a simple one-off transaction, empowerment is vital. Employees should be able to identify and respond flexibly to customers' changing needs over time, something which may be inhibited by a tightly scripted control approach.

3 **Technology:** If the technology involved in service delivery simplifies and industrializes the tasks of employees, a production line approach is more appropriate than empowerment. However, where the technology is non-routine or complex, empowerment is more appropriate.

4 **Business environment:** Some environments are more variable than others, for example the operating environment of an airline is more variable than that of a fast-food restaurant. A company may make its environment more complex, for example an airline may offer to cater for special meal and accessibility requirements, or such complexity may be forced on it by generally held expectations within the market. A production line approach is more appropriate where customer requirements are simpler and more predictable.

5 **Types of employee:** Bowen and Lawler (1992) recognized that empowerment and control approaches require different types of employee. Employees most likely to be effectively empowered are those who have high growth needs and who need to have their abilities tested at work. Where empowerment requires teamwork, employees should have strong social and affiliative needs and good interpersonal and group skills. Empowerment requires 'Theory Y' type managers who allow employees to work independently to the benefit of the organization and its customers. The control approach requires 'Theory X' type managers who believe in close supervision of employees (McGregor 1960).

Even with highly empowered employees, some form of control system is necessary. Control systems are closely related to reward systems in that pay can be used to control performance – e.g. bonuses forfeited in the event of performance falling below a specified standard. In addition, warnings or ultimately dismissal form part of a control system. In an ideal organization which has well-developed strategies to increase employees' involvement, this by itself should lead to considerable self-control or informal control from their peer group. Where such policies are less well developed, three principal types of control are used – simple, technical and bureaucratic controls.

■ Simple controls are typified by direct personal supervision of personnel – for example, a head waiter can maintain a constant watch over junior waiters and directly influence performance when this deviates from standard.

■ Technical controls can be built into the service production process in order to monitor individuals' performance – for example, a supermarket checkout can measure the speed of individual operators and control action (e.g. training or redeployment) taken in respect of those shown to be falling below standard.

■ Bureaucratic controls require employees to document their performance, for example the completion of worksheets by a service engineer of visits made and jobs completed. Control action can be initiated in respect of employees who on paper appear to be underperforming.

In addition to these internal controls, the relationship which many front-line service personnel develop with their customers allows customers to exercise a degree of informal control. College lecturers teaching a class would in most cases wish to avoid the hostility from their class which might result from consistently delivering a poor standard of performance – in other words, the class can exercise a type of informal control.

8.10 INTERNAL MARKETING

Many organizations have sought to improve their internal effectiveness through a programme of internal marketing. Internal marketing came to prominence from the 1980s and describes the application of marketing techniques to audiences within the organization. An early definition of internal marketing provided by Berry (1980) was:

> . . . the means of applying the philosophy and practices of marketing to people who serve the external customers so that (i) the best possible people can be employed and retained and (ii) they will do the best possible work.

The term internal marketing is relatively new and best practice reflects much of what has been part of an organization's human resource management (HRM) strategy. In an attempt to clarify the concept of internal marketing Varey and Lewis (1999) have conceptualized a number of its important dimensions.

■ **Internal marketing as a metaphor:** Organization jobs and employment conditions are 'products' to be marketed and managers should think like a marketer when dealing with people. However, it is the employer that is both buyer and consumer in the employment relationship, rather than the employee.

■ **Internal marketing as a philosophy:** Managers may hold a conviction that human resource management requires 'marketing-like' activities. However, this does not address employees' divergent needs and interests which may themselves be quite different from those of the organization. This is especially the case if the 'marketing' activities are actually promotional advertising and selling of management requirements. Employees may merely be seen as the manipulable subject of managerial programmes.

■ **Internal marketing as a set of techniques:** Human resource management may adopt market research, segmentation and promotional techniques in order to inform and persuade employees. But internal marketing as the manipulation of the '4Ps' imposes management's point of view on employees and cannot be said to be employee (customer) centred. Therefore, it is employees that must change their needs or must understand the position of the employer as they respond to the market.

TGI Friday's restaurants have become a familiar sight throughout the world, with 735 outlets in 55 countries in 2005. The themed restaurant chain offers 'mass customization' by which it provides a basically standard service to all customers, but the customer can personalize their meal through an extensive range of menu permutations.

Employees are seen as the key to delivering high-quality service to customers. This applies not only to front-line staff who visibly contribute to customers' experience, but also backroom staff. The company's approach to managing employees combines elements of control with empowerment. The control element is facilitated by service target times which, for example, require that starters should be served within seven minutes of receipt of a customer's order. A computer programme helps managers to monitor the achievement of service times. These elements of the service encounter tend to be specified by head office, and branch managers are expected to achieve specified standards.

However, it is the manner in which TGI Friday's empowers its employees that distinguishes the chain from its competitors. Crucial to this is the empowering of employees to take whatever actions they see fit in order to improve customers' experience. Employee performance requires, therefore, more than the traditional acts of greeting, seating and serving customers. Employees have to be able to provide both the behaviours, and the emotional displays, to match with customers' feelings. Getting serving staff to join in a chorus of 'Happy Birthday' may not be easy to script, but spontaneous singing when a meal is served to a group of diners celebrating a birthday can make all the difference to customers' experience of their meal.

Recruitment of the right kind of people becomes crucial and prospective candidates are selected as much for their sense of fun as on the strength of their CV. Initial interviews take the form of 'auditions' in which potential recruits are set individual and group tasks to test their personality type. Opportunities are given for trained staff to express their personality and individuality, for example by wearing outlandish clothes that make a statement about their personality.

TGI Friday's has become a preferred place of employment for restaurant staff, who have enjoyed relatively good working conditions, above-average earnings for the sector – especially when tips are taken into account – and a sense of fun at work. The chain has won numerous awards as a good employer, including the UK's 15th best workplace according to the *Financial Times* 2004 Survey of Best UK Places to Work, and the only restaurant chain to be included on the list for a second year running. It was also the fourth most fun place to work according to the *FT*.

It may be fine for serving staff to sing to customers when times are quiet, but how can they do this and still meet their service delivery time targets when the restaurant is busy? A number of customers commenting at www.ciao.co.uk observed that service standards could decline when a restaurant becomes very busy. They also commented on very high prices charged by TGI Friday's, with more than one person describing them as 'rip-off prices'. But in order to get the best staff who can create a memorable experience, is it worth paying staff a little more and passing this on to customers as higher prices? Would this approach to staff work in a restaurant format where competition is based on price?

■ **Internal marketing as an approach:** There is an explicit symbolic dimension to human resource management practices, such as employee involvement and participation, and statements about the role of employees within the organization. These are used to bring about indirect control of employees. Nevertheless, the symbolism of internal marketing may reveal many contradictions. For example, individualism contradicts team working, and the service culture as defined by management may contradict attitudes towards employee flexibility and responsibility. The complexities of managing people and their actions and knowledge may be reduced to mere 'techniques' of symbolic communication.

Much debate surrounds just how internal marketing fits within traditional human resource management structures and processes. Hales (1994), for example, is critical of the 'managerialist' perspective on internal marketing and of the literature on internal marketing as an approach to human resource management. Viewed as an activity in isolation, internal marketing is unlikely to succeed. For that to happen, the full support of top management is required.

8.11 INDUSTRIAL RELATIONS

As we saw in Chapter 6, commercial organizations range from small family businesses to large multinational organizations and public-sector bodies, covering external environments which range from protected and regulated to highly competitive. In reflection of this diversity, there is great variety in the manner in which managements negotiate employment conditions with their workforces. For organizations employing large numbers of staff, much of the employment relationship has traditionally been conducted collectively between the employer and trades unions representing groups of employees.

The essential features of collective bargaining are threefold.

■ First, a collective bargaining system recognizes trades unions with whom management negotiates on substantive issues such as pay and procedural issues, e.g. discipline and redundancy. Collective bargaining formally recognizes the presence within the organization of an outside body – the trades union.

■ Second, the pluralist approach to the employment relationship emphasizes a divergence of interests between the employer and employees. This divergence is considered best settled via a process of compromise and negotiation.

■ Third, a recognition that industrial action of some type, for example overtime bans, 'go slows' and strikes, might be used in order to pursue employee interests. This third feature of collective bargaining is overexaggerated by the media, some academics and politicians. As an element in collective bargaining, it becomes a consideration only if the first two elements have failed. Nevertheless, many service sectors such as railways and airlines have periodically suffered bad disruption as a result of failures in collective bargaining. Because services cannot be stored, the effects can be felt by customers immediately.

Efforts to stress a closer identification with business objectives through increasing individuals' level of involvement at work do not sit easily with the presence of an outside body which stresses the significance of collective action. Organizations which do not feel secure with trades unions are likely to attempt to marginalize their impact through their de-recognition and the creation of organization-specific employee relations policies described below. Many organizations have moved on from the traditional view of industrial relations to the situation where they speak of 'employee relations'. Marchington and Parker (1990) identified three reasons for the use of the term 'employee relations'.

1 The term has become fashionable and appears to be less adversarial than industrial relations. Thus, there has been growth in the use of the term, although slippage in the use of the word occurs in some cases without any change in behaviour.

2 It is increasingly used by personnel managers to describe the part of their work which is concerned with the regulation of relations between employer and employees. The internal regulation of this relationship is seen in many organizations to supersede any external regulation, through collective bargaining and/or trades union membership. This can be the case even though trades union membership still exists in a particular organization.

3 Employee relations focuses on that aspect of managerial activity which is concerned with fostering an identification with the employing organization and its business aims. It therefore concerns itself with direct relations between employees and management – that is, independently of any collective representation by trades unions.

Refer back to Chapter 5 for more discussion on legislation governing employment.

8.12 REDUCING DEPENDENCE ON HUMAN RESOURCES

Employees are an expensive and difficult resource to manage and, furthermore, within the services sector, variability and poor quality of front-line employees' contribution can harm the sales and image of a company. Services organizations have therefore led the way in pursuit of strategies to reduce the human element of their production process. The aim of employee replacement schemes can be to reduce variability, to reduce costs, or both. Cost cutting could be important where an organization is pursuing a cost leadership strategy, allowing it to gain a competitive advantage.

A number of strategies to reduce dependency on the organization's employees can be identified.

■ At one extreme, the human element in a service production and delivery process can be completely replaced by automatic machinery. Examples include bank ATM machines, vending machines and automatic car washes. Constraints on employee replacement come from the limitations of technology (for example, completely automatic car washes can seldom achieve such high standards of cleanliness as those where an operator is present to perform some operations inaccessible to machinery); the cost of replacement equipment (it is only within the past few years that the cost of servers and access to the Internet has fallen to a point where retailers can move from labour-intensive telephone sales to automated online sales); and the attitudes of consumers towards automated service delivery (many segments of the population are still reluctant to use Internet banking services, preferring the reassurance provided by human contact).

■ Equipment can be used alongside employees to assist them in their task. This often has the effect of de-skilling their task by reducing the scope they have for exercising discretion, thereby reducing the variability in quality perceived by customers. In this way computerized accounting systems in hotels reduce the risk of front of house staff adding up a client's bill incorrectly. Similarly, the computer systems used by many airline reservation staff include prompts which guide their interaction with clients.

■ Companies often introduce self-service production by customers, which not only reduces the need to employ as many staff, but cost savings can be passed on to customers as low prices. In this way, most petrol service stations expect customers to fill their own cars with fuel, rather than have this task undertaken by the station's own staff. Many supermarket chains have experimented with customer-operated scanners which reduce the need to employ checkout staff.

THINKING AROUND THE SUBJECT: LONG-DISTANCE BUS DRIVERS?

In times of economic prosperity, it can be very difficult for some types of business to meet customers' needs because of difficulties in recruiting staff. The British Chamber of Commerce's spring 2005 quarterly survey showed that the proportion of companies having difficulty finding skilled employees had doubled during the past decade. In 1994, 21 per cent of companies complained that they were being affected by a skilled labour shortage, but by the end of 2004 this had risen to 43 per cent. The problem of labour shortage is particularly acute in affluent parts of the country where living costs are high. Bus operators have found it very difficult to recruit drivers during periods of prosperity, when plenty of equally paid jobs are available, but which do not involve unsocial working hours, a characteristic of many driving jobs. Unlike the manufacturing sector, which can often solve a labour shortage by outsourcing production to overseas countries such as India or China, service-based industries involving direct customer–employee contact must employ staff where their customers need them – in their home country. Many bus companies have therefore attempted to bring staff to the job, rather than take the job to low-cost countries overseas. British bus companies have for some time recruited drivers from Commonwealth countries such as Barbados and India. However, the expansion of the EU to include countries of Eastern Europe, where wages are low and unemployment levels high, has offered new opportunities for British bus operators. Some, such as Stagecoach, have recruited drivers from Poland to drive buses in towns such as Oxford and London, where staff shortages had become acute. In Britain, debate has continued about how much immigration should be allowed, with the voice of traditionalists keen to preserve the nature of Britain pitched against companies such as Stagecoach that seek to enlarge the pool of labour from which they can recruit drivers.

Although many labour-intensive service industries have relied on immigrant sources of labour, could there be a danger of cheap labour sources undermining attempts to develop technology-based solutions? Also, for the host economy as a whole, could an increased number of immigrant workers then create even more demand as immigrant workers themselves become consumers of labour-starved industries? And would their home countries – usually poorer developing countries – suffer as a result of losing skilled workers?

A 24/7 SOCIETY MAY BE GOOD FOR CUSTOMERS, BUT CAN EMPLOYEES COPE WITH THE STRESS?

What happens when a company's customers want access to its goods and services 24 hours a day, and they want immediate access, not a promise of delivery tomorrow or some time in the future? The sad fact is that one consequence is often stress at work for those that are charged with responding to a company's promises which it must make if it is to stay alive in a competitive business environment.

The 24/7 culture has had a big impact on employees' lifestyles, with many individuals having to adjust to varying and often unsocial shift patterns. Employees often have to accept that Saturdays and Sundays are part of their normal working week, and this trend looks set to continue. Research undertaken by the Future Foundation (2004) predicts that by 2020, over 13 million people in the UK will be operating in an out-of-hours economy (outside the traditional Monday–Friday hours of 9 a.m.–6 p.m.), compared to the 7 million who did so in 2003.

While flexibility serves the interests of those who can afford to exploit the 24/7 society, the supporting workforce may see little reward for the unsociable hours they put in. Managers and supervisors, under pressure to meet targets and boost sales, are also hard-hit, often working extended hours as unpaid overtime.

It is not just the highly visible retail sector where staff are expected to be flexible – many backroom jobs in other sectors have become more stressful. The entertainment sector, for example, increasingly employs casual contract workers to meet its needs. The BBC has struggled to compete against satellite and cable television services, all intent on meeting viewers' demand for entertainment 24/7. It now employs a large number of free-lancers who give it greater flexibility at lower cost.

Evidence is mounting of increasing levels of stress at work. The Future Foundation research indicated that 58 per cent of respondents believed the 24/7 culture is destructive to family life. Another study, by the Industrial Society, showed that juggling home and work demands was a major source of stress for 70 per cent of respondents, while half cited unrealistic deadlines and constant time pressures as an additional factor (Industrial Society 2001). And according to a survey carried out for the Institute of Stress Management's National Stress Awareness Day in 2004:

- 53 per cent of people had suffered from work-related stress in the past 12 months
- 52 per cent of those under stress felt it was damaging their health
- 72 per cent of those who are stressed blamed too much work
- 20 per cent had sought medical or other professional help.

Employers are increasingly having to recognize the sometimes hidden costs to their business of having high levels of stress in their workforce. Moreover, the law is now requiring them to take some responsibility for employees' stress at work.

In the UK, the Management of Health and Safety at Work Regulations 1999 (specifically Regulations 3, 4, 13 and 19) explicitly state that employers must assess the risk of their employees developing stress-related illness because of work.

Section 2 of the Health and Safety at Work Act 1974 requires all employers with five or more employees to have a written policy on health and safety of employees at work, and a stress management policy should be a part of this. A policy should prevent stress by identifying the causes, control stress so that it does not have a negative effect and rehabilitate employees who are having a problem

Although stress is all around us today, some would argue that the harmful consequences of the 24/7 society have been exaggerated. People may remember the stress of having to get to their bank before it closed at 3.30 in 'the afternoon – good for the banks' employees, but possibly stressful for its customers; or the rush to stock up with food from supermarkets just before a bank holiday, in the knowledge that they would be closed for a number of days over the holiday period.

One advantage of the 24/7 society is that there isn't as much pressure to have to buy something from the shops before they close. Another benefit is that it can offer the opportunity for people to choose the times they want to work, a great benefit for families with young children. And Sunday, previously held out as a day of rest for the family to spend together, is now a shared leisure day in which shopping as a family unit has replaced the previously solo shopping trips in which housewives took on the biggest burden.

Businesses, employees and consumers are all perpetuating the move towards a 24/7 economy, and inevitably there are winners and losers. The Future Foundation research found that it was the affluent who benefit most. A third of consumers who participate economically between the hours of 6 p.m. and 9 a.m. were those with a household income of £46,000 or more. Only a fifth of those with an income of £10,430 or less participated. But the flip side of a vibrant night-time economy is an army of low-paid staff, many working for little above minimum wage, often trying to juggle multiple part-time jobs with study or looking after children.

Who benefits from the 24/7 economy? To some critics, it is in the interests of neither the economically disadvantaged, who pick up the jobs that nobody else wants to do, nor the employed, who have little to do other than work harder to spend more money achieving their desired lifestyle. Or are we romanticizing the 'good old days' when Sunday was Sunday and everybody lived a happier, less stressful life?

QUESTIONS

1 Briefly summarize the causes and consequences of work-related stress in modern Western societies.
2 Critically assess the harm done to employees and businesses by stress as a result of the moved towards a 24/7 society. Should employers and employees accept that a certain level of stress may be good?
3 Identify measures that employers can take to reduce the costs they may incur as a result of stress at work.

SUMMARY

An organization's internal environment comprises its structures and processes, which are influenced by the dominant culture of the organization. Internal and external environments are inextricably linked, because the effectiveness of an organization's structures and processes can help or hinder the task of responding to environmental change. Where employees share the vision of management, they may be more likely to embrace external change, rather than fear it and become reactive rather than proactive. As we saw in the previous chapter, strong **leadership** can provide a focused effort at marshalling the resources of an organization to meet the challenges and opportunities posed by the external environment. Employees usually make up a critical element of the internal environment and this chapter has discussed methods by which organizations seek to gain the moral involvement of employees to share the challenges and opportunities of external change.

This chapter has only briefly mentioned the growing volume of legislation that affects employment. The legislation is discussed at greater length in **Chapter 5**. Noticeable differences in the internal environment are often present in different types of organization (**Chapter 6**), with the culture of a typical sole trader being very different to that of a public limited company or a charity organization. Differences are likely to occur where a company operates in overseas countries **Chapter 12**). Growth (**Chapter 7)** has often formed a central cultural value. Its opposite – contraction – can be difficult to manage. The treatment of employees is often considered to be an important element of an organization's social responsibility (**Chapter 9**). The political and legal environments have had major impacts on the nature of the internal environment, for example with respect to employees' rights (**Chapters 2** and **5**). The development of new technologies (**Chapter 4**) has changed the nature of many jobs and improved internal communications.

Key Terms

Control	(305)	Incentives	(296)	Staff development	(300)
Employee involvement	(291)	Industrial relations	(311)	Training	(300)
Empowerment	(306)	Internal marketing	(308)		
Flexible workforce	(294)	Leadership	(315)		
Functional organization	(281)	Matrix organization			
Human resource		structures	(288)		
management (HRM)	(308)	Motivation	(295)		

CHAPTER REVIEW QUESTIONS

1 Discuss the ways in which improvements in the internal environment of organizations can lead to more effective responsiveness to changes in the external environment.

2 Do you agree with the notion that a marketing department can actually be a barrier to the successful development of a marketing orientation? Give examples.

3 'Mission statements are the result of senior managers undertaking management development courses. They may have the language, but mission statements are invariably ignored by the very people who they are aimed at.' Is this a fair statement?

4 Every now and again management gurus develop new ideas for managing organizations, such as business process re-engineering. Is there too much hype in such prescriptions?

5 Discuss the ways in which a fast-food restaurant can increase the level of participation among its staff.

6 What are the main differences in implementing a market-orientated management structure within the public as opposed to the private service sector?

ACTIVITY

Consult the jobs section of your local newspaper and examine jobs advertised by local private- and public-sector services organizations. To what extent is the organization's communication through its job advertisements consistent with its communication to customers? Does the business environment of an organization influence the way it seeks new staff, for example is there a difference between private-sector, public-sector and not-for-profit sector organizations?

Useful Websites

General HRM Links

Nottingham Trent University's page provides useful links to various HRM websites.

http://www.nbs.ntu.ac.uk/depts/hrm/hrm_link.htm

Chartered Institute of Personnel and Development

Website of the UK association which represents human resource management professionals.

http://www.ipd.co.uk/

Institute of Directors

Website of the organization representing leaders of UK industry, which aims to improve the quality of leadership through the Institute's professional development programme.

http://www.iod.co.uk/

International Labour Organization (ILO)

This website provides information on employment statistics and practices throughout the world.

http://www.ilo.org

The Future of Work

Series of working papers provided by the University of Leeds that touch on the impact of the Internet on patterns of work.

http://www.leeds.ac.uk/esrcfutureofwork/output/papers.html

Further Reading

This chapter has discussed very briefly some of the basic principles of human resource management as they apply to service organizations. For a fuller discussion of these principles, the following texts are recommended:

Beardwell, I. and Holden, L. (2003) *Human Resource Management: A Contemporary Approach*, London, FT Prentice Hall.

Bratton, J. and Gold, J. (2003) *Human Resource Management: Theory and Practice*, Palgrave Macmillan.

The issue of organizational culture is well covered in the following:

Hofstede, G. (1991) *Culture and Organizations*, London, McGraw-Hill.

Stapley, L.F. (1996) *The Personality of the Organization: A Psycho-dynamic Explanation of Culture*, London, Free Association Books.

The following provide insights into the importance of leadership styles within organizations:

Landsberg, M. (2000) *The Tools of Leadership*, HarperCollins.

Prabhu, V. and Robson, A. (2000) 'Achieving service excellence: measuring the impact of leadership and senior management commitment', *Managing Service Quality*, Vol. 10, No. 5, pp. 307–17.

Internal marketing often goes under a number of names, and the following are useful introductions to the topic:

Ahmed, P. and Rafiq, M. (2003) 'Internal marketing issues and challenges', *European Journal of Marketing*, Vol. 37, No. 9, pp. 1177–86.

Naudé, P., Desai, J. and Murphy, J. (2003) 'Identifying the determinants of internal marketing orientation', *European Journal of Marketing*, Vol. 37, No. 9, pp. 1205–20.

Varey, R.J. and Lewis, B.R. (1999) 'A broadened conception of internal marketing', *European Journal of Marketing*, Vol. 33, No. 9/10, pp. 926–44.

The debate on control mechanisms and empowerment is covered in the following articles:

Melhem, Y. (2003) 'The antecedents of customer-contact employees' empowerment', *Employee Relations*, Vol. 26, No. 1, pp. 72–93.

Lashley, C. (2000) 'Empowerment through involvement: a case study of TGI Friday's restaurants', *Personnel Review*, Vol. 29, No. 6, pp. 791–815.

References

Ahmed, P. and Rafiq, M. (2003) 'Internal marketing issues and challenges', *European Journal of Marketing*, Vol. 37, No. 9, pp. 1177–86.

Arnett, D.B., Laverie, D.A. and McLane, C. (2002) 'Using job satisfaction and pride as internal marketing tools', *Cornell Hotel and Restaurant Administration Quarterly*, Vol. 43, No. 2, pp. 87–96.

Atkinson, J. (1984) 'Manpower strategies for flexible organizations', *Personnel Management*, August.

Bateson, J.E.G. (1989) *Managing Services Marketing – Text and Readings*, 2nd edn, Forth Worth, USA, Dryden Press.

Berry, L.L. (1980) 'Services marketing is different', *Business*, May–June, Vol. 30, No. 3, pp. 24–9.

Berry, L.L. (1995) 'Relationship marketing of services – growing interest, emerging perspectives', *Journal of the Academy of Marketing Science*, Vol. 23, No. 4, pp. 236–45.

Bowen, D.E. and Lawler, E.E. III (1992) 'The empowerment of service workers: what, why, when, and how', *Sloan Management Review*, Spring, pp. 31–9.

Bruhn, M., Kudernatsch, D. and Tuzovic, S. (2004) *Integrating the Balanced Scorecard Approach with the Concept of Customer-oriented Compensation Systems – The Need for Causality*, Proceedings of the 6th Australasian Services Marketing Workshop, Dunedin, University of Otago.

Denton, D.K. (1990) 'Customer focused management', *HR Magazine*, August, Lexington, MA, pp. 62–7.

Dolan, P. and Brierley, I. (1992) *A Tale of Two Bus Companies*, London, Partnership Research.

Drucker, P.F. (1973) *Management: Tasks, Responsibilities and Practices*, New York, Harper & Row.

Future Foundation (2004) *Life in the 24/7? The Shape of Things to Come*, London, Future Foundation.

Grönroos, C. (1982) *Strategic Management and Marketing in the Service Sector*, Helsingfors, Finland, Swedish School of Economics and Business Administration.

Gummesson, E. (2001) *Total Relationship Marketing*, London, Butterworth Heinemann.

Hales, C. (1994) 'Internal marketing as an approach to human resource management: a new perspective or a metaphor too far?' *Human Resource Management Journal*, Vol. 5, No. 1, pp. 50–71.

Handy, Charles B. (1989) *The Age of Unreason*, Boston, MA, Harvard Business School Press.

Hartline, M.D. and Ferrell, O.C. (1996) 'The management of customer contact service employees: an empirical investigation', *Journal of Marketing*, Vol. 60, October, pp. 52–70.

Herzberg, F. (1966) *Work and the Nature of Man*, Cleveland, World Publishing Co.

Industrial Society (2001) *Managing Best Practice No. 83: Occupational Stress*.

Jelinek, M., Smirich, L. and Hirsch, P. (1983) 'Introduction: a code of many colours', *Administrative Science Quarterly*, 28, p. 337.

Levitt, T. (1960) 'Marketing myopia', *Harvard Business Review*, July–August, pp. 45–56.

Lukas, B.A. and Maignan, I. (1996) 'Striving for quality: the key role of internal and external customers', *Journal of Market Focused Management*, Vol. 1, pp. 175–97.

Marchington, M. and Parker, P. (1990) *Changing Patterns of Employee Relations*, London, Harvester.

Maslow, A. (1943) 'A theory of human motivation', *Psychological Review*, Vol. 50, No. 4, pp. 370–96.

Mayo, E. (1933) *The Human Problems of Industrial Civilization*, New York, Macmillan.

McGregor, D. (1960) *The Human Side of Enterprise*, New York, McGraw-Hill.

Milkovich, G.T. and Newman, J.M. (2002) *Compensation*, 7th edn, New York, McGraw-Hill.

Taylor, F.W. (1985) *Principles of Scientific Management*, Easton, Hive (originally published 1911).

Varey, R.J. and Lewis, B.R. (1999) 'A broadened conception of internal marketing', *European Journal of Marketing*, Vol. 33, No. 9/10, pp. 926–44.

Widmier, S. (2002) 'The effects of incentives and personality on salesperson's customer orientation', *Industrial Marketing Management*, Vol. 31, No. 7, pp. 609–615.

Chapter 9

Corporate Social Responsibility and Ethics

Chapter Objectives

This chapter will explain:

- the stakeholders in organizations, and the interrelationship between stakeholders' interests and corporate interests

- principles of good corporate governance

- ethics and their application to business practice

- the ecological environment as a resource for business and an asset to be protected

9.1 INTRODUCTION

'The customer is king' is a traditional business maxim and, according to this, everything that a company does should be geared towards satisfying the needs of its customers. But should commercial organizations also have responsibilities to the public at large? The question is becoming increasingly important, as commercial organizations have never before been subjected to such critical assessment from those who are quick to identify the harmful side effects of their activities. From a purely internal perspective, there have been many recent cases of large organizations, such as Enron, WorldCom and Parmalat, that failed to govern themselves in a responsible manner, for example by exaggerating the value of their assets in a way that misleads investors and may ultimately leave suppliers with unpaid bills, customers with undelivered goods and services, employees without a job and government without tax revenues due.

In a wider sense, it is often suggested that business organizations should act in a responsible manner, not only to members of their immediate microenvironment, but also to society at large. There are philosophical and pragmatic reasons for this.

Philosophically, models of a responsible society would have companies doing their bit to contribute towards a just and fair society, alongside the contributions of other institutions such as the family and the Church. More pragmatically, commercial organizations need to take account of society's values because if they do not, they may end up isolated from the values of the customers, employees and investors that they seek to attract. In increasingly discriminating markets, buyers may opt for the more socially responsible company. Acting in an anti-social way may have a long-term cost for a company and ultimately not serve the needs of those customers who prefer to deal with a socially acceptable company. Anti-social behaviour by companies may also attract the attention of regulatory bodies which often have the power to add to a company's production costs, or to make it impossible to satisfy customer demand in the first place.

This chapter begins by identifying the key stakeholders in organizations, to whom, it is increasingly argued, organizations should have a responsibility. It then explores the complex ethical and practical issues behind the concept of corporate responsibility.

9.2 THE STAKEHOLDERS OF ORGANIZATIONS

It is common to describe stakeholders as those organizations and individuals that may not necessarily have any direct dealings with a company, but that are nevertheless affected by its actions. There is an argument that an organization has responsibility to these stakeholders which goes beyond the basic legal relationship that it has with customers, suppliers and employees etc. In turn, a company can be significantly affected by the actions of its stakeholders.

The following section identifies the principal stakeholders in business organizations. Some of these are primary, with direct impacts of the organization on the stakeholder, and vice versa. Others can be considered secondary in that their impacts are more indirect. Very often, stakeholders have different agendas and may disagree over what constitutes good behaviour by an organization. As stakeholders in local industry, local community groups may have quite different reactions to the prospect of a company planning to create a new distribution centre in their area. Some may welcome the increase in job opportunities which the new facility presents, while others may be against the proposal because of the additional traffic congestion that it will be likely to generate. Although Figure 9.1 presents a simple model of stakeholders, we

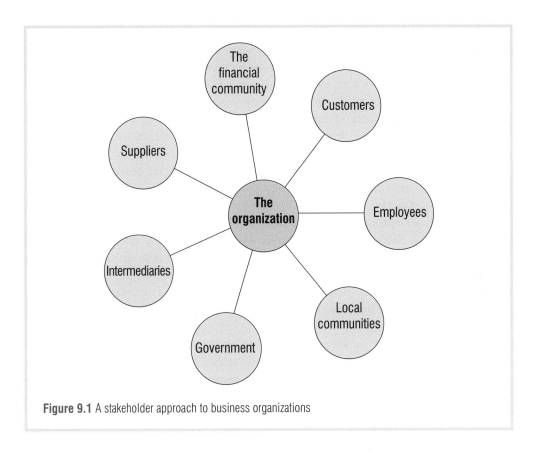

Figure 9.1 A stakeholder approach to business organizations

should always bear in mind that some stakeholders are more important than others, and this importance is likely to vary from one situation to another. Moreover, each group is not homogeneous and may present a variety of views about how an organization should behave.

9.2.1 Customers

There is an argument that the customer is *not* always right in the goods and services they choose to buy from a company. Customers may sometimes not be aware of their true needs or may have these needs manipulated by exploitative companies. Taking a long-term and broad perspective, companies should have a duty to provide goods and services which satisfy these longer-term and broader needs rather than their immediately felt needs. There have been many examples where the long-term interests of customers have been ignored by companies. Increasingly, legislation is saying that the customer is *not* always right and organizations have a duty to consider the long-term interests of customers as stakeholders. This has been very clearly seen in the mis-selling of endowment policies in the UK during the 1980s. Financial services companies, and their salespeople, were often over-eager to sell policies which were not right for the customer, for example many were sold a saving scheme which would not pay out until long after they required the lump sum payment in order to pay off their mortgage. Other elderly customers were sold endowment policies which would only have matured long after the age when statistically there was a high likelihood they would be dead. Customers may not have understood the fine detail of the policies, but salespeople invariably knew how lucrative selling endowment policies was for their bonus commission. In the short term, the financial services companies may have profited from selling such policies, but by the 2000s, the falling value of endowment policies compounded problems for homebuyers, whose endowment policies were no longer sufficient to pay off their mortgage loan. Faced with such mis-selling, regulatory authorities have acted to protect the wider interests of customers. The Financial Services Authority – the regulatory body – has fined companies for mis-selling and required compensation to be paid to customers.

There are many more examples of situations where customers are probably *not* right and their long-term interests have been neglected by companies, including:

- tobacco companies that have failed to impress upon customers the long-term harmful effects of buying and consuming their cigarettes
- manufacturers of milk for babies that should make mothers aware of the claimed significant long-term health benefits to children of using breast milk rather than manufactured milk products
- car manufacturers that add expensive stereo equipment to cars as standard equipment but relegate vital safety equipment to the status of optional extra.

In each of these cases, most people might agree that, objectively, buyers are being persuaded to make a choice against their own long-term self-interest. But on what moral grounds can society say that consumers' choices in these situations are wrong? According to some individuals' sense of priorities, an expensive music system may indeed be considered to offer a higher level of personal benefit than an airbag.

Customers as individual consumers usually fail to evaluate the external costs that they cause other consumers collectively to incur. External costs can be defined as the cost of consuming a product that is not borne directly by the consumer, and can take many forms, such as:

- congestion which one car driver causes to other drivers
- the pollution suffered by residents living near waste tips, caused by the disposal of fast-food packaging
- noise nuisance suffered by people living near a noisy nightclub.

In each case, market mechanisms have failed to make buyers of a good or service pay for the external costs that they have forced on others. Organizations that think strategically would recognize that socially unacceptable levels of external costs might bring pressure for legislation which results in higher costs, or prohibition of an activity completely. For the organization, this will have the effect of raising selling prices to customers or making impossible the provision of goods and services demanded by customers.

9.2.2 Employees

It used to be thought that customers were not concerned about how their goods were made, just so long as the final product lived up to their expectations. This may just have been true for some manufactured goods, but probably never was for services where production processes are highly visible. Today, increasingly large segments of the population take into account the ethics of a firm's employment practices when evaluating alternative products. If all other

THINKING AROUND THE SUBJECT: IRRESPONSIBLE SELLING OF PENSIONS?

The financial services industry throughout the 1980s and 1990s saw a lot of aggressive selling, as companies sought to increase their market share of a rapidly growing financial services market. By 2000, aggressive selling had been toned down as companies increasingly sought to act responsibly. In the 1980s and 1990s, many sales personnel earned a good living in the financial services sector. But can a salesperson be too successful? Have they put sales before responsibility? Many sales personnel have responded to bonus or other incentives offered by their employers to vigorously achieve sales which looked good at the time, but later came back to haunt the company. One of the key characteristics of a good salesperson is their ability to listen and to gain a good understanding of a buyer's needs. But what happens when the customer doesn't really have a very good understanding of their own needs? Furthermore, what happens when you couple this with a salesperson who would rather earn his sales commission as easily as possible than by probing the true needs of the customer? The result has been a series of mis-selling scandals that have tarnished the reputation of a number of business sectors, especially financial services.

The term *caveat emptor* ('let the buyer beware') has been used to excuse the situation where a salesperson sold a customer an item that was not at all suited to their needs. It was assumed to be the buyer's fault for buying wrongly, rather than the seller's fault for selling wrongly. The balance is now tilting in the customer's favour as society's expectations of sellers rise. This has been demonstrated through the mis-selling of a range of financial services during the 1980s and 1990s. Perhaps the most serious occurred where sales personnel employed by the big UK pensions companies persuaded employees to cash in the pension scheme which they had with their employer, and to take out a new scheme with their company. By 2003 the value of personal pensions had fallen sharply following a fall in stock market prices. Why did so many people give up a good employer's pension scheme for a much more dubious personal pension scheme? Many may have been tempted by a one-off payment from the government and the salesperson may have been tempted to sell personal pensions aggressively by a hefty commission payment on the sale. The customer may have thought that they were buying into a good deal, but most buyers were not able to understand the complexities of a pension scheme. In most cases the customer was badly advised and found that the pension that they had bought into was worth much less than the employer's pension that they had given up. The over-enthusiastic selling resulted in the big pensions companies being reprimanded by their industry watchdog and forced to pay millions of pounds in fines and compensation to customers. Worse still, the general public had come to mistrust pension policies in particular and financial services companies in general. At a time when the government was encouraging the public to save more for their retirement, how could the public be expected to heed this advice when they could see evidence of irresponsibility by pensions companies? Could the financial services industry as a whole be trusted to look after an individual's life savings, when it had an apparent record of irresponsibility?

things are equal, a firm that has a reputation for ruthlessly exploiting its employees, or not recognizing the legitimate rights of trades unions may be denigrated in the minds of many buyers. For this reason, some companies, such as Nike and Marks & Spencer, have gone to great lengths to challenge allegations made about the employment practices of their overseas suppliers.

Firms often go way beyond satisfying the basic legal requirements of employees. For some businesses, getting an adequate supply of competent workers is the main constraint on growth and it would be in their interest to promote good employment practices. This is true of many hi-tech industries. In order to encourage staff retention, in particular of women returning to work after having children, companies have offered attractive packages of benefits, such as working hours which fit around school holidays and sponsoring events which promote a caring image.

Can going beyond legal requirements for employees ever be considered altruistic rather than just good business? Quaker companies such as Cadbury's have a historic tradition of paternalism towards their staff. But could such altruism essentially be seen as an investment by an organization, which will have a payback in terms of better motivated staff?

9.2.3 Local communities

Market-led companies often try to be seen as a 'good neighbour' in their local community. Such companies can enhance their image through the use of charitable contributions, sponsorship of local events and being seen to support the local environment. Again, this may be interpreted either as part of a firm's genuine concern for its local community, or as a more cynical and pragmatic attempt to buy favour where its own interests are at stake. If a metal manufacturer installs improved noise reduction equipment, is it doing so in order to genuinely improve the lives of local residents, or merely attempting to forestall prohibition action taken by the local authority?

9.2.4 Government

The demands of government agencies often take precedence over the needs of a company's customers. Government has a number of roles to play as stakeholder in commercial organizations.

- Commercial organizations provide governments with taxation revenue, so a healthy business sector is in the interests of government.
- Government is increasingly expecting business organizations to take over many responsibilities from the public sector, for example with regard to the payment of sickness and maternity benefits to employees.
- It is through business organizations that governments achieve many of their economic and social objectives, for example with respect to regional economic development and skills training.

As a regulator which impacts on many aspects of business activity, companies often go to great lengths in seeking favourable responses from such agencies. In the case of many UK private-sector utility providers, promotional efforts are often aimed more at regulatory bodies than final consumers. In the case of the water industry, promoting greater use of water to final consumers is unlikely to have any significant impact on a water utility company, but influencing the disposition of the Office of Water Regulation, which sets price limits and required service standards, can have a major impact.

9.2.5 Intermediaries

Companies must not ignore the wholesalers, retailers and agents that may be crucial interfaces between themselves and their final consumers. These intermediaries may share many of the same concerns as customers and need reassurance about the company's capabilities as a supplier that is capable of working with intermediaries to supply goods and services in an ethical manner. Many companies have suffered because they failed to take adequate account of the needs of their intermediaries (for example, the Body Shop and McDonald's have faced occasional protests from their franchisees where they felt threatened by a business strategy which was perceived as being against their own interests).

9.2.6 Suppliers

Suppliers can sometimes be critical to business success. This often occurs where vital inputs are in scarce supply or it is critical that supplies are delivered to a company on time and in good condition. The way in which an organization places orders for its inputs can have a significant effect on suppliers. Does a company favour domestic companies rather than possibly lower-priced overseas producers? (Marks & Spencer has traditionally prided itself on buying the vast majority of its merchandise from UK producers, so a few eyebrows were raised when it announced in 1998 that it was to source a greater proportion from lower-cost overseas producers and to terminate relationships with some of its UK-based suppliers). Does it divide its orders between a large number of small suppliers or place the bulk of its custom with a small handful of preferred suppliers? Does it favour new businesses or businesses representing minority interests when it places its orders?

Taking into account the needs of suppliers is again a combination of shrewd business sense and good ethical practice.

9.2.7 The financial community

This includes financial institutions that have supported, are currently supporting or who may support the organization in the future. Shareholders – both private and institutional – form an important element of this community and must be reassured that the organization is going to achieve its stated objectives. Many company expansion schemes have failed because the company did not adequately consider the needs and expectations of potential investors.

9.3 PHILOSOPHICAL UNDERPINNINGS OF CORPORATE RESPONSIBILITY

There are essentially two views about why companies should act in a socially responsible manner.

1 In models of 'good' societies, organizations have a duty to think about the interests of society, and not just their own narrow interests.

2 More pragmatically, companies often support social causes because it is a cheap way of gaining attention and a unique selling proposition. In a market in which product offers are all broadly similar and with saturation advertising, support of socially valuable causes may allow a company to develop a unique identity for its products.

In practice, reasons for organizations acting in a socially responsible manner are a combination of the two.

THINKING AROUND THE SUBJECT:
IF THE COMMUNITY IS HAPPY, ARE THE PUBS CONTENT?

It seems that the business community has always included organizations that are prepared to reach out and help the communities they serve. Companies such as Cadbury and Rowntree have had a long tradition of caring for the needs of their workers when they left the factory. This may have been a case of genuine philanthropic concern by Quaker owners, or it could have been shrewd business practice. Most likely, it was a combination of the two.

What are we to make of a more recent example of big business's apparent philanthropy to less privileged groups in society? Tomorrow's People, a charitable trust, was launched in 1982 by Grand Met, the drinks group that subsequently merged with Guinness in 1997 to form Diageo, now the world's largest spirits company. The trust has funded a number of community projects, such as the Gateway Training Centre in south-east London which has helped to retrain unemployed young people.

At the time it was formed, Grand Met's board was responding to Britain's inner-city riots of 1981. It realized that the closure of breweries at a time of high unemployment could exacerbate social tensions. Since then, unemployment has fallen dramatically and the trust's attention has shifted to getting the long-term unemployed back into work. At the same time, mistrust by the public of big business has grown, and companies have to show that their claims of social responsibility actually mean something.

Over 20 years, Diageo has invested £25 million (at today's prices) as well as management time and resources in the trust. In total, the trust has made investments of £285 million, largely funded by government and the European Union. A study by Oxford Economic Forecasting calculated that economic and social benefits from the programme are worth an estimated £450 million – a return on investment of 160 per cent. These benefits include savings on welfare payments, additional tax receipts, and reductions in crime and healthcare costs. The study suggested that 35,000 people who had been through the trust's programmes had found work who would not otherwise have done so. Quite significantly, researchers found that return on investment in the trust's programmes was much greater than in publicly managed programmes offered through JobCentres.

The trust has moved with the times and, as unemployment has come down, it has targeted additional groups that are difficult to reach through conventional programmes, notably disabled people, older people and lone parents who it has helped back into work.

What is there in the trust's programme for Diageo? The project has helped staff to learn new skills and the company to strengthen its links with government. This latter point became particularly important in the first years of the twenty-first century, when the drinks industry came under intense scrutiny following widespread public concern about 'binge drinking'. At a more practical level, the parent company learnt a lot from the trust's partnering approach, and applied this to the way it trained its bar tendering staff. In 2005, it began introducing a partnership approach to bar tenders in the company's operations in Asia and Africa.

Can the benefits to Diageo of its involvement in the Tomorrow's People trust be quantified? Should they be? Is Diageo's involvement a cynical manipulation of public perceptions or a genuine attempt to act as a socially responsible organization?

Any discussion of corporate social responsibility should recognize that organizations typically produce a wide range of external costs. These represent resources (such as clean water or fresh air) that are used in the organization's production processes, but the costs of which are borne not by the company, but by somebody else. A simple example would be a factory emitting noxious fumes from its chimney. It could save on production costs by not cleaning its emissions, but in this case it has simply passed on some form of cost to its neighbours, who must now suffer an unpleasant environment. The precise costs may be very difficult to quantify, but could include short- and long-term health problems, and damage to buildings.

The opposite of external costs produced by organizations are external benefits. These are benefits that the organization produces, but for which it does not get any direct income benefit. A very simple example would be a company that puts a large clock on the outside of its building for the convenience of passers-by. This is an external benefit, in the sense that the company cannot charge users for the benefits of being able to tell the time.

As societies develop economically and socially, there are rising expectations about the level of external benefits that organizations should provide to society. At the same time, societies have become increasingly critical of organizations' external costs. Social pressure combined with legislation has had the effect of making organizations bear a higher proportion of their external costs, so that they become conventional internal costs. We will see below how, in the case of external costs caused by greenhouse gas emissions, a system of carbon trading has attempted to internalize the cost of emissions.

Rising consumer incomes have resulted in the external benefits provided by consumer purchases becoming a larger element of the total product offering, which consumers use to judge competing products in increasingly competitive markets. Consumers' changing evaluation of a company's external costs and benefits can be illustrated using the framework of Maslow's hierarchy of needs. This framework holds that individuals are motivated by their lowest level of unsatisfied need. According to Maslow, when individuals' basic physiological and social needs are satisfied, higher-order needs become motivators which influence their buying behaviour. Fifty years ago, a packet of washing powder would have largely satisfied a need to produce tangible cleanliness. With most of the population being able to afford cleaning powders which could produce this effect, emphasis moved to promoting washing powder on the basis of satisfying social needs. So one brand was differentiated from another by signifying greater care for the family or was seen to produce results which were visibly valued by peer groups. Today, manufacturers of washing powder recognize that a significant segment seeks to buy more than the packet of washing powder – they seek also to buy a chance to change the world by reducing ecological damage caused by washing powders containing high levels of harmful phosphates (Figure 9.2).

Criticisms of the concept of corporate responsibility take two forms: philosophical and pragmatic.

At a *philosophical level*, it has been argued by the followers of Milton Friedman that firms should concentrate on doing what they are best at – making profits for their owners. The idea of social responsibility by firms has been criticized as it would allow business organizations to become too dominant in society. By this argument, any attempt by firms to contribute to social causes is a form of taxation on the customers of their businesses. It would be better for firms to leave such money in the hands of their customers, so that customers themselves can

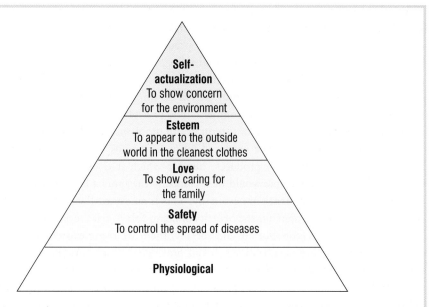

Figure 9.2 Maslow's hierarchy of needs model can be used to illustrate how changing levels of needs have affected the dominant factors that affected consumers in their purchase of washing powder. Increasingly, buyers are likely to avoid products that are associated with ecological and social harm, while preferring products which are ecologically friendly or produced in an ethical manner. In practice, as we will see later in this chapter, it can be quite difficult for consumers to evaluate the ecological and social credentials of a product. But this does not prevent some consumers feeling more comfortable in selecting products that are perceived as satisfying their higher-order needs for self-actualization or inner peace of mind.

decide what worthy causes they wish to support. Alternatively, donations to social causes should be handled by government which is democratically accountable, unlike business firms. There is particular strength in this argument where benefits are provided by private-sector organizations that have considerable monopoly power, such as utility companies. It may be too simplistic to say that customers voluntarily buy a company's products and therefore consent to the payment of social contributions. In reality, many markets are uncompetitive and customers may have very little choice.

At a *pragmatic level*, critics see corporate responsibility as being essentially about short-term and cynical manipulation by a company of its principal stakeholders. There is no such thing as altruism, and all corporate responsibility is done not for the benefit of society, but to improve corporate performance. As examples, litter bins sponsored by a fast-food restaurant, the provision of recycling points by supermarkets and donations to animal charities are not altruism but simply a new way of buying awareness of a company and liking of it, using values which are currently fashionable. It has been suggested that organizations may be quite keen to support good causes which are popular with the public in general, or the particular groups of customers that they target. Many consumer goods companies, for example, have supported child and animal welfare charities, knowing that this will be popular with their target audiences.

However, there may be other groups, such as refugees or the mentally ill, that represent even more deserving cases for an organization's activities, but in general these groups have been shunned by the corporate sector.

Governments have recently sought to pass on responsibility for many aspects of social provision (e.g. sponsorship of the arts). Is there a danger in expecting commercial organizations to undertake such a role? Commercial organizations tend to be very selective in which sections of society they support. It was noted above that firms have a habit of supporting causes which are popular, but may fail to protect minorities in society that command very little public prestige. For example, very few commercial organizations support activities in the fields of mental illness or freedom for political prisoners. It can be argued that responsibilities for such causes cannot be given up by the public sector and handed to private-sector organizations.

Collectively, consumers represent roughly the same group as the electorate. Electors have always expected government to act in the best public interest, otherwise – in the extreme – the government will not be re-elected. Consumers are developing similar expectations towards the suppliers of private-sector goods. If they do not feel the company is acting in the public interest, their goods will not be purchased. In taking on this role, some have suggested that private-sector companies are becoming more important than governments in setting the agenda for ecological reform. There are examples of where this has happened, such as the development of organically grown vegetables and the replacement of CFCs in aerosols. These initiatives originated primarily with the private sector rather than the government. However, there is a danger that corporate responsibility initiatives may follow short-term popular trends, rather than being based on a more rigorous scientific analysis.

9.4 CORPORATE GOVERNANCE

Free market ideology has traditionally held that companies were kept responsible to their stakeholders by the actions of customers and investors. If they became 'bad' citizens, they would be punished by customers not buying their products, and shareholders selling their shares in the company. The reporting system provided by the company's annual profit and loss account and balance sheet was the means of reporting to the world about its performance. Unfortunately, these have often proved insufficient to prevent companies being managed in such a way that investors have lost their money, customers have been let down and employees have lost their jobs unnecessarily. There is therefore growing concern with the concept of corporate governance – ensuring that an organization is run in a responsible manner with due regard to its key stakeholders.

For a long while, most people did not worry too much about how a company was internally governed, so long as shareholders received their dividends, customers were happy with its products and employees were thankful for a job. In the USA, Walt Disney Co. occupied a prominent place throughout the 1990s in *Business Week*'s rankings of America's worst corporate boards. Its board of directors were criticized for having too little management expertise, and exercising too little oversight of the company's chief executive officer. But with the company's share price climbing and shareholders happy, it more or less ignored the issue of governance, claiming that Disney's strong performance spoke for itself. That seemed to be how many investors seemed to regard corporate governance in the 1990s – in theory, a laudable goal, but one with only marginal relevance in the real world.

From the late 1990s, the business world was shaken by a series of corporate governance scandals, in which the executives of an organization took inappropriate care of the firms with which they were trusted. In America, Enron and WorldCom were brought down by a series of fraudulent deals which went unchecked. In Europe, the Italian company Parmalat – one of Europe's biggest food firms – was the subject of a corporate governance scandal. The company, which had sales in 2003 of around €9 billion, produced and sold milk, yoghurt, juice and other food products in Europe, the United States and around the world. It employed 36,000 people in 29 countries. After fraudulently certifying €8 billion in assets in its company's balance sheet, Parmalat entered bankruptcy protection in January 2004, and founder and former CEO Calisto Tanzi fled the country. It appeared that the employees of Bonlat, Parmalat's Cayman subsidiary, simply forged the documents the group required each quarter; furthermore, the company's auditors, Grant Thornton, appeared to be compliant in the process. One problem at Parmalat, which has also been a common feature of many corporate governance scandals, has been the close association between a company's board of governors and its chief executive. In the case of Parmalat, the company's founder Calisto Tanzi – who admitted personally siphoning around €470 million into family accounts – served as both chairman and chief executive of the group. Good corporate governance was not helped by the apparent lack of impartiality of the company's auditors, Grant Thornton, which helped to disguise the company's true financial position by hiding almost €14 billion worth of debt.

Is corporate governance becoming a bigger problem than previously, or are we simply more aware of misgovernance? If we go back 50 or even 100 years, people were behaving fraudulently without ever being exposed. The media is now taking a great interest in major companies whose internal style of governance appears to be inconsistent with their role as a trusted market-led organization. In addition to outright frauds, such as that which occurred at Parmalat, recent examples of poor corporate governance have included numerous cases of so-called 'fat cat' directors paying themselves large salary increases while worsening the employment conditions of their lower-paid employees. Many institutional investors have been dismayed to see senior staff in a company rewarded with very high financial bonuses, which are not consistent with poor financial performance by the company. As an example, many pension fund managers rose up against a proposal by retailer WHSmith to make a generous early retirement payment to its former chief executive who had presided over a period of falling profits and a falling share price.

In the UK, a number of blueprints for corporate governance have been developed (e.g. the Higgs Committee which reported in 2003). 'Good practice' in corporate governance is increasingly being defined in terms of the following.

- Having in place internal control systems which prevent an abuse of power by one individual or group of individuals. It is now regarded as poor practice for the role of chief executive and chairman to be combined in the same person. The chairman should act as an overseer of executives' actions, and should have authority and independence from the chief executive.

- Having an appropriate structure for the board of directors which combines full-time executive directors with non-executive directors brought in from outside.

- Striking a balance, when remunerating senior directors and employees, between the reassurance of a long-term salary and performance for results. The remuneration of senior staff

THINKING AROUND THE SUBJECT:
WHO SHALL WE BOYCOTT TODAY?

Is the public too demanding in how they expect business organizations to behave? It seems that companies can all too easily become the focus of a consumer boycott. The website http://www.ethicalconsumer.org/ summarizes current boycotts which have been organized by consumer groups. A look through a selection of companies that were facing boycotts in March 2005 indicated concerns which go from the mainstream and general to the highly focused and apparently fanatical.

- **Adidas:** boycotted for using kangaroo skin to make some types of football boots.
- **British Heart Foundation:** this leading medical charity was boycotted because it used animals in its research.
- **Colgate-Palmolive:** the focus of the boycott was the testing of household goods and their ingredients on animals.
- **DaimlerChrysler:** boycotted for its continued failure to pay adequate compensation for its use of slave labour in Germany during the Second World War.
- **Donna Karan:** the clothing company was boycotted for the alleged sweatshop conditions in its suppliers' factories.
- **Esso:** boycotted for its lobbying to sabotage international action on climate change.
- **Gap:** boycotted because of the controlling Fisher family's continued clearing of old growth forest in Mendocino County, USA.
- **GlaxoSmithKline:** boycotted for being one of the biggest customers of the Huntingdon Life Sciences animal testing laboratory.
- **Levi Strauss and Co:** boycotted for its failure to pay adequate compensation to workers who lost their jobs when a factory was relocated to Costa Rica.
- **Nestlé:** boycotted for its irresponsible marketing of breast milk substitutes.
- **Nike:** boycotted for its abuses of workers' rights in its factories in East Asia.
- **Procter & Gamble:** boycotted for its continued use of animal testing.
- **Shell:** boycotted because the people of the Ogoni region in Nigeria did not receive a fair share of profits from oil extraction, or adequate environmental standards.
- **Texaco:** boycotted for having the longest history of oil exploitation on tribal lands in Ecuador
- **UCI cinemas:** boycotted for involvement in the destruction of community parkland and woodland at Crystal Palace as part of a large development.

Some of these boycotts have come close to being mainstream in their appeal, for example many people who disagreed with Exxon's (Esso) attitude to global climate change may have quite happily driven past an Esso station to fill up at an apparently more benign oil company's filling station. But what support are some of the more obscure boycotts likely to achieve? When a young person sees a dress they like in Gap, will they be put off buying it because of a boycott which relates to the shop owner's actions in a forest far away? Who determines what are the important issues worthy of a boycott? Would somebody suffering a heart complaint support a boycott of the British Heart Foundation, when the focus of the boycott – the use of animals in research – could be a life-saver for them?

should be decided in an open manner, and a methodology should be used which avoids reciprocal agreements to pay each other more ('I support your claim for a higher salary if you support mine' may constitute a formal or informal understanding within an organization).

■ Recognizing employees as increasingly important stakeholders in organizations; there have been many initiatives, such as Investors In People, to promote the training and development of an organization's workforce.

■ The relationship between a company and its auditors should be at arm's length. Many corporate governance scandals have occurred where the relationship between auditors and companies has become too cosy. In the case of Enron, the company had a close 12-year relationship with its auditor, Arthur Andersen. Because Arthur Andersen did not want to jeopardize lucrative consulting as well as auditing fees, it was reluctant to call Enron to account over the use of special funding mechanisms to hide debt.

Although the USA and Britain are usually lumped together in their business practices, they have taken quite different approaches to corporate governance as far as accounting is concerned. The American way is a rule-based approach, whereas Britain takes a principle-driven approach. Critics of the US approach argue that the rule-based system allows companies and auditors to feel they have done their job so long as they can tick off boxes to say that they complied with certain rules. A principle-based system that insists on underlying substance over sometimes superficial formality is not so easily circumvented, its supporters claim.

Good corporate governance is culturally conditioned and what may constitute bad governance in one culture may be accepted as normal in others, reflecting economic, political, social and legal traditions in each country. Despite convergence, differences still predominate, for example in attitudes towards the disclosure of directors' salaries.

9.5 ETHICS

A common theme of the corporate governance scandals described above is the presence of unethical behaviour by some of the people involved. Was it ethical for Parmalat's auditors to carry out both auditing and management consultancy for the company? Might a conflict of interest have led it to condone accounting irregularities in its audit, fearing that if it were too rigorous, it might lose its lucrative consultancy work? What about some of the consumer boycotts listed earlier in this chapter: was it ethical of Nestlé to promote breast milk substitutes aware of evidence that natural breast milk is both better for the child and cheaper? Indeed, was it ethical of consumer groups to mount a boycott, knowing that some mothers may have had no alternative to the use of manufactured milk substitutes?

Ethics is essentially about the definition of what is right and wrong. However, a difficulty occurs in trying to agree just what is right and wrong. No two people have precisely the same opinions, so critics would argue that ethical considerations are of little interest to business. It can also be difficult to distinguish between ethics and legality, for example it may not be strictly illegal to exploit the gullibility of children in advertisements, but it may nevertheless be unethical.

Culture has a great effect in defining ethics and what is considered unethical in one society may be considered perfectly acceptable in another. In Western societies, ethical considerations confront business organizations on many occasions, as the following examples show.

- A food company may advertise a product and provide information which is technically correct, but omit to provide vital information about side effects associated with consuming the food. Should the company be required to spell out the possible problems of using its products, as well as the benefits?
- A dentist is short of money and diagnoses spurious problems which call for unnecessary medial treatment. How does he reconcile his need to maximize his earning potential with the need to provide what is best for his patient?
- In order to secure a major new construction contract, a salesperson must entertain the client's buying manager with a weekend all-expenses paid holiday. Should this be considered ethical business practice in Britain? Or in South America?

It is suggested that society is becoming increasingly concerned about the ethical values adopted by its business organizations. With expanding media availability and an increasingly intelligent audience, it is getting easier to expose examples of unethical business practice. Moreover, many television audiences appear to enjoy watching programmes which reveal alleged unethical practices of household-name companies. To give one example, the media has on a number of occasions focused attention on alleged exploitative employment practices of suppliers used by some of the biggest brand names in sportswear.

Firms are responding to increasing levels of ethical awareness by trying to put their own house in order. These are some examples of how firms have gone about the task.

- Many companies have identified segments of their market that are prepared to pay a premium price in order to buy a product which has been produced in an ethical manner, or from a company that has adopted ethical practices. Many personal investors are concerned not just about the return that they will get, but the way in which that return will be achieved. This explains the increasing popularity of ethical investment funds that avoid investing in companies which are considered to be of a socially dubious nature. In the food sector, many consumers would consider the treatment of cattle grown for meat to be inhuman and unethical and would be happy to buy from a supplier that they knew acted ethically in the manner in which the cattle were raised and slaughtered. Many with particularly strong convictions may refuse to buy meat at all.
- Greater attention to training can make clear to staff just what is expected of them, for example that it is unethical (and in the long term commercially damaging) for a pension company's sales personnel to try to sell a policy to a person which really does not suit their needs. Training may emphasize the need to spend a lot of time finding out just what the true needs of the customer are.
- More effective control and reward systems can help to reduce unethical practices within an organization. For example, sales personnel employed by a financial services company on a commission-only basis are more likely to try to sell a policy to a customer regardless of the customer's needs compared to a salaried employee who can take a longer-term view of the relationship between the company and its clients.

There are many documented cases to show that acting ethically need not conflict with a company's profit objectives, and indeed can add to profitability. For example, good safety standards and employment policies can improve productivity.

THINKING AROUND THE SUBJECT:
WOULD YOU INVEST IN AN ETHICAL FUND?

The 1980s and 1990s saw a great growth in investment funds which claimed to invest only in businesses which are run ethically. When ethical investment began in the UK in the 1980s, some City people described them as 'Brazil Funds' – they were simply 'nuts' . Such funds may have appealed to investors who seek to invest in companies which make a positive contribution to the world and who seek to avoid companies which harm the world, its people or its wildlife, but do they make any business sense?

Ethical investment funds started out as funds which merely excluded investment in specific activities or industries such as tobacco, gambling, alcohol and armaments. Other funds take a more proactive stance, actively looking to invest in companies involved in environmentally sound, socially progressive businesses.

A more recent approach, adopted from the late 1990s, goes further. It is based on the belief that ethical or socially responsible investment should go beyond the 'avoidance' or 'supporting' approaches described above. Often called an 'engagement' or 'influencing' approach, here the investment fund will not apply any screening criteria to its investment choices. Instead, fund managers undertake to create a dialogue with companies in their portfolio on a specific number of social and environmental issues. The aim is to encourage them to adopt the best business practices. Those companies which are already demonstrating a good performance in this area are encouraged to continue to set the highest standards.

Some commentators have been concerned about underperformance of ethical funds, relative to their non-ethical counterparts. Unfortunately, it is difficult to make a valid comparison, mainly because of the absence of larger companies in ethical funds. It has tended to be these larger companies which have driven the growth in popular share benchmarks such as the FTSE 100 Index. In an attempt to overcome problems of comparison, in July 2001, the FTSE4Good Index was launched. This measures the performance of companies that meet globally recognized corporate responsibility standards, and facilitates investment in those companies. It is claimed by Moneyworld (www.moneyworld.co.uk) that between 2001 and 2005, there was very little difference between the movement of the FTSE 100 Index and the FTSE4Good Index.

By 2005, ethical investment funds appeared to be becoming mainsream. According to the *EIRIS Guide to Ethical Funds* some 38 different fund management groups operated a range of more than 80 ethical funds, allowing investors to invest in a variety of unit trusts and open-ended investment companies, through life assurance funds to pension funds. However, some commentators remained critical of the whole idea of ethical investment. A report by the Social Affairs Unit was scornful of ethical investment, because ethics is about judgements on what people do with products. It cited the example of funds' refusal to invest in the nuclear industry, which implied that the industry was totally bad, despite the valuable role which nuclear radiation plays in medicine. Similarly, it is very much an individual judgement whether nuclear electricity generation is good or bad. So what is the role of ethical investment trusts? Ethics is very much about statements of what is right and wrong, and these vary between individuals, between cultures, and they change through time. Can an investment trust ever be said to represent the views of a society as a whole?

9.6 ECOLOGICAL RESPONSIBILITY

Issues affecting our natural ecology have captured the public imagination in recent years. The destruction of tropical rainforests, and the depletion of the ozone layer leading to global warming have serious implications for our quality of life, not necessarily today, but for future generations. Business is often seen as being in conflict with the need to protect the natural ecology. It is very easy for critics of business to point to cases where greed and mismanagement have created long-lasting or permanent ecological damage. Have the rainforests been destroyed partly by our greed for more hardwood furniture? More locally, is our impatience for getting to our destination quickly the reason why many natural habitats have been lost to new road developments?

There is argument about whether ecological problems are *actually* getting worse, or whether our perceptions and expectations are changing. Charles Dickens' description of Victorian London painted a grim picture of heavy manufacturing industry causing widespread pollution and using up natural resources in a manner which today would be considered quite profligate. Any comparison with industry today would probably leave the impression that environmental issues are lessening in their importance. Supporters of this view will point to the relatively clean air which we enjoy today, compared to the smogs which previously descended upon industrial areas, often for very lengthy periods. When salmon were caught in the River Thames in the 1990s for the first recorded time in over 50 years, it would be easy to gain the impression that the ecological environment was improving. Set against this is the worry that the actions that we are taking today could be storing up major ecological problems for the future. A lot of ecological change – such as the depletion of the ozone layer over Antarctica – is happening at a much faster rate than previously and there is no certainty about the magnitude of the consequences.

A market-led company cannot ignore threats to the natural ecology. Commercial organizations' concern with the ecological environment has resulted from two principal factors.

1 There has been growing pressure on natural resources, including those that directly or indirectly are used in firms' production processes. This is evidenced by the extinction of species of animals and depletion of hardwood timber resources. As a result of overuse of natural resources, many industry sectors, such as North Sea fishing, have faced severe constraints on their production possibilities.

2 The general public has become increasingly aware of ecological issues and, more importantly, some segments have shown a greater willingness and ability to spend money to alleviate the problems associated with ecologically harmful practices (see Laroche, Bergeron and Goutaland 2001).

At a macroenvironmental level, support for the ecological environment has sometimes been seen as a 'luxury' which societies cannot afford as they struggle to satisfy the essentials of life. As these necessities are satisfied, individuals, and society collectively, can move on to satisfy higher-order needs to protect what are seen as aesthetic benefits such as fresh air and a rich flora and fauna. The idea of environmentalism being a luxury is supported by the observation that countries with the strongest environmental movements, such as the USA and Germany, tend also to be the richest economically. And when consumers do take into account environmental concerns, they tend to focus on immediate threats, rather than longer-term issues.

In one survey, Gallup found that while 68 per cent of respondents mentioned pollution of drinking water as a great concern, acid rain (mentioned by 29 per cent) and global warming (34 per cent) generated less concern (Murray 2001). Many poorer countries tolerate poor environmental conditions in order to gain a competitive cost advantage over their more regulated Western competitors.

Is a commercial organization's pursuit of more consumption fundamentally opposed to ecological interests? Taken to its logical extreme, consumption of the vast majority of goods and services can result in some form of ecological harm. For example, the most ecologically friendly means of transport is to avoid the need for transport in the first place. The most ecologically friendly holiday is for an individual to stay at home. Individuals with a true concern for preserving their ecological environment would choose to reduce their consumption of goods and services in total. At the moment, such attitudes are held by only a small minority in Western societies, but the development of a widespread anti-consumption mentality would have major implications for marketers.

9.6.1 Assessing ecological impacts

It can be difficult for an organization to know just what is meant by the idea of being friendly to the ecological environment. Consumers may be confounded by alternative arguments about the consequences of their purchase decisions, with goods which were once considered to be environmentally 'friendly' suddenly becoming seen as enemies of the environment as knowledge and prejudice change. The following are recent examples which show how it can be difficult to evaluate the ecological credentials of a product.

- Recycling of old newspapers has traditionally been thought of as a 'good' thing, but recent thinking has suggested that there are greater environmental benefits from burning it and planting new trees to grow fresh materials, rather than using energy to transport and recycle used paper.
- In the 1980s, diesel was seen as a relatively clean fuel because it produced fewer greenhouse gases and diesel engines were more efficient than petrol engines. By the 1990s, particulates released into the environment by diesel engines had become linked with increasing levels of asthma and the environmental credentials of diesel were downgraded.
- Nuclear energy – for a long time the target for opposition by ecological pressure groups – has subsequently been accepted by many ecological campaigners because of its lower emission of greenhouse gases, compared with conventional fossil fuels; however, there is still no solution to the disposal of nuclear waste, which is a growing burden for future generations.
- Both supporters and opponents of proposals to build bypasses around towns use environmental arguments to support their arguments. Opponents argue that a new road in itself will create more road traffic which is environmentally harmful, while supporters argue that environmental impacts will be lessened by moving traffic out of town where it causes less harm.

Most members of the public are not experts on the technical aspects of ecological impacts of business activities. They may therefore be easily persuaded by the most compellingly promoted argument, regardless of the technical merit of the case. Very often, a firm may have a technically sound case, but fail to win the hearts and minds of consumers who seem intent on believing the opposite argument that is in accordance with their own prejudices. This was seen

THINKING AROUND THE SUBJECT:
WHAT SHOULD HAPPEN TO AN OLD CAR?

The last thing on most people's minds when they have just taken delivery of a new car is what will happen to the car when it reaches the end of its life. But the question is becoming an increasingly pressing one which has caught the attention off EU legislators.

A number of issues are raised when a car reaches the end its life. First, the old car will most likely be replaced by a new one, which will consume increasingly scarce resources. Not only are many metals becoming scarce, but the whole process of making a car and its components uses energy, invariably leading to the emission of greenhouse gases. Second, disposing of the old car poses problems. In days gone by, a local breaker's yard would remove as many usable parts as possible from an old car, such as door panels, starter motors and alternators. The remains would either be crushed for melting down or dumped in a landfill site. Unfortunately, cars have traditionally comprised many heavy metals which are potentially harmful if not disposed of carefully. Many components of a car, especially plastics, have not (until recently) been able to be recycled, so they have just filled up the increasingly scarce landfill sites.

In 2003, an EU directive on end-of-life vehicles came into force which required the vehicle industry to think much more seriously about its use of resources. The directive covered a number of points.

■ The use of certain heavy metals, such as lead, mercury and cadmium, in new vehicles was restricted from July 2003.

■ Manufacturers were required to mark certain vehicle components to aid recycling, and to make available dismantling information in respect of new vehicles.

■ Manufacturers must provide a free take-back for vehicles put on the market from 1 July 2002, if such vehicles have a negative value when scrapped.

■ The days of the local breaker's yard were limited by a requirement that end-of-life vehicles could be scrapped only by authorized treatment centres, which must meet tightened environmental standards.

The principle that the manufacturer of goods should have some responsibility for the whole life of their products is gaining ground, and has also been applied to household electrical items. Most consumers when they are buying a car or a fridge are unlikely to base their choice on the extent to which the product is recyclable. They will probably be just happy to take it to the dump and buy a new item, leaving the problem of disposal to 'somebody else', and potentially leaving the problem of leaching heavy metal residues to all of us as they find their way into watercourses.

The principle has been adopted that it should be the buyer of a new product that has to pay for its destruction, rather than the owner of the item when it reaches the end of its life. Otherwise could there be a problem where the cost of disposing of a car or a fridge becomes so great that owners are tempted to just abandon them illegally? In 2003, the government estimated that nearly half a million cars were just abandoned in the streets of the UK. Previously, the owners of vehicles at the end of their lives could have expected to sell their car and get £50 for it, regardless of condition. But since cars were classified as 'hazardous' waste, and their scrapping restricted to specially licensed sites, end-of-life cars came to be seen as a liability rather than an asset. For the hard-up car owner whose 12-year-old banger has finally given up on them, the principles of recycling may sound fine, but not if they have to pay.

clearly in debate about how to decommission Shell's *Brent Spar* oil platform. Government and the scientific community appeared to agree that environmental risks would be minimized by dumping the platform in deep water. Considerable risks would result from breaking it up on land, removing toxic materials and dumping the remains in landfill sites. Despite the backing that Shell received from the UK government and members of the scientific community, the public sympathy was with Greenpeace, which mounted a campaign against Shell. The public appeared to trust Greenpeace rather than a multinational oil company. Damage to the marine environment was easier for the public to conceptualize and become emotional about, compared to unrecognized risks on land which would occur 'somewhere else'. A highly effective campaign promoted Shell as the villain of the piece, causing great harm to its reputation. Because of this, Shell was forced to back down and settle for dismantling its platform on land.

Another issue is the presumed benefits for the ecological environment of new, efficient, low-energy products. In the car sector, opponents of further restrictions on car use have pointed out that cars are getting much more efficient, and therefore using less scarce fossil fuels and emitting fewer greenhouse gases. It is certainly true that for any class of car, the typical fuel consumption has dropped over the past decade or so. A family-sized car such as the Volkswagen Golf, which 20 years ago might have achieved 34 miles per gallon, today may achieve nearer to 40. Unfortunately, the falling costs of running a car which are associated with greater fuel efficiency have an income and a substitution effect. Falling costs mean that customers can now afford a bigger and better car, which will doubtless use more fuel. So over the past decade or so, the fastest growth in car sales to private consumers has been larger sports utility vehicles and multi-people vehicles. It is as if individuals have a set proportion of their income that they allocate to transport. If the cost per mile of running their vehicle comes down, they may trade up to the larger 'luxury' vehicle. This effect has been seen in a number of other sectors. The ecological benefits of increasingly fuel-efficient aircraft have been partly offset by the resulting lower prices of air transport, leading to more people taking short-break holidays. The Boeing 737-800 series aircraft not only uses much less fuel than the original Boeing-737 of 20 years ago, but this has also allowed budget airlines to develop a whole new market of low-cost air travel. It has been estimated that half a billion tonnes of carbon dioxide was emitted by aircraft into the atmosphere in 2002, up on previous years, despite the development of more efficient aircraft engines. The advent of budget airlines may also have brought tourists flocking to previously underdeveloped areas, causing ecological damage in the process.

9.6.2 How business can capitalize on 'green consumerism'

The green consumer movement can present businesses with opportunities as well as problems. Proactive companies have capitalized on ecological issues by reducing their costs and/or improving their organizational image, pursuing a green marketing strategy. Here are some examples of how firms have adapted to the green movement.

■ Many markets are characterized by segments which are prepared to pay a premium price for a product that has been produced in an ecologically sound manner. Some retailers, such as the Body Shop, have developed valuable niches on this basis. What starts off as a 'deep green' niche soon expands into a larger 'pale green' segment of customers who prefer ecologically sound products but are unwilling to pay such a high price premium.

THINKING AROUND THE SUBJECT:
FIRMS NEED TO PUT THEIR (GREEN) HOUSE IN ORDER

(Picture reproduced with permission of the Environment Agency)

This chapter has discussed some of the consequences of firms' depletion of natural resources and emission of pollutants into the atmosphere. Although the emphasis has been on the need for regulation to protect the environment against firms' activities, firms themselves need to be on their guard against environmental change. At least some of this change may be attributable to manufacturing activity, as in the case of climate change which has been linked to manufacturing industries' production of 'greenhouse gases'. There has been much debate about greenhouse gas emissions and their effects on weather patterns and sea levels. While there is still some debate about the causes and extent of such changes, it is evident that more businesses are likely to find themselves threatened by extreme weather conditions. This advertisement by the Environment Agency is designed to alert businesses to the dangers of flooding. Although firms may by themselves be unable to do much to reduce flooding in their area, they can nevertheless take actions that reduce the consequences for their operations, including the preparation of a flood plan.

- Being 'green' may actually save a company money. Often, changing existing environmentally harmful practices primarily involves overcoming traditional mindsets about how things should be done (e.g. using recyclable shipping materials may involve overcoming traditional one-way supply chain logistics).
- In Western developed economies, legislation to enforce environmentally sensitive methods of production is increasing. A company which adopts environmentally sensitive production methods ahead of compulsion can gain experience and hence competitive advantage ahead of other companies.

THINKING AROUND THE SUBJECT:
HOW GREEN IS A HOLIDAY?

Tourism is often seen as a clean industry, but marketers in the travel and tourism sector are having to address increasing concern about the environmental damage caused by tourism. In a typical year, 120 million glossy brochures are produced, of which an estimated 38 million are thrown away without being used. The growth of low-cost airlines has made it much easier for consumers to get away for a short break. Most people will probably feel very good about the low price they paid, but think much less about the CO_2 emissions emitted by their aircraft into the atmosphere. In resorts, the development of tourism frequently produces problems of waste and sewage disposal, while local residents find themselves competing for scarce water supplies. British travellers may worry about the damage that tourism causes to the environment, but recent surveys have shown that one in ten of them prefers to holiday in unspoilt or environmentally sensitive areas. Green Flag International, a non-profit-making organization, has been set up to promote conservation and to persuade tour operators that being 'green' can actually save them money. Among other things, it advocates using small, privately run guesthouses and hotels, shops and public transport, and employing local people as guides. Hotels are advised on saving water and electricity, for example by not changing room towels every day. The organization also seeks to educate tourists to evaluate the environmental impact of their visit before booking a holiday and urges tour operators to include in their brochures a statement of their environmental policies. Why do so few people who claim to be green still seek out the cheapest package holiday, regardless of its ecological impacts? And if being green doesn't always cost money, why do so many tour operators seem set in their ways?

CASE STUDY

CAN MARKET MECHANISMS REDUCE GLOBAL CLIMATE CHANGE?

Climate change has become one of the most talked about ecological issues facing business in the early twenty-first century. In the course of the twentieth century, the global temperature is thought to have increased by 0.6 degrees Celsius, and much of this rise has been attributed to human actions such as the burning of fossil fuels which release greenhouse gases (e.g. carbon dioxide) into the atmosphere. Greenhouse gases are blamed for causing climate change because they absorb infra-red radiation and prevent it from being dispersed into space, thereby having the effect of warming the Earth. This not only increases global average temperatures, but is also claimed to lead to increasingly unpredictable weather. Probable results of climate change include more frequent and fiercer storms, droughts and floods. If warming causes enough of the world's ice to melt, rises in sea levels could occur, leading to flooding in coastal areas. It is also claimed that melting ice from the Arctic could disrupt the flow and direction of the Gulfstream, having the effect of cooling parts of Europe.

Very few businesses can claim not to be affected by climate change. Bad weather, such as hurricanes, floods and gale-force winds, which have been attributed to climate change, affects companies when they come to renew their insurance policies. The storms which hits the UK in autumn 2000 are estimated to have cost UK insurers more than £1 billion, and these costs will ultimately be passed on to businesses and consumers in the form of higher premiums. Damage caused to property by storms can close down a company's factories and disrupt the supply of its raw materials. If the weather becomes more unpredictable, risk will increasingly have to be factored into business planning.

As well as being affected by climate change, companies are increasingly being called upon to take some of the responsibility for slowing the rate of greenhouse gas emissions. An important focus for these efforts was the Kyoto Treaty, drawn up in 1997. This requires developed countries to reduce their dependence on fossil fuels, which produce the greenhouse gases blamed for causing climate change. Kyoto binds developed nations to cut emission levels by 2012, compared with those of 1990.

One outcome of the Kyoto Treaty was the introduction in the EU in 2005 of a system of carbon trading. The scheme aims to lower the EU's emissions of greenhouse gases in line with the commitment of member states under the Kyoto protocol. It aims to achieve this reduction by imposing limits on emissions of carbon dioxide that certain energy-intensive industries are allowed to produce. Companies that produce less than their allowance (for example by improving their energy efficiency or investing in low-carbon technologies) can sell their excess allowances on an open market. Companies that exceed their allowances must buy additional allowances in the market, or face fines. All businesses in the UK covered by the scheme were allocated a share of the 756 million tonnes of carbon dioxide that the UK was allowed to produce.

The use of market mechanisms to solve the problem of global warming is an innovative way of trying to internalize companies' external costs. Rather than imposing a bureaucratic solution, a market-based system was seen by many as an attractive means by which businesses could overcome an ecological problem by a doing what they are good at – trading. Some advocates of the system have claimed that businesses face more opportunities than threats. There are opportunities for a wide range of businesses involved in technology and management consultancy. A report from management consultants Ernst & Young claimed that Britain and Spain were the world's two most attractive environments for investment in renewable energy technologies, such as wind and solar energy. In more general terms, more efficient use of energy and resources can benefit companies by bringing in cost savings.

However, critics have been quick to criticize the system of carbon trading set up as a result of the Kyoto agreement. In the first place, the United States, in 2000 the largest producer of emissions (an estimated 20.6 per cent of the world total), refused to sign the Kyoto agreement. Just as significantly, the agreement applied only to developed countries, but many commentators are concerned by the rapid growth in emissions from two of the fastest industrializing countries in the world – China and India. The US-based Pew Center on Global Climate Change estimated that in 2000, China was responsible for 14.8 per cent of the world's emissions, and this figure was expected to climb rapidly. Persuading developing countries to sign up to emissions reduction has been difficult. Many resent the idea that the developed world grew rich, fuelled by coal and oil, while the developing world might now be denied the chance to catch up.

In the UK, many companies have criticized carbon trading, although many have preferred not to be too vociferous for fear of appearing in the eyes of customers to be ecologically irresponsible. It has been claimed that some energy-intensive businesses, such as power generation and chemicals, will be at a competitive disadvantage compared to companies located in non-participating countries where CO_2 allowances do not have to be bought.

There is also an argument that such effort to combat climate change is wasted in any case. Not everyone agrees that climate change exists, or that it is necessarily a problem if it does exist. Although the great majority of mainstream scientific opinion maintains that the Earth's climate is changing as a result of human actions in burning fossil fuels, some sceptical scientists and lobby groups argue that there is little evidence of significant change to the global climate as a result of these actions. Sceptics have had considerable influence with the US federal government. Exxon Mobil has played a significant role in campaigning against the US government's adoption of the principles of the Kyoto agreement. In doing so, it has incurred the wrath of protest groups that have claimed it is putting corporate profits ahead of the global ecosystem. For its part, the company has claimed to be doing what is best for America and the vast majority of its customers, who simply want to buy the cheapest petrol.

QUESTIONS

1 To what extent is global climate change an issue for responsible buying decisions by consumers, rather than responsible production methods by business?

2 Why should a tourism business, such as a holiday hotel, be concerned by a global climate change?

3 Critically assess the opportunities and challenges for energy-intensive businesses, such as a metal manufacturer, resulting from the introduction of carbon trading.

SUMMARY

In a mature business environment, organizations must think beyond their own customers to society as a whole. There are good philosophical and pragmatic reasons why firms should act in a socially responsible manner. At a time of increasing competition in many markets, good social credentials can act as a differentiator in the eyes of increasingly sophisticated buyers. Although social responsibility by firms can achieve long-term paybacks, there can still be doubt about what is the most responsible course of action. But, as we have seen in this chapter, discussion about ecological issues and ethics is often muddied by lack of agreement on what is right and wrong.

The following key linkages to other chapters should be noted: ethics is founded upon what a society considers right and wrong, and social values are constantly changing (**Chapter 3**), reflected in legislation by governments (**Chapters 2** and **5**). Fierce competition within a market and a high degree of price sensitivity by buyers can encourage firms to engage in unethical practices (**Chapter 10**). New technologies are continually posing new challenges and opportunities for organizations in their efforts to act responsibly (**Chapter 4**). Expectations of responsibility by firms can differ markedly between countries (**Chapter 12**). Internally, ethical practice is closely linked to human resource management practices (**Chapter 8**).

Key Terms

Corporate governance	(329)	Ecological impacts	(336)	Green marketing	(338)
Corporate social responsibility	(327)	Ethics	(332)		
		External costs	(327)		

CHAPTER REVIEW QUESTIONS

1 Giving examples, explain what is meant by the term 'environmental lobbies'. Provide a resumé of the tactics you would advise a high-profile company to use in managing relations with special interest groups. (*Based on CIM Marketing Environment Examination*)

2 (a) Identify *two* stakeholder groups and briefly assess the nature and terms of their stake in the organization.

   (b) Prepare a brief for your marketing director outlining the concept of social responsibility and indicating how this might be applied to your customers and how it might be of overall benefit. (*Based on CIM Marketing Environment Examination*)

3 For what reasons might a fast-food restaurant company choose to act in a socially responsible manner? By adopting a responsible approach, is it really changing the way it does business?

4 Is it possible to define an ethical code of conduct which is applicable in all countries? How should a multinational company attempt to define a global ethical code of conduct?

5 What is meant by good corporate governance, and why has the topic become an important issue in many countries?

6 What should be the response of businesses to pressure groups' claims that their activities are causing ecological damage?

ACTIVITY

You are employed by a phone company as a commission-based sales assistant. The more people you get to sign up and switch from other phone companies, the more commission you will be paid. However, you know in your heart that most of the people you are selling to could get a much better deal with another company. Moreover, you realize that hidden in the small print of the contract are clauses which will result in additional charges to the customer which are not mentioned in the glossy, colourful brochure that you send out.

As a salesperson, would you consider yourself to be acting ethically by selling something when you know that buyers could get better elsewhere? Is it ethical not to alert buyers to the potentially disadvantageous terms contained in the small print, and just lure them to sign on the dotted line with the bait of free gifts and a glossy brochure?

What would you do?

Useful Websites

Business Ethics Discussion Group

The purpose of this list is to facilitate debate and discussion between members of the academic, research and business communities who are interested in the systematic study or practical investigation of the ethical issues facing business and industry.

http://www.jiscmail.ac.uk/lists/business-ethics.html

MIT Technology, Business and Environment Programme

MIT's Technology, Business and Environment site provides discussion and links to other sites concerning the links between business excellence and the environment.

http://web.mit.edu/ctpid/www/tbe.html

Greenpeace

Home page of Greenpeace.

http://greenpeace.org

Friends of the Earth

Home page of Friends of the Earth UK.

http://www.foe.co.uk

The Environment Council

This independent UK charity brings together people from all sectors of business, non-governmental organizations, government and the community to develop long-term solutions to environmental issues.

http://www.the-environment-council.org.uk/

Governance

Governance is an international monthly newsletter on issues of corporate governance, boardroom performance and shareholder activism. It provides analysis of key events, and publications and reports on corporate governance issues.

http://www.governance-news.com/index.htm

Further Reading

For a general review of 'environmentalism', the following texts provide a useful overview of the issues involved:

Lyon, Thomas P. and Maxwell, John W. (2004) *Corporate Environmentalism and Public Policy*, Cambridge University Press.

Daily, Gretchen C. and Ellison, Katherine (2003) *The New Economy of Nature: The Quest to Make Conservation Profitable*, London, Shearwater Books.

Newton, Lisa (2004) *Business Ethics and the Natural Environment*, Blackwell Publishing.

For a discussion of business ethics the following texts are useful:

Crane, Andy and Matten, Dirk (2003) *Business Ethics*, Oxford, Oxford University Press.

Bradburn, Roger (2001) *Understanding Business Ethics*, London, Thomson Learning.

Lovell, Alan and Fisher, Colin (2002) *Business Ethics and Values*, FT Prentice Hall.

Harrison, Robert, Newholm, Terry and Shaw, Deirdre (2005) *The Ethical Consumer*, London, Sage Publications.

The following provides insights to issues of corporate governance:

Monks, Robert A.G. and Minow, Nell (eds) (2003) *Corporate Governance*, Blackwell Publishing.

MacAvoy, Paul and Millstein, Ira (2003) *The Recurrent Crisis in Corporate Governance*, Basingstoke, Palgrave Macmillan.

Fahy, Martin, Weiner, Anastasia and Roche, Jeremy (2005) *Beyond Governance: Creating Corporate Value Through Performance, Conformance and Responsibility*, Chichester, John Wiley & Sons.

Harvard Business Review (2000) *Harvard Business Review on Corporate Governance*, Harvard Business School Press.

References

Anderson, P. (1982) 'Marketing, strategic planning and theory', *Journal of Marketing*, Spring, pp. 15–26.

Arbratt, R. and Sacks, D. (1988) 'Perceptions of the societal marketing concept', *European Journal of Marketing*, 22, pp. 25–33.

Laroche, M., Bergeron, J. and Goutaland, C. (2001) 'Targeting customers who are willing to pay more for environmentally friendly products', *Journal of Consumer Marketing*, Vol. 18, No. 6, pp. 503–20.

Murray, S. (2001) 'Green products: consumers count cost over ecology', *Financial Times*, 5 November, p. 4.

Part 4
Markets

Chapter 10
The Competition Environment

Chapter Objectives
This chapter will explain:

- the concept of market structure and the range of structures from atomistic competition to pure monopoly

- the dynamics of competition and how it impacts on an organization's activities

- the principles of atomistic competition as basic building blocks for understanding a firm's pricing and output decisions

- methods used by firms to avoid head-on competition

- the role of brands in providing product differentiation

- market imperfections and the steps taken by government agencies to counter abuse of monopoly power

10.1 INTRODUCTION TO THE COMPETITIVE ENVIRONMENT

Competition is a crucial fact of life to most organizations operating in a commercial environment. It usually arises when companies seek to attract customers from rival companies by offering better products and/or lower prices. Competition can also arise in the acquisition of resources, and where these are scarce relative to the demand for them, rival buyers will bid up their price. However, competition in customer and resource markets can be complex and a full understanding of each market is needed if the effects of competition on an organization are to be fully appreciated. This chapter begins by reviewing the fundamentals of competitive markets which are characterized by 'perfect competition' (sometimes referred to as 'atomistic competition'). In fact, perfect competition is the exception rather than the norm and most markets have imperfections which allow some organizations in the market to have undue influence over it. It is because of these imperfections that governments have intervened, believing that, in general, competitive markets are better for consumers.

Economists define markets in terms of the interaction between two groups:

1   those seeking to buy products
2   those seeking to sell them.

Economists distinguish between those economic influences that operate at the level of the individual firm and those that relate to the economy as a whole. The study of an organization and its customers/suppliers in isolation from the rest of the economy is generally referred to as *microeconomic* analysis. In this type of analysis, the national economy is assumed to be stable. However, this assumption is rarely true, so economists seek to understand the workings of the economy and, from this, the effects of changes in the national (and international) economy on individual organizations. This is generally referred to as *macroeconomic* analysis.

This chapter is concerned primarily with microeconomic influences as they affect the decisions made by individual firms, for example with regard to their pricing and production levels. The following chapter will return to macroeconomic analysis.

10.1.1 Market structure

The market conditions facing suppliers of goods and services vary considerably. Customers of water supply companies may feel they are being exploited with high prices and poor service levels by companies that know that their customers have little choice of supplier. On the other hand, customers are constantly wooed by numerous insurance companies that are all trying to sell basically similar products in a market that provides consumers with a lot of choice. Differences in the characteristics and composition of buyers and sellers define the structure of a market.

The term market structure is used to describe:

■ the number of buyers and sellers operating in a market
■ the extent to which the market is concentrated in the hands of a small number of buyers and/or sellers
■ the degree of collusion or competition between buyers and/or sellers.

An understanding of market structure is important to businesses, not only to understand the consequences of their own actions but also the behaviour of other firms operating in a market.

Market structures range from the theoretical extremes of perfect competition to pure monopoly. In practice, examples of the extremes are rare and most analysis therefore focuses on levels of market imperfection between the two extremes (Figure 10.1).

It is easy to take a static view of market structure but, in reality, markets are often in transition. This is most apparent in the economies of the former Soviet bloc countries, which until the late 1980s allocated resources according to their governments' central planning processes. Officially, market forces had little role to play, although they often existed discreetly, especially in the more liberal Soviet bloc countries such as Hungary. The collapse of communism brought about a major change in the way that resources were allocated in the national economy, with the interaction of supply and demand leading to the price mechanism being used as a means of allocating scarce resources, rather than government bureaucrats. In many countries which have emerged from communism, the transition to market forces has not been an easy one (see 'Thinking around the subject', below).

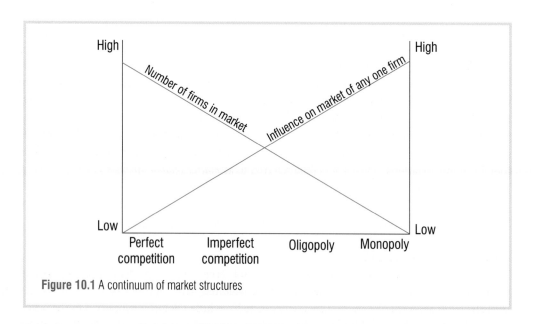

Figure 10.1 A continuum of market structures

By most measures of economic activity, the countries of the former Soviet bloc were lagging well behind most Western countries. The level of wealth generated per person, indicated by GDP per head, was typically much less than half of comparable economies in Western Europe. It seemed that central government bureaucrats were no match for market forces in stimulating the economy to produce more goods at lower cost. So long as factories and farms produced their quota of output, everybody seemed happy. The workers had little incentive to produce more output, and at a better quality, because they would not be rewarded for it. Producers simply didn't undertake any market research in order that they might make goods that customers actually wanted, rather than the goods which bureaucrats said should be produced. The result of this centralized planning process was a shortage of goods that people wanted, with 'black markets' often arising in order to satisfy customer demands which could not be met through an open market. Stories abounded of raw materials and agricultural produce which were left to rot on farms, either because there was little incentive to get them to consumers, or because the farms had simply grown too much of the produce which customers didn't want to buy.

The dismantling of communist government planning processes and the introduction of market forces came as a shock to most people of Eastern Europe – both as producers and as consumers. Producers were at first slow to learn the principles of marketing and the importance of understanding customers' needs. But, slowly, producers began to pick up signals from the market and started developing new and improved goods and services. In came modern bars and cafes to replace the previous dull outlets. Slowly, goods manufactured by Western companies began to appear in East European markets and were highly prized by consumers who could afford them. The presence of Western competitors gave manufacturers new standards which they had to compete against if they were to stay in business.

For consumers, centralized planning had previously meant allocation of resources by queuing. It was not uncommon, for example, to have to wait 20 years from ordering for a new Lada car to be delivered to the buyer. A 10-year wait for a new washing machine was typical for many consumer durables. With the introduction of market forces, prices rather than queuing became the method for allocating scarce resources. So prices of most goods and services shot up to a level way beyond what most consumers could afford. In any free-market economy, limited supply and almost infinite demand for goods and services can only lead to higher prices. The paradox was that consumers now had much more freedom and choice in the marketplace, but at market-determined prices the typical consumer did not have anywhere near enough money to pay for the goods and services which were now available. During the transition period, incomes struggled to keep up as factory closures led to rising unemployment. Meanwhile, inflation rates soared, and in many countries prices more than doubled each year.

A market-based economy was further frustrated by the presence in many countries of mafia-style groups that sought to control some aspect of the newly liberated markets. There were stories of gangsters and former Communist Party members using coercion to control the supply of many essential goods and services through the distribution chain. As an example, tomatoes grown in Bulgaria were being sold in shops in the country's capital, Sofia, for a higher price than those same tomatoes sold in export markets such as Britain and France. Retailing and distribution should have become a competitive business, helping to force down prices, but it seemed that the simple transition to a market-based economy was impeded by the presence of mafia-type groups. In the turmoil that accompanied the transition from centralized planning to market-based mechanisms, these groups saw a window of opportunity to re-establish a form of central power that had been lost with the demise of communism.

Competitive market forces may be a fine ideal, but this chapter and the next demonstrate how economies have a tendency to develop anti-competitive practices which undermine the power of markets to produce more output at low price.

10.2 ATOMISTIC (OR 'PERFECT') COMPETITION

This is the simplest type of market structure to understand and corresponds very much with most people's idea of what a very competitive market should be like. Government policy makers often pursue a vision of atomistic (or 'perfect') competition as the ideal market structure. Although perfectly competitive markets in their theoretical extreme are rarely found in practice, a sound understanding of the way they work is essential for understanding competitive market pressures in general.

Perfectly competitive markets are attributed with the following principal characteristics.

■ There are a large number of small producers supplying to the market, each with similar cost structures and each producing an identical product.

■ There are also a large number of buyers in the market, each responsible for purchasing only a small percentage of total output.

■ Both buyers and sellers are free to enter or leave the market, that is there are no barriers to entry or exit.

■ In a perfectly competitive market, there is a ready supply of information for buyers and sellers about market conditions.

Some markets come close to having these characteristics, for example:
■ wholesale fruit and vegetable markets
■ the 'spot' market for oil products
■ stock markets where shares are bought and sold (see Figure 10.2).

In reality, very few markets fully meet the economists' criteria for perfect competition and even those markets described above have imperfections (e.g. wholesale fruit and vegetable markets are increasingly influenced by the practice of large retailers contracting directly with growers or growers' intermediaries).

Perfect competition implies that firms are price *takers* in that competitive market forces alone determine the price at which they can sell their products. If a firm cannot produce its goods or services as efficiently as its competitors, it will lose profits and eventually go out of business. Customers are protected from exploitative high prices, because as long as selling a product remains profitable, companies will be tempted into the market to satisfy customers' requirements, thereby putting downward pressure on prices. Eventually, competition between firms will result in excessive profits being eliminated so that an equilibrium is achieved where loss-making firms have left the market and the market is not sufficiently attractive to bring new firms into it.

Probably the most important reason for studying perfect competition is that it focuses attention on the basic building blocks of competition: demand, supply and price determination.

10.2.1 Demand

Demand refers to the quantity of a product that consumers are willing and able to buy at a specific price over a given period of time. In economic analysis, demand is measured not simply in terms of what people would like to buy – after all, most people would probably want to buy expensive holidays and cars. Instead, demand refers to how many people are actually *able and willing* to buy a product at a given price and given a set of assumptions about the

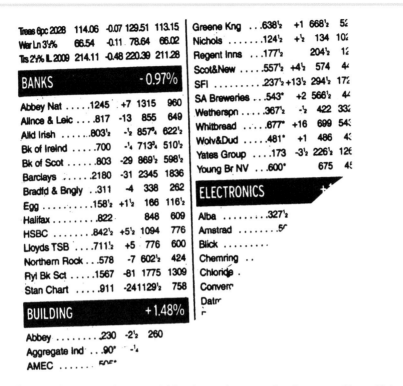

Treas 6pc 2028	114.06	-0.07	129.51	113.15
War Ln 3½%	66.54	-0.11	78.64	66.02
Tis 2½% IL 2009	214.11	-0.48	220.39	211.28

BANKS − 0.97%

Abbey Nat	1245	+7	1315	960
Allnce & Leic	817	-13	855	649
Alld Irish	......803½	-½	857¾	622½
Bk of Irelnd	700	-¼	713¾	510½
Bk of Scot	803	-29	869½	598½
Barclays	2180	-31	2345	1836
Bradfd & Bngly	..311	-4	338	262
Egg	.........158½	+1½	166	116½
Halifax	822		848	609
HSBC	.......842½	+5½	1094	776
Lloyds TSB	....711½	+5	776	600
Northern Rock	...578	-7	602½	424
Ryl Bk Sct	1567	-81	1775	1309
Stan Chart	911	-241	129½	758

BUILDING +1.48%

Abbey	230	-2½	260
Aggregate Ind	...90°	-¼	
AMEC	......505°		

Greene Kng	...638½	+1	668½	5
Nichols	.......124½	+½	134	10
Regent Inns	...177½		204½	1
Scot&New	.....557½	+4½	574	4
SFI	.........237½	+13½	294½	17
SA Breweries	..543°	+2	566½	4
Wetherspn	.....367½	-½	422	33
Whitbread	....677°	+16	699	54
Wolv&Dud	.....481°	+1	486	4
Yates Group	173	-3½	226½	12
Young Br NV	...600°		675	4

ELECTRONICS

Alba	........327½
Amstrad	5
Blick	....
Chemring	..
Chloride	.
Converr	
Datm	

Figure 10.2 Stock markets come close to satisfying the requirements of perfect competition, with large numbers of people buying and selling shares, resulting in daily movement in share prices. Regulators of stock markets go to great lengths to preserve the competitiveness of their markets, for example by requiring full disclosure by firms of information that might affect their share price. Where a buyer builds up a significant holding of a company's shares, stock market rules may require this fact to be disclosed.

product and the environment in which it is being offered. Demand is also expressed in terms of a specified time period, for example so many units per day.

In general, as the price of a product falls, so the demand (as defined above) can be expected to rise. Likewise, as the price rises, demand could be expected to fall. This relationship can be plotted on a simple graph. In Figure 10.3, a demand curve for medium-fat Cheddar cheese is shown by the line D1. This relates any given price, shown on the vertical axis, to the volume of demand, which is shown on the horizontal axis. Therefore, at a price of £8.00 per kg, demand is 10,000 units per period within a given area, while at a price of £4.00, the demand rises to 12,000 units.

It is important to note that the demand curve drawn here refers to total market demand from all consumers and is not simply measuring demand for one producer's output. The importance of this distinction will become clear later, as the implication of this is that firms have to make their price decisions based on overall market conditions.

The demand curve D1 is based on a number of assumptions. These include, for example, assumptions that the price of substitutes for cheese will not change or that consumers will not

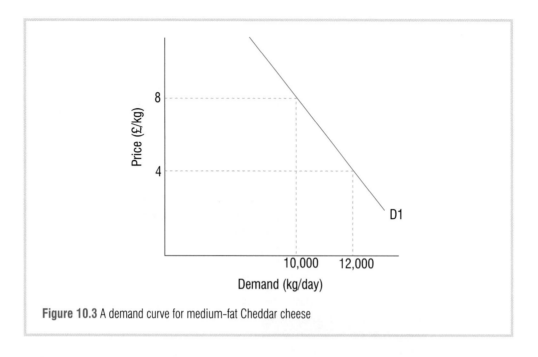

Figure 10.3 A demand curve for medium-fat Cheddar cheese

suddenly take a dislike to Cheddar cheese. Demand curve D1 measures the relationship between price and market demand for one given set of assumptions. When these assumptions change, a new demand curve is needed to explain a new relationship between price and quantity demanded.

In Figure 10.4, two sets of fresh assumptions have been made and new demand curves, D2 and D3, drawn based on these new sets of assumptions. For new demand curve D2, more cheese is demanded for any given price level (or, alternatively, this can be restated in terms of any given number of consumers demanding cheese being prepared to pay a higher price). There are a number of possible causes of the shift of the demand curve from D1 to D2.

1 Consumers could have become wealthier, leading them to demand more of all goods, including cheese.

2 The price of substitutes for Cheddar cheese (e.g. meat or other types of cheese) could have increased, thereby increasing demand for cheese.

3 Demand for complementary goods (such as savoury biscuits) may increase, thereby leading to an increase in demand for Cheddar cheese.

4 Consumer preferences may change. This may occur, for example, if Cheddar cheese is found to have health-promoting benefits.

5 An advertising campaign for Cheddar cheese may increase demand for cheese at any given price.

Similarly, a number of possible reasons can be put forward to explain the shift from demand curve D1 to D3, where for any given price level, less is demanded.

1 Consumers could have become poorer, leading them to demand fewer of all goods, including cheese.

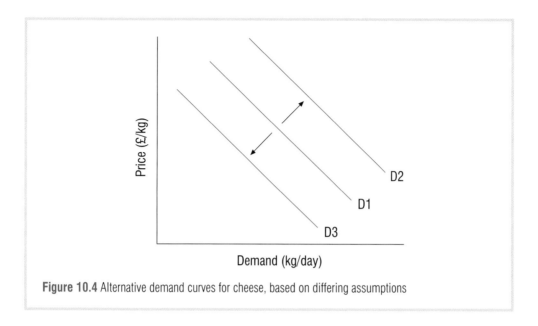

Figure 10.4 Alternative demand curves for cheese, based on differing assumptions

2 The price of substitutes for Cheddar cheese (e.g. meat or other types of cheese) could have decreased, thereby making the substitutes appear more attractive and reducing demand for Cheddar cheese.
3 Demand for complementary products may fall.
4 Cheddar cheese may become associated with health hazards, leading to less demand at any given price.
5 An advertising campaign for substitute products may shift demand away from Cheddar cheese.

The demand curves shown in Figures 10.3 and 10.4 have both been straight, but this is a simplification of reality. In fact, demand curves would usually be curved, indicating that the relationship between price and volume is not constant for all price points. There may additionally be significant discontinuities at certain price points, as where buyers in a market have psychological price barriers, above or below which their behaviour changes. In many markets, the difference between £10.00 and £9.99 may be crucial in overcoming buyers' attitudes that predispose them to regard anything over £10 as being unaffordable and anything below it as a bargain.

Actually collecting information with which to plot a demand curve poses theoretical and practical problems. The main problem relates to the cross-sectional nature of a demand curve, that is it purports to measure the volume of demand across the ranges of price possibilities. However, this kind of information can often only be built up by a longitudinal study of the relationship between prices and volume over time. There is always the possibility that, over time, the assumptions on which demand is based have changed, in which case it is difficult to distinguish between a movement along a demand curve and a shift to a new demand curve. It is, however, sometimes possible for firms to conduct controlled cross-sectional experiments where a different price is charged in different regions and the effects on volume recorded.

To be sure that this is accurately measuring the demand curve, there must be no extraneous factors in regions (such as differences in household incomes) that could partly explain differences in price/volume relationships.

The demand curves shown in Figures 10.3 and 10.4 slope downwards, indicating the intuitive fact that as price rises, demand falls and vice versa. While this is intuitively plausible, it is not always the case. Sometimes, the demand curve slopes upwards, indicating that as the price of a product goes up, buyers are able and willing to buy more of the product. Classic examples of this phenomenon occur where a product becomes increasingly desirable as more people consume it. A telephone network which has only one subscriber will be of little use to the first customer, who will be unable to use a telephone to call anyone else. However, as more customers are connected, the value of the telephone network becomes greater to each individual, who is correspondingly willing to pay a higher price. This phenomenon helps to explain why large international airports can charge more for aircraft to land than smaller regional airports. As the number of possible aircraft connections increases, airlines' willingness to pay high prices for landing slots increases.

Upward-sloping demand curves can also be observed for some products sold for their 'snob' value. Examples include some designer-label clothes where high price alone can add to a product's social status. Upward-sloping demand curves can be observed over short time periods where a 'bandwagon' effect can be created by rapidly rising or falling prices. For example, in stock markets, the very fact that share prices are rising may lead many people to invest in shares.

10.2.2 Supply

Supply is defined as the amount of a product that producers are willing and able to make available to the market at a given price over a particular period of time. Like demand, it is important to note that at different prices there will be different levels of supply, reflecting the willingness and/or ability of producers to supply a product as prices change.

A simple supply curve for medium-fat Cheddar cheese is shown in Figure 10.5. The supply curve slopes upwards from left to right, indicating the intuitively plausible fact that as market prices rise, more suppliers will be attracted to supply to the market. Conversely, as prices fall, marginal producers (such as those who operate relatively inefficiently) will drop out of the market, reducing the daily supply available.

It is again important to distinguish movements along a supply curve from shifts to a new supply curve. The supply curve S1 is based on a number of assumptions about the relationship between price and volume supplied. If these assumptions are broken, a new supply curve based on the new set of assumptions needs to be drawn. In Figure 10.6, two new supply curves, S2 and S3, are shown. S2 indicates a situation where, for any given price level, total supply to the market is reduced. This could come about for a number of reasons, including the following.

- Production methods could become more expensive, for example because of more stringent health and safety regulations. Therefore, for any given price level, fewer firms will be willing to supply to the market as they will no longer be able to cover their costs.
- Extraneous factors (such as abnormally bad weather) could result in producers having difficulty in getting their produce to market.
- Governments may impose additional taxes on suppliers (e.g. extending the scope of property taxes to cover agricultural property).

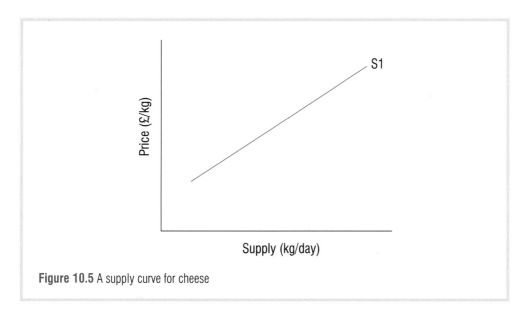

Figure 10.5 A supply curve for cheese

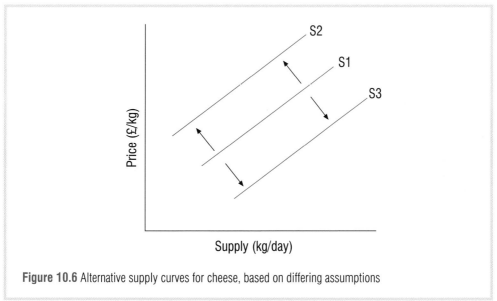

Figure 10.6 Alternative supply curves for cheese, based on differing assumptions

The new supply curve S3 indicates a situation where, for any given price level, total supply to the market is increased. This could come about for a number of reasons, including the following.

■ Changes in production technology that result in Cheddar cheese being produced more efficiently and therefore suppliers being prepared to supply more cheese at any given price (or, for any given volume supplied, suppliers are prepared to accept a lower price).

■ Extraneous factors (such as favourable weather conditions) could result in a glut of produce which must be sold and the market is therefore flooded with additional supply.

■ Governments may give a subsidy for each kilogram of cheese produced by suppliers, thereby increasing their willingness to supply to the market.

10.2.3 Price determination

An examination of the demand and supply graphs indicates that they share common axes. In both cases the vertical axis refers to the price at which the product might change hands, while the horizontal axis refers to the quantity changing hands.

It is possible to redraw the original demand and supply lines (D1 and S1) on a single graph (Figure 10.7). The supply curve indicates that the lower the price, the less cheese will be supplied to the market. Yet at these lower prices, customers are willing and able to buy a lot of cheese – more than the suppliers collectively are willing or able to supply. By following the supply curve upwards, it can be observed that suppliers are happy to supply more cheese, but at these high prices, there are few willing buyers. Therefore, at these high prices supply and demand are again out of balance.

Between the two extremes there will be a price where the interest of the two groups will coincide. This balancing of supply and demand is the foundation of the theory of market price, which holds that in any free market there is an 'equilibrium price' that matches the quantity that consumers are willing and able to buy (i.e. demand) with the quantity that producers are willing and able to produce (i.e. supply). Working out what this equilibrium price is, is called price determination.

In perfectly competitive markets, the process of achieving equilibrium happens automatically without any external regulatory intervention. Perfectly competitive markets do not need any complicated and centralized system for bringing demand and supply into balance, something

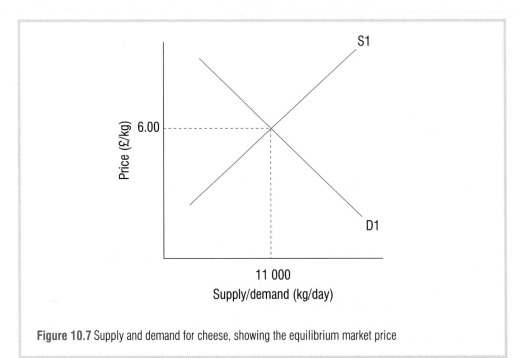

Figure 10.7 Supply and demand for cheese, showing the equilibrium market price

that is difficult to achieve in a centrally planned economy, such as those which used to predominate in Eastern Europe.

In Figure 10.7, supply and demand are brought precisely into balance at a price of £6.00. This is the equilibrium price and, at this price, 11,000 kg of cheese per day will be bought and sold in the market. If a company wants to sell its cheese in the market, it can only do so at this price. In theory, if it charged a penny more, it would get no business because everybody else in the market is cheaper. If it sells at a penny less, it will be swamped with demand, probably selling at a price that is below its production costs.

It is important to remember that in a perfectly competitive market, individual firms are price takers. The market alone determines the 'going rate' for their product. Changes in the equilibrium market price come about for two principal reasons:

1 assumptions about suppliers' ability or willingness to supply change, resulting in a shift to a new supply curve
2 assumptions about buyers' ability or willingness to buy change, resulting in a shift to a new demand curve.

The effects of shifts in supply are illustrated in Figure 10.8. From an equilibrium price of £6.00 and volume of 11,000 kg, the supply curve has shifted to S2 (perhaps in response to the imposition of a new tax on production). Assuming that demand conditions remain unchanged, the new point of intersection between the demand and supply lines occurs at a price of £6.50 and a volume of 10,500 kg. This is the new equilibrium price. A similar analysis

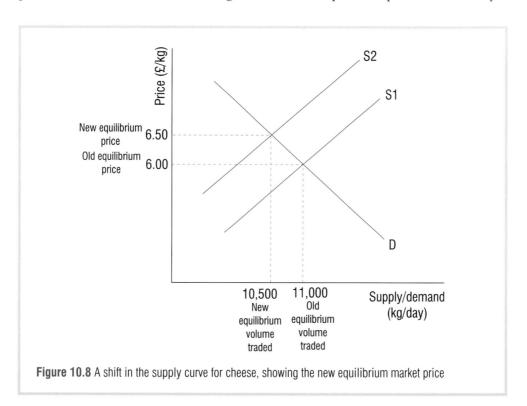

Figure 10.8 A shift in the supply curve for cheese, showing the new equilibrium market price

can be carried out on the effects of a shift in the demand curve, but where the supply curve remains constant.

New equilibrium prices and trade volumes can be found at the intersection of the supply and demand curves. In practice, both the supply and demand curves may be changing at the same time.

The speed with which a new equilibrium price is established is dependent upon how efficiently a market is working. In pure commodity markets where products are instantly perishable, rapid adjustments in price are possible. Where speculators are allowed to store goods, or large buyers and sellers are able to unduly influence a market, adjustment may be slower. The extent of changes in price and volume traded is also dependent on the elasticities of demand and supply, which are considered in the following sections.

Figure 10.9 In many town centres, clusters of restaurants offer a 'dish of the day' at roughly the same price. The meal is likely to be quite generic (such as fish and chips or chicken tikka masala) and prices for one restaurant will be established by reference to what other restaurants are charging. Restaurants may take a 'going price' from the market and design their meal offering around this price. Just what can they offer for the going rate of £6.00? Although the price of standard set menus may be very strongly determined by competitors' prices, each restaurant may nevertheless offer more specialized meals for which it faces less direct competition and therefore has greater discretion in setting its prices. Differentiation as a means of avoiding direct price competition is discussed later in this chapter.

THINKING AROUND THE SUBJECT:
PENNY WISE OR POUND FOOLISH?

One of the assumptions of a competitive market is that buyers have a good awareness of prices within the market. But survey after survey has shown consumers in fact typically have a very distorted knowledge of prices, reflecting individuals' own experiences and background. For example, a survey carried out in 2005 by ICM Research asked young people to estimate the price of a range of goods and services. Two-thirds knew how much a 6GB Apple iPod Mini should cost, within just a few pounds of the actual price charged by most retailers (£179). However, three-quarters of the people interviewed had no idea about the price of a pint of milk. An earlier survey by the telephone company BT had found knowledge of telephone prices to be particularly bad, probably reflecting the plethora of price plans which have emerged in recent years. Respondents gave the average price of a five-minute peak national call as £2.15, whereas in fact it was only 44p. Another sector with confusing price structures is railways. Here, respondents estimated the price of a second-class 'Saver' ticket from London to Edinburgh at £54, compared to the actual price of £64.

Supermarkets have long known that consumers are typically able to compare prices on a range of regularly purchased staple items, such as baked beans, potatoes and bread, so price cutting has often been focused on these items. Meanwhile, they are likely to be less knowledgeable about infrequently purchased items, and supermarkets may be tempted to let prices of these rise, in the knowledge that consumers would have little idea about whether the price was a good one or not. Of course, there are lots of other ways in which businesses may deliberately or inadvertently make prices difficult for consumers to understand, as witnessed by the complexity of pricing for gas and electricity supply. This reminds us again that it may be fine in theory to talk about competitive markets, but in practice, without consumers' knowledge of prices available in a market, a market cannot work efficiently.

10.2.4 Elasticity of demand

Elasticity of demand refers to the extent to which demand changes in relation to a change in price or some other variable such as income. What is important here is to compare the proportionate (or percentage) change in demand with the proportionate (or percentage) change in the other variable, over any given period of time.

The most commonly used measure of elasticity of demand is price elasticity of demand. Information on this is useful to business organizations to allow them to predict what will happen to the volume of sales in response to a change in price. This section is concerned with the responsiveness of a whole market to changes in price. It will be recalled that in a perfectly competitive market, firms must take their selling price from the market, so the only elasticity that is of interest to them is the elasticity of the market as a whole.

Price elasticity of demand refers to the ratio of the percentage change in demand to the percentage change in price. In other words, it seeks to measure how the sales of a product respond to a change in its price. This can be expressed as a simple formula:

$$\text{Price elasticity of demand} = \frac{\text{change in demand (\%)}}{\text{change in price (\%)}}$$

Where demand is relatively unresponsive to price changes, it is said to be inelastic with respect to price. Where demand is highly responsive to even a small price charge, demand is described as being elastic with respect to price.

Two demand curves are shown in Figure 10.10. D1 is more elastic than D2, as indicated by the greater effect on volume of a change in price, compared with the effects of a similar price change with D2.

A number of factors influence the price elasticity of demand for a particular product. The most important is the availability of substitutes. Where these are readily available, buyers are likely to switch between alternative products in response to price changes. The absolute value of a product and its importance to a buyer can also influence its elasticity. For example, if infrequently purchased boxes of matches increased in price by 10 per cent from 10p to 11p, buyers would probably not cut back on their purchases. However, if the price of television sets increased by the same percentage amount from £300 to £330, many buyers may pull out of the market.

For any measure of elasticity, it is important to consider the time period over which it is being measured. In general, products are much more inelastic to changes in price over the short term, when possibilities for substitution may be few. However, over the longer term, new possibilities for substitution may appear. This explains why petrol is very inelastic over the short term but much more so over the long term. Faced with a sudden increase in petrol prices (as happened following the Gulf War), motorists have little choice other than paying the increased price. However, over the longer term, they can reduce their purchases of petrol by buying more fuel-efficient cars, rearranging their pattern of life so that they do not need to travel as much, or by sharing cars.

Further measures of elasticity of demand can be made by considering the responsiveness of

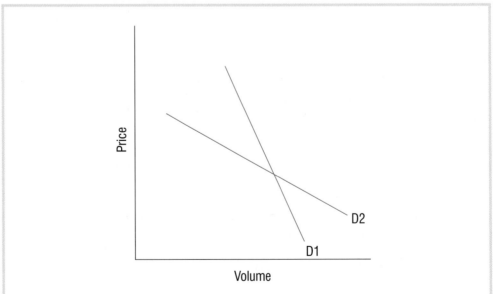

Figure 10.10 A comparison of a relatively elastic demand function (D1) with a relatively inelastic one (D2)

demand to changes in the assumptions on which the demand curve is based. The most important of these is income elasticity of demand, which measures the responsiveness of demand to changes in buyers' combined incomes and can be expressed in the following way:

$$\text{Income elasticity of demand} = \frac{\text{change in demand (\%)}}{\text{change in income (\%)}}$$

In general, as a population's income rises, the demand for particular products rises, giving rise to a positive income elasticity of demand. Where there is a particularly strong increase in demand in response to an increase in incomes (or vice versa), a product can be said to have a high income elasticity of demand. This is true of luxuries such as long-haul air holidays and fitted kitchens, whose sales have increased during times of general economic prosperity, but declined during recessionary periods. On the other hand, there are some goods and services whose demand goes down as incomes increase. These are referred to as inferior goods; examples in most Western countries include local bus services and household coal.

It is useful for business organizations to understand income elasticity of demand in order to plan a response to anticipated changes in aggregate income. If, for example, a general rise in consumer income looks likely to reduce the sales of a product that has a negative income elasticity, a business may seek to shift its resources to making products with a positive income elasticity. In trying to plan for the future, businesses rely on their own historical information about sales/income relationships, and also government and private forecasts about current and future levels and distribution of income.

A third measure of demand elasticity to note is a product's cross-price elasticity of demand. This refers to the percentage change in demand for product A when the price of product B changes. Where products are very close substitutes, this may be a very important measure to understand consumer demand. For example, the price of butter can have a significant effect on demand for margarine.

It is possible to identify numerous other ad hoc measures of elasticity of demand. Firms may be interested in the responsiveness of demand to changes in some measure of the quality of their product. For example, a railway operator may be interested in the effects on demand of improvements in service reliability or a bus operator may be interested in establishing the percentage increase in passenger demand resulting from a given percentage increase in frequency of a bus route.

10.2.5 Elasticity of supply

The concept of elasticity can also be applied to supply, so as to measure the responsiveness of supply to changes in price. Elasticity of supply is measured by the formula:

$$\text{Elasticity of supply} = \frac{\text{change in supply (\%)}}{\text{change in price (\%)}}$$

If suppliers are relatively unresponsive to an increase in the price of a product, the product is described as being inelastic with respect to price. If producers increase production substantially as prices rise, the product is said to be elastic.

In theory, high market prices act as a signal for companies to enter that market, or to increase the volume they supply to it. But in practice, there can be lengthy delays before firms are able to respond to these market signals, and the market for organic vegetables during the late 1990s illustrates this point. A combination of rising incomes, greater awareness of health issues and a string of food safety scares had led to rapid growth in demand for organic produce throughout Europe. But how can farmers grow organically on land which has been saturated by decades of artificial fertilizer use? The Soil Association, which operates a widely recognized accreditation scheme for organic produce, required that farmland should be free of artificial fertilizer for at least five years before any crops grown on it could be described as organic. So despite the rapid growth in demand and the price premiums that customers were prepared to pay, retailers found it difficult to satisfy demand. Furthermore, with a difficult and intermittent supply, could retailers risk their brand name by being seen as an unreliable supplier of second-rate produce? Marks & Spencer launched a range of organic vegetables in 1997, only to withdraw them soon afterwards, blaming the difficulty in obtaining regular and reliable supplies. However, by 2004, producers that had earlier taken their signals from the market and prepared themselves for organic production were finally able to increase the volume supplied to the market. But with a sharp increase in supply relative to demand, the price premiums available for organic produce fell.

As with price elasticity of demand, time is crucial in determining the elasticity of supply. Over the short term, it may be very difficult for firms to increase supply, making it very inelastic with respect to price. In the case of markets for agricultural products, elasticity is determined by the growing cycle and new supply may only be forthcoming in time for the next season. For many manufacturing processes, supplies can eventually be increased by investing in new productive capacity and taking on additional workers. Over the longer term, supply is more elastic.

10.2.6 Limitations of the theory of perfect competition

Although government policy makers often view perfectly competitive markets as an ideal to aim towards, the automatic balancing of supply and demand at an equilibrium price, as described above, is seldom achieved in practice. The following are some of the more important reasons why perfect competition is rarely achieved in practice.

- Where economies of scale are achievable in an industry sector, it is always possible for firms to grow larger and become more efficient, and thereby able to exercise undue influence in a market. In general, perfect competition applies only where production techniques are simple and opportunities for economies of scale few.
- Markets are often dominated by large buyers that are able to exercise influence over the market. The domestic market for many specialized defence products may be competitive in terms of a large number of suppliers, but demand for their products is dominated by one government buying agency.

- It can be naïve to assume that high prices and profits in a sector will attract new entrants, while losses will cause the least efficient to leave. In practice, there may be a whole range of barriers to entry which could cover the need to obtain licences for production, the availability of trained staff and access to distribution outlets. Also, there are sometimes barriers to exit where firms are locked into long-term supply contracts or where it would be very expensive to lay off resources such as labour.
- A presumption of perfectly competitive markets is that buyers and sellers have complete information about market conditions. In fact, this is often far from the truth. On the simple point of making price comparisons, much research has been undertaken to show that buyers often have little knowledge of the going rate for a particular category of product. For example, the use of bar code scanning equipment by retailers has resulted in many products no longer carrying a price label, weakening customers' retained knowledge of prices. Sometimes, as in the case of telephone call tariffs or credit card interest charges, prices are very difficult to comprehend.

In Chapter 13 we will look at dynamic models of competitive market forces. In this respect, Michael Porter identified five forces which contribute to competition within a market: the power of suppliers, the power of buyers, the threat of new entrants, the threat of substitute products and the intensity of rivalry between competing firms. It should be stressed again that so far in this chapter we have merely looked at the basic building blocks by which we begin to understand competition within markets.

10.3 MONOPOLISTIC MARKETS

At the opposite end of the scale to perfect competition lies pure monopoly. In its purest extreme, monopoly in a market occurs where there is only one supplier to the market, perhaps because of regulatory, technical or economic barriers to entry which potential competing suppliers would face. Literally speaking, a monopoly means that one person or organization has complete control over the resources of a market. However, this rarely occurs in practice. Even in the former centrally planned economies of Eastern Europe, there have often been active 'shadow' markets which have existed alongside official monopoly suppliers. Sometimes, monopoly control over supply comes about through a group of suppliers acting in collusion to form a 'cartel'. As with the pure monopoly, companies would join a cartel in order to try to protect themselves from the harsh consequences (for suppliers) of competition. Probably the best example of a cartel is OPEC (Organization of Petroleum Exporting Countries) which during the 1970s and 1980s had significant monopoly power over world oil price and output decisions.

Government definition of a monopoly is less rigorous than pure economic definitions. In the United Kingdom, two types of monopoly can occur:

1 a scale monopoly occurs where one firm controls 25 per cent of the value of a market
2 a complex monopoly occurs where a number of firms in a market together account for over 25 cent of the value of the market and their actions have the effect of limiting competition.

It can, however, be difficult to define just what is meant by 'the market'. While in Britain there may be just a few companies that between them have a near monopoly in the supply of bananas, when looked at in the context of the fruit market more generally, monopoly power

THINKING AROUND THE SUBJECT:
EFFECTS OF INCREASED GOVERNMENT REGULATION

Many industry sectors have complained of the burden of increased government regulation. Consider the following recent examples.

- **EU Directive on Traditional Herbal Medicinal Products:** The directive requires traditional, over-the-counter herbal remedies to be made to assured standards of safety and quality. Some small-scale producers have not been able to justify the elaborate testing that the directive would require, and have ceased production.
- **Financial Services and Markets Act 2000:** Required all businesses selling insurance to be registered with the Financial Services Authority and to meet its criteria from January 2005. Some small travel agents, which previously sold travel insurance as an ancilliary part of a holiday, decided that the cost of compliance was too great and withdrew from selling insurance.
- **Housing Act 1996:** Introduced a discretionary local authority licensing scheme for houses in multiple occupation. To obtain a licence, landlords would need to satisfy a number of standards, for example in relation to fire exits. Some landlords decided that the cost of improvements to their property could not be justified by the likely returns on their investment.
- **Disability Discrimination Act Part III – Access to Goods and Services:** From 2004, companies were required to take 'reasonable measures' to ensure equality of access to a company's goods and services for disabled people. Some organizations are reported to have closed facilities to the public rather than spend money in upgrading them.

The effects of these regulations can be asseseed using supply–demand analysis. Each of these regulations may have the effect of increasing producers' costs – some producers more than others. This can be shown as an upward shift in the supply curve. How much of the increase in cost will be passed on to customers? This will depend on the elasticity of demand for the product in question. A highly elastic demand curve may result in customers buying substitute products instead – for example, buying mainstream medicines rather than herbal medicines. If the regulation applies to the whole sector, firms are likely to differ in their ability to absorb additional costs, with smaller companies often hit harder than larger ones which can spread higher fixed costs over a higher volume of output. The least efficient producers may be forced out of the market because the market price for their product is now below their cost of production.

Try showing the effects of each of the regulations described above on a supply–demand graph and observe what is likely to happen to the equilbrium price.

diminishes. Also, is it most appropriate to confine attention to the UK market or to include overseas markets in a definition of monopoly? A firm may have a dominant market position at home, but may face severe competition in its overseas markets. In fact, the European Union now takes a Europe-wide perspective for assessing monopoly power for many products which can only sensibly be marketed Europe-wide. Therefore, although BAe Systems (formerly British Aerospace) has a dominant position in a number of its UK markets, when seen in a European context, it does in fact face severe competitive pressure.

10.3.1 Effects on prices and output of monopoly

A monopolist can determine the market price for its product and can be described as a 'price maker' rather than a 'price taker'. Where there are few substitutes for a product and where demand is inelastic, a monopolist may be able to get away with continually increasing prices in order to increase its profits.

In a pure monopoly market, consumers would face prices that are higher than would have occurred in a perfectly competitive market. Furthermore, because prices are higher, a downward sloping demand curve would indicate that output would be lower than in a competitive market. It is therefore commonly held that monopolies are against the public interest by leading to higher prices and lower output. Although there are occasionally circumstances where monopoly yields greater public benefit than free competition (discussed later in this chapter), the general policy of governments towards monopolies has been to restrict their power.

10.3.2 Implications of monopoly power for a firm's marketing activities

In a pure monopoly, a firm's output decisions would be influenced by the elasticity of demand for its products. So long as demand is inelastic, it could continue raising prices and thereby its total revenue. While a firm may have monopoly power over some of its users, it may face competition if it wishes to attract new segments of users. It may therefore resort to differential pricing when targeting the two groups. As an example, train-operating companies have considerable monopoly power over commuters that need to use their trains to arrive at work in central London by 9.00 a.m. on weekdays. For such commuters, the alternatives of travelling to work by bus or car are very unattractive. However, leisure travellers wishing to go shopping in London at off-peak times may be much more price sensitive. Their journey is optional to begin with and their flexibility with respect to their time of travel is greater. For them, the car or bus provides a realistic alternative. As a result, train operators offer a range of price incentives aimed at off-peak leisure markets, while charging full fare for its peak period commuters.

Organizations that think strategically will be reluctant to fully exploit their monopoly power. By charging high prices in the short term, a monopolist could give signals to companies in related product fields to develop substitutes that would eventually provide effective competition. Blatant abuse of monopoly power could also result in a referral to the regulatory authorities (see below).

10.4 IMPERFECT COMPETITION

Perfectly competitive markets may be ideal for consumers because they have a tendency to minimize prices and maximize outputs. However, lower prices are not attractive to suppliers because, for any given level of output, lower prices mean lower revenue and therefore lower profit. It is not surprising therefore that firms seek to limit the workings of perfectly competitive markets – this section looks at imperfect competition. It could be argued that most firms would like to be in the position of a monopolist and able to control the price level and output of their market. This is an unrealistic aim for most firms, but, in practice, firms can create imperfections in markets that give them limited monopoly power over their customers.

One of the assumptions of perfect competition is that products offered in a particular market are identical. An entrepreneur can seek to avoid head-on competition with its

THINKING AROUND THE SUBJECT:
COMPETITION CUTS THE COST OF CALLING

As recently as the mid-1990s most people regarded a mobile phone as something expensive, to be used sparingly. Since then, the cost of using a mobile phone has been falling. This can partly be explained by improving technology which has allowed handsets to be made for a fraction of the cost of two decades ago, and the tumbling costs of providing network capacity through fibre-optic and microwave links. But in addition to the technological drivers of price cuts, competition has played a very big part.

A report published in 2004 by the Organization of Economic Co-operation and Development (OECD) examined the effects of market structure on prices charged to users of mobile phones in OECD member states. Its statistics revealed a strong link between competition and prices. Countries with the cheapest phone services tended to have a larger number of operators. Those at the expensive end of the table had just two or three operators. The cheapest country in which to own a mobile phone was Denmark, where a typical total annual cost was £130. The most expensive was Poland, at £520, with Britain at £310, sitting at number 22 in a league table of 29 countries. It appeared to be no coincidence that Denmark had a fiercely competitive market, with a number of 'virtual' networks competing for custom, while Poland still had a very regulated market which was dominated by the previous government telephone monopoly.

Within Britain, the appearance of additional entrants has often been accompanied by renewed competitive pressures. When the Hong Kong company Hutchison Whampoa launched its '3' network in 2003, it precipitated ferocious price-cutting as it sought to build its market share from a customer base of zero. A decade earlier, the launch of Orange and One-to-One (now T-mobile) had brought price pressure on the then duopoly of BT Cellnet and Vodafone.

Even with apparently high levels of competition, there is still a role for government regulation. In June 2004, the UK regulator Ofcom ordered mobile phone networks to reduce the cost of incoming calls to mobiles, and the cost of making calls to rival operators. It seemed that a competitive market existed in the price of handsets and the per minute cost of dialling out from a mobile phone, which were commonly used by customers to evaluate one phone network against another. However, very few people evaluated the cost of making a call to somebody else and the mobile phone companies were in no hurry to cut incoming call costs.

The OECD report suggested that the price of using a mobile phone in Britain had delayed the move from fixed lines to mobile phones for voice calls. It estimated that by 2007, over half of all voice calls worldwide would be made using mobile phones. However, the higher costs of using a mobile in Britain relative to land lines would mean this point would not be reached in Britain until 2009.

Despite falling costs and an apparently competitive market, many observers of the UK mobile phone market have suspected an oligopoly in which none of the established operators wanted to 'rock the boat' and destabilize prices. With just five networks, is this sufficient to ensure competition?

competitors by trying to sell something that is just a little bit different compared to its competitors. Therefore, in a market for fresh vegetables, a vegetable trader may try to get away from the fiercely competitive market for generic fresh vegetables, for which the price is determined by the market, by slightly differentiating its product. The following are some possible differentiation strategies in respect of the sale of potatoes that it could pursue.

- The trader might concentrate on selling specially selected potatoes, for example ones that are particularly suited to baking.
- A delivery service might be provided for customers.
- The potatoes could be packed in materials that prevent them being bruised.
- The trader might offer a no-quibble money-back guarantee for people who buy potatoes that turn out to be bad.
- The potatoes could be baked and offered with a range of fillings.
- The potatoes might be processed into tinned or dried potatoes.
- As a result of any of the above actions, the trader could develop a distinct brand identity for the potatoes, so that buyers do not ask just for potatoes but for 'Brand X' potatoes by name.

In the example above, the trader has taken steps to turn a basic commodity product into something that is quite distinctive, so it has immediately cut down the number of direct competitors that it faces. In fact, if its product really was unique, it would have no direct competition; in other words, it would be a monopoly supplier of a unique product. However, it must not be forgotten that although the way the trader has presented the potatoes may be unique, they are still broadly similar to the potatoes that everybody else is selling. The trader therefore still faces indirect competition, including competition from other foods such as rice and pasta which provide a substitute for potatoes.

If a trader has successfully differentiated its product, it is no longer strictly a price taker from the market. It may be able to charge 10p a kilo more than the going rate for its selected and packaged potatoes if customers think that the higher price is good value for a better product. It will be able to experiment to see just how much more buyers are prepared to pay for its differentiated product.

THINKING AROUND THE SUBJECT:
A TAXI, BUT ONLY IF IT'S BLACK

How do people choose a taxi? In London, the famous black cabs are highly regulated in terms of the standards of drivers, the vehicles themselves and prices charged. Drivers must pass a 'knowledge' test before being allowed to operate and cannot refuse to carry a passenger, except in clearly specified situations. Few people would bother spending much effort in selecting one cab from another – they have been reduced to a commodity whose consistent standards and fares are rigorously maintained by the licensing body, the Public Carriage Office.

Contrast this with the situation in towns where regulations are minimal and buyers may have little idea about the integrity of the car that they are getting into or the reliability of its driver. This is the classic opportunity for the development of brands which help to differentiate one company's taxis from another's and simplify the buyer's choice process. It is open to individual operators to develop a brand which is associated with reliability, safety and courteousness. Often, operators are allowed to set their own prices to reflect the strength of their brand. Next time a customer seeks a taxi, they may know which taxi companies to avoid and which to go for out of preference.

Debate has taken place between those who would like to see a free market in taxis and those who see regulation as vital to the public interest. What is the experience in your area? Of what value are brands in guiding the choices of taxi users?

10.4.1 The role of brands

The process of branding is at the heart of organizations' efforts to remove themselves from fierce competition between generic products. Summarizing previous research, Doyle (1989) described brand building as the only way for a firm to build a stable, long-term demand at profitable margins (see Figure 10.11). Through adding value that will attract customers, firms are able to provide a base for expansion and product development and to protect themselves against the strength of intermediaries and competitors. There has been much evidence linking high levels of advertising expenditure to support strong brands with high returns on capital and high market share.

Branding simplifies the decision-making process by providing buyers with a sense of security and consistency which distinguishes a brand from a generic commodity. There have been many conceptualizations of the unique positioning attributes of a brand. These usually distinguish between tangible dimensions that can be objectively measured (such as taste, shape, reliability) and the subjective values that can be defined only in the minds of consumers (such as the perceived personality of a brand). With increasing affluence, the non-functional expectations of brands have assumed increasing importance. A number of dimensions of a brand's emotional appeal have been identified, including trust, liking and sophistication, and it has been shown that products with a high level of subjective emotional appeal are associated with a high level of customer involvement (Laurent and Kapferer 1985). This has been demonstrated, for example, in the preference shown for branded beer compared to a functionally identical generic beer. As consumers buy products, they learn to appreciate their added value and begin to form a relationship with them. For example, there are many companies selling petrol and credit cards, but individual companies such as Shell and American Express have created brands with which customers develop a relationship and guide their choice in a market dominated by otherwise generic products.

Figure 10.11 Toblerone has removed itself from the fierce competition for chocolate by developing a distinctive brand. By developing a unique identity and maintaining high quality standards, the brand commands a premium price among those chocolate buyers who value its distinctive attributes.

The traditional role of branding has been to differentiate products, but brands have been increasingly applied to organizational images too. This has occurred particularly with services where the intangibility of the product causes the credentials of the provider to be an important choice criterion.

In recent years there has been a growth in the number of 'own label' or 'private label' products sold by retailers. The suggestion that the growth of generic products is challenging traditional product branding strategy can partly be explained by a shift in buyers' brand allegiance, away from those of manufacturers and towards those of intermediaries. Through continued investment, retailers have developed products that have comparable functional qualities to manufacturers' branded products. In many cases, retailers' own-label products have developed a sufficiently strong brand reputation that they can command a price premium over other manufacturers' branded products.

Many have argued that both the functional and emotional dimensions of brands have been facing growing challenges. Research has suggested that consumers are becoming increasingly critical of the messages of brand-building advertisements, especially those aimed at creating abstract brand personalities. It is also claimed that consumers are becoming increasingly confident, ready to experiment and to trust their own judgement, and less tolerant of products that do not contribute to their own values. The functional qualities of brands have come under pressure from increasing levels of consumer legislation. Characteristics such as purity, reliability and durability may have traditionally added value to a brand, but these are increasingly enshrined in legislation and therefore less capable of being used to differentiate one product from another. However, any casual search through a shop selling 'lifestyle' goods, such as sports clothing, will reveal the continuing emotional appeal of strong brands.

10.4.2 Imperfect competition and elasticity of demand

The analysis of price decisions for firms in a competitive market indicated that, for any one firm, price is given by the market. An individual firm cannot increase profits by stimulating demand through lower prices, nor would it gain any benefit by seeking to raise its prices. This changes in an imperfectly competitive market where a firm acquires a degree of monopoly power over its customers. Each firm now has a demand curve for its own unique product.

Firms face a downward-sloping demand curve for each of their products, indicating that, as prices fall, demand increases and vice versa. In fact, a number of demand curves describing a firm's market can be described, ranging from the general to the specific brand. For example, in the market for breakfast cereals, the demand curve for cereals in general may be fairly inelastic, on the basis that people will always want to buy breakfast cereals of some description (Figure 10.12). Demand for one particular type of cereal, such as corn flakes, will be slightly more elastic as people may be attracted to corn flakes from other cereals such as porridge oats on the basis of their relative price. Price becomes more elastic still when a particular brand of cereals is considered. To some people, Kellogg's corn flakes can easily be substituted with other brands of corn flakes, so if a price differential between brands developed, switching may occur. By lowering its price, a firm may be able to increase its sales, but what is important to firms is that they increase their total revenue (and, thereby, profits). Whether this happens depends upon the elasticity of demand for the product in question.

THINKING AROUND THE SUBJECT:
MARKETING OR MARKETS?

Is marketing a natural ally of free markets, or is it really an enemy? To many people, marketing is all about bringing together customers who want to buy with sellers who want to sell. By carefully studying what buyers want to buy, marketers contribute towards the efficient operation of a market. Advocates of marketing would contrast the benefits of having marketers controlled by market disciplines with the inefficiency of having a central bureaucracy making resource allocation decisions.

However, marketers are not always so benign in their thoughts about markets. While most marketers would publicly endorse the power of free markets, many of their activities, consciously or unconsciously, undermine the spirit of free markets. Consider three of the defining characteristics of competitive markets which were discussed above: a homogeneous product; freely available information; and freedom of entry to and exit from the market. Now consider some common marketing strategies.

The idea of all companies selling a homogeneous product is anathema to one of the basic philosophies of marketing which is to add value to products through differentiation. This chapter has discussed ways in which companies use branding to try to differentiate their product from those of the competitors. Faced with shelves of slightly differentiated bottled water carrying different brand names, can this be said to be a market in a homogeneous product? Is there any meaningful difference between many of the brands?

Information available in a market is often difficult to assimilate, and some people have accused marketers of making their information even more difficult to understand. Try comparing mobile phone calling plans, or different tariffs offered by gas and electricity companies, and you could come to the conclusion that the companies' information may be freely available to all, but extremely complicated. Some would accuse marketers of engaging in 'confusion marketing' to try to make informed comparisons more difficult.

Marketers often do their best to reduce the ease of entry to or exit from a market. One consequence of the recent trend towards 'relationship marketing' has been to try to tie customers to the company through a long-term contract. Customers of mobile phone companies cannot easily leave their existing supplier if they are committed to a 12-month contract. Many manufacturers have sought exclusivity contracts with retailers which makes it difficult for new competitors to enter the market.

Karl Marx once observed that capitalism was essentially all about *reducing* risk rather than *taking* risk. Could marketing be more about trying to undermine the value of markets rather than trying to make them work more efficiently?

Total revenue is a function of total sales multiplied by the selling price per unit. Figure 10.13 summarizes the effects on total revenue of changes in price, given alternative assumptions about elasticity.

10.4.3 Oligopoly

One step on from imperfect competition is a market structure often referred to as an oligopoly. It lies somewhere between imperfect competition and pure monopoly. An oligopoly market is one that is dominated by a small number of sellers that provide a large share of the

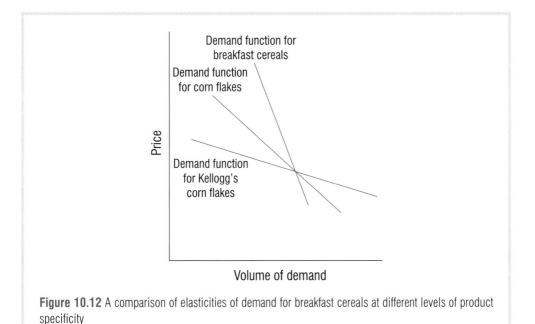

Figure 10.12 A comparison of elasticities of demand for breakfast cereals at different levels of product specificity

Price elasticity of demand	Price change	Revenue effect
High (elastic demand)	+	−
	−	+
Low (inelastic demand)	+	+
	−	−

Figure 10.13 Effects of elasticity of demand and price changes on total revenue

total market output. The crucial point about oligopoly markets is that all suppliers in the market are interdependent. One company cannot take price or output decisions without considering the specific possible responses of other companies.

An oligopoly is a particularly important market structure in industries where economies of scale are significant. They are typical of oil refining and distribution, pharmaceuticals, car manufacturing and detergents. Customers of oligopoly organizations may not immediately appreciate that the products they are buying come from an oligopolist as such firms often operate with a variety of brand names (the detergent manufacturers Unilever and Procter & Gamble between them have over 50 apparently competing detergent products on sale in the United Kingdom).

Oligopolists generally understand their relationship to one another and there is often a reluctance to 'rock the boat' by upsetting the established order. One firm is often acknowledged as the price leader and firms wait for their actions before adjusting their prices. In the UK car market, it has often been suggested that other manufacturers wait for Ford to adjust their prices before making their own price decisions. It has been suggested that firms may not match upward price movements, in the hope of gaining extra sales, but they would match downward price changes for fear of losing market share. Price wars between oligopolists can be very expensive to participants, so there is a tendency to find alternative ways to compete for customers, such as free gifts, coupons, added value offers and sponsorship activities.

Oligopolists have often been accused of collusion and creating barriers to entry for newcomers (such as signing exclusive distribution rights with key retailers). It has therefore been suggested that an oligopoly market structure is against the public interest. Against this argument, the public interest may benefit from economies of scale which allows products to be made at a lower unit cost than would be achievable by smaller-scale companies. Furthermore, while oligopolists may have a cosy market in their home country, they may face severe competition as an outsider in overseas markets. The benefits of scale in their domestic market can give them the resources and low unit costs with which to tackle an overseas market, thereby helping a country's balance of trade and creating additional employment.

At a local level, it has frequently been suspected that groups of building contractors, school bus contractors, solicitors and estate agents covertly agree not to 'rock the boat' by agreeing to conform to guidelines for pricing and tendering. The existence of trade and professional associations may provide a legitimate cover for such relationships and understandings to develop. In societies where business life is closely intermingled with social standing, the temptation to conform may be strengthened, and studies of Eastern trading systems have highlighted this influence (Fock and Woo 1998; Tsang 1998). Some evidence of this can be seen in the extensive network of co-operative *keiretsu* and relationships among Japanese distributors that has led selling prices to consumers to be higher than in comparable overseas markets.

10.5 COMPETITION POLICY

The vision of competitive markets that bring maximum benefit to consumers is often not achieved. The imperfections described above can be summarized as resulting from:

- the presence of large firms that are able to exert undue influence over participants in a market, for example through scale economies
- collusion between sellers (and sometimes buyers) which has the effect of restricting price competition and the availability of products
- barriers to market entry and restraints on trade which may prevent a company moving into a market (e.g. a manufacturer may prevent a retailer from selling competing manufacturers' products)
- rigidity in resource input markets which prevent supply moving to markets of strong demand (e.g. labour inflexibility may prevent a company from exploiting markets that have high levels of profitability).

Because of the presumed superiority of competitive markets, the law of most developed countries has been used to try to remove market imperfections where these are deemed to be against the public interest. This section initially considers the common law of England as a method by which anti-competitive practices have been curbed. More significantly, a growing body of legislation based on statute law is now available to governments and organizations seeking to curb anti-competitive practices.

10.5.1 Common law approaches to improving market competitiveness

Common law evolves over time on the basis of case judgments which set a precedent for subsequent cases to follow (see Chapter 5). In the UK, there is case law that holds that agreements between parties that have the effect of restraining free trade are unlawful. Sometimes, it may appear to be sensible for a business person to make a contract with another company by which he or she agrees to limit the parties with whom they can trade in the future. In return for an exclusivity clause, the business person may receive preferential treatment from the other party. Such agreements have often been referred to as 'solus agreements' and have been frequently used, for example, in contracts between oil companies and petrol station owners. Such an agreement normally contains a tying covenant by which the station owner agrees, in return for a rebate on the price, to sell only the supplier's brand of petrol, a compulsory trading covenant that obliges the garage owner to keep the garage open at reasonable hours and a continuity covenant that requires him or her, if the business is sold, to obtain the acceptance of the agreement by the purchaser. In one important case, a garage owner had two garages and a solus agreement in respect of each, one for $4\frac{1}{2}$ years and the other for 21 years. The garage owner felt that the actions of the oil company were threatening its profits and sought to obtain its petrol from a cheaper source, in defiance of his agreement. The case came before the House of Lords, which held that the essence of the solus agreements was to unreasonably restrict the garage proprietor's freedom of trading.

It is important to note the word 'reasonable'. In deciding whether the agreement between the oil company and petrol station owner was reasonable and therefore valid, the Law Lords stressed the importance of taking into account the public interest and held the $4\frac{1}{2}$-year agreement reasonable but the 21-year agreement too long and therefore unreasonable and invalid. The petrol station owner was therefore free to buy his fuel from another source, regardless of the agreement.

The 'public interest' is important in deciding whether a restrictive agreement is reasonable or not. The courts may feel that by tying a company to a supplier for 21 years, effective competition in a market is reduced, thereby resulting in higher prices for everybody.

While the case of the petrol station dated from the 1960s, more recent examples have been reported of firms seeking to rely on the common law to break free from a restrictive agreement. In the United Kingdom, tenants of pubs owned by breweries and pub companies often sign agreements that prevent them buying much of their beer or soft drinks from third parties, in return for which the landlord may provide support for the tenant. A number of tenants have approached the courts to have clauses restricting their rights to make third-party purchases of beer set aside, on the grounds that they have the effect of unreasonably restricting trade. To independent brewers seeking new outlets for their beer, it is important that such restraints on trade are removed to allow them access to the market.

A claim of restraint of trade can also be made against a company buying a business that restricts the future business activity of the person from whom they have bought the business. An individual who has set up a successful business may often be tempted by a takeover bid from another company. The acquiring company may be keen to grow so that it can achieve economies of scale, or it may simply want access to the target company's customers. Whatever the reason for the takeover, the acquiring company will often seek a clause restricting the seller of the business from going straight back into the marketplace and setting up another business which is in competition with the one that it has just sold. The owners of such businesses are usually required to agree to a clause that limits their rights to set up another estate agency business in competition with that of the acquiring company. Again, any clause has to be 'reasonable'. A clause prohibiting the seller of an estate agency business from setting up a new estate agency within a 25-mile radius of its base for a period of three years from the date of sale would almost certainly be considered reasonable. A clause prohibiting the seller from entering into any form of business anywhere in the country within 10 years would almost certainly be deemed to be unreasonable. If a clause in an agreement is deemed by a court to be unreasonable, it may remove it from the contract. It can, however, be difficult to know what a court will consider to be 'reasonable' in the circumstances of a particular case.

10.5.2 Statutory intervention to create competitive markets

Common law has proved inadequate on its own to preserve the competitiveness of complex, well-developed markets. Common law has therefore been supplemented by statutory legislation – that is, laws passed by government as an act of policy. One outcome of statutory intervention has been the creation of a regulatory infrastructure, which in the United Kingdom includes the Office of Fair Trading, the Competition Commission and regulatory bodies to control specific industries. However, much of the current regulatory framework in the UK is based on the requirements of Articles 85 and 86 of the Treaty of Rome.

10.5.3 Articles 85 and 86 of the Treaty of Rome

Article 85 of the Treaty of Rome prohibits agreements between organizations and arrangements between organizations that affect trade between member states of the European Union and in general prohibits anti-competitive practices, such as price fixing, market sharing and limitations on production. However, Article 85(3) provides for exemptions where restrictions on competition may be deemed to be in the public interest.

Article 86 prohibits the abuse of a dominant market position within the European Union in so far as it may affect trade between member states; the fact that a business has a monopoly position is not in itself prohibited.

The European Commission – which oversees the implementation of Articles 85 and 86 – can prohibit mergers where the combined turnover exceeds €200 million or where the company will have over 25 per cent of a national market and the merger will have an adverse effect on competition.

The European Commission is playing an increasingly important role in the policing of competition. As an example, the EU Commission's competition directorate conducted a five-year investigation into the close relationships between the Coca-Cola Company and its European intermediaries. The Commission held that many of the company's practices were harmful to consumers. These practices included: exclusivity clauses restricting the company's intermediaries from selling competitors' products; the right of first refusal clauses; and preferential shelf-space allocation clauses. The Commission accepted an offer from the company to desist from certain anti-competitive practices in the EU's €17 billion ($21 billion) carbonated drinks market (*International Law Update* 2004).

The requirement contained in Articles 85 and 86 of the Treaty of Rome that competition shall not be distorted implies the existence in the market of *workable competition*. This can be interpreted as the degree of competition necessary to ensure the observance of the basic requirements and attainment of the objectives of the Treaty, in particular the creation of a single market achieving conditions similar to those of a domestic market. Workable competition reflects an economic pragmatism. *Perfect* competition where producers respond instantly and inevitably to consumer demand and where the efficient allocation of resources is ensured, is in practice an illusion. *Workable* competition is concerned to achieve the most efficient resource allocation available given the constraints of a modern economy where consumer choice cannot be perfectly expressed (Weatherill 1996).

The EU often has difficulty in reconciling the need for a firm to operate globally at a large scale, and the resultant domination of the EU market by that firm. Proposed mergers between European airlines (e.g. the merger between Air France and the Dutch airline KLM) have raised the issue of whether it was justifiable to sacrifice competition on a small number of domestic routes in order to give an enlarged, efficient carrier a chance of taking on American carriers that were already operating at a large scale.

10.5.4 UK competition legislation

Domestic legislation is used to control anti-competitive practices where their effects are confined within national boundaries. In the UK, the 1998 Competition Act reformed and strengthened competition law by prohibiting anti-competitive behaviour. The Act introduced two basic prohibitions: a prohibition of anti-competitive agreements, based closely on Article 85 of the EC Treaty; and a prohibition of abuse of a dominant position in a market, based closely on Article 86 of the EC Treaty. The Act prohibits agreements which have the aim or effect of preventing, restricting or distorting competition in the UK. Since anti-competitive behaviour between companies may occur without a clearly delineated agreement, the prohibition covers not only agreements by associations of companies, but also covert practices. The Enterprise Act 2002 strengthened the Competition Act by including provision for a new Competition Appeal Tribunal (CAT) and its supporting body the Competition Service. The Act introduced criminal sanctions with a maximum penalty of five years in prison for companies that operate agreements to fix prices, share markets, limit production and rig bids. The voice of consumers was strengthened with designated consumer bodies able to make 'super-complaints' to the Office of Fair Trading.

In addition, a number of organizations are active in either using legislation to protect the competitiveness of markets (such as public utility regulators), or by drawing attention to abuses in monopoly power. At a local level, Trading Standards Departments have powers to prosecute companies using misleading prices, among other things. Consumer champions that can draw attention to anti-competitive practices include Citizens Advice Bureaux, Ombudsmen and the media (discussed in more detail in Chapter 5).

The Competition Commission has no power to initiate its own investigations but investigates alleged anti-competitive pricing practices referred to it by a number of designated bodies, including the Secretary of State for Trade and Industry, the Office of Fair Trading and industry regulatory bodies.

10.5.5 Evaluating claims of anti-competitive practice

A fine balance often exists between the co-operation among firms which leads to lower prices/better products for consumers, and co-operation which leads to collusion and a reduction in consumers' choice. There is diversity in interpretation of the notion of the 'public interest', which may be explained partly by cultural/political factors, and developments in our understanding of the consequences of market imperfection. It is evident, for example, that contemporary interpretations of anti-competitive practices differ significantly between Japanese and European systems of government regulation.

An investigation by the Competition Commission is normally completed within three months. The Commission has power only to make recommendations to the referring body. It is up to the latter whether the recommendations should be implemented. In the case of existing or potential monopolistic situations, the Commission can recommend divestment of assets or other action to reduce the undesirable elements of monopoly power.

Regulatory bodies are increasingly recognizing that co-operative relationships between companies can become anti-competitive. The following examples give an indication of recent thinking in the UK.

- In a 2003 report, the Competition Commission concluded that a monopoly situation existed for the supply of extended warranties for electrical goods. This had resulted in a lack of choice, excessive prices, insufficient information and lack of competition at the point of sale, leaving customers unduly pressurized to agree to disadvantageous terms. The Commission estimated that the five top providers of extended warranties – Dixons Group, Comet, Powerhouse, Littlewoods and Argos – had collectively made between £116 and £152 million more profit each year than they would have done had they been operating in a competitive market environment. The Commission accordingly recommended a series of actions to overcome this market imperfection, including making prices clearer at the outset, providing written quotations and allowing cancellation within 30 days.

- In February 2001, a report by the OFT uncovered evidence of anti-competitive behaviour and price fixing within the legal, accountancy and architectural professions. The OFT made recommendations to end a variety of restrictive practices within the professions, for example the Bar rule which prevented members of the general public briefing barristers direct without going through a solicitor first.

- The Competition Commission doesn't just involve itself with national organizations – it also investigates local abuse of monopoly power. Since the deregulation of the UK bus industry, the Commission has investigated several alleged anti-competitive practices by bus companies. For example, during an investigation of bus services in Darlington, the Commission found a scale monopoly that acted in favour of the Stagecoach and Go-Ahead Northern bus companies. It found that Stagecoach recruited most of the drivers of the ailing Darlington Transport Company, registered services on all its routes and then ran free services causing the sale of the municipal bus company to fall through and the company to collapse. The Director General of Fair Trading sought undertakings from Stagecoach and Go-Ahead Northern that they would maintain fares and service frequencies for three years after a competitor withdrew from a route, if their lower fares or increased frequencies had

THINKING AROUND THE SUBJECT:
CONSUMERS SMELL A RAT RATHER THAN PERFUME

A typical bottle of perfume may cost only pennies to make, but can end up selling for £20–£30 in UK stores. Inevitably, consumer groups have cried foul, accusing perfume companies of fixing prices. The companies' critics have pointed to the low prices charged for identical products in overseas markets where buyers are more price sensitive and the companies cannot sustain high prices. They also point to the refusal of the companies to supply perfumes to discount stores such as Tesco and Asda, which are pledged to lower the prices charged to consumers. This all sounds like a very anti-competitive situation that the Office of Fair Trading should seek to eradicate. But in fact, the OFT investigated the perfume sector in 1997 and amazed some of its critics by giving the perfume companies a clean bill of health. Restricting sales to discount chains could be justified because such shops do not have trained staff to give advice about the company's products. More importantly, the OFT recognized that price often adds to the perceived value of a perfume. If a perfume became known for being low in price, the cachet associated with wearing it would be lost. People like to flaunt the fact that they have an expensive perfume.

Undaunted, discount retailers sought to obtain supplies of perfumes from the 'grey' (unofficial distribution channels) market in countries overseas where price levels are generally lower. Who is right? Should we be able to buy low-price designer fragrances from the retailer that is prepared to obtain the best price? Or will the low price in the long run destroy the value of the item that we seek?

been responsible for the competitor withdrawing. The Commission eventually recommended a 12-month fares and frequencies freeze, despite protests by both companies that their behaviour had been in the public interest, pointing to their investment in new vehicles and staff training.

10.5.6 Control on price representations

One of the assumptions of a perfectly competitive market is that participants in it have complete information about competing goods and services. In reality, buyers may find it very difficult to judge between competing suppliers because prices are disclosed in a deceptive or non-comparable manner. Legislation, such as the Consumer Protection Act 1987, makes it illegal for a company to give misleading statements about the price of goods or services. This not only helps to protect consumers from exploitation, but also helps to preserve the competitiveness of a market. Consumer protection legislation was considered in more detail in Chapter 5.

10.5.7 Regulation of public utilities

During the 1980s, the privatization of many UK public-sector utilities resulted in the creation of new private sector monopoly companies, including those providing gas, water, telephones and electricity. The United Kingdom led the way in privatizing public utilities and many other countries have now followed its example.

To protect the users of these services from exploitation, the government's response has been twofold.

1 First, government has sought to increase competition, in the hope that the invisible forces of competition will bring about lower prices and greater consumer choice. In this way, the electricity generating industry was divided into a number of competing private suppliers (National Power, Powergen, Nuclear Electric, Scottish Power and Scottish Hydro), while conditions were made easier for new generators and distributors to enter the market. The problem here is that there may be very real barriers to entry in markets where the capital cost of getting started can be very high. For many of the newly privatized monopolies, effective competition proved to be an unrealistic possibility. It has not been possible, for example, to develop a competitive market for domestic water supply.

2 Where competition alone has not been sufficient to protect the consumers' interest, government has created a series of regulatory bodies which can determine the level and structure of charges made by these utilities. The regulatory bodies can determine the pattern of competition within a sector by influencing relationships between competitors and easing barriers to entry. These are some of the more significant regulatory bodies in the United Kingdom:

    – Ofcom, regulates the telecommunications and broadcasting sectors
    – Ofgem, regulates the gas and electricity sectors
    – Ofwat, regulates the water supply sector.

In general, private-sector companies operating in monopoly utility markets require a licence from their regulator to do so. The regulator takes a view as to what constitutes the public interest when reviewing operators' licences to trade. Prices charged, standards of service and speed of service are all factors that the regulator can insist the companies implement if they are to carry on trading. Unresolved issues can be referred from a regulator to the Competition Commission.

In utility markets where competition is absent, regulators have to balance what is desirable from the public's point of view with the companies' need to make profits, which will in turn provide new capital for investment in improvements. Over the long term, favouring consumers with short-term price constraints may result in lower investment in a sector, leading to supply shortages. Regulators are trying to combine market forces with a degree of centralized planning and there have been concerns about the difficulties of achieving this.

Even within the apparently more competitive telecommunications sector, the regulator has frequently intervened with instructions to operators to reduce specific categories of prices. In 2003, Ofcom published the result of an investigation by the Competition Commission into the 'termination charges' levied by mobile phone operators for calls coming in from other networks. The regulator found evidence of overcharging and ordered termination costs to be cut (White 2003).

10.5.8 Control of government monopolies

Although the UK government has gone a long way in privatizing and deregulating markets that were previously the preserve of state organizations, there are still many services that

Better information about prices may help to improve the competitiveness of markets. Within the gas and electricity supply sectors, the UK government has been concerned that relatively few private customers have switched their supplier, possibly because of confusion about the true cost of competing companies' supplies. Some give introductory discounts, some give high-user or low-user discounts and many give discounts for payment by direct debit. The energy regulator Ofgem has encouraged comparison websites

such as this one operated by www.buy.co.uk. Ofgem has approved its comparison methodology which guides consumers through all the gas and electricity choices available and identifies which supplier and price plan is best for them. It is claimed that an average family that switches suppliers on buy.co.uk or uSwitch.com saves £140 on their annual energy bills. (Reproduced with permission of buy.co.uk)

cannot be sensibly privatized or deregulated. It is difficult, for example, to privatize roads or to expose consumers to serious competition for road space. It would be almost impossible to deregulate social services or the police force. It used to be thought that because the government actually provided the service, the public interest was thereby automatically protected. Government and the public were considered one and the same thing. However, with an increasingly consumerist society, it has become clear that what government thinks is good for the public is not necessarily what the public actually wants. Therefore, where it is impractical to privatize publicly provided services, government has taken a number of measures to try to protect consumers from exploitation. The following are some of the methods that have been used.

■ **Arm's length organizations:** It was noted in Chapter 2 that agencies which operate at 'arm's length' from government have grown in number in recent years. With these types of organization, managers are given defined targets which are intended to reflect the interests of the users of the service, rather than just the narrower interests of government. The separation of operational issues from policy issues allows such agencies to focus more single-mindedly on meeting policy objectives, even if this means making politically unpopular decisions in the process.

■ **Market testing:** Sometimes, local and central government test the market to see whether part of the work of a department can be subcontracted to an outside organization, or whether internal production represents 'best value'. Even some specialized services, such as accounting, architectural and legal services, have been put out to market tender. It is sometimes argued that a clear producer–buyer division makes it much easier for the body providing money for a service to exercise control over standards of performance and to create a market at the point of production, even if not at the point of consumption. For example, a local authority producing its own refuse collection services has to balance the needs of consumers with its need for good industrial relations. By contracting out the service, the authority can concentrate single-mindedly on ensuring that the contractor is performing to the agreed standard.

3 **Customers' 'charters':** These have become popular as a method of providing consumers of public services with standards of service which government organizations are expected to meet. They have been introduced to protect health service patients and parents of schoolchildren, among others, against poor service provided by a public-sector monopoly organization. Cynics have dismissed them as government hype which conceals underlying expenditure cuts and unnecessarily raises consumers' expectations. However, by setting out standards of performance, a charter gives a clear message to the management and employees of a state organization about the standards that users expect of them.

THINKING AROUND THE SUBJECT: HOW MUCH IS THAT BIT OF ROAD?

Governments are usually monopoly providers of roads, and users generally have no choice of service provider. Furthermore, roads are usually paid for out of general taxation, with no direct link between the price of using a road and the decision whether or not to use road space. This has arisen largely because of the impracticality of road pricing and issues of equity between users. However, with improved technology and growing realization of the social and economic costs of traffic congestion, there has been a move towards pricing the use of roads. The London Congestion Charge, introduced in 2003, provides evidence that pricing a public service can change consumers' behaviour, with traffic volumes reported to have fallen by 16 per cent in the months following the introduction of the charge.

GREATER COMPETITION OR MORE MANIPULATION? APPLYING INFORMATION TECHNOLOGY TO PRICE DETERMINATION AT AMAZON.COM

Among many of the early hopes at the dawn of the Internet age was a belief that it would make pricing more transparent. The Internet would allow small companies to enter a marketplace without high set-up costs, and they could use this low-cost communication tool to stimulate competition. Buyers would quickly and easily be able to compare prices between different suppliers. With diminishing barriers to entry, a homogeneous product and freely available information, it seemed that the Internet would re-energize the competitiveness of markets. The emergence of auction sites such as eBay where buyers compete against one another to establish a market price for a product sounded like a return to the basic principles of freely competitive markets.

Like many of the earlier expectations of the Internet, the reality has been quite different. First, the idea of the small entrepreneur challenging established companies in a market from their low-cost garage or spare room turned out to be an urban myth. There were a few notable successes, such as lastminute.com and Screwfix.com, but even these required large amounts of capital to secure them a long-term place in the market. However, a survey by Gartner Research in 2004 found that rather than liberating the small entrepreneur, the Internet was consolidating the position of the big players in most markets. It seemed that the old rule of size mattering carried just as much weight on the Internet as it always had previously.

More serious was the challenge to the assumption that the Internet would make for more transparent pricing information. In fact, many companies seized on the power of the Internet to practise price discrimination, often unknown to visitors to their site. The idea of charging different prices for a basically similar product had been around for some time, and airlines had frequently used this practice to fill their aircraft. Now, through the use of 'cookies', companies have even greater power to manipulate prices.

There are dangers in practising price discrimination too avidly, as the online retailer Amazon.com found to its cost. In September 2002, the company attempted to implement a differential pricing structure by tracking customers' online purchasing behaviour, in order to charge loyal customers higher prices for its DVDs. Consumers were quick to discover the price differences and complaints followed. Amazon customers on DVDTalk.com, an online forum, reported that certain DVDs had three different prices, depending on the cookie a customer received from Amazon. Cookies are small files that websites transfer to customers' hard drives through the browsers they use. These files allow sites to recognize customers and track their purchase patterns. Depending on previous purchases, a DVD such as *Men in Black* could cost $33.97, $25.97 or $27.97. The list price was $39.95. One customer is reported to have ordered the DVD of Julie Taymour's *Titus*, paying $24.49. The next week he went back to Amazon and saw the price had jumped to $26.24. As an experiment, he stripped his computer of the electronic tags that identified him to Amazon as a regular visitor and the price fell to $22.74. One angry message posted on DVDTalk.com stated, 'Amazon apparently offers good discounts to new users, then once they get the person hooked and coming back to their site again and again, they play with the prices to make more money' (cited in Bicknell 2000). Loyal, repeat customers were particularly incensed.

Amazon.com quickly issued reports claiming that it had been presenting different prices to different customers but denied that it had done so on the basis of any past purchasing behaviour at Amazon. A spokesman stated that the company had just been carrying out a simple price test and was not discriminating against loyal customers. However, the company later admitted that it had been carrying out discriminatory pricing, justifying its use by the fact that the practice was commonplace among both Internet and bricks and mortar companies. Faced with vociferous criticism from its loyal customers, the company quickly ended its use of cookies to discriminate between customers and refunded the difference to customers who had paid the higher prices. Amazon.com may have had to retreat on this occasion, but the case emphasizes the power of the Internet to adjust prices to the state of demand. In addition, to yield management systems which put up the prices of airline seats and hotel rooms during periods of peak demand, the Internet provides a continuous feedback loop about individual customers' behaviour. The more a customer buys from a website, the more the site knows about him or her and the weaker his or her bargaining position is. As one commentator put it, 'It's as if the corner drugstore could see you coming down the sidewalk, clutching your fevered brow, and then doubled the price of aspirin.'
(Based on Streitfeld 2002)

QUESTIONS

1 Is the use of cookies to determine prices charged to individuals an ethical practice?
2 What, if any, is the similarity between the use of database-informed pricing decisions and the traditional haggling that goes on in Eastern bazaars? Are there any important points of difference?
3 To what extent has information technology contributed to the dissemination of information, and therefore to the development of more competitive markets? Have there been any negative consequences for the development of competitive markets?

SUMMARY

This chapter has reviewed the variety of market structures that exist, and the effect market structure has on a firm's pricing and product decisions. Perfectly competitive markets are presumed to favour consumers, but can limit the revenues of profit-seeking firms. In their purest extreme, this market structure is unusual. Product differentiation is a means by which a firm can avoid head-on competition and can be strengthened with the development of distinctive brands and the application of new technologies to develop new products (**Chapter 4**). The trend towards globalization of business (**Chapter 12**) is having the effect of making markets more competitive. This chapter has taken a microeconomic perspective on pricing and competition. Pricing is also affected by macroeconomic factors and these are discussed in **Chapter 11**. Public policy usually seeks control of anti-competitive practices and the legal framework for controlling such practices is discussed further in **Chapter 5**.

Key Terms

Anti-competitive practices	(376)	Elasticity of demand	(361)	Monopoly	(365)
Brands	(370)	Elasticity of supply	(363)	Oligopoly	(372)
Competition Commission	(376)	Imperfect competition	(367)	Perfect competition	(352)
Demand	(352)	Market structure	(349)	Price determination	(358)
		Markets	(373)	Supply	(356)

CHAPTER REVIEW QUESTIONS

1 In the context of market structure analysis, what are the options available to firms in a highly competitive market to improve profitability?

Select one of the options and discuss it, making clear how lasting the profit improvement is likely to be in the long run.
(*Based on CIM Marketing Environment Examination question*)

2 Identify the impact and discuss the likely marketing response to two of the following environmental changes affecting a major oil refining and distributing company:
- the introduction of a carbon tax
- a breakthrough in cost-effective solar power stations

- a well-financed new entrant entering its main market
- teleconferencing and telecommunications growing rapidly
- cut-price supermarket petrol sales expanding significantly.

(*Based on CIM Marketing Environment Examination question*)

3 You have been asked by your marketing director to provide a brief report analysing the profitability of your industry.
(a) Selecting an industry of your choice, identify the key elements of its structure and summarize the forces that determine its long-run profitability.

(b) Append your recommendations on the strategies a company could adopt in order to maintain or improve profitability.

(*Based on CIM Marketing Environment Examination question*)

4 (a) Show, using diagrams, what would happen to the market price of compact discs if a new technological development suddenly allowed CDs to be produced at a much lower cost than previously.

(b) What factors might cause the demand curve for CDs to shift upwards?

5 In a medium-sized English town, one bus company recently agreed to buy the operations of another operator, giving the acquiring company over 80 per cent of the local market for scheduled bus services. In view of a possible referral of the takeover by the Office of Fair Trading to the Competition Commission, assess the advantages and disadvantages to the public of the existence of a local monopoly.

6 Summarize the problems facing the government in its attempts to control the price of public water supply.

ACTIVITY

Collect information on prices charged for the following products: a top 10 DVD film to buy; car insurance quotes; mobile phone charges. What do the prices tell you about the competitiveness of these markets? Identify strategies that companies have pursued in order to reduce the effects of direct competition.

Useful Websites

DTI: Building the knowledge driven economy

Background paper relating to the government's White Paper *Our Competitive Future: Building the Knowledge Driven Economy*. The paper covers issues of knowledge as a means towards competitive advantage.

http://www.dti.gov.uk/comp/competitive/an_reprt.htm

Competition Commission

Home page of the UK Competition Commission, providing links to previous cases investigated by the Commission.

http://www.competition-commission.gov.uk/

Further Reading

This chapter has provided only a very brief overview of the principles of economics as they affect pricing. For a fuller discussion, one of the following texts would be useful:

Lipsey, R.G. and Chrystal, K.A. (2003) *Economics*, 10th edn, Oxford University Press.

Begg, David and Ward, Damian (2004) *Economics for Business*, Maidenhead, McGraw-Hill.

The following provide a more applied approach to price determination:

Hanna, N. and R. Dodge (1997) *Pricing*, Macmillan.

Nagle, Thomas, Holden, Ted and Holden Reed, K. (eds) *The Strategy and Tactics of Pricing: A Guide to Profitable Decision Making*, London, Prentice Hall.

The following article examines the impacts of the Internet on price awareness, and levels of competition within a market:

Sinha, I. (2000) 'Cost transparency: the net's real threat to prices and brands', *Harvard Business Review*, March, Vol. 78, No. 2, pp. 43–7.

There is now extensive literature on the benefits of brand building and how they add value to consumers:

Aaker, David A. and Joachimsthaler, Erich (2002) *Brand Leadership*, Free Press.

de Chernatony, L. and McDonald, M. (2003) *Creating Powerful Brands*, Butterworth-Heinemann.

Competition policy and law is reviewed in the following texts:

Motta, Massimo (2004) *Competition Policy: Theory and Practice*, Cambridge University Press.

Crew, Michael A. (2000) *Expanding Competition in Regulated Industries (Topics in Regulatory Economics and Policy)*, Kluwer Academic Publishers.

Beato, Paulina and Laffont, Jean-Jacques (eds) (2003) *Competition Policy in Regulated Industries: Approaches for Emerging Economies*, The Johns Hopkins University Press.

Furse, M. (2001) *Competition Law of the UK and EC*, Blackstone.

References

Bicknell, C. (2000) 'The Amazon story', *Wired News*, 21 July.

Doyle, P. (1989) 'Building successful brands: the strategic options', *Journal of Marketing Management*, Vol. 5, No. 1, pp. 77–95.

Fock, H. and Woo, K. (1998) 'The China market: strategic implications of Quanxi', *Business Strategy Review*, Vol. 7, No. 4, pp. 33–43.

International Law Update (2004) 'Coca-Cola agrees to desist from anti-competitive practices in European Union', October.

Laurent, Giles and Kapferer, Jean-Noel (1985) 'Measuring consumer involvement profiles', *Journal of Marketing Research*, Vol. 22 (February), pp. 41–53.

OECD (2004) *Mobile Baskets*, April 2004.

Streitfeld, D. (2002) 'Ads on web don't click', *Washington Post*, 29 October, p. 1.

Tsang, W.K. (1998) 'Can Quanxi be a source of sustained competitive advantage for doing business in China', *The Academy of Management Executive*, Vol. 12, No. 2, pp. 64–74.

Weatherill, S. (1996) *Cases and Materials on EC Law*, 3rd edn, London, Blackstone Press Ltd.

White, D. (2003) 'Mobile pricing riles operators', *Daily Telegraph*, London, 18 January.

Chapter 11

The National Economic Environment

Chapter Objectives

This chapter will explain:

- the structure of national economies, distinguishing between consumer, producer and government sectors

- methods of measuring activity within the economy

- the business cycle – causes and consequences for business organizations

- government economic policy objectives

- methods used by governments to manage the national economy

11.1 MACROECONOMIC ANALYSIS

In the previous chapter, microeconomic analysis of a firm's competitive environment made a number of assumptions about the broader economic environment in which the firm operates. In the analysis of supply and demand in any given market, changes in household incomes or government taxation were treated as an uncontrollable external factor to which a market responded. For most businesses, a sound understanding of this broader economic environment is just as important as understanding short-term and narrow relationships between the price of a firm's products and demand for them.

An analysis of companies' financial results has often indicated that business people attribute their current success or failure to the state of the economy. For example, a retail store that has just reported record profit levels may put this down to a very high level of consumer confidence, while a factory that has just laid off workers may blame a continuing economic recession for its low level of activity. Few business people can afford to ignore the state of the economy because it affects the willingness and ability of customers to buy their products. It can also affect the price and availability of its inputs. The shop that reported record profits may have read economic indicators correctly and prepared for an upturn in consumer spending by buying in more stocks or taking on more sales assistants.

This chapter is concerned with what has often been described as macroeconomic analysis. Although the workings of the economy at a national level are the focus of this chapter, it must be remembered that even national economies form part of a larger international economic environment. Issues of international economic analysis are discussed in Chapter 12.

This chapter begins by analysing the structure of the national economy and the interdependence of the elements within this structure. The national economy is a complex system whose functioning is influenced by a range of planned and unplanned forces. While unplanned forces (such as turbulence in the world economic system) can have significant impacts on the national economic system, organizations are particularly keen to understand the planned interventions of governments that seek to influence the economy for a variety of social and political reasons.

11.2 THE STRUCTURE OF THE ECONOMY

Most analyses of national economies divide the productive sectors into three categories.

1 The primary sector which is concerned with the extraction and production of basic raw materials from agriculture, mining, oil exploration, etc.
2 The secondary sector which transforms the output of the primary sector into products that consumers can use (e.g. manufacturing, construction, raw material processing, etc.).
3 The services sector, which comprises consumer services such as hairdressing and business services such as accounting.

Comparisons can be drawn between the three sectors described above and value chains (described in Chapter 1). In general, these three sectors add progressively higher levels of value to a product.

A further division in the economy occurs between the productive sector and the consumption sector. Intervening as both a producer and a consumer, government provides a third element of an economy. The relationship between producers and consumers is the basis for models of the circular flow of income, discussed later in this chapter.

11.2.1 Measures of economic structure

The relative importance of the three productive sectors described above has been changing. Evidence of this change is usually recorded by reference to three key statistics:

1 the share of gross domestic product (GDP) which each sector accounts for
2 the proportion of the labour force employed in the sector
3 the contribution of the sector to a nation's balance of payments.

A key trend in Britain, like most developed economies, has been the gradual decline in importance of the primary and manufacturing sectors and the growth in the services sector. The extent of the change in the UK economic structure, when measured by shifts in GDP and employment, is indicated in Figure 11.1.

While the statistics in Figure 11.1 appear to show a number of clear trends, the figures need to be treated with a little caution for a number of reasons.

1 Fluctuations in the value of GDP for the primary sector often have little to do with changes in activity levels, but instead reflect changes in world commodity levels. Oil represents a major part of the UK's primary sector output, but the value of oil produced has fluctuated from the very high levels of the early 1980s to the very low levels of the 1990s, largely reflecting changes in oil prices.
2 The level of accuracy with which statistics have been recorded has been questioned, especially for the services sector. The system of Standard Industrial Classifications (SICs) for a long while did not disaggregate the service sector in the same level of detail as the other two sectors.
3 Part of the apparent growth in the services sector may reflect the method by which statistics are collected, rather than indicating an increase in overall service level activity. Output and

	1969	1979	1989	1995	2000	2002
Primary						
Share of GDP (%)	4.3	6.7	4.2	4.4	4.1	3.7
Workforce (%)	3.6	3.0	2.1	1.4	1.5	1.3
Secondary						
Share of GDP (%)	42.0	36.7	34.5	29.4	25.5	24.5
Workforce (%)	46.8	38.5	28.9	18.3	20.8	19.2
Services						
Share of GDP (%)	53.0	56.5	61.3	66.2	70.4	71.8
Workforce (%)	49.3	58.5	69.0	76.5	77.7	79.5

Figure 11.1 Composition of the UK productive sector

Source: compiled from 'Economic Trends', *Employment Gazette*

employment is recorded according to the dominant business of an organization. Within many primary and secondary sector organizations, many people are employed in service-type activities, such as cleaning, catering, transport and distribution. Where a cook is employed by a manufacturing company, output and employment is attributed to the manufacturing sector. However, a common occurrence during recent years has been for manufacturing industry to contract out many of these service activities to external contractors. Where such contracts are performed by contract catering, office cleaning or transport companies, the output becomes attributable to the service sector, making the service sector look larger, even though no additional services have been produced – they have merely been switched from internally produced to externally produced.

Nevertheless, the figures clearly indicate a number of significant trends in the economy.

1 The primary sector in the United Kingdom, like most developed economies, has been contracting in relative importance. There are supply and demand side explanations for this trend. On the supply side, many basic agricultural and extractive processes have been mechanized, resulting in them using fewer employees and thereby consuming a lower proportion of GDP. Many primary industries have declined as suppliers have been unable to compete with low-cost producers in countries that are able to exploit poor employment working conditions. On the demand side, rising levels of affluence have led consumers to demand increasingly refined products. In this way, consumers have moved from buying raw potatoes (essentially a product of the primary sector) to buying processed potatoes (e.g. prepared ready meals) which involve greater inputs from the secondary sector. With further affluence, potatoes have been sold with added involvement of the service sector (e.g. eating cooked potatoes in a restaurant).

2 Output of the secondary sector in the United Kingdom fell from 42 per cent of GDP in 1969 to 24.5 per cent in 2002, reflecting the poor performance of manufacturing industry (the comparable figure for the 25 EU countries was 25.8 per cent). This can again partly be explained by efficiency gains by the sector, requiring fewer resources to be used, but more worryingly by competition from overseas. The emergence of newly industrialized nations with a good manufacturing infrastructure and low employment costs, rigidities in the UK labour market, declining research and development budgets relative to overseas competitors and the effects of exchange rate policy have all contributed to this decline.

3 In respect of its share of GDP, the services sector saw almost continuous growth during the period 1969–99, with banking, finance, insurance, business services, leasing and communications being particularly prominent. In 2004, the services sector accounted for 71.8 per cent of UK GDP, up from 53 per cent in 1969.

11.2.2 Towards a service economy?

There is little doubt that the services sector has become a dominant force in many national economies. According to Eurostat, services accounted for 71.1 per cent of GDP in the 25 EU countries in 2004 (Eurostat 2005). Between 1970 and 1997, it is reported that about 1.5 million new jobs per year were created in the services sectors within the EU – twice the average for the rest of the economy (Eurostat 1998).

The United Kingdom, like many developed economies, has traditionally run a balance of trade deficit in manufactured goods (i.e. imports exceed exports) but has made up for this with a surplus in 'invisible' service 'exports'. In 2003, while the UK's visible balance was in deficit by £47.4 billion, there was an invisible surplus of £15.6 billion.

During periods of recession in the manufacturing sector, the service sector has been seen by many as the salvation of the economy. Many politicians have been keen to promote the service sector as a source of new employment to make up for the diminishing level of employment within the primary and secondary sectors. A common argument has been that the United Kingdom no longer has a competitive cost advantage in the production of many types of goods and therefore these sectors of the economy should be allowed to decline and greater attention paid to those service sectors that showed greater competitive advantage. The logic of this argument can be pushed too far, as outlined below.

- A large part of the growth in the service sector during the 1980s and 1990s reflected the buoyancy of the primary and secondary sectors during that period. As manufacturing industry increases its level of activity, the demand for many business-to-business services such as accountancy, legal services and business travel increases. During periods of recession in the manufacturing sectors, the decline in manufacturing output has had an impact on the services sector, as evidenced, for example, through lower demand for business loans and export credits.

- The assumption that the United Kingdom has a competitive cost advantage in the production of services needs to be examined closely. In the same way that many sectors of UK manufacturing industry lost their competitive advantage to developing nations during the 1960s and 1970s, there is evidence that the once unquestioned supremacy in certain service sectors is being challenged. Financial services markets, which achieved prominence in London when the United Kingdom was the world's most important trading nation, are increasingly following world trade to its new centres such as Frankfurt. High levels of training in some of Britain's competitor nations have allowed those countries to firstly develop their own indigenous services and then to develop them for export. Banking services which were once a net import of Japan are now exported throughout the world.

- Over-reliance on the service sector could pose strategic problems for the United Kingdom. A diverse economic base allows a national economy to be more resilient to changes in world trading conditions.

11.2.3 International comparisons

There appears to be a high level of correlation between the level of economic development in an economy (as expressed by its GDP per capita) and the strength of its services sector. It is debatable whether a strong services sector leads to economic growth or is a result of that economic growth. The debate can partly be resolved by dividing services into those that are used up in final consumption and those that provide inputs to further business processes (see below).

According to the International Labour Organization (ILO 2004), over three-quarters of workers in most Western developed economies are employed in the services sector (e.g. United States 74.7 per cent and the United Kingdom 74.6 per cent). Western countries which are considered to be less developed have proportionally fewer employed in their serv-

> **THINKING AROUND THE SUBJECT:**
> **SERVICES ARE NOT JUST ABOUT RESTAURANTS AND HAIRDRESSERS –**
> **THEY ARE VITAL TO PRODUCTIVITY IN THE WHOLE ECONOMY**

The services sector includes businesses whose output is vital for improving the efficiency of other businesses within the national economy. Transport and communications are often cited as vital service activities, and the lack of transport infrastructure has held back many developing countries. This road haulier acts as part of many manufacturing firms' production process, moving raw materials and semi-manufactured components between factories. The road haulage industry adds value for private households by making the goods of manufacturing companies locally available. Increasingly, consumers are buying the services of road haulage companies as a 'luxury', by having goods delivered direct to their door. The road haulage sector does not exist in isolation from the government sector. Hauliers rely on government expenditure to provide adequate road capacity, and many would argue that cutbacks in government road expenditure have added to the operating costs of road hauliers. The government also collects taxation from the sector, only part of which is passed back to the sector, with the remainder being used to fund other government spending programmes.

ices sector, for example Poland (53 per cent) and Portugal (55.1 per cent), The lowest levels of services employment are found in the less developed countries, for example Morocco (35.6 per cent) and Bangladesh (27.6 per cent).

11.2.4 Consumer, producer and government sectors

Consumer goods and services are provided for individuals who use up those goods and services for their own enjoyment or benefit. No further economic benefit results from the consumption of the product. In this way, the services of a hairdresser can be defined as consumer services. On the other hand, producer goods and services are those that are provided to other businesses in order that those businesses can produce something else of economic benefit. In this way, a road haulage company sells services to its industrial customers in order that they can add value to the goods that they produce, by allowing their goods to be made available at the point of demand.

The essential difference between production and final consumption sectors is that the former creates wealth while the latter consumes it. Traditionally, economic analysis has labelled these as 'firms' and 'households' respectively. The discussion later in this chapter will indicate problems that may arise where an apparently prosperous household sector is not backed by an equally active production sector.

There has been continuing debate about the role of government in the national economy which has led to shifts in the proportion of GDP accounted for by the public sector. During the 1980s, the UK government regarded the public sector as a burden on the country and set about dismantling much of the state's involvement in the economy. Privatization of public corporations and the encouragement of private pensions were just two manifestations of this. By the mid-1990s, the proportion of UK government expenditure as a proportion of total GDP appeared to have stabilized in the range 38–42 per cent, with increasing social security spending offsetting much of the reduction in expenditure accounted for by state-owned industries. Figure 11.2 illustrates the cyclical nature of public spending and taxation as a proportion of UK GDP.

Governments do not always take such a 'hands-off' approach. The economies of Eastern Europe have in the past been dominated by central planning in which the government determined the lion's share of income and expenditure in the economy. Even in Britain shortly after the Second World War, the government assumed a very major role in the economy, with the nationalization of many essential industries. Even today, there are variations within Western

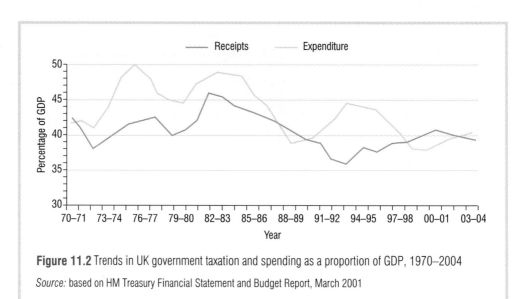

Figure 11.2 Trends in UK government taxation and spending as a proportion of GDP, 1970–2004

Source: based on HM Treasury Financial Statement and Budget Report, March 2001

Europe in the proportion of GDP accounted for by the government sector. Many Scandinavian countries, for example, have higher proportions than the UK, reflecting, among other things, a general acceptance by their populations that taxation revenues will be wisely spent on socially necessary expenditure.

Organizations need to keep their eyes on political developments which shift the balance of resources between public and private sectors. A company that is involved in the marketing of health service products, for example, will be very interested in the government's view about the respective roles to be played by the private sector and the National Health Service.

11.3 THE CIRCULAR FLOW OF INCOME

Households, firms and government are highly interdependent and the level of wealth created in an economy is influenced by the interaction between these elements. To understand the workings of a national economy, it is useful to begin by developing a simple model of a closed economy comprising just two sectors – firms and households – which circulate money between each other.

The simplest model of a circular flow of income involves a number of assumptions.

- Households earn all their income from supplying their labour to firms.
- Firms earn all their income from supplying goods and services to households.
- There is no external trade.
- All income earned is spent (i.e. households and firms do not retain savings).

In this simple model, the income of households is exactly equal to the expenditure of firms, and vice versa. It follows that any change in income from employment is directly related to changes in expenditure by consumers. Similarly, any change in sales of goods and services by firms is dependent upon employment. In this simplified economy, income, output, spending and employment are all interrelated (Figure 11.3). Of course, this simplified model of the economy is almost impossible to achieve in practice, because most economies are affected by factors that upset this stable equilibrium pattern of income and expenditure.

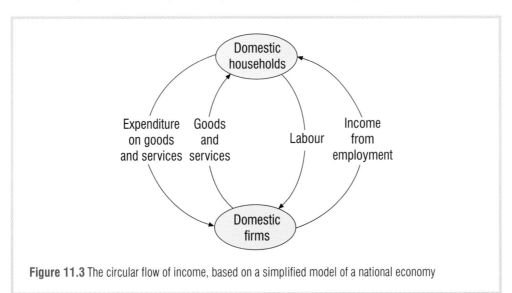

Figure 11.3 The circular flow of income, based on a simplified model of a national economy

Instability in this static model can come about for two principal reasons: additional money can be injected into the circular flow, while money currently circulating can be withdrawn. Injections have the effect of increasing the volume and speed of circulation of money within this flow, while withdrawals have the opposite effects.

Withdrawals can take a number of forms:

■ savings by households which occur when income is received by them but not returned to firms.

■ government taxation, which removes income received by households and prevents them from returning it to firms in the form of expenditure on goods and services; taxation of businesses diverts part of their expenditure from being returned to households

■ spending on imported goods and services by households means that this money is not received by firms, which cannot subsequently return it to households in the form of wages.

The opposite of withdrawals are **injections** and these go some way to counterbalancing the effects described above in the following ways.

■ Firms may earn income by selling goods to overseas buyers. This represents an additional source of income which is passed on to households.

■ Purchases by firms of capital equipment which represents investment as opposed to current expenditure.

■ Instead of reducing the flow of income in an economy through taxation, governments can add to it by spending on goods and services.

A revised model of the circular flow of income, incorporating these modifications, is shown in Figure 11.4.

This modified model of the economy still involves a number of fairly unrealistic assumptions (e.g. that consumers do not borrow money). In addition, it is unrealistic to assume that

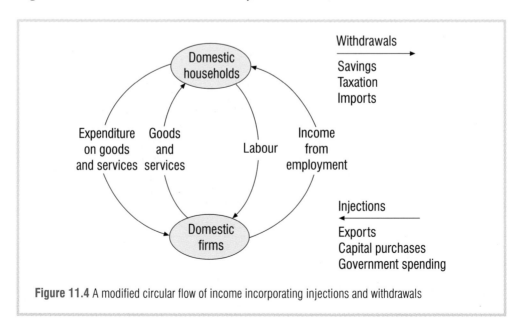

Figure 11.4 A modified circular flow of income incorporating injections and withdrawals

households only earn income from employment activity. They also receive it from returns on investments, property rentals and self-employment. However, it serves to stress the interdependence of the different sectors of the economy and the fact that, through this interdependence, changes in behaviour by one group can result in significant changes in economic performance as a whole. Of particular interest to government policy makers and businesses alike is the effect on total economic activity of changing just one element in the circular flow.

11.3.1 The Phillips machine model of the economy

In an attempt to demonstrate the workings of the economy, the Phillips machine model draws on the principles of fluid dynamics. The basic principle of the model is that water circulates around the machine's tubes in an analogous way to money circulating around the economy (Figure 11.5).

One starting point for the machine is to consider the holding tank which contains the total amount of money available for transactions. The fuller the tank, the greater the amount of money that flows into the neighbouring chamber as incomes. These are then pumped to the top of the machine from where they cascade down through the machine's central chambers. Some of this is taken out of the flow as government taxation, while additional money re-enters the flow as government expenditure. Further amounts are drawn off as some households choose to save some of their incomes. These savings flow into a tank holding households' surplus balances, some of which are used to finance spending on investment, which re-enters the main flow later. The higher the level of surplus balances available for investment, the lower

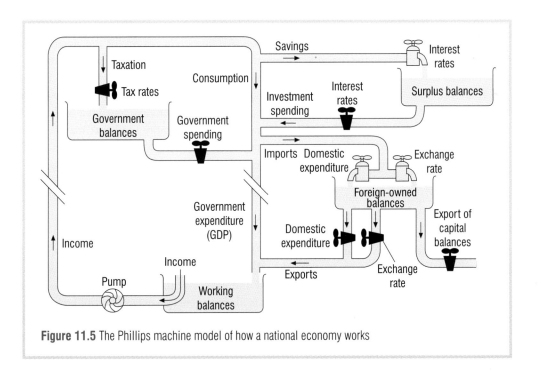

Figure 11.5 The Phillips machine model of how a national economy works

the interest rate and the greater the amount of new investment. Interest rates can be held constant by drawing some of the surplus funds into a spare tank at the back of the machine. The main flow now comprises consumers' spending, some of which goes on imports, thereby building up foreigners' holdings of sterling in another tank, thereby lowering the value of sterling. The fuller the tank, and therefore the lower the exchange rate, the greater the flow out of the pipe at the bottom which comprises exports.

The main flow now represents total national expenditure, which equals total national income. It falls back into the bottom tank from which it started, thereby topping up balances available for transactions. The flow throughout the system can be modified by inserting partial blockages at strategic points.

11.3.2 The multiplier effect

The multiplier effect can be compared to the effects of throwing a stone into a pond of water. The impact of the stone with the water will cause an initial wave to be formed, but beyond this will be waves of ever-decreasing strength. The strength of these ripples will lessen with increasing distance from the site of original impact and with the passage of time. Similarly, injecting money into the circular flow of income will have an initial impact on households and businesses directly affected by the injection, but will also be indirectly felt by households and firms throughout the economy.

The multiplier effect can be illustrated by considering the effects of a major capital investment by private-sector firms or by government. The firm making the initial investment spends money buying in supplies from outside (including labour) and these outside suppliers in turn purchase more inputs. The multiplier effect of this initial expenditure can result in the total increase in household incomes being much greater than the original expenditure. A good example of the multiplier effect at work in the United Kingdom is provided by the Millennium Dome project at Greenwich, opened in 2000. An important reason for the government supporting this project was the desire to regenerate an economically depressed part of London. Government expenditure initially created expenditure during the construction of the Dome and from employment within the Dome itself. This expenditure then rippled out to other business sectors, such as hotels and transport. The level of activity generated additional demand for local manufacturing industry, for example visitors require food that may be produced locally, the producers of which may in turn require additional building materials and services to increase production facilities. On an even larger scale, the Mayor of London, supported by central government, bid to host the 2012 Olympic Games, largely on the basis of the multiplier benefits that would result.

The extent of the multiplier effects of initial expenditure is influenced by a number of factors. Crucial is the extent to which recipients of this initial investment recirculate it back into the national economy. If large parts of it are saved by households or used to buy imported goods (whether by firms or by households), the multiplier effects to an economy will be reduced. In general, income that is received by individuals that have a high propensity to spend each additional pound on basic necessities is likely to generate greater multiplier benefits than the same money received by higher-income households that have a greater propensity to save it or to spend it on imported luxuries. The implications of this for government macro-economic policy will be considered later.

The multiplier effect can be used to analyse the effects of withdrawals from the circular flow as well as injections. Therefore, if firms spend less on wages, household income will fall as a direct result, leading indirectly to lower spending by households with other domestic firms. These firms will in turn pay less to households in wages, leading to a further reduction in spending with firms, and so on.

Multiplier effects can be studied at a local as well as a national level. Government capital expenditure is often made with a view to stimulating areas of severe unemployment (as in the case of the Millennium Dome and grants given by Regional Development Agencies to support private-sector investment in Tyneside). The presence of a university in a town usually generates strong multiplier benefits, and it has been estimated, for example, that Newport's University College, with a turnover of around £30 million per annum, employs between 800 and 900 people and generates multiplier benefits to the local economy of around £80 million per annum. However, whether the local economy is helped will depend upon how much subsequent expenditure is retained within the area. In one study of the regional multiplier effects of siting a call centre for British Airways in a deprived part of Tyneside, it was found that a high proportion of the staff employed commuted in from other, more prosperous areas, thereby limiting the multiplier benefits to the deprived area.

As well as examining the general macroeconomic effects of spending by firms on household income and vice versa, multiplier analysis can also be used to assess the impact of economic activity in one business sector upon other business sectors. Many economies suffer because vital economic infrastructure remains undeveloped, preventing productivity gains in other sectors. The availability of transport and distribution services have often had the effect of stimulating economic development at local and national levels, for example following the improvement of rail or road services. The absence of these basic services can have a crippling effect on the development of the primary and manufacturing sectors – for instance, one reason for Russian agriculture not having been fully exploited has been the ineffective distribution system available to food producers.

One approach to understanding the contribution of one business sector to other sectors of the economy is to analyse input–output tables of production and data on labour and capital inputs. In one study (Wood 1987) these were used to estimate the effects that productivity improvements in all of the direct and indirect supply sectors had on the productivity levels of all other sectors. Thus, some apparently high productivity sectors (such as chemicals) were shown to be held back by the low productivity of some of their inputs. On the other hand, efficiency improvements in some services, such as transport and distribution, were shown to have had widespread beneficial effects on the productivity contribution of other sectors. This is reflected in the common complaint among manufacturing businesses in the UK that their productivity is severely reduced by traffic congestion which adds to their delivery costs and the costs of their supplies.

11.3.3 The accelerator effect

Changes in the demand for consumer goods can lead, through an accelerator effect, to a more pronounced change in the demand for capital goods. This accelerator effect occurs when, for instance, a small increase in consumer demand leads to a sudden large increase in demand for plant and machinery with which to satisfy that demand. When consumer demand falls by a small amount, demand for plant and machinery falls by a correspondingly larger amount.

The accelerator effect is best illustrated by reference to an example (Figure 11.6) based on consumers' demand for air travel and airlines' demands for new aircraft. In this simplified example, an airline operates a fleet of 100 aircraft and during periods of stable passenger demand buys 10 new aircraft each year and retires 10 older aircraft, retaining a stable fleet size of 100 aircraft. Then, some extraneous factor (e.g. a decline in the world economy) may cause the airline's passenger demand to fall by 3 per cent per annum. The airline responds to this by reducing its capacity by 3 per cent to 97 aircraft (assuming that it can reschedule its aircraft so that it is able to accommodate all its remaining passengers). The easiest way to achieve this is by reducing its annual order for aircraft from 10 to 7. If it continued to retire its 10 oldest aircraft, this would have the effect of reducing its fleet size to 97, in line with the new level of customer demand. What is of importance here is that while consumer demand has gone down by just 3 per cent, the demand facing the aircraft manufacturer has gone down by 30 per cent (from 10 aircraft a year to 7). If passenger demand settles down at its new level, the airline will have no need to cut its fleet any further, so will revert to buying 10 new aircraft a year and selling 10 old ones. If passenger demand picks up once more, the airline may seek to increase its capacity by ordering not 10 aircraft but, say, 13.

11.3.4 Inflation

It should be apparent that multiplier effects are associated with injections to the circular flow of income, causing more money to chase a fixed volume of goods and services available for consumption. This leads to the classic case of demand-pull inflation, when excessive demand

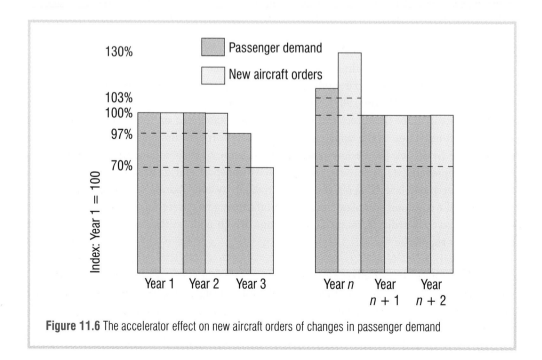

Figure 11.6 The accelerator effect on new aircraft orders of changes in passenger demand

for goods and services relative to their supply results in an increase in their market price level. Demand-pull inflation can result from an increase in the availability of credit, excessive spending by government and tax cuts that increase consumers' disposable incomes, so allowing them to buy more goods and services.

An alternative cause of inflation is referred to as cost-push inflation. On the supply side, increases in production costs (such as higher wage costs, rising raw material costs, higher overheads, additional costs of health and safety legislation) may push up the price at which companies are prepared to supply their goods to the market, unless they are offset by increases in productivity.

An inflationary spiral can be created where higher wages in an economy result in greater spending power, leading to demand-pull inflation. The resulting higher cost of consumer goods leads workers to seek wage increases to keep them ahead of inflation, but these increases in wage costs add a further twist to cost-push inflation, and so on. Because markets are seldom perfectly competitive and therefore unable to correct for inflation, governments are keen to intervene to prevent inflationary processes building up in an economy (see below).

11.3.5 Complex models of the economy

The simple model of the economy presented above is based on many assumptions which need to be better understood if model making is to make a useful contribution to policy making. It is important for governments to have a reasonably accurate model of how the economy works so that predictions can be made about the effects of government policy. A model should be able to answer such questions as the following.

- What will happen to unemployment if government capital expenditure is increased by 10 per cent?
- What will happen to inflation if income tax is cut by 2p in the pound?
- What will be the net effect on government revenue if it grants tax concessions to firms investing in new capital equipment?

Companies supplying goods and services also take a keen interest in models of the economy, typically seeking to answer questions such as the following.

- What effect will a cut in income tax have on demand for new car purchases by private consumers?
- How will company buyers of office equipment respond to reductions in taxation on company profits?
- Will the annual budget create a feeling of confidence by consumers which is sufficiently strong for them to make major household purchases?

Developing a model of the economy is very different from developing a model in the natural sciences. In the latter case, it is often possible to develop closed models where all factors that can affect a system of interrelated elements are identifiable and can be measured. Predicting behaviour for any component of the model is therefore possible, based on knowledge about all other components. In the case of economic models, the system of interrelated components is open rather than closed. This means that not only is it difficult to measure components, but it can also be difficult to identify what elements to include as being of significance to a national economy. For example, few models accurately predicted that a sudden rise in oil prices by OPEC producers would have a major effect on national economies throughout the world. Furthermore, it is very difficult to develop relationships between variables that remain constant through time. Whereas the relationship between molecules in a chemistry model may be universally true, given a set of environmental conditions, such universal truths are seldom found in economic modelling. This has a lot to do with the importance of attitudes of firms and consumers which change through time for reasons that may not become clear until after the event. For example, a 2 per cent cut in income tax may have achieved significant increases in consumer expenditure on one occasion, but resulted in higher levels of savings or debt repayment on another. The first time round, factors as ephemeral as good weather and a national success in an international football championship could have created a 'feel good' factor which was absent the following time round.

11.4 THE BUSINESS CYCLE

From the discussion in the previous sections, it should become quite apparent that national economies are seldom in a stable state. The situation where injections exactly equate withdrawals can be described as a special case, with the normal state of affairs being for one of these to exceed the other. An excess of injections will result in economic activity increasing, while the opposite will happen if withdrawals exceed injections. This leads to the concept of the business cycle which describes the fluctuating level of activity in an economy. Most developed economies go through cycles that have been described as:

- recession–prosperity
- expansion–contraction
- stop–go, and
- 'boom and bust'

Figure 11.7 shows the pattern of the business cycle for the United Kingdom, as measured by fluctuations in the most commonly used indicator of economic activity – the gross domestic product (described below).

11.4.1 Measuring economic activity

Gross domestic product (GDP) is just one indicator of the business cycle. In fact, there are many indicators of economic activity that may move at slightly different times to each other. Some 'leading' indicators may be used as early warning signs of an approaching economic recession, with other indicators – if not corrected by government intervention – following a similar trend in due course. Some of the more commonly used indicators of the business cycle are described below.

Gross domestic product

This index measures the total value of goods and services produced within the economy and can be used to compare economic performance over time and to compare performance between countries (see Figure 11.8). In a typical year, the economies of Western European countries may expand by 2–3 per cent per annum, although this has reached 4–5 per cent in boom years, while GDP has fallen during recessionary periods. Much more rapid growth in

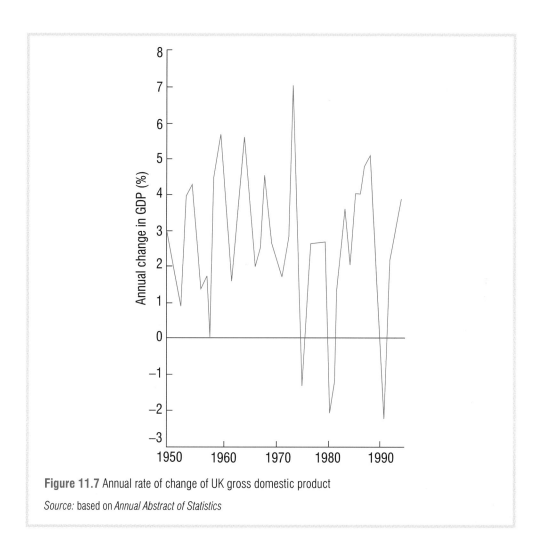

Figure 11.7 Annual rate of change of UK gross domestic product

Source: based on *Annual Abstract of Statistics*

gross domestic product has been seen in emerging economies, such as China, where annual growth in GDP in the early years of the twenty-first century was averaging about 9 per cent a year. One derivative of the crude GDP figure is a figure for GDP per capita. Therefore, if GDP is going up by 2 per cent a year and the population is constant, it means that, on average, everybody is 2 per cent better off. Whether this is true in reality, of course, depends not only on how the additional income is distributed but also on an individual's definition of being better off (GDP takes no account of 'quality of life'). Since GDP depends on both prices and quantities, an increase in prices will also increase GDP (this is also referred to as nominal GDP). This is not a particularly good measure of economic well-being, so a GDP deflator removes the effects of price changes by calculating real GDP, expressed using a constant set of prices.

Unemployment rates

Because of the profound social and economic implications of high levels of unemployment, governments normally monitor changes in unemployment levels closely. Unemployment tends

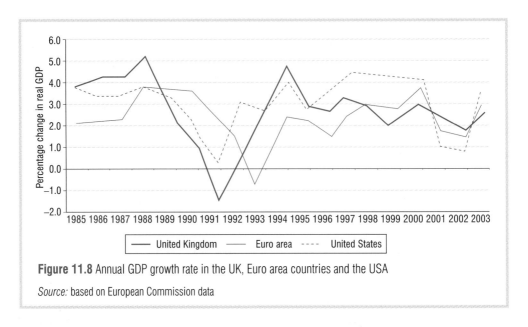

Figure 11.8 Annual GDP growth rate in the UK, Euro area countries and the USA

Source: based on European Commission data

to rise as the economy enters a general economic recession and falls as it enters a period of recovery. Unemployment occurs where firms are unable to sell their output and seek to scale back their workforce, either by laying off existing workers or not recruiting new ones. This results in less spending by the growing number of unemployed people, thereby exacerbating firms' sales difficulties. Actually measuring trends in unemployment over time can be difficult, as definitions used by governments frequently change. Cynics would say that this is done to hide the true level of unemployment, for example by excluding people that are on job training schemes.

Output levels

The output of firms is an important indicator of the business cycle, and is closely watched because of its effects on employment, and the multiplier effects of firms producing less and therefore spending less with their suppliers. In the United Kingdom, the government's Business Monitor publishes regular indicators of outputs for different sectors. Another widely quoted source of data on output is the Confederation of British Industry (CBI), which publishes monthly and quarterly surveys on industry's output, investment and stock levels. This provides a good indication of changes in different sectors of the economy and possible future business trends. In addition to these widely used and formalized methods of measuring output, a number of ad hoc approaches have been used, which it is claimed give early indicators of an economic recovery or downturn. Examples include the following.

- Sales of first-class tickets by train-operating companies, where a fall in sales is often an early indication of firms cutting back expenditure ahead of major cuts in output.
- The number of commercial vehicles crossing the Severn Bridge between England and Wales has been correlated with output of the manufacturing sector in general.
- Sales of Ford Transit vans have been associated with a revival in fortunes by the small business sector and rising sales of heavy trucks with growing confidence by firms to invest in capital equipment.

Average earnings

Unemployment figures record the extreme case of workers that have no employment. However, underemployment can affect the national economy just as significantly as unemployment as workers are put on short-time working or lose opportunities for overtime working. Conversely, average earnings may rise significantly during the early years of a boom as firms increase overtime working and bid up wage rates in an attempt to take on staff with key skills.

Disposable income

Average disposable income refers to the income that individuals have available to spend after taxation. It follows that as taxes rise, disposable income falls. A further indicator of household wealth is discretionary income, which is a measure of disposable income less expenditure on the necessities of life, such as mortgage payments. Discretionary income can be significantly affected by sudden changes in the cost of mortgages and other items of expenditure, such as travel costs, which form a large component of household budgets.

Consumer spending

Trends in consumer spending may diverge from trends in discretionary income on account of changes in consumers' propensity to borrow or save. When consumer spending runs ahead of discretionary income, this can be explained by an increase in borrowing. Conversely, spending may fall faster than discretionary income, indicating that consumers are repaying debts and/or not borrowing additional money. There are numerous indicators of consumer spending, including the government's Family Expenditure Survey. More up-to-date information is supplied by the Credit Card Research Group (CCRG), an organization representing the main UK credit card issuers. After making a number of assumptions about changing card-using habits, CCRG is able to monitor changes in the volume of consumer spending using credit cards. It is also able to monitor consumer borrowing using credit cards and net repayments of credit card debts.

Savings ratio

The savings ratio refers to the proportion of individuals' income that is saved rather than spent. Saving/borrowing levels are influenced by a number of factors, including the distribution of income in society (poorer people tend to save less, therefore any redistribution of income to this group would have the effect of reducing net savings) and consumers' level of confidence about the future (see below). During periods of high consumer confidence, savings ratios tend to fall as consumer borrowing rises. This was true of the expansionary period of the late 1980s when the proportion of household income saved reached a low point of 2.8 per cent. During the recessionary years of the mid- to late 1990s, savings ratios increased sharply, reaching a high point of 12 per cent in 1996 before gradually falling again to 5.8 per cent in the more prosperous year of 2003. Businesses look to a fall in savings ratios as an early indicator of increasing consumer confidence.

Confidence levels

Private individuals and businesses may have a high level of income and savings, but there is no guarantee that they will spend that money or take on new debt in making purchases of expensive items. They may only be happy about making major spending decisions if they feel confident about the future. Higher confidence levels may result, for example, from consumers feeling that they are not likely to be made unemployed, that their pay is going to keep up with inflation and that the value of their assets is not going to fall. A number of confidence indices are now published, for example by Chambers of Commerce and the CBI, covering both private consumers and businesses. The organization GfK publishes a monthly Consumer Confidence Barometer for the European Commission.

Inflation rate

Inflation refers to the rate at which prices of goods and services in an economy are rising. A commonly used general indicator of inflation in the United Kingdom is the Consumer Prices Index (CPI). In January 2004, the Bank of England's Monetary Policy Committee replaced the previous Retail Prices Index (RPI) with this European-derived measure of inflation. Like the RPI, it is based on information collected about the prices of goods and services consumed by an average household. This is a commonly used 'headline' rate of inflation which is frequently used by employees as a basis for wage negotiations and is used by the UK government for adjusting the value of a number of social security benefits. The CPI is itself due to be replaced in 2005 by another index devised by the European Union's statistical service Eurostat, which will include an element of housing costs.

The problem with a general index such as the Consumer Prices Index is that it may be too general to be of relevance to the spending patterns of certain individuals or organizations, so there are numerous alternative indices covering specific sectors. Many building societies, for example, produce indices of house price inflation, while specialized indices are available for new car purchases and construction costs, among others. The government publishes a monthly producer prices index which measures changes in the prices of goods bought by manufacturing firms. A rise in this indicator can signal later increases in the CPI when the components are incorporated into finished goods bought by households. Inflation affects different groups of consumers in different ways. During a period of falling interest rates and fuel prices, a home-owning, car-using household may experience negative inflation, leaving it with greater discretionary income. At the same time, the cost of public transport and rented housing may be increasing, leaving groups dependent on public transport and paying rents to a Housing Association facing a high level of inflation, thereby leaving less discretionary income.

A 'normal' level of inflation is often considered to lie in the range of 1–3 per cent per annum. Where prices are falling, the opposite case of deflation occurs, which can have economic consequences just as serious as very high inflation (see Chapter 2 for a discussion on government policy objectives).

Interest rates

Interest rates represent the price that borrowers have to pay to a lender for the privilege of using their money for a specified period of time. Interest rates tend to follow a cyclical pattern which is partly a reflection of the level of activity in the economy. During periods of recession, the supply of funds typically exceeds demand for them (caused, for example, by consumers being reluctant to spend, thereby building up their savings, and by the unwillingness of consumers and firms to borrow to pay for major expenditure items). In these circumstances, interest rates have a tendency to fall. During a period of economic prosperity, the opposite holds true, and interest rates have a tendency to rise. Rates are also influenced by government intervention, as governments have frequently use them as a tool of economic management. In general, low interest rates are seen as desirable because they reduce the cost of firms' borrowings and increase consumers' level of discretionary income through lower mortgage costs. However, during periods of unhealthily excessive demand in the economy, governments use high interest rates to try to dampen down demand from firms and consumers.

Overseas trade figures
The monthly overseas trade figures indicate the difference between a country's imports and exports. A lot of attention is given to the 'current account' which measures overseas transactions in goods and services but not capital (discussed further in Chapter 12). In general, a current account surplus is considered good for an economy, suggesting that an economy's production sector is internationally competitive. A detailed analysis of overseas trade figures indicates trends that can often be related to the business cycle and can be used to predict future levels of activity in the economy. At the height of a boom cycle, imports of manufactured goods may rise much faster than corresponding exports, possibly suggesting unsustainable levels of household consumption. Rising imports of capital equipment may give an indication that firms are ready to invest in additional domestic productive capacity following the end of a period of recession.

Exchange rates
The exchange rate is the price of one currency in terms of another (e.g. an exchange rate of £1 = $1.85 means that £1 costs $1.85). A number of factors influence the level of a country's exchange rate, but as an economic indicator the rate is often seen as an indication of the willingness of overseas traders and investors to hold that country's currency. Falling rates of exchange against other currencies may be interpreted as overseas investors losing their confidence in an economy or its government, leading them to sell their currency holdings and thereby depressing its price. The theory of exchange rate determination and the implications for business are discussed in more detail in Chapter 12.

Government borrowing
During periods of economic prosperity, government income streams from taxation tend to be buoyant, while many of its costs in respect of social welfare payment may be reduced, on account of lower levels of unemployment and low incomes. The reverse tends to be true during periods of economic recession. In this sense, government borrowing is not so much an indicator of the business cycle, but rather a consequence of it. The Labour governments from 1997 to 2005 adopted a 'golden rule' on borrowing – to use borrowing only to finance investment and not to pay for day-to-day spending. Borrowing fell during the prosperous years up to 2004, and then started to rise, rising by £500 million a month in late 2004 as a weakening business environment caused government revenues to fall. By January 2005, total government debt had reached over £400 billion, and doubts began to be expressed about the ability of the government to borrow only to invest over the economic cycle.

THINKING AROUND THE SUBJECT:
BOOM AND BUST FOR EVER?

Throughout much of the 1990s, growth of the US economy seemed almost unstoppable. Was this the dawn of the 'new economy' in which governments had managed to manipulate economies so effectively that the historical pattern of 'boom and bust' had become a thing of the past? Sadly, towards the end of 2000, the US economy came back down to Earth.

What causes such long and sustained booms, such as the US economy had just enjoyed? Can we learn anything from previous booms that might help us to understand future business cycles?

The economic historian Angus Maddison undertook an analysis of the world economy over the past millennium and noted just three periods of rapid advance in incomes per head. The most rapid occurred from 1950 to 1973, when average global real incomes per head rose at a compound annual rate of 2.9 per cent. The other two periods were 1973–98 and 1870–1913. In the latter two periods, average real incomes per head rose at a compound average annual rate of 1.3 per cent.

Interestingly, these periods of prolonged economic boom appeared to have three things in common.

1 Each of these periods was associated with a process of rapid international economic integration, with trade and global capital flows growing faster than world output, for example between 1973 and 1998, world exports rose from 10.5 per cent of world GDP to 17.2 per cent.

2 All three periods were associated with significant catching up by laggard economies with world leading economies. Between 1870 and 1913, the catching up was by Western Europe, the USA and some former European colonies, on the UK; between 1950 and 1973, it was by Western Europe, Japan and a few small east Asian countries, on the USA; and between 1973 and 1998, it was by much of the rest of Asia (including China), again on the USA. It was noted that the bigger the gap between the laggards and the leaders, the faster the rate of convergence has been.

3 The final feature of these periods has been a historically unprecedented rate of technological advance, generating rising real incomes per head in the world's most advanced economies.

The declining costs of transport and communications undoubtedly lie behind much of the development of the global economy over the last several centuries. The Internet should be seen as just the latest innovation which continues a long historical sequence.

But what about the future? Over the past couple of decades, the world's two most populous countries, China and India, with 2.25 billion people between them (or just under 40 per cent of the total world population), have been growing faster than both the world as a whole and its economic leaders. Should this lead us to believe that economic growth will continue? Can the rate of technological advance be sustained? Between 1973 and 1995, the rate of US growth in labour productivity per hour fell to just under 1.5 per cent a year, from 3 per cent between 1950 and 1973. Even with the development of the Internet, are rates of growth in productivity sustainable? Looking ahead, what new scientific and technological advances are likely to sustain a continued growth in productivity?

11.4.2 Tracking the business cycle

It is easy to plot business cycles with hindsight. However, businesses are much more interested in predicting the cyclical pattern in the immediate and medium-term future. If the economy is at the bottom of an economic recession, that is the ideal time for firms to begin investing in new productive capacity. In this case, accurate timing of new investment can have two important benefits.

1 Firms will be able to cope with demand as soon as the economy picks up. At the end of previous economic recessions, demand has often initially outstripped the restricted supply, leading many domestic firms and consumers to buy from overseas. Firms have often only invested in new capacity once overseas competitors have built up market share, and possibly created some long-term customer loyalty too.

2 At the bottom of the business cycle, resource inputs tend to be relatively cheap. This particularly affects wage costs and the price of basic raw materials such as building materials. Good timing can allow a firm to create new capacity at a much lower cost than it would incur if it waited until it was well into the upturn, when rising demand would push up resource costs.

Analysing **turning points** in the business cycle has therefore become crucial to marketers. To miss an upturn at the bottom of the recession can result in a firm missing out on opportunities when the recovery comes to fruition. On the other hand, reacting to a false signal can leave a firm with expensive excess stocks and capacity on its hands. A similar problem of excess capacity can result when a firm fails to spot the downturn at the top of the business cycle.

It is extremely difficult to identify a turning point at the time when it is happening. Following the recession of the early 1990s, there were a number of false predictions of an upturn, some politically inspired by governments keen to encourage a 'feel good' factor ahead of an election. There was a widespread feeling in 1994 that the UK economy had reached a turning point and many companies began investing in new stock and capacity in expectation of this upturn. When the predicted revival in domestic consumer expenditure failed to transpire, companies in product fields as diverse as cars, fashion clothing and electrical goods were forced to sell off surplus stocks at low prices.

Getting out of a trough in the business cycle is very dependent upon the confidence of firms and individuals about the future. Cynics may argue that governments are acting in a politically opportunistic way by talking about the onset of recovery. However, if the government cannot exude any confidence for the future, there is less likelihood of firms and individuals being prepared to invest their resources for the future.

Firms try to react to turning points as closely as possible in a number of ways.

■ Companies that are highly dependent on the business cycle frequently subscribe to the services of firms that have developed complex models of the economy and are able to make predictions about future economic performance. Some of these models (such as those developed by major firms of stockbrokers) are general in their application and based on models of the economy used by government policy makers in the Treasury. Specialized models seek to predict demand for more narrowly defined sectors, such as construction.

■ Companies can be guided by key lead indicators which have historically been a precursor of a change in activity levels for the business sector. For a company manufacturing heavy trucks, the level of attendance at major truck trade exhibitions could indicate the number of buyers that are at the initial stages in the buying process for new trucks.

■ Instead of placing all their hopes in accurate forecasts of the economy, companies can place greater emphasis on ensuring that they are able to respond to economic change very rapidly when it occurs. At the bottom of the cycle, this can be facilitated by developing flexible production methods, for example by retaining a list of trained part-time staff that can be called on at short notice, or having facilities to acquire excess capacity from collaborating firms overseas at very short notice. At the top of the cycle, the use of short-term contracts of employment can help a company to downsize rapidly at minimum cost. The development of 'efficient customer response' systems seeks to simplify supply chains so that orders can be fulfilled rapidly without the need to carry large stockholdings.

THINKING AROUND THE SUBJECT:
SPENDING CUT AS 'FEEL GOOD' FACTOR FADES

What happens to consumers' spending patterns in the shops when recession sets in? After a number of years of sharp rises in house prices, the property market cooled towards the end of 2004, and Christmas 2004 saw many retailers reporting falling sales. It seemed that higher interest rates and a lessening of the 'feel good' factor had led shoppers to be more cautious in their spending. The more expensive retailers insisted that quality would always shine through, even in hard times, while discount retailers argued that they would win business from more expensive competitors. The out-of-town shopping centres may claim that they are a natural destination for bargain hunters and will attract families that are watching their pennies. By contrast, their high-street rivals say that cash-strapped families will be spending in dribs and drabs and will make the occasional shopping trip to town but will not have enough discretionary income to justify a visit to an out-of-town centre.

Amidst this hype and speculation, a survey by HSBC bank identified furniture, cars and DIY goods as the first casualties of a downturn. HSBC estimated that for every 1 per cent drop in consumer spending, sales of vehicles would drop by 4.64 per cent, furniture and electrical goods by 1.87 per cent and DIY sales by 1.61 per cent. The sectors most protected are utilities which should suffer only a 0.32% fall for every 1 per cent drop in spending, newspapers and books (0.32 per cent), and food (0.36 per cent). This is borne out in the financial performance of retailers during the recession of the early 1990s, when companies such as Harveys Furnishings, Dixons and Wickes DIY all suffered falls in profit, while Boots' and WHSmith's profits actually rose.

Despite the analysis of spending patterns during previous recessions, doubts often remain that things will be the same next time around. Could DIY stores actually benefit as people trade down from paying people to do their maintenance and building work for them? And what about food? Could people actually increase their spending as they substitute premium ready prepared meals for more expensive eating out at restaurants?

11.5 MACROECONOMIC POLICY

The national economy has been presented as a complex system of interrelated component parts. To free market purists, the system should be self-correcting and need no intervention from governments. In reality, national economies are not closed entities and equilibrium in the circular flow can be put out of balance for a number of reasons, such as:

- increasing levels of competition in the domestic market from overseas firms that have gained a cost advantage
- changes in a country's ratio of workers to non-workers (e.g. the young and elderly)
- investment in new technology which may replace firms' expenditure on domestic wages with payments for capital and interest to overseas companies.

Most Western governments have accepted that the social consequences of free market solutions to economic management are unacceptable and they therefore intervene to manage the economy to a greater or lesser extent.

11.5.1 Policy objectives

This section begins by reviewing the objectives governments seek to achieve in their management of the national economy.

Maintaining employment

However unemployment is defined, its existence represents a waste of resources in an economy. Individuals who have the ability and willingness to work are unable to do so because there is no demand from employers for their skills. Workers' services are highly perishable in that, unlike stocks of goods, they cannot be accumulated for use when the economy picks up. Time spent by workers unemployed is an economic resource that is lost for ever. Most developed economies recognize that unemployed people must receive at least the basic means of sustenance, so governments provide unemployment benefit. Rising unemployment increases government expenditure. As well as representing a wasted economic resource, unemployment has been associated with widespread social problems, including crime, alcoholism and drug abuse. High levels of unemployment can create a divided society, with unemployed people feeling cut off from the values of society while those in employment perceive many unemployed as being lazy or unwilling to work.

In general, governments of all political persuasions seek to keep unemployment levels low in order to avoid the social and economic problems described above. However, many suspect that governments with right-wing sympathies are more likely to tolerate unemployment on the grounds that a certain amount of unemployment can bring discipline to a labour market which could otherwise give too much economic bargaining power to workers. An excess of labour supply over demand would result in wages paid to workers falling, at least in a free market. This may itself be seen as a desirable policy objective by lowering prices for consumers and increasing firms' competitiveness in international markets.

In their attempts to reduce unemployment, governments must recognize three different types of unemployment, each requiring a different solution.

1 Structural unemployment occurs where jobs are lost by firms whose goods or services are no longer in demand. This could come about through changing fashions and tastes (e.g. unemployment caused by the closure of many traditional UK seaside hotels); because of

competition from overseas (for example, many jobs in the textile, ship building and coal mining industries have been lost to lower-cost overseas suppliers); or a combination of these factors. Where a local or national economy is very dependent upon one business sector and workers' skills are quite specific to that sector, the effects of structural employment can be quite severe, as can be seen in the former ship building areas of Tyneside or coal mining areas of South Wales. Governments have tackled structural employment with economic assistance to provide retraining for unemployed workers and Regional Assistance Grants to attract new employers to areas of high unemployment.

2 Cyclical unemployment is associated with the business cycle and is caused by a general fall in demand, which may itself be a consequence of lower spending levels by firms. Some business sectors, such as building and construction, are particularly prone to cyclical patterns of demand, and hence cyclical unemployment. The long-term cure for cyclical employment is a pick-up in demand in the economy, which governments can influence through their macroeconomic policy.

3 Technological unemployment occurs where jobs are replaced by machines; it has had widespread implications in many industrial sectors such as car manufacture, banking and agriculture. Governments have to accept this cause of unemployment, as failure to modernize will inevitably result in an industry losing out to more efficient competition. For this reason, attempts to subsidize jobs in declining low-technology industries are normally doomed as overseas competitors gain market share, and eventually lead to job losses which are greater than they would have been had technology issues been addressed earlier. Where a low-technology sector is supported by import controls, consumers will be forced to pay higher prices than would otherwise be necessary. Where the goods or services in question are necessities of life, consumers' discretionary income will effectively fall, leading to lower demand for goods and services elsewhere in the economy. Although technological unemployment may be very painful to the individuals directly involved, the increasing use of technology usually has the effect of making necessities cheaper, thereby allowing consumers to demand new goods and services. One manifestation of this has been the growth in services jobs, as consumers switch part of their expenditure away from food and clothing (which have fallen in price in real terms) towards eating out and other leisure pursuits.

Stable prices

Rapidly rising or falling prices can be economically, socially and politically damaging to governments. Rapidly rising prices (inflation) can cause the following problems.

▪ For businesses, it becomes difficult to plan ahead when selling prices and the cost of inputs in the future are not known. In many businesses, companies are expected to provide fixed prices for goods and services which will be made and delivered in the future at unknown cost levels.

▪ Governments find budgeting difficult during periods of high inflation. Although many government revenues rise with inflation (e.g. value added tax), this may still leave an overall shortfall caused by higher costs of employing government workers and higher contract costs for new capital projects.

▪ Inflation can be socially divisive as those on fixed incomes (e.g. state pensioners) fall behind those individuals who are able to negotiate wage increases to compensate for inflation. Inflation also discriminates between individuals that own different types of assets. While some physical assets such as housing may keep up with inflation, financial assets may be eroded by inflation rates that exceed the rate of interest paid. In effect, borrowers may be subsidized by lenders.

- High levels of inflation can put exporters at a competitive disadvantage. If the inflation level of the United Kingdom is higher than that of competing nations, UK firms' goods will become more expensive to export, while the goods from a low inflation country will be much more attractive to buyers in the United Kingdom, all other things being equal. This will have an adverse effect on UK producers and on the country's overseas balance of trade (assuming that there is no compensating change in exchange rates).

High levels of inflation can create uncertainty in the business environment, making firms reluctant to enter into long-term commitments. Failure to invest or reinvest can ultimately be damaging for the individual firm as well as the economy as a whole.

This is not to say that completely stable prices (i.e. a zero rate of inflation) are necessarily good for a national economy. A moderate level of price inflation encourages individuals and firms to invest in stocks, knowing that their assets will increase in value. A moderate level of inflation also facilitates the task of realigning prices by firms. A price reduction can be achieved simply by holding prices constant during a period of price inflation. Where price inflation causes uncertainty for firms purchasing raw materials, this uncertainty can often be overcome by purchasing on the 'futures' market. Such markets exist for a diverse range of commodities such as oil, grain and metals and allow a company to pay a fixed price for goods delivered at a specified time in the future, irrespective of whether the market price for that commodity has risen or fallen in the meantime.

The opposite of inflation is deflation, and this too can result in social, economic and political problems.

- Individuals and firms that own assets whose value is depreciating perceive that they have become poorer and adjust their spending patterns accordingly. In Britain during the early 1990s, many individuals saw their most important asset – their house – falling in value as part of a general fall in property prices. In extreme cases, individuals felt 'locked' into their house as they had borrowed more to buy it than the house was currently worth. They therefore had difficulty trading up to a larger house, thereby possibly also creating demand for home-related items such as fitted kitchens. More generally, falling property prices undermined consumer confidence, in sharp contrast to the 1980s when rising house prices created a 'feel good' factor, fuelling spending across a range of business sectors.

- Individuals and firms will be reluctant to invest in major items of capital expenditure if they feel that, by waiting a little longer, they could obtain those assets at a lower price.

- Deflation can become just as socially divisive as inflation. Falling house prices can lead many people who followed government and social pressures to buy their house rather than renting to feel that they have lost out for their efforts.

Economic growth

Growth is a goal shared by businesses and governments alike. It was suggested in Chapter 7 that businesses like to grow, for various reasons. Similarly, governments generally pursue growth in gross domestic product for many reasons.

■ A growing economy allows for steadily rising standards of living, when measured by conventional economic indicators. In most Western economies, this is indicated by increased spending on goods and services that are considered luxuries. Without underlying growth in GDP, increases in consumer spending will be short lived.

■ For governments, growth results in higher levels of income through taxes on incomes, sales and profits. This income allows government to pursue socially and politically desirable infrastructure spending, such as the construction of new hospitals or road improvements.

■ A growing economy creates a 'feel good' factor in which individuals feel confident about being able to obtain employment and subsequently feel confident about making major purchases.

Economic growth in itself may not necessarily leave a society feeling better off, as economic well-being does not necessarily correspond to quality of life. There is growing debate about whether some of the consequences of economic growth, such as increased levels of pollution and traffic congestion, really leave individuals feeling better off. There is also the issue of how the results of economic growth are shared out between members of a society.

THINKING AROUND THE SUBJECT: WHAT VALUE ON QUALITY OF LIFE?

One of the paradoxes of Western developed economies is that despite increased prosperity, as measured by GDP, people appear to be more stressed and increasingly unhappy. Despite better healthcare, rising incomes and labour-saving devices, surveys repeatedly show people are no happier than they were in the 1950s. This seems far from the economist JM Keynes' prediction in the 1930s that once the 'economic problem' of satisfying basic material needs was achieved, people would not have to work so hard and would devote their spare time to trying to live well.

People appear to be inconsistent in their statements about what would make them happy. They may say that a shorter travelling time to work would make them happy, yet more and more people travel longer distances to their place of employment in order to work harder to earn more money for more goods which in the end do not make them feel any better.

One explanation for this apparent paradox is that people compare themselves with others. If everyone is getting richer, people do not get happier – they do so only if they get richer relative to their peers. A BMW 3 series car can be a status symbol only if few people can afford it. When incomes rise and more people can afford the luxury brand, individuals become motivated to work harder to afford an even better model. This mechanism is a driving force behind economic growth, but it has the effect of constantly undermining the underlying benefit of economic progress.

Politicians tend to focus on economic growth figures, but should they instead be concentrating more on indices of happiness? Indices of depression and mental illness have been rising sharply in most Western countries in the past couple of decades, and seem to be closely correlated with economic growth. According to Lord Layard, author of a book on happiness, one in six people in the UK is thought to suffer from some form of mental illness. He has argued that a course of cognitive behavioural therapy can alleviate depression in 60 per cent of cases and typically costs about £1000. Is £1000 spent on relieving someone's depression, so they benefit in terms of happiness, a better investment by the government than £1000 spent increasing the competitiveness and efficiency of manufacturing industry?

Distribution of wealth

Governments overtly and covertly have objectives relating to the distribution of economic wealth between different groups in society. In the United Kingdom, the trend since the Second World War has been for a gradual convergence in the prosperity of all groups, as the very rich have been hit by high levels of income, capital gains and inheritance tax, while the poorer groups in society have benefited from increasing levels of social security payments. During periods of Labour administrations, the tendency has been for taxes on the rich to increase, tilting the distribution of wealth in favour of poorer groups. However, the period of the Conservative governments in the 1980s saw this process put into reverse as high-income groups benefited from the abolition of higher rates of income tax and the liberalization of inheritance taxes. At the same time, many social security benefits were withdrawn or reduced in scope or amount, leaving many lower- or middle-income groups worse off. The post-1997 Labour government has tended to reverse this trend, for example by intro-ducing a statutory minimum wage and increasing a number of benefits paid to disadvantaged groups.

The effects of government policy objectives on the distribution of income can have profound implications for an organization's marketing activities. During most of the post-war years, the tendency was for mid-market segments to grow significantly. In the car sector, this was associ-ated with the success of mid-range cars such as the Ford Escort and Mondeo. During periods of Labour administration, the sale of luxury cars had tended to suffer. The boom of the late 1980s and mid-1990s saw the rapid rise in income of the top groups in society, resulting in a significant growth in luxury car sales. Manufacturers such as BMW, Mercedes-Benz and Jaguar benefited from this trend.

Improving productivity

Productivity growth, alongside high and stable levels of employment, is central to long-term economic performance and rising living standards. Increasing the productivity of the economy has become a key objective of successive UK governments. Government approaches to improving long-term productivity have followed two broad strands: maintaining macroeco-nomic stability to enable firms and individuals to plan for the future, and implementing micro-economic reforms to remove the barriers which prevent markets from functioning efficiently. These microeconomic reforms address historic weaknesses in competitiveness, investment, research and development, innovation and entrepreneurship.

Stable exchange rate

A stable value of sterling in terms of other major currencies is useful to businesses that are thereby able to accurately predict the future cost of raw materials bought overseas and the ster-ling value they will receive for goods and services sold overseas. Stable exchange rates can also help consumers, for example in budgeting for overseas holidays. It is, however, debatable just what the 'right' exchange rate is that governments should seek to maintain (this is discussed further in Chapter 12).

An important contributor to maintaining a stable exchange rate is the maintenance of the balance of payments. Governments avoid large trade deficits, which can have the effect of lowering the exchange rate. From a business perspective, balance of trade surpluses tend to benefit the economy through the creation of jobs, additional economic growth and a general feeling of business confidence. Surpluses created from overseas trade can be used to finance overseas lending and investment, which in turn generate higher levels of earnings from overseas in future years.

THINKING AROUND THE SUBJECT:
PENSIONS CRISIS – WHAT PENSIONS CRISIS?

To many commentators, a crisis is looming as retiring people find that their pensions are not sufficient to allow them to lead the lifestyle that they had expected. But research published by the Future Foundation in 2004 cast some doubt about the scale of any such 'crisis', and highlighted differences in wealth between different age groups.

Its International Longevity Centre UK study showed that the average amount of wealth for those aged 55 has reached a record £130,000. This was on top of the money they may have in their pension funds. The report challenged the traditional perception of all older people as needy, pointing out that a significant number of middle-aged people were 'over-saving' for their retirement. Increases in home ownership coupled with the house-price boom and greater participation in company and private pensions among those now in their 40s and 50s were largely responsible for the emergence of the golden generation, with inequalities emerging between affluent, property-owning retirees and those who had low lifetime earnings and lived in rented accommodation.

The study also indicated that although levels of unsecured debt were high among younger people — peaking at £5000 to £6000 for those in their early 20s — by the age of 44 levels of consumer debt declined sharply as individuals prepared for retirement by paying off their loans and building up their savings and investments. By retirement, very few individuals had any unsecured debt. The study also shows that key transition from becoming a mortgage-holder to an outright homeowner occurs when people are aged between 55 and 59. People from 45 to 59 are the most likely to benefit from inherited wealth.

The Future Foundation had earlier reported that there is likely to be a significant growth in the wealth of the richest 20 per cent of the UK population, largely made up of '60s generation' people who are typically individualistic and liberal minded. Individuals with readily disposable assets (excluding houses and pension policies) of more than £50,000 were expected to exceed 5 million by 2005, and have been dubbed the 'mass affluent'. Typical members of this group are retired professionals, married but with no dependent children, and who inherited property from parents and received windfalls from privatized utilities and building society conversions. They are also likely to have a substantial occupational pension.

For businesses, the attractions of such a group are enormous and many financial services companies, for example, have targeted this group with products that meet their needs. For governments, the emergence of this mass affluent group raises a number of issues. Should policy seek to reduce the imbalances which are inherent in a society where some people have a good pension and others don't? Should this group be excluded from means-tested benefits, simply because they have saved for their retirement whereas others have either chosen or not been able to save for theirs? Should this group be expected to provide its own healthcare, or should the state continue to provide a service for all, regardless of wealth?

Government borrowing

Government borrowing represents the difference between what it receives in any given year from taxation and trading sources and what it needs in order to finance its expenditure programmes. The difference is often referred to as public sector net borrowing (PSNB). The level of PSNB is partly influenced by political considerations, with right-wing free market advocates favouring a reduced role for the government, reflected in a low level of net borrowing. Advocates of intervention are happier to see the PSNB rise. Government borrowing tends to rise during periods of economic recession and fall during periods of boom. This can be explained by income (especially from income and profits taxes) rising relative to expenditure during a boom and expenditure (especially on social security benefits) rising relative to income during a recession. Taxes and public spending tend to be quite cyclical, reflecting political ideology and the state of the national and international economy and trends, as discussed earlier (see Figure 11.8). Figure 11.9 shows a breakdown of total government budgeted income and expenditure by category for the year 2004–5.

11.5.2 Government management of the economy

From government policy objectives come strategies by which these policy objectives can be achieved. This is an area where it can be possible to line up a dozen economists and get a dozen different answers to the same problem. Sometimes, political ideology can lead to the strategy being considered to be just as important as the policy objectives, with supporters of alternative strategies showing very strong allegiance to them.

In trying to reconcile multiple objectives, governments invariably face a dilemma in reconciling all of them simultaneously. Of the three principal economic objectives (maintaining employment, controlling inflation and economic growth), satisfying objectives for any two invariably causes problems with the third (see Figure 11.10). It is therefore common for governments to shift their emphasis between policy objectives for political and pragmatic reasons. However, many surveys of business leaders have suggested that what they consider important above all else is stability in government policy. If the government continually changes the economic goal posts or its economic strategy, businesses' own planning processes can be thrown into confusion.

Sometimes, policy can be implemented in pursuit of one objective, only for adverse side effects to appear, leading to policy being directed to solving this second problem. During much of the 1990s, UK governments put the reduction in inflation as the top economic policy priority and achieved this through high interest rates and a strong value of sterling, among other things. However, high interest rates and a strong pound created recessionary conditions, signified by falling demand, rising unemployment and reduced levels of investment. Resolving these problems then became a priority for government policy.

Two commonly used approaches to economic management can be classified under the headings of:

1 fiscal policy, which concentrates on stimulating the economy through changes in government income and expenditure
2 monetary policy, which influences the circular flow of income by changes in the supply of money and interest rates.

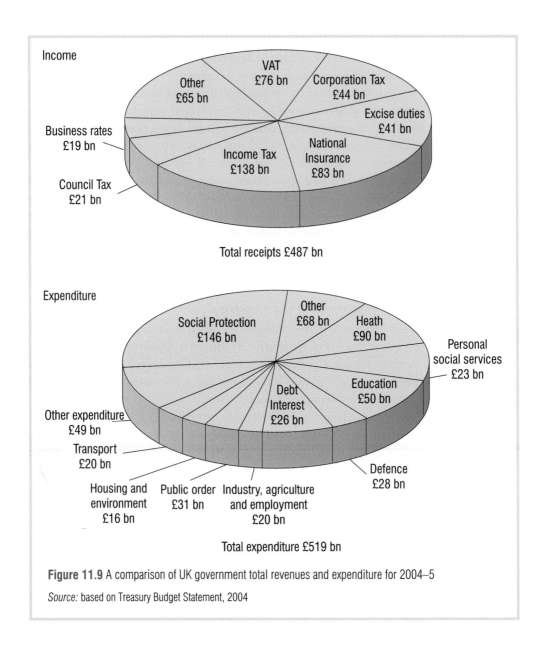

Figure 11.9 A comparison of UK government total revenues and expenditure for 2004–5

Source: based on Treasury Budget Statement, 2004

Fiscal policy

Government is a major element of the circular flow of income, both as tax collector and as a source of expenditure for goods and services and payments to households. Increases in government spending have the effect of injecting additional income into the circular flow and, through the multiplier effect, thereby increasing the demand for goods and services. Reductions in government spending have the opposite effect. Changes in taxation can similarly affect the circular flow of income (e.g. a cut in income tax effectively injects more money into the economy).

	Policy goals		
Possible effects of policy goals	Economy: steady increase in GDP	Employment: maintain ful employment	Inflation: maintain stable currency
Economy	—	Full employment contributes to GDP growth	Desire to retain low level of inflation may curb economic growth
Employment	Rapid GDP growth can lead to 'over-full' employment and skill shortages	—	Desire to retain low level of inflation may limit employment opportunities
Inflation	Economic growth may lead to excessive demand relative to supply, resulting in inflation	Full employment can lead to an inflationary spiral of wage increases	—

Figure 11.10 Problems in reconciling conflicting economic policy objectives

The use of fiscal measures to regulate the economy achieved prominence with the economist John Maynard Keynes, whose followers are generally referred to as Keynsians. Keynes developed his ideas as a means of overcoming the high levels of unemployment and falling commodity prices which were associated with the Great Depression of the 1930s. Conventional economics had failed to return resource markets to equilibrium, largely because of rigidities that had built up in markets. Instead, Keynes advocated the use of fiscal policy to increase the level of aggregate demand within the economy. Through a multiplier effect, spending by workers employed on government 'pump-priming' projects would filter through to private-sector suppliers, who would in turn employ further workers, thereby eventually eradicating unemployment. If the economy showed signs of becoming too active, with scarcity in resource markets and rising price levels, suppression of demand through fiscal actions would have the effect of reducing inflationary pressures (Figure 11.11).

In the 1930s, fiscal measures were considered quite revolutionary and resulted in such projects as the electrification of railways and the construction of the National Grid being undertaken not just for the end result but also for the multiplier benefits of carrying out the construction tasks. More recently, road building and government-funded construction in general have been used as a regulator of the economy, on account of their high employment content and low levels of initial 'leakage' to imported supplies. This has, however, served to increase the cyclical pattern of demand facing the construction sector.

Critics of fiscal policy have argued that fiscal intervention is a very clumsy way of trying to return the economy to equilibrium and a method that achieves temporary rather than permanent solutions to underlying economic problems. Keynsian policies call for bureaucratic civil

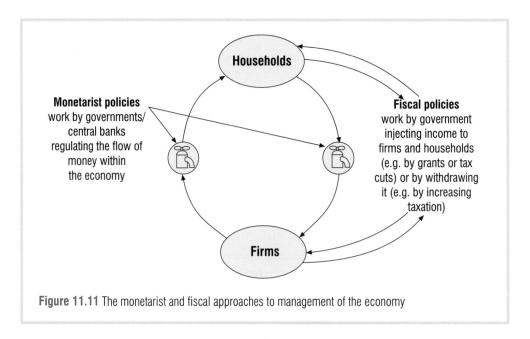

Figure 11.11 The monetarist and fiscal approaches to management of the economy

servants to make quasi-commercial decisions, which they are generally ill-equipped to do. There is much evidence of failed fiscal policy at a local level where government grants and tax incentives have been given to attract industry to depressed areas, only for those industries to close down after a few years (e.g. car factories built in Northern Ireland, Merseyside and Glasgow with government grants and tax concessions have often proved to be commercial failures). The Keynesian notion that business cycles could be eliminated by fiscal policies of taxing and spending were severely challenged by the 'stagflation' of the late 1970s, when high inflation combined with rising levels of unemployment, despite policy makers seemingly doing all the right things according to Keynes.

Critics of fiscal policy look to monetarist policies as an alternative.

Monetary policy

Although Keynes' general theory influenced the world for decades, it has now largely been replaced by the works of Adam Smith, Milton Friedman, Robert Lucas and Paul Samuelson, whose approach advocates change in the volume of money supply to influence aggregate demand in the economy. The basic proposition of monetarism is that government need only regulate the supply of money in order to influence the circular flow of income. From this, adjustments in the economy happen automatically by market forces without the need for intervention by government in the running of business organizations (Figure 11.11). If government wishes to suppress demand in the economy, it would do this by restricting the volume of money in circulation in the economy (e.g. by raising interest rates or restricting the availability of credit). It would do the opposite if it wished to stimulate the economy.

Monetarism appeals to free market purists because of the limited government hands-on intervention that is required. However, governments have found it politically unacceptable to pursue monetarist policies to their logical conclusion. Suppressing demand by controlling the availability of money alone could result in unacceptably high levels of interest rates.

11.5.3 Limitations of government intervention in the national economy

At a practical level, critics of both monetarist and fiscal approaches to economic management have pointed to their failure to significantly influence the long-term performance of an economy. More recently, the fundamental concept of government intervention has been challenged in an emerging body of theoretical and empirical research which is commonly referred to as rational expectations theory. Proponents of the theory claim that it is too simplistic to regard government economic intervention in terms of simple stimulus–response models. It is naïve, for example, to assume that private companies will take an increase in government capital spending as a cue to increase their own productive capacity. Instead, firms rationally assess the likely consequences of government intervention. Therefore, an increase in government capital expenditure may lead to an expectation of eventually higher interest rates and inflation. Faced with this rational expectation, firms may decide to cut back their own expenditure, fearing the consequences for their own business of high inflation and interest rates. This is the opposite of the government's intended response. The theory of rational expectations holds that business people have become astute at interpreting economic signals and, because of this, government's ability to manage the national economy is significantly reduced.

11.5.4 The central bank

A nation's central bank plays an important role in the management of the national economy. In the United Kingdom, the Bank of England acts as a lender of last resort and has responsibility for regulating the volume of currency in circulation within the economy. Through its market operations, it intervenes to influence the exchange rate for sterling. The Bank of England also has a supervisory role in respect of privately owned banks within the United Kingdom.

Countries differ in the extent to which powers of the central bank are separated from government. In the United States and Germany, for example, granting the central bank a quasi-autonomous status and allowing it freedom to make decisions on monetary policy has for a long time been regarded as a means of guaranteeing prudent management of the money supply against political intervention for possibly short-term opportunistic objectives. Against this, the argument is put forward that central banks should be politically accountable and should be influenced by the social and political implications of their actions and not just the more narrowly defined monetary ones. In the United Kingdom, the Bank of England has traditionally been influenced by the Treasury, and seen to be effectively a branch of government decision making. However, the incoming Labour government in 1997 decided to give autonomy to much of the Bank's activity through a newly formed Monetary Policy Committee (MPC), made up of a panel of eight economics experts, plus the Governor of the Bank of England who acts as Chair. The Monetary Policy Committee is free to set interest rates at a level which it considers prudent and in the best interests of the country. Opinion remains divided on the relative merits of a politically influenced central bank and one that is above sectional political interests. While there is evidence that the MPC has acted with integrity, business leaders have sometimes accused it of being dominated by academics and financiers who are unable to empathize with the problems faced by businesses. Employers' pressure groups, such as the CBI, feel less able to put pressure on the MPC than they previously could on Treasury ministers.

Throughout the EU, the development of a single currency has placed much greater control over monetary policy in the hands of the European Central Bank (ECB). The power of individual member states to determine their own interest rates and monetary policy is handed over to the ECB which also handles member states' currency reserves. The subject of the single European currency is discussed further in Chapter 12.

CASE STUDY

BOOM AND BUST IN CHINA?

Ideas about the best way to manage national economies have changed over time. This chapter has discussed how Keynsian policies have tended to give way to monetarist policies as dominant paradigms for managing the economies of Western developed countries. Monetarist policies work best where markets are deregulated, and the effects of monetary change can rapidly be taken on board by firms and households through adjustments to their savings and expenditure. In reality, the economic framework of many emerging economies poses quite a different challenge for economic management, as a study of China demonstrates.

China is an emerging economy with an underdeveloped financial system. The period from the 1990s had been one of almost continuous boom, with the annual growth rate of GDP averaging about 9 per cent. The country manages to combine very tight centralized political control by the Communist Party with thriving capitalism in its Special Economic Development Zones. But by 2005, the strength of the Chinese economy was being questioned by many, and it seemed that the economy was overheating. Would this centralized control by the Communist Party be strong enough to prevent a Western-style boom and bust cycle? Or had the country gone down the route of economic liberalization which laid it open to the type of economic cycle that the West had experienced repeatedly during the previous century?

China traditionally adopted the sort of approach to economic management favoured in the West in the 1950s and 1960s, when currencies were fixed to the dollar and credit controls were used to regulate unemployment and inflation. As a result, China has been less prone to economic or financial crisis than those emerging countries where financial liberalization allowed hot money to flow in and out of the country quickly, precipitating a currency crisis which eventually impacts on the rest of the economy.

China has a very high level of savings by households, which are typically invested in government-owned banks. But these state-run banks lend mainly to state-run firms without being subject to market-based disciplines. As a result, there was an evident massive overinvestment in productive capacity, with little regard for return on capital. It seemed that the Chinese economy, where state planning co-exists with market forces, had difficulty in adjusting to change. In the case of privately owned companies, when demand begins to fall (for example, in response to a fall in demand from Western countries), the companies cut their investment. However, in the case of state-controlled companies, political factors dominate and investment is not necessarily cut back when demand falls.

Traditional reaction of the Chinese government in its management of the economy has been to use administrative arrangements to change capacity. However, in a sign that

China was moving further to a capitalist-based system, in January 2005, it announced an increase in interest rates. The decision to increase interest rates not only raised the possibility that the economy would slow sharply during the following year but also suggested that a revaluation of the Chinese currency – the yuan – was less likely. A revaluation would have made China's exports more expensive in overseas markets, posing a further threat to the expansion plans of domestic producers. This in turn would affect the performance of companies producing goods and services for the expanding domestic market. Although the Chinese economic boom of the 1990s was based on export-led growth, by 2005 there were strong signs that the economy was becoming increasingly driven by domestic demand. A growing number of middle-class people were now earning a level of income which triggered a range of purchases which had previously been considered to be unaffordable luxuries. It seemed that the Chinese business cycle would increasingly be influenced by international and domestic market factors. The export-led nature of the economy had made the country quite dependent on the wealth of those countries that its manufacturers exported to. It was no coincidence that China's period of great economic growth also coincided with a period of great economic prosperity in the United States and Europe. But with the development of the domestic economy, an additional cyclical factor would set in. Faced with falling export orders, domestic employment would be likely to fall, and consequently the number of people earning a level of income that triggers 'luxury' purchases would fall. There would therefore be not only a primary effect of falling exports, but also a secondary effect from falling demand for domestic producers.

QUESTIONS

1 To what extent is it possible, or desirable, for governments to manage a national economy through centralized planning systems of the type that have traditionally been practised in China?
2 Summarize the macroeconomic factors that will influence demand in China for consumer durables such as cars and televisions over the next decade.
3 What are the key consequences for the Chinese economy of the business cycle?

SUMMARY

This chapter has reviewed the structure of national economies and the flow of income between different elements of the economy. Producers, consumers and government are interrelated in the circular flow of income. Business cycles occur because the speed of the circular flow of income temporarily increases or decreases. Although governments seek to limit the magnitude of the business cycle, the cycle can pose problems (and opportunities) for business organizations. The rate at which an organization can grow can be constrained by the rate at which the national economy is growing (**Chapter 7**). This chapter has reviewed economic indicators that companies can read in order to better understand and predict the environment in which they operate. A good information system (**Chapter 4**) should be able to analyse leading indicators of the economy rapidly and effectively.

The state of the economic environment is very much influenced by politicians, and the interaction between the economic and political environments is developed further in **Chapter 2**. This chapter has recognized that the national economic environment is part of the international economic environment and international economic issues are discussed in **Chapter 12**.

Key Terms

Accelerator effect	(399)	Fiscal policy	(419)	Multiplier effect	(398)
Borrowing	(407)	Gross domestic product		Public sector net borrowing	
Business cycle	(402)	(GDP)	(402)	(PSNB)	(417)
Central bank	(421)	Inflation	(400)	Recession	(392)
Circular flow of income	(395)	Injections	(396)	Retail Prices Index (RPI)	(406)
Competitive cost		Interest rates	(406)	Savings ratio	(405)
advantage	(392)	Invisibles	(392)	Turning point	(409)
Confidence level	(406)	Macroeconomic analysis	(389)	Unemployment	(403)
Deflation	(406)	Models	(401)	Withdrawals	(396)
Disposable income	(405)	Monetarism	(420)		
Economic structure	(390)	Monetary Policy			
Exchange rate	(407)	Committee	(421)		

CHAPTER REVIEW QUESTIONS

1 'Economic policy is the product of the conflicting desires of governments for price stability and full employment stability.' Discuss this statement in the context of your government's economic policies. (*Based on CIM Marketing Environment Examination question*)

2 What would be the marketing implications of your present government's current economic policies? (*Based on CIM Marketing Environment Examination question*)

3 During 1997, the UK government announced that it would fund the creation of a new university campus in a deprived part of Belfast. What multiplier benefits are likely to be associated with this project?

4 Identify some of the consequences for a UK vehicle manufacturer of a UK inflation rate of 5 per cent per annum, compared to an EU average of 2 per cent.

5 Contrast the effects of 'tight' fiscal and tight monetary policies on the construction sector.

6 In the context of 'rational expectations' theory, what evidence could you suggest to indicate that business people 'see through' the short-term implications of government economic policies?

ACTIVITY

You and your friends spend £200 on a night out at a nightclub, drinking beer, having a meal beforehand and taking a taxi home. Use the multiplier model to assess the effects on the local economy. What is the overall benefit locally? How much leaks out of the local economy?

Useful Websites

Institute of Economic Affairs

The IEA's aim is to explain free market ideas to the public, including politicians, students, journalists, businessmen, academics and anyone interested in public policy.

http://www.iea.org.uk/

The Institute for Fiscal Studies

The IFS is an independent research organization that aims to provide high-quality economic analysis of public policy. The IFS home page provides links to analysis of topical economic issues, government budgets, IFS surveys and other online economics and social sciences resources.

http://www1.ifs.org.uk

Business Cycle Indicators

The Conference Board is a not-for-profit, non-advocacy, business research and membership organization with 2800 companies and other enterprises in 63 counties. It provides timely research on management practices and economic trends and is a frequently quoted private source of business information.

http://www.tcb-indicators.org/

Confederation of British Industry

The CBI represents companies from all sectors of UK business and is the premier organization speaking for companies in the UK. Its website provides details of CBI surveys and discussion of topical economic issues.

http://www.cbi.org.uk/home.html

Centre for Economic Performance

The CEP was established by the Economic and Social Research Council. Based at the London School of Economics and Political Science, it is now one of the leading academic research centres in Europe and a world leader in economic research. Its website provides discussion on causes of countries' and firms economic performance.

http://cep.lse.ac.uk

UK Treasury

Home page of HM Treasury that includes analysis of recent government economic measures, revenue and expenditure.

http://www.hm-treasury.gov.uk/

The European Central Bank

Home page of the ECB that provides European economic analysis.

http://www.ecb.int/

Further Reading

Macroeconomics can be a complex subject and this chapter has reviewed only the key elements of the macroeconomic system. For a fuller discussion of the subject, the following texts are useful:

Burda, M. and Wyplosz, C. (2001) *Macroeconomics: A European Text*, 2nd edn, Oxford University Press.

Griffiths, A. and Wall, S. (eds) (2004) *Applied Economics: An Introductory Course*, 10th edn, London, Prentice Hall.

Sawyer, M. (ed.) (2004) *The UK Economy: A Manual of Applied Economics*, Oxford University Press.

For a review of the UK economy, the following statistical data are published regularly by the Office for National Statistics:

UK National Accounts (The Blue Book): the principal annual publication for national account statistics, covering value added by industry, the personal sector, companies, public corporations, central and local government, published annually.

Economic Trends: a monthly compendium of economic data which gives convenient access from one source to a range of economic indicators.

References

Eurostat (1998) *Eurostat Yearbook 1998*, Luxembourg, Statistical Office of the European Communities.

Eurostat (2005) *Eurostat Yearbook 2005*, Luxembourg, Statistical Office of the European Communities.

Future Foundation (2004) *Asset Accumulation and Lifestage Report*, London, Future Foundation.

ILO (International Labor Organization) (2004) Bureau of Statistics, http://laborsta.ilo.org/, accessed 17 April 2004.

Wood, P.A. (1987) 'Producer services and economic change, some Canadian evidence', in *Technological Change and Economic Policy*, K. Chapman and G. Humphreys (eds), London, Blackwell.

Chapter 12

The International Business Environment

12.1 THE TREND TOWARDS A GLOBAL BUSINESS ENVIRONMENT

At some point, many business organizations recognize that their growth can continue only if they exploit overseas markets. However, entering overseas markets can be extremely risky, as evidenced by examples of recent failures where companies failed to foresee all the problems involved.

■ The mobile phone company MMO_2 invested over £1.5 billion in the Dutch mobile phone operator Telfort but failed to achieve higher than fifth ranking in the Dutch market. In April 2003 the company admitted defeat and sold the entire Dutch operation for just £16 million.

■ The grocery retailer Sainsbury's pulled out of Egypt in 2001, only two years after investing in a chain of 100 supermarkets. Sainsbury's had gone out on a limb in Egypt, which had no tradition of supermarket shopping, and the company was not helped by persistent rumours of links with Jewish owners. Sainsbury's two years of involvement in the Egyptian market had incurred a loss of over £100 million.

■ Even the fast food retailer McDonald's initially failed to make profits when it entered the UK market in the 1970s and had to rapidly adjust its service offer in order to achieve viability.

Nevertheless, a company which has successfully developed its business strategy should be well placed to extend this development into overseas markets. There are many examples of companies that have successfully developed overseas markets, including the following.

■ The retailer Tesco successfully reduced its dependence on the saturated UK grocery market by developing outlets in the Far East and Eastern Europe.

■ The mobile phone company Vodafone has expanded from its UK base and now provides service in 30 countries, reducing the company's unit costs through economies of scale, and offering seamless, added value services to international travellers.

■ The Irish airline Ryanair started life with a route network which focused on Dublin. With successful expansion of its route network, most of its services now do not call at its Irish base.

■ Carphone Warehouse was the brainchild of entrepreneur Charles Dunstone and after a small-scale start in London, it has successfully expanded to operate more than 1100 stores throughout Europe, operating under the Carphone Warehouse banner in the UK and the Phone House in France, Spain, Germany, Sweden and the Netherlands.

Many of the fundamental principles of environmental analysis which have been applied to a firm's domestic market will be of relevance in an international setting. The processes of identifying market opportunities and threats, developing strategies, implementing those strategies and monitoring performance involve fundamentally similar principles as those which apply within the domestic market. The major challenge to companies seeking to expand overseas lies in sensitively adapting business strategies which have worked at home to the needs of overseas markets whose environments may be totally different to anything previously experienced.

Globalization of the business environment has occurred because of a number of developments.

■ There has been a tendency for barriers to international trade to be removed, facilitated by the efforts of the World Trade Organization.

■ A tendency towards cultural convergence has reduced the differences between national market characteristics, thereby reducing the cost of adapting products to specific national markets.

■ Improved communications (e.g. the telephone, air travel and the Internet) have reduced the cost of dealing with faraway places.

■ The growth of large multinational corporations has facilitated the process of seeing the world as one global market.

Nevertheless, new challenges face companies doing business internationally. According to Naomi Klein, global service brands such as Shell, Wal-Mart and McDonald's have become metaphors for a global economic system gone awry, as evidenced by growing concern about the pay and conditions of Third World workers. She believes that brands and their multi-national owners, rather than governments, will increasingly become the target for activists (Klein 2000).

At a macroenvironmental level, success in international trade can help to explain the emergence and growth of many of the countries that have achieved economic pre-eminence in the world, during both modern and ancient history. The Venetians, Spaniards and later the British, Americans and Japanese all saw periods of rapid domestic growth coincide with the growth of their trade with the rest of the world.

International trade is becoming increasingly important, representing not only opportunities for domestic producers to earn revenue from overseas but also threats to domestic producers from overseas competition. Taking the UK as an example, while the value of GDP increased by 21 per cent between 1995 and 2002, the value of exports increased by 31 per cent. The international trade of a nation is made up of the sum total of the efforts of its individual producers and consumers who decide to buy or sell abroad rather than at home. To gain a general overview of the reasons why trade between countries takes place, explanations can be found at two levels:

1 at a micro-level, individual firms are motivated to trade overseas
2 at a macro-level, the structure of an economy and the world trading system can either inhibit or encourage international trade.

We will consider first the micro reasons which lead firms to enter international trade, and then the aggregate macroenvironmental reasons why international trade takes place.

12.1.1 Firms' reasons for going global

For an individual company, exporting to overseas markets can be attractive for a number of reasons. These can be analysed in terms of 'pull' factors, which derive from the attractiveness of a potential overseas market, and 'push' factors, which make an organization's domestic market appear less attractive.

■ For firms seeking growth, overseas markets represent new market segments, which they may be able to serve with their existing range of products. In this way, a company can stick to producing products that it is good at. Finding new overseas markets for existing or slightly modified products does not expose a company to the risks of expanding both its product range and its market coverage simultaneously.

■ Saturation of its domestic market can force an organization to seek overseas markets. Saturation can come about where a product reaches the maturity stage of its life cycle in the domestic market, while being at a much earlier stage of the cycle in less-developed overseas markets. While the market for fast food restaurants may be approaching saturation in a number of Western markets – especially the United States – they represent a new opportunity in the early stages of development in many Eastern European countries.

■ As part of its portfolio management, an organization may wish to reduce its dependence upon one geographical market. The attractiveness of individual national markets can change in a manner that is unrelated to other national markets. For example, costly competition can develop in one national market but not others, world economic cycles show lagged effects between different economies, and government policies – through specific regulation or general economic management – can have counterbalancing effects on market prospects.

■ The nature of a firm's product may require an organization to become active in an overseas market. This particularly affects transport-related services such as scheduled airline services and courier services. For example, a UK scheduled airline flying between London and Paris would most likely try to exploit the non-domestic market at the Paris end of its route.

■ Commercial buyers of products operating in a number of overseas countries may require their suppliers to be able to cater for their needs across national boundaries. As an example, a company may wish to engage accountants that are able to provide auditing and management accounting services in its overseas subsidiaries. For this, the firm of accountants would probably need to have created an operational base overseas. Similarly, firms selling in a number of overseas markets may wish to engage an advertising agency which can organize a global campaign in a number of overseas markets.

■ Similarly, there are many cases where private consumers demand goods and services that are available internationally. An example is the car hire business, where customers frequently need to be able to book a hire car in one country for collection and use in another. To succeed in attracting these customers, car hire companies need to operate internationally.

■ Some goods and services are highly specialized and the domestic market is too small to allow economies of scale to be exploited. Overseas markets must be exploited in order to achieve a critical mass, which allows a competitive price to be reached. Specialized aircraft engineering services and oil exploration services fall into this category.

■ Economies of scale also result from extending the use of brands in overseas markets. Expenditure by a fast food company on promoting its brand to UK residents is wasted when those citizens travel abroad and cannot find the brand that they have come to value. Newly created overseas outlets will enjoy the benefit of promotion to overseas visitors at little additional cost.

In addition to gaining access to new markets, individual firms may enter international trade to secure resource inputs. The benefits of buying overseas can include lower prices, greater consistency of supply, higher quality, or taking advantage of export subsidies available to overseas suppliers. Manufacturing has become a highly specialized business, and the traditional approach of companies attempting to make as much of their product locally in-house has long since gone. Today there is increasing separation of the assembly of products from the manufacture of components, which are likely to be outsourced to other subsidiaries within the same multinational company, or to other specialized businesses. With global communications and reliable logistics, outsourcing is a global activity which seeks out suppliers based on factors such as low cost, high skills or manufacturing capacity. In the case of raw materials that are not available in the domestic market, a firm may have little choice in its decision to buy from overseas.

12.1.2 Macroenvironmental reasons for globalization

From the perspective of national economies, a number of reasons can be identified for the increasing importance of international trade.

- Goods and services are traded between economies in order to exploit the concept of comparative cost advantage. This holds that an economy will export those goods and services that it is particularly well suited to producing and import those where another country has an advantage. The principles of comparative cost advantage are discussed more fully in Section 12.2.1.

- The removal of many restrictions on international trade (such as the creation of the Single European Market and the activities of the World Trade Organization) has allowed countries to exploit their comparative cost advantages. Nevertheless, restrictions on trade remain, especially for trade in services.

- Increasing household disposable incomes result in greater consumption of many categories of luxuries, such as overseas travel, which can only be provided by overseas suppliers. Against this, economic development within an economy can result in many specialized goods and services which were previously bought in from overseas being provided by local suppliers. Many developing countries, for example, seek to reduce their dependence on overseas banking and insurance organizations by encouraging the development of a domestic banking sector.

12.1.3 Cultural convergence?

It has often been claimed that a major driver of international trade is cultural convergence, implying that individuals are becoming more alike in the way that they think and behave. Improved communications and increasing levels of overseas travel have undoubtedly led to homogenization of international market segments. Combined with the decline in trade barriers, convergence of cultural attitudes allows many organizations to regard parts of their overseas markets as though they are part of their domestic market. Advocates of the concept of cultural convergence remind us that needs are universal and therefore there should be no reason why satisfaction of those needs should not also be universal. If a Big Mac satisfies a New Yorker's need for hygienic, fast and convenient food, why should it not satisfy those similar needs for someone in Cairo? Against this, many observers have noted individuals' growing need for *identity* in a world which is becoming increasingly homogenized. Support for regional breakaway governments (e.g. by the Kurdish and Basque people) may provide some evidence of this. During the build-up to the Iraq War in 2003, many consumers in Arab countries used purchases of Muslim products to identify themselves with an anti-American cause. Many Western service brands have become despised by some groups as symbols of an alien identity. Banks in many Muslim countries have reported increased interest in syariah-based banking services, which do not charge interest based on the traditional Western banking model (*Business Times* 2002).

Figure 12.1 For many developing countries such as Indonesia, there is a long tradition of fast food provided by hawkers' stalls, such as this one, which provide traditional, low-cost food. As economies develop, hawkers' stalls have tended to decline, but where will the growing number of wealthy consumers choose to spend their money? Will they patronize new Western-style fast food outlets? Or will they invest in home cooking equipment which allows them to store food and prepare a wider selection of food quickly and efficiently? The introduction of fast food restaurants has not always been an immediate success in developing countries, and even in the developed economy of Singapore, cultural traditions have led to a continuing role for organized 'hawkers' markets'.

THINKING AROUND THE SUBJECT:
LOOKING FOR LESS SATURATED BURGER MARKETS?

A saturated domestic market is often the spur for companies to seek new foreign markets. But is there a moral case against companies seeking to promote a Western style of service consumption in countries with well-established and sustainable lifestyles? Fast food companies have stepped up their efforts to develop new foreign markets as Western markets for fast food become saturated. Is it responsible to promote burgers, which are high in saturated fats, to people whose diets are inherently healthier? Is it right that fast food companies should develop low-fat burgers for the American market, partly out of fear of litigation, while selling higher-fat burgers to less developed countries where legislation and consumer awareness of health issues are more lax? Defenders of fast food companies point to the fact that they are providing hygienic food prepared in conditions which may be far superior to the norm in many developing countries. It is claimed that they have offered jobs to individuals which can be the envy of peer groups. Should the solution be greater education of consumers in healthy eating, rather than more regulation? Is greater education a realistic prospect in a culture where fast food has become a cultural icon?

12.2 THEORY OF INTERNATIONAL TRADE

Today, the United Kingdom, like most industrialized countries, is dependent on international trade to maintain its standard of living. Some products that buyers have become accustomed to, such as tropical fruits and gold, would be almost impossible to produce at home. For products such as these, the UK economy could overcome this lack of availability in three possible ways.

1 By using alternative products (which can be produced at home) in place of those that cannot be produced domestically. For example, faced with a domestic shortage of aluminium, many users could switch to domestically produced steel.

2 The domestic economy could try to produce the product at home. This is often impossible where key elements of production are missing (e.g. uranium cannot be produced in the United Kingdom because it is not a naturally occurring substance). In other cases, such as the production of tropical fruits, domestic production can be achieved, but only at a very high cost.

3 The third alternative is to import goods from a country which is able to produce them.

A similar analysis could be made of the options facing all other countries, not just the United Kingdom. Rather than producers in the United Kingdom growing bananas at great expense for domestic consumption, while a producer in a tropical country attempted to grow temperate fruits, both could benefit by specializing in what they are good at and exchanging their output. This is the basis for the theory of comparative cost advantage.

12.2.1 Comparative cost advantage

The theory of comparative cost advantage can be traced back to the work of Adam Smith in the late eighteenth century and broadly states that the world economy – and hence the economies of individual nations – will benefit if all countries:

■ concentrate on producing what they are good at and export the surplus

■ import from other countries those goods that other countries are better able to produce than themselves.

The principles of comparative cost advantage can be illustrated with an example. For simplicity, the following example will assume that there are only two countries in the world – Britain and the 'rest of the world'. A second assumption is that only two products are made in the world – food and coal.

It is possible to draw up a table showing the hypothetical food and coal production possibilities of the two countries.

■ If Britain used all of its natural resources to produce coal, then it could produce 40 tons per year, but no food. It could, on the other hand, use all of its resources to produce 40 tons of food per year, but no coal.

■ By contrast, the rest of the world could produce 160 tons of food a year or 40 tons of coal. The different ratios reflect the fact that Britain and the rest of the world possess different combinations of resources.

■ The maximum possible world output of food is therefore 200 tons or 80 tons of coals.

This can be summarized in a production possibility table (Figure 12.2).

	Food	or	Coal
Britain	40	or	40
Rest of world	160	or	40
World production total	200	or	80

Figure 12.2 Production possibility table: food and coal

Neither country is likely to produce solely coal or food. For Britain to give up 1 ton of coal production will result in an increase in food production of 1 ton. However, if the rest of the world gives up 1 ton of coal production, it can increase food production by 4 tons. In this example, Britain should continue to produce coal, because the comparative cost of giving up land for food is lower than the rest of the world. For Britain, the cost of 1 ton of food is 1 ton of coal. For the rest of the world, the cost of 1 ton of coal is 4 tons of food foregone. The rest of the world has a comparative cost advantage in the production of food (because the 'opportunity cost' of the resources used is lower than in Britain).

The next stage of analysing comparative cost advantages is to consider how production of coal and food may actually be divided between Britain and the rest of the world, and, from this, the pattern of trade that could take place. It is again assumed that there are only two countries in the world, that these are the only two goods traded and that total world production equals total consumption (i.e. stocks are not allowed to accumulate). An additional assumption will be made here that coal is more valuable than food. For the moment, it is assumed that 1 ton of coal is worth 5 tons of food.

Figure 12.3 illustrates two situations:

1 where both countries divide their resources equally between food and coal production, without engaging in trade

2 a revised trade pattern where each country specialises in the product for which it has a comparative cost advantage.

On the basis of the assumptions made, Figure 12.3 indicates that the world as a whole is better off as a result of the two countries specializing in doing what they are good at. Total wealth has gone up from 300 units to 360 units. This pattern would hold so long as the relative costs of production and the terms of trade remained the same. Of course, both of these could, in practice, change. Increased costs in Britain could change its comparative cost in producing food compared to the rest of the world. The pattern would also change if the value of coal went down in relation to the value of food, for example if 1 ton of coal was worth only half a ton of food, and not 5 as in this example.

Of course, this has been a very simple example using quite unrealistic assumptions. However, it does show how international trade can benefit all nations. In reality, substitutions take place between large numbers of countries and an almost infinite range of products. Nevertheless, the underlying principles of exporting what a country is good at and importing

	Original production pattern – no trade		Revised production pattern – specialization	
	Food	Coal	Food	Coal
Britain	20	20	0	40
Rest of world	80	20	160	0
World production total	100	40	160	40
Value of 1 ton of food = 1 unit				
5 ton of coal = 5 units	100	200	160	200
Total wealth	300 units		360 units	

Figure 12.3 Effects on a national economy of specialization based on comparative cost advantage

those products that can be made more cheaply elsewhere still hold true. To give modern examples of what this actually means for the UK economy, Britain is good at producing pharmaceuticals which are sold abroad in large volume. It is not so good at producing labour-intensive textiles which are imported in large amounts from the relatively low wage countries of the Far East.

Although the concept of comparative cost advantage was developed to explain the benefits to total world wealth resulting from each country exploiting its comparative cost advantages with regard to access to raw materials and energy supplies, it can also have application to the services sector. In this way, a favourable climate or outstanding scenery can give a country an advantage in selling tourism services to overseas customers, a point that has not been lost on tourism operators in the Canary Islands and Switzerland respectively. Another basis for comparative cost advantage for services can be found in the availability of low-cost or highly trained personnel (cheap labour for the shipping industry and trained computer software experts for computer consultancy respectively). Sometimes the government of a country can itself directly create comparative cost advantages for a service sector, as where it reduces regulations and controls on an industry, allowing that industry to produce services for export at a lower cost than its more regulated competitors (e.g. many 'offshore' financial services centres impose lower standards of regulation and taxation than their mainstream competitors).

12.2.2 Limitations to the principle of comparative cost advantage

Unfortunately, the principles of comparative cost advantage may sound fine in theory, but it can be difficult to achieve the benefits in practice. In reality, the global ideals described above can become obscured by narrower national interests. Consequently, the full benefits of comparative cost advantage may not be achieved.

▪ Imports can be seen as a threat to established domestic firms. Short-term political pressure to preserve jobs may restrict the ability of firms and individuals to import from the country that is best placed to produce specific products.

- Governments seek to pursue a portfolio of activities within their economies in order to maintain a balanced economy. Also, governments may protect industries in order to create greater employment opportunities for particular social or regional groups of the population.
- Governments may seek to temporarily protect fledgling new industries during their development stage in the hope that they will eventually be able to become strong enough to compete effectively in world markets. Competition early on could kill such infant industries before they are able to develop.
- Trade may not take place in some products – or may be made more difficult – because the requirements of different markets vary. National regulations on matters such as food purity and electrical safety may make it uneconomic to produce special versions of a product for an overseas market.
- Transport costs act as a deterrent to international trade. Although it may be cheaper to produce building materials in southern Europe than in the United Kingdom, the very high transport costs of getting them to the UK market will limit the amount that actually enters international trade.
- National governments often artificially stimulate exports by giving export subsidies, allowing domestic producers to compete in world markets against more efficient producers. The European Union, for example, has frequently been accused of subsidizing the export of agricultural products such as grain and meat to protect European farmers against competition from more efficient and less subsidized American and Australian farmers.
- International politics may severely limit the trade that a country has with the rest of the world. Although the trade barriers that existed within Europe are now disappearing, there is increasing concern that the creation of the EU and other trading blocs, such as the North American Free Trade Agreement area, will have the effect of reducing trade between Europe and the rest of the world.
- Sometimes governments have defence considerations in mind in restricting international trade (for example by restricting arms sales to hostile nations).
- Imports may represent a threat to the culture of a country and governments seek to prevent their import. This particularly affects films and publications (e.g. the governments of many Muslim countries make it difficult for films made in the West to be imported).

Despite a plethora of international agreements to facilitate trade between nations, minor, and sometimes major, trade disputes occur between nations. The countries involved may agree that the benefits of open markets and comparative cost advantage leading to benefits to all are fine in theory, but the actual short-term implications for them are too harmful. It could be that the government in one country is facing an election and restrictions on imports could gain rapid approval for the government. However, if one country is tempted to introduce some sort of control on imports from another country, it will almost inevitably result in retaliation by the other country. This can spiral, resulting in progressively declining world trade levels. The precise methods by which trade is restricted can take a number of forms.

- The extreme form of import control is for a country to ban imports of a product or class of products from one or more countries. For example, the EU has banned imports of food containing genetically modified organisms (GMOs). From 2003, the WTO approved such bans by countries where GMOs could have an adverse effect on human health or biodiversity.

- A tariff can be imposed on goods of a specified type. Governments have imposed tariffs on imports where they believed the product was being 'dumped' by the exporting country at below its production cost, thereby threatening domestic producers with unfair competition. As an example, the US government imposed tariffs of between 8 per cent and 30 per cent on certain kinds of foreign steel in 2002, claiming unfair competition from low-cost producers in countries such as Japan, Brazil and South Korea. A year later, the World Trade Organization judged that this tariff broke WTO rules.
- A quota on the volume of imports of a particular product can be imposed – imports of cars to the United Kingdom from Japan were restrained for a long time on the basis of a voluntarily agreed quota.
- Governments sometimes impose covert controls as an alternative to more formal controls, in order to try to diffuse attention and avoid retaliation. A country may unreasonably claim that an exporting nation's products do not meet quality or safety standards imposed by that country. Many countries used this type of argument – some would say unjustifiably – to ban imports of British beef, claiming that outbreaks of the cattle disease BSE made meat from the United Kingdom potentially unsafe. Sometimes, import documentation and procedures are made so complex that they act to increase the costs of importers relative to domestic producers.

12.2.3 Multinational companies and the exploitation of comparative cost advantages

Multinational companies (MNCs) have been at the forefront of efforts to exploit comparative cost advantage differences between countries. There has been a tendency for MNCs to focus manufacture of one product line (e.g. a car model) in just one or a small number of factories, to serve the whole world. Such factories typically also benefit by being located in a country where production costs (e.g. through lower wage rates or taxation) are comparatively low.

Companies in fiercely competitive markets often calculate that it is cheaper to manufacture a product in a low-cost country such as China and to ship the finished product to the country where there is demand for it. Most British clothes companies now manufacture the bulk of their clothing in less developed countries where wages paid to staff can be a fraction of those that would be paid to UK staff. This can more than offset higher transport costs and allow the company to compete on price, especially where there are significant price points above which buyers will not buy an item. However, locating manufacturing facilities a long way from customers extends the time between a market need being identified and the delivery of goods to meet that need. While fashion for basic underwear and socks may not change much over time, outerwear tends to be much more volatile, with preferred styles and colours changing frequently. If it takes several months to get the latest 'hot' fashion from China to Chichester, it might just arrive in the shops as customers have moved on to a new 'hot' fashion. For this reason, manufacturers supplying goods to highly volatile markets are more likely to favour manufacturing facilities closer to home. In the world of consumer electronics, Sony surprised many people when it brought production of camcorders back from China to Japan (Nakamoto 2003). Digitization had made the product life cycle even shorter than before. Previously, because the market was growing, it was fine to make as many camcorders as the company had capacity for. But, by 2002, it became necessary to adjust product configuration as closely as possible to market demand, something Sony felt was easier to achieve in Japan. Furthermore, this move helped to reduce the company's electronics inventory from ¥923.4 billion in the third quarter of 2000 to ¥627.5 billion in the third quarter of 2001 and again to ¥506.5 billion in the third quarter of 2002. To a company such as Sony, inventory is a business risk in a fast-changing market.

In general, greater distances between focused factories and the end users lead to greater transport uncertainty, increasing the need for 'buffer stocks' to be held in the supply chain. The need to obtain customs clearance can also contribute to delays and variability. Also, breaking down bulk from a focused factory to individual national markets can be expensive. Options include shipping direct from each source to the final market in full containers; or consolidating from each source for each general geographic area, with bulk broken down into intermediate inventory ready for specific markets.

Some companies, such as the computer manufacturer Dell, have examined their value chain and calculated that there are opportunities for delaying the final configuration of a product until it is as close to the customer as possible. They can then achieve lower costs by shipping generic sub-assemblies to the local operation which typically provides finishing, local language packaging, and direct customer delivery. Dell therefore sources many of its components from China and Thailand, among other places, and serves its European markets by assembling them at a plant in Limerick, Ireland.

12.2.4 Exchange rates

Nation states generally have their own currency system which is quite distinct from the currency of their international trading partners. It follows, therefore, that the currency which a buyer wants to use as payment may not be the currency that a seller wants to receive as payment for goods or services. If a British customer buys a Japanese-built car, they would expect to pay for their car in pounds sterling and not Japanese yen. So the Japanese manufacturer must become involved in foreign exchange transactions by converting the sterling which it has received back into yen which it will need in order to buy components and to pay its workforce. The fact that different countries have their own currencies makes life for an exporter more complex and risky than for a company that just serves its domestic market.

The biggest problem arising from the use of multiple currencies for trade is that their value in relation to each other fluctuates through time. The value of one currency in terms of another currency is known as its exchange rate. The exchange rate of the yen to sterling will determine how many yen a Japanese car maker will receive for the sterling that it has received from its customers in the UK.

Currencies are just like any other commodity that is traded in a market. If the demand for a currency is great relative to its supply, then its 'price' (or exchange rate) will rise. The opposite will happen if there is excess supply of that currency. The principles of exchange rate determination are illustrated in Figure 12.4.

Changes in the supply of, or demand for, a currency can come about for a number of reasons.

- Changes in demand for a nation's currency can result from a significant change in exports from that country. If UK exports to Japan suddenly increase, UK firms would be left holding large volumes of yen from their Japanese customers. When the UK exporting

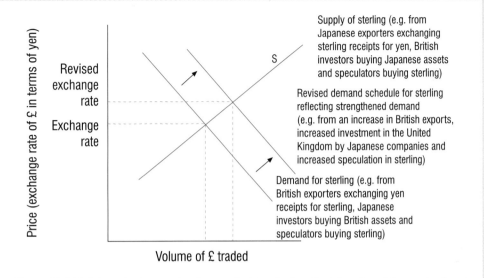

Figure 12.4 Market mechanisms and exchange rate determination: the interaction of the supply of, and demand for, a currency determines the exchange rate

company went to the currency markets to exchange its yen for sterling, its demand for sterling would have the effect of pushing up the price of sterling in terms of yen. While one company on its own may not have much impact on an exchange rate, the combined effects of many companies cause exchange rates to fluctuate.

■ An increase in imports by UK firms from Japan would have an opposite effect. Japanese firms would seek to change the sterling payments they have received into yen. Their supply of sterling will increase relative to demand for it and its price will fall. Of course, in this and the previous example, the actual transactions would normally be handled routinely by the companies' bankers and most trading firms' transactions would be too small on their own to significantly affect exchange rates. Large overseas orders or the collective effects of many buyers and sellers could, however, have a significant effect on exchange rates.

■ Demand for foreign currencies can similarly arise from transactions involving the purchase of assets overseas and the remission of profits and dividends overseas.

■ As in many commodity markets, demand for a currency at any given time is influenced by individuals' expectations about future price levels for a currency. Traders in currencies may use their reserves to buy currencies that they consider are likely to rise and sell those that they expect to fall. Expectations about changes in currency values can be based on factors such as the inflation rate in a country (which has the effect of reducing the purchasing power of its currency); growing imbalances between a country's imports and exports; and general government macroeconomic policy.

■ Intervention by government can affect the supply of, and demand for, its currency. For example, if a government seeks to raise the value of its currency in terms of other currencies (or at least prevent it falling), it can use its gold and foreign currency reserves to buy up its own currency, thereby raising its exchange rate.

From an importer's or exporter's point of view, fluctuations in exchange rates cause considerable uncertainty. Companies selling goods or services abroad may not be certain what revenue they will actually receive if they invoice in a foreign currency, since a change in the exchange rate – between agreeing the price and receiving payment – can earn them more or less than anticipated. Where imports are priced in a producer's currency, importers of goods or services may be uncertain about the final price of their purchases.

From a national government's perspective, a falling exchange rate creates inflationary pressures, since imports become relatively expensive (i.e. it takes more pounds to buy any given yen's worth of imported products). A falling exchange rate helps exporters to achieve overseas sales, because their products effectively become cheaper overseas. It also has the effect of making imports more expensive. Through both of these effects, employment opportunities in the domestic economy are enhanced by a relatively low exchange rate. Governments must balance the stimulus to companies that a low exchange rate brings with the inflationary pressure that it generally entails.

Individual companies can minimize their exposure to risks arising from exchange rate fluctuation in a number of ways.

- Where it is important for a firm to be certain of the future cost of materials imported from overseas, it can enter into forward currency contracts which provide it with a specified amount of foreign currency at an agreed time in the future, at an agreed exchange rate. So even if the value of a currency changes in the meantime, a company can buy its materials from overseas at its budgeted price, using an overseas currency whose value was fixed during its budgeting process.

- Where the buyer's or seller's currency has a history of volatility, they may decide to use a third currency which is regarded as a relatively stable, or 'hard', currency. Many sectors of international trade, such as oil and civil aviation, are routinely priced in US dollars, regardless of the nationality of the buyer and seller.

- The impact of currency fluctuations on large multinational companies can be reduced by trying to plan for expenditure (on components, etc.) in one currency to roughly equal the revenue it expects to earn in that currency. Any change in exchange rates therefore has an overall broadly neutral effect on the organization.

- Fluctuating exchange rates can become an opportunity for companies that can rapidly shift their resources to take advantage of imports from countries that have suddenly become advantageous. Commodity traders operating in 'spot' markets may be able to switch supply sources according to changes in exchange rates.

12.2.5 Fixed exchange rates

An alternative to market-based fluctuating exchange rates is a fixed exchange rate system. Here, countries agree to maintain the value of each other's currency, or at least to keep fluctuations within a very narrow range. Where necessary, governments take action to maintain the agreed rates of exchange.

Prior to the full launch of the euro in 1999, the Exchange Rate Mechanism (ERM) of the EU's European Monetary System (EMS) sought to fix member states' exchange rates relative to other participating members' currencies (the 'parity' rate). Countries achieved this by a variety of policy measures. If a country sought to increase its exchange rate to bring it back up to parity, it could: increase interest rates (which in the short term can attract 'hot money' into a currency, thereby pushing up its value); carry out open market operations where the government uses gold and foreign currency reserves to buy up its own currency; and generally increasing speculators' confidence in its economy (e.g. by reducing inflation or a balance of payments deficit). Although the EMS no longer exists in its original form, the principles are still used. Prior to adopting the euro currency, new members of the EU (and applicant members) have tended to fix the value of their currency in relation to the euro, using the methods described above. This has been true, for example, of Bulgaria which will join the EU in 2007, but has sought to maintain a fixed exchange rate between its lev and the euro since 2002.

12.2.6 European Monetary Union

In 1999, most of the major economies of the EU agreed to replace their own currencies with the euro currency. The development of the euro as a common currency has overcome problems of fluctuating exchange rates between traders in countries that have adopted the euro. Its use has reduced the costs of trade between EU member states and should allow for the develop-ment of a 'hard' currency backed by substantial reserves, and which is able to match the US dollar as a world currency. The UK did not join in the launch of the euro, arguing that a single currency reduces the scope for national governments to manage their economies. For a common currency to be stable over the longer term, it is important that all economies con-verge in terms of such factors as inflation rates and government spending. Without being able to adjust exchange rates and interest rates, national economic policy may be unable to tackle economic problems that are specific to a nation state. Despite the UK's reservations about joining the single European currency, it is likely that UK companies trading with other EU companies may nevertheless adopt the currency. For some, this may be a requirement of their EU trading partners, while others will see benefits in using a strong currency, in much the same way as the US dollar is used. The first few years of the euro saw its value gradually fall against major world currencies, suggesting that traders lacked confidence in the currency and/or the strength of the European economy. However, the value of most cur-rencies is cyclical and the strength of the euro could in due course increase against other world currencies.

It was noted in Chapter 2 that control over currency amounts to control over the economy and one reason for Britain's less than enthusiastic embrace of the euro has been the recogni-tion that the country's powers to take independent economic decisions will be greatly reduced. This has already been seen in the case of the Republic of Ireland, where in 2000 it appeared that a low centrally determined interest rate was inappropriate for the national economy which was showing signs of overheating with a rising rate of inflation, which could have been less-ened by a high interest rate.

Opinion has been divided about the effects of the euro on UK business organizations. Advo-cates of the euro point to the greatly reduced transaction costs involved in trading with other EU countries and the greatly reduced risk of adverse currency movements between agreeing a price and actually completing a transaction. In the early days of the euro, many UK exporters were keen to join the euro area, as sterling was perceived as being overvalued relative to the euro, putting their exports at a competitive disadvantage. Against these arguments, many

THINKING AROUND THE SUBJECT:
A COMMON CURRENCY, SO WILL THERE BE A COMMON PRICE?

Will the development of the single European currency eventually lead to uniform prices for a product throughout Europe? Advocates of the euro claim that this will be one of the currency's benefits, as price discrepancies become blatantly obvious and consumers shop around in the cheapest market. But what about price discrepancies that exist between different regions of the UK? The going rate for petrol in one town can be between 5 and 10 per cent different compared to a town just 20 or 30 miles away. This may seem remarkable considering the mobility of buyers and the ease of shopping around for petrol. Similarly, there is no immediately obvious reason why the price of used cars should vary between different regions of the UK. Similar price variations are present in the USA, which has much longer experience of a single currency. There, prices of most consumer goods tend to reach a high in the affluent north-east and are lowest in the relatively poor areas of the Deep South. Why should this be? And what hope is there of the single European market harmonizing prices when there are such discrepancies of commodity-type products within a single country?

businesses in the UK were initially disappointed by the failure of the euro to become a strong and stable reserve currency and for many businesses the US dollar retained this role. Many businesses also recognized that a large currency area does not in itself guarantee a strong and stable currency and critics of the euro have pointed out that the world's largest currency areas such as Russia, China, India and Indonesia (but with the exception of the USA) are among the weakest economies, while some of the smallest currency areas, such as Singapore and Switzerland, are among the most dynamic. Had the euro appreciated in value against sterling in its early days, instead of depreciating, the reaction of UK exporting businesses may have been that an independent currency had given new opportunities to gain competitive advantage against relatively high price euro area competitors.

12.3 OVERSEAS TRADE PATTERNS

The existence of comparative cost advantages and variations between countries in the types of goods and services demanded results in each country having its own distinctive pattern of overseas trade. The nature of a country's overseas trade can be described with respect to:

- the items that it imports and exports
- the countries it trades with.

Trade patterns throughout the world change in response to changes in the economic, political, technological and social environments. For example, during the first years of the twenty-first century, the rising GDP per capita of China has resulted in Chinese consumers purchasing increasing numbers of overseas holidays. At the same time, growing environmental protection legislation has resulted in many production processes being transferred from Western developed countries to less developed ones where regulations are relatively lax, leading to new export trade.

12.3.1 Measuring international trade

The difference between what a country receives from overseas and the amount it spends overseas is referred to as a country's balance of payments. Countries differ in the way in which they break down their overall balance of payments, but these can be broadly divided into:

- the purchase and sale of goods and services (usually described as current account transactions), and
- the acquisition and disposal of assets and liabilities abroad (referred to as capital account transactions).

Although it is common to talk about a country's overall balance of payments being in surplus or deficit, they must technically be balanced (Figure 12.5). If, for example, a country has a deficit in its current account, this has to be made up by running down one of its assets (e.g. by using holdings of foreign currencies to reduce a capital asset or borrowing from overseas and thereby increasing a capital liability). The opposite would be true if a country produced a current account surplus (holdings of foreign assets would increase or foreign liabilities would reduce).

Media headlines which describe a 'trade deficit' or 'surplus' generally refer to the current account element of the balance of payments. The components of the current and capital account elements are described below.

- The current account is generally further divided into two components: a visible trade balance and an invisible trade balance. Visible trade includes transactions in manufactured goods, raw materials and fuel products. Invisibles comprise intangible sales and purchases overseas. Invisible trade is made up of services (e.g. tourism, insurance and shipping), including government services (e.g. payments to overseas armed forces and diplomatic missions), and interest, profit and dividends receivable from or payable abroad.
- The capital account records outward and inward flows of capital for investment purposes (i.e. it excludes routine trading transactions). It includes payments made for long-term investment in tangible assets (e.g. new factories and equipment) and intangible assets (such as the purchase of shares in an overseas company). It also includes short-term movements of money between traders in the money markets (sometimes referred to as 'hot money').

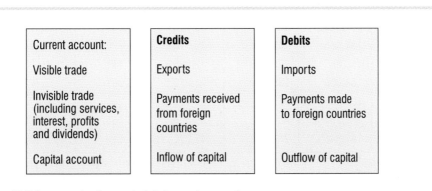

Figure 12.5 Components of a country's balance of payments

12.3.2 Measuring international transactions

Traditionally, the value of manufactured goods has been measured as they pass through Customs, and from this information, the total value of imports and exports has been calculated. In the case of capital transactions, governments generally make provisions for large transactions to be reported (e.g. many countries restrict the free movement of capital to a specified maximum amount per transaction). However, it is becoming increasingly difficult to measure the value and volume of overseas trade.

- It is very difficult to accurately measure trade in services, which are transacted through a variety of means (e.g. the sale of insurance and banking services using postal and telecommunication methods). In the case of earnings and expenditure on tourism, it can be difficult to measure the total expenditure of tourists whose spending can be dispersed through a variety of business sectors. Governments estimate such figures using various survey techniques. However, initial estimates frequently have to be subsequently revised.
- With the advent of the Single European Market, border controls on trade within the EU have largely been removed, so it is very difficult to get an accurate indication of the volume of imports and exports between EU member states. Again, overseas trade within the EU is measured using various survey techniques.

Having made these caveats, recent trends in the UK overseas current account are shown in Figure 12.6. The years for which data is shown correspond roughly to turning points in worldwide business cycles.

Year	Visible trade		Balance	Services balance	Current account surplus/deficit
	Exports	Imports			
1984	70,265	75,601	−5,336	4,205	−1,482
1986	72,627	82,186	−9,559	6,223	−864
1988	80,346	101,826	−21,480	3,957	−16,475
1990	101,718	120,527	−18,809	3,689	−19,293
1992	107,343	120,447	−13,104	5,051	−9,468
1994	134,465	145,059	−10,594	3,790	−1,684
1996	166,340	178,938	−12,598	7,142	−435
1998	164,056	185,869	−21,813	13,309	−3,792
2000	187,936	220,912	−32,976	13,246	−24,094
2002	186,257	232,712	−46,455	15,466	−18,222
2003	187,846	235,136	−47,290	14,617	−20,430

Figure 12.6 UK overseas current account (£000,000)

Source: based on *Annual Abstracts of Statistics*

12.3.3 Trends in UK international trade

A number of immediate observations can be made about the changing pattern of UK overseas trade, including the following.

- During the recent past, the United Kingdom has run a deficit in its visible balance, but partly made up for this by having a surplus in invisibles. Although the visible trade balance has deteriorated in recent years, growth in the invisible balance has not been sufficient to counteract the decline in visible exports.

- The UK balance of payments has been influenced over the past few decades by North Sea oil. High prices and volumes in the 1980s greatly helped the balance of payments, but declining reserves and a falling world oil price had a negative effect in the late 1990s, which has only partly been offset by the sharp rise in world oil prices that occurred in 2005.

The overseas trade balance of a nation is very much influenced by the structure of its domestic economy. For the UK economy, the deterioration of the visible balance is symptomatic of the declining competitiveness of its manufacturing industries. Indices of competitiveness reached a low point during the late 1980s as many industry sectors became dominated by products from low-cost producers, especially those in the Far East, which had more flexible labour markets and had invested in new productive capacity. More recently, however, there are signs that the United Kingdom has regained some of its competitiveness. This is manifested in the growing number of foreign manufacturers that have located factories in the United Kingdom. While part of the reason for their UK investment is the avoidance of EU external tariff barriers, their decisions also reflect the attractiveness of an increasingly flexible UK labour market and government support for inward investment. However, doubts have been expressed about the sustainability of this inward investment if the UK remains outside the single European currency area.

Some indication of the importance of international trade in services for the United Kingdom can be seen by examining trade statistics. In 2003, the United Kingdom earned a surplus of £14.6 billion from international trade in services, compared to a deficit of £47.2 billion in goods and raw materials. A closer examination of trade statistics indicates the relative importance of the main service sectors. The most important in terms of overseas sales continues to be insurance and financial services, which made a net contribution to the UK balance of payments of £15.5 billion in 2003.

The year-to-year pattern of overseas trade is influenced by business cycles at a national and international level. The downward phase of the world business cycle has the effect of reducing the total value of world trade (or at least slowing down its rate of growth). The business cycles of individual countries may lead or lag the general cycle, or various local reasons may mean that a country is not significantly affected by the worldwide business cycle. A consumer boom in a domestic economy often has the effect of sucking in manufactured imports. The economic boom in the United Kingdom during the mid- to late 1980s, coupled with a high exchange rate, resulted in a very large increase in manufactured imports. At the same time, the domestic manufacturing sector was becoming increasingly uncompetitive, leading to a capacity reduction which limited its opportunities for exports. This contributed to the record visible trade deficits of the early 1990s, which were corrected only as the economic recession caused a reduction in consumer goods imports and falling production costs once more stimulated exports of manufactured goods. During the mid-1990s, UK consumer expenditure remained fairly depressed, but exporters were able to seize opportunities in overseas markets which emerged from their recessionary cycle ahead of the United Kingdom.

An indication of the changing relative competitiveness of UK business sectors can be found by examining ratios of:

■ imports as a proportion of home demand, and
■ exports as a proportion of manufacturers' sales.

Department of Trade and Industry statistics indicate varying industrial performance. In the case of the imports, the most recent figures indicate a particular weakness in office machinery and data processing equipment and instrument engineering, and relatively limited penetration by imports in the case of food, drink and mineral products. For exports, transport equipment and chemicals performed strongly, while furniture, timber and paper products achieved low proportions of exports.

Trade patterns can also be analysed in terms of the origin and destination of a country's transactions. Recent years have witnessed a number of changes in the pattern of the UK's trading partners.

■ UK trade has become increasingly focused on the EU, accounting for 51.9 per cent of all imports to the United Kingdom in 2003 and 55.3 per cent of exports.
■ An increasing proportion of the UK's international trade is with developed economies, accounting in 2003 for over 80 per cent of total trade. The share of trade with developing economies has fallen, reflecting a growing self-sufficiency on the part of the latter.
■ Trade with the United States has gradually become a smaller proportion of the UK's international trade, accounting for about 10.1 per cent of imports and 15.5 per cent of exports in 2003.
■ The share of imports accounted for by oil-exporting countries has fluctuated with the growth and subsequent fall of North Sea oil production.

12.3.4 Prospects for UK international trade

The post-war years have generally been disappointing for the UK's balance of trade, with a worsening deficit in visible trade being only partly offset by surpluses in services and North Sea oil. In view of its extensive ownership of overseas assets, the United Kingdom can afford to continue running a moderate trade deficit, but governments have sought to keep deficits within tolerable limits. Very high deficits would probably lead to a fall in the value of sterling, which itself would be inflationary and may lead to an increase in interest rates. Governments would prefer to avoid the social, economic and political consequences of a large trade deficit.

League tables of international competitiveness have shown the United Kingdom slipping. The World Economic Forum regularly produces league tables of competitiveness, based on such factors as resource costs, flexibility of resources and taxation. The top 10 list of most competitive countries (Figure 12.7) shows the UK behind a number of countries, including the USA, Japan, Singapore and many of the Scandinavian nations.

Prescriptions for the UK's future prosperity in international trade have focused on a number of issues, including the following.

■ Continuing to improve the cost structure of UK industry, particularly through deregulation of the economy and improvements in the flexibility of labour.

Country	2004 ranking	2002 ranking	2000 ranking
Finland	1	1	1
United States	2	2	2
Sweden	3	3	9
Taiwan	4	6	7
Denmark	5	4	14
Norway	6	8	6
Singapore	7	7	4
Switzerland	8	5	15
Japan	9	16	21
Ireland	10	12	11
UK	11	11	12
Netherlands	12	13	8
Germany	13	14	17
Australia	14	10	5
Canada	15	9	3

Figure 12.7 Ranking of most competitive countries for business

Source: based on data presented to the World Economic Forum, Davos, 2004

■ Exploiting service-sector competitive advantages, especially within the fields of banking and insurance. However, although the United Kingdom has historically achieved surpluses in these fields, competition from newly developed countries has intensified. Many comment-ators have predicted that if the United Kingdom does not join the single European currency area, its role as a financial centre of Europe will be further weakened. Similarly, the UK should exploit opportunities in new and emerging sectors when they arise, for example bio-technology.

■ Many have pointed to the valuable role played by governments, such as the Japanese, in promoting a country's exports. In the United Kingdom, the emphasis of government policy has tended to lie in improving supply-side efficiency rather than promoting specific sectors overseas.

■ It is argued that many UK companies have failed to invest in new capacity during periods of recession in order to meet an upturn in the world economy. The consumer boom of the 1980s resulted in imports of goods such as agricultural equipment for which domestic pro-duction capacity had been cut during the previous recession and not subsequently replaced.

■ The proportion of GDP spent by the United Kingdom on research and development is low by international standards, placing doubts on the ability of its manufacturers to become world leaders in new product fields (refer back to Chapter 4).

■ Finally, many commentators have pointed to the poor training in marketing and management skills of UK managers, which leaves them badly placed to aggressively tackle overseas markets, or even to protect their domestic markets from import competition. Worse still, many people suspect an anti-industry culture in which the best talent finds its way to the professions such as law and consultancy rather than management.

Many commentators have suggested that the UK is well positioned to take advantage of developments in the Internet. A study undertaken by Merrill Lynch in 2000 suggested that the UK was the second best placed country to benefit from the 'new' Internet-based economy, just behind the United States, and ahead of Sweden, Switzerland, Finland, Ireland and the Netherlands.

It must not be forgotten that market mechanisms in themselves have a tendency to correct trade imbalances. A country with long-term trade deficits based on structural weaknesses in its economy will experience a weakening in the value of its currency, which will have the effect of making exports cheaper and imports dearer. Through a substitution effect in its domestic markets, domestic manufacturers will gain competitive advantage over importers, thereby reducing a trade deficit. Similarly, exports will become cheaper in overseas markets, again reducing a trade deficit. For countries which run continuing trade surpluses, market forces will tend to reduce the surplus. Continuing surpluses will cause a rise in the value of a country's currency, making exports more expensive and imports cheaper. Eventually, exports may become so expensive (when priced in buyers' currencies) that the country's exporters will establish factories overseas, and may even find it cheaper to assemble products overseas for import to its domestic market.

12.4 INTERNATIONAL TRADE INSTITUTIONS AND AGREEMENTS

The exploitation of comparative cost advantages through free trade may sound fine in theory, but is often difficult to achieve in practice, for the reasons described earlier in this chapter. There have therefore been many attempts to develop international agreements for the free movement of trade. At their simplest, international trade agreements comprise bilateral agreements between two countries to open up trade between the two. Sometimes, groups of countries join together to form trading blocs in which trade between member states is encouraged at the expense of trade with non-bloc members. There are also multilateral agreements between nations to develop free trade. Some of the more important are described below.

12.4.1 European Union and the Single European Market

A principal aim of the European Union has been the removal of barriers to trade between member states. The most significant step towards this was achieved through the EU's Single European Market programme and the development of the European Economic Area, which extended the principles of the single market to include members of the European Free Trade Area (EFTA). Since 1993 there has been a progressive easing of trade within the European Economic Area and the following are some of the benefits achieved.

■ The removal or reduction of institutional barriers to trade (e.g. reduced import/export documentation), thereby reducing travel times.

- The technical harmonization of product standards, allowing for greater economies of scale and competition using a standardized product which is able to compete in multiple domestic markets.
- The ability for companies with licences to operate in their home market to be able to extend these rights to other EU markets.
- The liberalization of capital movements.
- The removal of discriminatory public purchasing policies.
- Establishment of the euro currency.

The benefits of the single market will be achieved through a combination of reduced costs and increased competition, which will have the effect of reducing local national monopoly power enjoyed by some suppliers. A number of UK sectors have been identified as likely beneficiaries of more open markets, able to exploit their comparative cost advantages. These include pharmaceuticals, the food and drink industry, insurance and civil aviation.

Despite the efforts of the Single European Market programme, a number of barriers to trade within the EU remain.

- There is debate about the extent to which cultural variations within Europe will eventually be homogenized. Some of these variations are based on geographical factors (e.g. lifestyles and attitudes of people living in the relatively hot southern climate countries differ markedly from those of northern countries) and may be difficult to change.
- Although harmonization of product standards has proceeded a long way, some problems remain. For example, the UK's non-standard design of electrical plugs or its practice of driving on the left may never be harmonized to a European standard.
- It is still often necessary for individuals or firms to obtain licences before they can operate in another member state. Although removal of such barriers is on the EU agenda for reform, free trade in services has generally been harder to open up to cross-border trade than dealings in manufactured goods. In 2005, Germany and France rejected a proposed Services Directive which would have allowed any service provider that is registered in its home country to practice its trade or profession in any other EU member country.

Nevertheless, the Single European Market has become a major trading bloc which has made trade within the bloc easier, while creating common policies with respect to trade with the rest of the world.

12.4.2 Other regional trading blocs

A number of other trading blocs exist in the world with aims which are similar to those of the EU. These include the North American Free Trade Agreement (NAFTA), the Gulf Co-operation Council (GCC) and the Association of South East Asian Nations (ASEAN). In the case of NAFTA, the United States, Canada and Mexico have sought to reduce barriers to trade between their countries so that each can exploit its comparative cost advantage. Some measures are already in place, but the creation of the single market will have increasing effect in the future. Inevitably, while trade is made easier within the free trade area, there is a danger of other outside countries being disadvantaged.

When does a requirement for rigorous staff training amount to a restrictive international trade practice? The French authorities have insisted that all guides accompanying groups on the country's ski slopes should take a test which is one of the toughest in Europe, citing the increased safety of groups which results. British tour operators have in the past provided ski guides who are generally assessed by companies for their basic mountain awareness abilities. They have assumed more of a social role than that of an expert guide in difficult terrain. British tour operators claim that their customers prefer the social informality of their guides rather than the formality of the French ski instructors.

Is this an example of a covert restriction on international trade by the French authorities, keen to give preference to their own politically important local guides? Or does their action represent a genuine concern for safety (if not consumer preferences) which is neutral in terms of its effects on

12.4.3 Organization for Economic Co-operation and Development (OECD)

The OECD was originally set up in 1947 to administer America's Marshall Aid programme in Europe, but subsequently turned increasing attention to the developing world. The OECD now has 21 members, including most European countries, the United States, Canada and Japan. It works by trying to co-ordinate the economic policies of members, to co-ordinate programmes of economic aid and by providing specialized services, especially information.

12.4.4 The World Bank

The World Bank (officially known as the International Bank for Reconstruction and Development) acts as an adviser to governments in the provision of international finance. The main role of the World Bank is to provide capital on favourable terms to aid the economic reconstruction of countries. In cases where it advances loans to overseas governments, it may require its advice to be incorporated into government policy as a condition of its loan.

12.4.5 The International Monetary Fund (IMF)

The IMF shared its origins with the OECD and World Bank in that all three institutions were created in the immediate post-Second World War period and were seen as a means towards world economic regeneration. The IMF is essentially a world forum for international negotiations on governments' fiscal policies. Its original aims of regulating and stabilizing exchange rates have been somewhat undermined by the ability of traders and multinational companies to influence exchange rates, often having a bigger impact on markets than policies agreed by the IMF.

12.4.6 The World Trade Organization (WTO)

The WTO has its origins in the General Agreement on Tariffs and Trade (GATT) of the early post-war period. The signatories to the agreement sought to achieve greater international economic prosperity by exploiting fully the comparative cost advantages of nations by reducing the barriers that inhibited international trade. All the signatories agreed not to increase tariffs on imported goods beyond their existing levels and to work towards the abolition of quotas which restricted the volume of imports. The WTO has proceeded to reduce tariffs and quotas through several negotiating 'rounds'. It has also tried to redress the distortion to world trade and the unfair competitive advantage given to subsidized exporters of agricultural products.

Many critics of the WTO's attempts to liberalize trade in goods and services claim that they will create disadvantages for developing countries (for example, it may be plausible for FedEx to run a privatized Indian Post Office, but could there really be much chance of the Indian Post Office challenging FedEx on its home ground?).

12.4.7 Other international agreements and institutions

A wide range of other agreements and institutions affect international trading companies. Some of these will be very general in nature and affect a wide range of businesses. An example in this category is the agreement to set up a European Bank for Reconstruction and Development, aimed at helping the restructuring of the emerging East European economies. Improved access to loans may help a wide range of exporters of capital equipment. There are many examples of bilateral agreements between countries which can influence the operations of business organizations. Agreements between countries on how the taxation of multinational companies should be handled can have serious implications for businesses, leading to the possibility of double claims for taxation where this possibility is not specifically excluded by a bilateral government agreement.

There are also very many agreements and institutions covering specific industries. An example of an institution that has a direct effect on an industry is the International Civil Aviation Organization (ICAO) to which most countries belong and which has agreed international safety standards for civil aviation. In other cases, agreements between countries can have an indirect effect on a market, as with an international agreement signed to restrict international trade in ivory.

12.5 EVALUATING OVERSEAS BUSINESS OPPORTUNITIES

Overseas markets can represent very different opportunities and threats compared to those that an organization has been used to in its domestic market. Before a detailed environmental analysis is undertaken, an organization should consider in general terms whether the environment is likely to be attractive. By considering in general terms such matters as political stability or cultural attitudes, an organization may screen out potential markets for which it considers further analysis cannot be justified by the likelihood of success. Where an exploratory analysis of an overseas environment appears to indicate some opportunities, a more thorough analysis might suggest important modifications to a product format which would need to be made before it could successfully be offered to the market.

This section first identifies some general questions which need to be asked in assessing the business environment of overseas countries and then considers specific aspects of researching such environments.

12.5.1 Macro-level analysis of a foreign business environment

The combination of environmental factors that contributed to success within an organization's domestic market may be absent in a foreign country, resulting in the failure of export attempts. In this section, questions to be asked in analysing an overseas business environment are examined under the overlapping headings of the political, economic, social and technological environments.

The political environment

At a national level, individual governments can influence attractiveness to business in a number of ways.

- At the most general level, the stability of the political system affects the attractiveness of a particular national market. While radical change rarely results from political upheaval in most Western countries, the instability of many African governments can lead to uncertainty about the economic and legislative framework in which goods and services will be traded.

- Licensing systems may be applied by governments in an attempt to protect domestic producers. Licences can be used to restrict individuals practising a particular profession (e.g. licensing requirements for accountants or solicitors may not recognize experience and licences obtained overseas) or they can be used to restrict foreign owners setting up an overseas operation.

- Regulations governing product standards may require an organization to expensively reconfigure its products offer to meet local regulations, or may prohibit their sale completely.

- Controls can be used to restrict the import of manufactured goods, requiring a company to create a local source of supply, leading to possible problems in maintaining consistent quality standards and also possibly losing economies of scale.

- Production possibilities can be influenced by government policies. Minimum wage levels and conditions of service can be important in determining the viability of an overseas operation. For example, many countries restrict the manner in which temporary or seasonal staff can be employed. This could make the operation of a seasonal holiday hotel inflexible and uneconomic.

- Restrictions on currency movements may make it difficult to repatriate profits earned from an overseas operation.

- Governments are major procurers of goods and services and may formally or informally give preference in awarding contracts to locally owned organizations.

- Legislation protecting trade marks varies between companies. In some countries, such as Russia and Thailand, the owner may find it relatively hard to legally protect itself from imitators.

The economic environment

A generally accepted measure of the economic attractiveness of an overseas market is the level of GDP per capita. The demand for most products increases as this figure increases. However, organizations seeking to sell goods and services overseas should also consider the distribution of income within a country which may identify valuable niche markets. For example, the relatively low GDP per head of South Korea still allows a small and relatively affluent group to create a market for high-value overseas holidays.

An organization assessing an overseas business environment should place great emphasis on future economic performance and the stage that a country has reached in its economic development. While many Western developed economies face saturated markets for a number of products, less developed economies may be just moving on to that part of their growth curve where a product begins to appeal to large groups of people.

THINKING AROUND THE SUBJECT:
CHINA – A LOT OF PEOPLE, BUT A LOT OF DIFFERENCES

Many Western companies have set their sights on the potential of China, the world's most populous country and one which can bewilder Westerners. But is it good enough to simply lump all of China together as one homogeneous business environment? With 22 provinces (23 if Taiwan is included), three municipalities and five autonomous regions, there is tremendous diversity in business environments. Exporters seeking success in China must analyse the country carefully and choose the most promising area as their point of entry.

There is a significant income difference between urban and rural areas and between coastal and inland areas, with cities (especially the coastal cities) generally being much richer than rural areas. Examples of cities at the top of this purchasing power list are Shenzhen, Guangzhou, Shanghai, Beijing, Tianjin, Hangzhou and Dalian.

Exporters are particularly interested in the distribution of 'trigger' levels of income, above which an individual's needs for necessities are satisfied and they can become purchasers of imported Western luxury goods. It has been suggested that a per capita purchasing power of US$1000 per annum is the critical figure above which Chinese people typically start buying colour TVs, washing machines and imported clothing.

Rapid economic growth is bringing a wide variety of goods within reach of a growing number of consumers. China's per capita GDP was $1100 in 2003, equivalent to $5500 when adjusted for purchasing-power parity. By 2010, 40 million households will earn more than 48,000 renminbi ($6000) per year, equivalent to $24,000 in terms of purchasing-power parity and enough to qualify a household as middle class by US standards. Income varies widely, however. At $5600 per capita, GDP in Shanghai is more than five times higher than it is in Chongqing, in the interior of the country (Chen and Penhirin 2004).

However, care needs to be taken in interpreting official figures about wealth in China. The actual purchasing power of a dollar in China compared to the West is higher because many Chinese do not report all their income. There are also distortions caused by hidden savings and allowances received from family members living abroad. Furthermore, the Chinese typically pay very low or no rent, spend little on healthcare and education due to subsidies and are allowed to have only one or two children. There is also a booming black market in labour, goods, services and foreign exchange which further distorts official statistics of wealth.

For exporters to China, getting their product to the market, at the right time and at the right place, can be very difficult, given the limitations of the communications infrastructure. This is especially true of the inland provinces and emphasizes the need for exporters to focus their marketing and distribution efforts on just a few of the richest areas. It has been observed that not even the largest multinational companies have attempted to take on the whole Chinese market at once.

A crucial part of the analysis of an overseas business environment focuses on the level of competition within that market. This can be related to the level of economic development achieved within a country. In general, as an economy develops, its markets become more saturated. This is true, for example, of the market for household insurance which is mature and highly competitive in North America and most Western European countries, but is relatively new and less competitive in many developing economies of the Pacific Rim, allowing better margins to be achieved. In addition to competition for customers, a mature economy is also likely to experience stronger competition for labour resources, leading to higher wage costs.

The social and cultural environment

An understanding of cultural differences between markets is very important for businesses contemplating entering foreign markets. Individuals from different cultures not only buy different products but may also respond in different ways to similar products. Attitudes towards work can affect production efficiency. Examples of differing cultural attitudes and their effects on international trade in goods and services include the following.

- Buying processes vary between different cultures. For example, the role of women in selecting a product may differ in an overseas market compared to the domestic market, thereby possibly requiring a different approach to product design and promotion.
- Some categories of goods and services may be rendered obsolete by certain types of social structure. For example, extended family structures common in some countries have the ability to produce a wide range of services within the family unit, including caring for children and elderly members.
- A product that is taken for granted in the domestic market may be seen as socially unacceptable in an overseas market. Frequently encountered examples include pork products in Muslim countries and beef in Hindu countries.
- Attitudes towards promotional programmes differ between cultures. The choice of colours in advertising or sales outlets needs to be made with care because of symbolic associations (e.g. the colour associated with bereavement varies between cultures).
- What is deemed to be acceptable activity in procuring sales varies between cultures. In Middle Eastern markets, for example, a bribe to a public official may be considered essential, whereas it is unacceptable in most Western countries.
- Attitudes to work differ between cultures, for example with respect to the role of women and deference to authority.

The technological environment

An analysis of the technological environment of an overseas market is important for organizations that require the use of a well-developed technical infrastructure and a workforce that is able to use technology. Communications are an important element of the technological infrastructure – poorly developed telephone and postal communications may inhibit attempts to make credit cards more widely available, for instance.

12.6 SOURCES OF INFORMATION ON OVERSEAS MARKETS

The methods used to research a potential overseas market are in principle similar to those that would be used to research a domestic market. Companies would normally begin by using sec-

Hilton International, owner of many of the world's most prestigious hotels, has joined the race to build the first hotel on the moon. It has developed a project called the Lunar Hilton, which would comprise a complex with 5000 rooms. Powered by two huge solar panels, the resort would have its own beach and sea as well as a working farm. Experts disagree on the practicalities of life on the moon, but barriers seem to be diminishing as new discoveries are made.

'Space tourism' received a boost in April 2001 when the determined multi-millionaire Dennis Tito paid $20 million for a round-trip ticket to the International Space Station. Such is the interest in exploiting the moon for tourism that there is now a Space Tourism Association and a lot of national pride is at stake. The Russians placed the first man in space and now the first tourist in space. In Japan, the Kinki Nippon Tourist (KNT) Company, the country's second largest wholesale tour opera- tor set up a space travel club in 2002. Back in 1998, KNT helped a Japanese Pepsi franchisee launch a sweepstake for a sub-orbital flight. The company received 650,000 applications for five tickets, each valued at $98,000. The company is convinced that excursion-class spaceships will become a driving force for the travel industry in the twenty-first century.

Three Japanese companies have between them already spent £25 million on development work for their own moon projects. Compared to this, Hilton's expenditure to date of £100,000 looks quite modest. Is the company mad in believing that people will want to visit the moon? Or is this just the kind of long-term strategic thinking that so many businesses lack? With the world becoming smaller and increasingly saturated with goods and services, does the moon offer a unique opportunity for expansion?

ondary data about a potential overseas market which are available to them at home. Sources that are readily available through specialized libraries, government organizations and specialist research organizations include Department of Trade and Industry information for exporters, reports of international agencies such as the Organization for Economic Co-operation and Development (OECD), Chambers of Commerce and private sources of information such as that provided by banks. Details of some specific sources are shown in Figure 12.8.

Initial desk research at home will identify those markets that show greatest potential for development. An organization will then often follow this up with further desk research of materials available locally within the short-listed markets, often carried out by appointing a local research agency. This may include a review of reports published by the target market's own government and specialist locally based market research agencies.

Just as in home markets, secondary data have limitations in assessing market attractiveness. Problems in overseas markets are compounded by the greater difficulty in gaining access to data, possible language differences and problems of definition which may differ from those with which an organization is familiar. In the case of products that are a new concept in an overseas market, information on current usage and attitudes to the product may be completely lacking. For this reason, it would be difficult to use secondary data to try to assess the likely response from consumers to large out-of-town superstores in many Eastern European countries.

| **Government agencies** |
| Department of Trade and Industry market reports |
| Overseas governments - e.g. US Department of Commerce |
| Overseas national and local development agencies |

| **International agencies** |
| European Union (Eurostat, etc.) |
| Organization for Economic Co-operation and Development (OECD) |
| World Trade Organization (WTO) |

| **United Nations (UN)** |
| International Monetary Fund (IMF) |
| Universal Postal Union |
| World Health Organization (WHO) |

| **Research organizations** |
| Economic Intelligence Unit |
| Dun & Bradstreet International |
| Market research firms |

| **Publications** |
| *Financial Times* country surveys |
| *Business International* |
| *International Trade Reporter* |
| Banks' expert reviews |

| **Trade associations** |
| Chambers of Commerce |
| Industry-specific association – e.g. ICAO |

| **Online resources** |
| Eurostat |
| Mintel Online |
| FT Online |

Figure 12.8 Sources of secondary information on foreign markets

Primary research is used to overcome shortcomings in secondary data. Its most important use is to identify cultural factors which may require a product format to be modified or abandoned altogether. A company seeking to undertake primary research in a new proposed overseas market would almost certainly use a local specialist research agency. Apart from overcoming possible language barriers, a local agency would better understand attitudes towards privacy and the level of literacy that might affect response rates for different forms of research. However, the problem of comparability between markets remains. For example, when a Japanese respondent claims to 'like' a product, the result may be comparable to a German consumer who claims to 'quite like' it. It would be wrong to assume on the basis of this research that the product is better liked by Japanese consumers than German consumers.

Primary research is generally undertaken overseas when a company has become happy about the general potential of a market, but is unsure of a number of factors that would be critical for success, for example whether intermediaries would be willing and able to handle their product or whether traditional cultural attitudes will present an insurmountable obstacle for a product not previously available in that market. Prior to commissioning its own specific research, a company may go for the lower-cost but less specific route of undertaking research through an omnibus survey. These are surveys regularly undertaken among a panel of consumers in overseas markets (e.g. the Gallup European Omnibus) which carry questions on behalf of a number of organizations.

12.7 MARKET ENTRY STRATEGIES

A new foreign market represents both a potential opportunity and a risk to an organization. A company's market entry strategy should aim to balance these two elements.

The least risky method of developing a foreign market is to supply that market from a domestic base. This is often not a cost-effective method of serving a market, and may not be possible in the case of some inseparable services where producer and consumer must interact. Where an exporter needs to set up production facilities overseas, risk can be minimized by gradually committing more resources to a market, based on experience to date. Temporary facilities could be established that have low start-up and close-down costs and where the principal physical and human assets can be transferred to another location. A good example of risk reduction through the use of temporary facilities is found in the pattern of retail development in East Germany following reunification. West German retailers that initially entered East Germany in large numbers were reluctant to commit themselves to building stores in specific locations in a part of the country that was still economically unstable and where patterns of land use were changing rapidly. The solution adopted by many companies was to offer branches of their chain in temporary marquees or from mobile vehicles – these could move in response to the changing pattern of demand. While the location of retail outlets remained risky, this did not prevent retailers from establishing their networks of distribution warehouses which were considered to be more flexible in the manner in which they could respond to changing consumer spending patterns.

Market entry risk reduction strategies also have a time dimension. While there may be long-term benefits arising from being the first company to develop a new product field in a foreign market, there are also risks. If development is hurried and launched before consistent quality can be guaranteed to live up to an organization's international standards, the company's long-term image can be damaged, both in the new foreign market and in its wider world market. In the turbulent business environment of Eastern Europe in the late 1980s, two of the world's principal fast food retailers – McDonald's and Burger King – pursued quite different strategies. The former waited until political, economic, social and technological conditions were capable of allowing it to launch a restaurant that met its global standards. In the case of Burger King, its desire to be first in the market led it to offer a sub-standard service, giving it an image from which it was difficult to recover.

An assessment of risk is required in deciding whether an organization should enter a foreign market on its own or in association with another organization. The former maximizes the strategic and operational control that the organization has over its overseas operations, but it exposes it to the greatest risk where the overseas market is relatively poorly understood. A range of entry possibilities are considered below.

12.7.1 Exporting

It is often possible for a company to gain a feel for a foreign market by exporting to it from its home base. Where economies of scale in production are high and transport costs are low, this is often a very cost-effective solution. To minimize risks associated with an unknown market, an exporter would often employ an export agent at home or an import agent in the overseas target market. The use of an agent may also be more cost-effective for the company than creating its own overseas sales force. If initial export attempts succeed, a company may then consider setting up its own production base overseas. As an example of this strategy of gradual commitment, the Müller yoghurt company initially exported its premium yoghurts from Germany to the United Kingdom, until its market had grown to such an extent that it felt confident about committing resources to a new UK production centre.

Exporting is likely to be the less satisfactory option for manufacturers that produce high-volume, low-value products for which transport costs could put them at a competitive disadvantage in overseas markets. Exporting is generally not possible in the case of services that demand a high level of interaction between a company and its customers at the latter's home base (e.g. with high-contact services such as street cleaning subcontracting cannot be very easily exported without creating a base in the customer's home country).

Although the use of export/import agents may initially minimize risks for an exporter, their use also brings potential problems. Where an import agent acquires exclusive rights to market a product in a country, conflict can occur between the agent and exporter on marketing policy issues (e.g. in the early 1990s there was an acrimonious disagreement on policy between Nissan and its UK sole importer AFG).

12.7.2 Direct investment in a foreign subsidiary

This option gives an organization maximum control over its foreign operations, but can expose it to a high level of risk on account of the poor understanding that it may have of the overseas market. A company can either set up its own overseas subsidiary from scratch (as many UK hotel companies have done to develop hotels in overseas markets), or it can acquire control of a company that is already trading (such as the acquisition of the UK electricity supplier Powergen by the German utility group Eon).

Where the nature of the product offer differs relatively little between national markets or where it appeals to an international market (e.g. hotels), the risks from creating a new subsidiary are reduced. Where there are barriers to entry and the product is aimed at an essentially local market with a different culture to the domestic market, the acquisition of an established subsidiary may be the preferred course of action, although even this is not risk free.

12.7.3 Global e-commerce

The development of the Internet has offered new opportunities for organizations to enter foreign markets, especially services companies whose transactions are essentially intangible. At the business-to-business level, a lot of backroom service processing, such as invoicing, data entry and software development, can now be carried out in parts of the world where there is a plentiful supply of low-cost, skilled workers, and the results sent back to the customer by a data link (see case study). At the consumer level, many service providers now promote themselves to global audiences through the Internet. A consumer in the UK, for example, could find a hotel in Australia and book a room online without the hotel needing to use an intermediary. The costs to service providers of reaching global audiences in this way can be low.

Travel-related services and financial services have seen major developments in global e-commerce. However, the limitations of the Internet in gaining access to foreign markets should be recognized. For many private consumers, purchasing through the Internet is perceived as being very risky, and this riskiness is likely to increase when the supplier is based overseas. In the case of Internet banking services offered in the UK from overseas, customers may find themselves not protected by legislation which protects customers of UK-based banks. Some service providers are careful about how they make their services available globally through the Internet in order to preserve price discrimination. For this reason, airlines often restrict sales of tickets through the Internet to local national markets, to prevent customers buying in the cheapest global market.

Finally, it should be remembered that the Internet is becoming increasingly cluttered with websites and it is not sufficient for a global trader to simply have a website. One of the biggest challenges is to get a potential customer to a company's site. In the case of many consumer goods and services, the only sensible solution may be to pay one of the many information intermediaries that act as a cyber exchange between often geographically separated buyers and

Figure 12.9 We are all familiar with buying clothing and shoes made in countries such as China and India where production costs are low. The production of goods in a low-cost country can be separated from their consumption in a high-income country. This opportunity for separation has not generally been possible for services, as the consumer and producer normally need to interact with each other. The development of telecommunications is allowing new opportunities to lessen the effects of service inseparability. Many service companies have located call centres in low-cost countries such as India, and customers may be quite unaware that their call is being answered several thousand miles away. (Reproduced with permission of Iserve Systems Ltd)

THINKING AROUND THE SUBJECT:
GUIDING CUSTOMERS THROUGH INTERNATIONAL CYBERSPACE

The Internet can be a jungle. Getting a next-door neighbour to visit your website may be difficult enough, but how do you get a potential customer from the other side of the world to visit?

The theory is simple – if you have a product to sell, put it on the Internet and search engines will find you. This cheap form of promotion would allow small businesses around the world to promote themselves without the need to print and distribute expensive brochures.

Of course, life is not so simple. Type into the search engine Google a term which describes many common consumer products and you will probably get thousands of hits. So firms often resort to paying intermediaries to try to raise their ranking in Google's listing, or selling through the site of an intermediary which has already achieved a high ranking.

Being close to the top of a search engine's listing has become an important part of international business strategy. Consider the case of a company that specializes in buying redundant manufacturing machinery from factories that have closed down, and reselling it to buyers looking for second-hand equipment. Addressing global markets is often key to success here. After all, if a shoe factory that has just closed down in Leicester is selling off its injection moulding equipment, it is unlikely that there will be many potential buyers for the equipment in Leicester or indeed the UK. If one company in the UK couldn't profitably use the equipment, then it is likely that no UK companies will be able to. But the equipment may be just what an entrepreneur in Romania is looking for. How can a UK-based trader in second-hand equipment get its site to the top of the list that the Romanian is looking at? Relying on searches for 'machinery' or even 'second-hand machinery' is unlikely to be very fruitful – after all, there are likely to be thousands of sites in this category across the world. But including market-specific terms such as 'injection moulding' and 'shoes' in the web page text and meta-tags will help to put a company's site higher in a specialized search category. Having several pages with different titles, text and meta-tags provides more opportunities to target specific international market segments. And there's another trick that many companies use to get overseas buyers to their site. It costs relatively little to produce a foreign-language version of the main pages of a company's site. If a Romanian entrepreneur entered 'прессформа впрыски' in a search engine instead of 'injection moulding' or 'shoes', the seller's site would probably come very close to the top of the search results.

sellers. Online service intermediaries such as expedia.com and ebookers.com have become important service sectors in their own right. For many service companies entering a foreign market, it may be safer and more cost-effective to work through these, rather than acting alone. The Internet is undoubtedly offering new opportunities for firms to enter foreign markets, but basic rules of foreign market entry still apply and many of the successful uses of global e-commerce have involved more traditional approaches based on joint ventures and strategic alliances.

12.7.4 Licensing/franchising

Rather than setting up its own operations in an overseas market, a company can license a local company to manufacture and sell a product in the local market. This is commonly used, for example, by soft drinks manufacturers that sell the right to companies to market a branded product in a foreign market. The licensee must usually agree to follow a product formulation closely and to maintain consistent standards of quality and brand image.

While exporters of manufactured goods frequently license a foreign producer to manufacture and sell their products, a company developing a service overseas is more likely to establish a franchise relationship with its overseas producers, which gives it greater control over the whole service production process. As with the development of a domestic franchise service network, franchising can allow an organization to expand rapidly overseas with relatively low capital requirements. While a clearly defined business format and method of conducting business is critical to the success of a foreign franchise operation, things can still go wrong for a number of reasons. The service format could be poorly proven in the home market, making overseas expansion particularly difficult. Unrealistic expectations may be held about the amount of human and financial resources that need to be devoted to the operation of a foreign franchise. Problems in interpreting the spirit and letter of contractual agreements between the franchisee and franchisor can result in acrimonious misunderstanding. In 1997, for example, the Body Shop took back control of its French franchises, claiming that they had been performing poorly in the hands of its local franchisees.

12.7.5 Joint ventures

An international joint venture is a partnership between a domestic company and a foreign company or government. A joint venture can take a number of forms and is particularly attractive to a domestic firm seeking entry to an overseas market where:

- the initial capital requirement threshold is high, resulting in a high level of risk
- overseas governments restrict the rights of foreign companies to set up business on their own account, making a partnership with a local company – possibly involving a minority shareholding – the only means of entering the market
- there may be significant barriers to entry which a company already based in the foreign market could help to overcome (for example, access to local intermediaries)
- there may be reluctance on the part of consumers to deal with what appears to be a foreign company; a joint venture can allow the operation to be fronted by a domestic producer with whom customers can be familiar, while allowing the overseas partner to provide capital and management expertise
- a good understanding of local market conditions is essential for success in an overseas market; it was noted above that the task of obtaining marketing research information can be significantly more difficult abroad as compared to an organization's domestic market; a joint venture with an organization already based in the proposed overseas market makes the task of collecting information about a market, and responding to it sensitively, relatively easy
- taxation of company profits may favour a joint venture rather than owning an overseas subsidiary outright.

Some recent examples of joint ventures are shown in Figure 12.10.

Venture partners	% holding	Subsidiary/purpose
Equity joint ventures		
GfK ORG-Marg	40 60	Creation of ORG-GfK Marketing Services, based in Bangalore, India, to monitor monthly retail sales in retail outlets for the consumer technology markets
Siemens AG 3M Corp	50 50	Creation of enterprise to deliver converged voice and data products to businesses
International Power Malakoff	20 80	Operation of gas-powered electricity generation in Malaysia
Non-equity joint ventures		
Commercial Union Credito Italiano (Italy)		Agreement for CI to sell and distribute CU's life and non-life insurance policies in Italy
Hambros Merchant Bank Bayerische Vereinsbank (West Germany)		Co-operation agreement in cross-frontier merger and acquisition finance
Barclays Bank Tokyo Trust (Japan)		Agreement gave Barclays Bank a banking licence to operate in Japan to provide trust management and securities handling in collaboration with its partner

Figure 12.10 Recent examples of international joint ventures

Strategic alliances

These are agreements between two or more organizations where each partner seeks to add to its competencies by combining its resources with those of a partner. A strategic alliance generally involves co-operation between partners rather than joint ownership of a subsidiary set up for a specific purpose, although it may include agreement for collaborators to purchase shares in the businesses of other members of the alliance.

Strategic alliances are frequently used to allow individual companies to build upon the relationship that they have developed with their clients by allowing them to sell on services that they do not produce themselves but that are produced by another member of the alliance. This arrangement is reciprocated between members of the alliance. Strategic alliances have become important within the airline industry, where a domestic operator and an international operator can join together to offer new travel possibilities for their respective customers.

International strategic alliances can involve one organization nominating a supplier in related product fields as a preferred supplier at its outlets worldwide. This strategy has been used by car rental companies to secure a link-up with other transport principals, to offer what the latter sees as a value-added service. An example is the agreement between Hertz Car Rental and Eurotunnel to provide a new facility for customers of each company called 'Le Swap'. By the agreement, customers are able to rent a right-hand-drive car in the United Kingdom, travel through the tunnel by train and swap to a left-hand-drive car at the other end, and vice versa.

Figure 12.11 With the globalization of markets, strategic alliances are becoming increasingly crucial in order to facilitate international growth. In the airline sector, an alliance such as the oneworld alliance allows one airline's services to be marketed by all other alliance members. For customers, British Airways is able to offer 'seamless' travel around the globe on services of fellow alliance members. For the company, there are opportunities to rationalize its operations in foreign countries. (Reproduced with permission of oneworld alliance)

12.7.6 Management contracting

Rather than setting up its own operations overseas, a company with a proven track record in a product area may pursue the option of running other companies' businesses for them. This is particularly important for services-based organizations. For a fee, an overseas organization which seeks to develop a new service would contract a team to set up and run the facility. In some cases, the intention may be that the management team should get the project started and gradually hand over the running of the facility to local management. This type of arrangement is useful for an expanding overseas organization where the required management and technical skills are difficult to obtain locally. In countries where the educational infrastructure offers less opportunity for management and technical training, a company (or in many cases, overseas governments) can buy in state-of-the-art management skills. Developments in Eastern Europe have resulted in many opportunities for UK-based service companies, including the management of hotels, airlines and educational establishments (e.g. the former hotel group Forte was contracted to set up and operate a number of hotels in Eastern Europe and the University of Strathclyde was contracted to set up and run a business school in Poland).

12.8 ADAPTING TO FOREIGN BUSINESS ENVIRONMENTS

Having analysed an overseas market and decided to enter it, an organization must make decisions that will allow it to successfully enter and develop that market. Decisions focus on the extent to which the organization should adapt its products to the needs of the local market, as opposed to the development of a uniform product that is globally applicable in all of its markets. In this section, we first consider decisions relating to product configuration, and then decisions about its pricing and promotion and, finally, decisions in respect of production methods.

12.8.1 Product decisions

Sometimes, products can be exported to a foreign market with little need for adaptation to local needs. Improved communications and greater opportunities for travel have helped create much more uniform worldwide demand for products. McDonald's and Coca-Cola, for example, now appeal to people from Boston to Beijing and from Manchester to Moscow (although in both of these examples, the company's products have been subtly adapted to local markets). Products often need to be adapted for a number of reasons.

■ The law of an overseas country may set differing product standards. For example, regulations specifying vehicle lighting standards mean that cars often have to be re-specified for foreign markets. Within the EU, harmonization of product standards is making this task much simpler for traders.

■ Despite convergence of cultural values, inertia often results from centuries of tradition. It has taken time, for example, for the idea of fast food to take hold in France where the culture stresses eating as a pleasurable social experience. Tastes may take time to change, which helps to explain why McDonald's restaurants offer different menus in many of the markets that it serves.

■ There are often good geographical reasons why products would need to be adapted. The hotter climates of southern Europe result in different patterns of demand for ice cream, car design and clothing, for example.

**THINKING AROUND THE SUBJECT:
IS LESS ALWAYS MORE?**

How does a large American hotel chain adapt to the Japanese market? Hotels operated by Hilton International in the USA have bedrooms which to many visitors from overseas are surprisingly large. But what would an American think of a typical Japanese hotel? Land prices in America are generally fairly low outside the main metropolitan areas, hence the relatively spacious facilities offered. But in Japan, space is at a premium and has given rise to all sorts of miniaturized hotel formats, aimed at keeping prices at an affordable level. How could Hilton International remain affordable yet retain its generic brand values? Following extensive research, the company developed a hotel format which was appropriate to the Japanese market. To avoid the problem of visitors from America being shocked by the relatively cramped hotels, Hilton International developed a separate brand format, 'Wa No Kutsurogi', providing comfort and service the Japanese way.

■ Socio-economic factors may call for product reformulation. For example, high incomes and low petrol prices combine with long travel distances to boost demand in the United States of America for large, well-specified cars, at the expense of small hatchbacks which are popular in the United Kingdom.

Against the tendency towards local adaptation, the development of a globally uniform product can also have its advantages. The use of a common brand name in overseas markets yields benefits from economies of scale in promotion. Standardization of the product can also yield economies of scale in market research and large-scale, centralized production methods.

12.8.2 Promotion decisions

A promotional programme that has worked at home may fail miserably in a foreign market. Usually, this is a result of the target country's differing cultural values, although legislation can additionally call for a reformulation of promotion. The following are a few of the reasons why promotion reformulation may be needed.

■ The law on promoting goods and services that are considered socially harmful varies between countries. For this reason, television advertising is not available in some countries for promoting some medicines, alcohol and children's products.

■ The availability of promotional media varies between countries. While Internet advertising is now widely used in the United Kingdom, the low levels of Internet access in some less developed countries may limit the potential for this form of communication.

■ Different cultures respond to promotional messages in different ways, reflecting different attitudes towards hard-sell, brash and seductive approaches, for example.

■ Certain objects and symbols used to promote a product might have the opposite effect to that which might be expected at home (e.g. animals that are successfully used to promote a product at home may be viewed with disgust in some markets).

■ Sometimes, the brand name to be promoted will not work in the overseas market, so it may be changed. There are many examples of brand names that fail overseas. The Spanish brand of 'Bum' snacks would probably not sell well in English-speaking countries, for example.

■ There can also be problems where legislation prevents an international slogan being used. In France, for example, law no. 75–1349 of 1975 makes the use of the French language compulsory in all advertising for goods and services – this also applies to associated packaging and instructions, etc.

In practice, a combination of product and promotion modification is needed in order to meet differing local needs and differences in local sensitivity to advertising.

12.8.3 Pricing decisions

A common global pricing policy will help to project a company as a global brand. However, the reality is that a variety of factors cause global organizations to charge different prices in the different markets in which they operate. There is usually no reason to assume that the pricing policies adopted in the domestic market will prove to be equally effective in an overseas market. Furthermore, it may be of no great importance to customers that comparability between different markets is maintained.

There are a number of factors that affect price decisions overseas.

■ Competitive pressure varies between markets, reflecting the stage of market development that a service has reached and the impact of regulations against anti-competitive practices.

■ The cost of making a product may be significantly different in foreign markets. For services that employ people-intensive production methods, variations in wage levels between countries will have a significant effect on total costs. Personnel costs may also be affected by differences in welfare provisions that employers are required to pay for. Other significant cost elements which often vary between markets include the level of property prices or rental costs. The cost of acquiring space for a retail outlet in Britain, for example, is usually significantly more than in southern or Eastern Europe.

■ Taxes vary between different markets. For example, the rate of value added tax (or its equivalent sales tax) can be as high as 38 per cent in Italy compared to 17.5 per cent in the United Kingdom. There are also differences between markets in the manner in which sales taxes are expressed. In most markets, these are fully incorporated into price schedules, although on other occasions (such as in Singapore) it is more usual to price a service exclusive of taxes.

■ Local customs influence customers' expectations of the way in which they are charged for a product. While customers in the domestic market might expect to pay for bundles of goods and services, in an overseas market consumers might expect to pay a separate price for each component of the bundle. For example, UK buyers of new cars expect features such as audio equipment to be included in the basic price of a car, whereas buyers in many Continental European countries expect to buy these as separate items.

■ For some service industries, it is customary in many countries to expect customers to pay a tip to the front-line person providing a service, as part of the overall price of the service.

■ Formal price lists for a service may be expected in some markets, but in others the prevalence of bartering may put an operator that sticks to a fixed price list at a competitive disadvantage.

■ Government regulations can limit price freedom in overseas markets. In addition to controls over prices charged by public utilities, many governments require 'fair' prices to be charged in certain sectors and for the prices charged to be clearly publicized.

■ A product that is considered quite ordinary in its domestic market may be perceived as exclusive in an overseas market and therefore it will adopt a higher price position. For example, the price position of the retailer Marks & Spencer is middle market in its domestic UK base, but the company has positioned its stores in Indonesia as upmarket with a high price position relative to local competitors. By contrast, a company with a strong brand in its home market may have to adopt (initially at least) a lower price position when it launches into a competitive overseas market.

12.8.4 Distribution decisions

Market entry strategies were discussed earlier at a strategic level. It is also crucial to consider more operational issues of how a company is going to get its products through to the final consumer. The following factors should be taken into account.

■ Consumers' attitudes towards intermediaries may differ significantly in overseas markets. What is a widely accepted outlet in one country may be regarded with suspicion in another. For example, the idea of buying cosmetics from a grocery store may be viewed with suspicion in many countries, although it is now accepted in most Western European countries.

■ The extensiveness of outlet networks will be influenced by customers' expectations about ease of access, which in turn may be based on social, economic and technological factors. The proliferation of many small-scale distributors in less developed economies, for example, can partly be explained by the lack of domestic refrigeration, which may favour frequent replenishment of household supplies from a local store rather than less frequent bulk buying from a large centralized store.

■ Differences in the social, economic and technological environments of a market can be manifested in the existence of different patterns of intermediaries. As an example, the interrelatedness of wholesalers and retailers in Japan can make it much more difficult for an overseas retailer to get into that market compared to other overseas opportunities. In some markets, there may be no direct equivalent of a type of intermediary found in the domestic market – estate agents on the UK model are often not found in many markets where the work of transferring property is handled entirely by a solicitor.

■ The technological environment can also affect distribution decisions. The relatively underdeveloped postal and telecommunications services of many Eastern European countries make direct availability of goods and services to consumers relatively difficult.

■ What is a legal method of distributing goods and services in the domestic market may be against the law of an overseas country. Countries may restrict the sale of financial services, holidays and gambling services – among others – to a much narrower set of possible intermediaries than is the case in the domestic market.

12.8.5 People and production decisions

Where a company is planning to manufacture its products in a foreign market, it will need to ensure that its production methods comply with local regulations. Adaptation to local regulations governing employment is particularly important for labour-intensive service industries.

Where goods or services produced overseas involve direct producer–consumer interaction, a decision must be made on whether to employ local or expatriate staff. The latter may be preferable where a service is highly specialized and may be useful in adding to the global uniformity of the service offering. In some circumstances, the presence of front-line expatriate serving staff can add to the appeal of a service. For example, a chain of traditional Irish bars established on the Continent may add to their appeal by employing authentic Irish staff.

For relatively straightforward goods and services, a large proportion of staff would be recruited locally, leaving just senior management posts filled by expatriates. Sometimes, an extensive staff development programme may be required to ensure that locally recruited staff perform in a manner that is consistent with the company's global image. This can, in some circumstances, be quite a difficult task – a fast food operator may have difficulty developing values of speed and efficiency among its staff in countries where the pace of life is relatively slow.

CASE STUDY

INDIAN CALL CENTRES CREATE A NEW INTERNATIONAL TRADE SECTOR

Dial an 0800 customer helpline in the UK and your call may be answered not in Bradford or Birmingham, but quite likely in Banagalore or Bombay. Operating call centres on behalf of western clients has become an important new source of international trade for some less developed countries that have previously been associated with manufacturing cheap clothes and electrical items. In September 2004, over 250 call centre providers from around the world exhibited at Call Centre Expo to try to sell their services. In India alone, the value of handling overseas clients' telephone calls was estimated by Datamonitor to be $4.64 billion in 2004, plus another $1.16 billion from data work – for instance, reconciling bills, passing invoices and correcting errors in customer statements. Such international trade would have been almost unthinkable only 20 years ago.

Handling customer service requirements emerged as a new international trade sector in the 1990s. Organizations of all kinds found increasing need to enter information into computerized databases – records of customer sales, services performed, details of rolling stock movements, to name but a few. In the early days, most firms regarded this as a backroom function which they could perform most cost effectively by using their own staff at their own premises. With time, an increasing volume of data to be analysed, the growing popularity of customer telephone support services and the growing sophistication of data analysis systems, many service companies emerged to take the burden of data processing off of client companies.

At first, most data processing and call handling companies operated close to their clients. However, by the late 1980s, this activity began entering international trade, to be processed by companies in foreign countries where costs were lower, working regulations more relaxed and trades unions often non-existent. An important factor accounting for this development in international trade was the rapid pace of technological developments. Processed data and voice calls could now be transmitted very quickly and cheaply using satellites and fibre-optic links.

Data processing and customer telephone support have established a firm foothold as exportable services in areas such as India, the Caribbean and the Philippines. Each of these countries is characterized by relatively low wage rates with skills that are at least as good as those of workers in many more developed countries.

In India, the outsourced call centre industry has been growing at double-digit rates from the late 1990s. According to Datamonitor's estimates, during 2004–05, the sector achieved a growth of around 44.4 per cent, with total revenues touching approximately US$5.8 billion. Furthermore, the industry has shown a compound Annual Growth Rate of 56.4 per cent over the 2000–05 period, higher than any other industry sector in India.

The development of Grecis illustrates the way in which international trade can be developed. Grecis started as a customer-support centre for USA-based General Electric in 1997. The company was looking for ways of cutting the cost of its customer support operations and backroom operations. In 2004, the company employed about 18,000 people worldwide including more than 12,500 in India, and also has customer-contact centres in China, Hungary, Mexico and Romania. Although General Electric accounted for 93 per cent of Grecis sales in 2004, the company has an expansion strategy to increase the proportion of third-party client work that it undertakes. Its target third-party clients have focused on companies that deal with debt collection, insurance and human resources.

Wages at Indian call centres such as those operated by Grecis are much lower than they would be in Britain. It is reported that many staff in 2004 would have earned as little as £2.90 a day and the total pay for an eight-hour shift could be below the minimum wage for one hour's work in Britain. Handling calls often involves anti-social hours, with night-time shifts a common feature of employment. National holidays such as Republic Day and religious festivals like Diwali and Holi are usually ignored by call centre companies working for UK and USA-based clients. As for trades unions, these hardly exist.

Although wages would be considered low by Western standards, a job in a call centre has been seen by many in less developed countries as highly prized. It has been reported that call centre wages are typically double what a fully qualified local teacher can earn, allowing individuals to buy previously unattainable luxuries.

Despite the rapid growth of Indian call centres, many challenges are emerging. Most importantly, costs are rising, and appear to be following the pattern of developing countries gradually losing their competitive edge in a sector to even lower-cost countries. Staff turnover has become a major issue, with reports of annual staff turnover reaching 60 per cent. The UK's Financial Services Authority (FSA) in a study in 2005 found that the staff turnover at Indian call centres was approaching that in the UK, and that managers were demanding comparable wages to their UK counterparts. Retaining women after they marry is a problem not generally encountered in the UK. Some staff have been deterred by the abuse they can face from callers, who may hold them personally responsible for the delay in getting their computer repaired or their insurance claim being settled.

The FSA also warned that overseas calls centres posed 'a material risk' to its aim of cutting financial crime, protecting consumers and retaining confidence in Britain's financial markets. The industry was not helped by reports in 2005 of Indian call centre workers stealing customers' details and selling them on to third parties. Overcoming these fears will inevitably involve more regulation, further forcing up Indian call centre operators' costs, and cutting their international competitive advantage.

Some UK companies, such as the insurer Norwich Union, have enthusiastically extended their support operations in India. But it seems that polarization has been occurring, with a Gartner Research report suggesting that two-thirds to three-quarters of those who already use overseas call centres plan to increase their use, while the majority of companies would not consider sending any of their operations overseas. Some, such as NatWest Bank, have proudly proclaimed in their advertising that their telephone calls are actually answered in the UK.

India, like most developing countries, has a long way to go before it becomes a predominantly service-based, rather than an agricultural- or manufacturing-based economy. In the case of data processing, new communications technologies have allowed production to take place in a totally different location to the customer, thereby overcoming the problem of inseparability. The continuing fall in telecommunications costs has led to call centres located several thousands of miles away from a client becoming a financially attractive proposition. There are clearly limits on developing countries' abilities to export services, but marketers in these countries will be looking for new opportunities to separate production and consumption, and export the benefits to relatively wealthy Western clients. Meanwhile, the development of these countries' domestic economies will doubtless lead to growing demand for services from the growing business sector and for consumer services from the emerging middle classes. In India, call centres have acquired a momentum of their own and one of their biggest recent sources of growth has been demand for services from local Indian companies. According to NASSCOM Research, the call centres generated revenues in excess of US$600 million from the domestic Indian market during 2004–05.

QUESTIONS

1 Why has data processing and call centre handling emerged as a major new activity in world trade?

2 What are the advantages and disadvantages to a Western European-based insurance company of outsourcing its call centre operations to a supplier in India?

3 What are the advantages to the Indian economy of developing its call centre industry? Are there any disadvantages?

SUMMARY

This chapter began by discussing the reasons why international trade takes place. Despite the theoretical benefits of the free movement of goods and services between countries, barriers to achieving such benefits remain. Currency fluctuations remain a major risk for international traders, although the single European currency alleviates this risk for traders within the EU. The overseas business environment is likely to be very different to that experienced at home, and therefore it is essential that appropriate exploratory research is carried out. This chapter has discussed methods of overseas market entry that balance the need for risk reduction against the need to maintain control over an overseas venture.

This chapter has brought together many of the issues discussed in previous chapters and applied them specifically to the needs of an overseas market. For any market, it is important to study its competitiveness (**Chapter 10**), the state of its national economy (**Chapter 11**), its political system (**Chapter 2**), its social and cultural values (**Chapter 3**), and attitudes towards social responsibility (**Chapter 8**). Good information becomes particularly important for planning and controlling an overseas operation (**Chapter 4**).

Key Terms

Balance of payments	(443)	International trade	(433)	Trading blocs	(436)
Barriers to trade	(448)	Invisible trade	(443)	Visible trade	(443)
Comparative cost		Multinational companies	(437)	World Trade Organization	(428)
advantage	(433)	Strategic alliances	(462)		

CHAPTER REVIEW QUESTIONS

1 What is the nature of the gains arising from trade liberalization and why is it such a painful process?
(*Based on CIM Marketing Environment Examination*)

2 Explain who will be the winners and losers as a result of trade liberalization in your own country. Summarize what advice you would give to any company to ensure it ends up on the winning side.
(*Based on CIM Marketing Environment Examination*)

3 (a) Your consultancy firm has decided to produce a brief booklet, in bullet-point format, to provide advice to marketing clients who are considering establishing overseas operations.

(b) Using relevant headings and points, produce an outline draft for this booklet, including a bibliography and useful sources of information.
(*Based on CIM Marketing Environment Examination*)

4 Summarize the advantages and disadvantages to a British capital goods manufacturer of possible UK adoption of the euro.

5 Suggest how the UK insurance industry can avoid going the same way as the motorcycle industry and losing out to overseas competition.

6 What cultural differences might cause problems for a hotel chain developing a location in India?

ACTIVITY

Choose two or three international service providers from the following sectors: hotels, airlines, fast food, car rental, accountancy services. Go to their websites and click through to a selection of their national sites in countries with a different socio-economic profile to your own. Analyse points of difference and similarity between the different countries. Have the companies succeeded in being local 'global companies'?

Useful Websites

World Trade Organization

This site provides information on international trade developments, statistics, WTO documents and policies.

http://www.wto.org/

Trade Partners UK

Advice and information from the Department of Trade and Industry for exporters. Provides information on overseas markets by region.

http://www.tradepartners.gov.uk/

International Monetary Fund

Site contains IMF news, publications and international economic information.

http://www.imf.org/

Economist Intelligence Unit

Selected free access is provided to global business intelligence reports.

http://www.eiu.com/

World Link

The online magazine of the World Economic Forum with a searchable archive.

http://www.worldlink.co.uk/

EU Euro Website

The official EU website on the euro includes documents, legislation, links to other websites and a search engine. It provides access to basic information and documentation on the euro.

http://europa.eu.int/euro/html/entry.html

Infonation

An interactive statistical database for the member states of the United Nations.

http://www.un.org/Pubs/CyberSchoolBus/infonation/e_infonation.htm

Annual Barclays Country Reports

Country reports contain data on market analysis, economic policy, the political environment, recent trends and outlooks.

http://www.corporate.barclays.com/go/cms.nsf/lookup/188151117A7375FB8025690D004C0021

Country Risk Analysis

A rich source of historical data about world trading markets. Discusses economic, financial and political events which impact on international trade.

http://www.duke.edu/~charvey/Country_risk/couindex.htm

Financial Times

The newspaper's archive includes country reports.

http://www.ft.com

CIA World Publications: *The World Fact Book*

Published by CIA World Publications, this website gives access to facts and statistics on more than 250 countries and other entities.

http://www.odci.gov/cia/publications/ factbook/index.html

UK Overseas Trade Statistics

The site includes a summary of recent trade statistics.

http://www.statistics.gov.uk

US International Trade Statistics

US orientated, but contains a lot of data on world markets.

http://www.census.gov/ftp/pub/foreign-trade/www/

Organization for Economic Co-operation and Development (OECD): International Trade

The OECD's database on international trade shows the value of each member country's exports and imports of goods and services by type.

http://www.oecd.org/std/serint.htm

International Business Resources on the WWW

Michigan State University's site provides many useful links to statistical data and information resources.

http://www.ciber.msu.edu/busres/Static/ Statistical-Data-Sources.htm

Further Reading

For a general overview of trends in international business, consult the following:

Overseas Trade, a DTI–FCO magazine for exporters published 10 times per year by Brass Tacks Publishing Co., London.

World Trade Organization, *Annual Report*, published annually.

World Trade Organization, *Trade Policy Review* (serial).

For statistics on the changing pattern of UK trade, the following regularly updated publications of the Office for National Statistics provide good coverage:

Economic Trends, a monthly publication which includes statistics relating to international trade performance.

Overseas Direct Investment, detailed breakdown of UK overseas direct investment activity, outward and inward, by component, country and industry.

For a general overview of international marketing management, the following texts provide a more detailed analysis of many of the points discussed in this chapter.

Keegan, W.J. (2003) *Global Marketing*, FT Prentice Hall.

Lowe, Robin and Doole, Isobel (2004) *International Marketing Strategy*, London, Thomson Learning.

For a review of the development of the European Economic Area, the following are useful sources:

Bulletin of the European Commission.

Bulletin of Economic Trends in Europe (published by Eurostat).

McCormick, John (2002) *Understanding the European Union*, 2nd edn, Palgrave Macmillan.

Green-Cowles, Maria and Dinan, Desmond (eds) (2004) *Developments in the European Union 2*, Palgrave Macmillan.

Strategic alliances are becoming increasingly important and the following text provides greater insight into their operation:

Mockler, R.J. (2000) *Multinational Strategic Alliances*, Chichester, John Wiley.

References

Business Times (2002) 'More local banks now offer Islamic products and services', February, p. 12.

Chen, Y. and Penhirin, J. (2004) 'Marketing to China's consumers', *McKinsey Quarterly*, December, pp. 62–73.

Klein, N. (2000) *No Logo*, Flamingo.

Nakamoto, M. (2003) 'A speedier route from order to camcorder', *Financial Times*, 12 February, p. 11.

Part 5

Bringing it Together: Environmental Analysis

Chapter 13
The Dynamic Business Environment

Chapter Objectives

This chapter will explain:

- how to bring together the analysis of various elements of a company's business environment in a way that is actionable by managers

- the role of information in allowing managers to understand their operating environment

- models used to try to forecast future environmental change and strategies by which companies can respond to such change

- frameworks for assessing risk in the business environment

13.1 THE IMPORTANCE OF ENVIRONMENTAL KNOWLEDGE

Information represents a bridge between the organization and its environment and is the means by which a picture of the changing environment is built up within the organization. Management is responsible for turning information-based knowledge into specific business plans.

According to Nonaka, 'In an economy where the only certainty is uncertainty, the one sure source of lasting competitive advantage is knowledge' (Nonaka 1991). A firm's knowledge base is likely to include, among other things, an understanding of the precise needs of customers; how those needs are likely to change over time; how those needs are satisfied in terms of efficient and effective production systems and an understanding of competitors' activities. We are probably all familiar with organizations where knowledge seems to be very poor – the over-optimistic sales forecast which results in unsold stockpiles; the delivery which does not happen as specified, or junk mail which is of no interest at all. On the other hand, customers may revel in a company which delivers the right service at the right time and clearly demonstrates that it is knowledgeable about changes in consumers' preferences. The small business owner may have been able to achieve all of this in his or her head, but in large organizations, the task of managing knowledge becomes much more complex. Where it is done well, it can be a significant contributor to a firm's sustainable competitive advantage.

Let us define the terms 'knowledge' and 'information'. Even though in some senses they may be used interchangeably, many writers have suggested that the two concepts are quite distinct. In fact, knowledge is a much more all-encompassing term which incorporates the concept of beliefs that are based on information (Dretske 1981). It also depends on the commitment and understanding of the individual holding these beliefs, which are affected by interaction and the development of judgement, behaviour and attitude (Berger and Luckmann 1966). Knowledge has meaning only in the context of a process or capacity to act. Drucker noted that 'There is no such thing as knowledge management, there are only knowledgeable people. Information only becomes knowledge in the hands of someone who knows what to do with it' (Drucker 1999). Knowledge, then, is evidenced by its association with actions and its source can be found in a combination of information, social interaction and contextual situations which affect the knowledge accumulation process at an individual level.

Here we need to distinguish between knowledge at the level of the individual, and at the level of the organization. Organizational knowledge comprises shared understandings, is created within the company by means of information and social interaction, and provides potential for development. It is this form of knowledge that is at the heart of knowledge management. Organizational progress is made when knowledge moves from the domain of the individual to that of the organization.

Two different types of knowledge about the environment can be identified. First, there is knowledge which is easily definable and is accessible, often referred to as 'explicit' knowledge. This type of knowledge can be readily quantified and passed between individuals in the form of words and numbers. Because it is easily communicated, it is relatively easy to manage. Knowledge management is concerned with ensuring that the explicit knowledge of individuals becomes a part of the organizational knowledge base and that it is used efficiently and contributes where necessary to changes in work practices, processes and products. This, however, is not the limit of knowledge management. The second type of knowledge comprises the accumulated knowledge of individuals which is not explicit, but which can still be important to the successful operation of an organization. This type of knowledge, often known as 'tacit' knowledge, is not easy to see or express, it is highly personal and is rooted in an individual's experiences, attitudes, values and behaviour patterns. This type of tacit knowledge can be much more difficult to formalize and disseminate within an organization. If tacit knowledge can be captured, mobilized and turned into explicit knowledge it would then be accessible to others in the organization and enable the organization to progress rather than have individuals within it having to continually relearn from the same point. The owner of a small business could have all of this information readily available to him in his head. The challenge taken on by many large corporations is to emulate the knowledge management of the small business owner. One outcome of a knowledge-based organization has often been referred to as the learning organization in which the challenge is to learn at the corporate level from what is known by individuals that make up the organization.

The transition from individuals' information about the business environment to corporate environmental knowledge requires sharing of knowledge by all concerned. The extent to which this is achieved is influenced by internal environmental factors, which were discussed in Chapter 8. A knowledge management programme is needed to break down a laissez-faire attitude, and would typically include the following elements:

- a strong knowledge-sharing culture, which can only emerge over time with the development of trust
- measures to monitor that sharing, which may be reflected in individuals' performance reviews
- technology to facilitate knowledge transfer, which should be as user-friendly as possible
- established practices for the capture and sharing of knowledge – without clearly defined procedures, the technology is of only limited value
- leadership and senior management commitment to sharing information – if senior management doesn't share information, why should anybody else bother?

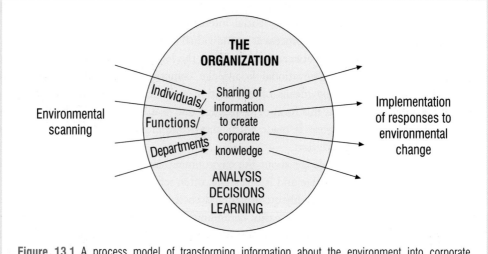

Figure 13.1 A process model of transforming information about the environment into corporate knowledge which can be acted upon

Information and knowledge have to be seen in the context of the inter-functional dynamics of an organization. A timely supply of appropriate information provides feedback on an organization's performance, allowing actual performance to be compared with target performance. On the basis of this information, control measures can be applied which seek – where necessary – to put the organization back on its original targets. Organizations also learn from the past, in order to better understand the future. For making longer-term planning decisions, historical information is supplemented by a variety of continuous and ad hoc studies, all designed to allow better-informed decisions to be made. Information cannot in itself produce decisions – it merely provides data which must be interpreted by managers. As an inter-functional integrator, a management information system draws data from all functional areas of an organization, and increasingly from other members of an organization's value chain.

As information collection, processing, transmission and storage technologies improve, information is becoming more accessible not just to one particular organization, but also to its competitors. Attention is therefore moving away from how information is collected, to who is best able to make use of the information. It is too simple to say that managers commission data collection by technical experts and make decisions on the basis of these data. There has been research interest in the relationship between managers and market researchers, focusing on the role of trust between the two and how its presence helps to reduce risk (Moorman, Zaltman and Deshpande 1992).

Recent technological innovations – for example, electronic point of sale (EPOS) systems – have enabled companies to greatly enhance the quality of the service they provide in terms of speed, accuracy and consistency. In turn, the resulting increase in operational efficiency, combined with the additional information which it is now possible to generate, has allowed organizations to improve other areas of their product offer – such as the development of customer loyalty programmes – as a means of gaining competitive advantages. Organizations must also understand the effects of macroenvironmental factors such as the state of the local or national economy. Without this broader environmental information, routine pieces of market research information – such as the market share held by a company's brands over the past year – cannot be interpreted meaningfully.

To summarize, information allows management to improve its strategic planning, tactical implementation of programmes and its monitoring and control. A practical problem is that information is typically much more difficult to obtain to meet strategic planning needs than it is to meet operational and control needs. There can be a danger of managers focusing too heavily on information which is easily available (typically internal information) at the expense of that which is needed (typically macroenvironmental information).

13.2 INFORMATION SYSTEMS

Many analyses of organizations' knowledge-creating activities take a systems perspective. The sub-components of a management information system typically include marketing, production, financial and human resource management systems. In a well-designed management information system, the barriers between these sub-systems should be conceptual rather than real – for example, sales information is of value to all of these sub-systems to a greater or lesser extent (see Figure 13.2).

THINKING AROUND THE SUBJECT:
WHAT PRICE KNOWLEDGE?

The knowledge-based firm is founded on an assumption that it is able to obtain a ready supply of information about customers, actual and potential, so what happens when those customers tire of giving information about themselves? After all, if information has value in the hands of firms, consumers might reasonably think that it has value if they retain the information about themselves. As more and more organizations try to gather information about their customers' changing needs, there is a danger of 'survey fatigue' setting in. Just how many times can you ask customers questions about their preferences and attitudes, before the whole process of carrying out a survey spoils the enjoyment of a service itself? Do customers think that their comments will ever be taken notice of by management? A report prepared in 1998 by the Future Foundation found that only 50 per cent of consumers were happy to provide personal information to firms with which they deal, down from over 60 per cent in 1995. A core of people appear not to be interested in taking part in data collection exercises at all, and won't fill in questionnaires. Careful organization of surveys can improve response rates. Stopping people when they are in a hurry to get away will not make an interviewer popular, but catching them when they are captive with nothing else to do (e.g. waiting at the baggage carousel at an airport) may be more successful. Some companies have tried to make the whole process of carrying out a survey enjoyable. The airline Virgin Atlantic uses its seat-back entertainment system to provide an interactive electronic questionnaire which passengers can complete at their leisure.

Many companies offer prize incentives in return for completion, but does this encourage people to skip through the questions without much thought, simply in order to qualify for the prize incentive? If companies leave questionnaires for self-completion with no price incentive and no intervention by an interviewer, how can they be sure that they get a representative sample of respondents? It has often been noted that customers who are very happy or very dissatisfied are the most likely to volunteer information. But what about the mass of people who hold average views about an issue? These are likely to be under-represented and a challenge for businesses to learn about.

For most organizations operating in a competitive environment, a crucial role is likely to be played by the marketing information system. This can conceptually be seen as comprising four principal components, although in practice they are operationally interrelated.

1 Much information is generated internally within organizations, particularly in respect of operational and control functions. By carefully arranging its collection and dissemination, internal data can provide a constant and up-to-date flow of information at relatively little cost, useful for both planning and control functions.

2 Marketing research is that part of the system concerned with the structured collection of marketing information. This can provide both routine information about marketing effectiveness – such as brand awareness levels or delivery performance – and one-off studies, such as changing attitudes towards diet or the pattern of income distribution.

3 Marketing intelligence comprises the procedures and sources used by managers to obtain pertinent information about developments in their marketing environment, particularly competitor activity. It complements the marketing research system, for whereas the latter

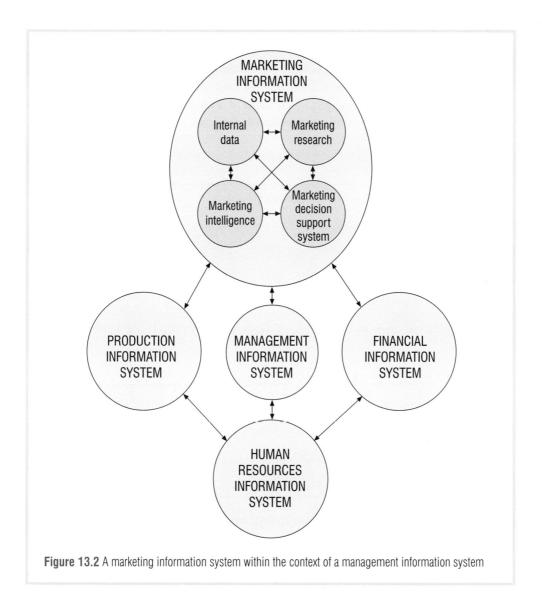

Figure 13.2 A marketing information system within the context of a management information system

tends to focus on structured and largely quantifiable data collection procedures, intelligence gathering concentrates on picking up relatively intangible ideas and trends. Marketing management can gather this intelligence from a number of sources, such as newspapers, specialized cutting services, employees that are in regular contact with market developments, intermediaries and suppliers to the company, as well as specialized consultants. Figure 13.3 shows some commonly used secondary (i.e. previously collected) sources of information which are used for environmental scanning.

4 Decision support systems comprise a set of models that allow forecasts to be made. Information is both an input to such models – in that data is needed to calibrate a model – and an output, in that models provide information on which decisions can be based.

Models are frequently used by companies when deciding on where to locate new distribution outlets. Historical data may, for example, have established a relationship between one variable (e.g. the level of sales achieved by a particular service outlet) and other variables (e.g. pedestrian traffic in a street). Predicting the sales level of a proposed new outlet then becomes a matter of measuring pedestrian traffic at a proposed site, feeding this information into the model and calculating the predicted sales level.

National media – e.g. *Financial Times* industry surveys

Trade, technical and professional media – e.g. *Travel Trade Gazette*, *Marketing Week*

Government departments and official publicattions – e.g. *Annual General Household Survey*, transport statistics

Local chambers of trade and commerce

Professional and trade associations – e.g. Association of British Travel Agents, Law Society

Yearbooks and directories, e.g. *Dataquest*

Subscription services, providing periodic sector reports on market intelligence and financial analyses, such as Keynote, MEAL, Mintel

Subscription electronic databases, e.g. Mintel OnLine

Competitors' websites and publications

Figure 13.3 Secondary sources of information commonly used for scanning the marketing environment

THINKING AROUND THE SUBJECT:
IS THE GLASS HALF FULL OR HALF EMPTY?

The chairman of Bata, the shoe manufacturer, is famously quoted for his analysis of a foreign market for his firm's shoes. Two employees were despatched to research a potential market in Africa and noticed that very few people were wearing shoes. 'No hope here – the people don't wear shoes' was the response of one. But the other saw it quite differently 'What an opportunity – just think what this market will be worth when these people start wearing shoes!' Facts alone will not make marketing decisions – the facts must be interpreted and this interpretation can lead to quite diverse conclusions.

For those organizations that have set up marketing information systems, a number of factors will determine their effectiveness.

- *The accuracy with which the information needs of the organization have been defined* – needs can themselves be difficult to identify and it can be very difficult to draw the boundaries of the firm's environments and to separate relevance from irrelevance. This is a particular problem for large multi-product firms. The mission statement of an organization may give some indication of the boundaries for its environmental search; for example, many banks have mission statements which talk about becoming a dominant provider of financial services in their domestic market. The information needs therefore include anything related to the broader environment of financial services rather than the narrower field of banking.
- *The extensiveness of the search for information* – a balance has to be struck between the need for information and the cost of collecting it. The most critical elements of the marketing environment must be identified and the cost of collecting relevant information weighed against the cost that would result from an inaccurate forecast.
- *The appropriateness of the sources of information* – information for decision making can typically be obtained from numerous sources. As an example, information on changes in social trends can be measured using a variety of quantitative and qualitative techniques. Companies often rely on the former when only the latter can give a depth of understanding that makes for better management decisions. Successful companies use a variety of appropriate sources of information.
- *The speed of communication* – the information system will be effective only if information is communicated quickly and to the people capable of acting on it. Deciding what information to withhold from an individual and the concise reporting of relevant information can be as important as deciding what information to include if information overload is to be avoided.

13.3 FORWARD PLANNING WITH RESEARCH

It should never be forgotten that the overriding purpose of all the material that has been presented in this book is to allow an organization to better understand its future. The organization will not normally be able to change the external environment that it faces, but at least it can try to understand the likely change and be prepared for it. But even the best informed companies have had difficulty knowing how to respond when there are so many uncertainties in their business environment. Consider some recent cases of business plans which failed to accurately predict the future.

- Initial take-up of cable television services in the UK was very slow, and forecasts based on American models of consumer take-up failed to take account of the quality of alternative media available in the UK, among other things.
- Many tourist attractions, such as London's Millennium Dome, have attracted far fewer visitors than originally expected, due to a misunderstanding of the attractiveness of competing attractions and the general state of the economy (see Figure 13.4).

On the other hand, some organizations may have been too cautious in their interpretation of the business environment and underestimated likely demand for their new products

THINKING AROUND THE SUBJECT:
KNOWLEDGE FROM THE SHOP FLOOR?

This chapter has described a number of formalized approaches to bridging the gap between senior management and the external environment. Many of these techniques build up a picture through reports containing numbers, or sometimes verbal descriptions of the environment. But could large organizations learn from the knowledge-gathering techniques used by typical small business owners?

A small business owner, such as a self-employed decorator or builder, is in a good position to understand their environment – and customers' perceptions of the environment – from the comments which they receive back directly from customers. In the large multi-outlet corporation, this opportunity for direct feedback is not available on a regular basis to key corporate decision makers. Many large organizations have therefore developed programmes for sending their senior staff back to the front line in order that they can understand at first hand the expectations of customers and the actual performance of the company.

'Management by walking about' has become a popular way in which senior executives try to gain knowledge about aspects of their operations which are not immediately apparent from structured reporting systems. Archie Norman, when head of the retailer Asda, is reported to have introduced a number of innovations learnt during his regular visits to the company's shop floors. Some companies have adopted a formal system of role exchanges where senior executives spend a period at the sharp end of their business. Even the vice chancellors of some universities have taken the bold step of trying to live the student life for a day or a week, and experiencing classrooms and lectures at first hand. Many have hoped that this would give vice chancellors a better understanding of the day-to-day issues which are of greatest concern to students. Although many organizations have developed similar programmes for their senior management, others have been critical of the idea. Is management by walking about no more than a gimmick? Are supporters of the scientific management approach correct in their claim that the time of a highly paid executive is spent more cost-effectively in the boardroom rather than doing relatively unskilled work on the shop floor?

■ When the Prudential Assurance company launched its new Egg e-savings account, it experienced an unexpectedly high level of take-up, resulting in delays and frustration for potential customers. With Internet banking being a new phenomenon, the company had very little knowledge about how consumers would react to doing their banking online. Would consumers be worried about security? Would they take the trouble to log on and find out?

■ Many people in the industry expected the launch of Freeview digital television services in 2002 to be a flop, following the previous low levels of take-up of ITV digital services. In fact, Freeview quickly became very popular, with reports of shortages of set-top adapter boxes.

As a planning tool, marketing research provides management with market and product-specific information, which allows it to minimize the degree of uncertainty in planning its business activities. This risk minimization function can apply to the whole of the business operations, or to any of its constituent parts, such as advertising. At a macroenvironmental level, simple extrapolation of trends may be acceptable where the business environment is stable. However, extrapolation often proves inadequate where major economic, social, political or technological change occurs. For example, extrapolation breaks down when events such as wars, new health scares and medical discoveries dramatically change the price and availability of a product or of competing products.

For some products, markets have historically shown very little turbulence and are unlikely to alter dramatically in the future. The market for undertakers' services will probably remain stable and simple demand forecasting techniques may be appropriate. However, many industries involving high technology are extremely turbulent, with rapid changes in technology occurring, sometimes overshadowing existing products. As an example, typesetting and telex bureaux saw steady growth during the 1980s but then saw a rapid contraction following the widespread advance of low-cost personal computers. Historical trends could not be relied upon to predict the future.

Forecasting the future involves a combination of scientific analysis and artistic judgement. No element of the business environment can be seen in isolation, and forecasts can be made only with a holistic understanding of the environment.

Figure 13.4 London's Millennium Dome, open to the public for just one year in 2000, proved to be a disappointment in terms of visitor numbers. Against forecasts of 12 million paying visitors, only about half this figure actually visited. Forecasts were made difficult because of so many uncertainties in the business environment and the absence of comparable previous projects which might give some idea of the likely take-up. What other 'millennium' projects would be launched to compete with the Dome? In fact, the London Eye, a competing attraction, beat its forecast of visitor numbers and doubtless took day trip visitors away from the Dome. What would be the effects of the limited local transport infrastructure? Would visitors be prepared to use public transport to get to the Dome? What would be the state of the national economy during millennium year and how would this impact on visitor numbers? And what would be the effects on public perceptions of press reviews after the Dome was opened?

13.4 FRAMEWORKS FOR ANALYSING THE BUSINESS ENVIRONMENT

There are two aspects to be considered when describing an analytic framework with which to analyse the business environment:

1 a definition of the elements that are to be included in the analysis, and
2 the choice of methods by which these input elements are to be used in predicting outcomes.

The nature of the framework used bears a relation to the nature of the dominant business environment at the time. In the relatively stable environment that existed during the middle years of last century, management could control its destiny by controlling current performance. As the business environment has become more turbulent, control becomes dependent upon management's ability to predict the future and respond to change.

Diffenbach (1983) has argued that detailed environmental analysis became important only in the mid-1960s. Prior to that, the business environment was analysed primarily for the purpose of making short-term economic forecasts. The developments to include a longer-term appreciation of the wider economic, technological, demographic and cultural elements of the environment came about in three stages.

1 An increased appreciation of environmental analysis was encouraged by the emergence of professional and academic interest in the subject.
2 Awareness of the concepts of environmental analysis led to academic analysis of the subject.
3 Eventually, the concepts that had been vindicated by subsequent academic analysis were taken on board by business organizations and used as a routine tool for strategic decision making.

As frameworks for analysis have developed in sophistication, so has the paradox that, by the time sufficient information has been gathered and analysed, it may be too late for the firm to do anything about the opportunities or threats with which it is faced. Ansoff (1984) has put forward a framework that helps to overcome this decision-making dilemma. His model allows the firm to respond rapidly to problems whose precise details are a surprise, but whose general nature could have been predicted. Ansoff's model of strategic issue analysis is shown in Figure 13.5. The central feature of the model is the continued monitoring of the firm's external and internal environments for indicators of the emergence of potentially strategic issues that may significantly influence the firm's operations in future. The focal point for Ansoff's analysis is the issue, such as the emergence of environmentalism, rather than the conventional headings of the economic, technological environments, etc. The model allows for a graduated response: as soon as weak signals are picked up, steps are taken to allow for the possibility of these issues developing further. Responses become more precise as the signals become more amplified over time. In other words, Ansoff's model avoids the need for a firm to wait until it has sufficient information before taking a decision; it responds gradually as information emerges.

13.4.1 Choice of framework

A range of analytic frameworks is available for companies to use in analysing their business environment and for making strategic marketing decisions. The choice of framework will depend upon four factors.

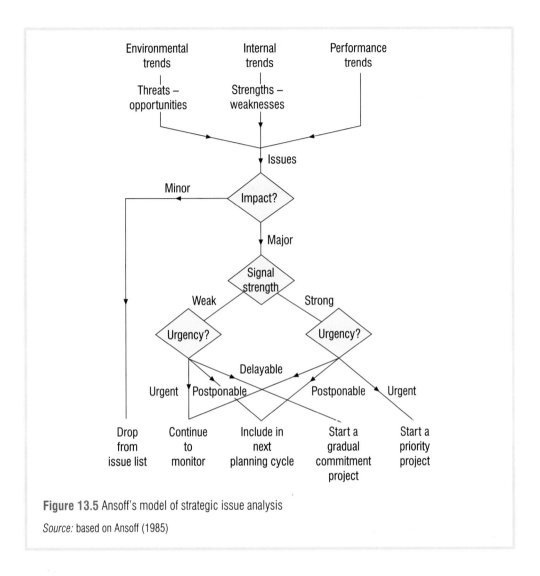

Figure 13.5 Ansoff's model of strategic issue analysis

Source: based on Ansoff (1985)

1 The level of turbulence in the marketing environment will vary between firms operating in different markets. For example, the marketing environment of an undertaker has not been, and in future is even less likely to be, as turbulent as that of an electronic goods manufacturer. An extrapolation of recent trends might be adequate for the former type of business, but the latter must seek to understand a diverse range of changing forces if it is to be able to accurately predict future demand for its products.

2 The cost associated with an inaccurate forecast will reflect the capital commitment to a project. A clothing manufacturer can afford to trust his or her judgement in running off a small batch of jackets. The cost of making a mistake will probably be bearable, unlike the cost of building a chemical refinery on the basis of an inaccurate forecast. The latter situation calls for relatively sophisticated analytic techniques.

3 More sophisticated analytic techniques are needed for long-timescale projects where there is a long time lag between the planning of the project and the time it comes into production. The problem of inaccurate forecasting will be even more acute where an asset has a long lifespan with few alternate uses.

4 Qualitative and quantitative techniques may be used as appropriate. In looking at the future, facts are hard to come by. What matters is that senior management must be in the position to make better-informed judgements about the future in order to aid decision making and planning.

We begin our discussion of frameworks with two basic building blocks of environmental analysis – the marketing audit and SWOT analysis.

13.4.2 The marketing audit

It has been customary for business organizations to undertake financial audits to check on their financial health. Increasingly, the principles of the independent and objective audit are being applied to examine how effective an organization has been in addressing the markets which it serves. The tool used for this has often been referred to as a marketing audit, which has been defined by Kotler (1997) as:

> a comprehensive, systematic, independent and periodic examination of a company's or business unit's marketing environment, objectives, strategies and activities with a view to determining problem areas and opportunities and recommending a plan of action to improve the company's marketing performance.

The marketing audit is not itself a means of making decisions. It is essentially a set of procedures by which an organization explicitly asks questions, about the internal and external environments in which the business operates, as well as the performance of the marketing functions themselves (such as the firm's distribution and pricing effectiveness). The process begins by the appointment of an independent person to undertake the audit. This could be a consultant from outside the organization or somebody from another position within the firm, either sideways or above the function being audited. A self-audit could be undertaken, but at the risk of a loss of objectivity. However, a number of books containing checklists and questions are published which will aid objectivity.

A large part of the audit is devoted to an objective analysis of the micro- and macro-environment. In the case of the macroenvironment, the audit would independently verify or challenge any assumptions that the company had been making; for instance about the likely rate of economic growth or the speed of change in the technological environment. In the case of the microenvironment, the person undertaking an audit of the distribution environment could proceed by asking retailers themselves about how they perceive the company's products and future trends in retailing for that type of product.

The marketing audit would also look inward to examine the relationships within the marketing function and between it and other functional areas of the firm. Organizational structures and decision-making procedures would be objectively assessed for effectiveness.

The availability of good-quality, timely information is crucial to undertaking a marketing audit.

13.4.3 SWOT analysis

A method widely used in marketing audits is a grid used to plot internal strengths and weaknesses in one half of the grid and external opportunities and threats in the other half. The terms opportunities and threats should not be viewed as 'absolutes' for, as Johnson and Scholes (2004, p. 77) pointed out, what might appear at first sight to be an opportunity may not be so when examined against an organization's resources and the feasibility of implementing a strategy.

A SWOT analysis summarizes the main environmental issues in the form of opportunities and threats (O&T) facing an organization. With this technique, these are specifically listed alongside the strengths and weaknesses of the organization (S&W). The strengths and weaknesses are internal to the organization and the technique is used to put realism into the opportunities and threats. In this way, the environment may be assessed as giving rise to a number of possible opportunities, but if the organization is not capable of exploiting these because of internal weaknesses then they should perhaps be left alone.

The principles of a SWOT analysis are illustrated in Figure 13.6 by examining how an airline which has an established reputation as a charter carrier could use the framework in assessing whether to enter the scheduled service market between London and Paris.

13.4.4 Trend extrapolation

At its simplest level, a firm identifies a historic and consistent long-term change in demand for a product over time. Demand forecasting then takes the form of multiplying current sales by a historic growth factor. In most markets, this can at best work effectively only in predicting long-term sales growth at the expense of short-term variations.

Trend extrapolation methods can be refined to recognize a relationship between sales and one key environmental variable. An example might be an observed direct relationship between the sale of new cars to the private buyer sector and the level of disposable incomes. Forecasting

Strengths	Weaknesses
Strong financial position	Has no allocated take-off or landing 'slots'
Good reputation with existing customers	at main airport
Has aircraft that can service the market	Poor network of ticket agents
	Aircraft are old and expensive to operate
Opportunities	**Threats**
Market for business and leisure travel is	Channel Tunnel may capture a large share
growing	of market
Deregulation of air licensing allows new	Deregulation will result in new competitors
opportunities	appearing
Costs of operating aircraft are falling	Growth in air travel will lead to more
	congestion

Figure 13.6 SWOT analysis for a hypothetical airline considering entry to the scheduled London–Paris air travel market

the demand for new cars then becomes a problem of forecasting what will happen to disposable incomes during the planning period. In practice, the task of extrapolation cannot usually be reduced to a single dependent and independent variable. The car manufacturer would also have to consider, among other things, the relationship between sales and consumer confidence, the level of competition in its environment and the varying rate of government taxation.

While multiple regression techniques can be used to identify the significance of historical relationships between a number of variables, extrapolation methods suffer from a number of shortcomings. First, one variable is seldom adequate to predict future demand for a product, yet it can be difficult to identify the full set of variables that have an influence. Second, there can be no certainty that the trends identified from historic patterns are likely to continue in the future. Trend extrapolation takes no account of discontinuous environmental change, as was brought about by the sudden increase in oil prices in 1973 or the effects on world business confidence following the terrorism attacks of 11 September 2001. Third, it can be difficult to gather information on which to base trend analysis; indeed, a large part of the problem in designing a business information system lies in identifying the type of information that may be of relevance at some time in the future. Fourth, trend extrapolation is of diminishing value as the length of time used to forecast extends. The longer the time horizon, the more chance there is of historic relationships changing and new variables emerging.

Trend extrapolation as applied by most business organizations is a method of linking a simple cause with a simple effect. As such, it does nothing to try to understand or predict the underlying variables, unless extrapolation is applied to these variables too.

At best, trend extrapolation can be used where planning horizons are short, the number of variables relatively limited and the risk level relatively low. A retailer may use extrapolation to forecast how much ice cream will be demanded in summer. A historic relationship between the weather (quantified in terms of sunshine hours or average daily temperatures) may have been identified, on to which a long-term relationship between household disposable income and the domestic freezer population has been added. The level of demand for ice cream during the following month could be predicted with reasonable accuracy; with input from the Meteorological Office on the weather forecast, from the Treasury's forecast of household disposable incomes (relatively easy to obtain if the forecast period is only one month), and from statistics showing recent trends in household freezer ownership (available from the Annual General Household Survey).

13.4.5 Expert opinion

Trend analysis is commonly used to predict demand where the state of the causative variables is known. In practice, it can be very difficult to predict what will happen to the causative variables themselves. One solution is to consult expert opinion to obtain the best possible forecast of what will happen to these variables.

In Diffenbach's (1983) study of American corporations, 86 per cent of all firms said they used expert opinion as an input to their planning process. Expert opinion can vary in the level of speciality, from an economist being consulted for a general forecast about the state of the national economy to industry-specific experts. An example of the latter are the fashion consultants that study trends at the major international fashion shows and provide a valuable source of expert opinion to clothing manufacturers seeking to know which types of fabric to order, ahead of a fashion trend.

Expert opinion may be unstructured and come either from a few individuals inside the organization or from external advisers or consultants. The most senior managers in companies of reasonable size tend to keep in touch with developments by various means. Paid and unpaid advisers may be used to keep abreast of a whole range of issues such as technological developments, animal rights campaigners, environmental issues, government thinking and intended legislation. Large companies may employ MPs or MEPs (Members of the European Parliament) as advisers, as well as retired civil servants. Consultancy firms may be employed to brief the company on specific issues or monitor the environment on a more general basis.

In today's economy, it is essential that businesses monitor not only the domestic environment but also the European Union and the international environment: as much legislation affecting UK companies comes from the EU as from the UK government. Legislation passed in the United States can have an indirect effect on UK companies, even though their products may not be intended for sale in America. What is happening in America today may be happening in Europe next year.

Relying on individuals may give an incomplete or distorted picture of the future. There are, however, more structured methods of gaining expert opinion. One of the best known is probably the Delphi method. This involves a number of experts, usually from outside the organization, who (preferably) do not know each other and who do not meet or confer while the process is under way. A scenario (or scenarios) about the future is drawn up by the company. This is then posted out to the experts. Comments are returned and the scenario(s) modified according to the comments received. The process is run through a number of times with the scenario being amended on each occasion. Eventually a consensus of the most likely scenario is arrived at. It is believed that this is more accurate than relying on any one individual because it involves the collected wisdom of a number of experts who have not been influenced by dominant personalities.

13.4.6 Scenario building

Scenario building is an attempt to paint a picture of the future. It may be possible to build a small number of alternative scenarios based on differing assumptions. This qualitative approach is a means of handling environmental issues that are hard to quantify because they are less structured, more uncertain and may involve very complex relationships.

Often the most senior managers in a company may hold no common view about the future. The individuals themselves are likely to be scanning the environment in an informal way, through conversations with colleagues and subordinates within the organization and through business acquaintances and friends outside. The general media, and business and technical publications will also shape a person's 'view' of the future. Individuals will vary in their sensitivity to the environment. Such views may never be harnessed in any formal way, but they may be influencing decisions taken by these individuals. Yet the views each person holds may never have been exposed to debate or challenge in a way that would allow the individual to moderate or change his or her view.

Scenario building among senior management will help individuals to confirm or moderate their views. A new perspective may be taken on issues or forthcoming events. A wider perspective may be taken by individuals who may become more sensitive to the environment

THINKING AROUND THE SUBJECT:
SHELL DRAWS UP LIKELY FUTURE OIL SUPPLY SCENARIOS

How do you predict the future demand for oil products? Simple techniques based on extrapolation of previous trends have been found lacking by events such as wars in the Middle East. The traditional approach used by Shell, like most of the major oil companies, was to forecast the amount of refinery capacity which it would need to meet consumer demand for refined oil-based products by extrapolating recent patterns of demand. It assumed that recent trends would by and large continue, and was caught largely unawares in 1973 by the actions of OPEC. OPEC, a cartel of Middle Eastern oil producers, had used its monopoly power to reduce the supply of crude oil and thus force up crude oil prices threefold. This represented a very severe discontinuity in recent trends, and left most oil companies facing much lower levels of demand than they had previously planned for. Most oil companies were not much better prepared for the second sudden OPEC price rise that occurred in 1983.

Today, Shell tries to manage its future by developing a range of possible scenarios of future business environments. From these scenarios, managers can develop plans of action to meet each eventuality that could be envisaged. Identifying the nature of scenarios can be a challenge to management's creativity.

One example quoted by Shell to justify its scenario-based approach to planning is the oil price collapse which occurred in 1986. In 1984, crude oil prices stood at $28 a barrel. Other oil companies using trend extrapolation predicted that oil prices would stabilize over the next two years at the $25–$30 a barrel level. The prospect of it falling to $15 may have seemed far fetched to many planners yet, in February 1986, the world market price of oil fell first to $17 a barrel, before drifting down to a low point of $10 two months later.

Shell claimed it was much better prepared for this price collapse as it had envisaged a scenario in which this occurred and developed a contingency plan of action in the event of it taking place. This covered, for example, alternative plans for investment in new energy sources and renewal plans for its shipping fleet. For most of its activities, Shell was trading in commodity markets in which product differentiation was either very difficult or impossible. The ability to learn and react rapidly to environmental change gave Shell its only major advantage over its competitors.

More recently, Shell's approach to scenario building demonstrated its value during the 2003 Iraq War. Although Shell had not foreseen the details of the conflict which followed the invasion of Iraq by Allied Forces, it had envisaged a scenario in which there was a serious disruption to oil supplies in the Gulf region, whether this came by war, accident or another cause. Contingency plans allowed the company to rapidly replace oil supplies from alternative sources and to redeploy its tanker fleet. The speed with which the company could adjust the forecourt price of petrol to the consumer in response to volatile spot market prices had been increased with improved internal communications.

For the future, Shell has stated that attitudes towards the environment represent an opportunity for alternative scenario building. The company has developed two scenarios. In the first scenario, the world moves towards sustainable growth, with a change in attitudes towards consumption among consumers throughout the world and increasing controls on pollution-creating processes. The second scenario envisages a drop in environmentalism as an issue, with increasing emphasis on the need to generate economic wealth at a national level. Governments may seek to stimulate employment even if this results in greater environmental damage, while concern for worldwide approaches to the control of pollution may give way to increasing trade barriers as countries struggle for short-term economic survival. The contingency plan for the 'sustainable' scenario might include shifting resources to increase production of wind-generated electricity or biodegradable packaging. For the 'economic stimulation' scenario, expanding output and reducing production costs may be more appropriate.

The development of scenario-building methods has seen increasing importance attributed within Shell to the forecasting of business environments. The company has attributed its high and stable level of profits to this approach. The first business environment planners at Shell were seen by many as eccentric mavericks whose conclusions were relatively marginal to achieving the short-term aims of most managers. Today, the findings of the business environment planners at Shell are communicated within the organization more effectively and managers attach much more significance to the scenarios presented by drawing up their own response plans.

and the impact it can have on business. A more cohesive view may be adopted by senior management which may help strategy formulation and planning. The scenarios may be built up over a number of meetings which may be either totally unstructured or semi-structured, with each meeting focusing on different aspects of the environment. The approach may be used at different levels of management in a large organization; a multinational company may build scenarios at the global, regional and country level. For example, Shell UK Ltd is widely reported to have used this approach on a number of occasions. In the early 1980s it was used as part of the company's methodology for attempting to assess the demand for oil depending on a number of alternative scenarios (see 'Thinking Around the Subject', about the Shell oil company). Chapter 12 discussed the UK government's Foresight Programme, which aims to bring together experts from industry, academia and government in an attempt to identify and evaluate trends in technological developments.

13.4.7 Influence diagrams and impact grids

A more applied approach is to assess the likely impact of specific aspects of environmental change on the business. One method is to construct influence diagrams (Narchal *et al.* 1987) so that a better understanding of the relationships between environmental forces can be obtained. If the price a company has to pay for raw materials is a critical factor then the forces that influence the price of raw materials will be of interest to it. By monitoring these it will have an earlier warning about price rises than if it were to wait until its supplier told it of the price increase. In the influence diagram (Figure 13.7), a positive relationship means that if the value of one force rises then the pressure on the dependent factor will be in the same direction. A negative relationship means that if the value of the environmental force rises then the pressure on the dependent factor is in the opposite direction, downwards.

A number of specific influence diagrams may be used to improve understanding of how forces in the environmental may influence particular aspects of the business. To gain a broader view, environmental impact grids can be constructed. Specific environmental forces or events are identified and their impact on particular aspects of the business assessed (see Jenster 1987). Weighting the assessment on a simple scale, say 0 equals no effect and 10 equals substantial or critical impact, will help decision making. A simple grid can then be constructed (Figure 13.8).

For those companies that wish to structure the environmental analysis in a more detailed way, there are two different but complementary methods of impact analysis. The simplest is

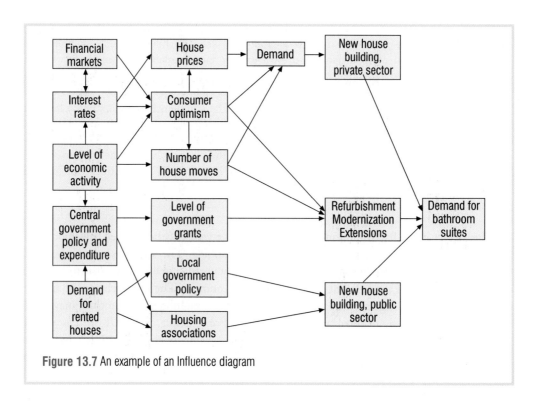

Figure 13.7 An example of an Influence diagram

Environment change Impact on UK car market	UK government raises VAT	EU directive to limit exhaust emissions	EU announces plans for single currency	Japanese car makers abandon voluntary limits on imports to Europe	Technological breakthrough for battery car
UK demand	8				
EU demand	0				
UK production levels	4				
Prices	8				
Production costs					
Marketing costs					

Figure 13.8 An environmental impact grid, where 0 = no effect and 10 = substantial or critical impact

trend impact analysis (TIA), where the movements in a particular variable are plotted over time and the projected value is assessed (Figure 13.9).

A further development of trend impact analysis is cross-impact analysis (CIA), which is used in an attempt to assess the impact of changes in one variable on other variables. This is much more difficult to do but at the minimum it will help managers to understand the possible relationships between forces in the environment. At best, it will provide key information in order to aid strategic decision making (see Figure 13.10). It is reported that the General Electric Company (USA) uses these impact grids as an aid to writing scenarios.

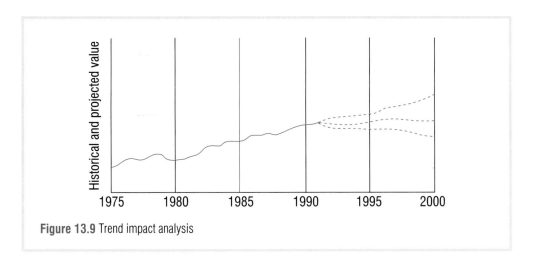

Figure 13.9 Trend impact analysis

Wild cards \ Possible events	OPEC forces price of oil to $30/barrel	OPEC falls out: oil drops to $12/barrel with oversupply	Economic downturn becomes recession and lasts 5 years	Government increases car and petrol taxes
Clean-burn petrol engine developed				
Japanese launch first mass-produced battery-powered car				
Environment deteriorates suddenly; car drivers in Western world limited to 30 miles per day				

Figure 13.10 Cross-impact analysis

A scenario for the early 2000s may be that the use of personal phones is set to grow very rapidly as the technology improves and prices continue to fall. Will young single professional people decide that they do not need a traditional fixed phone in their apartment? One mobile phone may be all they need. Newly married couples are likely to have his-and-hers personal phones rather than install a fixed phone in the home. A cross-impact study undertaken by British Telecom may reveal a serious threat to its traditional domestic fixed-line business. What is more, it is likely that the high-income, high-use customers will be the first to desert traditional suppliers. An alternative scenario is that while the personal mobile phone becomes the dominant mode for voice and text communications, the domestic fixed line business will be used mainly for Internet connections. Or could wireless broadband Internet services, combined with hand-held PDA devices, result in a new generation of Internet-based mobile phones?

13.4.8 Environmental threat and opportunity profile (ETOP)

A marketing opportunity is an attractive situation for a company which could present the company with a competitive advantage. Opportunities should be assessed for their attractiveness and success probability. Attractiveness can be assessed in terms of potential market size, growth rates, profit margins, competitiveness and distribution channels; other factors may be technological requirements, degree of government interference, environmental concerns and energy requirements. Set against the measure of attractiveness is the probability of success. This depends on the company's strengths and competitive advantage; such issues as access to cash, lines of credit or capital to finance new developments. Technological and productive expertise, marketing skills, distribution channels and managerial competence will all need to be taken into account. A simple matrix (Figure 13.11) can be constructed to show the relationship between attractiveness and success probability.

An environmental threat is a challenge posed by an unfavourable trend or development in an organization's environment that could lead to the erosion of the organization's sales or

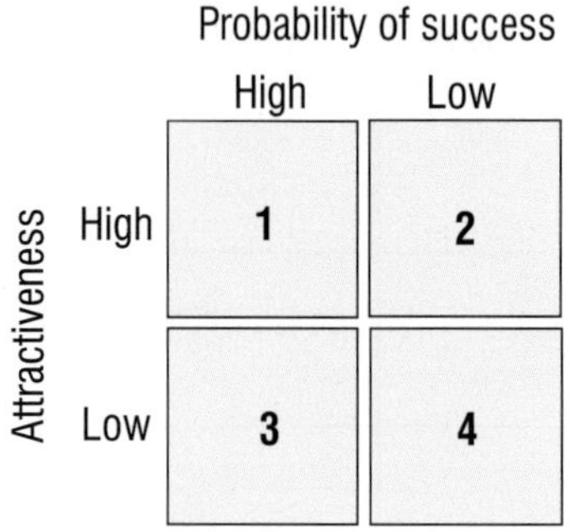

Figure 13.11 An opportunity matrix:
1 attractive opportunity which fits well with company's capabilities
2 attractive opportunity, but with low probability of success
3 high probability of success; poor fit with company's capabilities
4 let's forget this one

profitability. In this case the threats should be assessed according to their seriousness and the probability of occurrence. A threat matrix can then be constructed (Figure 13.12).

In order for the environmental analysis to have a useful input into the business planning process, a wide range of information and opinions needs to be summarized in a meaningful way. This is particularly so if a number of the techniques described in this chapter have been used in a wide-ranging analysis. The information collated from the detailed analysis needs to be simplified and summarized for planning purposes. The environmental threat and opportunity profile (ETOP) provides a summary of the environmental factors that are most critical to the company (Figure 13.13). These provide a useful report to stimulate debate among senior management about the future of the business. Some authors suggest trying to weight these factors according to their importance and then rating them for their impact on the organization.

13.4.9 Porter's Five Forces model of industry competitiveness

The business environment of most organizations is dynamic, with new organizations and technologies emerging to challenge a company's position. A widely used framework for analysing the dynamism of the business environment is Porter's Five Forces model (Porter 1985). This model helps managers identify the factors that affect the intensity of competition within a particular industry, and illustrates the relationship between different players and potential players in the industry. The five forces requiring evaluation are: the power of suppliers, the power of buyers, the threat of new entrants, the threat of substitute products and the intensity of rivalry between competing firms (Figure 13.14).

1 **The power of suppliers:** The power of suppliers is likely to be high if the number of suppliers are few and/or the materials, components and services are in short supply. The suppliers of microprocessor silicon chips have in the past held a powerful market position due to their dominance of technology and high demand for their products relative to available supply.

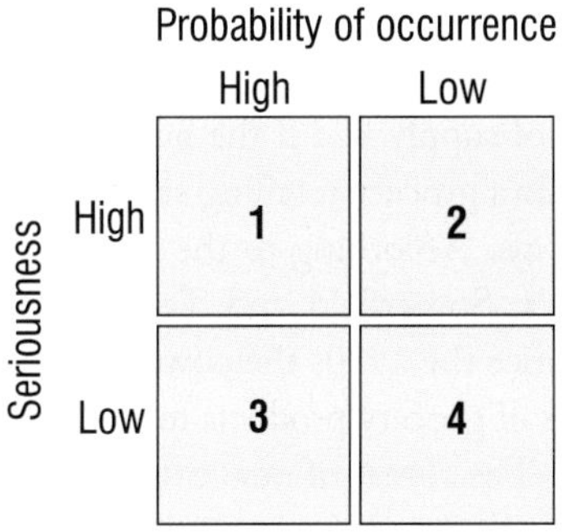

Figure 13.12 A threat matrix:
1 competitor launches superior product
2 pound sterling rises to $3
3 higher costs of raw materials
4 legislation to cover 'environmentally friendly' claims on labels

Factor	Major opportunity	Minor opportunity	Neutral	Minor threat	Major threat	Probability
Economic Interest rates rise to 15%					✓	0.8
£ falls to $1.40	✓					0.4
Disposable incomes do not rise for 5 years				✓		0.3
Political Change of political party – more spending on education and public transport			✓			0.9
Legal EU bans flavouring additives in snacks				✓		0.1
Market Competitor launches major TV campaign				✓		0.5

Figure 13.13 Environmental threat and opportunity profile (ETOP): probability scale from 0.1 (very unlikely to happen) to 0.9 (very likely to happen)

2 **The power of buyers:** Buyer power is likely to be high if there are relatively few buyers, if there are alternative sources of supply and if the buyer has low switching costs. During the past couple of decades, Britain's grocery retailing sector has become increasingly dominated by five very large organizations. According to the Nielsen Grocery Service (Mintel 2004), Asda, Morrisons, Sainsbury's, Somerfield and Tesco held over three-quarters of market share by turnover in 2003. Since the 1970s the power in the marketplace has steadily shifted away from the manufacturers of grocery products to the grocery retailers.

3 **The threat of new entrants:** The threat of new entrants will be higher if there are low barriers to entry. New entrants may already be in the industry in another country but decide to move into your geographic market. A number of South Korean car manufacturers, including Hyundai and Kia, moved into the UK and other European markets during the 1990s. Some Indian motorcycle and car manufacturers (who have a very strong home market and low costs of production) are beginning to show interest in European markets. Alternatively, new entrants may arrive from outside the industry. Bic, whose technology base was plastic moulding, made disposable ball-point pens. Some years ago it was able to successfully

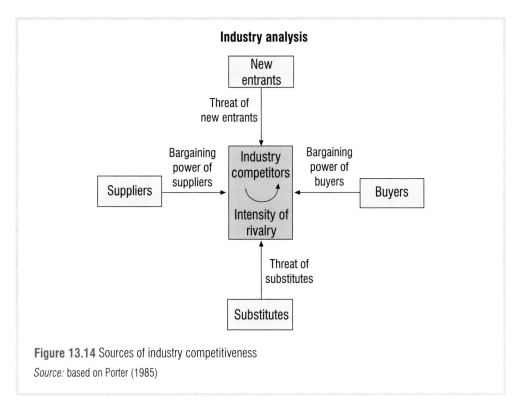

Figure 13.14 Sources of industry competitiveness

Source: based on Porter (1985)

diversify into the wet shave razor market with plastic disposable razors, thus challenging established market leaders such as Gillette and Wilkinson in their core business.

4 **The threat of substitute products:** Substitute products are likely to emerge from alternative technologies, particularly as the economics of production change. Initially the new technology may have high costs associated with it. However, as the technology and experience develops, the level of investment rises and production volumes increase, then costs of production will fall with economies of scale. Manufacturers will then look for more and more applications. Artificial sweeteners for sugar, lighters for matches, plastic containers for glass, polyester for cotton and personal computers for typewriters are obvious examples. These substitutes may change the whole economics of an industry and threaten the survival of the traditional product providers.

5 **Intensity of rivalry between competing firms:** The intensity of rivalry may be high if two or more firms are fighting for dominance in a fast-growing market. For example, this occurred in the UK's personal phone market during the mid-1990s. There may also be a fight to establish the dominant technology in a sector, something that occurred in the early 2000s in the MP3 portable music sector, and previously in the fight between three competing technologies, VHS (the UK winner), Betamax and U-matic to establish the dominant format for domestic VCR players. The need is to become established as the dominant technology or brand before the industry matures. Companies are likely to engage heavily in promotional activity involving advertising and promotional incentives to buy. In a mature industry, particularly if it is characterized by high fixed costs and excess capacity, the

intensity of competitive rivalry may be very high. This is because manufacturers or service providers need to operate at near maximum capacity to cover overhead costs. As the industry matures or at times of cyclical down-turn, or when a number of companies have invested in new capacity, firms fight to maintain their maximum level of sales. Price cuts and discounting may become commonplace and profits will be eroded. Low-cost producers with high brand loyalty have the best chance of survival.

Porter's Five Forces model of industry competitiveness helps understanding of the microenvironment. Monitoring these forces will provide managers with some insight into trends in competitive rivalry within their industry.

13.5 FORMING A VIEW OF ENVIRONMENTAL INFLUENCE

The pace at which senior managers believe the environment is changing and the nature of that change is likely to influence their decision making and planning. Four broad patterns of environmental change may be considered, as shown in Figure 13.15. In part (a) of the figure senior management believes that there is a stable environment with little change. In part (b) senior management believes that there is incremental change at a known and pre-

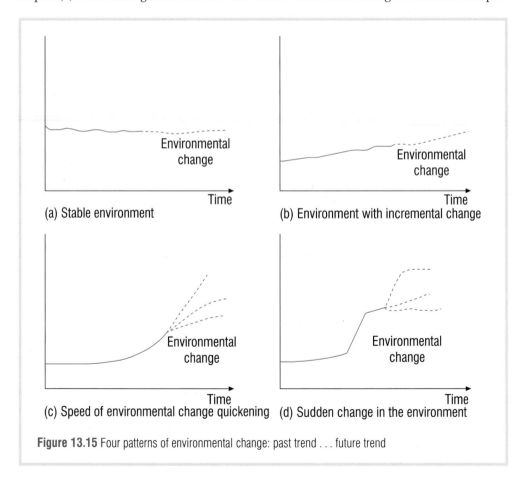

Figure 13.15 Four patterns of environmental change: past trend . . . future trend

dictable pace. In part (c) the pace of change is quickening and becoming harder to anticipate. In part (d) the environment may be subject to sudden change as a major factor has a dramatic impact on other environmental forces, for example sudden steep increases in oil prices.

Other considerations for senior management are whether the environment is simple or complex and stable or dynamic (Figure 13.16). Here it is the relationship between the company and its environment that is in question and whether this is changing. Is the environment moving from being simple to becoming more complex, for example? Or is it moving from a period of stability into one of dynamism? The same environmental change may be seen as an opportunity by one company and a threat by another. The view taken will be influenced by the analysis undertaken, the views of senior management and the ability of the company to respond.

Chapter 1 introduced the three basic components of the marketing environment. The organization's internal environment refers to internal structure, processes and activities and the relationships between business functions. This is the controllable environment. The external environment is the uncontrollable element and has two components. The microenvironment is composed of all organizations and individuals that directly or indirectly affect the activities of the organization. This is sometimes referred to as the industry or task environment. It is thus necessary for the organization to track the behaviour of the market, its competitors, customers, channel members and suppliers. The macroenvironment is composed of those forces that influence the international and domestic economy and society as a whole. These forces are sometimes summarized as sociological, technological, economic and political, and are often abbreviated to STEP, or PEST, to aid memory.

Having completed an analysis of the business environment, ideally by means of a marketing audit, the information needs to be distilled into a SWOT summary (Figure 13.17). The strengths and weaknesses are in respect of the organization's internal environment and the opportunities and threats come from the external environment.

Management needs to be able to answer the questions 'Where are we now?' and 'Where are we likely to go?' given the present performance and future environment. The SWOT summary, then, provides a key input to the planning process. If we assume that we are preparing a business plan for a strategic business unit (an SBU may be a subsidiary or division of a larger

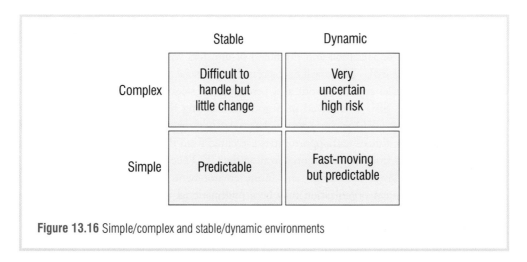

Figure 13.16 Simple/complex and stable/dynamic environments

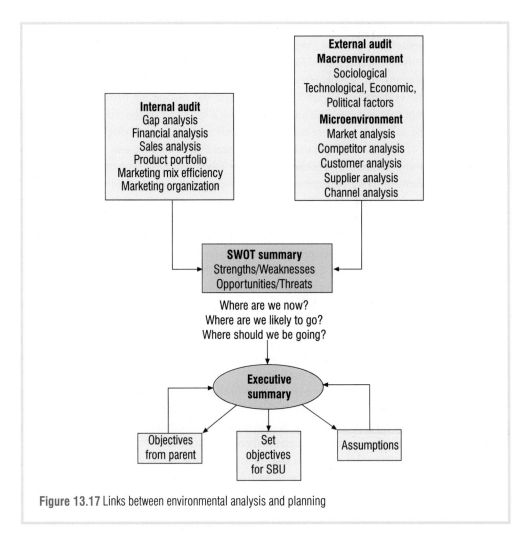

Figure 13.17 Links between environmental analysis and planning

organization), then the chief executive officer (CEO) has to set the business objectives for the coming financial year. In arriving at a decision the CEO has to balance a number of conflicting demands. The parent organization and the board of directors will have expectations regarding the performance of the SBU. These will be expressed in financial terms such as return on capital employed (ROCE), sales revenue, profit as a percentage of sales and rate of growth, etc. The chief executive of the SBU is involved in negotiations during the setting of these objectives. During the process the CEO is conscious of the recent performance of the business (from the internal audit) and the threats and opportunities presented from the external audit. In accepting the financial objectives from the parent organization the CEO needs to ensure that they are realistic and achievable, given the current and future environment. This may seem obvious but remember that the parent organization may be a multinational with a head office in another country or continent. The environmental forces to which the head office managers and directors are exposed may be quite different from those influencing the local SBU.

In negotiating the objectives with the parent and in setting the SBU objectives it is beneficial to state explicitly the key assumptions made. Therefore, if the growth rate of the economy will directly influence your business it is necessary to state what level you have assumed over the planning period. Likewise for interest rates, levels of disposable income, business confidence indices and exchange rates. These would all be primary assumptions. If your business is dependent on others then some secondary or derived assumptions may need to be stated. If 80 per cent of your business is sales to the automotive industry then specifying the assumed level of car sales would be important. Likewise, if you manufacture bathroom suites and fittings your business is directly dependent on sales of new housing and the refurbishment of existing housing stock, both of which are influenced by the level of interest rates.

Planning in larger businesses is a complex activity. Once the business operates over a number of product groups, industries and international markets, then an environmental analysis needs to be conducted at the local level as well as the SBU and corporate level. Forming a cohesive view about the environment becomes much more difficult. In managing a business, senior executives have to balance the immediate requirements of existing operations against the longer-term requirements of shaping and developing the future business. Where does the organization wish to be in five and ten years' time? Since the organization cannot change the business environment it would be wise to attempt to monitor and predict it and then to shape the business to maximize the opportunities and minimize the threats posed by the environment.

13.6 MANAGING OPERATIONAL RISK

So far, risk and uncertainty have been discussed at a strategic level. But in addition to making decisions at a macro level, businesses must increasingly address the issue of risk at a much more operational level. While operational risks may not normally pose such a threat to the survival of an organization as strategic risks, they can nevertheless have serious consequences for an organization. The subject of risk assessment has become an increasingly important item on businesses' agenda, and there are now numerous consultants that undertake, for a fee, risk assessments of an organization's activities.

Risk assessment has become increasingly important at an operational level for a number of reasons.

- Western societies have become more litigious (see Chapter 5), with consumers' rights increasingly being enshrined in legislation. Consumers now have more grounds for obtaining legal redress against a company that has failed to deliver its promises, in contrast to previous times when organizations might have been able to get away with their failings. In the field of financial services, for example, a series of mis-selling scandals has changed the focus from buyers who bought wrongly to sellers who sold wrongly, and organizations must increasingly bear the risk of mis-selling.
- The volume of government regulation of business has increased. We saw in Chapter 2, for example, that organizations are increasingly required to protect the ecological environment. Risk arises from the fines which may be imposed on a company if its fails to meet regulatory requirements.
- The rights of employees have tended to increase, and organizations must assess the risk of disadvantaging individual employees or groups of employees who could potentially have a claim against the organization.
- With the growing importance of consumer brands, it has become increasingly important for

an organization to preserve its image. Even though a company might not have broken any law, its association with unethical practices may do incalculable harm to the organization.

■ Threats of terrorism have increased in recent years and pose a challenge for continuity of business operations. Sometimes a terrorist group may be campaigning against a company specifically. This has been the case, for example, with the direct action taken against organizations that supplied goods and services to Huntingdon Life Sciences, a company that undertakes experiments on live animals. At other times, an organization may simply represent the values of a group which terrorists are opposed to, and an attack is a means of making this point publicly and with maximum impact. When a group bombed a branch of the British-owned HSBC Bank in Istanbul in January 2004, it probably did not have any particular grudge against the bank, but the bank symbolized a set of Western values and intervention in the world which the group was opposed to.

How should organizations respond to operational risk? They need to reconcile the potential benefits of an activity with the downside risk of certain undesirable events happening. Many approaches to risk assessment seek to develop a risk profile of an activity, and estimate the cost to the company if an event occurs, and the probability that it will actually occur. An organization can therefore choose between alternative courses of action on the basis of their expected cost (defined as the total cost of an event happening, multiplied by the probability of it happening). Of course, calculating these values can be quite speculative. For a food manufacturer, for example, how does it estimate the probability of terrorist groups sabotaging its factories or environmental campaigners blockading its distribution depots? It may be even more difficult to calculate the cost to the organization of such events occurring. The costs of physical damage may be relatively easy to assess, and may easily be covered by insurance. But it is much more difficult to assess the damage to a company's reputation. Would the activities of a protest group provide a negative association with the company which will live on in people's minds? Or would an attack on the company promote sympathy from its customers?

In choosing between alternative operational plans, organizations must take into account a number of considerations.

■ Should the organization be taking part in this type of activity at all? If a service process or manufactured good offers too many opportunities for the company to make mistakes, it may be better for the organization to drop that line of activity completely. Should a train operator provide a left luggage service at its stations, when the risk of injury from a terrorist bomb is great in relation to the revenue generated? Many airlines have discontinued taking 'unaccompanied minors' on their flights, because the risk of failing to provide an adequate service is too great, relative to the profitability of this type of activity.

■ Will reconfiguration of a product in order to reduce risk make it unattractive to some consumers, who will no longer buy it? For example, there has been a suggestion that increased delays at airports due to security screening have led some people to believe that the hassle of flying is too great, and so they have chosen other means of transport, or not travelled at all.

■ By contrast, rigorous measures may be perceived by some customers as a price worth paying in order to ensure that they can consume the product without fear (for example, the Israeli airline El Al is acknowledged to have the strictest security of any airline, and this has been used by the airline to promote reassurance to consumers).

Terrorist attacks can affect manufacturers as well as service organizations, but their effects on service organizations can be very much greater. Manufacturing companies can take steps to protect the security of their production facility by controlling access only to employees. Cases of deliberate damage to manufactured goods are rare, and manufacturers have taken steps to reduce this risk throughout their distribution channels, for example by introducing tamper-evident packaging. This is in contrast to service organizations, where customers typically enter the production process and cannot easily be screened out in the way that unauthorized entry to a factory can be prevented. Indeed, the whole point of most services is for customers to enter the service 'factory' so, with relatively open access, risks are much greater.

THINKING AROUND THE SUBJECT:
IS A COMEDIAN TOO RISKY TO HANDLE?

Airlines have had to face up to the operational challenge of reducing risks from terrorism. An aircraft loaded with fuel, owned by a national flag carrier and flying over some of the world's great cities is a potent weapon for terrorists to take control of. But how should airlines assess the risks they face as they try to operate an efficient and welcoming service?

Consider the case of the entertainer Jeremy Beadle, who was reportedly denied boarding a London to Glasgow flight in January 2004 because he did not have any formal identity papers. The check-in staff appeared to be in doubt that he was actually the entertainer who had been seen by millions of people each week on television. Many nearby fans were apparently able to vouch for his identity. But without the right bit of paper to prove that he was in fact the well-known entertainer, he could not proceed.

In many service industries, staff would use their common sense and weigh up the situation and come to a decision. But the security industry is labour intensive and there can be fierce competition between security service providers that operate on low margins. Staff tend to be paid the minimum wage level and opportunities for choosing top-quality staff and training them in judgement skills are limited. So, in order to comply with government requirements, it is easier for companies to rely on strict rules-based blueprint approaches to security checking.

Fans of Jeremy Beadle who were waiting in Glasgow for him to perform may have been disappointed when he did not turn up. Disappointment may also have been experienced by the thousands of frail little old ladies that have innocently tried to take nail scissors and knitting needles on board an aircraft, but have had them confiscated because 'those are the rules'. Despite the 'rules', a smart and determined terrorist might have developed a much more ingenious method of smuggling harmful objects on board the aircraft.

Often, the appearance of a strictly enforced security policy may give some reassurance to customers that management is taking measures to avoid a terrorist attack. But sometimes the visible appearance of security may be a front for much deeper flaws. While there may have been few reported cases of little old ladies using their knitting needles as weapons to overpower cabin crew, it may be easier to imagine a determined terrorist breaking a glass bottle to use as a much more lethal weapon. Little old ladies with their needles may be an easy and visible sign that security is being treated seriously by an airline, but would airlines voluntarily enforce a bottle ban, thereby annoying even more passengers, and causing a loss of valuable duty-free sales in airport shops?

OUTSOURCING OVERSEAS MAY LOOK CHEAP, BUT HOW DO YOU ASSESS THE RISK?

In a competitive business environment, companies survive and prosper by cutting their costs faster than competitors, or delivering better-value goods and services to customers. Risk is an inherent part of firms' survival strategies. If they cut costs too greatly, will the quality of their products suffer to such an extent that customers drift away to the competition? If they manage to attract customers on the basis of product quality, will the cost of such high quality lead to a financial loss?

In many industry sectors, markets are very dynamic, with new technologies and customer preferences emerging. If market leadership is to be maintained, companies must take risks in order to bring down their costs and/or improve the quality of the goods and services that they supply. But history is littered with examples of firms that have unsuccessfully cut their costs so that, instead of improving their profitability, they have alienated customers. Companies that save money by reducing the level of stocks that they keep run the risk of alienating disappointed customers who may simply go to a competitor with a higher level of stock availability. Replacing a metal component with a plastic one may reduce manufacturing costs, but will customers remain loyal when the plastic component performs badly?

Many Western companies have moved their production facilities to cheaper, less developed countries in an attempt to cut their costs. In price-sensitive markets, failure to move to cheaper sources of production could result in long-term decline, as the retailer Marks & Spencer found when its over-reliance on domestically produced clothes put it at a competitive disadvantage to retailers that sourced their clothes predominantly from the Far East.

The process of transferring production to overseas countries is often referred to as 'offshoring', and the presumed cost savings often come with associated risks. The political risks range from major political threats such as terrorism, political violence and war to more subtle threats, including politically discriminatory regulations. Few countries are likely to unilaterally confiscate a company's assets, but unexpected renegotiation of a licence to operate in the country can remain a danger.

China and India have become popular countries for companies seeking low-cost production. However, their stability is not assured and, in 2005, many businesses were concerned when China said that it could declare war on Taiwan. Only two years previously, there was widespread alarm at the prospect of a nuclear war between India and Pakistan.

The risk of disruption through terrorism has increased for companies that transfer production to lower-cost countries. The security consultant Arrow has noted that at the beginning of the twentieth century the number of non-state armed political groups probably numbered no more than a dozen. By the middle of the last century, this figure was around 100, and at the turn of this millennium it had risen to over 480. Just to add to the threats facing businesses, an increasing number of attacks are being carried out by loosely formed clan-based groups and disgruntled individuals.

Numerous risk management companies assess risks associated with different countries.

The insurance company Aon's risk assessment for each country takes into account threats from terrorists, nationalists, separatists and other extremists. In 2005, it identified India, Pakistan, Israel, Palestine, Saudi Arabia and Colombia as high-risk countries. Western Sahara, Mongolia, Cameroon, Togo and Gabon were among the least risky countries.

How can companies overcome risks of taking their production overseas? A thorough analysis of a country is an important prerequisite, but too much analysis can lead to paralysis. Should a company avoid China just because of the fear of war with Taiwan? Taking risks is an important element of gaining cost advantages.

Companies often choose to take out insurance against specified risks. Coverage can provide compensation of up to £1 billion in the event that a company's assets are confiscated by the government. Premiums are dependent upon the nature of a company's business and the political stability of the host country. Companies can also insure against more common threats which could disrupt their business, for example a long business interruption caused by a failure of the telephone network. With climate change believed to be the cause of increasingly volatile weather patterns, insurance is often arranged to cover the risk of damage caused by hurricanes and floods, such as the hurricane that hit a number of Caribbean islands in 2004.

But insurance cannot cover all the risks of operating in a low-cost foreign country. It may cover disruption caused by bad weather, interruption to production caused by failure of infrastructure, theft from the business and even fraud. However, insurance is less likely to cover losses which arise as a result of cultural risks. It is reported that Capital One, the credit card company, was harmed by staff at an Indian call centre misleading customers with false offers of credit. It is reported that the computer manufacturer Dell was forced to shift a number of customer support jobs back to the United States because many customers had complained that they had difficulty understanding Indian accents. Other companies have suffered petty thefts and absenteeism which are not considered abnormal by the host cultures.

Rather than going it alone in an offshore venture, many companies choose to go into partnership with a local company, although even here there may be problems between cultures in interpreting the partnership agreement. The UK insurer Aviva is reported to have created 3700 call centre jobs in India, on the basis that this would give it a competitive advantage in the fiercely competitive UK general insurance market. The company went into partnership with a local company called EXL. Having a local partner provided important knowledge to Aviva about local control standards. A partnership agreement was structured in such a way that Aviva could take back control if its standards were not met.

All life involves some risk, and any innovation brings risk as well as reward – so a firm's priority must be to manage risks better. It will rarely be possible for governments to eliminate risks entirely. In the first years of the twenty-first century, offshoring appeared to be a relatively low-risk strategy for businesses. But should companies put all their eggs in the one basket of the cheapest producer, or should they spread their risk around different countries with differing levels of political risk? Should they keep some operations back home in order that they can set benchmarks more effectively?

QUESTIONS

1 Summarize the strategic risks facing a UK-based insurance company in its attempts to set up a call centre in a less developed country.

2 Develop an environmental threat and opportunity profile (ETOP) for a UK company seeking to develop an overseas call centre in India.

3 For a manufacturer of domestic electrical equipment, compare the risks, costs and benefits of manufacture at home with the alternative of manufacturing in a low-cost developing country.

SUMMARY

Information is becoming increasingly important as a means by which organizations gain advantage in a competitive business environment. With recent advances in a firm's ability to collect data, greater attention is now paid to the effective use of information. 'Keeping in touch' drives a firm's information collection and it is important that methods of data collection, analysis and dissemination are appropriate to this task. As firms grow, their information management activities tend to become more complex. Numerous frameworks are available for analysing the business environment. The choice of framework will depend, among other things, on the complexity of the environment, the speed of change and the cost of inaccurately predicting change in the environment.

There are close linkages between this chapter and **Chapter 10** where we discussed the nature of competition. In all but the most 'perfect' markets, understanding competitors is crucial to market success. An important consideration in predicting the future is the likely consequence of any change in the political and legal environments (**Chapters 2 and 5**), where change can occur quite suddenly. Change in the social and demographic environment (**Chapter 3**) tends to be more gradual. Finally, **Chapter 4** discussed developments in information technology which are improving organizations' ability to gather and analyse information about their business environment.

Key Terms

Audits	(488)	Five Forces model	(497)	Risk assessment	(503)
Decision support systems	(481)	Forecasting	(485)	Scenario	(491)
Environmental impact		Knowledge management	(477)	SWOT analysis	(489)
grids	(493)	Learning organization	(478)	Trend analysis	(490)
Environmental scanning	(481)	Management information			
Expert opinion	(490)	system	(479)		

CHAPTER REVIEW QUESTIONS

1 What factors make an organization's environment so complex?

Using an industry example, suggest relevant sources of information it might access to help it understand its complexity. (*Based on CIM Marketing Environment Examination*)

2 Your government has approached an independent group of economic forecasters to undertake a SWOT analysis of the national economy. Prepare a short series of relevant slides to support the forthcoming presentation of this analysis. (*Based on CIM Marketing Environment Examination*)

3 All the industries listed below experienced a turbulent business environment during the 1990s. Select one of these industries (or any other industry with which you are familiar) and identify the changes encountered.

Telephones, TV, hospitals, electricity, computing, retailing.

4 Choose an industry and look ahead about three to five years; build three scenarios for the future.

5 Construct an influence diagram for a product category of your choosing. Some ideas are:
   (a) retirement apartments (private sector for sale or rent)
   (b) children's bikes
   (c) conservatories
   (d) fabric material (used for curtaining and furniture coverings)
   (e) computer-controlled document-handling machinery (for handling, collating and folding documents or leaflets and stuffing envelopes)

6 For those of you in work, attempt to construct an 'environmental impact grid' for your business.

7 Cars propelled by traditional fuels such as petrol and diesel are claimed to pollute our cities and damage the environment. Investigate the alternative fuels under development and evaluate their benefits and limitations. What environmental forces may speed up or slow down the introduction of alternative fuels? It may be technically possible to produce cars which run on alternative fuels but how could you persuade the market to accept them?

ACTIVITY

Genetically modified (GM) ingredients are now appearing in food sold in UK supermarkets. Agri-businesses and some food manufacturers believe there are substantial benefits to using genetically modified crops (and possibly animals in the future). Some food manufacturers claim *not* to use GM ingredients. Some pressure groups and customers believe they should be made illegal. Most customers are unsure and possibly confused. Supermarkets are treading cautiously. This is a complex business–environmental problem. Technology makes it possible. Government legislation appears not to cover the issue. Main players in the markets are unsure. There is potentially a new industry worth billions of pounds in an embryonic state. It potentially affects us all.

Conduct an environmental audit on this topic. Look at the issues from the point of view of different players: producers, manufacturers, retailers, consumers and government. (If there is more than one group in your class, each could take up the position of one of the players.)

Useful Websites

Impact of E-Business on Office Work

A Canadian website offering useful overviews of how office support work processes are changing, and the skills and labour market knowledge that office workers are likely to need in the future.

http://www.ont.hrdc-drhc.gc.ca/ english/lmi/eaid/occ.info/ ebusReport/full_e.html

The Ernst & Young Center for Business Innovation

The Ernst & Young Center for Business Innovation website contains downloadable knowledge management publications, surveys, details of the 'Knowledge Advantage 1998' and a discussion on 'Managing the Knowledge Organization'.

http://www.businessinnovation.ey.com/

The WWW Virtual Library on Knowledge Management

A comprehensive site containing links, online forums, articles, magazines, analyses and news.

http://www.brint.com/km/

Shell

This site provides a useful description of the way the Shell oil company uses scenario building in its business planning.

http://www.shell.com/royal-en/content/ 1,5028,25432–50913,00.html

Business Information Discussion Site

Business-Information-All is a forum for teachers and researchers working in the area of business information management, business information systems or business information technology.

http://www.jiscmail.ac.uk/lists/business- information-all.html

Further Reading

There are many texts on the subject of marketing management which focus on how an organization can implement measures to respond to a changing external environment. The following are useful:

Kotler, P. (2003) *Marketing Management: Analysis, Planning, Implementation and Control*, 11th edn, Hemel Hempstead, Prentice Hall International.

Piercy, N. (2002) *Market-led Strategic Change*, 3rd edn, Butterworth-Heinemann.

Competition within the Internet environment is discussed in the following:

Porter, M.E. (2001) 'Strategy and the Internet', *Harvard Business Review*, March, pp. 63–78.

For a general discussion of the principles of marketing research, the following texts are recommended:

Hague, P. and Hague, N. (2004) *Market Research in Practice: A Guide to the Basics*, London, Kogan Page.

Proctor, T. (2003) *Essentials of Marketing Research*, London, FT Prentice Hall.

Wilson, A. (2002) *Marketing Research: An Integrated Approach*, London, FT Prentice Hall.

The important role played by information in business planning is discussed in the following:

Antal, A., Child, J. and Nonaka, I. (eds) (2003) *Handbook of Organizational Learning and Knowledge*, Oxford University Press.

Davenport, Thomas H. and Prusak, Laurence (2000), *Working Knowledge: How Organizations Manage What They Know*, Harvard Business School Press.

References

Ansoff, H.I. (1984) *Implementing Strategic Management*, Englewood Cliffs, NJ, Prentice Hall.

Ansoff, I.C. (1985) *Corporate Strategy*, London, Penguin.

Berger, P.L. and Luckmann, T. (1966) *The Social Construction of Reality*, Garden City, NY, Doubleday.

Diffenbach, J. (1983) 'Corporate environmental analysis in US corporations', *Long Range Planning*, Vol. 16, No. 3, pp. 107–16.

Dretske, F. (1981) *Knowledge and the Flow of Information*, Cambridge, MA, MIT Press.

Drucker, P.F. (1999) *Management Challenges for the 21st Century*, New York, Harper & Row.

Jenster, P.V. (1987) 'Using critical success factors in planning', *Long Range Planning*, Vol. 20, No. 4, pp. 102–9.

Johnson, G., Scholes, K. and Whittington, R. (2004) *Exploring Corporate Strategy*, 7th edn, Hemel Hepstead, FT Prentice Hall International.

Kotler, P. (1997) *Marketing Management: Analysis, Planning, Implementation and Control*, 9th edn, Hemel Hempstead, Prentice Hall International.

Mintel (2004) *Food Retailing – UK*, London, Mintel.

Moorman C., Zaltman, G. and Deshpande, R. (1992) 'Relationships between providers and users of market research: the dynamics of trust within and between organizations, *Journal of Marketing Research*, Vol. 29 (August), pp. 314–28.

Narchal, R.M. *et al.* (1987) 'An environmental scanning system for business planning', *Long Range Planning*, Vol. 20, No. 6, pp. 96–105.

Nonaka, I. (1991) 'The knowledge-creating company,' *Harvard Business Review*, Vol. 69, No. 6, pp. 96–104.

Porter, M.E. (1985) *Competitive Advantage*, New York, Free Press.

Case Studies

Five case studies are presented here which bring together a number of issues discussed in previous chapters. All the cases focus on organizations that have faced significant changes in their business environments. Their challenge has been to first identify the change that was occurring, to understand its impact on their business, and then to make decisions about how they could most effectively respond to the change. For each case study, a number of discussion questions are posed. The cases represent a range of different business environments, as outlined below.

■ **CD Marketing Services Ltd** was operating a low-tech door-to-door leaflet distribution service that was being challenged by sophisticated targeting services using computerized databases. Should the company capitalize on its strengths in its established sector? It knew this sector well, but did this sector face oblivion? What strengths did it have to take on its much larger rivals if it wished to move into the much more hi-tech and growing customer profiling and database management sector?

■ **Bass Brewers Ltd** entered the Czech Republic shortly after the end of the communist era, where it found a highly fragmented market for beer and a very different social environment compared to the UK. Bass saw opportunities to use its skills in brand development and distribution to bring about the profitable consolidation of the Czech beer market. But with very low beer prices, overcapacity and a well-financed Japanese competitor also seeking dominance of the market, how could Bass earn profits? Eventually, Bass pulled out of the Czech market, having never made a profit.

■ **Ford Motor Company** is generally associated with car manufacturing but, as this case study demonstrates, it earns a high proportion of its profits from selling services. The case picks up on the point made in Chapter 11 that developed economies tend to be increasingly dominated by services. Here we discuss how Ford has addressed the challenges and opportunities of a service-based economy.

■ **Bus operators** in Britain have faced tremendous change in their business environment. At a political level, they have had to respond to a change from a tightly regulated environment to an almost completely unregulated environment, and now face a gradual trend towards more government regulation. At the same time, social and economic change, which resulted in long-term decline in bus use, has now been partly reversed, with bus operators seeing the first increase in usage for many years.

■ The **Co-operative Bank** has successfully carved a niche market for itself. At a time when many people are sceptical about banks' practices, the Co-operative Bank has adopted an ethical positioning. It has developed a charter that defines sources and uses of funds that it deems to be ethically unacceptable. Adopting an ethical positioning has helped to reverse the decline in the Co-operative Bank's customer base.

CASE 1: CD MARKETING SERVICES – RIDING THE CREST OF THE INFORMATION REVOLUTION

Companies have always tried to know more about their customers in order to help their segmentation, targeting and positioning strategies. In recent times, more companies have sought to communicate directly with their customers, rather than relying on indirect communication through advertising media. The technology to enable this has been developing rapidly. Fifty years ago, few people would have imagined that large amounts of consumer profile data would be bought and sold by companies. But today, the collection, analysis and dissemination of marketing information have led to the emergence of a whole new information services sector. A seemingly bewildering array of organizations has developed a previously unimaginable range of information services which help client companies to get their message to customers more cost-effectively than their competitors.

One company that has ridden the crest of the information wave is Circular Distributors Ltd. It has been in business for over half a century as a supplier of targeted messages, acting on behalf of numerous goods and services suppliers. Like most companies in the services sector, it has found its marketing environment changing at an increasingly rapid rate. The company has been deeply affected by technological developments, which affect the way it operates, the expectations of its customers and the activities of its competitors.

The company is essentially in the business of supplying direct marketing services. As a proportion of all firms' promotional expenditure, direct marketing has been increasing its share, giving rise to exciting opportunities for companies that had developed a sound knowledge of techniques for dealing with customers on a one-to-one basis. Some indication of the shift in promotional expenditure is shown in Figure 14.1. When the direct mail component of this expenditure is examined more closely, it is evident that the business-to-consumer element has been expanding more rapidly than the business-to-business element (Figure 14.2).

A low-tech start
Circular Distributors was founded as a very low-tech distributor of leaflets from door to door. One of its early achievements was to deliver 10 million free samples of soap for Lever Brothers in the first ever door-to-door distribution of its

kind. From a scattergun approach to distribution, the company had gradually refined its techniques to deliver promotional leaflets and sample offers of products that typically included shampoo, tea bags and soap. Fifty years ago, many manufacturers of fast moving consumer goods (fmcg) would have been more than happy with the company's approach which by today's standards would be considered quite simplistic. It was essentially putting a fairly generic product into the hands of a fairly homogeneous market to encourage trial and hopefully a subsequent purchase. Over time, markets have become more fragmented, as distinctive lifestyle groups have emerged. In response to this, companies have sought to differentiate their products to appeal to ever-smaller niche segments. The fairly generic, low value added service that Circular Distributors was selling had become too blunt an instrument for fmcg companies, which now had an exciting range of value-added marketing services available to them to target customers more cost-effectively. Nevertheless, door-to-door distribution remained big business and in 2002 the Direct Marketing Association estimated that over 8 billion items were delivered through consumers' letterboxes – an average of 304 items per household. Of that total, a substantial 31 per cent consisted of unaddressed material, the result of door-drop marketing. The total turnover of the industry in the UK was estimated at over £576 million.

Circular Distributors' management team, headed by Nick Wells and three fellow directors, had taken control of the company in 1991 in a £1.1 million management buy-out. An important part of the new management's business development plan during the 1990s was to concentrate on services that were able to target smaller groups of consumers. Groups that were at transition points in their lives represented particularly promising opportunities, because

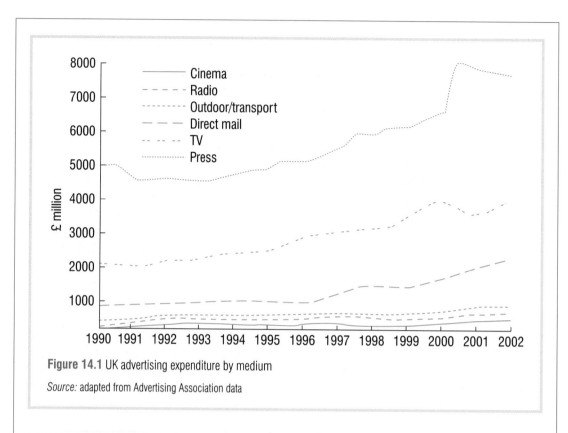

Figure 14.1 UK advertising expenditure by medium

Source: adapted from Advertising Association data

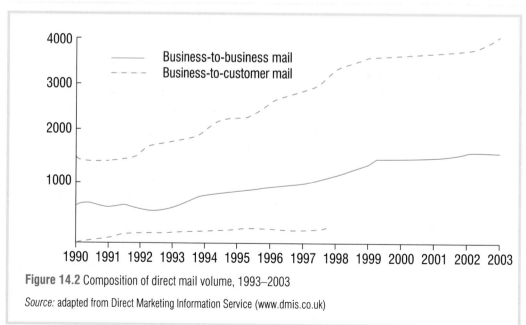

Figure 14.2 Composition of direct mail volume, 1993–2003

Source: adapted from Direct Marketing Information Service (www.dmis.co.uk)

such groups were likely to be very receptive to messages about types of purchases which were still new to them. Mothers-to-be (who faced many new types of purchase decision) were seen as a very promising target for the company's strategy. An important part of its strategy was subsequently based on a publication called *Emma's Diary*, launched in 1992 and produced in association with the Royal College of General Practitioners. The 132-page booklet is a week-by-week guide to pregnancy and is given out by GPs and midwives to women when their pregnancy is confirmed. The company's research has claimed that 78 per cent of expectant mothers and 81 per cent of first-time mothers-to-be read it. This gives *Emma's Diary* higher readership than all of the competing 13 parenting magazines combined.

Advertising in the bi-annual publication by producers of baby-related products has accounted for almost a third of *Emma's Diary*'s revenue. A further third of revenue comes from companies paying for the distribution of product samples in the mother's gift pack, which is distributed free to readers through selected shops. The mother's gift pack is an effective marketing medium, collected in 1999 by 400,000 of the total of 720,000 expectant mothers. The remaining one-third of revenue comes from sales of consumer information, which is gathered when expectant mothers register to qualify for the mother's pack.

Slow growth

By 1999 the company appeared to be moving along at a very pedestrian pace. In the information age, too much of its energies still appeared to be directed at stuffing envelopes, and too little to the collection, analysis and sale of marketing information. The one-third of revenue for *Emma's Diary* that came from data sales had highlighted the possibilities for the company, but it seemed to be moving at a much slower pace than other companies such as Claritis and Experian, which were growing rapidly through the sale of consumer information. In June 1999 *The Sunday Times* ran an article on the company and the expert commentators consulted were not over-impressed. Ray Perry of the Chartered Institute of Marketing described Circular Distributors as 'a flat and stagnant company' that needed 'a new lease of life and a new identity'. John Eggleston of KPMG said its managers 'need to take action quickly, accept that growth demands some risk and develop firm and practical plans' to seize opportunities for growth. Managers were criticized for focusing too much on internal issues and lacking the drive to respond to market changes. The article concluded: 'If Circular Distributors is to maintain its profits, it needs to provide door-to-door services of a higher value. It must change its image from a letter-box-stuffing operation to a distributor of marketing materials and services. Ultimately it may need to change its name to attract the right clients.'

The criticism implicit in the *Sunday Times* article goaded the company into a more adventurous approach to its business. For a start, the company changed its name from Circular Distributors to CD Marketing Services and developed Lifecycle Marketing as a brand in its own right to distinguish it from the relatively low-value letterbox distribution service. The Circular Distributors name was retained for the door-to-door distribution service. This part of the business was still very large and in 1999 delivered a total of more than 1.5 billion items throughout the UK. However, within its portfolio of services, the sale of consumer information may have been the star or growth service, but door-to-door distribution was in danger of going from being a cash cow to a dog.

Investment in the future

During 1999 the company invested heavily in new technologies aimed at giving it a competitive advantage in the growing field of data analysis. The immediate effect of this investment was to reduce profits by about £400,000, but within two years this expenditure contributed to an increase in annual sales to £33 million and profits to £2.4 million in 2002. CD invested heavily in developing more sophisticated services than stuffing promotional material and product samples through letterboxes.

Among the new services developed by CD were CD Microtargeting, which can pinpoint precisely where a target market lives in units of just 700 households; CD Newshare, offering high-speed 'with-newspaper' distribution, providing delivery within just three days – CD itself delivered over 3 million free newspapers each week; and the Solus scheme, which undertakes targeted door-to-door mailshots. Virgin Holidays used the Solus scheme in 2002 to deliver more than half a million leaflets personalized by shop name to the catchment areas of Co-op Travel and Travelcare stores, which offer Virgin Holidays. The door-drop activity ran alongside an integrated media campaign including radio, new media and point of sale.

In developing these more specifically targeted products, the company had subtly changed its core business. The emphasis was now as much on collecting information about consumers as on distributing product samples.

With regard to *Emma's Diary*, the focus of the company's service offer had shifted from distribution to information management. By 1999 CD already had a database of 3.5m families. It was now collecting data on 600,000 families each year, with 100,000 being 'cleansed' to remove those that change address. The aim was to build Britain's largest database of families with young children.

What was the nature of the service being offered by the company's Lifecycle Marketing division? Segmented lists of consumers created by the company could be rented by organizations for one-off use. The company also sold licences by which other organizations could include CD's data in their own databases. As a further service, CD offered its clients the chance to include specific questions in its publications, for which the client would have exclusive rights to use the data generated. Given the growing difficulty of getting consumers to respond to questionnaires, and the high response rates achieved by CD's targeted publications, this service was highly valuable in its own right.

Who were the customers for CD's lifecycle information services? The two most important groups of customers were financial services and home-shopping businesses, which each accounted for about 30 per cent of data sales. Remaining sales were spread between suppliers of baby products, child book clubs and various other types of business. All of these clients were attracted by the fact that readers of the company's publications were going through some form of life change, such as becoming a parent or getting married, or having a child starting school. Each of these life changes is typically associated with new spending priorities and, in the absence of previous knowledge about these new types of purchases, mailshots may be particularly welcomed by individuals. Client companies particularly valued the high coverage of the target segments, and the low wastage rate within the lists.

What business is CD Marketing Services in?

The company knew the door-to-door business inside out and had carved a valuable niche for itself where it could offer unrivalled coverage, flexibility and economies of scale. But now that it was moving into the supply of information services it was competing on territory already staked out by much larger competitors. Companies such as Claritas and Experian had already built up massive databases of consumer information, not just on new mothers. They could also offer services in many of the overseas markets that their clients operated in. It was not good enough for CD to claim that it had superior knowledge of a small number of niche market segments, because its larger competitors had been steadily building up ever more sophisticated databases of consumer niches. The company saw a major problem in convincing clients to defect from its larger competitors to use its own information services. Would CD always be seen as a low-value letterbox stuffer or could it use its long-standing relationships with many fmcg companies to add information services to its service offer? The company needed to build trust and confidence among clients that had never used its services or only perceived the company as a provider of lower-value door-to-door distribution.

At the same time, the company was aware that it should not lose sight of its core letterbox market, which was still profitable. A number of initiatives to raise the value of services offered to clients were attempted, for example offering a weekend distribution service. The company had previously operated only a weekday service, but had identified that clients' messages could be more effective if they were delivered to a target customer on the day when they have most time to read them. New types of client appeared for the door-to-door service, such as Internet service providers that sought distribution of free CD-ROMs to targeted households. The company also extended its gift pack concept by delivering it door to door, without the need to collect it from a designated retail outlet. During 2000, a trial took place to distribute children's school packs door to door. Each pack consisted of a plastic bag containing a back-to-school calendar (carrying advertising messages), a CD-ROM from an Internet service provider, and samples of products aimed at children aged between 5 and 14. A response card sought to increase the volume of information that the company could sell on to its clients.

International expansion

CD also sought to expand into mainland Europe. It formed strategic alliances with a number of companies that were members of the European Letterbox Marketing Association, so that it was now able to offer its UK clients a 'one-stop-shop' distribution service to 140 million homes in France, Germany, Spain and Italy. As evidence that it was taking European expansion seriously, it recruited three multilingual sales staff to handle European sales. By having the ability to offer Europe-wide distribution, the company hoped that it would be able to cater for clients such as L'Oréal, Kimberley-Clark and Gillette, which have pan-European marketing operations.

The company had moved into areas of expertise which were previously unknown to it, and thereby taken big risks. But in the rapidly changing market for information services, it could not afford to stand still. New methods of distributing information to target customers are appearing all the time, with recent examples being the Internet, digital television and WAP mobile phones. How widely should CD spread its resources? Which new media are worth investing in, and which ones may disappear as quickly as they appeared? Could it afford to become involved in marketing through new 'third generation' mobile phones? How far can the company's brand be stretched? There is a great danger that any investment in emerging media may be too little to be effective. It could simply end up having some representation with all media, but being effective in none. The company has taken steps into the Internet by setting up a website for *Emma's Diary*, and has gained some information about visitors to the site. It has also earned revenue from 'click throughs' to advertisers on the site. But to be in this business seriously, the company needs to devote serious amounts of time and resources to it. With an ever increasing number of Internet service providers offering portals which seek users and advertisers, CD is just one of many minnows in a crowded marketplace.

Future focus?

Circular Distributors has moved from providing a low-value service in a slowly growing market to providing higher-value services in rapidly expanding markets. Although the information age has produced many opportunities, it has also produced many casualties among companies that have expanded too fast and failed to deliver a credible value proposition to their customers. During early 2000, 'dotcom' fever appeared to reach a peak with large amounts of money being poured into new ventures seeking to gain more information about consumers. Should CD have taken a bolder approach, or was caution more appropriate? And what about door-to-door distribution, the bread and butter of CD's business – shouldn't the company focus on what it knows best? For the future, one of the main problems facing the company is knowing just where the next threat to its business would come from. What, for instance would the effect of 3G mobile phones be on consumer information services? Which new technologies should the company invest in? What new services should it seek to offer? Where does the traditional service of door-to-door distribution fit into its portfolio?

With so many calls on the company's investment capital, and the opportunities of Contin-

ental Europe beckoning, it seemed that some form of alliance, beyond membership of the European Letterbox Marketing Association, was needed to ensure a prosperous future. After looking at a number of alternative strategies, the company agreed in 2001 to a takeover by TNT Post Group (TPG), which includes the Dutch Post Office (Royal PTT Post) and TNT. The deal, which gave TNT a 90 per cent stake, would strengthen TNT's position in the UK market and formed part of the group's strategy to become the leading European supplier for mail-related services. TNT set about applying to the UK postal regulator Postcomm for an interim UK postal service licence, something that would have been very difficult for CD Marketing Services to achieve on its own.

Source: based on Circular Distributors Ltd website (http://www.cdltd.co.uk) and http://www.Emmasdiary.co.uk; Direct Mail Information Service (http://www.dmis/keystats/html); *Sunday Times* Enterprise Network (2000), Section 3, 21 May, p. 17.

QUESTIONS

1 What business is CD Marketing Services in? What business should it be in?

2 Draw a product/market expansion matrix identifying the growth options for CD Marketing Services. How would you assess the risk of each identified growth option?

3 On what bases can CD position itself relative to its competitors? What position would you recommend it adopt? What do you consider to be the most important sources of sustainable competitive advantage for CD?

4 What methods should the company use to scan its environment for new opportunities/threats? How should they be assessed?

5 There is a view that information technology

will increasingly allow CD's clients to do much of the data analysis that they currently buy in from CD. In such a scenario, how can CD add value to its service offer?

6 Critically assess CD's opportunities for overseas expansion. What factors should influence the company's overseas expansion strategy?

CASE 2: PLENTY OF BEER IN THE CZECH REPUBLIC, BUT WHERE'S THE PROFIT?

It would seem like a hopeless case of a drunken hangover. Why would Western brewers want to enter the beer market in the Czech Republic, a country that was awash with famous local brands, with the legendary quality of its beers, intense loyalty to regional brands, and among the lowest beer prices in Europe? True, the Czechs also had one of the highest rates of consumption in the world, which in 1997 stood at an average of 165 litres per person per year, beaten only by Bavaria. But even this high consumption was falling, as traditional hard-drinking working men cut back on their consumption. In fact, consumption fell steadily to 158 litres in 2004. To lovers of real ale, the Czech Republic may have been heaven, but why should Western brewers have been so keen to move into an apparently saturated market with low prices and falling consumption? To the UK-based Bass Breweries (as it was then known), the Czech market represented an opportunity waiting to be developed. However, a study of its venture into the Czech Republic illustrates that understanding the environment of an emerging market can involve a lot of risks, and in Bass's case, it ultimately failed to achieve all its ambitions.

In the communist era, Czech breweries operated within a system of production allocations determined by central state planners, with each brewery allocated a geographical area of distribution. This provided for very little competition within a given region, and capital investment into the modernization of production facilities was low. However, the quality of Czech beers was preserved on account of the professional honour of the brewer. The Czech Republic has a long tradition of brewing, with some of the world's oldest and most respected beers, including the Staropramen, Ostravar and Vratislav brands. One of the reasons for the high consumption of beer has been its high quality and low price. The price of a litre of beer in 1997 was typically less than a quarter of what a comparable litre would have cost in the UK, the low price reflecting low taxes and low margins for producers.

With the collapse of the communist government in 1989, central planning and state ownership gave way to a private, market-driven economy. In this reorientation, Czech breweries found themselves in a new business environment. With government financing severed, breweries were forced to privatize. Profitability, competition and marketing became paramount, as regional brewers' hold over local customers was weakened.

Czech beer drinkers had become used to a mentality of taking what was available, rather than seeking the best product to suit their needs and preferences. Bass saw that the fragmented market was ripe for consolidation. In 1997, the three largest breweries held only 55 per cent of the market, with another 25 per cent being made up of small regional brewers, none of whom had a national market share of over 3 per cent. Even Budwar, possibly the best-known Czech beer in the UK, accounted for just 3 per cent of the domestic market. Many of the Czech Republic's near neighbours had similar structural problems and opportunities in their beer sector and, like other Western investors, Bass saw the country as a platform for expansion into the rest of Eastern Europe.

In addition to exploiting the Czech market, Bass also saw an opportunity to develop global markets for the high-quality beers that were currently confined to the domestic Czech market. Bass could use its global distribution network to exploit the brands in a way that would have been impossible to domestic companies.

Bass first invested in the Czech Republic in 1994, with a 34 per cent stake in Prague Breweries, later increasing this to 46 per cent. This brought Bass three Prague-based breweries that would have seemed quite small and unsophisticated by UK standards. In 1995 it bought 78 per cent of Vratislavice nad Nisou (with two breweries in North Boherrda) and 51 per cent of Ostravar, a brewery in North Moravia. In 1996 Bass acquired a controlling interest in Prague Breweries when it increased its stake to 51 per cent. In 1997, the three companies in which it had invested were merged under the name Prague Breweries, in which Bass has a 55 per cent stake. This made Prague Breweries the second-biggest brewer in the Czech Republic, but it still had only a 14 per cent market share. The market leader, Prazdroj, had 27 per cent. Bass had started the process of consolidation in the industry, but it still had a long way to go if it was to match progress in Western Europe.

A further approach to making the Czech market profitable was the development of strong brands that could be sold at higher margins. Importantly, the 'typical' Czech beer drinker appeared to be changing, as the heavy-drinking male gave way to a rising number of young, relatively affluent professionals.

Bass's first new product development in the country was a premium lager called Velvet, developed and brewed in the Czech Republic, but with the help of Bass in the UK. From the beginning, Bass sought to position Velvet as something quite different to commodity beers.

It had a distinctive smooth, creamy head and Bass commissioned special glasses for it to be served in. To add to its differentiation, Bass provided training for bar staff on how to pour and serve it. Velvet was aimed at high-income consumers and promoted through bars and restaurants with targeted tastings. Promotional support was provided by advertising in *Elle*, *Harper's Bazaar* and *Esquire*, and by a dedicated sales team. Despite the conservatism of Czech drinkers, Bass had successfully found a niche market – the emerging middle classes in stylish bars. Bass's strategy has been to invest heavily in brands for the long term. In developing a brand, the company started with a research programme among consumers to learn more about their preferences, followed with research on respondents' perceptions of competing brands. It then undertook lifestyle segmentation, something previously unheard of in the Czech Republic.

Another strength of Bass in its home market was distribution and this represented another opportunity in the Czech market. By the end of 1997, a new sales, marketing and distribution structure was in place, making it possible to distribute national brands efficiently and effectively. The structure included national marketing, key account and business development teams, along with a unified sales force and distribution network. In three years, one result of this reorganization had been to increase distribution of the company's products from 50 to 80 per cent of all retail outlets in the country.

Overcoming the cultural barriers of the Czech people proved to be one of the biggest challenges for Bass. It seemed that many people found change to a market-based system difficult to cope with after 40 years of centralized planning. The whole idea of customer focus seemed to lack credibility among employees who had been used to customers having no choice. While Bass might have been expert at brewing, branding and distribution issues, it underestimated how much time it would have to spend on change management issues and instilling Western values into staff. Problems were encountered in getting people to make decisions, motivating them to act on their decisions and then having to check that agreed actions were actually being undertaken. Recruitment, appraisal and reward increasingly stressed a number of key attitudes of mind: being customer focused, results-driven and innovative, behaving with integrity, treating people with respect, and showing respect for the community. As an example of the problems that had to be overcome, salespeople had a pride that prevented them from listening to retailers, fostered by years of production orientation.

Bass never managed to achieve profitability in the Czech market. Despite being an early mover in the consolidation of the Czech beer market, it was increasingly threatened by other international brewers that had gone through the same process of evaluating overseas markets and decided to enter the Czech market.

Most significant was the advance of the world's second-largest brewer, SAB Miller, which by 2003 had about 50 per cent of the domestic market, and employed 2700 people in three breweries (Plzen, Nosovice and Velke Popovice) and 13 distribution centres.

Back home, all the major UK breweries were undertaking reviews of what business they should be in, and Bass decided that its future should lie in the growing leisure sector (where it owned restaurants, hotels and fitness centres), rather than brewing. It came to an agreement for the Belgian brewer Interbrew SA to acquire all of Bass's brewing operations. Although the takeover of Bass's UK operations was blocked by the Department of Trade and Industry on competition grounds, Interbrew's acquisition of Bass's non-UK businesses was cleared by the European Commission. Bass was subsequently renamed Six Continents and in 2003 split its pub operations into a new company, Mitchells and Butler.

Interbrew already had a significant part of its business in Central and Eastern Europe, with operations in Russia, Ukraine, Hungary, Croatia, Romania, Bulgaria, Montenegro and the Czech Republic. It had a long-term vision for Bass's brands and, following the acquisition of Bass's Czech assets, earmarked 3 billion Czech koruna for development of Prazske Pivovary. Could it succeed where Bass had not been able to earn a profit?

Meanwhile, third position in the Czech beer market was taken by Budejovicky Budvar which, despite a wave of privatization and consolidation in the Czech beer industry since the end of communism in 1989, remained in state hands.

The presence of two major international brewers in the Czech market helped to focus attention on exports at a time when domestic consumption of beer was steadily falling. Domestic consumption was stagnating as beer faced increasing competition from other types of drink, particularly wine.

The accession of the Czech Republic and nine other countries into the EU in May 2004 helped to integrate the country's brewing industry into the wider European marketing environment. Accession meant the easing of export administration, long border queues and prohibitive import duties in some countries. Countries such as Hungary, Poland and the Baltics previously had restrictively high customs duties, so accession opened up new markets for brewers with an interest in the Czech Republic. The retail price of beer was claimed to be two to three times higher in most EU countries, so exporting appeared to be more profitable than domestic sales. SAB Miller set out to make the Prazdroj's brand Pilsner Urquell its flagship label worldwide. In

2004 around one-third of the 1.5 million hectolitres brewed was sold abroad. It saw that, as the Czech market had reached maximum consumption, the only room for growth was through exports.

Meanwhile, cultural and economic convergence between the Czech Republic and the rest of the EU continued to present new opportunities for imported beers. Interbrew claimed that a growing number of retailers were coming to appreciate that stocking niche brands such as its Staropramen brand could create a clear point of difference in a crowded market, and encouraged consumers to trade up. Belgium's Stella Artois was introduced to the Czech Republic, targeting upwardly mobile, educated and well-travelled young people. Some claimed that it was sacrilege, but others saw it as normal market development when Czech brewers diversified into alcoholic fruit drinks and alco-pops.

Source: based on Johnstone, C. (2005) 'Major breweries invest in controversial beer concept for Czech drinks market', *Prague Post*, 7 July; 'Interbrew to invest £1m in Staropramen as sales soar', The Publican.com, 30 June 2005; 'Czech brewers see the world as their oyster', www.eubusiness.com, 26 March 2005; Hamm, Jennifer (2002) 'Foreign beer enters local market', *Prague Post*, 18 December.

QUESTIONS

1 With hindsight, critically evaluate Bass's decision to enter the Czech beer market.
2 Review the alternative market entry strategies that were open to Bass and assess each for its level of risk.
3 Critically assess the problems and opportunities for Interbrew's investment in the Czech Republic arising from further integration of the country into the European Union.

CASE 3: DOES FORD MAKE CARS OR SELL SERVICES?

In Chapter 11, we looked at the structure of national economies and made a general observation that services have become the dominant element of most developed economies. In the UK and USA, for example, the services sector accounts for about three-quarters of GDP. But what exactly do we mean by the services sector? And how have individual organizations adapted to the service-dominant economy?

There are many examples of companies that have made the transition from being predominantly manufacturing based to being predominantly service based. WPP, one of the world's largest advertising agencies and perhaps the best example of a 'pure' intangible service industry, actually started life as a manufacturer of shopping baskets (WPP originally stood for Wire Plastic Products). But it soon understood the needs of its customers, and the fact that they were buying its shopping baskets and trolleys in order to boost sales. From there it was a small step to selling in-store promotional displays, and then on to advertising. WPP moved from being an essentially manufacturing-based company to a service-based company.

Service companies have emerged not just from the manufacturing sector, but also from the agricultural sector. By 2002, 58.3 per cent of UK farmers were engaged in some form of diversified activity, to the extent that nearly one in five diversified holdings now had no conventional agricultural production (Centre for Rural Research 2003). The idea of adding value to agricultural products was nothing new to farmers; after all, many had undertaken some processing of the food that they had grown, such as turning milk into cheese. Many more had ventured into services by selling the produce that they had grown through their own farm shops. These had developed from simple roadside stalls that operated only at harvest time to become fully fledged service activities in their own right. It was no longer good enough to simply have the right fruit and vegetables, but also opening hours, car parking and customer facilities that met buyers' rising expectations. Some farm shops have even developed into mini out-of-town visitor centres which families visit to eat, go shopping and provide entertainment for children. In an attempt to get a higher price for their produce, some farmers have developed innovative service-based methods of delivery. Vegetable box schemes have become very popular, with some segments of food buyers preferring to pay a premium price for freshly delivered local produce. Barcombe Organic Nurseries in Lewes, Sussex, is typical of many farms that have developed a vegetable box scheme by offering buyers Internet-based ordering, home delivery and food preparation advice.

Returning to the manufacturing sector, many organizations that we may instinctively think of as being manufacturers are really driven by services. The case of car manufacturers is an interesting one to examine in detail. To many people, cars are the classic example of a manufactured product, made in factories from the combination of thousands of components. But recent experience from the car sector suggests that car manufacturers may be rather more enthusiastic to describe themselves as service-orientated companies. Indeed, the modern car buyer is buying a bundle of service benefits, just as much as the tangible components of the product offer.

The days are long gone when a car manufacturer would sell a car on the strength of its design features, and then forget about the customer until the time came to replace the car three years later. Car manufacturers realized that car buyers sought more than the tangible offering – important though that was. Over

time, they have moved increasingly into the services sector in an attempt to gain a larger share of car buyers' wallets.

In the UK, Ford has led the way in many aspects of this increasing service orientation. It saw an opportunity in the 1970s – with the liberalization of consumer credit regulations – to offer car buyers loan facilities with which to make their car purchase. Not only did this make it easier for middle-income groups to a buy their cars, but it also allowed Ford to retain the margins that would otherwise have gone to banks, which were the main alternative source of car loan finance. Ford Motor Credit has become a licensed credit broker and a major profit centre within the company.

The next major attempt to gain a greater share of car buyers' wallets came through selling extended warranties on the cars it sold. Traditionally, new cars had come with just 12 months' warranty, but Ford realized that many buyers wanted to buy peace of mind that they were not going to face unexpected repair bills after their initial warranty had expired. Increased competition from Japanese importers, and the improving reliability of its new cars, encouraged this development.

By the mid-1990s, Ford came round to the view that many of its customers were buying transport solutions, rather than a car per se. So it came up with schemes where customers paid a small deposit, followed by a fixed amount per month, in return for which they received comprehensive finance and warranty facilities. In addition, it promised that the company would take back the car after three years and replace it with a new one. Marketed under the 'Options' brand name, Ford was soon selling nearly half its new cars to private buyers using this method. Over time the scheme was developed to include facilities for maintaining and insuring the car.

Repairs and maintenance have always been

important service activities in the car sector, but manufacturers tended to lose out on much of the benefits of this to a fragmented dealership network. Customer databases for maintenance and new car sales were often not co-ordinated and Ford found that it had very little direct communication with the people that bought its cars. By the 1990s, the dealership network was becoming more closely integrated with Ford's operations and new opportunities were seized for keeping new car buyers within the system. Recent buyers could be alerted of new services available at local dealers, using a database managed centrally by Ford. Numerous initiatives were launched, such as Ford's own mobile phone service. Ford sought to make it easy for customers to get back on the road when their own car was taken in for servicing, so the provision of car hire facilities contributed to the service ethos. In 1996 the company linked up with Barclaycard to offer a Ford-branded credit card, so Ford found itself providing a service to its customers that was quite removed from the tangible cars that it sold (although points accrued by using the card could be used to reduce the price of a new Ford car).

By 2000, volume car manufacturers had ceased to make big profits in the UK. In 2002, Ford, with 18 per cent of the market made just £8 million in profits on its European operations. Falling profit margins on selling new cars were partly offset by profits made on service-based activities. In the same year, the company made £1.38 billion worldwide from its credit arm, which arranged finance for about 40 per cent of all new cars that it sold. But adding services is not a guaranteed route to increased profitability. In the mid-1990s, Ford had acquired the Kwik-Fit tyre-fitting chain, hoping to further develop its service base with a chain that would appeal to all car owners, and not predominantly those who owned a Ford-manufactured car. But

Kwik-Fit failed to be a success for Ford and it was later sold back to its founder at a price well below what Ford had paid for it. It seemed that the market for tyre replacements was cut-throat and suffering overcapacity, with many existing players having had long experience in this service-based sector. Meanwhile, many of Ford's newly acquired luxury car brands, including Jaguar and Volvo, were not making money and many commentators had criticized the design of these model ranges. Could this have been a warning that Ford's core competencies lie in engineering and design, rather than running labour-intensive service businesses?

REFERENCE

Centre for Rural Research (2003) Farm Diversification Activities: Benchmarking Study 2002. Final Report to Defra. CRR Research Report 4. Centre for Rural Research, University of Exeter, and Tourism Research Group, University of Plymouth.

QUESTIONS

1 Given the evidence of Ford, is it still appropriate to talk about the manufacturing and service sectors being quite distinctive?

2 What business is Ford in? What business should it be in?

3 Discuss the view that Ford should do what it is good at – designing cars – and leave services to other companies.

CASE 4: THE BUS INDUSTRY RIDES THROUGH A CHANGING BUSINESS ENVIRONMENT

As you stand waiting for a bus to come along, it can be easy to lose sight of the complex environmental forces that have influenced the bus that eventually arrives. People that have used bus services in different countries may begin to wonder why standards appear to vary so much between countries. The Netherlands and

Germany are noted for their impeccable bus services, which are clean and reliable, and generally cheap and frequent. Anybody that has tried to use a bus in India or Indonesia may think they are taking their lives in their hands with a chaotic service noted for unreliability and overcrowding. Britain's bus services may represent a compromise between these two extremes. But in all these cases, the nature of the bus service is a reflection of the underlying business environment. When the nature of bus services changes, this invariably results from the change in the underlying business environment.

In the UK, the social and economic environment has been a major factor in the operation of bus services. Before the Second World War, buses were the dominant form of transport, in an era where car ownership was low and generally reserved for the wealthy. But from the 1950s onwards, continued economic prosperity led to a sharp rise in car ownership. For a new car owner, the car represented freedom to travel where they wanted and when they wanted, without having to share a bus with up to 70 other people, and being restricted to the times that the bus ran. Owning a car became a status symbol, and bus use gradually acquired a stigma. The young, elderly and disadvantaged came to rely on bus services, while the upwardly mobile acquired status and convenience from their ownership of a car. Bus usage in Britain has fallen steadily from a high point in the early 1950s and has only recently been reversed – especially in London – largely on account of increasing traffic congestion and priority measures that have been given to buses in many town centres. Demographics have also affected the fortunes of bus companies, with periods of rising numbers of young and elderly people helping bus operators.

But in addition to the social and economic environment, bus operators have been deeply affected by changes in the political environment, both at a central and local government level. The political environment of the UK has turned full circle, from reliance on free market forces until the 1920s, then strict regulation until the 1980s, which was followed by a return to a political obsession with competitive markets. More recently, the cycle has appeared to be starting all over again, with calls for increased regulation of the sector.

The UK bus industry of the early 1920s saw large numbers of small entrepreneurs operating in competition with each other, resulting in sometimes wasteful and dangerous competitive practices. The dominant political attitude shifted during the 1920s, away from a pure laissez-faire approach to one where state intervention in the economy was becoming more acceptable. Against this changing background, government was able to recognize that public transport was an important public service by passing the Road Traffic Act 1930. This required all bus routes to be licensed. Route licences gave the holder substantial monopoly power and large bus-operating companies emerged during the 1930s by acquiring the licences of their smaller competitors. The companies thereby acquired territorial monopolies that made it even more difficult for a small company to prove the need for a new service and acquire a route licence. In these conditions, bus companies tended to be production rather than marketing led. A further recognition that public transport was an essential public service came when a large section of the bus industry was nationalized by the Labour government in 1948.

By the 1960s bus operation had ceased to be profitable outside the main urban areas and the busy inter-urban routes, mainly due to increasing levels of car ownership. Faced with a deterioration in the quantity and quality of bus services, the Labour government of the late 1960s again intervened with the acquisition of the largest private-sector group of companies, and the subsequent formation of the National Bus Company and Scottish Bus Group. These were given responsibility for running most of the large bus operators outside the major cities. The two companies were given strict financial rather than social objectives, although government did later intervene in a manner which appeared to make the companies an instrument of wider government policy. For example, they had been asked to keep fare increases down to help the government's anti-inflation policy.

Local authorities in a number of areas had for many years operated their own bus fleets for various reasons. Making profits to help keep down the level of rates charged to ratepayers was one objective but, in addition, local authorities provided bus services out of civic pride and to ensure that a high standard of public service was provided. By the 1960s, local authority bus operations had also become generally unprofitable. They were often allowed to lose money if councillors decided that the service being provided justified being subsidized out of rates income.

By the 1970s, a highly regulated system of route licensing and companies having large territorial monopolies resulted in the business environment being very production rather than marketing orientated. Promotion was aimed almost entirely at existing users – providing basic information rather than trying to create a favourable image among potential users. Faced with an inelastic demand, bus companies would set fares as high as politically possible with the regulatory Traffic Commissioners. Innovation in new products was nearly always reactive rather than proactive. Most innovation was aimed at cutting production costs – such as reducing the need to employ conductors through a one-person operation – rather than meeting the needs of consumers, such as providing faster journey times or a reliable service.

At the same time as the market for scheduled bus services appeared to be going into decline, the market for contract hire by schools, factories and private groups remained buoyant. In this market there were no quantity restrictions on operator licences, only the quality controls that applied equally to operators of scheduled bus services. The market was dominated by a large number of small firms aggressively competing against each other on price and the quality of service provided. It would be difficult for a production-orientated company to survive in this environment for long.

By the 1980s the question was being asked whether the unregulated environment that had encouraged a marketing orientation in the contract service sector could also be applied to the scheduled services sector to achieve the same effect. The traditional argument against deregulation was that licence holders that had a territorial monopoly provided some element of social service – they used profits generated on one route or at one time of day to cross-subsidize loss-making routes or less profitable evening and weekend services. The National Bus Company used this argument to defend itself, even though it had been given clearly defined profit rather than social goals by the government.

The political environment for bus operators changed significantly during the 1980s. The first change was brought about by the Conservative government's ideological belief that free and unregulated markets were inherently better than regulation, which was presumed to stifle innovation. The government therefore abolished the need for route licences in most parts of the country. Any company could now operate a bus service subject to satisfying safety criteria. In addition, subsidies from local authorities to provide socially necessary but unprofitable bus services were put out to competitive tendering, rather than being allocated to the existing licence holder.

The second major change was the restructuring and gradual dismantling of public-sector bus operations. The ideology of the time considered that the state was bad at providing marketable goods and services compared to the private sector. Where a social service was considered desirable, this should be explicitly identified by policy makers in government and satisfied by market mechanisms. The first step was the breaking up of the National Bus Company and sale to the private sector. Many of the individual companies which it comprised were sold on favourable terms to their management and employees, fulfilling another wish of the Conservative government of the late 1980s – widespread capitalism. Local authorities, which had frequently operated their bus fleets as a quasi-social service, were forced to restructure their operations by forming limited companies to which a board of directors was appointed with a view to eventual sale to the private sector.

Changes in the political environment had totally transformed the market for bus services during the 1980s. Marketing tools that had been used by the fast moving consumer goods sector for many years, but ignored by this section of the bus industry, became widely used. Tactical pricing was used aggressively to gain market share, particularly by new entrants to a route that frequently charged very low fares to attract initial custom. Market-led new service developments occurred, such as high-frequency minibus services. Much more attention was paid to product quality, including reliability, availability of service information, training of staff and the appearance of vehicles. Corporate identity increasingly took as its starting point the values of the target customers rather than those of management.

Local monopolies of bus services had until the 1980s been seen as beneficial by the government, recognizing the implicit public service obligations of licence holders. However, in a sudden about-turn, bus operators were now subject to the same vetting for anti-competitive practices as most other industries. The Office of Fair Trading was constantly investigating claims that companies were trying to restore their monopoly status by driving their competitors off the road by using practices that were reminiscent of the 1920s. The powers of the OFT were weak and investigations often took a long time, allowing competitors to be driven out of a market in the meantime.

The early years of deregulation were characterized by a lot of competition between small and medium-sized firms. However, by the mid-1990s, consolidation of the industry was beginning to create large companies, such as Stagecoach and First Group, which had significant local monopoly power. As numbers of passengers continued to fall and fares continued to rise, cynics argued that a publicly regulated monopoly had effectively been replaced by private, unregulated monopolies, which the incoming Labour government of 1997 sought to address with tighter regulation. The government was reluctant to legislate for greater control and, besides, did not want to commit government money to buying back the privatized bus companies. However, it has encouraged local authorities to work together with bus operators to create Quality Partnerships and increased funding available for innovative services. Furthermore, there were some signs that after the initial turbulence of deregulation, some real benefits were beginning to be evident. In 2004, the Confederation of Passenger Transport (CPT) reported that more people were using buses in the UK than at any point in the previous 10 years, with a total of 4.5 billion journeys made in 2004 – a 2 per cent rise on the previous year. Passengers also enjoyed improved facilities, as the average fleet age has come down from 9.6 years to 8 years.

QUESTIONS

1 Summarize the main macroenvironmental factors that have affected the fortunes of the bus industry in your country during the past 50 years.

2 To what extent has government policy towards the bus industry reflected the dominant political ideology of the time?

3 Briefly summarize the main marketing implications of a change from regulation to free competition for bus services.

CASE 5: TAKING AN ETHICAL LINE AT THE CO-OPERATIVE BANK

To most people, banks may be a necessity of life, though they remain unloved and frequently despised by the groups that they seek to serve. Most people would be able to recount claims that banks have overcharged them, and have taken seemingly extortionate fees for providing a slow and very simple service. At a general level, many people have accused banks of being the unacceptable face of capitalism. Overpaid bank executives have been perceived as making decisions that help their own personal betterment, rather than benefit society at large. Banks may get rich by selling arms and investing in technologies that produce climate change, but where are they when it comes to lending money to disadvantaged groups in poor areas? Add to this the occasional scandal involving misuse of information, undeserved bonuses for chief executives and sometimes outright corruption, and it is easy to see why banks rate low in many people's estimation of ethical business practices.

The banking sector in the UK has been dominated by the 'big four' banks – Barclays, Lloyds TSB, HSBC and the Royal Bank of Scotland – which are often seen as indistinct in terms of their practices. But one relatively small bank, the Co-operative Bank, has actively adopted an ethical positioning in its bid to gain market share. The use of a distinct promotional positioning has been the key to the Co-operative Bank's survival and expansion in a competitive and consolidating marketplace.

The Co-operative Bank was founded in 1872 by the Co-operative Wholesale and Retail Societies, which had a vision of providing all the goods and services that an individual would need from cradle to grave, free from capitalist profiteering. By the mid-1980s the bank had enjoyed a period of steady growth and the number of branches passed the 100 mark, helped by several innovative new services such as free in-credit banking, extended opening hours and interest-bearing cheque accounts. However, the bank found its market position being steadily eroded by increased competition from the major clearing banks and particularly the larger building societies. Following deregulation of the UK banking sector in the 1980s, these had been able to enter the personal banking sector and many had established their own personal cheque accounts. Partly as a result of this new competition, the Co-operative Bank saw its market share fall from 2.7 per cent in 1986 to 2 per cent by 1991. Alongside this trend the bank faced a changing customer profile. Traditionally the bank had attracted a high proportion of its customers from the more affluent ABC1 social groups. By 1992 an increasing number of new accounts were being attracted from the C2DE social groups, while at the same time the bank was losing its core ABC1 accounts. This trend was diluting its position as a more upmarket bank and reducing its potential to cross-sell more profitable financial products such as insurance and personal loans.

The bank's research showed that, outside its customer base, it lacked a clear image, being seen mainly as rather staid and old-fashioned, and with left-wing political affinities. Many people linked the image of the bank with the Co-op shops, which in the 1980s were often looking tired alongside their more dynamic competitors. Furthermore, spontaneous recall of the Co-operative Bank name had fallen steadily despite extensive advertising of its innovative new products.

The bank realized that immediate action was necessary to rebuild its image and stem the loss of its ABC1 accounts. BDDH was appointed as advertising agency to devise a promotional campaign. The agency carried out an audit of the Co-operative Bank to identify any distinctive competencies that it could build a campaign upon. It soon found that the bank's heritage offered a unique positioning opportunity against other mainstream banks. This derived in particular from its sourcing and distribution of funds, which had been governed by an unwritten ethical code, with the effect that the bank never lent money to environmentally or politically unsound organizations. BDDH set out to transform the results of its audit into a relevant and motivating proposition that would appeal beyond the bank's current customer base. A key strategic decision was made to target promotional activity at the growing number of 'ethical consumers' who, importantly, were found to have a more upmarket ABC1 profile.

The 'ethical bank' formed the foundation upon which BDDH built its campaign. Initially this was tested on the bank's existing customers, where it gained a high level of approval. The bank recognized that advertising claims must be met by actual practice and incorporated its ethical stance into its customer charter. The bank was well aware that the media enjoys making trouble for companies that claim to be ethical but in fact are caught out undertaking unethical practices. Advertising was initially used to raise awareness of the bank's positioning. The creative work was deliberately provocative and motivating, while at the same time maintaining the bank's credentials as a high-street lender. The creative images used were often simple and stark.

The key objectives of the campaign were:
(i) build customer loyalty and so stem the outflow of ABC1s
(ii) expand the customer base, targeting ABC1s
(iii) expand the corporate customer base.

National press and regional television in the bank's 'northern heartland' were the primary media used in the initial stages of the campaign. Cinema advertising was used as the campaign progressed.

The marketing objectives were exceeded as a result of the promotional campaign. The bank established a strong and differentiated brand platform that it subsequently used to launch new services, including its 'Smile' Internet banking operation (www.smile.co.uk). The campaign was targeted carefully with the aim of achieving maximum impact, which enabled the message to be delivered cost-effectively. The case clearly demonstrates how effective promotional activity, linked closely to business and marketing objectives and strategy can provide a long-term sustainable competitive position in the marketplace.

In 2004, the bank reported its tenth year of increased profits, up in 2003 to £130 million. Although the bank's margins had been falling, it remained prudent in its lending, with a mortgage loan-to-value ratio of 50 per cent – considered good for the industry, and further evidence that the bank was not reliant on poorer socio-economic groups that tend to borrow a higher proportion of a property's value. Of course, the bank's rising profitability could not be entirely attributed to its ethical positioning, but the bank's success can be put down to a clear understanding of its customer base and its own unique competencies.

QUESTIONS

1 Identify a programme of research that might indicate whether the Co-operative Bank's ethical positioning has been effective.

2 How sustainable is an ethical positioning by a bank? To what extent have the Co-operative Bank's rivals sought to establish their ethical credentials? What barriers prevent an even wider uptake of an ethical position?

3 What – if any – new challenges or threats arise for the Co-operative Bank's ethical promotion as a result of greater use of online banking services?

Glossary

Accelerator effect – When a small change in demand for consumer products has a much larger effect on demand for capital goods manufacturers

Acquisition – When a company acquires the share capital of another company

Act of Parliament – A law passed by the UK parliament

Age structure – The composition of a population, defined in terms of the proportions contained within defined age ranges

Anti-competitive practices – Actions by companies that have the effect of reducing the amount of competition in a market

Article numbering – An industry-wide standardized system for allocating a unique number to each product

Attitudes – An individual's consistently favourable or unfavourable feelings about an object, person or idea

Audits – Evaluation of an activity, e.g. a financial audit checks the accuracy and integrity of a company's accounting procedures

Balance of payments – A record of all transactions between domestic consumers and firms and those based overseas

Barriers to trade – Formal and informal obstacles that prevent trade taking place between countries

Best value – A term used in UK local government to describe the process of ensuring that the services it provides are provided as efficiently and as effectively as best practice available in the open market

Birth rate – The number of births in a population, per 1000 members of the population

Borrowing – Temporarily having the use of somebody else's financial resources

Branding – The process of creating a distinctive identity for a product that differentiates it from its competitors

Building societies – Organisations registered under the Building Societies Acts that are owned by their savers and borrowers

Business cycle – Fluctuations in the level of activity in an economy, commonly measured by employment levels and aggregate demand

Buyer–seller relationships – A buyer and seller consider their current transaction in the context of previous transactions, and their expectations for future transactions

Cabinet – The senior executive of the UK government, headed by the prime minister

Cash flow – The amount of cash available to a business at any particular time

Cellular household – A household unit in which the members of the household live their lives with a significant amount of independence from other members

Central bank – In the UK, a lender of last resort, and responsible for setting monetary and interest rate policy; in the UK, this is the Bank of England (the European Central Bank for the EU)

Census of Population – A 10-yearly survey of population characteristics

Channels of distribution – A 'route to market' for a company and a means of getting its goods and services to the final consumer

Charities – In the UK, organizations registered in accordance with the Charities Acts whose primary aim is to benefit a good cause, rather than profit-seeking shareholders

Charter mark – A UK government scheme to recognize excellent quality in public services

Circular flow of income – The means by which money circulates in an economy between households and firms

Civil Service – Paid government officials who are responsible for implementing government policies

Codes of practice – A set of rules, usually drawn up by an industry or trade association, specifying the behaviour expected of members

Companies Acts – Legislation governing the creation and operation of limited liability companies

Comparative cost advantage – When it costs a company fewer units of resources to produce a unit of output compared with its competitors

Competition Commission – UK regulatory body responsible for ensuring that markets remain competitive and in the long-term interest of consumers

Competitive cost advantage – A firm has a marketing mix that the target market sees as meeting its needs better than the mix of competing firms

Computer-aided design (CAD) – The use of IT in the design of new products

Computer-aided manufacturing (CAM) – The use of IT to make better-quality products at lower unit cost

Common law – A law that emerges through precedents created in previous judgments by courts

Confidence level – In the context of consumer expenditure, the confidence felt by individuals about their personal future welfare and/or national economic prosperity

Contract – An agreement between two or more parties

Co-operatives – Associations of producers or consumers to share the benefits of co-operation

Co-operative society – UK organization owned by customers

Corporate governance – Procedures adopted for the internal management of an organization

Corporate social responsibility – an organization takes into account the interest of all stakeholders who may be affected by its activities

Cultural convergence – The idea that distinctive characteristics of different cultures are becoming less significant

Culture – The whole set of beliefs, attitudes and ways of behaving shared by a group of people

Debentures – Loans secured against the assets of a company

Decision support systems – Techniques and processess used to facilitate better decisions by managers

Deflation – A falling level of prices

Demand – Consumers' ability and willingness to pay for a product

Demand-techology life cycle – A demand-technology life cycle will have a history of emergence, rapid growth, slower growth, maturity and decline, but over a shorter period than the more sustainable longer-term demand cycle

Demography – The study of population characteristics

Directives – Instructions by the EU to member states to introduce changes to their domestic legislation

Directors – Members of a limited company who have responsibilities for governing the company

Discrimination – Making a distinction between two or more otherwise similar phenomena

Diseconomies of scale – When unit costs increase as output increases

Disposable income – Income available to individuals after they have made allowance for essential, non-discretionary spending

Diversification – When an organization enters new markets and/or new products which are not closely related to its current activities

Duty of care – The legal responsibility of an individual or a company not to harm others

Ecological impacts – The effects of organizations' activities on ecological systems

Economic structure – The composition of an economy in terms of the number and types of buyers and sellers it comprises

Economies of scale – Costs per unit fall as output rises

Elasticity of demand – The change in volume of demand for a product in response to a change in some parameter, e.g. the price of the product

Elasticity of supply – The extent to which the amount supplied to a market varies following a change in price

Electronic commerce – Transactions of goods or services for which payment occurs over the Internet or other wide area networks

Electronic Data Interchange (EDI) – Proprietary systems for transferring data between organizations

Electronic point of sale (EPOS) – A system for recording details of individual sales

Employee involvement – Making employees feel a sense of ownership in their job

Empowerment – Expecting employees to use their own discretion to solve a problem, rather than closely following instructions

Environmental scanning – A systematic method of monitoring changes in an organization's business environment

Environmental set – The complete list of organizations that have impacts on a business

Ethics – A culturally determined sense of what is right and wrong

Ethnic minorities – Small groups in a population who are distinctive in terms of their racial and cultural background

Equity capital – The shareholders' interest in a business, representing risk capital

European Commission – Administrative executive of the European Union

European Council of Ministers – Ministers representing each of the EU member states

European Court of Justice – The supreme court within the EU

European Economic Area (EEA) – A common market area comprising the EU plus affiliate nations

European Union (EU) – The 25 states of Europe that belong to an economic and political union

Exchange rate – The price of one currency expressed in terms of another

Externalities – Costs that are not borne by the organization that causes them

External costs – Product costs that are borne by individuals or firms who are not compensated for the costs they incur

Family roles – Expectations of the behaviour of different members of a family unit

Fiscal policy – Government policy on public borrowing, spending and taxation

Five Forces model – Porter's model of the competitive environment of any firm, which comprises the threat of new entrants and substitute products, the bargaining powers of customers and suppliers, and competition among current competitors

Flexible workforce – When a workforce that is expected to be flexible in its working practices, and also possibly to be hired and laid off at short notice

Flotation – When a company seeks to raise capital on a stock market

Forecasting – Estimating the future value of a given phenomenon

Franchising – A company sells the right for another organization or individual to use its business processes and brand name

Functional organization – An organization that organizes its internal management around the functions that they perform

Geodemographic analysis – The study of consumer behaviour based on an individual's area of residence

Globalization – A tendency to treat the world as though it were part of an organization's domestic market

Green marketing – Marketing that seeks to be ecologically responsible

Gross domestic product (GDP) – A measure of the value of goods and services produced in an economy during a specified period

Horizontal integration – Merging of firms' activities at a similar point in a value chain

Household structure – The composition of a household unit in terms of the number and relationship of its members

Human resource management (HRM) – Management activity related to the effective and efficient recruitment, training, motivation, reward and control of an organization's employees

Ideology – A guiding set of beliefs

Imperfect competition – A market that is competitive, but does not meet the criteria for perfect competition, e.g. because of variations in product features and information availability

Incentives – Things that motivate an individual to achieve a goal

Industrial relations – Relationships between employees and their employers, often mediated through trades unions

Inflation – A rise in the general level of prices of goods and services

Injections – Money received by households that does not come from firms, and money received by firms in the circular flow of income

Intellectual property rights – Ownership of the rights to intangible ideas

Interest rates – The cost of borrowing money (or the return from lending money)

Intermediaries – Individuals or organizations who are involved in transferring goods and services from the producer to the final consumer

Internal environment – The processes and structures internal to an organization that facilitate or impede its response to change in its external environment

Internal marketing – The application of the principles and practices of marketing to an organization's dealings with its employees

International trade – Imports/exports to/from other countries

Internet – Computers connected through a common platform

Invisible trade – Overseas trade in services, as distinct from 'visible' goods

Invisibles – Imports and exports to/from a country, which comprise intangible services

Joint ventures – An agreement between two or more firms to exploit a business opportunity, in which capital funding, profits, risk and core competencies are shared

Judiciary – Legal structures and processes

Just-in-time (JIT) systems – Reliably getting products to customers just before they need them

Knowledge management – Processes for collecting, analysing and distributing information to people in an organisation who can act on it

Leadership – The ability to effectively take charge of and direct a team

Legislature – The body responsible for passing legislation

Learning organization – An organization that learns about its environment and adapts to change through effective information-sharing and decision-making activities

Life stages – Distinctive patterns of behaviour associated with periods in individuals' lives

Lifestyle – A set of distinctive attitudes and behaviours

Limited company – An organization that has a separate legal personality from that of its owners

Liquidation – When a company is broken up and its assets sold off in order to pay off creditors and to return any surplus to shareholders

Lobbying – Seeking to influence decisions by other individuals/organizations

Local government – Government at the level of town or county

Macroeconomic analysis – economic analysis

Macroenvironment – The forces in an organization's environment that have an indirect impact on it (e.g. demographic and legislative change)

Management buy-out – When the management of a company agrees to buy all or part of a business from the owners

Management information system – A systematic method of collecting, analysing and distributing information that can be used by management decision makers

Market structure – A definition of a market in terms of the number of sellers relative to the number of buyers

Markets – A place (actual or virtual) whre buyers and sellers meet to exchange things of value

Matrix organization structures – An organization structure that relies on co-ordination of management functions, rather than a strict hierarchical functional control

Mergers – The amalgamation of two or more organizations

Microenvironment – The immediate environment of an organization, with which it comes into contact directly (e.g. its customers and suppliers)

Migration – Movements of people from one country/region to another

Misrepresentation – When a false representation is made about goods or services

Mission statement – A statement of the essential purpose of an organization

Models – A representation of reality that identifies key variables and relationships between the variables

Monetarism – A view of the national economy that attributes instability in the economy to issues of money supply

Monetary Policy Committee – UK committee of the Bank of England responsible for developing and maintaining monetary policy

Monopoly – A market in which there is only one supplier; rarely achieved in practice, as most products have some form of substitute

Motivation – The desire to achieve personal goals

Multinational companies – Companies operating in multiple markets/countries

Multiplier effect – The addition to total income and expenditure within an economy resulting from an initial injection of expenditure

Nationalized industry – State-owned trading organization

Negligence – Harm caused to others through failure to exercise a duty of care

New product development (NPD) process – A sequential (sometimes concurrent) process for getting ideas for new products, developing, testing and launching them

Non-Departmental Public Bodies (NDPBs) – Organizations that are essentially owned by the government and are part of the public sector, but operate at 'arm's length' from their sponsoring government department; also commonly referred to as 'quangos' (see below)

Oligopoly – A market dominated by a few interdependent suppliers

Organic growth – A virtuous circle of business growth in which success leads to growth, which leads to further success and further growth

Organizational culture – Shared values within an organization which help to distinguish one organization from another

Organizational life cycle – The stages that organizations go through from initial launch, through growth, maturity and eventuality to decline and possible closure

Organizational objectives – A statement of where an organization wants to be at some defined point in the future (e.g. in terms of sales levels or profitability)

Outsourcing – When a company engages another organization to provide services (e.g. IT maintenance, office cleaning)

Partnership – An agreement between individuals to operate a business together, and to share risks and rewards, usually in agreed proportions

Patents – A right for a company to prevent others copying a product whose unique intellectual property has been recognized by the Patent Office

Perfect competition – A market in which there are no barriers to entry, no one firm can dominate the market, there is full information available to all buyers and sellers, and all sellers sell an undifferentiated product

Political parties – Groups of people who share a political ideology seek to advance their cause through an organization referred to as a political party

Pressure groups – Groups that are formed to promote a particular cause

Price determination – The method of determining prices in a marketplace through the interaction of supply and demand

Privatization – Government policy to transfer economic activity from the public to the private sector

Product life cycle – The stages that a product goes through from initial launch, through growth, maturity and eventuality to decline and possible deletion from a company's product portfolio

Profit maximization – When firms seek to achieve the maximum possible level of profit

Prospectus – An official document issued by a company seeking to raise fresh capital

Private Finance Initiative (PFI) – Private-sector capital, risk and management expertise is brought in to manage government assets and/or services

Public limited company – A company owned by its shareholding members, which has to satisfy additional criteria regarding capital, membership and reporting, compared with an ordinary limited company

Public–private partnership (PPP) – A general term to cover joint agreements between public- and private-sector organisations, including Private Finance Initiatives (see above)

Public sector net borrowing (PSNB) – The amount of money owed to lenders, less the amount that government has lent to others

Quango – A governmental organization that operates at 'arm's length' from its sponsoring department (quasi-autonomous non-governmental organization), also known as non-departmental public bodies

Receivership – When a company is not a going concern and a process is initiated of breaking up the company and distributing its assets to creditors (also shareholders if there are sufficient funds)

Recession – A period when the size of the national economy is declining, or at least not growing

Regional government – In the UK, government for Scotland, Wales and Northern Ireland

Regulation – Restricting the freedom of operators in a market to protect the interests of users and/or the community in general

Reference groups – Groups that an individual makes reference to when making decisions about his/her own behaviour

Research and development (R&D) – Investment in new products, or new methods of making existing products

Retail Prices Index (RPI) – A measure of the percentage change in prices charged by shops for a basket of goods during a specified period

Rights issue – When a company seeks to raise additional equity capital from its existing shareholders

Risk assessment – An analysis of the probability of an event happening and the seriousness of its effects

Roles – Behaviour that is expected of an individual

Satisficing – performing to a satisfactory level, rather than the highest achievable level

Savings ratio – The proportion of households' available income that is saved rather than spent

Scenario – A hypothetical picture of an environment that may occur in the future

Share capital – The equity capital of a company, representing owners' interests in the business

Shareholders – Investors who take a risk in purchasing a company's shares

Social class – A method of dividing a population into groups based on their social background

Social exclusion – When groups of a society are prevented by formal or informal barriers from taking a full part in the life of the community

Social objectives – An organization pursues objectives that will benefit the wider community at large, and not just its own members

Sole trader – A business, the identity of which is indistinguishable from that of its owner

Staff development – Investment in employees that is aimed at developing their general abilities, rather than specific skills

Stakeholders – Any person with an interest in the activities of an organization (e.g. customers, employees, government agencies and local communities)

Statute law – Legislation created by government

Stock exchange – A market in which a company's shares are bought and sold

Strategic alliances – An agreement between two or more companies to share their resources, e.g. operational resources and access to customers

Subculture – Elements within a culture with a distinctive set of values and behaviours

Supply – The volume of a product that firms are prepared to bring to a market, at a given price, and within a specified time period

SWOT analysis – An organization's internal strengths and weaknesses, matched against its external opportunities and threats

System – A relationship between interdependent components

Takeover – When one company seeks to acquire control of another

Task forces – Teams focused on tackling a specific problem

Technological fusion – The merging of different technologies

Technology transfer – The process of disseminating new technologies between sectors and products

Tort – Law relating to the liability of individuals and organizations to others in respect of their negligent actions

Trade marks – Legal protection given to an organization for its distinctive logos and brand names

Trading blocs – An agreement between a group of nations to make trade between members easier than trade with other countries

Training – Development of skills in a workforce

Transformation process – When low-value inputs are turned into relatively high-value outputs

Trend analysis – Studying past trends as a basis for predicting future activity (e.g. of sales or costs)

Turning point – A point in a business cycle when recession turns into expansion, or vice versa

Unemployment – Unused or under-utilised potential workers in a population

Values – A deep-seated set of beliefs

Value chain – The sequence of activities and organizations involved in transforming a product from one that is of low value to one that is of high value

Vertical integration – The extension of a firm's activities to prior or subsequent points in a value chain

Virtual organization – An organization that has no physical manifestation, but is made up of formal and informal networks of parties

Visible trade – Overseas trade in manufactured goods

Withdrawals – Money in the circular flow of income that should flow from households to firms or vice versa, but that is instead withdrawn from circulation (e.g. through savings or taxation)

World Trade Organization – An international organization that seeks to facilitate trade between nations by, among other things, removing trade barriers

Index